Routledge Revivals

The Manor and the Borough

The Manor and the Borough

Sidney and Beatrice Webb

Volume I

Routledge
Taylor & Francis Group

First published in 2011 by Read Books Ltd.

This edition first published in 2018 by Routledge
2 Park Square, Milton Park, Abingdon, Oxon, OX14 4RN
and by Routledge
52 Vanderbilt Avenue, New York, NY 10017, USA

Routledge is an imprint of the Taylor & Francis Group, an informa business

© 2011 by Taylor & Francis

Publisher's Note
The publisher has gone to great lengths to ensure the quality of this reprint but points out that some imperfections in the original copies may be apparent.

Disclaimer
The publisher has made every effort to trace copyright holders and welcomes correspondence from those they have been unable to contact.

A Library of Congress record exists under ISBN:

ISBN 13: 978-0-367-14944-4 (hbk)
ISBN 13: 978-0-367-14947-5 (pbk)
ISBN 13: 978-0-429-05407-5 (ebk)

The Manor and the Borough

SIDNEY and BEATRICE WEBB

VOL I

British Library Cataloguing-in-Publication Data
A catalogue record for this book is available from
the British Library

Beatrice Potter Webb

Beatrice Potter Webb was born in Gloucester, England in 1858.

Both her mother and brother died early in her childhood leaving her to be raised by her father, Richard Potter. He was a successful businessman with large railroad interests and many influential friends in politics and industry whose company the young Beatrice would become accustomed to.

Educated at home by a governess, she also travelled widely and, due to this, gained a keen interest in sociology. Using the valuable resource of her father's library, studying became a passion, and she soon began to conduct her own sociological investigations. However, it was a time she spent with relatives in Lancashire, that Beatrice had her first glimpse of the working classes and their way of life. This early experience shaped her ideas on class inequality and the working conditions of the lower classes.

Upon reaching adulthood, Potter moved to London and helped her cousin, Charles, a social reformer, research his book *The Life and Labour of the People in London*. It was during this time that she was introduced to Sidney James Webb, who later became her husband and collaborator.

Beatrice and Sidney published many works together, but her solo titles include *Cooperative Movement in Great Britain* (1891), *Wages of Men and Women: Should they be equal?* (1919), *My Apprenticeship* (1926), and *Our Partnership* (1948).

In 1913, along with her husband, Beatrice created the New Statesman, which grew to become an incredibly influential publication. They also founded the London School of Economics and Political Science in 1895.

The Webb's, together, wrote eleven volumes of work which arguably shaped the way subsequent scholars thought about sociology. They also collaborated on more than 100 books and articles on the conditions of factory workers, and the economic history of Britain, among other subjects.

In 1928 Potter retired to Liphook, Hampshire with her husband. Webb passed away on 30 April 1943, and her ashes are buried in Westminster Abbey as a mark of respect for her valued work in the field of social reform.

CONTENTS

BOOK III

THE MANOR AND THE BOROUGH

PART I

CHAPTER I

CHAPTER II

CHAPTER VI

CHAPTER VII

BOOK III

THE MANOR AND THE BOROUGH

INTRODUCTION

IN a preceding volume [1] we have dealt with two main forms of English Local Government, the Parish and the County; organisations which existed from one end of the kingdom to the other. But to the rule of the County—to some slight extent also to the rule of the Parish—there were, up and down England, numerous exceptions, out of which had developed, as it happens, not the least important, and, as some may think, the most picturesque parts of the Local Government of England between the Revolution and the Municipal Corporations Act, namely, those connected with the Manor and the Borough. It does not lie within our province to inquire whether some or all of these exceptions to the uniform organisation of Parish and County may not represent a once universal government, either Manorial or of Village Community character. Whether or not this was the case, the continued existence of these forms after 1689 compels us to devote a volume to the various Exemptions, Immunities, and Franchises which enabled the inhabitants of particular localities to exclude the authority of the County at large, or that of one or other of its officers; and thereby to enjoy, within their own favoured areas, some peculiar forms of self-government.[2]

---

[1] *English Local Government from the Revolution to the Municipal Corporations Act*, vol. i.—*The Parish and the County*, 1906.

[2] It may occur to the student that there was, between 1689 and 1835, another kind of definitely localised local governing body, not based on immunities or exemptions, but wielding, within its area, new and specialised powers. Such authorities were, for instance, the Turnpike Trustees or the various types of Street Commissioners, established by Local Acts. With all these authorities we deal in another work. It must suffice here to note that, although affecting limited areas, they did not constitute exceptions to the rule of the County. They might, in fact, without inconsistency with the County or with each other, have been multiplied so as to cover the whole area.

The proportion of the Local Government of England that was, in 1689, carried on, whether by prescription, by Charter, or by statute, in the form of exemptions from or exclusions of County jurisdiction, was far larger than is commonly supposed.

Thus, with a few insignificant exceptions, the whole force of police that then existed owed its appointment neither to the Parish nor the County, but to Manorial Courts or Municipal Corporations; whilst the magistracy of the large towns was provided, not by the Commission of the Peace, but by the Mayors, Aldermen, and Recorders. The suppression of nuisances, which comprised at that time nearly the whole regulative activity of local authorities, was practically monopolised by the Leets of private Lords and of enfranchised Boroughs; for the recovery of small debts, the Court Baron of the Lord, or its municipal analogue, often called the Court of Record or the Court of Pleas, had largely ousted the Court of the Sheriff of the County at large. Markets and fairs were matters neither of Parish nor of County concern, but were under the control of the individual or Corporate owners of Franchises; whilst many lay and clerical Lords, and most Municipal Corporations, had their own gaols, if no longer their own privileges of "pit and gallows." More important than these common services, which, in 1689, were still small in extent, was the administration of the land, a service not now usually connected with Local Government. But even at the end of the seventeenth century, no small fraction of the surface of the Kingdom was still managed by or in connection with those local governing authorities that we class as Seignorial Franchises and Municipal Corporations. In thousands of rural Manors the rotation of crops, the dates at which the various agricultural operations should be undertaken, the management of the pastures, quarries, and fisheries, the care of the cattle, and the breeding of stock formed part of the business of the same open "Court" that suppressed nuisances, fined minor offenders, chose the local officers, and tried petty actions for debt and damages. In hundreds of urban districts the Manorial Courts or the Municipal Corporations were administering not only the remnant of the ancient commons, but also dwelling-houses, wharves, docks, quays, piers, shambles, and market places. The tolls and dues levied by these authorities, whether by Charter, prescription, or mere ownership of the soil, formed in the aggregate no unworthy rivals of the various County and Parish Rates. By 1835, it is true, the agricultural business of these local governing bodies had, with the progress of inclosure, shrunk into insignificance. The importance of the urban properties and the revenue from tolls had, on the other hand, in many places greatly increased.

In our history of the County we showed that, in 1689, practically its whole business, from one end of England to the other, was transacted by judicial process, in open Courts of Justice, in the guise of enforcing fixed personal obligations. By 1835, as we have seen, this had been silently transformed into administration by committees, meeting in private, appointing, instructing, and controlling a salaried staff of officers according to a variable policy decided on from time to time by the committees themselves. The Seignorial Franchises and Municipal Corporations seem, at first sight, to admit of no such simple generalisation. We shall, indeed, describe the successive stages of what appears to us to be an analogous evolution. But instead of being able to trace this evolution, within the very period with which we are dealing, in the life-history of one vigorous organism, what we have is rather a collection of apparently heterogeneous individuals, showing signs of having been arrested in their development at different stages of their growth; some remaining in a rudimentary state; some even reverting to simpler types; and some, again, standing still at what seems full maturity. Those local governing authorities that we describe in our chapters on "The Lord's Court" and "The Court in Ruins" never developed, from first to last, anything beyond the machinery of a judicial tribunal, designed to enforce pre-existing rights and obligations. In subsequent chapters we shall describe, under the terms the "Lordless Court," the "Lord's Borough," and the "Enfranchised Manorial Borough," organisations marked by the possession of specialised administrative structure of various grades of complexity, from the mere creation of one or two new officers and the custody of a common purse up to a full equipment of Mayor, Aldermen, and Common Councillors, but exhibiting during the whole century and a half little or no development, and in some cases even retrograding to the simpler form of a Lord's Court. The more highly organised bodies that we analyse in our various chapters on Municipal Corporations— usually, we may observe, exhibiting no great tendency to develop — have in their constitutions the administrative structure predominant, whilst the judicial tribunals and judicial processes have sunk to a subordinate, and sometimes to an insignificant position. It adds to the complexity, and, as we think, to the impression produced of arrested development, that, so far as the period between 1689 and 1835 is concerned, we find all the different types coexisting in each successive decade. In 1835 there were still rural Manors in which the archaic Lord's Court provided the local services by the enforcement of ancient personal obligations. Already, in 1689, the Corporation of the City of London was transacting its extensive business by an administrative apparatus more highly developed than that of the most advanced County a hundred and fifty years later—apparatus more complicated than any modern constitution can show.

Yet in face of this apparent heterogeneity, and of what we may call the sluggishness of development among our various individuals, the very multitude of the specimens, and their variety in detail, enables us to set them out in such an order that they are seen, alike in constitution and in function, to pass almost imperceptibly one into another. Nor is it only between the separate organisms themselves that there are no sharp dividing lines. In particular instances we may see the Court Leet and View of Frankpledge becoming inextricably confused with the General Sessions of the Peace; the Court Baron or Customary Court with the Borough Court of Record or Court of Pleas; and the Jury of either or both of these Manorial Courts with the Court of Common Council. The student, we suggest, will find it impracticable to regard the various individuals otherwise than as members of one and the same genus; nor, we must add, otherwise than as units in an ascending series. There is, in fact, no logical stopping point, when all the specimens are reviewed, between the most insignificant Court of a petty Lord of the Manor, held once or twice a year at his Hall, for the admission of a new tenant or the appointment of the Constable, and the many-chartered Corporation of the Mayor, Aldermen, and Commonalty of the

City of London; an all-embracing government in perpetual session; a County of itself, controlling the services of the most important mercantile port in the world; administering a revenue of regal magnificence; and exercising judicial and even legislative functions, asserted to be independent of the High Court of Parliament itself.

We do not wish to assert that this ascending series of surviving specimens necessarily represents the successive stages in the life-history of the most fully-developed Chartered Municipality. Such a hypothesis we leave to be tested by the historians of the Manor and the Borough. It is, indeed, plain, even on a survey of what existed between 1689 and 1835, that part of the Municipal structure and some Municipal functions are not to be found, even in germ, in any Manorial origin. The historian must take account of those ancient shire towns distinguished by heterogeneity of tenure.[1] Also the remnant of Gild organisation clinging to many eighteenth century Municipalities—possibly even the frequent admission to the Freedom of the Corporation by Servitude of Apprenticeship—points to an ancestry unconnected with the Manor. We must, moreover, not forget the working of the imitative faculty, and of the tendency to assimilation. A constitution which had, by custom and by law, developed out of one form of association may be subsequently adopted by, or imposed upon, other groups of persons associated together for quite other reasons. But whether or not our classification suggests any plausible theory of the growth of the Manor and the development of the Borough, some such classification of the ascending series of franchises and immunities, exemptions and privileges, customs and powers, that existed between 1689 and 1835 outside the County and over and above the Parish, is indispensable to any adequate survey of English Local Government.

A thoroughly intelligent description of these Seignorial Franchises and Municipal Corporations, even as they existed in 1689, would require an historical erudition that we do not possess. Already in the seventeenth century these mediæval institutions had fallen more or less into decay, leaving, in the

---

[1] *Township and Borough*, by Prof. F. W. Maitland, 1898; *The Domesday Boroughs*, by A. Ballard, 1906.

majority of cases, only disconnected fragments of what we may assume to have once been a complicated if not a systematic structure. Without an adequate knowledge of what exactly was the Manor in its prime, and of the part played by the Borough in the local government of the twelfth century, it is difficult, and sometimes impossible, to trace and to understand the significance of such remnants as remained at the end of the seventeenth century. Our lack of knowledge of what the organism in its maturity was and did necessarily hampers our interpretation of its remains. A further difficulty is caused by the fact that these remnants, in many cases, did not remain unaltered. In the Municipal Corporation in particular, the new growths of the seventeenth and eighteenth centuries are often found inextricably twined about the old structure—the gain by accretion coming, in some specimens, to be more than equivalent to the loss by decay. In the case of some of the larger and more populous Chartered Municipalities, such as Norwich and Bristol, Nottingham and Southampton, the development of a Corporate Magistracy so completely submerged the more ancient structure, whether Gild or Manorial, that we might almost have described them as particular varieties of a specialised form of the County; whilst in the exceptional instance of the City of London, one or more of its outgrowths—its so-called Commission of Sewers, if not also its Corporation of the Poor—might, in addition, have conveniently been classed with the Statutory Bodies for Special Purposes that we shall describe in the succeeding volume.

CHAPTER I

THE LORD'S COURT

In many parishes of England, town as well as country, we find existing, in the latter part of the seventeenth century, a sort of local governing authority that was neither Parish Vestry nor County Justices, neither Statutory Body nor Municipal Corporation, but one or other tattered remnant of the old jurisdiction of the Manor.   Here and there would be found public officers exercising peculiar functions under strange titles.   An Aleconner or a Pinder, a Swine-ringer or a Burleyman, a Common Driver or a Constable—sometimes even a vaguely influential potentate called a Portreeve or a Boroughreeve—derived his authority neither from the meeting of the inhabitants in Vestry assembled, nor from the Justices of the Peace ; neither from Statute nor from Charter. Once or twice a year a "Court" would be held, to which people would resort, for purposes they scarcely knew what. At this "Court Leet," or "Halmot Court," or "Soke Court," or "Court Baron," or "Forest Court," or "Hundred Court," or "Swainmoot," or "Lawday," as it was variously styled in different instances, all sorts of matters of common interest, as well as questions connected with individual property rights, might be dealt with.   In one place all transfers of copyhold property, on death or on alienation, would be registered with quaint ceremonies, accompanied by the exaction of customary fines and fees.   In another, various arrangements about the commonfield agriculture, the "town bull and boar," the use of the "town's plough," or the management of the common pasture would form the bulk of the business.   In others, again, the presentment of nuisances and the condemnation

of offenders to a fine would seem to fill the greatest place.
It was in such a Court, as Butler tells us in *Hudibras*, that
the villagers would

> . . . impeach a broken hedge,
> And pigs unringed ; at Vis. Franc. Pledge,
> Discover thieves, bawds, and recusants,
>   .   .   .
> Tell who did play at games unlawful,
> And who filled pots of ale but half-full.[1]

What was invariable in such a Court was the appointment of
one or more officers ; and the plain citizen, to whom the
Manor had seemed but a harmless antiquity, might discover
that he had been summarily chosen to discharge some onerous
public function without fee or reward, or that he had been
condemned to pay a small fine for this or that offence against
the well-being of the little community.[2]

---

[1] *Hudibras*, by Samuel Butler, Canto II. It will be remembered that
Shakespeare makes Christopher Sly, in his " very idle words "—

> Rail upon the hostess of the house
> And say *you would present her at the Leet*
> Because she brought stone jugs and no seal'd quarts.
>   (*Taming of the Shrew*, Induction, Scene ii.).

[2] We know of no adequate study of the Lord's Court, as an organ of Local
Government, from the beginning to the end of its development. By far the
most authoritative, as well as the most interesting, account of its actual form
and working is to be gathered from the various writings of Professor F. W.
Maitland ; notably his *Select Pleas in Manorial and other Seignorial Courts*,
1889, and *The Court Baron*, 1891, both volumes of the Selden Society ; and
The History of English Law, by Sir F. Pollock and F. W. Maitland, 1895,
vol. i. For the latest discussion of the conflicting views see *Surveys Historic
and Economic*, by Prof. W. J. Ashley, 1900, and *The Growth of the Manor*, by
Professor Vinogradoff, 1905. Useful bibliographies will be found in Miss F. G.
Davenport's *Classified List of Original Materials for English Manorial and
Agrarian History*, 1894 ; and *The Manor and Manorial Records*, by N. J.
Hone, 1906. Bacon gives a clear account of the functions of the Court Leet in
his *Answers to Questions proposed by Sir Alexander Hay touching the Office of
Constable*, 1608, and in vol. vii. pp. 748-754 of the 1858 edition of his *Works* ;
and its relation to other judicial institutions is well stated in *The History of
English Law*, by Professor W. S. Holdsworth, 1903. Among the numerous
legal treatises and manuals for Stewards—not to speak of half-a-dozen archaic
works of the sixteenth century—we may mention *The Order of Keeping a Court
Leet and Court Baron*, by Jonas Adames, 1593 ; *Jurisdictions, or the Lawful
Authority of Courts Leet, etc.*, by John Kitchin, 1598 (and about fourteen other
editions in English or French down to 1675) ; *The Complete Copyholder*, by Sir
Edward Coke, 1630 (and half-a-dozen other editions down to 1764) ; *The
Relation between a Lord of the Manor and the Copyholder his Tenant*, by Charles
Calthorpe, 1635 ; *The Court-Keeper's Guide, etc.*, by William Sheppard, 1641

(a) The Lawyer's view of the Lord's Court

The common bewilderment as to the meaning of the Lord's Court was not shared by the authors of the elaborate manuals of its jurisdiction and procedure, prepared for the instruction of Stewards and others who had the duty of "keeping Courts." In these popular manuals we find displayed a clear-cut theory of the origin, exact constitution, and precise functions of the Courts of Lords of Manors, asserted with an assurance that may usefully be contrasted with the modesty of conjecture of such modern investigators as Professors Maitland and Vinogradoff. We may, in the twentieth century, doubt whether "the methodically learned John Kitchin of 1 Gray's Inn, Esquire, and Double Reader"

(and about eight other editions down to 1791); *Treatise of the Antiquity, Authority, Uses, and Jurisdiction of the Ancient Courts of Leet*, by Robert Powell, 1642, 1688; *The Authority . . . of . . . County Courts, Courts Leet, and Courts Baron*, by William Greenwood, 1st edition, 1668, 9th edition, 1730; *Lex Custumaria*, by S. C[arter], 1701 (other editions to 1796); *Practice of Courts Leet and Courts Baron*, by Sir William Scroggs, 1st edition, 1714, 4th edition, 1728; *The Complete Court-Keeper*, by Giles Jacob, 1st edition, 1713, 8th edition, 1819; *Lex Maneriorum*, by W. Nelson, 1728; *History of the High Court of Parliament . . . and . . . of Court Baron and Court Leet*, by T. Gurdon, 1731; *The Complete Steward*, by John Mordant, 1761; *Jurisdiction of the Courts Leet*, by Joseph Ritson, 1791; *Practical Treatise on Copyhold Tenure, etc.*, by R. B. Fisher, 1794, 1804; *Treatise on Copyholds*, by Charles Watkins, 1st edition, 1797, 4th edition, 1825; *Laws respecting Copyhold and Court-Keeping, etc.*, by Henry Fellowes, 1799; *Practical Treatise on Copyhold Tenure*, by John Scriven, first edition, 1816, seventh edition, 1896; *Copyhold and Court-keeping Practice*, by Rolla Rouse, 1837; *The Law of Copyholds*, by Leonard Shelford, 1853; and especially *The Law of Copyholds*, by C. I. Elton and H. J. H. Mackay, 2nd edition, 1893. The last-named work (with those of Watkins and Scriven) we have found the most useful. An admirable account of a mediæval Manor will be found in *The Economic Development of a Norfolk Manor*, 1086-1565, by Miss F. G. Davenport, 1906. For references to MS. Manor Rolls, see p. 116. The most complete series of published records of a Court Leet, extending from 1552 to 1846, is *The Court Leet Records of the Manor of Manchester*, edited by J. P. Earwaker, twelve vols., 1884-1890. *The Durham Halmote Rolls* (Surtees Society) and *Leet Jurisdiction in the City of Norwich*, by Rev. W. Hudson, 1892 (Selden Society), may be consulted for earlier proceedings. The best descriptions known to us of the actual proceedings of Courts Leet in the nineteenth century are those of the Court at Ashton-under-Lyne in 1844 (Health of Towns Commission, First Report, Appendix, vol. ii. pp. 71-73); of the Court at Berkeley in 1890, in *Gloucestershire Notes and Queries*, vol. iv. 1890, p. 27; and of the Court at Durham in 1805, in *Memorials of S. Giles', Durham*, edited by J. Barmby, 1896, p. 7. See also *History of the English Landed Interest*, by R. M. Garnier, 1892, ch. xxix. and xxx. We know of no work describing the part played by the Lord's Court between 1689 and 1835.

knew quite as much about the origin and early development of the Court Leet and Court Baron as he supposed. Even what he described as its contemporary nomenclature and procedure was, as we shall presently show, unlike the actual facts of many of the Courts that were being held around him. But such treatises as Kitchin's *Jurisdictions* and Jacob's *Complete Court-Keeper* had a significance not possessed by any similar handbooks for parish officers or Justices. The Overseers of the Poor and the Surveyors of Highways, like the Clerk of the Peace, could turn to numerous statutes authoritatively defining their powers and duties. But the Lord's Court was not the creation of any Act of Parliament. There was not even a Royal Charter prescribing its constitution or procedure. In default of any authoritative document, the Steward whom the Lord appointed to hold his Court naturally accepted the guidance of the contemporary legal manuals. Hence the perpetual republishing and elaborating of these manuals by a succession of legal experts can hardly have failed to have tended gradually to transform the Courts as they were into the Courts as the lawyers thought they ought to be. Moreover, the legal theory of the seventeenth century has, for us, a further value. It preserves some of the spirit which had inspired the Manorial Courts in their prime, without some understanding of which their function can hardly be appreciated. Before describing the fragments of Manorial Jurisdiction actually forming part of English Local Government between 1689 and 1835, we think it, therefore, convenient to give in outline the constitution, procedure, and functions attributed to the Lord's Court by the contemporary legal authors.

We note, first, that, in the lawyer's view, we have before us not one Lord's Court, but several; with different constitutions and functions, different procedures and officers. There is evident a tendency to elaboration, one learned authority making out as many as five different Courts.[1] But this

---

[1] In R. B. Fisher's *Practical Treatise on Copyhold Tenure*, 1794, these are given as the Court Leet, the View of Frankpledge, the Court Baron, the Customary Court, and the Court of Survey. But there is no evidence that there was ever a separate Court called the View of Frankpledge, this being merely a duty undertaken by the Sheriff's Turn and afterwards by the Lord's Court (as Court Leet). The Court of Survey (occasionally called also "Court

elaboration and distinction was largely, if not entirely, analytic. The models for procedure offered to Stewards constantly assumed that the various kinds of Court would be held at one and the same time, as connected parts of what was in fact a single sessions of one and the same tribunal. We are unable to find—contrary to a common impression—that even the most punctilious lawyer asserted that the several Courts which he analytically distinguished ought, as a matter of law, always to be held at different times or at different places. So far as analytic distinction was concerned, the Courts resolved themselves, in the lawyer's view, into two sharply contrasted tribunals, the Court Baron and Customary Court on the one hand, and the Court Leet and View of Frankpledge on the other.[1]

(b) The Court Baron

The Great Court of the Manor, or Court Baron, was, in the lawyers' view, essentially a private Court of the Lord, necessarily incident to every Manor, having for its object the maintenance of the rights of the Lord against his tenants and of the privileges of the tenants against the Lord, together with the settlement of their mutual differences and the organisation of their common affairs. It was not a Court of Record, but a private jurisdiction forming part of the estate and property of the Lord. The Court was to be summoned by notice given by the Steward to the Reeve or Bailiff, and by him affixed to the Church door, or handed to the Parish Clerk to be read in Church, according

---

of the Supervisor"—see *Seven Somerton Court Rolls*, by A. Ballard; *Transactions of Oxfordshire Archæological Society*, 1906) was only a special sitting of the Court Baron, at which every tenant of the Manor had to produce his title, and special inquiry was made of the mutual rights and privileges of Lord and tenants. It was "generally held immediately upon the descending of a Manor to a new Lord, or upon the purchase of a Manor, to inform the new owner of every respective estate which he has a right to as Lord, and the tenure and customs by which they are held" (*The Laws respecting Copyholds and Court-keeping*, by Henry Fellowes, 1799, p. 43). Elaborate details of what a Court of Survey should inquire into are given in *The Surveyor's Dialogue*, by John Norden, originally published in 1607, and in a fourth edition in 1738 (see pp. 120-213).

[1] That the legal manuals from the thirteenth century onward distinctly contemplated the holding, in one undivided sessions, of all the two, three, four, or even five Courts that they analytically distinguished, will be clear to any one who examines the model agenda for the sessions that most of them supply. In this agenda the items belonging to the several Courts are inter-

to local usage.[1]   It was to be presided over by the Lord or
his Steward, and had to be attended by all the tenants of the
Manor, whether freeholders or copyholders.   Neglect to attend
the Court—subtraction, or non-performance of suit of Court—
was punishable in the absence of an "essoin," or excuse
admitted as sufficient, by a fine, and theoretically even by

mingled; and one Jury after another is to be sworn and charged.   As in the
Court rolls, so in "the manuals for Stewards which come to us from the
thirteenth and fourteenth centuries, we cannot discover two Courts or two
methods of constituting the Court" (*History of English Law*, by Sir F. Pollock
and F. W. Maitland, 1895, vol. i. p. 581).   The later manuals are to the
same effect.   "After the Steward has gone through his charge to the jurors
of the Court Leet," says Sir William Scroggs, "he may proceed to his charge
to the Homagers or Court Baron" (*The Practice of Courts Leet and Courts Baron*,
by Sir William Scroggs, 4th edition, 1728, p. 22).   Even Sir Edward Coke
alludes to Courts "of this double nature."   The common practice "where
a Court Leet and Court Baron are held together" is referred to (*ibid.* p. 11;
Lex Custumaria, by S. C[arter], 1701, p. 73); or "where the three Courts are
held at the same time" (*Practical Treatise on Copyhold Tenure*, by R. B. Fisher,
1794, p. 167).   The five necessary attributes of the Lord's Court, according to
a widely read authority, were "The Lord is chief to command and appoint,
the Steward to direct and record, the freeholders to affeer and judge, the
copyholders to inform and present, the Bailiff to attend and execute"—thus
merging the Customary Court with the Court Baron (*The Authority, Jurisdiction, and Method of Keeping County Courts, Courts Leet, and Courts Baron*, by
W. Greenwood, 9th edition, 1730, pp. 309-405).   So, too, in the hundred
pages of "customs" of particular Manors given by Watkins, the items belonging
to the Court Baron, Customary Court, and Court Leet are not distinguished
one from another (*A Treatise on Copyholds*, by Charles Watkins, 4th edition,
1825, vol. ii. pp. 477-576).   "The various Courts," says an able antiquary,
"were conducted very much on the same lines in all Manors; that is, all
business connected with the transfer of land was duly settled, presentments
were made of the tenants for various offences, as trespass, assault, blood-
drawing, drunkenness, pound - breaking, disorderly conduct, etc., and for
disobeying sanitary regulations in not cleansing ditches.   Actions between
tenants were tried, an immense boon to them, for they had a Court of Justice
in their own locality, acquainted with the parties to the suit and the witnesses"
(*The History of Dulwich College*, by W. Young, 1889; vol. ii. ch. ii., on the
Court Rolls, by F. B. Bickley, p. 266).   In fact, any careful student of the
lawyers' treatises, as of the Court Rolls, will, notwithstanding all the analytic
differentiation, have no difficulty in inferring of the Courts which they are
describing that—as Professor Maitland tells us of those of the thirteenth
century—"the Court which had been enforcing the customs of the Manor did
not become some other Court when it turned to punish breaches of the peace
or to adjudicate upon actions of debt between the tenants; a lawyer might
analyse its powers, might insist that some were royal franchises, while others
were not, but all its powers, whatever they might be, were used in the mass
and apparently with little thought as to the various titles by which they had
been acquired" (*Select Pleas in Manorial and other Seignorial Courts*, by
Prof. F. W. Maitland, 1889, p. xviii; see also *History of English Law*, by Prof.
W. S. Holdsworth, 1903, pp. 68-69).

[1] *Practical Treatise on Copyhold Tenure*, by John Scriven, 1816, pp. 433-449.
It was said that at least sixteen days' notice ought to be given (*The Order of
Keeping a Court Leet and Court Baron*, by Jonas Adames, 1593, p. 1).

forfeiture of the tenement. The "free suitors," or freehold tenants of the Manor, holding of the Lord, in fee simple, land liable to escheat to him, were assumed to constitute the Homage ; and the presence of at least two such freeholders, if not three,[1] was declared to be indispensable to a legal Court Baron. But as subinfeudation had been forbidden since the Statute of Quia Emptores in 1290 there were, by 1689, few Manors in which this condition could be complied with ; and the lawyers had been driven to assert that a "Customary Court Baron" could be held in the presence of copyholders only, who themselves constituted the Homage.[2] And by special custom, there might be separate Homages or Juries, sometimes of freeholders and copyholders respectively, having distinct functions. "If," said a writer of 1656, "the custom of the place be to make two or more Juries, or one Grand Jury and divers Petit Juries, it is good to observe it."[3]

The Court was to be opened by formal proclamation and summons to all concerned to attend. The roll of those owing "suit of Court" had to be read, and the names noted of those who were present. The "essoins" of the absentees were to be received and considered, and the defaulters to be fined. The Homage or Jury was then to be sworn, four at a time ; and the Steward had to address to them a formal "charge." The judgments of the Court were made either by the whole "Homage," or by a Jury of Homagers,[4] and they were embodied in the form of presentments to the Court, which were accepted and pronounced by the Steward.

The principal business of the Court was to declare and enforce the ancient customs of the Manor, which, whether relating

---

[1] In the Manor of Dymock (Gloucestershire) the legal quorum was, by custom, three ; see the "customs" as elaborately recorded in an indenture of 1565, enrolled in Chancery in 1657 ; mentioned in *Jurisdictions*, by John Kitchin, in 1598 ; and given in *A Treatise on Copyholds*, by C. Watkins, 4th edition, 1825, vol. ii. pp. 487-491.

[2] *The Relation between the Lord of the Manor and the Copyholder his Tenant*, by Charles Calthorpe, 1635, p. 72.

[3] *The Court-Keeper's Guide*, by William Sheppard, 1656, p. 20. "In some cases," said the lawyers, "the Steward may impanel a second Jury to inquire into the concealments of the first, and fine them" (*The Practice of Courts Leet and Courts Baron*, by Sir William Scroggs, 4th edition, 1728, p. 16).

[4] "Out of the copyholders choose your Homage," says a manual (*Laws respecting Copyholds and Court-keeping*, by Henry Fellowes, 1799, pp. 32-43).

to the incidents of land tenure, or to the use of the common fields or waste, were legally binding on both the Lord and his tenants.   At one Court annually, the Manorial officers were to be appointed——the Reeve or Greave, or Bailiff, who collected the Lord's quit-rents and heriots, his " fines certain " and "fines arbitrary," his " work silver " and his "customary penny," his " chevage " and " childwite," his " boscage " and "foldage "; the Beadle, who gathered in the fines and amercements;   the Hayward, who had in charge the common or waste;[1] some-times a Common Driver or a Herdsman, a Hog-ringer or a Swineherd, a Woodward or a " Greave of the Moors," a " Sur-veyor of Hedges " to see that the tenants enclosed during seed-time and harvest,[2] or other officers connected with the customary privileges of the community.   These officers were in the vast majority of cases "presented by the Homage "— sometimes several persons for the Steward to choose one. The question of liability to service in the several offices, and of the remuneration, if any, for such service, was deter-mined by the ancient customs of the Manor in each case. Moreover, the Court was said to have a vaguely defined power to enact By-laws, binding on all the tenants of the Manor, at least in matters, such as the use of the waste, in which they had a common interest.   It was the business of the Homage or Jury also to make presentments of escheats and surrenders of tenements, and of the death of any tenant of the Lord ; of dower and freebench, of " waste," " emblements," and " botes."   New tenants had also to be admitted by the Steward, on payment of the customary fees and fines, and with due per-

[1] It does not seem possible to accept Mrs. Grote's simple etymology which made Hayward = hogwarden (*Some Account of the Hamlet of East Burnham*, by a Resident, *i.e.* Harriet Grote, London, 1858, p. 28) ; nor is the later identifi-cation of Hayward with hedgewarden more trustworthy.   The duties of the mediæval Hayward, harvestman or reaper (in Latin, *messor* or *messarius*), a mere farm servant, "who seems to have acted sometimes as pounder," are fully described by Walter de Henley ; see also pp. xxv and xxxiii of *The Durham Halmot Rolls* (Surtees Society, 1889), and at p. 140 of *The Court Baron* (edited by F. W. Maitland and W. P. Baildon for the Selden Society, 1891).   The word is used for shepherd in the "Journal of a Gloucestershire Justice, 1715-1756," in *Law Magazine and Review*, vol. ix. p. 280.   But in the sixteenth and seventeenth centuries the Hayward might act in almost any capacity as an officer of the Lord's Court.   Kitchin gives the title as synonymous with Greave or Beadle (*Jurisdictions, etc.*, by John Kitchin, p. 93 of edition of 1675).

[2] As at Gnossall (Staffordshire) ; see *The Manor and Manorial Records*, by N. J. Hone, 1906, p. 193.

formance of the ancient ceremonies of the Manor.[1] The Court, moreover, had the important function of hearing plaints and deciding disputes. It had, said Kitchin, been "ordained to determine injuries, trespasses, debts, and other actions,"[2] at any rate among the tenants of the Manor, and by immemorial custom, also actions against mere residents within the Manor ; but in all cases limited, by the judges' construction of an ambiguous statute, to actions for less than forty shillings.[3] It might or might not examine witnesses, as the freeholders, who were both the judges and the jurymen, chose to decide.[4] The Court could be held anywhere within the Manor, or, by custom,

[1] See the extensive collection of the customs of particular Manors recorded in *A Treatise on Copyholds*, by Charles Watkins, 4th edition, 1825, pp. 477-576.

[2] *Jurisdictions, etc.*, by John Kitchin, 1598, p. 6. "A Court Baron," says another authority, "consisteth of the Lord, Tenants, Steward, and Bailiff within the Manor, and is sometimes called the Copyholders' Court, especially when it is for trial of titles of their lands, for taking and passing estates, surrenders, admittances, and grants ; and herein the Lord or his Steward is judge (as the custom of the place is) ; yet this Court is sometimes called the Freeholders' Court, when the actions and proceedings are for trial under 40s., and is something like a County Court, and the proceeding much the same, and was without doubt granted to the Lord originally by the King ; but now most are by prescription, and are commonly held once in three weeks, and may be as often as the Lord or Steward thinks fit, who is supreme judge in law and equity" (*The Practice of Courts Leet and Courts Baron*, by Sir William Scroggs, 4th edition, 1728, pp. 39-40).

[3] The Statute of Gloucester, 1278, limiting actions in the King's Courts to cases in which not less than 40s. was at issue, was construed by the judges as forbidding such actions in the County Court and Court Baron (*Select Pleas in Manorial Courts*, by F. W. Maitland, p. lvi). At Dover, by custom, the Lord's Court had jurisdiction without limit of 40s. (*Jurisdictions*, by John Kitchin, 1598) ; and in at least several scores of Manors—possibly those once connected with such ecclesiastical corporations as the Knights of St. John—the Court had jurisdiction in probate and testamentary cases (*Treatise on the Law of Copyholds*, by John Scriven, 7th edition, 1896, p. 423). The wills proved in nearly fifty such Courts, between 1562 and 1815, are now deposited at Somerset House, London, or at various diocesan registries (see the list in *The Manor and Manorial Records*, by N. J. Hone, 1906, pp. 22, 302).

[4] *The Practice of Courts Leet and Courts Baron*, by Sir William Scroggs, 4th edition, 1728, p. 3. Whether the Court had anciently heard counsel or allowed appearance by attorney is not clear. That it did so in places in the eighteenth century is plain, but we suspect that this was exceptional. We read in 1731 of "the Freeholders' Court having lost most of its business, lawyers and attorneys not finding an account in giving attendance there for one or two cases, and the parties finding it difficult to have the assistance of lawyers there" (*The History of the High Court of Parliament . . . and . . . of Court Baron and Court Leet*, by T. Gurdon, 1731, vol. ii. p. 610). Occasionally even leading counsel would appear. At a "Baronial Court" held in the archiepiscopal Manor of Lambeth in 1828, with a Jury of copyholders, both the Attorney-General and Henry Brougham were engaged for the several parties in a copyhold case (Angell *v.* Angell ; see *Times*, January 7, 1828).

in one Manor for other Manors belonging to the same Lord. It could be called together whenever the Lord or his Steward chose, without unreasonably inconveniencing the tenants; but usually, by custom, it was to be held every three weeks—a period apparently derived from a Writ of Henry III. to the Sheriff of Lincoln, authorising the Courts of the Lords to be so held,[1] whence they were frequently termed Three Weeks' Courts. Finally, as was eventually decided by the Court of King's Bench in 1822, neither the right to hold such a Court, nor its jurisdiction in petty actions, was lost by mere non-user; so that it could be revived after a lapse of half a century.[2]

We have said above that the lawyers declared the Court Baron to be a private jurisdiction of the Lord of the Manor, and not a public tribunal. But we must warn the student against a misunderstanding by which we ourselves were long misled. When it was held that the Court Baron was of private, not of public nature, those words were used in a sense very different from that nowadays given to them. All that the lawyers meant was that the Court Baron was not a Court of the King, to be held only by his authority or subject to his will. What the modern student has to bear in mind is that the Court Baron, however little of its power it may have owed to the King, had within its sphere no small part of the administration of the common affairs of the inhabitants of the Manor. It was, in fact, an organ of local government, alike legislative, executive, and judicial in function, with attributes that we shall, in our subsequent analysis, find of considerable interest. It was the Court Baron, and not the Court Leet, that had jurisdiction over the commonfield agriculture that survived, in many cases, down to the nineteenth century, and over the common pastures and wastes that were destined in certain places to become streets of dwelling-houses, market-places, wharves, and docks. It was the Court Baron, and not the Court Leet, that could claim authority over fisheries and weirs, and generally over the banks and channels of rivers and estuaries, out of which

[1] Close Roll of 18 Henry III.; see *The Law of Copyholds*, by C. I. Elton and H. J. H. Mackay, 2nd edition, 1893, p. 300.

[2] R. *v.* Steward of Manor of Havering atte Bower, 1822; in *Reports of Cases, etc.*, by E. V. Barnewall and E. H. Alderson, 1822, vol. v. pp. 691-692; *Reports of Cases, etc.*, by James Dowling and A. Ryland, 1823, vol. ii. pp. 176-177.

might spring prescriptive rights to tolls and dues. It was the Court Baron, and not the Court Leet, that provided the tribunal for the trial of petty actions for debt and trespass, which we shall see figuring prominently among the Courts by which the autonomy of Manorial Boroughs and Municipal Corporations was built up. It was the Court Baron, and not the Court Leet, that chose the Reeve, the chief local officer of the little community, who became responsible for collecting the money tributes due to the Lord of the Manor, exactly as the chief officer of the Manorial Borough[1] was responsible to the Lord for his quit-rents, or as the Mayor of the fully-developed Municipal Corporation was answerable for the "farm" of the Borough to the King. Finally, it was the Court Baron, not the Court Leet, that contributed what became the predominant principle of eighteenth-century Local Government—common consent and local autonomy— the Homage being, unlike the Leet Jury, themselves the judges of the Court, interpreting, and therefore developing, the Customs of the Manor as if these concerned themselves alone, without the intervention of the Lord or his Steward, and without reference to the interests of the rest of the community. To the lawyer the Court Baron of the Manor might seem essentially a law court, "the lowest judicial unit of the Kingdom." But "in practice though primarily a law court, the Manor Court would also serve as the administrative and, in some sense, as the legislative organ of the community of the Manor."[2] "The majority of homagers," noted a learned Steward of the seventeenth century, "sworn at the Lord's Court, for the better preservation of order, have, time beyond memory of all men, used, with the Lord's consent, to make By-laws, as well for the stinting and limiting the number, as for appointing times for the putting the tenants' cattle into the common pastures, wastes, and commons of the Manor. And such By-laws, made with reasonable penalties, and clauses for distress for such penalties, have, by the time aforesaid, been binding and concluding to all the tenants of the Manor. The like orders and consent bind for the mending

---

[1] See Chap. III. "The Manorial Borough."
[2] *History of Municipal Government in Liverpool*, by Prof. Ramsay Muir, 1906, p. 2.

of tenants' ways, and for the establishment of the common
good, and preventing of public annoyances, provided that such
orders crossed not the law or statutes of the Kingdom."[1]   It
may be that it was the Court Leet and View of Frankpledge
that gradually assumed the greater prominence in those places
in which the Lord's Court continued, without further development, to be the local governing authority.   But it is the
constitution and legal attributes of the Court Baron that we
shall presently find of equal, if not of greater, significance
in our description of the Manorial Boroughs and our analysis
of the Municipal Corporations.

Such being the importance of what we may term the
Court Baron aspect of the Lord's Court, we may be pardoned
for drawing the attention of the sociological student to one
of its attributes, unnoticed by the lawyers, which had, we
suggest, an adverse influence on its eighteenth-century development.   The common agreement upon which rests the authority
of a modern Municipality is that of inhabitants at large—that
is, of the consumers of its services.   The Court Baron, on
the other hand, was essentially the organ, not of the citizens
or consumers as such, but of the occupying owners of
agricultural land—that is to say, it belonged to the genus of
Associations of Producers.[2]   The student of other types of
Associations of Producers will not be surprised to find the
Homage resenting the intrusion of "foreigners" and the
invasion of the commons by "landless residents."   The same
spirit led to the exaction of tolls and dues in the market and
at the landing stage from those who had not been admitted
as tenants of the Manor ; and led, even in unincorporated
villages, to the Reeve, as representative of the Homage,

---

[1] *History and Antiquities of Lewes*, by T. W. Horsfield, 1824, vol. i. p. 179
(quoting a document of 1662).

[2] By the term "Associations of Producers" we mean societies or communities of persons who are engaged in the production of commodities or
services, and who themselves own or control the whole or part of the material
instruments of production, or are otherwise self-directing.   The best known
examples of such associations are the Merchant and Trade Gilds of the Middle
Ages and, in our own generation, what are called Productive Co-operative
Societies or "self-governing workshops" (to be distinguished from the so-called
Distributive Co-operative Societies or "stores," which do also much production,
and are Associations of Consumers).   See, on the whole subject, *The Co-
operative Movement in Great Britain*, by Beatrice Potter (Mrs. Sidney Webb),
1900.

charging a fee to such persons for the privilege of opening a shop. It was, we suggest, the fact that the Court Baron had the attributes that belong to an Association of Producers, that caused it, as we shall see in our account of the Manorial Boroughs, to develop into a close body, renewing itself by co-option, from which the ordinary inhabitant was excluded.

(c) *The Court Leet*

The Court Leet [1] and View of Frankpledge was, so the lawyers held, not a private incident to a Manor, but a public jurisdiction, a Franchise assumed to have been obtained by Royal Grant to the Lord of the Manor, with a view to spare his tenants the trouble of attending the Sheriff's Turn. Such a grant can seldom be traced except in Charters to Boroughs; but in Manors in which a Court Leet had actually been held time out of mind the grant was presumed. The Court Leet, unlike the Court Baron, was a Court of Record, and the Steward who presided was not merely its officer but an integral part of the Court itself, [2] empowered summarily to punish by fine any contempt committed in Court, and even to commit the offender to prison in default of payment. He could take a recognisance of the peace; [3] and, in fact, "in matters within the jurisdiction of the Leet, the Steward," so the lawyers held, "had [in Court] powers equal with the Justices" themselves in their own Courts. [4] It was a char-

---

[1] "The word Leet... is not to be found either in the Saxon law or in Glanvil, Bracton, Briton, Fleta, or the Mirror (our most ancient law writers), nor in any statute prior to 27 Edward III. c. 28" (*The Jurisdiction of the Courts Leet*, by J. Ritson, 3rd edition, 1816, p. 1; *A Short Treatise of the History and Antiquities and Jurisdiction of all the Courts of Law*, by Henry Aldridge, 1835, p. 193). The word seems to be of East Anglian local usage. "Towards the end of the thirteenth century the word Leet (leta), which seems to have spread outward from the East Anglian counties, was becoming a common name for such a Court" (*History of English Law*, by Sir F. Pollock and F. W. Maitland, vol. i. book ii. ch. iii. sec. 5, p. 568; see also *Leet Jurisdiction in the City of Norwich*, by Rev. W. Hudson, 1892; *Select Pleas in Manorial Courts*, by F. W. Maitland, 1889, pp. xvi and lxxiii; *The Coventry Leet Book*, by M. D. Harris, 1907).

[2] Holroyd *v.* Breare and Holmes, in *Reports of Cases, etc.*, by E. V. Barnewell and E. H. Alderson, 1822, vol. ii. p. 473.

[3] 7 Henry VI. c. 12 (1429); 10 Henry VI. c. 8 (1432); 11 Henry VI. c. 7 (1433).

[4] *Practical Treatise on Copyhold Tenure*, by John Scriven, 7th edition, 1896, p. 441. For instances of the Court Leet becoming indistinguishable from the Petty or General Sessions of the Peace, see pp. 350-352.

acteristic feature of this Court that it had to be attended by the people at large. In legal theory the obligation to attend and, if required, to take part in the proceedings extended to every male resident within the Manor over twelve—some said over sixteen—years of age, who had dwelt there for a year and a day. It was, perhaps, with reference to this obligation that the 42nd section of Magna Charta had provided that these Courts were "to be held but twice a year, a month after Michaelmas and Easter." But though any " View of Frankpledge " or enrolment in tithings had long since been obsolete, the roll of the inhabitants was, in 1689, still supposed to be called over, and every one had to answer to his name.[1] New residents (or perhaps only new freeholders)

---

[1] "You must call to the Constable for a Leet Bill, which should comprehend all inhabitants of the Leet within the precinct above the age of 16 " (*The Practice of Courts Leet and Courts Baron*, by Sir William Scroggs, 4th edition, 1728, p. 18). The Statute of Marlborough (52 Henry III. c. 10) excused from attendance at the Sheriff's Turn, and impliedly at the Lord's Court, peers, ecclesiastics, and women. Prior to that statute it seems that every one over 12, including servants and women, had to attend (*Practical Treatise on Copyhold Tenure*, by John Scriven, 7th edition, 1896, p. 438). But tenants in Ancient Demesne were always held to be exempted (*The Law of Ancient Demesne*, by J. P. Yeatman, 1894 ; *Villainage in England*, by P. Vinogradoff, 1892, p. 89 ; *The Manor and Manorial Records*, by N. J. Hone, 1906, ch. vii.). How long the View of Frankpledge was kept up is uncertain. Long after the Lord's Court had lost its power of trying felonies, a great authority incidentally tells us that it "retained the duty of viewing the frankpledges . . . which it exercised, it is said, as late as 10 Henry VI. (1432) in Cornwall " (*The Tenures of Kent*, by C. I. Elton, 1867, p. 154). We owe to Mr. Seebohm an even later example. In 1470 we see the Court at Hitchin (Herts) still admitting men into "the tithing of the Lord the King"; and presenting that "John Crouche is of the age of 12 years and more, and has resided within the precinct of this View for one year and beyond, and is out of the tithing of the Lord the King. Therefore he is in mercy, and it is ordered to distrain him to put himself on the tithing of the Lord the King" (translation from MS. Court Rolls, Hitchin, portfolio 177, No. 60, in Public Record Office). We do not know whether this fining of absentees from the Lord's Court, as we see it in the eighteenth century, can be connected with the mediæval chevagium (see *Select Pleas in Manorial Courts*, by Professor F. W. Maitland, 1889, p. xxxi). "The strict theory of the law," we are told, "seems to have required that all the frankpledges should attend the view"; but as a matter of fact it was usual for none but the Chief Pledges to attend ; often, however, they had to bring with them a sum of money which was accepted in lieu of the production of their tithings " (*History of English Law*, by Sir F. Pollock and F. W. Maitland, 1895, vol. i. p. 557). It may be, as has been suggested, that the Leet Jury was composed of, or in some way represents, the Headboroughs, and that these were the heads of tithings, or Capital Pledges. In some cases, however, there seems to be no connection between the Jury and either Headboroughs or Capital Pledges ; and the fining of all tenants of the Manor seems often to be unconnected with the Leet Jury. These and other customary payments to the Manor require further study. There is, for instance, the frequent custom of

were then "sworn to be faithful and loyal to the King," all absentees being subject to a fine. Here the legal function of the ordinary inhabitant ceased. But the Bailiff or Reeve had to summon not only the inhabitants generally, but also two or three dozen of the more respectable and substantial residents to serve as jurymen, either for the occasion of the coming Court or Lawday, or, according to local custom, sometimes during the ensuing twelve months. The principal functions of this Jury were inquisitorial and judicial. It was "charged" on its appointment to discover all persons who had committed any offence against the commonweal, whether contrary to the lawful customs of the Manor or to the law of the land; and to "present" such offenders to the Court. For though the Court Leet was practically the Court of the Lord of the Manor, and was presided over by his Steward, it administered, so the lawyers said, not the Lord's will but the King's justice, and the Lord himself could be "presented" in his own Court for a breach of the law and condemned accordingly. The Court Leet was, in fact, a local criminal court—as the lawyers said, the King's Court holden by the Lord,—but the King did not

"common fine," payment made annually either by every tenant or resident, whether present in Court or not, or by the officers of particular townships on behalf of their townships. There is much reason to suppose, as Ritson declared, that this "common fine," or "certum letæ," was a payment made to excuse all the suitors but the Chief Pledges from appearing at the Court (*Jurisdiction of the Courts Leet*, by J. Ritson, 3rd edition, 1816, p. 120). At the Easter Leet of the Manor of Wimbledon (Surrey) "the Headboroughs pay a Common Fine, for Putney, 6s. 8d.; Roehampton, 2s.; Mortlake, 8s. 4d.; Barnes, 5s.; Wimbledon, formerly 8s. 4d., but abated by reason of the parsonage to 6s. 8d." (*The Law of Copyholds*, by C. Watkins, 4th edition, 1825, vol. ii. pp. 554-556). In a case brought before the Court of King's Bench a customary exaction of ten shillings each from the jurymen as Chief Pledges was upheld (*Term Reports*, vol. ii. p. 42; *Jurisdiction of the Courts Leet*, by J. Ritson, 1816, p. 100). On the other hand, this view does not explain the cases in which a payment is exacted from all and sundry, whether they attend or not. "Cert Money and Common Fine," says an eighteenth-century writer, "is a fine paid by resiants or residents of several Manors to the lords thereof, for the certain keeping of the Leet, and sometimes to the Hundred (as the Manor of Hook in Dorsetshire pays Cert Money to the Hundred of Egerdon). And Common Fine is a certain sum of money which the residents within the View of some Leets paid to the Lord thereof, called in divers places Headsilver, in others Cert Money and Headpence; and was first granted to the Lord towards the charge of his purchase of the Court Leet, whereby the residents had now the liberty of doing their Suit Royal nearer home, and not be compelled to go to the Sheriff's Turn. As in the Manor of Sheapshead in the County of Leicester, every resident pays a penny per head to the Court held after Michaelmas, which is there called Common Fine" (*The Complete Steward*, by John Mordant, 1761, vol. i. p. 37). Other synonyms were "King's Silver," "Headmoney," and "Chief Silver."

interfere either by appointing judges or other officers, or by reviewing or controlling its proceedings. It was the Lord's own Steward who presided over the Court, selected the inhabitants who were to serve as the Jury, instructed them as to their duties, and appointed, on their nomination, the Constable, the Aleconners, and the other public officers of the Manor, whilst all the fines imposed went into the pocket of the Lord, or were the perquisites of the Manorial officers.

The Court Leet differed, however, markedly from a modern criminal court both in its procedure and in the practical range of its jurisdiction. The Court, it was assumed, would act without instigation from any prosecutor, and needed to issue no summons to a defendant. Everybody was, in fact, presumed to be in attendance. The Jury presented offenders out of their own knowledge, sometimes aided by the reports of the various officers, and their presentments apparently condemned such offenders, even in their absence. There was no necessity to hear witnesses, and neither attorney nor counsel would be present,[1] though the Court would listen to a defendant in extenuation or denial of the accusation. In their presentment the Jury not only declared the defendant guilty of the offence mentioned, but also indicated the appropriate penalty. As the Court had no gaol at its command, and, as seventeenth-century lawyers held, no power of imprisonment,[2] this penalty nearly always took the form of a money

---

[1] "When they are discharged the same day," says Ritson, "it would seem necessary for them to proceed chiefly upon evidence, and indeed there is generally, if not always, a proclamation for that purpose. . . . The proceedings . . . are without expense, the suitor pays no fees, and advocates or attorneys of course never enter it" (*Jurisdiction of the Courts Leet*, by J. Ritson, 3rd edition, 1816, pp. 23-24). But, as above mentioned, lawyers did sometimes attend the Lord's Court, which was at once Court Baron and Court Leet.

[2] Coke, who always took a limited view of the power of the Lord's Court, seems first to have asserted this (*The Compleat Copyholder*, by Sir E. Coke, 1630), and it became accepted. "The Court Leet," says a law book of 1745, quoting Sir William Scroggs, "is the only Court which may fine but not imprison" (*The Justice of Peace*, by Theodore Barlow, 1745, p. 159). The stocks for drunkards (4 James I. c. 5), the pillory and tumbril for bakers and brewers (51 Henry III. st. 1, c. 6), and the ducking-stool and brank (or scold's bridle) were, however, available, and seem to have been lawfully inflicted as punishments by the Court Leet (*Jurisdiction of the Courts Leet*, by Joseph Ritson, 1816, p. 12), at any rate in the Middle Ages (see for a case in 1290, *Select Pleas in Manorial Courts*, by F. W. Maitland, 1889, p. 98). Ritson complained that Coke had taken an unduly limited view of the Court's powers (*Jurisdiction of the Courts Leet*, by Joseph Ritson, 1816, p. 19).

fine or "amercement." The presentment was then referred by the Steward to two Affeerors,[1] or officers appointed to "affeer" the amercement, by which was to be understood its final assessment at a definite money penalty, usually less than the maximum indicated for the particular class of offence. Such a fine, if not at once paid in Court, had to be collected by the Bailiffs, or Beadles, or "Serjeants" of the Manor, or, if no such officers had been appointed, by the Constable, who, with or without a Manorial distress warrant from the Steward, had power to distrain on the goods of defaulters.[2] The presentment of the Jury, made in one form and received by the Steward in Court, might be "retired" or reversed the same day, if the Steward chose to allow it, by another Jury; but was, so the lawyers held, "the day passed, as true and sacred as the Gospel," not subject to traverse or appeal, in that or any other Court.[3] Even more peculiar in modern eyes was the scope of the Court Leet's jurisdiction. As we see it in the legal text-books of the sixteenth and seventeenth centuries, it had already lost its authority over the great majority of criminal offences. "Petty treasons and felonies," says Kitchin, "are

---

[1] Whether the affeerors were chosen by the Steward or by the Jury is not clear. In the Manor of Worplesdon (Surrey) it was customary, "for the Lawday," for "one to be a freeholder, but if a Court without a Lawday" for both to be copyholders (*Treatise on Copyholds*, by C. Watkins, 4th edition, 1825, vol. ii. pp. 559-561).

[2] "A Steward may by parole command a Bailiff to make distress" (*Treatise of the Antiquity . . . of the Ancient Courts of Leet*, by Robert Powell, 1642, p. 83). "The Lord may have an action of debt or distrain for it of common right; and such distress may be taken in the streets, and be sold" (*The Justice of Peace*, by Theodore Barlow, 1745, p. 159).

[3] *Jurisdiction of the Courts Leet*, by Joseph Ritson, 1816, pp. 9-10. But though not subject to appeal, or, strictly speaking, to traverse, a presentment that affected the party's freehold property might be made the subject of complaint to the Court of King's Bench, which that Court would try. Moreover, that Court's jurisdiction in other matters was not ousted by the fact that they had been dealt with in the Lord's Court. Thus, when the Jury of the Lord's Court of the Manor of St. Giles's in the Fields on complaint of the keeping of over 400 hogs by a distiller near St. Giles's Pound, with a stench that was abominable, had formally presented that this was no nuisance, such a decision did not prevent an indictment being brought in the Court of King's Bench, when the Jury found that it was a nuisance (R. *v.* Smart, 1784; see notes of trial among the Hardwicke MSS.; *Life of Lord Chancellor Hardwicke*, by G. Harris, 1847, vol. i. pp. 265-270). The lawyers drew a distinction between offences. It was said by Hale, "that if there be a presentment in a Leet for a personal misdemeanour it is a conviction, and conclusive; but if it be for a nuisance or any matter that concerns freehold, the party may come up afterwards and traverse" (*Jurisdiction of the Courts Leet*, by J. Ritson, 1816, p. 140).

enquirable and presentable in a Leet, but not punishable there." All matters of indictment had, indeed, been transferred to the assizes by a statute of Edward IV. The Court Leet, meeting only once or twice a year, with its cumbrous machinery of universal attendance and its inability to impose sentences of imprisonment, was obviously unfitted for dealing with petty police cases. The whole business of the conservancy of the King's peace, including, therefore, every case of assault, was, in fact, taken over by the Justices of the Peace in Petty or Quarter Sessions. It was to these Justices, and not to the Court Leet, that Parliament throughout the sixteenth and seventeenth centuries confided the jurisdiction with regard to the new statutory offences, which were superseding so many of the old Common Law misdemeanours. Thus, by 1689, there remained to the Court Leet, in the lawyer's view, little more than the petty delinquencies connected with the Assize of Ale, the Manorial market, and the use of the highways, together with the wide and elastic offence denoted by a common nuisance.

To the modern student, the Suppression of Nuisances seems a comparatively insignificant part of Local Government. But to the lawyer and the administrator of 1689 it comprised, along with the Relief of the Poor, practically the whole of local administration. As we shall see in the subsequent volume, in which we deal with the Suppression of Nuisances, this was the root out of which sprang such services as the Maintenance of Roads, the Drainage of Towns, the Paving and Cleansing and Lighting of Streets, and the whole of what we now call Public Health. "A common nuisance," says a contemporary lawyer, "seems to be an offence against the public, either by doing a thing which tends to the annoyance of all the King's subjects, or by neglecting to do a thing which the common good requires." [1] When we come to describe the regulative activity sanctioned by this definition we shall see that it covers an amazing range of requirements, both positive and negative; each generation—with or without express direction from the Legislature—dropping out some offences and adding others, the categories now swelling, now contract-

---

[1] *Justice of the Peace*, by R. Burn, 6th edition, 1758, vol. ii. p. 432; citing a dictum of Hawkins.

ing, so that the volume of individual personal activity dealt
with was always varying.   Thus, in the Courts Leet of the
fifteenth and sixteenth centuries, we find the Stewards directing
the Juries to present persons guilty of " eavesdropping " or
" theftbote," of maintenance or barratry, of " being a common
and turbulent brawler " or " a common scold," of " selling
unbaited beef " or " gashing hides."   In the seventeenth and
eighteenth centuries the more common " annoyances of all the
King's subjects," to which the Juries directed their attention,
were unscoured ditches or unmended highways, trees over-
hanging the road, refusing to pave the street in front of one's
house, or declining to serve as Ale-taster, Dog-muzzler, or
Scavenger.   From the middle of the eighteenth century down
to the very end of the period with which we are dealing, we
find, in the roll of presentments, quite other kinds of personal
conduct stigmatised as common nuisances — such as the
emission of smoke, heaping refuse on unoccupied land, permitting privies and cesspools to drain into the newly-made
sewers, leaving cellar flaps open and unguarded, retaining
hanging signs, permitting dangerous bulls to go at large,
keeping mastiffs unmuzzled, or allowing pigs to roam in the
streets.   In fact, it is difficult to find any kind of personal
conduct, whether intrinsically innocent or plainly criminal,
and whether or not expressly included among statutory
offences, which might not, at one period or another, have
found its way, as a common nuisance, into the presentments
of a Court Leet Jury.

Closely connected with this judicial business was the
power assumed to be possessed by the Court Leet, equally
with the Court Baron, of making new By-laws, binding on all
the residents within the Manor.   The earlier legal writers
found the Court Leet making such By-laws, and accepted this
function as warranted by tradition.   Gradually it became of
undoubted authority.   " It seemeth that of common right,"
wrote Dr. Burn in 1756, " any Court Leet, with the assent of
the tenants, may make By-laws under certain penalties, in
relation to matters properly within the cognizance of such
Court, such as reparation of the highways and the like." [1]
Within what limits this By-law-making power would have

---

[1] *Justice of the Peace*, by Dr. R. Burn, vol. iii. p. 240 of edition of 1820.

been, in any particular generation, upheld by the King's
Courts must remain uncertain, as the point cannot be said
to have been very definitely determined. But whether or not
the King's Courts would have upheld their dicta, we find the
legal manuals unhesitatingly advising the Stewards that such
By-laws might be made.

The Court Leet exercised also another important function
which we do not nowadays associate with a criminal tribunal.
It had the duty of appointing whatever staff of public officers
to attend to the government of the locality that custom
required. There were, first of all, the officers charged with
"conserving" the King's peace within the Manor. In a small
rural Manor this meant only the appointment, year by year, of
one of the residents to serve as Constable. In larger parishes
there might be several Constables for different hamlets or
tithings; they might be called "Chief Pledges," "Boroheads,"
"Borsholders," "Tithingmen," "Deciners," "Headboroughs,"
"Thirdboroughs," or by other ancient titles of which the
original meaning had been forgotten; but their duty was
always to preserve order in the little community. The legal
form seems to have been for the Jury to present one or more
persons as liable to serve the particular office, and for the
Court—that is the Steward—to appoint one or more of the
persons so presented. In addition to these officers, particular
Manors had, by custom, to appoint such others as Aleconners
cr Ale-tasters, Carnivals or Carnals, the Pinder, Pinner, or
Poundkeeper, the Dyke-reeve or Moss-reeve or Wall-reeve, and
the Burleymen or Bylawmen. Sometimes in an old "forest"
district the Court had to appoint a "Greave of the Forest,"
and various subordinate forest officers. In the numerous
unincorporated market towns it was the Court Leet that had
to appoint the Bread-weighers and Viewers or Inspectors of
Weights and Measures, the Market-lookers, the Searchers and
Sealers of Leather, the Pecksealers, and the indispensable
Bellman or Town-crier; whilst in populous towns there might
also be Town Scavengers, Dog-muzzlers, Clerks of the Wheat,
Fish, and Butchery Markets, or even, as at Lewes, a "Clerk of
the Spars and Withs."[1] The whole official staff of a Court

---

[1] *The History and Antiquities of Lewes*, by T. W. Horsfield, 1824-32,
p. 174.

Leet might thus be very numerous—in exceptional cases even
exceeding a hundred.[1] In all these offices service was compulsory upon all adult male residents within the Manor, and
could be enforced by summary fine and distraint on any
recalcitrants. It was taken for granted by the lawyers that
every respectable male resident was liable under legal obligation to serve the Manor in his turn,[2] without salary or other
remuneration. It was, in fact, no part of the conception of
local government, at the time when the Court Leet was in its
prime, that there should be anything that we should now call
the Municipal administration of public services, that is to say,
the employment of paid officers to do positive services for the
common enjoyment. Every service requisite for the simple
life of the little community was a duty imposed, as a condition
of tenure or an obligation of status, upon some individual
resident or another. If every man did his duty in obeying
the law of the land and the customs of the Manor—if he
neither broke the King's peace nor committed a public
nuisance—all would be well. But as men were perverse and
weak, there would be defaulters unless some one was responsible
for seeing that the Law and the By-laws were adhered to. In
the old system of frankpledge, the " Capital Pledge " was
apparently held responsible for his " tithing," or group of
inhabitants, on all counts. In the Court Leet, as we find
it in the eighteenth and nineteenth centuries, each Manorial
officer was technically responsible for presenting the commission of one specified offence throughout the whole Manor.
The Jury was responsible, on the information given by these
officers, for presenting and amercing all offenders. " The soul
of the system," says a learned antiquary, " consisted in the
universal obligation of every member of a tithing [that is, in
theory, every adult male] to disclose and bring to punishment
every breach of the laws and customs by which the community

---

[1] *The Court Leet Records of the Manor of Manchester*, vol. vi. p. 241 (Court
of 5th October 1686, when 110 officers were appointed).

[2] By Common Law, the Deputy Steward of the Salford Court explained in
1835, the choice of persons to serve as Constable rested with the Court, unless
there was a valid custom to the contrary. Such a custom existed in the township of Urmston, the "nomination of Constables by house-roll, so that each
person in the township bears the burden in his turn " (*Manchester Times*,
1835).

was bound." [1]　It is this note of the social obligation of every citizen, pervading both the legislation and the legal manuals of the sixteenth century, that we find characterising, in particular, the government of numerous little communities by the Court Leet of the King holden by the Lord of the Manor.

[1] *Leet Jurisdiction in the City of Norwich*, by Rev. William Hudson, 1892, p. lxxv.

CHAPTER II

WE now pass from the clear-cut theories of contemporary lawyers to the actual constitution and working of the Lord's Court between 1689 and 1835. It will be at once apparent that we are dealing with an institution that is nowhere in its prime, but in every instance falling into decay. In some Manors the Lord's Court still provided the principal machinery of Local Government; in others there survived only a mere shred of a constitution. In many districts it is the management of the land that has passed away; in others, the function of trying petty cases of debt and trespass; in others, again, it is the power of fining nuisance-mongers or of appointing Constables that has been lost. What will become abundantly clear is that the Lord's Court, as it actually existed, differed widely from the lawyer's view of what it ought to have been. In many of the cases that we shall describe there was no separation, either in constitution or procedure, between what the lawyers termed the Court Baron of the Lord, and the Court Leet of the King. In these cases we see one and the same Court, in a single undivided sitting, transacting, through one set of officers and one Jury, without distinguishable order or precedence, all the business of the little community, whether this business related to the maintenance of the Lord's rights, the conveyance of a plot of land from seller to purchaser, the mutual arrangement of the common rights of the tenants, the keeping up of fences and dykes, the crops to be sown in particular fields, the dates at which the various agricultural operations were to begin, the trial of civil actions, the present-ment of public nuisances and minor crimes, the fining of

offenders, and the choice and appointment of an indefinite
variety of local public officers. We find, in fact, in the
majority of our examples, simply an Undifferentiated Court.
This absence of the theoretical differentiation between Court
Baron and Court Leet will become apparent to the reader of
the descriptions alike of the Courts of the Hundred, Honour, or
Barony, and those of the Manor or Borough—in the Middle
Ages, it may be said, all tribunals were Undifferentiated Courts
—but we shall recur to it specifically when we come to the
Court of the Manor.

(a) *The Hierarchy of Courts*

The actual constitution of the Lord's Court was, however,
in some places more complicated than is described by the
lawyers. We discover still existing in some parts of the
country between 1689 and 1835 a curious array of Courts
above Courts, and jurisdictions within jurisdictions. We come
across Hundred Courts, Honour Courts, Soke Courts, Barony
Courts, Knight's Courts, or Forest Courts, wielding authority
over large districts within which are also various distinct
Halmote Courts, Courts Baron, Courts Leet, or Borough Courts.
In the ruinous condition into which these Courts had, by 1689,
everywhere fallen, we cannot with any certainty unravel what
relationship they had once borne to each other, except that
the smaller Courts stood in a certain position of inferiority
to those of wider jurisdiction. We cannot, for instance, say
that the relationship was ever one of Courts of First Instance
and Courts of Appeal—there was, we imagine, in mediæval
jurisdiction, taking the form of punishing defaults, nothing
corresponding to the customary modern right of a defendant
in a civil action to appeal against a decision of a Court of
First Instance.[1] Nor do we find evidence of any right of

---

[1] Whether such a right of appeal had ever existed we do not assume to
decide. In one great ecclesiastical jurisdiction, at least, such a right of hearing
appeals was, in 1284, strenuously asserted on behalf of the Hundred Court,
and as strenuously denied on behalf of the Court of the Manor. At Crondal,
in Hampshire, where the Manor belonged to a priory, it was claimed by the
Bishop of Winchester, as Lord of the Hundred Court, that "where the Prior
and his Steward and his other ministers, for a bribe, or through partiality, or
in any other manner, refuse to do justice [in the Court of the Manor] to any
plaintiff of the Hundred of Crundale, the Lord Bishop of Winchester and his
Steward have power at the first Hundred [Court] at Blackheathfield to inquire,
terminate, and amend this wrong." To this the Convent, as owner of the Manor,

appeal to an outside or higher jurisdiction in the civil suits between tenants of the Manor. But it seems clear that, in some cases at any rate, the presentments of the inferior Courts were enforced by actions taken at the head Court; moreover, there is reason to believe that the head Court did not always refrain from dealing with cases which might have been within the jurisdiction of the inferior Court; and it certainly had some sort of jurisdiction in default.[1] "It seems a good prescription," says Sir William Scroggs, "for a Grand Leet (to which other inferior Leets may be subordinate, as that to the Torn) to oblige the Chief Pledges and a certain number of the resiants or inhabitants of every town, etc., within its precinct to appear at every such Grand Leet, to inquire into such offences as were not inquired into in the inferior Leet."[2] We may perhaps infer that if an offence had not been presented in the Court of a petty Manor, it might be presented in the Court of the Honour or Grand Leet of some wider jurisdiction, if such existed; and if not presented at any subordinate Court, then at the Court of the Hundred.[3] Hence, we venture—though without desiring in any way to imply a complete subordination of one to the other—to describe these interesting series as Hierarchies of Courts.

made answer "that it is altogether to be denied, because he [the Bishop] has no right to intrude himself in the Prior's Courts; because if bondmen, they have no refuge except to their Lord, and if freemen, the King alone and his Justices ought to hear and terminate complaints of a false judgment." It was admitted that the tenants of the Manor owed suit and service to the Bishop's Hundred Court, which held the View of Frankpledge for the whole Hundred; and it was eventually agreed that the tenants should not be called to account in the Court of the Manor for anything already dealt with by the Hundred Court. We gather that the jurisdiction in appeal or in default was left undecided (*Records and Documents relating to the Hundred and Manor of Crondal*, by F. J. Baigent, Hampshire Record Society, Part I. p. 16).

[1] Ritson seems to have been unable to conceive of a Hierarchy of Courts. He asserts that the jurisdiction of the "Leet of the Hundred" was only over so much of the Hundred as was not within the jurisdiction of the Court Leet of a Manor; and similarly with the Sheriff's Turn (*Jurisdiction of the Court Leet*, by J. Ritson, 3rd edition, 1816, p. 5).

[2] *The Practice of Courts Leet and Courts Baron*, by Sir William Scroggs, 4th edition, 1728, p. 3; see *History of English Law*, by F. W. Maitland, 1895, vol. i. p. 569.

[3] *Practical Treatise on the Law of Copyholds*, by John Scriven, 7th edition, 1896, p. 436. It is noteworthy that, in the sixteenth century, the Hundred was still regarded as the jurisdiction next above that of the Manor. In 1555, when it was provided that the Courts Leet should deal with offences under the first Highways Act (2 and 3 Philip and Mary, c. 8), the Stewards of Leets were to render returns of all estreats and fines, not to the Justices of the Peace or to any County officer, but to the Bailiff or High Constable of the Hundred.

For the most remarkable of these Hierarchies of Courts we must go to the West of England. The wide area of the Vale of Berkeley, comprising the ancient Hundred of that name in the County of Gloucester, had been ruled over, time out of mind, by a series of mutually related Courts of the Lord of Berkeley Castle. There was, first, the Hundred Court for the whole area; then the numerous Halmotes or Halimotes, the Lord's Courts for the separate Manors within the Hundred; and, finally, certain differentiated Courts, called Borough Courts or Leets, held in and for certain favoured townships, which had, by ancient seignorial grants, been constituted Boroughs.[1]

In 1689 this Hierarchy of Courts, which had existed " time out of mind," was still in full, though somewhat formal, operation. Twice a year the Lord's Steward issued his precept to the Bailiff of the Hundred, directing him to summon to the Court of the Hundred and Honour of Berkeley—also called the Court Leet or Law Day—" to be holden at the Booth Hall in the town of Berkeley "; to command the attendance of the persons who were to form the Jury—these in 1733 were thirty in number; in 1734, forty-two; drawn from a score of different Manors,—and to require the Constables of the Manors and the Tithingmen of the several parishes and townships that " they give notice of holding the same in the respective parish churches on the Sunday next before the Leet," in order that not they only, but also all who

---

[1] For information as to the Courts of the Hundred of Berkeley we are indebted to the courtesy of the Earl of Berkeley, of his land steward, Mr James Peter, and of Mr Hutton, steward of his Lordship's Courts, who kindly permitted consultation of the records in the muniment room at Berkeley Castle; as well as to our friend Miss Hadley, Archivist to the London County Council, who was good enough to devote part of a holiday to the work. A detailed description of the Hundred Court at Berkeley in 1890 will be found in *Gloucestershire Notes and Queries*, vol. iv. p. 27; and some account of the Hundred Rolls in *ibid.* vol. v. pp. 85-88. See also Fifth Report of Royal Commission on Common Law Courts, 1833; House of Commons Returns of Hundred Courts, 1839, and of Courts of Request, 1840; *The Berkeley Manuscripts*, by Sir John Maclean, 3 vols., 1883-85 (Bristol and Gloucester Archæological Society); and (for the two Boroughs) First Report of Municipal Corporation Commissioners, 1835, Appendix, vol. i. p. 19; Report of Royal Commission on Unreformed Corporations, 1880; *History of the Town of Berkeley*, by Rev. John Fisher, 1856 and 1864; "Corporation Insignia," in *Notes and Queries*, 2nd ser. vol. v. p. 519; and " Extinct Corporations of Wotton and Berkeley," in *Notes and Queries*, 7th ser. vol. ii. p. 64; *A New History of Gloucestershire*, by Samuel Rudder, 1779, pp. 846-854; and *Historical Notes relating to the Borough of Wotton*, by W. H. Wright, 1872 (in Cheltenham Public Library).

had business at the Court, might be present. The Tithingman of Stinchcombe—we know not why—had to bring with him two men. In the manuscript "Precedent Book," which has been the guide of many generations of Stewards, we can almost see before us the whole procedure of this ancient tribunal. The Steward opens the Court by calling on the Bailiff for a return of the Jury, which, together with that of the Tithingmen and Constables of Manors, is formally called over, and the absentees fined; for attendance is compulsory, and right down to the middle of the nineteenth century the fines are enforced. The Constable of Bevington comes into Court near the Steward, and, half-bent, prays for the prosperity of the noble family of the Berkeleys. The Tithingman of Woodmancote brings a "tag" with which to tie up Lord Berkeley's "writings" under penalty of ten shillings fine. The Jury is sworn, in groups of four, one Bible being supplied to be held by each group, and the King's Proclamation against Profaneness and Immorality is read. The Steward delivers his charge to the Court, directing the Jury to inquire into every conceivable offence committed within the Hundred, from manslaughter down to the robbing of hen-roosts, from the unlawful pursuit of game to conspiracies by artificers, from felony to forestalling and regrating—all still declared to be "presentable" in this Court, even if successive Stewards have felt obliged to substitute that word for "punishable." Then the Jury examines into the state of repair of the highways and bridges, the stopping-up or diversion of footpaths and watercourses, and the obstruction of the roads by encroachments or laying of timber. All those who can give information relating to any of these delinquencies are commanded to give it then and there in Court. Various officers of the Hundred continue to be appointed, at any rate the Bailiff of the Hundred and the Haywards of the several Manors, even after the appointment of others had been discontinued. Various Acts of Parliament are solemnly read and proclaimed. The presentments made at the last previous Court are read over, and those which are reported to have been complied with are crossed off. Meanwhile the Jury has completed its new presentments, which are written out by the Bailiff, and signed by the several jurymen. The Constables make their returns, and are sworn to the truth thereof. The Steward, with such formal solemnity as he can command, then closes the Court. Other sittings of the Court are held by the Steward every three weeks, to which the subordinate Manors owe no attendance, though the freehold tenants of the Barony are supposed to be present and to form the Court. The business of these three-weekly sittings, for which a Jury of householders was summoned when required, was, at any rate in the nineteenth century, confined to the trial of civil actions for debt arising anywhere within the Hundred of Berkeley. Throughout the whole of the eighteenth and nineteenth centuries this ancient Court continued to be held, its formalities and ceremonies gradually dropping off one by one—its criminal jurisdiction already gone before 1700, its presentments of nuisances hardly lasting beyond 1800,[1] its hearing of civil suits passing in the middle of the nineteenth century to the new County Court, its fines for non-attendance[2] not surviving the third quarter of the nineteenth century; until, in 1900, the thousand-years' record is broken, and the Court is silently discontinued.

We pass now to the Halimotes, or Courts Baron, held on behalf of the Lord of Berkeley in the several Manors of the Hundred. These were either "General Halimotes," held normally once a year, or "Special Halimotes," held when required for some urgent business. These Courts, we are informed, dealt during the eighteenth century only with admissions of new copyholders, transfers of property,[3] and

---

[1] In 1801 the owners of the land adjoining a road, and the owner of a footbridge over a brook were presented for not repairing these highways ; and the latter was amerced in forty shillings, leviable on his goods and chattels (MS. Entry Book, Berkeley Hundred Court, October 1801).

[2] "We present that it appears by the oath of John Neale, Bailiff of the said Hundred, that he, the said Bailiff, did, on 16th April, go to the dwelling-house of N. W. of Cambridge in the Parish of Slimbridge within the said Hundred, to levy on his goods and chattels the sum of five shillings, being an amercement imposed on him for not attending at the last Court Leet for the said Hundred to serve on the Jury. And we present that it further appears to us by the oath of the said Bailiff that R. U.—brother to the said N. U.—did on the said 16th April instant pay to the said Bailiff the sum of five shillings in discharge of such amercement for the use of the said Lord of the said Hundred " (MS. Entry Book, Berkeley Hundred Court, 18th April 1803). A similar entry occurs six months later.

[3] Here is a typical entry. "N. W., gentleman, came to this Court by warrant of attorney from W. W. H., and surrendered a close of pasture late Symonds, held by the life of the said W. W. H., and the estate of W. W. H., after which proclamation was made and J. H., the life in reversion, came and was admitted " (MS. Court Rolls, Wotton, 20th October 1732).

purely Manorial offences.   The Steward presided, the rest of
the Court consisting of what was called "the Homage," being
all the copyhold tenants of the particular Manor, who sat
without individual summons by virtue of their tenancy.   In
the score or more of such Courts actually held in the year
1733, we noticed that the Homage numbered from two to
about a dozen.   Attendance was compulsory, under penalty of
a fine of five shillings, which was usually "affeered" to one
shilling.[1]   It is interesting, as bearing on the relationship of
the several Courts in this Hierarchy, to find it expressly stated
that the fines imposed by the Manor Courts were recovered
by action in the Berkeley Hundred Court at one of its three-
weekly sittings.[2]   So far as we have ascertained, the only
business of these Halimotes during the eighteenth century
that can be said to relate to Local Government was their
appointment of a Reeve of the Manor, who had power to
distrain on the cattle of the lands of any copyhold or leasehold tenant of the Manor for any amercement imposed by the
Court.[3]   Service as Reeve was compulsory on the copyhold
and leasehold tenants in rotation, "the furthest behind in
serving the office of Reeve" being always appointed, even if
a woman, or a group of officials like the Overseers of the
Poor, when these happened to have a copyhold or leasehold
workhouse.[4]   But the office could always be served by a

---

[1] MS. Precedent Book, Berkeley. At a Court Baron at Ham Manor
defaulters were amerced half a crown, affeered to one shilling (MS. Entry Book,
Court Baron, Ham, 14th October 1797); but at one at Cam, ten shillings,
affeered to two (*ibid.* Cam, 7th October 1833).

[2] *Gloucestershire Notes and Queries*, vol. iv. pp. 27-30.

[3] "The Homage also present that the Reeve of this Manor in virtue of his
office may distrain for rent or for any amercement imposed in the Lord's Court
upon any copyholder or leaseholder, as well as the cattle of such copyholders or
leaseholders as of any other renting or occupying the copyhold or leasehold
land or tenements of such leaseholder or copyholder, provided the cattle be found
feeding upon the same copyhold or leasehold estate ; and further that the Reeve
is not bound to ascertain whose cattle those they may so distrain are, but
finding the same in or upon such copyhold or leasehold lands or tenements may
lawfully distrain them, as now and at all times out of memory hath been
accustomed to do" (MS. Entry Book, Courts Baron of many Manors, October
1810).

[4] A woman is appointed Reeve "as being furthest behind," and serves by
deputy (MS. Court Roll Book, Court Baron of Hurst Manor, 14th October 1799).
"The Homage present that the Overseers of the Poor of this tithing are the
furthest behind in serving the office of Reeve for the house called the workhouse
on Berkeley Heath" (MS. Court Roll Book, Court Baron of Berkeley, 5th
October 1833).

"sufficient deputy."[1]   Right down to the very end of the nineteenth century these Manor Courts were still being held, the Juries were presenting encroachments and Manorial defaults, and petty officers were being appointed.[2]

The third sort of Courts held within the Hundred of Berkeley were those of the townships or so-called "Boroughs" of Berkeley and Wotton. These were each styled "Court Leet with View of Frankpledge and Court Baron," and separate records were apparently in each case kept. But what was actually held in each of these picturesque little towns was only one Court. Once a year the Steward issued his precept to the "Serjeant of the Borough," requiring him "to summon all such persons as owe suit to the Court Leet and Court Baron of the Borough," and to "warn a sufficient number of the most able in the Borough to serve on the Grand Jury." On the appointed day the Steward opened the Court by calling on the Constable to read first the "Resiant Roll," with loud proclamation to "all who live within the jurisdiction of this Court" to come forward and do the suit they owe, and then the "Jury Panel," those who did not answer to their names being amerced. The jurymen were then sworn, in the same groups of four that we have already described in the Hundred Court. At each of these Courts there were two distinct Juries, each usually exceeding a dozen in number—the Homage, composed of freehold, leasehold, and copyhold tenants of the Manor; and the "Grand Jury" or "Leet Jury," made up merely of residents. The Juries both made presentments, those of the Homage relating to surrenders and admissions, conveyances and other property business, together with purely Manorial defaults, such as suffering a messuage to decay, allowing water from a new well to injure a neighbour's house, or removing a gate and not replacing it, for which small

[1]   "At this Court it was found and presented by the Homage that G. S. is the furthest behind in serving the office of Reeve for a close called Rowles Court Leaze.   We therefore order the said G. S. to take upon him the said office, either by himself or his sufficient deputy, in one month's time under the penalty of £5, to be levied upon his goods and chattels, or to be recovered by action of debt for the use of the Lord of the said Manor " (MS. Entry Book, Court Baron of Slimbridge Manor, 12th October 1797).

[2]   See, for instance, the interesting description of the proceedings in 1887 of " the Court for the Manor of Wotton Foreign," being so much of the Parish of Wotton as lies outside the Borough, in *Gloucestershire Notes and Queries*, vol. iv. pp. 27-30.

amercements are imposed. The Grand Jury or Leet presented all manner of nuisances relating to highways and water-courses; unlicensed alehouses, scolds and eavesdroppers; the delinquencies of butchers and bakers; pound breach and rescue of cattle; and encroachments on the streets. The officers appointed at the previous Court then made their returns of offenders against the laws and Bylaws concerning their several departments —handing in small scraps of paper on which we fear they had too often perfunctorily written " omnia bene," or words to that effect.[1] But the Court would sometimes insist on the office being executed. " We present E. C. and E. S.," reports the Grand Jury of Wotton in 1713, " for neglecting their office, particularly not taking up vagrants. We do fine them ten shillings each." [2] Then the officers of the Borough for the ensuing year were appointed, the Grand Jury presenting three names as suitable persons to be Mayor, and two names in the case of other officers, for the selection of one by the Steward. For each of the two Boroughs the Court appointed a Mayor, a Serjeant, a Constable, and one or two Ale-tasters, Carnivals, and Searchers and Sealers of Leather.[3] Sometimes other officers—a Scavenger or a Surveyor—are mentioned as acting under the appointment and direction of the Mayor. At Berkeley it was the custom—we observe it still in force between 1797 and 1804—for the Court to recite and declare every year a string of heterogeneous rights or By-laws, on the presentment, be it noted, of the Homage Jury. No pigs are to go at large, under penalty of three and fourpence, the Hayward being ordered to impound any found wandering and to take his own fee of twopence; no " soil, dung, apple must, or any other stinking matter " is to be deposited in

---

[1] " We have served the office to the best of our knowledge and we have found it all well " (Return of Searchers and Sealers of Leather, Court Rolls of Wotton, 2nd October 1714). " We present that we have found no flesh nor fish that have been brought to our market and exposed for sale, upon our vigilant search, but what hath been fit and wholesome for the body of man; and that we have nothing more to present at this time " (Return of Carnivals, *ibid.* October 1709). " We have took care that the bulls have been baited, ere that the meat hath been sold for the same, and we have carefully looked after all other meat and fish " (*ibid.* 30th September 1710).

[2] MS. Court Rolls, Wotton, 3rd October 1713.

[3] Aldermen are mentioned (among the Leet Jury) both in Berkeley and in Wotton (MS. Entry Book, Wotton Court, 20th October 1737 ; Berkeley Court, 21st October 1745). These were (in 1833 at Berkeley) the twelve members of the close Town Council.

Berkeley streets, under penalty of a pound, and the Scavengers are ordered to sweep up all dirt into heaps every Saturday, for the officers of the Lord to carry it out of the Borough; no timber or other obstruction is to be put in the streets; the common pasturage on Berkeley Heath is not to be usurped or surcharged; every person coming into the Borough to carry on business or set up a household—we gather without having been born or perhaps apprenticed within the Borough—is to pay the Mayor six and eightpence as of old; nobody but the Mayor shall put up any stall in the Market or Fair; the right of all persons to a free wharf or landing place on the river is declared and perpetuated; and there is a stern prohibition of taking in "inmates" to be a nuisance to the Borough. On the other hand, at Wotton, it is the Grand Jury that we see making presentment of stopped-up watercourses, broken gullies, and filth thrown down the gutter in "a time of flood to the great annoyance of" a certain mill. A butcher is presented, on the knowledge of one of the jurymen, "for putting stinking meat to sale in our market"; and other frequenters for selling goods "by weight unlawful being too light." So, too, we find the Grand Jury ordering that no persons shall stand with goods in a certain passage on market day, that posts and rails be set up for the protection of foot passengers, that obstructive encroachments be removed, and that certain unlawful windows that overlook the almshouses be stopped up.[1]

Another case of a Hierarchy of Courts continuing in active existence is presented by the great Manor of Taunton, extending over nearly the whole of Taunton "Deane," or Vale, in Somerset.[2] Here the Manor transcended even the Hundred,

---

[1] "Item, we order that for the future no person shall lay dung . . . in the street called . . . (MS. Court Rolls, Wotton); all persons that do claim any right to the Chipping Well shall pay their proportion toward the repairing the same, upon the pain of five shillings" (ibid.).

[2] *The Customs of the Manor of Taunton and Taunton Deane*, by Richard Locke, 1785; *The Ancient Customs of Taunton Deane*, by H. B. Shillibeer, 1821; *History of Taunton*, by Joshua Toulmin, 1st edition, 1791, 2nd edition, edited by James Savage, 1822; *History of Somerset*, by John Collinson, 1791, vol. iii. pp. 225-240; *General Account of West Somerset*, by Edward Jeboult, 1873—Part II. *The Valley of the Tone*, Part III. Taunton; *On the Origin of Gilds, with a Notice of the Ancient Gildhall of Taunton*, by J. H. Pring, 1883; "The Customs of the Manor of Taunton Deane," by W. A. Jones, in *Somerset Archaeological and Natural History Society*, vol. xviii. pp. 76-99; House of Commons Return of Courts of Request, 1840, p. 140.

the Lord's Court at the head of the Hierarchy, which continued to be held down to Victorian times, exercising jurisdiction over no fewer than five Hundreds and many tithings and parishes. Besides this Court, there existed minor Courts for the Liberty (by which we understand the precinct of the Castle), and for the " Hundred of Taunton Market "; which (like Berkeley and Wotton) had been granted exceptional autonomy, under the name of a Borough.[1] The "ancient customs of the Manor," formally presented and recorded in 1647 and again in 1817, enable us to gain some vision of this interesting Hierarchy. The highest Court seems to have rejoiced in a number of different names or nicknames, according to the date at which or the purpose for which it was held. In 1647 it sat as a Court of Survey. Twice a year it was the Court Leet or Lawday. On the occasion on which, once a year, the Manorial officers were chosen it was the " Choice Court." The sitting " next after Michaelmas Lawday " was the " Fulfilling Court," when two tenants in each Hundred were sworn to view the list of amercements for the past year, and to " affeer " them; it may be that there was a second " Fulfilling Court " in the spring. There was the " Ossinge Court," or " Penn Court," of which the meaning is unknown to us. Finally there was the " Three Weeks' Court," called also the Court Baron, held every three weeks, primarily as a petty debt court,[2] though it dealt also with defaults. This score or more of Courts— incidentally referred to as " Tenants' Courts "[3]—all held in the Great Hall of the Castle of Taunton, before the Steward or, in the case of the Three Weeks' Court, by the Clerk of the Castle—had to be attended by all the customary tenants of the Manor, but these, if not specially summoned as jurymen, could escape on payment of small fines—a penny each time, or eightpence for the year, bought exemption from the Court Baron or Three Weeks' Court, and threepence each time did the same for the others. At the Leet or Lawday, twice a year,

---

[1] "Outfaring Courts" are also mentioned (*The Customs of the Manor of Taunton and Taunton Deane*, by Richard Locke, 1785), which were perhaps those held for the "Outfaring" part of the Vale, sixteen parishes which had been alienated from the Manor by William I. (*History of Taunton*, by Joshua Toulmin, 1822, p. 45).

[2] House of Commons Returns of Hundred Courts, 1839, and of Courts of Request, 1840.

[3] *Customs of the Manor of Taunton and Taunton Deane*, by R. Locke, 1785.

there was summoned a "Grand Jury," which seems not only to have presented nuisances and Manorial offences, but also to have heard and decided disputes relating to copyhold tenements. At one of the two Leets or Lawdays the Grand Jury presented suitable persons to serve as High Constable for the Hundred of Taunton Deane, and as Tithingmen for one or two of the tithings. It is not apparent how the numerous Petty Constables or Tithingmen for the other tithings were appointed, though it is stated that these all had to attend the Court Baron or Three Weeks' Court to present defaults; and also to attend the two Leets or Lawdays. That this attendance had fallen into desuetude, may be inferred from the fact that it was recorded in 1647 that the Tithingmen of twenty-seven tithings had to pay a shilling each yearly to be excused from bringing in their bushel measures to be tried by the standard on the two Lawdays.[1] At the Choice Court, the tenants had to make a choice of persons to be appointed as "Receiver to receive the Steward at the two Leets or Lawday Courts; and one several Reeve for every Hundred to gather the Lord's rents; and Beadles to serve the Lord's Courts, and to gather the amercements and customary works, and to make account thereof to the Reeve as hath been accustomed within every Hundred."[2] The office of Reeve had to be served in turn by the "bond-land" tenants—those having houses on their holdings—according to a rotation known as "the Recognition of the Manor." There were "certain plots of ground in each Hundred, the profits of which are appointed to the Reeves for the time being."[3] Two tenants had also to be appointed annually as Viewers, and sworn to present any customary tenant neglecting to keep his house in repair.[4]

Among the minor Courts of the Hierarchy, we know

---

[1] *Ancient Customs of Taunton Deane*, by H. B. Shillibeer, 1821, Appendix, p. 9.

[2] *Ibid.* By 1821 the Bailiff had, it seems (in all the Hundreds except one), superseded the Reeve in the collection of the Lord's rents and dues. It is to be noted that, between 1781 and 1801, these included six heriots, varying from £42 to £84 each (*ibid.* pp. 92-93).

[3] *Ibid.* p. 114.

[4] *Ibid.* p. 107. Other officers of the Manor in 1647 were the Constable of Taunton Castle, the Bailiff of the Castle, the Clerk of the Castle, and the Porter, or Keeper of the Gate of the Castle—all, we assume, appointed by the Lord or his Steward; the Woodward and the Overseers or Surveyors of the Water-works, Wears, and Banks, of whom we know nothing (*ibid.* Appendix).

nothing of the two Lawdays per annum and the "Three Weeks' Courts," which the Clerk of the Castle is said to have held for the Liberty of the Precinct of the Castle, nor of the "Outfaring Courts," of which we have a bare mention. But in the Borough of Taunton the Clerk of the Castle held not only a "Borough Court" every fortnight, presumably for petty debt business, but also two "Lawday Courts" annually, at which were chosen, right down to Victorian times, the two Portreeves, who collected the Lord's quit-rents in the Borough and enjoyed the privilege of letting for their own profit the standings in the market-place;[1] two Bailiffs, who seem to have been[2] the chief executive officers of what had become a flourishing market centre; together with two Constables, six Tithingmen, and one or more Ale-tasters. The two Constables did much of the administrative work of the town under the Bailiffs: billeting soldiers, managing the almshouses, and distributing various dole charities. In return they enjoyed the patronage, presided at an annual "Constables' Feast," kept the profits of the market scales, and succeeded to the more lucrative office of Portreeve.[3] But the real rulers were the Bailiffs, who had, by the end of the eighteenth century, made themselves virtually permanent, and, after 1792, were recognised by Parliament as the returning officers for the Borough. "The Jury year after year empanelled are," we are told in 1821, "called the Packed Jury. . . . One of the Bailiffs . . . did publicly assert that the Bailiffs going out of office always took care to assemble such persons as jurors as would return the nominees of themselves. . . . It is notorious that some years ago a Jury was summoned, and it being rumoured that they meant to alter the succession of Bailiffs, they were immediately dismissed, and another Jury empanelled. . . . For a succession of years four individuals only have filled the office of Bailiffs, two of them taking the same in alternate years."[4] This Court of the Borough of Taunton had in fact attained to a measure of autonomy, the Jury electing the Bailiffs and the

[1] *History of Taunton*, by Joshua Toulmin, 1821, p. 277.

[2] Before 1627 and after 1792—the interval having been filled by a Chartered Municipal Corporation.

[3] *General Account of West Somerset*, by Edward Jeboult, 1873, Part III., Taunton, pp. 24-26.

[4] *Ancient Customs of Taunton Deane*, by H. B. Shillibeer, 1821, p. 130.

Bailiff selecting the Jury, without the interference of the Lord's Steward. It had, moreover, developed a certain amount of administrative structure. As such it falls into our class of Manorial Boroughs, to be dealt with in a subsequent chapter. We mention it here merely to complete our survey of the Hierarchy of Courts.

Hierarchies of Courts were, of course, not confined to the South and West of England. In Northumberland, for instance, there continued to be held, down to the middle of the nineteenth century, a whole array of Courts on the wide domains of the Duke of Northumberland.[1]

[1] We were unable to examine the MS. records of these Courts, but there seem to have been (*a*) Great Courts of the Baronies of Alnwick, Tindale, and perhaps Prudhoe ; (*b*) Halmote Courts or Courts Baron for particular Manors, of which fifteen were still being held in 1839, for petty debt cases, and possibly other business ; and (*c*) a Court for the Manor of the Borough of Alnwick, nominally every three weeks, but actually only half-yearly, at which Burgesses or Freemen were admitted, nuisances presented, Bylaws made, offenders amerced, copyhold properties transferred, and the Borough officers formally appointed and sworn. With the struggle of this Borough Court for autonomy we shall deal later, when we describe the Manorial Borough of Alnwick. It would be interesting to discover what exactly were the functions and the relations of the highest members of these Northumberland Hierarchies. For instance, we hear of a "Knight's Court," or "curia militaris," held at Alnwick Castle, nominally attended by the great freehold tenants, and exercising jurisdiction over the entire barony of Alnwick. Such Courts, though apparently disused between 1741 and 1791, were being held in the latter part of the seventeenth and the beginning of the eighteenth centuries ; dealing, we infer, primarily with successions and admissions, disputes between free tenants of different Manors, encroachments of one Manor on another, and defaults not duly presented in the inferior Courts. At the Knight's Court held in 1707, for instance, "the tenants of Chillingham, Fawdon, and Swinhoe were amerced 20d. each township, who owe service to His Grace for watching the Fair according to ancient custom," for their default in not sending in the men whom they had to furnish to guard the Borough of Alnwick at the great Alnwick Fair. Latterly, at any rate, the "Knight's Court" appointed Constables for various Manors, for which Courts were not held, and dealt with many minor offences and defaults throughout a wide district. The Court of the Barony of Tindale, on the other hand, held at Wark, seems to have survived down to 1846 as a petty debt Court, meeting three times a year, and resorted to only in cases in which the defendants did not reside within the jurisdiction of any subordinate Courts (MS. Records of the Corporation of Alnwick, 1594-1835 ; *Feudal and Military Antiquities of Northumberland and the Scottish Borders*, by Rev. C. H. Hartshorne, 1858 (being vol. ii. of "Memoirs of the Archæological Institute of Great Britain, etc.," for 1852) ; *History of Alnwick*, by George Tate, 1869 ; *History of Northumberland*, vol. i., by E. Bateson ; Fifth Report of Royal Commission on Courts of Law, 1833, pp. 170-171 ; House of Commons Returns of Hundred Courts, 1839, and of Courts of Request, 1840).

We do not even know whether the Alnwick "Knight's Court" is to be identified with the Capital Court of the Barony, stated in 1483 to be held every twenty days, harvest excepted. The term "Knight's Court" (curia militaris)

In the "Liberty of the Hundred of Macclesfield," in Cheshire, where the Earl of Derby held sway, we find an intricate series of jurisdictions within jurisdictions. There was the Court for the Hundred of Macclesfield, held annually as the "Court of Great Leet" and monthly as a Court Baron or "Court of Trials," exercising authority over the whole of the Liberty of the Hundred. The records of its annual Leet sessions show it appointing Constables for those townships which had no Courts of their own, and receiving presentments from these Constables as well as from its own "Grand Jury," relating to offences throughout the Hundred outside the Forest and the Borough of Macclesfield—selling ale without licence, various public-house disorders, breaking the Assize of Bread, failure to repair pavement, "keeping two mongrel curs unmuzzled," breaking the peace and making an affray, encroachments on the waste, "keeping a gun," and "keeping a brace of greyhounds and killing a hare in Birtles; is a great killer and destroyer of hares," adds the Constable.

At its nominally monthly sessions, or "Court of Trials" —which gradually came to be only two or three times a year—the same Steward presided with the same Officers, but an entirely different Jury was empanelled, the "Jury for Trials," by which pleas of debt and trespass to an unlimited amount were dealt with. Meanwhile the Forest of Macclesfield, comprising part of the Hundred—nine of the townships being, in fact, partly in the Forest and partly outside it—had its own Courts. We do not know whether a Swainmote was held later than that of 1616, of which we have seen the records, but throughout the eighteenth century and down to

is unusual, but not unknown elsewhere. In the Honour of Forncett in Norfolk, comprising several Manors having their own Courts, there was held, in the fifteenth century, an Honour Court or "Knight's Court" (*The Economic Development of a Norfolk Manor, 1086-1565*, by F. G. Davenport, 1906, Appendix I.). In the Isle of Wight, right down to the middle of the nineteenth century, there continued to be held the "Knighton Court or Knight's Court," by the Steward of the Governor of the Island, in the Town Hall of Newport, every three weeks. Its functions became restricted to petty debt suits, in which it exercised jurisdiction over the whole island except the Borough of Newport. After the end of the eighteenth century even this function became disused, and the Court continued in form only (House of Commons Return of Courts of Request, 1840, pp. 46-47). The Archbishop of York held a "curia militaris" for the Liberty of Ripon from, at any rate, the fourteenth right down to the nineteenth century. In 1840 it was a Court for civil actions, unlimited in amount (*ibid.* pp. 174-175).

the middle of the nineteenth we find a "Halmote Court," called subsequently "Court of Record for the Manor and Forest of Macclesfield," held by the same Steward as the Hundred Court, and eventually on the same day as the latter. At the six-monthly meetings of this Court for the Manor and Forest it acted also as a Court Leet, appointing Constables for the several townships in the Forest. At the other sittings of the Court conveyances of copyholds were made and an extensive business was done in the trial of civil actions, without limit of amount. Finally, there were also held, at least in the sixteenth century, two separate Courts for the Borough of Macclesfield, both using the Town Hall—one the "Portmote," or "Great Leet of the Borough," by Lord Derby's Deputy Steward, which seems to have dealt with the usual nuisances and affrays, false weights and measures, the regulation of the common, and the trial of civil actions; and the other "the Mayor's Court," held by the Mayor of the Borough, apparently for the trial of civil actions in which both parties were Burgesses. How exactly these several Courts had come into existence, and what was the precise demarcation among them all, we have been unable to ascertain. What is interesting is that all the resiants of the Hundred, including those in the Manor of the Forest and those in the Borough, owed suit and service to the Hundred Court; while all those in the Borough, including the Mayor and Corporation, owed suit and service also to Lord Derby's Portmote. A dispute between the Earl of Derby and the Borough in 1569, as to the relations of the two competing Borough Courts, led to an award by two judges attempting to define their several spheres, and giving separate keys of the Town Hall to the Mayor and the Steward respectively. We gather that Lord Derby's "Portmote," or "Town Leet," was discontinued sometime in the seventeenth century, leaving the Mayor's Court in possession of the field. This continued, as the "Borough Court," to try personal actions without limit of amount. Meanwhile the ordinary business of a Court Leet, formerly done by Lord Derby's Portmote, was apparently silently absorbed by the Mayor, ex-Mayor, and two Aldermen, sitting as Justices for the Borough. A Charter of Charles II. had made them Justices, and given power to hold general

Sessions of the Peace, but not to try felonies. This amounted to little, if any, more jurisdiction than had been possessed by the Portmote; and what we have, in fact, is a Court Leet passing insensibly into what was called a Court of Quarter Sessions. Thus in 1761-1762 we see the Borough Justices in what they called Quarter Sessions appointing the Burley-men, the Fish and Flesh Wardens, the Moss Lookers of Densmoss (a part of the Borough Common), the Searchers and Sealers of Leather, a Scavenger, a Pig-catcher, a Beadle, and the two Common Lookers; and dealing indiscriminately with assaults and affrays, trespasses on the Common, wrongful enclosures of the waste of the Borough, false weights and measures, and exposing unwholesome meat for sale.[1]

How far this hierarchical organisation of the Lord's Court still existed in 1689, and how quickly the surviving remnants disintegrated, we have been unable to ascertain. From the scanty records that we have been able to consult, we infer that it continued over large parts of England during the eighteenth century, but everywhere becoming more formal than real, and everywhere falling rapidly into decay.[2]

[1] MS. Records, Macclesfield Hundred Court, 1688-1835; MS. Court Books of ditto, 1698-1808; MS. Records, Court Leet and Halmote Court of Macclesfield Manor and Forest, 1684-1835; MS. Award of 1569; MS. Records, Macclesfield Portmote, 1591; MS. Records, Macclesfield Borough Court, 1761; MS. Quarter Sessions Rolls, 1761-1762 (all in Lord Derby's Macclesfield Estate Office); House of Commons Returns of Petty Debt Courts, Hundred Courts, and Courts of Request, 1828, 1839, and 1840; Fifth Report of Royal Commission on Courts of Law, 1833, p. 35a; ·Report on Certain Boroughs, by J. T. Hogg, 1838, pp. 51-74; *History of Macclesfield*, by John Corry, 1817; *Macclesfelde in ye Olden Time*, by Isaac Finney, 1873; *Contributions towards a History of . . . Prestbury*, by F. Renaud (Chetham Society, 1876); *East Cheshire*, by J. P. Earwaker, 1880, vol. ii. pp. 459-525; *History of the County Palatine of Chester*, by Geo. Ormerod, 2nd edition, 1882, vol. iii. pp. 739-757.

[2] We catch glimpses of a similar Hierarchy of Courts in the great episcopal domains in various dioceses. The Hundred Court of Farnham, in Surrey, for instance, still held, but shrunken to the mere copyhold business of Farnham itself, apparently once had jurisdiction over a wide stretch of the Bishop of Winchester's domains (see *Collections of Records and Documents relating to the Hundred and Manor of Crondal*, by F. J. Baigent, Hampshire Record Society, 1891; *The Manor of Manydown, Hampshire*, by G. W. Kitchin, 1895; *Victoria County History of Hampshire*, vol. ii. 1906, pp. 579-586), including the Manorial Boroughs of Farnham and Alresford, the latter to be subsequently described. As late as 1718 a "Court of the Bishopric" was held, at which representatives of a score of Manors attended (MS. Manor Rolls, Farnham, 1718). We do not know in what connection stood the "Cheyney Court," which we find held throughout the eighteenth and for the first third of the nineteenth century; latterly, at least, at Winchester, within the cathedral precincts, and exercising jurisdiction throughout the Bishop's temporalities, extending to over two hundred towns and

We suggest that it may possibly be that in the former existence of a Hierarchy of Courts we have the explanation of some
of the quaint instances in which the representation of a small
hamlet has survived in a comic form. In Dorsetshire, for
example, we read that "the Tithingman of Combe Keynes is
obliged to do suit at Winfrith Court ; and after repeating the

villages. In 1833 its business was confined to hearing petty debt cases (Fifth
Report of Royal Commission on Courts of Common Law, 1833, p. 88a).
Similarly, in the diocese of St. Albans, the Manor Rolls of Winslow (Buckinghamshire) in the time of Edward III. show that "in case of a dispute a Court
was held under the great ash tree at St. Albans, and the decision of this
superior Manorial Court of headquarters settled the question" (The English
Village Community, by F. Seebohm, 1883, p. 31). So the Abbot of Gloucester
in the thirteenth century held a "Libera Curia" for his great freehold tenants,
whilst each separate Manor had its own Halmote (Select Pleas in Manorial
Courts, by F. W. Maitland, 1889, p. xix). We may likewise infer a Hierarchy
of Courts in the great Honour of Clitheroe, of which "the customs of the copyholds" were "ascertained by the Jury of Survey within the forest of Pendle in
the Manor of Igtenhill, 1666." Throughout the wide extent of the Honour
there were "Hamlet Courts" twice a year, which we may interpret as Halmote
Courts. There was also a Court of the Honour, attended by all the tenants. The
Homage or Jury presented a Greave or Bailiff. There was also a Deputy Greave,
elected in open Court by a majority of the tenants. All "real" plaints were
to be tried in this Court, by a Jury of twenty-four tenants (The Law of Copyholds, by C. I. Elton and H. J. H. Mackay, 2nd edition, 1893, Appendix VIII.
p. 511). There was, moreover, within the Honour at least one Manorial Borough,
that of Clitheroe, where a "Court of Record" sat weekly under a Recorder
(House of Commons Return of Courts of Request, 1840, pp. 68-69), and independent administrative structure had been developed, to which we subsequently
refer (pp. 156, 205). Another instance of a Hierarchy of Courts, with subordinate Manors and Boroughs of various degrees of independence, is presented by a
Welsh Lordship—typical, we suspect, of other Welsh jurisdictions. The Manor
paramount of Cantref Moelynaidd comprehends four Hundreds of Radnorshire
and twelve mesne Manors. The Boroughs of Knighton, Cnwelas, New Radnor,
and Rhayader, together with the obsolete Boroughs of Pain's Castle and
Presteign, are also included in it. The Manor paramount continued, throughout the eighteenth century, and indeed through most of the nineteenth, to exercise
jurisdiction over them all, except the Borough of New Radnor. The Steward
held a Court Baron for the whole lordship every three weeks, the business of
which had become confined to petty debt cases, for which a Jury of six men
was summoned when required. Courts Leet were also held within the mesne
Manors, and also (at least in the Bailiwick of Gladestry and Colfa) a Court
Baron monthly for small debts. Within the Boroughs, the Steward of the
Lordship also held Courts Leet, at which Juries of Burgesses nominated new
Burgesses, who were admitted and sworn and thereby became entitled to the
Parliamentary franchise for these Boroughs. The two ancient Boroughs of
Pain's Castle and Presteign either lost, or had never possessed, such Courts, and
the House of Commons disallowed in 1690 the claims of their Burgesses to vote.
The Borough of New Radnor (p. 236), on the other hand, had become largely independent of the Hierarchy, getting a Royal Charter establishing a close Corporation, and holding its own Courts (History of Radnorshire, by Rev. J. Williams,
in Archæologia Cambrensis, 3rd ser. vols. iii. p. 26, and iv. p. 1, 1857-58 ; First
Report of Municipal Corporation Commission, 1835, vol. i. pp. 357-362).

following incoherent lines, pays threepence and goes out without saying another word :—

" With my white rod,
  And I am a fourth post,
  That threepence makes three,
  God bless the King, and the Lord of the Franchise,
  Our Weights and Measures are lawful and true,
  Good-morrow, Mr. Steward, I have no more to say to you.

" On default of any of these particulars the Court Leet of Combe is forfeited." [1] It does not appear to be an unwarranted inference that the Tithing of Combe Keynes, though possibly having a minor Court of its own, had not been granted the privilege of standardising its own weights and measures, and had to do suit at the superior Court at Winfrith by four men, of whom the Tithingman was the leader, and eventually the proxy for the others, paying a penny each for their absence. The attendance of the Tithingmen of the whole Hundred was (as we have seen at Taunton) usual at the Hundred Court. "If there be more than one Tithingman, as always is in the Hundred Court," says a widely circulated manual, "swear them all in like manner, and receive from them the Common Fine or King's Silver. Then take from them their resiant rolls or lists of their tithings; call them over and mark them that answer thus, 'appears.'" [2] The attendance even of the Tithingman might be dispensed with, his staff or rod of office being sent to represent him. Thus in the Hundred of Twyford, in Kent, "there was," we read, "till of late years a singular though a very ancient custom kept up of electing a Deputy to the Dumb Borsholder of Chart, as it

[1] *History and Antiquities of Dorset*, by John Hutchins, 1774, vol. i. p. 127 ; *Ancient Customs of Taunton Deane*, by H. B. Shillibeer, 1821. Can "post" be derived from "prepositus," the word used for Reeve ?

[2] *The Complete Courtkeeper, or Land Steward's Assistant*, by Giles Jacob, 1st edition, 1713 ; 8th, 1819, p. 30. We may catch a glimpse in 1774 of such attendance of the Tithingman at the Court of the Hundred at Whitchurch in Dorsetshire, comprising nineteen tithings. At the Court of this Hundred the residents in all the tithings were supposed to attend, and (as in the Hundred of Berkeley) to serve on its Juries. Two Constables were regularly appointed for the Hundred. But subordinate Courts were also held in some, at any rate, of the Manors within the Hundred, at which Petty Constables for these Manors (or apparently for the tithings) were appointed. Only in twelve out of the nineteen tithings did the Hundred Court appoint the Petty Constable (R. v. Genge, in *Reports of Cases, etc.*, by Henry Cowper, 1783, pp. 13-17).

was called, claiming liberty over fifteen houses in the precinct of Pizeinwell, every householder of which was formerly obliged to pay the keeper of this Borsholder one penny yearly. This Dumb Borsholder was always first called at the Court Leet holden for the Hundred of Twyford, when its keeper, who was yearly appointed by that Court, held it up to his call, with a neckcloth or handkerchief put through the iron ring fixed at the top, and answered for it. This Borsholder of Chart, and the Court Leet, has been discontinued about fifty years, and the Borsholder who is put in by the Quarter Sessions for Wateringbury claims over the whole parish. This Dumb Borsholder is made of wood, about three feet and half an inch long, with an iron ring at the top, and four more by the sides near the bottom, where it has a square iron spike fixed, four inches and a half long, to fix it in the ground, or on occasion to break open doors, etc., which used to be done "—it is said down to 1748—" without a Warrant of any Justice on suspicion of goods having been unlawfully come by and concealed in any of these fifteen houses." [1]

(b) *The Court of the Hundred*

The Hierarchy of Courts that we find so well preserved in the Vale of Berkeley and at Taunton Deane, and less perfectly elsewhere, throws, we think, some light on the nature and origin of the various other Courts, up and down the country, that we find existing under the name of Hundred Courts, without any apparent connection with separate Courts of minor jurisdiction. When, in the fourteenth century, the Hundred Courts were merged in the County Courts of the Sheriffs—if that is what happened—those Hundred Courts which had already passed, as valuable Franchises, into private hands were not affected.[2] Not infrequently, therefore, these continued to be held, and it may be that they went on without intermission into the eighteenth century; sometimes

---

[1] *History and Survey of Kent*, by Edward Hasted, 1797, vol. v. p. 107 ; *Observations on Popular Antiquities*, by John Brand, vol. i. p. 132 of 1841 edition ; *Kent's Capital*, 1906. So, too, we read that, in Essex, "Lambourn Manor was held by service of the Ward Staff" (*i.e.* the Constable's or Watchman's staff), which was carried into Court with quaint ceremonies (*Ancient Manorial Customs in the County of Essex*, by R. S. Charnock, 1870, pp. 17-22).

[2] *Lex Maneriorum*, by W. Nelson, 1728, p. 190.

held, as of old, like that of Fawsley, "beneath the spreading branches of an enormous beech tree."[1] We are inclined to doubt, however, whether the few specimens of which we have particulars are all of the same species. In some cases the surviving Hundred Court appears simply to have outlived the Hierarchy, whilst often itself combining with the Court of its principal Manor. In other cases we may suspect that the term Hundred Court never has denoted the superior member of any Hierarchy of Courts, and that it represents much the same jurisdiction as was elsewhere exercised by the ordinary Manor Courts. In rare instances, again, a so-called Hundred Court is found among the various Courts held by Municipal Corporations in and for their Boroughs, with no wider jurisdiction than a Borough Court.[2] As such it will fall to be described in subsequent chapters.

What appears to be a common feature of the so-called Hundred Courts between 1689 and 1835 is their extreme attenuation of function. The majority of those that survived into the eighteenth century seem to have been little more than Courts for the trial of petty civil actions for debt and damages, and, as such, hardly come within the scope of Local Government as we have defined it. Other Hundred Courts, whilst retaining traces of the Court Baron side, appear

---

[1] This Hundred Court was thus held in Fawsley Park until the beginning of the eighteenth century, when it was removed to Everdon (*History and Antiquities of Northamptonshire*, by George Baker, 1822, vol. i. p. 238; *Victoria County History of Northamptonshire*, vol. i. 1902, p. 298).

[2] Such was the Colchester "Hundred and Foreign Court." Such, too, was the "Hundred Court" of Kidwelly, in Carmarthenshire; and such were those in the Cinque Ports (p. 378).

Less clear is the case of the Hundred Court of Gloucester, which continued, as its Minutes show, to be nominally held by adjournment weekly before the Mayor and the two Sheriffs of the City. What it did is not apparent, as the Minutes contain, after 1680, little more than a perpetual repetition of the names of the suitors, who were the owners of certain estates in Gloucestershire and Herefordshire, the jurisdiction over which had, somehow or another, come to belong to the Corporation of Gloucester. It swore in Constables (*infra*, p. 341). During the whole period there was held also the Court Leet of the City of Gloucester half-yearly, before the Steward of the two Sheriffs, the MS. Minutes of which, between 1784 and 1819, show it to be making presentments of the usual kind. Whether the "Hundred Court" of Gloucester was merely held by the Corporation by right of its ownership of a Hundred, just as the Corporation of the City of London held the Bailiwick of Southwark; or whether, as Mr. Adolphus Ballard has suggested, it was a Court of the owners of those lands within the County which had to maintain the city wall, we must leave for antiquarian research.

chiefly as emasculated Courts Leet, appointing Constables and occasionally presenting nuisances. Our general impression is that these isolated Hundred Courts had once been undifferentiated Courts, dealing with all sorts of business indifferently, at one and the same Court, by one set of officers;[1] and that the appearance of specialisation has resulted from the unevenness of the decay into which their various functions were falling. Pending further study of the records of the various Hundred Courts from the fourteenth to the nineteenth century, we can do no more than set forth such particulars as we have been able to glean of those which existed after 1689.

A remarkable case of survival of an ancient Hundred Court, detached from the Manor Courts within the Hundred, is that of Salford,[2] in Lancashire, where we find the Steward of the Earl of Sefton, throughout the eighteenth, and down even to the middle of the nineteenth century, continuing to hold "the Court Leet, View of Frankpledge, and Court of Record of our Sovereign Lord the King for his Hundred or Wapentake of Salford." This Court evidently represented an ancient tribunal of which the jurisdiction extended nominally to the whole of the modern Hundred of Salford—perhaps

---

[1] Thus we are told that the "Hundred Court of Perveth" in Cardiganshire seems to have been held as a "Court Leet and Law Day" twice a year, and as a "Court Baron" fortnightly; it maintained the stocks and regulated the common, dealt with presentments and heard civil actions, and appointed both Constable and Reeve (prepositus or "major")—see *Treatise on Copyholds* by C. Watkins, 4th edition, 1825, p. 503.

[2] The archives of Salford, long neglected, scattered, and destroyed, are only now being collected and studied. Some records of the Lord's Court from 1597 to 1669—apparently the active Court of the Seignorial Borough, comparable with that of Berkeley or Wotton—have lately been published (*The Portmote, or Court Leet, Records of the Borough or Town and Royal Manor of Salford*, by J. G. de T. Mandley; Chetham Society, vols. xlvi. and xlvii., 1902). Stray records of Salford Courts exist, both of earlier and later date, some being preserved among the archives of the modern Salford Hundred Court of Record in Manchester, while those from 1828 to 1867 are in a thick, leather-bound volume now in the Salford Public Library. See also the particulars in House of Commons Return of Courts of Request, 1840; and Fifth Report of Royal Commission on Courts of Common Law, 1833; and the occasional reports in the newspapers, especially *Manchester Guardian*, 4th May 1833, 8th October 1836, 18th October 1837; *Manchester Chronicle*, 4th May 1833; *Manchester Times*, 19th December 1835; and, on the whole subject, *Mediæval Manchester and the Beginnings of Lancashire*, by James Tait, 1904, p. 9. The Manchester Municipal Code, vol. v., 1899, gives the Acts and Orders in Council, 1868-1893, with a short memorandum on the history of the Court (pp. 267-268).

to the whole of the ancient " Salfordshire,"—still described as
" the King's Manor of the Hundred of Salford," of which the
Earl of Sefton was not styled Lord but Steward, and which
included some fifty parishes or townships, among them being
Oldham, Bolton, Bury, and Manchester itself.[1]   Judging from
such fragmentary records as have survived, the Court of the
Hundred of Salford was in fact once as all-embracing as the
Court of the Hundred of Berkeley, having under it many
other Courts ; perhaps even the Court of the Barony of
Manchester itself, with its own subordinate Halimotes or
Courts Baron of the separate Manors, which we may assume
to have been undifferentiated Courts, or (in the case of Salford
and Manchester at any rate), like Berkeley or Wotton, the
Leets or Moots of favoured townships which seignorial Charters
had made into so-called Boroughs.   We shall describe
presently the vigorous life of the Manchester Court Leet.
In the sixteenth and seventeenth centuries there had been
another such Borough Court held at Salford itself, called the
Portmote, presumably under the charter of the Earl of
Chester and Lincoln of 1231.   At some period between
1669 and 1828—apparently between 1738 and 1800—
it seems to have coalesced with or been merged in the
Hundred Court, which presumably had continued to exercise
a wider jurisdiction.[2]   When we are again enabled to take

[1] Roger the Poitevin retained the township of Salford in demesne when he
enfeoffed under-tenants for the rest of his estate, a separation which had
lasting consequences.   "A stroke of a Norman baron's pen divorced Manchester
and Salford in all but their devotions, and what he sundered no one has been
able to bring together again, though they have long since ceased to be separated
by green fields sloping down to a trout stream.   A stranger who found himself
in Deansgate, and wanted to know why two types of tram-car were running in
what seemed to him a single city, would be mightily astonished if we told him
that this was the doing of a foreign Count of the eleventh century.   But so
it is.   It may be doubted whether it occurred to any citizen of Manchester
resident in Broughton, who, during the recent deadlock between the two
tramway committees, was turned out of the car at the city boundary, and had
to walk several hundred yards in the rain to catch a Salford car, to curse the
memory of Count Roger the Poitevin.   He might have done this with some
justice" (*Mediæval Manchester and the Beginnings of Lancashire*, by James
Tait, 1904, p. 10).

[2] We imagine that in many other cases the Court of the Hundred had
become combined with that of its principal Manor.   Thus, in the Hundred of
Crewkerne in Somerset, which constituted a single "Lordship," extending over
seven tithings, in the sixteenth, seventeenth, or eighteenth centuries, there was
only one Court held, called the Hundred Court and Court Baron.   At the
principal sessions of this Court each year the Lord nominated not only the

up the story in 1828, it is not the Portmote of the Borough
but the "Court Leet, View of Frankpledge, and Court of
Record . . . for the Hundred or Wapentake of Salford"
that is being held in Salford. By this time the Court, so
far as the area outside Salford Borough was concerned, had
ceased to stand in any relation whatever to such Manor
Courts as were still held within its ancient jurisdiction. In
1833, for instance, the Deputy Steward explained—probably
on the authority of Joseph Ritson's learned book—that " the
business of this Court solely applied to townships which had
not the benefit of Courts Leet of their own. This being
the Hundred Court Leet, it was their duty, therefore, to elect
Constables in such cases . . . and in the event of proper
persons not being returned by the townships to the Court,
or where two lists were presented, they must elect such
persons as would faithfully discharge the duties of the office."[1]
We accordingly find the Salford Hundred Court in 1828
attended every half-year by the Constables, Deputy Constables,

Bailiff of the Hundred, but also the Portreeve of the little town of Crewkerne,
who collected the profits of its fair and market. The suitors of the Court
elected the Reeve, who was responsible for collecting the quit-rents and fines
due from the tenants. The other sessions held during the year were known as
the Three Weeks' Courts, and at these the Tithingmen of the several districts
were bound to attend, each bringing with them four of their neighbours, who
were called " four posts," and who had to make presentments (*The Book of
the Axe,* by G. P. R. Pulman, 4th edition, 1875, pp. 247-250 ; quoting an
MS. Survey of the Manor in 1599). Possibly a similar case is .that of the
"Manor, Hundred, and Borough" of Bradford in Wiltshire, which we see
holding its "Court Leet, View of Frankpledge, and Court Baron" in 1819, and
appointing a Constable and an Assistant Constable for the Hundred, together
with a factotum, who combined in himself " the five offices of Bailiff of the
Hundred, Assistant Constable of the Hundred, Haywarden, Tithingman of
the Old Town and Tithingman of the New Town of Bradford." It is reported
to the Home Office that the new and zealous Constable has presented this
pluralist for making false presentments to the Quarter Sessions, swearing that
the roads were in good repair when they were not (Home Office Domestic State
Papers in Public Record Office, No. 10, 13th April and 1st May 1819, and
January 1820).

[1] Report of Proceedings of Salford Court Leet, *Manchester Chronicle,* 4th
May 1833. This view was upheld by the Court of King's Bench in 1822,
as against the inhabitants of the Township of Failsworth, who claimed to meet
annually to elect their own Constable, but failed definitely to allege that they
did this by prescription. The action of the Salford Court in appointing a
Constable for this Township was confirmed (R. *v.* Lane, in *Reports of Cases, etc.,*
by E. V. Barnewall and E. H. Alderson, 1823, vol. v. pp. 488-489). Ritson
had said that the Leet of a Hundred had jurisdiction only over such parts of
the Hundred as were not within the jurisdiction of the Court Leet of any
Manor (*Jurisdiction of the Courts Leet,* by J. Ritson, 3rd edition, 1816, p. 5).

and Assistant Constables of forty out of the fifty townships included within the Hundred; and enabling such nuisances in these townships as noxious smells and smoke from factories, obstructions of the highway, leaving roads unfenced in dangerous places, foul ditches, exposing unwholesome food for sale, and using false weights or measures to be presented and fined.[1] The Court was always held at Salford. We gather that the jurymen were chosen from residents of the so-called "Borough" of Salford, not, as at Berkeley, from the various Manors of the Hundred; the so-called Burgesses of Salford Borough were required to attend under penalty of sixpence, and inhabitants of the Borough not being Burgesses, under penalty of threepence; new Burgesses had to be sworn in; and it is evident that the principal business of the Court related to that Borough, for which, besides the officers of the Hundred, it appointed annually a Boroughreeve, two Constables, a Dog-muzzler, an Ale-taster, Bylaw-men and Inspectors of Flesh and Fish. The Hundred Court seems, in fact, to have been the only active "police and sanitary authority" which the township of Salford enjoyed, until the rise, early in the nineteenth century, of a democratic Open Vestry, and the advent, in 1829, of a statutory body of Police or Street Commissioners; and the fact that this Court appointed the Boroughreeve, gave it complete authority in what had already become a crowded and insanitary factory town.

Meanwhile there was being continuously held at Salford another series of Courts, from three weeks to three weeks, also

---

[1] See, for instance, MS. Minutes, Salford Hundred Court Leet, 9th April 1828. We add two examples as typical: "The jurors of our Lord the King upon their oaths present that at Ancoats Bridge within Ardwick in the said Hundred of Salford . . . is a manufactory for making sal ammoniac next to the King's common highway there leading from Manchester to Ashton . . . which emits great quantities of noisome and noxious fumes and vapours to the great nuisance of all the King's subjects passing and travelling there, by the default of Ebenezer Breillatt. . . . Therefore he is in mercy. . . . And they amerce him in five shillings, and he is commanded to abate the same within two months under the pain of one hundred pounds" (ibid. 9th April 1828). In 1833 the Deputy Constable of Pendleton said he had been requested by the respectable inhabitants of that township to present a number of owners and occupiers of property abutting "the Black ditch . . . full to overflowing of refuse of dyehouses . . . causing an intolerable stench . . . the most intolerable nuisance in the neighbourhood." The Jury thereupon presented the offenders (ibid. April 1833).

purporting to be those of the Court of the Salford Hundred or Wapentake. Every third Thursday one or other of the three Deputy Stewards, whom the Earl of Sefton had appointed for this special purpose,[1] held his Court for the trial of actions for debt or damages under forty shillings within the wide limits of the Hundred. Over a thousand such actions a year were being dealt with by this Court in 1835,[2] notwithstanding the concurrent existence as petty debt tribunals of the Court Baron of Manchester and of statutory Courts of Requests in and for Manchester, Oldham, Bury, and Rochdale.[3]

Amid the political agitation of 1829-32, the Radicals began to chafe against the "self-elect" constitution of the Salford Hundred Court, by which they meant exclusively the half-yearly sessions for the appointment of Borough officers. They recalled the fact that the Earl of Sefton, as a Whig peer, had supported the Reform Bill; and some of them urged him to be true to his faith in representative government, and to cause his Deputy Steward to leave off packing the Jury with Tories. Lord Sefton fell in with this view, and from 1835 onward the jury-

---

[1] In 1835, at any rate, and for many years previously, these Deputy Stewards were the members of one of the leading firms of solicitors at Manchester, and quite distinct from the Deputy Steward, a barrister, whom the Earl appointed to hold the half-yearly Courts.

[2] House of Commons Return of Courts of Request, 1840 ; Fifth Report of Royal Commission on Courts of Common Law, 1833, pp. 26a, 53a, 61a, 78a, 108a, 132a, 1b, 10b.

[3] Somewhat akin to the position of the Salford Hundred Court was apparently that of Bradford at Wellington in Shropshire. This Court, held by the Duke of Cleveland under Royal Letters Patent of 1672, had once exercised full jurisdiction over the whole Hundred. By the nineteenth century, however, it had come to exercise what we may call Leet jurisdiction, and to appoint Constables only for those Manors within the Hundred which no longer held Courts of their own. It continued, however, to sit fortnightly for the preliminary stages of civil actions, and twice a year for the trial of causes arising anywhere within the Hundred. At the two general Courts (one of them being utilised for the appointment of Constables, etc.) it is said that the Constables of the Hundred had to attend (Fifth Report of Royal Commission on Courts of Common Law, 1833, pp. 106a, 167a, 168a ; House of Commons Return of Hundred Courts, 1839, p. 5 ; and of Courts of Request, 1840, pp. 132-133). Here, too, we may mention the Court of the Hundred of Whitchurch (Dorset), which did not try civil suits, but appointed two Constables for the Hundred and Tithingmen for such of the nineteen Tithings within the Hundred as did not have Courts of their own. When a resident in one of the Tithings for which a Manor Court was held had been appointed Constable for the Hundred by the Hundred Court, he appealed to the Court of King's Bench for exemption, on the plea that the Hundred Court had no right to appoint a resident "within a private Leet." But he was held liable to serve the Hundred (R. v. Genge, 1774, in Reports of Cases, etc., by Henry Cowper, 1783, pp. 13-17).

men at the half-yearly meetings were taken by lot from a list of the five hundred highest rated inhabitants.[1]   At the same time it became taken for granted that this Jury should accept, for the offices of Boroughreeve and Constables, the nominations made by the open Vestry Meeting.[2]   Under these circumstances there seems to have been no popular objection to the continu- ance of the formal participation of the Hundred Court in the Local Government of the Borough, and its half-yearly sessions accordingly went on being formally held, and its annual appoint- ments of Boroughreeve and other officers being made, down to 1867.   No objection seems ever to have been made to the three-weekly trial of civil actions, under which form, by virtue of successive Acts of Parliament, and with only the slightest change of name, the ancient Court of the Wapentake or Hundred of Salford survives to this day.[3]

On the South Coast of England we find, right down to 1855, at Brighton, in Sussex, the Court of the Hundred of Whalesbone, or more properly, Wellesbourne.   This was de- scribed as "the Leet or Lawday and View of Frankpledge," not for any one Manor but for the whole of the Hundred, the

---

[1] The reformer who secured this change was one J. S. Ormerod, who was pre- sented with a gold snuff-box by his admirers. His reply contains the following passages, which we give as specimens of the feeling that prevailed. "When I first thought of making an effort to prevent the Borough of Salford . . . from being ruled and governed in its Municipal constitution by men who had nothing to recommend them but superstition and bigoted Toryism ; when I found also that these men were chosen by a class of individuals who were self-elected from men possessing precisely the same politics as themselves ; when I found that these men were so ignorant as to boast of having been upon that Jury thirty years, some for more than twenty, others for twenty "—he determined to approach Lord Sefton, who made inquiry and directed his Deputy Steward to adopt a new plan (*Manchester Times*, 19th December 1835).

[2] See, for instance, *Manchester Guardian*, 8th October 1836.

[3] In 1846 its jurisdiction was preserved and enlarged, so as to enable it to deal with actions up to £50, by 9 and 10 Victoria, c. 126.   In 1868 it was amalgamated with the Court of Record held by the Manchester Corporation under its Charter of 1838 and 17 and 18 Victoria, c. 84, and given the new title of the Salford Hundred Court of Record (31 and 32 Victoria, c. 130). The Earl of Sefton was thereby continued as High Steward, with a right to receive one-third of the fees arising from such cases as would have been within the jurisdiction of the old Salford Court, less a proportion of the expenses, but in no case to amount to less than two hundred guineas a year (sec. 35).   The Boroughs of Oldham, Bolton, Heywood, and Rochdale successively got them- selves exempted from the jurisdiction of the Salford Hundred Court, in all matters in which the modern County Court has cognizance (Orders in Council of 30th December 1878, 16th August 1886, and 15th March 1893, and the Oldham Corporation Act 1886, 49 and 50 Victoria, c. 117).

Lord or Steward of the Hundred being the Earl of Abergavenny.   The Hundred of Whalesbone comprised the parish
of Brighthelmston (now Brighton) with the "Boroughs" or
hamlets of Preston and Patcham—a much smaller area than
the Hundred of Berkeley.   Within the Hundred there were,
however, a number of reputed Manors and parcels of Manors,
inextricably confused by partitions and alienations.   Brighthelmston itself, in the days when its importance lay in its
fishing, had had an important Manor Court of its own, of which
the "ancient customs" had been of sufficient consequence to
be investigated by a special Royal Commission of 1580.[1]
What Lord's Courts were held in the eighteenth century within
the Hundred, and exactly for what purposes, we have been
unable to ascertain.[2]   But the Hundred Court continued
vigorously to exist, though, as we gather, principally, if not
entirely, for the purpose of appointing annually at Easter the
various officers of the Hundred: the High Constable, twelve
Headboroughs or Assistant Constables,[3] an Aleconner, and a
Searcher and Sealer of Leather.   It had apparently only one
Jury, summoned by the Deputy Steward.   It seems not to
have dealt with actions for debt or damages.   Of the history
of this ancient jurisdiction during the eighteenth century we
know nothing.   We find it after the Parliamentary election of
1825 coming into sharp conflict with the Vestry, which refused
to pass the High Constable's accounts.   The items objected to
related to the swearing in of special constables "during the late
county election," and the payments to private persons for
apprehending suspected criminals and vagrants.[4]   These items
appeared, in accordance with the provisions of 18 George III.
c. 19 (1779), in the Overseers' accounts, and as it had never
become quite clear whether the consent of the Vestry was
necessary to their validity, the County Magistrates did not
scruple to pass the Overseers' accounts containing the items

---

[1] *History of Brighthelmston*, by J. A. Erredge, 1862 ; *Compendious History of Sussex*, by M. A. Lower, 1870, vol. i. pp. 77-84 ; *Sussex Archæological Collections*, vol. ii. p. 38.   We recur to this in the following chapter (p. 173).

[2] There is evidence that Manorial Courts were held for property business ; see, for instance, the reference to the surrender of certain tenements by the Churchwardens of Brighthelmston "at a General Court Baron for the Manor of Allingworth" (MS. Vestry Minutes, Brighton, 3rd February 1806).

[3] *Brighton Herald*, 9th April 1825.

[4] *Ibid.* 17th September 1825 and 29th July 1826.

objected to.[1] The friction between the Vestry and the Hundred Court continued; and in 1828 the Vestry sent an elaborate memorial to the Earl of Abergavenny, as "the Lord of the Leet of the Hundred of Whalesbone," protesting against "the great, notorious, and crying abuse," that the outgoing High Constable packed the Jury summoned to elect his successor, and "the choice has consequently not been congenial to the wishes of the inhabitants."[2] It appears that the same little set of the Vicar, the County Justices resident in the town, and other Tory magnates had appeared as jurymen year after year, the Vicar acting always as Foreman. In answer to this memorial the Steward addressed to the Vestry a long and able description of the procedure of the Hundred Court. In future, he adds, "I shall require the High Constable to return to me . . . a list of at least fifty of the most respectable inhabitants . . . and I shall advise that such list be made known to the public. . . . From this list I shall select by ballot 23 to form a Jury. . . . If any reasonable and fair objection shall be stated in Court . . . to any gentleman so summoned . . . I shall not hesitate to dispense with the attendance of that juryman."[3] The result was that within a short time the Vestry and the High Constable became on excellent terms,[4] and the Hundred Court continued to be held for nearly another generation.[5]

[1] MS. Minutes, Quarter Sessions, Sussex, 20th October 1825. Such a case had then recently occurred at the Cheshire Quarter Sessions, where the Constable of Ashton-under-Lyne had laid his accounts before the Vestry, and had an item disallowed (the expense of prosecuting a Dissenting Minister for preaching in the streets); two Justices had nevertheless allowed the Overseers' Accounts including this item. One out of the eight Overseers appealed to Quarter Sessions, which confirmed the allowance. The Court of King's Bench dismissed an appeal on the ground that it was not promoted by a majority of the Overseers, without, therefore, deciding that the action of the Justices had been wrong (R. v. Justices of Lancashire, in *Reports of Cases, etc.*, by E. V. Barnewall and E. H. Alderson, 1823, vol. v. pp. 755-758).

[2] *Brighton Herald*, 2nd February 1828.

[3] MS. Vestry Minutes, Brighton, 25th January and 22nd February 1828.

[4] *Ibid.* 20th January 1831.

[5] For the so-called Hundreds of Sussex and Kent, and their relations to the "Rapes" or "Lathes" of these Counties, see "The Hundred of Eastbourne and its Six Boroughs," by Rev. William Hudson, *Sussex Archæological Collections*, vol. xlii. p. 189, 1899, and "Liberties and Franchises within the Rape of Hastings," by W. D. Cooper, *Sussex Archæological Collections*, vol. vi., 1853, pp. 57-70. "In Sussex," we learn of the thirteenth century, "each Hundred seems to have had a Beadle, that is, a summoner, who was called an Alderman," and who sometimes performed the suit of court due by the tenants of the Hundred at superior Courts (*History of English Law*, by Sir F. Pollock and F. W. Maitland, 1895, vol. i. p. 545). At Swanborough, one of these

The Hundred Courts which remained in private hands are scarcely to be distinguished from the Courts of Franchises, Liberties, Lordships, or Honours which had obtained exemption from the jurisdiction of, or concurrent jurisdiction with, the County Court. The Franchise or Liberty often included several Hundreds. In the " Seven Hundreds " of Cirencester in Gloucestershire, for instance, which had for five or six centuries enjoyed great exemptions from the Sheriff of the County, there continued to be held, in the eighteenth century, a three-weekly Court under the Steward of Earl Bathurst. Its business seems to have been exclusively the trial of small civil suits, personal actions, and debts under forty shillings. It was, we are told, regarded as " vexatious, dila-tory, and expensive," and so was superseded in 1792 by the effect of a Local Act, which created a Court of Requests, under seventy-five Commissioners, who took it in turn to sit as judges.[1]

In Kent the " Seven Hundreds " constituted a Franchise, having a Court of its own, held by the Bailiff. This Court

"Hundreds," which belongs to the Marquis of Abergavenny, and comprises several parishes, " Boroughs," and Manors, the ancient Court of the Hundred was held right down to our own day. There attended the Constable and Alderman of the Hundred, the Headboroughs of the Parishes, and one or two dozen jurymen. Annoyances and defaults were presented and amerced, and civil suits under forty shillings were tried. The Jury presented persons to serve as Constable and Alderman of the Hundred (down to 1860) and Head-boroughs of the various parishes (down to 1842), of whom the Steward chose one ("The Hundred of Swanborough," by J. Cooper, in *Sussex Archæological Collections*, vol. iv., October 1890). See also *The Perambulation of Kent*, by W. Lambard, 1576, p. 21 ; *Robinson on Gavelkind*, 5th edition, by C. J. Elton and H. J. H. Mackay, 1897, p. 211. Of the village of Lamberhurst we read that "a fair is held here yearly on 10th October for toys and pedlary, the profits of which the Portreeve of the Hundred of Milton receives of ancient custom, which officer executed within this Hundred the office of Clerk of the Market in all points whilst the Market was held, but it has been disused time out of mind" (*History of Kent*, by E. Hasted, 1797 to 1801, vol. vii. p. 53). For Tenterden Seven Hundreds, see *History of the Weald of Kent*, by R. Furley, 1871, vol. i. pp. 315-324, vol. ii. p. 555 ; *History of the Weald of Kent*, by T. D. W. Dearn, 1814, pp. 162, 233-245 ; House of Commons Return of Courts of Request, 1840.

[1] *History of Cirencester*, by K. J. Beecham, 1887, pp. 162-170. This Court of Requests was, like others, itself superseded after 1846 by the new County Courts. We may mention here (though we have no information as to their Courts) the analogous " Seven Hundreds " of Worcestershire, which had of old such extensive immunities ; the Hundreds of Windsor Forest, and, best known of all, the Chiltern Hundreds (Desborough, Stoke, and Bray in Buckinghamshire), of which the Stewardship—remaining, as it does, in the gift of the Chancellor of the Exchequer—has become a minor part of the machinery of Parliamentary procedure (see *The Stewardship of the Chiltern Hundreds*, by F. S. Parry, a privately printed Treasury Memorandum of 1893 ;

was held during the eighteenth century, and only discontinued after the whole Franchise had been sold by the Crown in 1817 to a private landowner. Within the Franchise, as we learn from a survey of the time of the Commonwealth, "there belongeth to each Hundred a Court Leet, where the Constables and Borsholders are elected, and all nuisances are amerced by the Steward and Jury, which Court is held whenever the Lord or Steward may appoint." In six of these "Seven Hundreds" the Court used to be held by the Steward or Bailiff for the profit of the Crown. In the seventh, comprising Tenterden, the chief town, the ownership of this so-called "royalty of the Court of the Bailiwick of the Seven Hundreds" was vested in the Mayor and twelve Jurats of the Municipal Corporation, by whom the Court was, in 1814, still being held.

Throughout the wide area of Yorkshire there were Courts in every Wapentake, the division corresponding with the Hundred. We catch a glimpse of these Courts in 1641 in the notebook of a Yorkshire farmer. "The baily [Bailiff] of every Wapentake," he says, "is to keep a Court, which is called the Wapentake Court, Three Weeks' Court, or Sheriffs' Turn, where any petty cause or small trespass may be heard and ended once within three weeks." In at least two Wapentakes these Courts continued to be held for more than two centuries much as Henry Best describes them; some remnants lingering until the middle of the nineteenth century.[1]

In Cheshire there continued to be held an active Hundred Court for the Hundred of Wirral, which includes the town of Birkenhead. This was held on lease from the Crown until 1819, when it reverted to the Commissioners of Woods and Forests, by whom it was sold in 1820 for £500 to a Liverpool attorney. The Court continued for another generation to do an extensive business in petty debt cases, especially those arising in the rapidly growing town of Birkenhead.[2]

"The Ancient Hundreds of Buckinghamshire," by Morley Davies, in *Home Counties Magazine*, vol. vi. pp. 134-144; article by J. H. Round in *Victoria County History of Buckinghamshire*, vol. i. 1905, p. 225).

[1] *Rural Economy in Yorkshire in 1641*, by Henry Best, Surtees Society, vol. xxxiii., 1857, p. 91; House of Commons Return of Courts of Request, 1840, pp. 170-171.

[2] Fifth Report of Royal Commission on Courts of Common Law, 1833; House of Commons Returns of Hundred Courts, 1839, and Courts of Request.

At least a score of other Hundred Courts continued to be held in different parts of the country throughout the eighteenth, and down to the middle of the nineteenth, century,[1] principally as tribunals for the trial of small civil suits. We find them also, here and there, appointing not only Bailiffs and Constables for the Hundred or Liberty itself,[2] but also Constables and Haywards for Manors within the Hundred, but not exercising any other functions of the mediæval Courts. Similarly, there existed down to the same period a score of Courts of Honours, Lordships, or Liberties,[3] which were not styled Hundred Courts,

1840 ; *History of the Hundred of Wirral*, by W. Mortimer, 1847 ; *Liverpool Courier*, 9th April 1869.

[1] Among these other surviving Hundred Courts the principal were those for the other Hundreds of Lancashire, Amounderness (held by a Steward for the Duchy itself), West Derby (held by the Earl of Sefton), Lonsdale (held by the Earl of Lonsdale) ; that held by the Duke of Richmond for "Richmondshire," comprising five Wapentakes of the North Riding of Yorkshire ; those of Scarsdale and Chesterfield in Derbyshire, held by the Duke of Devonshire under a grant of 1631 ; that of Bucklow (Cheshire), held on lease from the Crown by the Egertons of Tatton ; that of Grumbald's Ash (Gloucestershire), held by the Duke of Beaufort under lease from the Crown down to 1835, until which date it appointed Constables and Haywards for the Manors within the Hundred, as well as tried petty debt cases ; those of Chew Magna (Somerset), which ceased to be held about 1836 ; Keynsham (Wiltshire), Portbury (Wiltshire), Whitstone (Wiltshire), Offlow (Staffordshire), Durnford (Sussex) ; St. Briavel's (Gloucestershire), held by a Steward for the Crown ; Henbury (Gloucestershire), Thornbury (Gloucestershire) ; Huntingstone (Huntingdonshire), belonging to the Earl of Sandwich ; Penwith (Cornwall), Pain's Castle (Radnor), and the Duke of Beaufort's Court Baron for the Hundred of Crickhowell (Breconshire). Some particulars as to their activity in 1830-40 may be gathered from the Fifth Report of the Commission on Courts of Common Law, 1833, and the House of Commons Returns of Hundred Courts, 1839, and Courts of Request, 1840.

[2] "Bailiffs and Constables of Hundreds are chosen annually at the Courts Leet for the several Hundreds and Liberties within the County" (*A Guide to the Practice of the Court of Quarter Sessions for the County of Somerset*, by J. Jesse, 1815, p. 20).

[3] Such as the Nottinghamshire Peverel Court, held by Lord Middleton as Steward, and exercising jurisdiction, concurrently with the two County Courts, within the whole of the Counties of Nottinghamshire and Derbyshire except the Corporate towns ; Tutbury Honour Court, held by the Duke of Devonshire at Tutbury (Staffordshire) every three weeks for civil actions by residents within the Honour, which included parts of no fewer than six Counties and had its own Coroner as well as its own Bailiff (*Three Centuries of Derbyshire Annals*, by J. C. Cox, pp. 71-84) ; the Court Baron of the Honour of Pontefract (Yorkshire), with jurisdiction over 350 townships, in a district of 600 square miles, and held twice a year each at Leeds, Bradford, and Huddersfield ; Allertonshire Liberty Court (Yorkshire), held by the Bishop of Ripon every three weeks, for the thirty-two townships within the Liberty ; the Court of the Liberty and Honour of Pickering Lythe (Yorkshire), held twice a year only ; Skipton Honour Court (Yorkshire), held under Letters Patent of 1307 by the Earl of Thanet as Lord of the Honour ; Whitby Strand Liberty Court, held by the Cholmleys as Bailiffs

but which exercised jurisdiction over areas within which there were at least several Manors, and which occasionally extended to hundreds of square miles. We cannot help regretting that so little examination has been made of the sixteenth, seventeenth, and eighteenth century records of these Hundred Courts, and other Courts of wider jurisdiction than that of a Manor, from which additional light might be thrown on the relations of the different Courts of the ancient Hierarchy.[1]

of the Liberty, in succession to the Abbots of Whitby (Yorkshire); Kidwelly Honour or Lordship and Liberty Court, held by the Earl of Cawdor for three "commotes" of Carmarthenshire, comprising nineteen Manors and sixteen Parishes; Perfeth Court Baron, also held by the Earl of Cawdor, as Lord of the Lordship; the Court of Pleas for the Honour of Leicester, held by a steward for the Duchy of Lancaster, in some connection with the Courts Leet of nine Manors within the Honour; the Ramsey Court of Pleas, held under ancient charters by the Lord of the Liberty of Ramsey (Huntingdonshire); Ampthill Honour Court (Bedfordshire), not held for the trial of actions after the eighteenth century; Bromfield and Yale Lordship Court (Denbighshire), held at the beginning of the eighteenth century by the Grosvenors as Lords of the Lordship; and various other Welsh Lordship Courts, such as Chirk, which ceased to be held in consequence of an adverse judgment of the Court of King's Bench about 1827 (Williams *v.* Lord Bagot, *Reports of Cases*, by Barnewall and Cresswell, vol. iii. pp. 235, 772, etc.). With these should perhaps be classed the great Wakefield Court Baron held by the Lord of the extensive jurisdiction of Wakefield, which included, by 1835, a quarter of a million inhabitants, and exercised important functions in connection with weights and measures, as well as dealing with a couple of thousand civil actions annually. Some information about them in 1830-40 may be gathered from the House of Commons Returns of Hundred Courts, 1838, and Courts of Request, etc., 1840, and the Fifth Report of the Royal Commission on the Courts of Common Law, 1833.

[1] We cannot pretend to deal with the various Forest Courts, held under picturesque names in districts which were technically royal forests. The special forest laws (as to which the various editions of John Manwood's *Forest Laws*, from 1598 to 1665, were authoritative) apparently ceased to be enforced after the Commonwealth, the Act "for the limitation of Forests," 16 Charles I. c. 16 (1640), having practically brought the old system to an end. Some attempt was made to revive the Courts on the Restoration; but we do not actually know that either the six-weekly "Court of Attachment" or "Woodmote," the "Court of Regard" every third year, or the "Court of Justice Seat" was held after the Revolution (*Life of Lord Justice Guilford*, by the Hon. Roger North, 1808, vol. i. p. 75; *The Rural Life of England*, by William Howitt, 1838, vol. ii. p. 59). But Courts continued to be held, sometimes under the ancient forest name of "Swainmote" or "Swanimote," sometimes under that of Halmote Court, in various forest districts, especially in the Forest of Dean, though they seem to have decayed rapidly after the first quarter of the eighteenth century, and to have become often formal only. To this day, however, in the Forest of Dean, the Steward of the Crown holds his Court annually at the "Speech House," wearing a cocked hat, and equipped with a sword. We may yet read *The Rights of His Majesty's Forest Asserted, in a Charge given at a Swanimote Court held . . . before the Verderers of the Forest of Windsor*, 1717, by Nathaniel Boothe, Steward of the Court, 1719; and

(c) The Court of the Manor

The Court of the Hundred, where it continued into the eighteenth century, retained, as we have seen, little beyond its function as a tribunal for petty actions of debt, combining with this, in a few instances, the more or less formal appointment of Constables and other officers. This was not the case with the innumerable Manor Courts that existed in 1689, many of which continued, right into the nineteenth century, to be active local authorities, managing the commonfields and pastures, suppressing nuisances, providing the police, and trying cases of debt and trespass in the little communities over which they had jurisdiction.[1] It is, in fact, the existence of the humble Court of the Manor, much more than that of the enigmatical and pretentious Courts of the Hundred, Honour, Barony, or Forest, that compels us to include the Lord's Court in our survey of English Local Government between 1689 and 1835.

It is significant that this Court of the Manor, as we find

"The Rolls of the Court of Attachment of the Royal Forest of Waltham" between 1713 and 1848 are printed as vol. v. of the Report of the Epping Forest Commissioners, 1873. See *Select Pleas of the Forest*, by G. J. Turner (Selden Society, 1901); *Remarks on Forest Scenery*, by W. Gilpin, 1791, with a good list of Forests; *Historical Inquiries concerning Forests and Forest Laws*, by Percival Lewis, 1811; the statutes of 1817 and 1829; an able article in *Edinburgh Review*, April 1902; *The Royal Forests of England*, by J. C. Cox, 1905; and *A History of English Law*, by Prof. W. S. Holdsworth, 1903, pp. 340-352. Also the various reports of the Commissioners of Woods, Forests, and Land Revenues, especially those of 1788 and 1853; that of the House of Commons Committees on the Forest of Dean, 1874, and on the Woods and Forests, 1889 and 1890; Report on the Forest of Dean, by H. C. Hill, published by the Stationery Office, 19th July 1887; *The Forest of Dean*, by H. G. Nicholls, 1858; an exceptionally well-informed article in *The English Historical Review*, vol. xxi., 1906, pp. 445-459; *The History of the Forest of Dean in Gloucestershire*, by John Nisbet; *History of Knaresborough*, by Eli Hargrove, 1798; *History of the Forest of Rossendale*, by T. Newbigging, 1868; *The Honour and Forest of Pickering*, by R. B. Turton (North Riding Record Society, N.S., vols. i.-iii., 1894-96); *The Forest of Essex*, by W. R. Fisher, 1887; *Annals of the Ancient Royal Forest of Exmoor*, by E. J. Rawle, 1893; *The Great Forest of Brecknock*, by John Lloyd, 1905; vol. ii. of the *Victoria County History of Hampshire*, 1905, pp. 409-470, for the New Forest; and chap. iv., "Forest Police," in *The History of Police in England*, by Captain Melville Lee.

[1] "Every Manor," it was said, "is a little Commonwealth whereof the tenants are the members, the land the body, and the Lord the head" (*The Surveyor's Dialogue*, by John Norden, 4th edition, 1738, p. 44).

it existing after 1689 from one end of England to the other, is an Undifferentiated Court. Whatever it may be termed by the Steward, it combines and confuses in its actual procedure and work the attributes which the sixteenth-century lawyer ascribed to his three or four distinct tribunals. In the vast majority of the Manors that we have examined, we see the Steward giving notice, once or twice a year, that he would hold, not the various separate Courts given in the text-books, but, under one name or other, simply the Lord's Court. This might be held in the open air, beneath some aged tree;[1] it might, as at Selborne in Hampshire, be in an ancient barn of the Manor farm;[2] it might be at the Lord's Manor-house (perhaps for this reason in Southern England often called a Court);[3] or occasionally in some old building in the village known as the Court House,[4] or even, in a few cases, the Town Hall, or Gild Hall.[5] It was a common practice to "open the Court" at the ancient place and then instantly to adjourn to the largest room of the village inn.[6] There would be a customary date for holding the Court, which would be seldom departed from—it might be soon after Michaelmas or Easter; it might, as at Coggeshall in Essex, be on Whit Monday;[7] it might, as at Andover in Hampshire, be "the Sunday next before St. Michael";[8] in many of the Manors of the Bishop of Winchester we read of "the Turn of St. Martin," or "the

---

[1] *Treatise on Copyholds*, by Charles Watkins, 4th edition, 1825, vol. ii. p. 9. At Newton (Norfolk), in 1531, it was "under the oak" (*The Manor and Manorial Records*, by N. J. Hone, 1906, p. 132).

[2] *Practical Treatise on Copyhold Tenure*, by R. B. Fisher, 1794, p. 59.

[3] Or "place," which may be from "placitum" (*Treatise on Copyholds*, by Charles Watkins, 4th edition, 1825, vol. ii. p. 11). Mr. Seebohm connects "Court" with "curtis," which is "so often applied to the later Manor-house"; and with the "cohortes" around a Roman villa (*English Village Community*, by F. Seebohm, 1883, p. 263).

[4] So at Epworth in Lincolnshire (see *History and Topography of the Isle of Axholme*, by Rev. W. B. Stonehouse, 1839, pp. 143-149).

[5] At Coggeshall in Essex the Court was always held at the Shambles in the market-place (*Treatise on Copyholds*, by C. Watkins, 4th edition, 1825, vol. ii. p. 574). At Bungay it was held "in the Corn Cross," until the demolition of that building in 1810 (*History of Suffolk*, by Rev. A. Suckling, 1846, p. 129).

[6] *Treatise on Copyholds*, by C. Watkins, 4th edition, 1825, vol. ii. p. 9. At Yardley Hastings, in Northamptonshire, the Court was always formally opened in an ancient hall in the village, and then adjourned to the village inn (*Practical Treatise on Copyhold Tenure*, by John Scriven, 1816, p. 5).

[7] *Treatise on Copyholds*, by C. Watkins, 4th edition, 1825, vol. ii. p. 574.

[8] *Firma Burgi*, by Thos. Madox, 1726, p. 210; *Treatise on Copyholds*, by Charles Watkins, 4th edition, 1825, vol. ii. p. 477.

Turn of Hock";[1] it might even be, as in a Manor near Rochford, Essex, "at cockcrowing, before the day was well light."[2] At such a Court — in different Manors called indifferently the View of Frankpledge, the Court Baron,[3] the Turn, the Court Leet, the Lawday, the Leet, or simply the Great Court or the Little Court—there would attend most of the men of the village, whether freeholders or copyholders, leaseholders or cottagers. In Manor after Manor we find evidence that some sort of roll of names was read over, and defaulters fined. Thus at Standon in Staffordshire, during the eighteenth century, the fine for non-attendance was a shilling for freeholders, sixpence for leaseholders and other tenants of the Manor, and twopence for cottagers.[4] Elsewhere it often seems to have been only the freehold or copyhold tenants of the Manor whose attendance was insisted on. At Braintree in 1653 the tenants who did not appear were severally fined three shillings; in 1665, freeholders two shillings and copyholders one shilling; whilst in 1732 the absent freeholders had to pay only a shilling each and the copyholders half a crown.[5] At Devonport, about 1800, we read that "all the tenants are obliged to attend, or be amerced two and sixpence."[6]

---

[1] See MS. Manor Rolls, Farnham, Surrey, 8th October 1717, for one of many examples.

[2] "The Honour of Rayleigh in Essex . . . hath a Custom Court kept yearly the Wednesday next after St. Michael's Day; the Court is kept in the night and without light but as the sky gives, at a little hill without the town called the King's Hill, where the Steward writes only with coals and not with ink. And many men and Manors of great worth hold of the same, and do suit unto this strange Court, where the Steward calls them with as low a voice as possible he may; giving no notice when he goes to the Hill to keep the same Court; and he that attends not is deeply amerced if the Steward will" (*The Surveyor's Dialogue*, by John Norden, 4th edition, 1738, p. 161). How much truth and how much significance there was in this account of what was apparently nicknamed "the Lawless Court" we cannot say (see *Law Dictionary*, by John Cowell, 1727, under this appellation; *Treatise on Copyholds*, by Charles Watkins, 4th edition, 1825, vol. ii. p. 9).

[3] Court Baron is clearly "curia baronis," and the meaning of "curia baronis" is significantly explained by the variant "curia nobilis viri R.R." that we find as the title of the Braintree Court in the earliest roll (1616). It was simply the Lord's Court. There seems to have been every variety in the name borne by the Court in different Manors, and we can trace little connection, in the period 1689-1835, between these variations of name and the equally great variations in function.

[4] *The History of Standon*, by Edward Salt, 1888.

[5] MS. Manor Rolls, Braintree (Essex).

[6] *The Plymouth Dock Guide*, p. 28 (*circa* 1800). At Leamington the Earl of Aylesford, as Lord of the Manor, revived the Lord's Court in that Manor in

An indisputable element in the Lord's Court, and the *primum mobile* upon which all its action depended, was the Jury or Homage, the sample of the inhabitants by which the community as a whole was represented. The Jury was always formally summoned by the Bailiff or Beadle, at the command of the Steward, but exactly in what way the important task of selection was performed is seldom to be discovered. It may be that, in some cases, the tenants of the Manor were supposed to be taken haphazard in rotation. In some Manors, as we have reason to believe, the choice was controlled by the Steward. In the Manor of Dymock, Gloucestershire, by ancient custom recorded in 1565 and 1657, the Steward chose one " free-bencher " and the tenants another, these two jointly selecting the twelve tenants who were to form " the Lord's Homage." In case of their disagreement, the Steward decided.[1] On the other hand, a learned lawyer writes in 1825 that, " So far at least as my own experience extends, the Steward of the Court is totally ignorant even of the names of the jurors until the delivery to him by the Bailiff of the persons summoned as jurymen, together with the resiant roll, or names of those who are liable to perform suit to the Lord at the particular Court." [2]

The Jury was sometimes appointed to serve until the holding of the next Court, and sometimes appointed, sworn, and discharged at each Court.[3] The number varied, twelve

1828, after ninety years' desuetude. " Over 900 householders answered to their names and paid their fines " (*Complete History of Royal Leamington Spa*, by T. H. B. Dudley, 1896-97, pp. 188-89). A Steward who holds Courts in many Manors in the Southern Counties informed us (1906) that when he first took in this duty he frequently found the villagers swarming to the Court, though it was called a Court Baron, and they were neither freeholders nor copyholders. These residents presented themselves as of old, believing vaguely that they had some right or were under some obligation to attend ; and they were sometimes much aggrieved at being told that they had no part in the ceremony.

[1] *Treatise on Copyholds*, by C. Watkins, 4th edition, 1825, vol. ii. pp. 487-491.

[2] *Treatise on Copyholds*, by John Scriven, 2nd edition, 1823, vol. ii. p. 845.

[3] " The Jurymen," says Ritson, " in some Manors continue in office for a whole year, while in others they are sworn and discharged in the course of the day " (*Jurisdiction of the Courts Leet*, by Joseph Ritson, 1816, p. 9). " In some Manors it is not the practice to summon a fresh Jury whenever a Court is held, but the same tenants are summoned for successive Courts, vacancies in the list being filled from time to time by the Steward, or by the permanent Foreman and the Steward together " (*Law of Copyholds*, by C. I. Elton and H. J. H. Mackay, 2nd edition, 1893, pp. 197-198).

or more being the most frequent. Here again, whilst we find some of the names used by the lawyers, we seek in vain for some of their distinctions. In the Court at Braintree the well-kept records make it clear that there was only one Jury, which consisted, as the names reveal, of the ordinary house-holders of the little town; and which made all the present-ments of the Court. In the Court of the "Honour and Manor" of Hampton Court, between 1800 and 1808, we find the twelve to fourteen jurors described as "the jurors as well for the Court Leet as for the Court Baron and Customary Court"—there being, in fact, only one Jury for what was, in practice, a single undifferentiated Court. So, in many scores of Manors in ecclesiastical hands, within the dioceses of Canterbury, London, and Winchester, of which we have been permitted to consult the Manor Rolls, we find that the Jury was sworn as the Jury of the King and the Lord; though where business affecting property had to be done it was frequently styled also the Homage. On the other hand, at Epworth, in Lincolnshire, there were, in 1776 at any rate, clearly two Juries, but these were not called the Homage and the Leet Jury respectively; nor did their several functions correspond with the lawyer's distinctions. They are referred to as the Grand Jury and the Copyhold Jury. The "Grand Jury and Inquest of the Manor"—termed in 1587 "inquisitio magna," when thirty persons were sworn—apparently dealt indifferently with pleas of debt, successions to property, pre-sentments of such public nuisances as short weight in bread, presentments of such common misdemeanours as assaults and affrays, and presentments (in 1631) of such Manorial offences as "trespasses in the sown fields" by wandering beasts. "The Grand Jury," it was solemnly recorded in 1776, "may settle disputes on freehold lands, as to the boundaries, etc., and the Copyhold Jury may do the same on copyhold lands. The Grand Jury may make Bylaws, and compel observance of the same." We gather that "offences within the Manor," including public nuisances, were presented indifferently by either Jury.[1]

---

[1] "Notes from the Court Rolls of the Manor of Epworth," by Charles Jackson, *The Reliquary*, vol. xxiii., 1883, pp. 44-48, 89-92, and 174-175; *History and Topography of the Isle of Axholme*, by Rev. W. B. Stonehouse, 1839, pp. 143-149. On the other hand, we find the term Grand Jury used

The presentments of the Jury, when accepted by the Steward, and (in the case of amercements) "affeered" or revised by the affeerors, became the findings of the Court. These presentments appear to have comprised indifferently the recital of the customs of the Manor, the making of new By-laws, the appointment of officers, the verdicts in the civil actions tried, and the conviction and the fining of offenders, whether in respect of public nuisances, Manorial defaults, breaches of By-laws, or such misdemeanours as assaults, affrays, and even petty larcenies. These presentments were made by the Jury, either "on their own view and knowledge," or upon the testimony of one or other of the officers of the Court or other witnesses;[1] or, in civil suits, after hearing the parties to the suits, and, it may be, their counsel and witnesses. We imagine that, in many instances, the presentments were discussed by the Jury, then and there, in open Court, and written down by the most practised scribe among them. On the other hand, there is reason to believe that these presentments were sometimes drawn up and signed by the Jurymen in a separate meeting. "For the most part," writes an experienced lawyer at the end of the eighteenth century, "they generally come ready prepared with them, and deliver a copy of them signed by the several tenants to the Steward to enter in the Court rolls"[2]—a duty which he sometimes neglected to perform.

The officers of the Court might be few or numerous, and they differed from Manor to Manor, in their numbers and in their titles, far more according to the size and character of the community than with any relation to the particular name of the Court. The Lord's Steward summoned and presided over the Court whatever it was called. The Bailiff, though this title is sometimes used as synonymous with Reeve or Greave, was always the Lord's man, selected by the Steward. The residents or homagers whose presence was specially required as jurymen were warned to attend by the

simply for a Court Leet Jury ; as, for instance, in *Jurisdiction of the Courts Leet*, by J. Ritson, 3rd edition, 1816, p. 8.

[1] Where the Jury "are discharged the same day," says Ritson, "it should seem necessary for them to proceed chiefly upon evidence ; and, indeed, there is generally, if not always, a proclamation for that purpose" (*Jurisdiction of the Courts Leet*, by J. Ritson, 3rd edition, 1816, p. 24).

[2] *Treatise on Copyholds*, by C. Watkins, 4th edition, 1825, vol. ii. p. 383.

Bailiff whether the Court was styled Court Baron or Court Leet. We find Reeves, Haywards, and Herdsmen appointed at the same Court, whatever its appellation, as Constables, Ale-tasters, and Scavengers. We find Courts calling themselves nothing but Courts Baron nevertheless appointing Headboroughs, Constables, Ale-tasters, and Scavengers; making presentments on all sorts of subjects; and seizing light weights and short measures.[1] We find Courts calling themselves nothing but Courts Leet nevertheless appointing Reeves and Haywards and a variety of functionaries whose business it was to manage the common pasture. It is extremely rare to find any definite salary assigned to any of these officers[2]—the Court had, indeed, normally no Corporate funds out of which such a salary could be paid—but we suspect that some small provision for the remuneration of some of them was not infrequent. Thus we read of "Constable's acres," "Reevewick lands," and "Beadlewick lands," which were either held by the tenure of service in turn as Constable or as Reeve and Beadle respectively, or else were enjoyed for the year by those who served in those offices.[3] Sometimes there was a particular profitable right attached to one of the offices, such as the profits of the pound, the forfeitures of swine found unringed or at large, or the money penalties incurred for breach of stint of common. More usually, however, the officers found such remuneration as they got in their power to exact small customary fees. The profitable character of the Steward's fees is often alluded to. "Court-keeping" on behalf of Lords of Manors, or as deputy for their Stewards, was, at any rate in the seventeenth century, one of the recognised means of

[1] As, for instance, at Torquay; see *History of Torquay*, by J. T. White, 1878, p. 134.

[2] The leading instance of a Lord's Court having salaried officers, and, down to 1780, levying its own rate for their payment, is that of Manchester, which we subsequently describe in detail (p. 99). In the Manors of Stepney and Hackney, in 1622, then almost entirely rural in character, the Reeve was in each case entitled to a salary of £2 : 13 : 4 and £3 : 6 : 8, together with a piece of cloth for a coat (*Treatise on Copyholds*, by C. Watkins, 4th edition, 1825, vol. ii. pp. 508-533).

[3] *The Village Community*, by G. L. Gomme, 1890, pp. 274-275. We note that in the fourteenth century, in Forncett Manor, there were 20 acres designated "Reeveship lands," and 15 acres "Messorship lands," which were charged with an annual burden of two shillings per acre for the benefit of the two tenants serving those offices (*The Economic Development of a Norfolk Manor*, 1086-1565, by F. G. Davenport, 1906, pp. 50-51).

livelihood for the young barrister.[1] But there were evidently other fees. The Bailiff or Beadle of the Court might, for instance, get a fee for administering the oath to persons newly appointed. " He had been sworn in as a Pig-ringer by the Court Leet, and paid fourpence for his oath," deposed one of the parties to a settlement case in 1792, when the judges held that this office was one " of great antiquity and serviceable to the parish." [2] Whether the Court of the Manor, calling itself either Court Leet or Court Baron, had any legal authority to levy any compulsory tax, was never decided by the Superior Courts. But it was not uncommon for the Jury, in order to provide the Reeve or Hayward or Fieldsmen with the small sums necessary to effect petty improvements in the commonfields, or to carry out certain necessary repairs, to order that a levy of a few pence or a few shillings per beast should be made, the amount being collected from all the users of the common lands by the officers concerned.[3] We occasionally see this simple financial transaction expanding into a system of buying and selling " stints," or rights of common, either for the common benefit or for the convenience of individual owners. We may even find instances (as at Great Tew) of the levy being made, not per beast, but on the annual value of all the tenements, like the Poor Rate.[4]

The Undifferentiated Court, as it existed between 1689 and 1835, might conceivably be the result of a gradual coalescence and merging of previously existing separate Courts ; or it might, as we are inclined to believe, be a continuance of

---

[1] 1 James I. c. 5 (1603) ; see the *Autobiography of the Hon. Roger North,* edited by Rev. A. Jessopp, 1887, for a good description of " court-keeping " about 1680. " Some few years ago there was a design of bringing a Bill into Parliament for regulating the fees of Stewards of Manors, but the Legislature thought it much too delicate a matter to interfere in, and the design was dropped " (*Treatise on Copyholds,* by C. Watkins, 4th edition, 1825, vol. ii. p. 454).

[2] R. *v.* Inhabitants of Whittlesey, 4 J.R. 807 ; *Fenland Notes and Queries,* vol. i. p. 253. In London, in the nineteenth century, the unfortunate householder compelled by a surviving Manorial Court to serve as Constable was sometimes mulcted of half a crown by the officer of the Court who administered the oath (Second Report on the State of the Police in the Metropolis, 1817, p. 394).

[3] To cite one example out of many, the Court of Hitchin in 1819 levied fifteen pence per beast (*English Village Community,* by F. Seebohm, 1883, pp. 443-453).

[4] In a few exceptional cases, of which we shall subsequently describe Manchester and Lewes as the chief, this levy by the Lord's Court became a substantial rate for the purposes of urban government (pp. 103, 173).

a simple tribunal, in which the process of differentiation had not yet begun. But it is not uncommon to find, where two or more sessions of the Court are held each year, a certain difference made between the business done at these several occasions. What we have called the property business—the admissions and surrenders, and the receipt of fines and heriots —took place, if required, apparently at every Court. The trial of civil actions took place, apparently, from three weeks to three weeks, or whenever the Court was held, a Jury being summoned only when required. The appointment of officers, whether Reeve, Beadle, or Hayward on the one hand, or Constable, Ale-taster, or Scavenger on the other, occurred only once a year, normally at the Michaelmas Court. Sometimes the presentment of nuisances and other specifically Court Leet business is confined to the same occasion, which is often designated as the Lawday,[1] the View of Frankpledge, or the Leet.[2] In the Manor of Wistow (Yorkshire) the particular Sessions of the Lord's Court that was held at Lammas was "the fearing (*i.e.* affeering) Court," at which apparently the amercements of offenders were assessed.[3] During the eighteenth century we meet with a certain number of cases in which the Steward has plainly attempted to distinguish between the business done by this Court. Thus at Braintree, from 1709 onwards, the Steward tries to make a distinction in his records between the Court Leet on the one hand and the Court Baron and Customary Court on the other. There is still only one Court held, and only one Jury summoned. But the appointment of Constables and other officers, together with the presentments of nuisances, are entered in the book under the heading "Visus franc plegum cur."; whilst a separate heading on the same

---

[1] Thus the customs of the Manor of Worplesdon in Surrey prescribed that Courts were to be held twice a year, once with a Lawday (*Law of Copyholds*, by Chas. Watkins, 4th edition, 1825, vol. ii. p. 559). At Braunton in Devonshire there used to be "Monthly Courts" for dealing with civil suits, and four times a year a "Law Court," at one of which a Reeve, Ale-tasters, Pound-keeper, Crier, Beadle, and "Gatewardens" (perhaps from gate, meaning a lane) were appointed ("The Customs of the Manors of Braunton," by R. Dymond, in *Transactions of the Devon Association*, vol. xx., 1888, pp. 254-303).

[2] In the Manor of Wimbledon (Surrey) the Easter Court was the one designated as the Leet, when the Headboroughs of the several tithings had to attend (*Law of Copyholds*, by C. Watkins, 4th edition, 1825, vol. ii. pp. 554-556).

[3] *History of the Parishes of Sherburn and Cawood*, by W. Wheater, 1882, p. 281.

page, "Modo d. Cur. Baron et Customar," precedes the formal presentment and fining of absent freehold and copyhold tenants of the Manor, the admissions of new tenants, and the recording of property transfers.[1] In the Manor of Hitchin, where the rolls of 1471 describe the Court simply as "the View of Frankpledge, with the Court held there," those between 1721 and 1819 reveal a Court which styles itself Court Leet and Court Baron, but having only one Jury, called the Homage, doing all the business that was done —appointing Herdsmen and "Pit-keepers," regulating the common herd and the enjoyment of the common pasturage, levying a rate of fifteenpence per beast, and presenting dangerous footpaths and other nuisances.[2] At the beginning of the nineteenth century the language of the entries changes. We hear not only of the Homage, but of "jurors for our Lord the King," who make presentments of encroachments, digging gravel on the common, and other offences for which fines are imposed and made payable to "the Lord of the Leet." But this same Jury is presently found equally presenting the deaths of tenants of the Manor and the admission of new ones. From 1819 onward the proceedings become still more differentiated according to the lawyers' formula. The Court—still held as one Court only—is now styled "the Court of the View of Frankpledge of our Sovereign Lord the King with the General Court Baron of W. W., Esquire." There are both "jurors of our Lord the King" and "the Homage of this Court." They jointly declare "the

---

[1] This is the common form adopted by the Stewards of some scores of Manors in the South of England belonging to Bishops and chapters, of which, by the kind permission of the Ecclesiastical Commissioners, we have been enabled to examine the rolls. But these Stewards have usually grouped, along with the Leet presentments of the "Jury of the King and of the Lord," other presentments which clearly form part of the Court Baron business, such as those of the deaths of freeholders of the Manor and of encroachments on the Lord's waste— confining those under the heading "Modo d. Cur. Baron" to other property business. We may here note that these ecclesiastical Manor rolls were mostly kept in Latin down to the middle of the eighteenth century, or several generations later than was elsewhere customary.

[2] MS. Manor Rolls, Hitchin (Herts), for 1470-1471, in Public Record Office (portfolio 177, No. 60); and those from 1721 onward, in possession of the Commissioners of Woods and Forests, to whom we are indebted for the privilege of inspection. The roll for 1819 is printed in *The English Village Community*, by F. Seebohm, 1883, pp. 443-453; see also *History of Hertfordshire*, by N. Salmon, 1728, p. 162; *The Royal Manor of Hitchin*, by Wentworth Huyshe, 1906.

boundaries, extent, rights, jurisdiction, and customs of the said Manor." The Lord, they assert, has "Court Leet and View of Frankpledge" twice a year, and also "General and Special Courts Baron and Customary Courts at his will." The Court Leet appoints two Constables, six Headboroughs, two Aleconners, two Leather Searchers and Sealers, and one Bellman, who acts also as Watchman and Crier. The Leet Jury presents various nuisances. The Homage has its own presentments about the customs relating to property, the freedom of the market from tolls, and the obligation of the Lord to provide the pound and stocks. Can we believe that this new and sudden elaboration of what had, for three centuries at least, been a single undifferentiated Court, with a single Jury, indicates anything more than the historical knowledge and antiquarian zeal of a new Steward of the Manor?

Whatever was the Court, its business was, it is clear, of the most varied kind. Thus, in the little town of Braintree in Essex, which we have already described as being ruled by an enigmatical Select Vestry, or "Four and Twenty,"[1] we see the Lord's Court, between 1616 and 1813, appointing Constables, Ale-tasters, Fish and Flesh Tasters, and Leather Searchers; presenting nuisances as distinguished from Manorial defaults; enforcing the Assizes of Bread and Ale; punishing the usual market offences; acting down to 1713 in conjunction with the Company of the Twenty-four that we have already described as the Parish Vestry; and even levying rates on the inhabitants for repairing the common pump and scavenging the streets. At the same meetings of the Court we have the admission of new tenants of the Manor, the transfer of properties on death or alienation, and, by the same Jury, the presentment of encroachments on the Lord's waste, and the defaults of tenants in not scouring ditches. In the little Manor of Standon, for which the rolls exist from 1338 to 1773, we see the Lord's Court, down to the first quarter of the eighteenth century at any rate, equally combining both Court Baron and Court Leet business—making presentments of highway and other nuisances and forbidding the harbouring of vagrants—and also dealing with admissions, heriots, convey-

---

[1] *English Local Government*, Vol. I. *The Parish and the County.*

ances, encroachments on the waste, defaults of tenants, and other property matters.[1] So in the interesting Lord's Court at Epworth that we have already mentioned, the "customs" elaborately recorded in 1776 reveal a tribunal at which By-laws were made, nuisances were presented, the common pasturage was regulated, officers were appointed, offenders were fined, new tenants of the Manor were admitted, the fines for copyhold alienations were fixed, and civil suits between tenants of the Manor were determined.[2] At Devonport, as we are told by a local chronicler about 1800,[3] the Lord's Court "has the privilege of Court Leet and Court Baron, which is annually held some time in the month of October. . . . It has the power of fines and even of imprisonment for small offences ; and all horses, cattle, implements, and utensils of any kind which shall appear to a Coroner's Jury to have occasioned the death of any person within the Manor, be it of whatever kind or value, are liable to be forfeited to the Lord of the Manor."

A less familiar function of the Lord's Court, and one that we suspect was, even in 1689, still of greater public interest to every inhabitant of the village than those hitherto described, was the management of the agricultural operations of the little community. In nearly every Manor there were common pastures ; sometimes woods into which the tenants of the Manor might send their pigs ; sometimes valuable hay-meadows shared by lot or by a primitive scramble ; more frequently large open "commons" of coarse herbage ; and invariably roadside strips and odds and ends of unoccupied land forming part of "the Lord's waste." The simple acts of administration which the enjoyment of these common rights involved formed part of the business of every Manor Court. We see appointed

---

[1] *History of Standon,* by Edward Salt, 1888.

[2] *History and Topography of the Isle of Axholme,* by Rev. W. B. Stonehouse, 1839, pp. 143-149.

[3] *The Plymouth Dock Guide* (*circa* 1800), p. 28. The right of the Lord of the Manor to deodand, or forfeiture of any article causing the death of a human being, was not abolished until 1846 (9 and 10 Victoria, c. 62 ; see *The King's Coroner,* by R. H. Wellington, 1905, p. 169). Besides knives and bludgeons, horses and cattle, the wheel of a vehicle and a mill-wheel have been thus forfeited. In 1841, after an accident on the Great Western Railway at Sonning, a railway carriage is said to have been taken by the Lord of the Manor as a deodand. In 1840 the deodand was valued by the Jury at £2000 in the case of an accident on the London and Birmingham Railway (*Monthly Law Magazine,* vol. x., 1841, p. 15).

such officers as Herdsmen,[1] to drive out and home, and watch over, the pigs, sheep or cattle, horses or asses that the individual proprietors contributed to the common herd or flock. There are Common Drivers [2] to see that only the cattle and horses of the tenants of the Manor use the commons, and these only up to the permitted number, or "stint of common," free from disease and properly marked. There are Pig-ringers, whose duty it is to prevent any swine wandering on the wastes without being properly ringed. There is a Pinder or Pound-keeper, who arrests stray beasts or animals found at large in contravention of any of the regulations of the little community, and confines them in the Pound, until the owner redeems them by the customary small fine or fee. It is part of the business of the Lord's Court not only to appoint these officers, but also to supervise their work, to make and revise the By-laws that they enforce, and to give them any necessary instructions from time to time.

The agricultural functions of the Lord's Court extended, however, to much more than the administration of the common pastures. The England of 1689 was still, in the main, a country of "common fields"—wide expanses of arable land, divided into innumerable narrow strips called "pieces," "selions," or "lands," all in separate ownership, but thrown open after harvest to common pasture; cultivated severally by their owners upon a uniform system, usually that of the well-known three years' course.[3] Each Manor had its particular order of cultivation, by which, for instance, approximately one-third of its arable area was devoted, in rotation, to "tilthgrain" or winter corn, "etchgrain" or spring corn, and fallow. This "open field" system of agriculture involved a great deal of collective regulation, which fell, as we shall show, to the Jury at the Lord's Court, acting through officers for whom the most significant title was that of Fieldsmen.[4]

---

[1] Termed also Swineherds, Hogreeves, Neatherds or Noltherds, Common Herds, Shepherds, etc. At Hornsea there was a "Nowtherd, whose office it was to look after the sheep in the pastures" (*An Account of Hornsea in Holderness in the East Riding of Yorkshire*, by E. W. B., 1847-64).

[2] Or Common Keeper; often, we suspect, called Haywards, Pinders, etc.

[3] See, for instance, the evidence yielded by "the Elizabethan Village Surveys," described by W. J. Corbett in *Transactions of Royal Historical Society*, N.S. ix., 1897, pp. 67-87.

[4] Or Burleymen or Bylaw-men. In the Manor of Hornsea, four "sworn

We do not think that the extent and complication of this agricultural business of the Lord's Court has been at all adequately realised. Professor Maitland, for instance, to whom we in common with all students of English institutions owe the deepest gratitude, suggests that "so far as the arable land is concerned, the common field husbandry, when once it has been started, requires little regulation. . . . The truth is that if you have cut up a field into acre strips, given a parcel of dispersed strips to each of many men, and given to each man a right to turn out his beasts on the whole field during a certain part of the year, you have made an arrangement which maintains itself with unhappy ease. These men must follow the accustomed course. If one man strives to break through it, he must straightway trample on his neighbour's crops or suffer his own to be trampled on, for only as a rare exception is there a beaten way to a strip. . . . We underrate the automatism of ancient agriculture and of ancient government."[1] However true may be this suggestion about the common agriculture of the English Manor of the thirteenth century— and on this we offer no opinion—it was, we think, certainly not true of many an English Manor between 1689 and 1835. By that time, at any rate, even the simplest three-course system included some variety and choice among crops. Moreover, even the smallest Manor was divided into more than three parts,[2] and these parts necessarily differed among themselves in their requirements. The actual operations to be performed during the year at the various parts of the area of the Manor, were, even in 1689, not very different in number or diversity from those performed over the same area to-day. We suggest, in fact, that the Manor had, somehow or another, to arrive at nearly as many separate small decisions in the

tenants of the Manor were annually appointed at the Court as Bylaw-men, commonly two for Hornsea Fields and two for Southorp. Their office was, among other things, to look after the stocking of the pastures by the farmers and owners of common rights ; and they also directed the employment of 'the Town's plough' or 'Common plough'" (*An Account of Hornsea in Holderness in the East Riding of Yorkshire*, by E. W. B., 1847, p. 64).

[1] *Township and Borough*, by F. W. Maitland, 1898, p. 25.

[2] This was the case even in earlier times. Thus, in the Manor of Forncett, Norfolk, in the fourteenth century, "the rolls contain no clear indication that there were within the vill three great fields. . . . 'Campi' are mentioned, but they were numerous and small" (*The Economic Development of a Norfolk Manor*, 1086-1565, by F. G. Davenport, 1906, p. 27).

course of the year as those which occupy the time and thought of a modern farmer. It had to be settled each year which seed—wheat, barley, oats, rye, sainfoin, turnips, grass, clover, rye-grass, "thetches" or peas[1]—should be sown in each of the numerous subdivisions of the great fields. The dates at which these separate sections were to be opened and closed to common pasture had to be fixed. There were different kinds of common pasture to be arranged for in varying proportions, according to the common needs—sheepfolds in such and such a field, up to such and such a date; horses in such and such a field; the "cow common" to be in such and such a place; the "horse hitching" in another. In order to keep the various parts of the land in good condition, the kind, and still more the degree, of use to which they might be severally put had each year to be determined with considerable care, and portions set apart from time to time to be allowed to lie a summer unused, in order that they might recover. The various offences against the order of the Manor—the trespasses on each other's strips, the illicit use of the pasturage, the straying of animals into the corn, neglecting fences, or disobeying the orders as to the course or the dates of cultivation—had all to be prosecuted and tried at the Court.[2] The

---

[1] Even in the fourteenth century at least four crops were regularly cultivated in England, and a choice had therefore to be made. "The areas assigned to the different kinds of crops varied somewhat from year to year" (*ibid.* p. 28).

[2] We must own to being surprised at the paucity of the records of the actual presentment and punishment of such predial offences. We imagine that the village may have known how to compel obedience to the communal decisions by sanctions less formal and less dilatory than the tardy amercement by the Michaelmas Jury. But many examples can be found in the records of Manor Courts if they are sought for. Thus the MS. rolls of the Court of the Manor of Hitchin for 1470-71 record the presentment and amercement of persons for allowing a hedge to grow on to a lane, ploughing up a greenway, encroaching on a greenway, ploughing up a balk, and ploughing the end of a "Land" to harm (Court Rolls in Public Record Office, portfolio 177, No. 40; an example that we owe to the kindness of Mr. Seebohm). The rolls of the Court held at Gnossall, Staffordshire, in the sixteenth century contain many references to similar offences (*The Manor and Manorial Records*, by N. J. Hone, 1905, pp. 188, 191, 192, 195, 198, 201). So, at Epworth, at the end of the seventeenth and beginning of the eighteenth century we see the Court fining persons for allowing their cattle to stray into the cornfield, for suffering their fences to lie down, for keeping sheep in the cornfield after the date fixed for their removal, and for riding over the cornfield ("Notes from the Court Rolls of the Manor of Epworth," by C. Jackson, in the *Reliquary*, vol. xxiii., 1883, pp. 44-48, 89-92, 174-175). In our subsequent account of the Manorial Borough of Godmanchester we shall give other examples (p. 184).

common bull and boar had to be provided, and regulations made for their use.[1] There were always gaps in the hedges to be repaired, gates to be mended, paths and roads to be put in order, ditches to be scoured, and the walls of the pound to be kept up. There might even be, as at Hornsea in the East Riding of Yorkshire, the "town's plough" or "common plough" to be looked after and managed. This, we are told, "was an implement of great size, used for making deep furrows in the fields for drainage; and for this purpose, when the ground was in a proper condition, the Bylaw-men, at their discretion, called on the farmers for the requisite force for managing the plough; this was six or eight or more oxen (at that time much used for draught), headed by two horses, with several men and boys."[2] We shall, in subsequent chapters, describe the large part that agricultural management of this sort played in the business transacted by such a Manorial Borough as Godmanchester, and by such a Municipal Corporation as Berwick-on-Tweed. Here we shall confine ourselves to one leading instance of similar business performed, on no inconsiderable scale, by the Court of the Manor.

The Manor of Great Tew in Oxfordshire, apparently co-extensive with the Parish of the same name, distinguished in history as the home and place of burial of Falkland, had, during the eighteenth century, probably about as many inhabitants as it has to-day, namely, between three and four hundred. These three or four score of families were, nearly all of them, engaged in and dependent on the cultivation of the three thousand acres of the Manor. The management of these agricultural operations—nowadays performed individually

[1] The provision of the Manor Bull and Boar is frequently made the subject of presentments. In the Manor of Fulham the obligation was declared by the Lord's Court to be on the Rector, in respect of his great tithes (Presentments of 1550 and 1680, in *Fulham Old and New*, by C. J. Feret, 1900, vol. ii. pp. 120-121). So it was in 1819 at Hitchin (*English Village Community*, by F. Seebohm, 1883, pp. 443-453). The following is a common form of presentment in Manors of the South of England among the Court Leet business. "We do present A. B., being a tenant of the Lord of the Manor, shall keep a bull or a boar for the tenants" (MS. Manor Rolls, "Court of View of Frankpledge," Caddington, Essex, 22nd May 1713, among the archives of the Ecclesiastical Commissioners). The custom is referred to in Shakespeare's *Henry IV.*, Act ii, scene 2, and in the last chapter of Sterne's *Tristram Shandy*.

[2] This interesting survival continued, as one of the regular functions of the Lord's Court, down to the local Inclosure Act of 1809 (*An Account of Hornsea in Holderness in the East Riding of Yorkshire*, by E. W. B., 1847, pp. 64-65).

by the half a dozen capitalist farmers as exclusively private concerns—formed, it is clear, the principal part of the business of the "Vis. Franc. Pledg. cum Cur. Baron. prehonorabilis Antonii dni. vice comit. de Falkland dni. Manerii," held every October. The presentments of the Jury of this Court, probably a majority of all the owners of the strips of land to be cultivated, give us a picture of the variety and intricacy of the decisions which had to be come to even in the Court of a tiny village. We see how numerous and complicated were these decisions, even in a normal year, without any alteration of the customary three years' course. But we are able to do more than that. We may even see the little community deciding, in 1761, on the revolutionary step of changing from a three to a nine years' course—at a date, be it noted, when many a capitalist farmer was still wedded to the old-fashioned routine,[1] thus indicating that agricultural administration by the Lord's Court was not necessarily so inefficient nor so unprogressive as is sometimes supposed. We append extracts from the Court rolls for the years 1692, 1756, 1759, and 1761 respectively.[2]

Orders of 21st April 1692

We do order to make a horse hich [hitching][3] for this year, and we do agree that it shall be from the Pool head up the pool

---

[1] A similar agricultural revolution is recorded of the village of Hunmanby in Yorkshire, some time prior to 1794. By unintelligent cultivation, the commonfields had become "worn-out." At last the co-owners of the strips were persuaded to adopt a six years' course of (1) turnips fed off by sheep, (2) seeds, (3) seeds, (4) seeds, (5) wheat, (6) oats or pease. The grass seeds, hurdles and nets, and wages of the shepherd were paid for, and the sheep supplied, by the co-owners in proportion to their holdings. The Field-reeves and Shepherd were appointed, regulations made, and the dates of the various operations determined, we are told, at meetings of those concerned, which may have been simply Courts of the Manor (*General View of the Agriculture of the East Riding of Yorkshire*, by Isaac Leatham, 1794, pp. 45-46; *The English Peasantry*, by Gilbert Slater, 1907, p. 88).

[2] We are indebted for these interesting records to Mr. M. E. Boulton, the present Lord of the Manor ; and (for those of the latter years) to Mr. Adolphus Ballard, M.A., Town Clerk of Woodstock, and Clerk to the Oxford Board of Guardians, author of *Notes on the History of Chipping Norton*, 1893 ; *Chronicles of the Royal Borough of Woodstock*, 1896 ; *The Domesday Boroughs*, 1905 ; *The Domesday Inquest*, 1907, etc. Mr. Ballard's stimulating researches lead us to look forward with interest to further historical work from his pen.

[3] For other uses of "hitching the fields," "hitchland," and "hatching ground," see *The English Peasantry*, by Gilbert Slater, 1907, pp. 23-30, 76, 81.

side to Hollo Lake, and up Hollo Lake to the upper side of William Watson's . . . and so along the hade [head ?] way to the end of William Reynold's headland end. And so it shall come for[e]lands [?] on the home side of the wat[e]ry balke in Millslads, and every Land into the great Pool the head shall go with the land ; he that maketh default shall forfeit to the Lord of the Manor for every default £1.

And we do further order that the aforesaid hichin[g] shall be tide [tied ?] with horses and e[a]ten of[f] by or before the 17th day of Aug. next, and none to be mowed or cut or carried away, . . .

We do order that the winter corn-field shall be from the horse hi[t]ching all up the west side of Wood Way, all up to the up[p]er side of Whete [Wheat ?] land.

We do order to keep ten sheep for a yard-land for this summer common and no more ; the defaulter shall forfeit to the Lord of the Manor 4d. for every sheep and 1 pen[n]y to the tellers for every default.

We do order to keepe the cow common on the 14th day of May and not before, and all the gaps in Down he[d]ge and . . . to be stopped sufficiently, every man his own gaps, by or befor the same day.

We do order to keep but one horse for the yard-land and no more, and there shall be no mare nor mares tide [tied] in the common field. . . .

We do order that no man shall ti[e] his horse or horses in the corn-field. . . .

We do order the sheep and folds to be reed [?] out of the corn-field by or before the 22nd day of this instant April. . . .

We do order that no man shall baite his horse or horses in hollters [halters ?] or out of hollters in the field, nor no man shall ti[e] his horse or horses on mowed ground till the horses hi[t]ching be reede [?]. . . .

And every man shall ty [tie] his own ground till a quarter of the field be reede [?] of the grain that it was laid for under the same fine.

And we do order that no man letteth any Land on the Sainfoin Hill to any out-town man, he or they, be them whom they will, shall have no more power after he hath taken of[f] his own crope to ty [tie] any horse or horses to bait any sort of catill [cattle] on the said grounds. . . .

We do order that every man shall scour up his trench at Hollo Lake by or before May day next, . . .

We do order that every man shall fence his own pe[a]se Lands from Butcher's Row he[a]d to Wood-way Ford and from Bryer

Lands ford to Tew Park corner, by or before the 7th day of May next. . . .

We do order the jury to mete [meet] on the 22nd day of this inst. April by 8 of the clock in the morning, at Preston Pool Hill. . . .

We do order the Fieldsmen and empower them [to set] 8 horse commons and no more, and they are to set to every husbandman that hath most need one apiece, to the millers 4 apiece if need be; 3/ to be for every common.

Orders of 28th October 1756

It is ordered by the Jury that no person shall keep more than eighteen sheep to the yardland this winter, and every person shall brand his sheep or mark them on or before 21st of November next, and to lay as many upon the turnips as they will, which shall not be deemed any part of the eighteen above mentioned; the defaulter to pay three shillings and fourpence.[1]

. . . that the cows shall break the hangings of Horse Hill in a fortnight after the Cow Hill is broke, and in a week after the hanging is broke to break the hanging of Chescomb Hill and the top of Chescomb Hill, or as the Fieldsmen shall direct; and the herd not to break without the Fieldsmen's direction, the defaulter for every default to forfeit to the Lord of the Manor three shillings and fourpence.

. . . that every Cow Common occupied by any person that has not at least a quartern of land in his occupation shall be deemed a Cottage Common, and every person that occupies more than a quarter of a Yardland and occupies more than two Cows Common [a] yardland, all that is over shall and is hereby deemed Cottage Commons; and it is ordered by 'the Jury that every Cottage Common, or the owner or occupier thereof, shall pay (in lieu of having the hanging of Horse Hill and the top and hanging of Chescomb Hill laid to the Cow Common this next Summer) the sum of five shillings, which money is hereby ordered to be paid to the Fieldsmen on or before the twelfth day of May next; and if any cottager shall not be able to sell his Common for fourteen shillings a common, the Fieldsmen, upon having notice thereof on the day aforesaid, he shall be obliged to pay him or them after the rate of nine shillings a Common at Gunpowder Treason [2] following,

---

[1] The opening and closing formal words of each subsequent order are omitted from the text for the sake of brevity. All the penalties for disobedience were increased from three and fourpence in 1756 and 1759 to ten shillings in 1761, the year of the revolution in the course of cultivation.

[2] Meaning, of course, the 5th November.

which money so raised by the five shillings on every Cottage
Common shall be laid out in scouring the damings [? dammings],
trenching the Cow Common, mending the rudaway [? roadway],
and doing other good husbandry throughout the Field without
regard to one's man ground rather than another, which nine
shillings a Common is to be rated upon the cattle that are laid
upon the Common, share and share alike. . . .

. . . that no person that is to occupy lands in the Common
Field of Great Tew shall have liberty to sell Sheep Commons to
any person that does not occupy at least a quarter of a yardland in
the Common Field, but if they have any Commons to sell they are
to give notice to the Fieldsmen a week before Martinmas next, and
if the Fieldsmen can't sell them to people that occupy at least a
quarter of a yardland, the Commons are ordered to be paid for
after the rate of ninepence a Sheep Common, to be raised by a levy
the same as the Poor's Levy.[1] . . .

. . . that the sheep shall be hained off the young sainfoin all
this winter, and the Park Hill sainfoin at Martinmas next; and the
Little Oxenden sainfoin [is] to lie to the Common till Mayday
next, and Chescomb Hill its hangings to lie to the Sheep Common
till Mayday next. . . .

. . . that the horses shall be hained out of the Commonfield
on or before the 31st day of December next. . . .

. . . that the Farr Hill shall be broke up this winter for
turnips, and that Upper Barnwell shall be winter ploughed and
sowed grass seeds with the spring grain to be sown thereon next
spring; and that the Hayward or Fieldsmen shall pound all
manner of cattle off the turnips the same as if the Farr Hill was
cornfield. . . .

. . . that the horse hitchin [? hitching] shall be from Park
Hill to London Way on the Old Hill next to Galleythorns, one
Land to a yardland, and that the remainder of the Hill shall lie for
a summer fallow, and Oxenden sainfoin to be fed with sheep next
summer with it. . . .

. . . that between the hedges, being the clover quarter, shall
be hained from the sheep on or before the Martinmas next, and
from all manner of cattle on or before the 31st day of December,
and the gaps in the Millway hedge and Alice hedge to be stopped
by the owners on or before the 31st day of December next; and
every person to mound their own Landsends. . . .

. . . that the Jury meet on Preston Pool Hill on the 16th
November next by ten o'clock to do such matters between tenant
and tenant and Lord and tenant as shall be wanting. . . .

. . . that Priest Croft and the Leys shall be added to the Cow

---

[1] Note the change from a levy per head of cattle, or per right of common
to a levy upon the annual value of each tenement.

Common for the year 1758, and the Northfields both to be laid to
the Cow Common the year 1759. . . .

The Jury appoints T. L. and W. L. to be Constables.

The Jury appoints G. L., J. B., T. L., and J. M. Fieldsmen for
the year ensuing.

The Jury appoints J. B. to be Hayward for the year ensuing.

The Jury presents the death of T. S., Quaker, by which there
is a yardland and a half, and a small close called the Longgreen,
fallen to the Lord of the Manor.

The Jury presents that Widow F.'s lifehold tenement (is) going
to decay, and that she ought to repair the same.

Orders of 22nd October 1759

It is Ordered by the Jury to sow all Little Oxenden, the
Furlong called the Plank Pitts, Ten Lands over Oxenden Bottom
next to Woodway, and Eight Lands next to Woodway in Ellden
Stump furlong, pease the next spring, being in the year 1760, and
in the spring 1761 to sow the same with barley, and to lay the
same down with ryegrass and clover, the defaulter for every
default to forfeit to the Lord of the Manor three shillings and
fourpence. . . .

. . . to sow turnips upon Wheatland, Piked and Broad Castors,
Hollow Marsh Hill, and to Alepath, except the furlongs next to
Woodway, the next spring, being the year 1760, and in the spring
1761 to sow the same barley and lay it down with ryegrass and
clover. . . .

. . . that Wheatland, Piked and Broad Castors, and Hollowmarsh Hill, and from Churchway to Alepath, to be hained from all
manner of cattle next summer on the 14th day next after Old
Midsummer. . . .

. . . that the Slad from the Brook by Woodway side up to
Hollow Marsh, and all the furlongs shooting into Woodway, including Mr. Nevill's Hadland [? headland] at Hoare's Stone, and all the
furlongs above Chipping Norton way from Woodway to Rattock,
be sowed thetches for a horse hitchin [? hitching] this next spring,
and to be sowed wheat as soon as the thetches are tied off, and in
the spring 1761 to be sowed barley and laid down with grass
seeds. . . .

. . . to sow Lent grain the next spring on the furlong below
Chipping Norton Way and all the rest part of the Westfield, and in
the spring or summer 1761 to sow the same turnips, and to hain
the said turnips from all manner of cattle on the 14th day next
after Old Midsummer 1761. . . .

. . . that the hangings of Horse Hill and the hangings of Chescomb Hill be pastured by the cows this next summer 1760, and that Forest Croft and the Leys be pastured by the cows in the summer 1761, and that the two North fields be pastured by the cows in the summer 1762. . . .

. . . that the Lands' ends on Chescomb Hill be mounded by the owners of the Lands; and gates to be hung on the road by the Constables on or before the 16th day of November next. . . .

. . . that the Lands' ends on Horse Hill be mounded by the owners of the Lands on or before a fortnight before Old Ladyday next; and that the gaps in Down Hedge against Horse Hill and the Hollow way side be mounded by the owners at the same time; and that the gates be put up by the Constable by the same time. . . .

. . . that all Park Hill, and all Oxenden (except what is before ordered to be sowed pease), ryegrass and clover this next spring. . . .

. . . that the occupiers of land in the Commonfield shall have the liberty of laying as many sheep on their turnips as they will carry, which said sheep are not to be deemed any part of the sixteen above mentioned.

But in case of wet weather while the sheep are at turnips they are to have the liberty of Great Oxenden and Little Oxenden before it is sowed and nowhere else; and no person that has sheep at turnips that does not occupy at least a quarter of a yardland shall have the liberty of coming upon either of the Oxendens in wet weather. . . .

. . . that the folds be hained out of the winter Cornfields on or before the 21st November next; and no person shall turn upon his neighbour's winter corn (except what is sowed amongst the turnips on the turnip division) after the 21st of November. . . .

. . . that the horses shall be hained out of the Commonfield on or before St. Thomas, Old Style, next. . . .

. . . that Farr Hill shall lie for a sheepwalk all next summer and that three sheep to a Yardland may be laid on the Farr Hill three weeks before May Day next, which three sheep shall be over and above the sixteen sheep laid upon the Winter Common, for the encouragement of them and an inducement to all occupiers of land that sow turnips. . . .

. . . that the Old Hill shall be mowed for hay next summer, and the sheep to have it afterwards till Martinmas then next following, and no longer. . . .

. . . that the Old Hill and Galleythorns be hained from sheep to-morrow, and all Park Hill from all manner of cattle and folds at the same time. . . .

. . . that Churchway be mounded on both sides from Ayleshedge to Woodway, by the Yardland, on or before a month before Martinmas. . . .

. . . that the gaps in Ayleshedge be mounded by the Owners on or before Ladyday next. . . .

It is Ordered by the Jury to mound the sainfoin from Woodstock Way to the Mill hedge, every Land's end by the owner of the Land; and where the furlong shoots up the brook, to be mounded by the two outside hides; and to mound the wheat at Huckerswell, every one their own Land's ends; and to mound the barley from Cloncil Corner to Barnwell Ford, every man his Land's ends; and the barley in Brook Furlong and Long Furlong to be mounded by the two outside hides; and the gaps to be stopped in Millway hedge on or before Mayday. . . .

Orders of 23rd October 1761

It is Ordered by the Jury that Horse Hill be mounded by the two outside hides and the owners of the Lands' ends, on or before the 16th day of November next; the defaulter for every default to forfeit to the Lord of the Manor ten shillings.

. . . that the grass seeds on Alepath Furlong, Hollowmarsh Hill, Wheatland and Broad Castors and Picked Castors, Little Oxenden, the Plank Pits, Eldenstump Furlong, and all Great Oxenden and Park Hill be hained from the sheep on the 22nd day of November next; and the said grass seeds and the sainfoin to be hained from all manner of cattle on the 21st day of December next, the defaulter for every default to forfeit to the Lord of the Manor ten shillings.

. . . that the Cow Common be hained from horses on the 21st day of December next, and the Cow Common and Chescomb Hill to be hained from all manner of cattle on the 23rd day of March next. . . .

. . . that the sheepfolds be hained out of the Cornfields on the 22nd of November next. . .

. . . that the horse hitchin [? hitching] be in the Fallowfield beginning at the side next Cuckoo's Holt, a yard to a Yardland; and that the horses shall not be hitched or tied on any other part of the Commonfield till after it is mowed, except on the highways. . . .

. . . that all Huckerswell be sowed turnips this next summer, 1762, and sowed barley with grass seeds, spring 1763; mowed for hay, summer 1764; sheepwalk, 1765; oats, 1766; fallow, 1767; wheat, 1768; pease, 1769. . . .

. . . that between the hedges shall be sowed turnips in summer 1763, and every year after for eight years after the manner of Huckerswell.

. . . that Upper Barnwell be sowed turnips, 1764, and every year after for eight years after the manner of Huckerswell.

. . . that the Lower side of Woodstock way beyond the Brook shall be sowed turnips, 1765, and every year after for eight years after the manner of Huckerswell.

. . . that Galleythorns and the Old Hill be sowed turnips, 1766, and every year after for eight years after the manner of Huckerswell.

. . . that Park Hill and Great Oxenden be sowed turnips, 1767, and every year after for eight years after the manner of Huckerswell.

. . . that Upper Oxenden, Plankpits, and Ten Lands next Woodway, in both Eldenstump Furlong and over Oxenden Bottom and Wheatland and Broad and Picked Castors and Hollowmarsh Hill to Alepath be sowed turnips, 1768, and every year after for eight years after the manner of Huckerswell.

. . . that from Alepath to the Great Pool be sowed turnips, 1769, and every year after for eight years after the manner of Huckerswell.

. . . that the Westfield from Alepath and Woodwayford be sowed barley or oats next spring, and ryegrass and clover; that it shall be mowed for hay, 1763; sheepwalk, 1764; oats, 1765; fallow, 1766; wheat, 1767; and pease, 1768. . . .

. . . that the grass seeds at Great Oxenden and Park Hill shall be broke for the sheep at Old Ladyday next and not before. . . .

. . . that all the grass seeds sowed last spring shall be mowed for and hay to Park Hill; and Great Oxenden to be sheepwalk, and all the grass seeds besides after they are mowed, except Chescomb Hill. . . .

. . . that the Hayward shall pound all horses, pigs, hogs, etc., that are found grassing about the waste in the town.

The Jury elect S. D. Hayward, and agree to pay him two shillings a yardland; and he is to keep the crows from off the wheat immediately that the wheat is out of danger; and to keep the crows five weeks before harvest from off the wheat till reaping time; and to keep the Field free from moles and wants,[1] and is to employ his whole time in doing the said duty.

This vivid picture of the administration of commonfield agriculture by the Lord's Court raises some interesting questions. How did the twelve or fifteen members of the Jury of Great Tew manage to formulate all these complicated orders? We learn from contemporary letters that

---

[1] *I.e.* hedgehogs.

their discussions were prolonged and tempestuous. In 1755 the Court had actually to be adjourned because these "fathers of the hamlet" could not arrive at an agreement by nightfall. When the spring came round there arose "a great demur amongst the town's people about some of them trespassing the last Court Order"; and the local representative of the Steward was obliged to send to him for the original document, or a copy of it, "for the Fieldsmen," who were to enforce it. In October the Lord of the Manor himself writes to his solicitor : "I am afraid I must trouble you to come and hold a Court here, though I doubt 'tis probable we shall be obliged to adjourn again as we did last year on account of squabbles." Within five years, as we have seen, the reformers got their way, and made the great revolution of adopting a nine years' course. That this did not do away with argument and discussion, we may realise from the fact that in 1763 the Lord of the Manor reports that they "could not finish the business of the Court till near ten this evening."[1]

The problem remains why we possess so little record of the agricultural decisions of the Lord's Court, which must, in thousands of Manors, have been formulating orders analogous to those of Great Tew. In Manor after Manor we find the books of records kept by the Stewards between 1689 and 1835 giving attention to little else than the admissions of new tenants, the surrenders of copyholds, and other conveyancing business. There is a growing attenuation of the record. Sometimes the appointment of officers is recorded, sometimes not. The presentments of nuisances die away. The pleas in debt and trespass, with the verdicts arrived at, are often not entered at all, or entered in a separate book. When, as at Great Tew, the Jury had long and elaborate presentments, they prepared these on separate sheets of paper, which they delivered, as we are elsewhere expressly told, "to the Steward to enter in the Court rolls."[2] It is plain that the Steward, who was not interested in the tenants' agricultural operations, omitted the very heavy task of copying

---

[1] MS. Letters from Great Tew to Edward Ryves of Woodstock, 9th April and 23rd October 1756 and 28th October 1763 ; in the possession of Mr. Ballard.

[2] *Treatise on Copyholds*, by C. Watkins, 4th edition, 1825, vol. ii. p. 383. The interesting presentments of the Jury of Great Tew are written on large sheets of paper, those of each year being entirely distinct from those of other years

these lengthy presentments into his book ; and the loose sheets, like the corresponding loose papers of the Vestry, the Municipal Corporation, and the Court of Quarter Sessions, have been far less perfectly preserved, and even less carefully looked for, than the bound volumes.[1]

We might leave at this point our account of the Court of the Manor, content with the foregoing generalised description of its constitution and procedure. But, to give greater actuality to our survey, we take from our collection half a dozen specimens for individual description. In these Manors the Courts will be seen to range from a wholly undifferentiated tribunal transacting all kinds of business, through Courts calling themselves by composite names, but transacting only one kind of business, up to Courts which correspond, in their duality, closely with the lawyers' view of what the Lord's Court ought to be. Whether this duality had always existed, or whether it was merely the product of a disintegration of function, we leave to the judgment of the historian.

(i.) *The Bamburgh Courts*

It has been observed that, in more than one respect, the County of Northumberland has, in the past, been a century or two later in constitutional development than the more settled parts of the South of England. Accordingly, it is to Northumberland that we turn for the best examples of Manorial Courts continuing in full and unrestricted activity throughout the eighteenth century. Along the six miles of wild rocks and sandhills from Budle Point to Beadnell Bay the little fishing villages and scattered agricultural hamlets were under the dominion of the Lord of the Castle of Bamburgh,[2] that rises to this day so picturesquely on its black rock from amid the sweeping stretches of sparkling white sand. Here we find a particularly full and varied Manorial

---

[1] For another instance, at Laxton (Notts), see *The English Peasantry*, by Gilbert Slater, 1907, ch. ii.

[2] In 1704 the Bamburgh Manors, which had belonged to the Forsters, were acquired by Lord Crewe, Bishop of Durham, and were on his death in 1720 left in trust for charitable purposes. We are indebted to the existing trustees, and to Mr. W. T. Hindmarsh of Alnwick, for access to the MS. records from 1695. See also the *History of Northumberland*, by E. Bateson, vol. i. (1893), in which some extracts are given (pp. 169-172).

jurisdiction extending throughout the whole of the period under our consideration. In the hall of the ancient castle two Courts were regularly held, the View of Frankpledge and Court Baron of the Manor of the Castle, with jurisdiction extending over the whole of the great Manor of about fifty square miles ; and the Court of the Manor of the " Borough " of Bamburgh itself, governing the little village that clustered round the fortress. The Court of the Manor of the Castle claimed, in 1689, the attendance of some two hundred suitors of various grades. There were, first of all, the free tenants of the Manor—great personages residing in Scotland and the South of England, who held lands of the Lord of Bamburgh, and who, between 1689 and 1835, were regularly summoned at his Courts, and as regularly "essoined." The real attendants at these Courts were the more assiduous or the more dependent of the eight or nine score of " Freeholders," " Copyholders," " Leaseholders," and " Cottagers " of the " demesnes " of Bamburgh and North Sunderland, and of the three vills or townships of Beadnell, Shoreston, and North Sunderland, together with the " Resiants in Bamburgh Castle " itself, all of whom are elaborately recited in the records. At this Court, which was held only once a year (with frequent omissions in the years between 1695 and 1774) all kinds of business was transacted. Constables, Pounders, and Ale-tasters were appointed for each of the three constituent townships. Minor offences—principally trespasses by animals in the common-fields, nuisances, assaults, and affrays—were presented and amerced. The townships themselves were amerced for non-repair of pinfolds and stocks.[1] New copyholders were admitted and successions to property registered. Occasional orders were made as to the management of the common pasture, the particular fields in which horses were to be tethered, the repair of the " headland," [2] and the obnoxious habits of some of the inhabitants of Beadnell, who had started extracting fish oil in the streets.[3] But the principal business of the Court

---

[1] MS. Court Rolls, Manor of the Castle of Bamburgh, 1707, etc.

[2] *Ibid.* 1st October 1705.

[3] " Ordered that none of the inhabitants of Beadnell shall boil or extract oil out of fish in the town streets, or within the houses there, the same being not only noxious and offensive, but also dangerous to the neighbourhood " (*ibid.* 22nd April 1719).

was the trial of civil actions between inhabitants of the
Manor for debts or damages not exceeding 39s. 11d. In the
earlier years of the eighteenth century there was always an
array of such actions to be dealt with at every Court. It
was, indeed, a serious offence in any inhabitant to bring before
any other tribunal, whether civil or criminal, any matter
which could be dealt with at the Court of the Manor. In
1705, for instance, we find two of the tenants fined 39s. 11d.
each, one for getting the other arrested on a writ issued
by the King's Court at Westminster, and the other for
indicting his adversary at Quarter Sessions.[1] Right down
to the middle of the nineteenth century this Manorial jurisdiction in civil actions and petty offences was maintained and
continued; though we note the stream of cases getting
gradually smaller, and all attempt at enforcing an exclusive
jurisdiction is abandoned.[2]

The whole of the business of this Court seems to have
been transacted by the dozen or so of jurymen summoned by
command of the Steward. Down to 1707 there was one
Jury only, described as the "Jury of Inquiry and of Trial
of Actions." From 1707 onward we find in the records
always two Juries sworn, a "Jury of Inquiry" and a "Jury
for the Trial of Causes." But the two Juries were, in fact,
the same persons, though the names usually occur in different
orders.[3] It is to be noted that the differentiation of the

---

[1] "Upon the oath of T. H. we present the said H. J. for causing T. H. to
be indicted at the General Quarter Sessions of the Peace for the county,
whereas if he had any cause of action or complaint against the said T. H. the
same might have been redressed and punished in this Court; for which he is
amerced 39s. 11d. Upon oath of H. J. we present T. H. for causing the said
H. J. to be arrested upon a writ out of some of the Courts at Westminster at
the said T. H.'s suit; whereas the cause of action being under 39s. 11d. . . .
and therefore cognisable in this Court, he might have had redress in this
Court; we do therefore amerce him 39s. 11d." (*ibid.* 1st October 1705).

[2] The Court appears to have been held usually once a year, even for civil
suits; but half-yearly meetings occasionally occur, and even (as between 1779
and 1786) other meetings. It was assumed in 1839 that it had the right to
three-weekly sessions, but was then, in fact, held only once a year, with an
average of only one or two cases (House of Commons Return of Courts of
Request, 1840, p. 114).

[3] We suspect that the Jury was appointed to serve for the year. A possible
cause of the nominal differentiation between its two main functions of presentment and of trial is suggested by an entry of 1748. "In the cause between
Mills and Taylor, A. A. sworn on Jury instead of George Taylor" (MS.
Court Rolls, Manor of Bamburgh, 6th July 1748). It was obviously convenient

Jury into two Juries bore no resemblance to the lawyers'
distinction between the Homage of the Court Baron and the
Jury of the Court Leet.　At Bamburgh the Jury of Inquiry
continued to act both as the Homage of the Lord and the
Jury for the King; admitting new copyholders, regulating
the commons, appointing Constables, and presenting public
nuisances.　The second Jury was, as its name implies,
restricted to the trial of "plaints and pleas " between parties.[1]

We pass now to the Manor of the Borough of Bamburgh,
for which the same Steward, assisted by the same Bailiff, held
entirely separate Courts.　Here again we have the elaborate
array of classes of persons owing suit and service—Free
Suitors, Freeholders, Cottagers, Leaseholders, and " Farmers,"
whatever may be meant by this term.[2]　But the Court is,
down to 1719, termed, in its records, a Court Baron only;
and we do not feel sure whether (as we shall subsequently
describe in the case of Alresford) the Lord had not retained
the View of Frankpledge and Court Leet when granting to
the " Borough of Bamburgh " the privilege of a separate Court.
The " Borough of Bamburgh " had had, indeed, a long and
eventful history.　For more than two hundred years it had
ranked as a " Free Borough," even receiving Royal Charters
and sending members to Parliament.　But it was practically
destroyed in the Scotch wars of the fifteenth century; and it
seems then to have reverted to a position of Manorial subordination, retaining of its former status nothing more than the

---

to be able to omit from the Jury for the Trial of Actions persons interested in a
particular suit, without necessarily omitting them from the Jury of Inquiry.

[1] It is to be noted that there are (as we have seen in the Courts at Hitchin
and elsewhere) distinct signs that the Stewards latterly tried to make their
Courts what the lawyers were saying that they ought to be.　Thus, from 1779,
we find the Jury which does all the main business termed the Jury for our
Lord the King, and the Jury which tries actions only is termed the Homage
Jury for the Trial of Causes (*ibid.* June and October 1779).

It is interesting to find that in the Manor of Blanchland, also belonging
to the Crewe Trustees, where the Courts were held by the same Steward as those
of Bamburgh, we find practically the same terms used.　There is the same
recital of Freeholders, Leaseholders, and Cottagers, as liable to suit and service ;
and the same "Jury of Inquiry and for Trial of Causes."　But in this remote
rural Manor there were, from 1785 at any rate, no "causes," and very few
presentments of nuisances, so that the holding of the Court was discontinued
after 1812, in spite of an urgent petition from the inhabitants (MS. Court Rolls,
Manor of Blanchland, 1785-1812).

[2] We did not notice any explicit mention of Copyholders, so that it is possible
that " Farmers" here mean "customary tenants " by copy of Court Roll.

name of Borough, and the separation of its Court from that of
the rest of the Manor.[1] In its decay the Manor of the Borough
passed to the Priory of Nostell in Yorkshire; which acquired
also the two neighbouring townships of Elford and Fleetham,
and apparently added them to the jurisdiction of the Borough
Court. At the beginning of the eighteenth century, the ownership of the Manor of the Borough was reunited with that of
the Manor of the Castle, and presently we find the Steward,
who held both Courts, giving them both the same title of View
of Frankpledge and Court Baron.[2] Both dealt, in fact, with
the same heterogeneous kinds of business, though in differing
proportions. The Court of the Borough, like that of the
Castle, actually empanelled only one set of jurymen for all
its business; and this remained as a single Jury until 1727,
when it became nominally differentiated into a Jury "ad
inquirendum" and a Jury "per treatione causae" (*sic*), but
nevertheless consisted always of the same twelve or thirteen
persons. The Court of the Borough had, however, its own
distinctive character, both in function and in structure.
It formally admitted new tenants to the "burgageship" of the
Manor of the Borough. It had far more presentments of
nuisances than the Court of the Castle, and these nuisances
were rather more distinctively urban in their character. It
dealt with weights and measures, with the mutual obligations
of millers and their customers, and with the clearing of the
lanes from loose stones.[3] It had to make a large number of
regulations· for the use of the "Burrow Yards" (or Borough
Yardlands, commonfields under plough), as well as for stinting
the common pastures.[4] What is, however, still more distinctive

---

[1] For Bamburgh as a Borough see *History of Northumberland*, by E. Bateson,
1893, vol. i. pp. 114-148. It is mentioned as a Borough in 1197; it received
Royal Charters in 1255, 1321, 1332, 1382, and 1405; it was represented
in the Parliament of 1295; and it was destroyed between 1419 and 1439.
Its population probably at no time exceeded a few hundreds, but it was divided
into four Wards, and elected four Bailiffs.

[2] MS. Court Rolls, Manor of the Borough of Bamburgh, 1719, etc.

[3] "Ordered that the several occupiers of the lands and grounds of Bamburgh
shall, upon notice from the Constables, assist to clear the lanes of stones and
molehills" (*ibid.* 23rd April 1719). "Every person within this Manor shall
grind at the mill they are accustomed to. . . . The miller shall wait on his
customers to carry the grist to his mill and back again within forty eight hours'
warning" (*ibid.* 4th May 1731).

[4] "None of the inhabitants of Bamburgh shall for the future put any of
their cattle to feed in any of the Burrow Yards (? Borough Yardlands) until all

is the fact that, throughout the whole proceedings, we are conscious of the " Freeholders of the Borough " in the background, as constituting a standing part of the government, with functions of their own. We have no records of the meetings of these Freeholders—we have not even any such reports from them brought into Court as those presented by the Jury of the Manor of Great Tew—but we learn something about them from the records of the Court itself. We must, of course, visualise them, not as the owners of freehold houses in a crowded city,[1] but as the owners of scattered strips of arable land in the " Borough yards," or common-fields, with rights of common pasturage. In 1705 we find them entering into a Corporate agreement with the Lord, duly ratified and recorded at the next Court, as to their " free liberty " to depasture on the Town Moor, to have " the eatage " of certain fields, and to drive their cattle in summer on the seashore, whilst, if the weather is very bad, they are to be free to use also the Castle demesne ground.[2] We see them authorised by the Court to make " a general rate or assessment " on themselves, in order to raise a sufficient sum to make good the fences ; and to collect the said rate or tax by one of themselves.[3] We even find them on one occasion directed to decide upon and, by a mere majority vote, to assess upon all the inhabitants of the Borough, for repairing and cleansing the well, a compulsory rate or tax, which the Court will enforce by distraint.[4] The

the corn growing thereon shall be led in " (*ibid.* 9th September 1760). "No stints of horses shall be kept for sheep, nor sheep for horses, and the stinting Day is to be 10th of May yearly " (*ibid.* 9th September 1760). " It is also ordered that the several rabbit cuts in the said moor ought to be filled up at the end of every hunting (*i.e.* shooting) season so prevent all mischiefs by the horses or cattle falling therein " (*ibid.* 23rd May 1775). "The several holds in the said moor which have been made for the purpose of burning for kelp ought to be filled up at the end of every burning season, and the stones surrounding the same to be removed " (*ibid.* 23rd May 1775).

[1] We do, however, read that "no person living out of a freehold mansion-house shall keep any horses upon Bamburgh Commons " (*ibid.* 13th October 1722).

[2] *Ibid.* 2nd October 1705.   [3] *Ibid.* October 1790 ; also 1794.

[4] "It is at this Court, by and with the consent of the Jury, thought fit and ordered that the Freeholders of the Town of Bamburgh do, some time before the next Court, . . . agree upon and lay an assessment upon every inhabitant or householder . . . for and towards.the repairing and cleansing the Kiln Well, as to the said Freeholders, or major part of them, shall seem fit and expedient." Any one refusing to pay was to forfeit one and eightpence, to be levied by distraint (*ibid.* 16th October 1696). On the other hand, the way to the well was ordered to be repaired, not by a tax, but by the tenants of the adjoining lands (*ibid.* 15th October 1699).

existence in the fourteenth century of a chartered Borough of Bamburgh makes it probable that the rights and privileges of the Freeholders of this Manor were but the remnants of a decayed autonomy. But for this historical probability, we might almost have seen in them the nascent germ of what, in other circumstances, developed into such Manorial Boroughs as Alnwick or Arundel, presently to be described.[1]

[1] The records of the "Court of View of Frankpledge with Court Baron" of the Manor of Tweedmouth and Spittal, between 1658 and 1663, with far less full minutes down to 1819, offer an exceptionally clear view of an Undifferentiated Court. This Manor, lying opposite the Borough of Berwick-on-Tweed, was purchased for £570 by the Municipal Corporation in 1652-1657, in order that the latter might be able to clear out "the numerous company of disorderly, uncivil, and lawless persons, principally Scotswomen of evil fame," who were harboured there. The MS. records of the Courts that continued to be held by the Corporate Lord of the Manor show the extreme heterogeneity of the business. The fifteen Jurymen who were invariably sworn at each six-monthly Court dealt indiscriminately, in their presentments, with the appointment of Constables and the amercement of nuisance-mongers, with actions for debt and the punishment of "a blood and affray," with the lack of a Pound and the admission of new copyhold tenants of the Manor, with defective weights and measures and the defaults of tenants in keeping their ditches scoured, with the harbouring of "inmates" and the keeping of ducks and geese "to abuse the water," with the grant of a portion of the waste and the ordering of the strangers to find security that they will not become chargeable, with prohibitions of the boiling of salmon in the village itself and the method by which "the assessment that was gathered for repairing the highways" (1663) was to be accounted for by the Bailiffs. The entries show that the Court passed higgledy-piggledy from one kind of business to the other, whether it was the presentment of a nuisance, the admission of a new copyholder, the appointment of a Constable, the verdict in an action on the case between two inhabitants, or the punishment of a common scold. But there are variations in the record. From 1658 to 1668 there are numerous and extremely heterogeneous entries in English, including many civil actions. From 1663 to 1732 the entries are in Latin, and relate exclusively to the property business of the Manor. We see no reason to suppose that the busy local tribunal came suddenly to an end, and we suspect that the presentments of the Jury (as at Great Tew) were written on separate loose sheets, which a new Steward neglected to copy into his book. From 1732 to 1764 the entries are in English, but still exclusively relating to conveyancing, etc. Between 1764 and 1771, whilst admissions and conveyances, etc., are recorded as by "the Homage"— evidently a new Steward had learnt that this was the legal formula—there are a certain number of "presentments of the Jury," and "orders of the Court," relating to the appointment of Constables, nuisances, and weights and measures, which the Jury went round to inspect. After 1771, again, we have nothing but conveyances recorded. The Steward makes no entry in this book of the findings of the Jury in civil suits. Yet we know that this very Court, which determined dozens of civil actions in the seventeenth century, was still determining them in the nineteenth century, and had doubtless been doing so continuously. Over 200 summonses were taken out in 1839, over 100 cases heard, and half a dozen judgments enforced by execution against property (House of Commons Return of Courts of Request, 1840, p. 125).

(ii.) The Court Leet of the Savoy

In contrast with the little fishing ports of Northumberland stands the so-called Precinct of the Savoy, in 1689 a tiny scrap of densely populated, extra-parochial territory around the ancient palace, prison, and chapel of the Savoy in Westminster. Here the Manorial rights have continued to belong to the Crown, in respect of the Duchy of Lancaster, and the Lord's Court—to be regarded, apparently, as exercising only Court Leet functions—has been held uninterruptedly for at least five centuries down to the present day.[1] Every year during the past five centuries the Steward, as of old, has held this ancient Court, the Bailiff formally notifying the residents to attend, and expressly summoning about a score of them to serve on the Jury. At the end of the seventeenth century, and (as the records show) throughout the eighteenth century, the Court was an effective local governing authority—in the absence of any effective Vestry, the only authority for the Precinct, other than the much-occupied Middlesex Quarter Sessions.[2] At the sessions of this Court were appointed the four Burgesses and the four Assistant Burgesses, each serving for life, a number to which the Precinct was entitled under the Act of 1585, in imitation of the constitution of the Court of Burgesses for Westminster. The Court also appointed annually from among the respectable householders four Constables, four Aleconners, and two Flesh-tasters, who were

[1] The early records of this Court, mentioned as held in 1399, have disappeared, but the proceedings between 1682 and 1789 are summarised in precise detail in the *Digest of the Proceedings of the Court Leet of the Manor and Liberty of the Savoy*, which Joseph Ritson, the learned antiquary, who was then the Steward, published in 1789. For its work since that date there is its great bound volume of current records, "The Court Book of the Manor and Liberty of the Savoy," for access to which (and much information) we are indebted to the courtesy of Mr. G. R. Askwith, the present Steward.

[2] The Precinct of the Savoy, as an extra-parochial place, had apparently for a long time no parish officers. We hear of a sort of Select Vestry in 1635 and 1732 (see Vol. I. *The Parish and the County*, p. 186), which may not have continued in authority. The inhabitants held annual meetings to choose Trustees for regulating the Nightly Watch under 14 George III. c. 90 (1774). A body of Paving Commissioners, similarly elected, was established by 5 and 6 William IV. c. 18 (1835). When at last the Precinct was required in 1855 to take rank among the Parishes of Westminster for the election of a member of the Metropolitan Board of Works, the election was also made at the meeting of ratepayers, which had by this time assumed to be an open Vestry.

required to serve their year of office, and severely fined in default.[1] These officers were required severally to make their presentments of nuisances and defaults to the next Court, when the Jury did not fail to inflict substantial fines on the offenders. Shopkeepers using fraudulent weights and measures,[2] residents keeping houses of ill-fame,[3] traders obstructing the streets by leaving timber, casks, or packing-cases about, or stopping up the footway by ladders;[4] owners allowing their premises to become structurally unsafe; soap-boilers conveying offensive soaplees along the Strand;[5] the Keeper of the Savoy Prison for ill-treating the military prisoners detained there[6]—even the proprietor of Exeter Change for "keeping a tiger carelessly secured in a shed on Savoy Hill to the great alarm of the neighbours"[7]—found themselves reprimanded, warned, and smartly fined for their delinquencies. During the eighteenth century the "Commissioners of the Pavement" and the "Commissioners of Sewers," both statutory authorities for the City of Westminster, were repeatedly presented for their neglect. The condition of the "Strand Bridge," of "Strand Lane Stairs," of "Essex Stairs," and of "Surrey Stairs" was perpetually exercising the minds of the Jury.[8] Nor did the Court lack its paid professional officers. Besides the Bailiff, whose remuneration lay in his fees, there was an Upper Beadle and an Under Beadle, each with a gorgeous staff of office, and (in 1795) an Assistant Constable. Year after year the proceedings go on, in the nineteenth century growing steadily more perfunctory. The advent of the new police in 1829 evidently accelerates the process of decay. In 1861 the Court petitions Parliament to be included, like the City of Westminster, in the abolition of the

---

[1] As lately as 1791 an inhabitant was summarily fined £7 for refusing to serve as Constable (MS. Records, Savoy Court, 1791).

[2] "Upon the return of the Aleconners, they present Mr. F., Cheesemonger, in Butcher Row, for having scales which they found deficient, and do amerce him in the sum of forty shillings" (MS. Records, Savoy Court, 1785). Similarly a baker, "for breaking the Assize of Bread," is fined forty shillings (*ibid.* 1792).

[3] *Ibid.* 1809 (very frequently also between 1682 and 1789).

[4] *Ibid.* 1795.

[5] *Ibid.* 1796, 1797, 1807, 1809, 1810 (£30 fine).

[6] 1795 and 1798; in 1810 the Jury visited the prison and found "all well" (*ibid*).

[7] *Ibid.* 1798.

[8] *Digest of the Proceedings of the Court Leet of the Manor and Liberty of the Savoy*, by J. Ritson, 1789.

"Annoyance Jury." After this date the officers' presentments cease, and the proceedings become formal only, though fines continued to be nominally inflicted on keepers of houses of ill-fame (as a method of driving them out of the Precinct) down to 1880. The Court still (1907) continues to be held, with elaborate ceremony, the Steward formally "charging" the Jury, and insisting on its attendance. The proceedings, however, are confined to a punctilious maintenance of ancient boundary marks, and the five-centuries-old "Court of the Steward, Bailiff, and Burgesses of the Manor and Liberty of the Savoy," fully alive and active in 1807, lingers in 1907 only as a shadow of the past.[1]

---

[1] We may mention another extra-parochial place in the Metropolis, governed, apparently, by a Lord's Court. The Tower of London has, time out of mind, been the nucleus of a "Liberty," or area exempted from some or all of the jurisdiction of the County. According to a statute of 1663 this Liberty of "the Tower Hamlets" included no fewer than twenty-one places, comprising Shoreditch, Hackney, and the whole eastern part of Middlesex, within which were many separate Manors. These were, at any rate for militia purposes, under the Constable of the Tower, who acted in many ways as Custos Rotulorum and Lord-Lieutenant. Whether anything in the nature of a Hundred Court was ever held we cannot tell ; but Courts of Quarter Sessions were regularly held in the Tower itself until the reign of James II., when they were removed, as the concourse of people within the fortress was deemed unsafe. Meanwhile a Court was being held in the Tower, exercising Leet jurisdiction over the "Liberties" of the Tower in a narrower sense, extending, in fact, only to "the circumference without the Tower" and to extra-parochial places close by, such as Little Minories, Old Artillery Ground, and Wellclose Square. We hear in the sixteenth century of the presentments of "Her Majesty's Inquest of the Tower." Those of the "Leet Jury" for 1679 are preserved. The official orders and Letters Patent of James II. expressly mention this Court Leet of the Tower, and confirm the immunity of the "Liberties" from the authorities of the Cities of London and Westminster. Whether this Court of the "Precinct" of the Tower, as this adjacent "Liberty" came to be called, in any way represented a shrunken Court for the whole of the Tower Hamlets, superior to the Courts of the Manors within them, we cannot ascertain. Even as the Court Leet of the Precinct, it apparently faded away early in the eighteenth century. From an interesting petition of 16th February 1727 (preserved in War Office Ordnance Records, Misc. No. 1, Entry Book re Tower Liberty, in Public Record Office), we gather that the Court was held under the Steward of the Constable of the Tower, and that the Jury presented persons to serve as officers of the Precinct, including, since 1601, two Overseers of the Poor, who accounted regularly to the Court. The Court disposed of various funds, including fees paid by publicans for licences ; the rent of a shed on Tower Hill built by the Court itself, and of another on Tower Wharf ; "the disposal of the Bulwark Bar" (apparently a toll) ; fines imposed for oaths ; fees on burials at the chapel of the Tower ; fees on licences to watermen to work the Tower ferries on Sundays ; voluntary contributions at the Chapel, and otherwise ; and, finally, a rate levied on the inhabitants of Tower Hill. With these revenues the Court relieved the poor and administered the government of the Precinct. Latterly, however, by the neglect of Governors and of the Court, " the late Gentleman Porter " has

(iii.) *The Court Leet and Court Baron of Manchester*

The Manor of Manchester affords an example of a Lord's Court continuing to serve as an active local governing authority for a vast population and one of the greatest of English provincial towns, not merely between 1689 and 1835, but right down to 1846, under conditions very different from those of the rural fishing villages of Bamburgh, and even from those of the Precinct of the Savoy.[1]

The first point that we notice is that at Manchester there

appropriated the income of the Bulwark Bar, and some of the other revenues have been left unclaimed, with the result that the rate on the inhabitants has been increased. The military authorities are therefore requested to restore the privileges of the Court Leet. We have been unable to trace any of the records of this Court or to find out when it actually ceased to be held (see *The Survey of London*, by John Stow, vol. i. p. 77, of Strype's edition of 1720 ; *History and Antiquities of the Tower of London*, by John Bayley, vol. ii. pp. 654-670, and Appendix, pp. 112 and 121 of 1st edition only, 1825).

[1] Owing to the public-spirited action of the Manchester Town Council the records of this Court from 1552 to 1846 have been printed in full (see *The Court Leet Records of the Manor of Manchester*, in twelve volumes, edited, with notes and introduction to each volume, by J. P. Earwaker, 1884-1890). Extracts from these rolls had already been edited by John Harland in two volumes of the Chetham Society's publications (1864 and 1865). The Town Council has also published *The Constables' Accounts of the Manor of Manchester* (1612-1776), three vols., edited by J. P. Earwaker, 1891-1892. For the early history of the Manor see the scholarly treatise by Professor James Tait, *Mediæval Manchester and the Beginnings of Lancashire*, 1904 ; which does not, however, clear up the complicated relationship between the Hundred and the Manor, the Manor and the Parish, and the Parish and the Townships. Something is to be gathered on these points from *Chapters from the Early History of the Barony, Lordship, Vill, etc., of Manchester*, by J. Harland, 1861-1862 (vols. 53, 56, and 58 of the Chetham Society) ; the article on " The Feudal Baronage," by W. Farrer, in the *Victoria County History of Lancashire*, vol. i., 1906 ; and from the series of histories of the several chapelries in course of publication by the Chetham Society, viz. those of *Denton*, by J. Booker (vol. 37) ; *Didsbury and Chorlton*, by J. Booker, 1857 (vol. 42) ; *Stretford*, by H. T. Crofton, 1899-1903 (vols. N.S. 42, 45, and 51) ; *Birch*, by J. Booker, 1857 (vol. 47) ; and *Newton*, by H. T. Crofton, 1904-5 (vols. 52-55), for some of which references we are indebted to Dr. W. E. Axon. See also *Didsbury, Sketches, Reminiscences, and Legends*, by Fletcher Moss, 1890. For incidental references to the Manorial Court, see the account of the customs enrolled in 1623 (*History of Boroughs*, by H. A. Merewether and A. J. Stephens, 1835, vol. i. pp. 541-545); *A Picture of Manchester*, by Joseph Aston, 1816, pp. 27-30, 168 ; *An Essay on English Municipal History*, by James Thompson, 1867, ch. xiv ; *Manchester Guardian*, 18th October 1817, 4th May and 19th October 1833, 12th October 1836, 25th October 1837, 13th January and 10th February 1838 ; *Manchester Courier*, 15th October 1836 ; and the case of Rutter *v.* Chapman, 1839. The close of its history is described in the introduction to vol. xii. of *The Court Leet Records of the Manor of Manchester*, by J. P. Earwaker, 1890 ; *Alderman Cobden*, by Sir E. W. Watkin, 1891 ; *Cobden as a Manchester Citizen*, by W. E. A. Axon, 1904.

was, at any rate in the nineteenth century, not one Lord's Court,
but a pair of Courts—two separate and distinct tribunals, held
in different places, at different times, by different officers of the
Lord of the Manor, served by different staffs of subordinates,
and preserving entirely distinct records.　There was the
"Court Baron of the Manor of Manchester," a "Three Weeks'
Court," of which the functions seem to have been confined to
the trial of civil actions under forty shillings.[1]　There was the
"Court Leet and View of Frankpledge held in and for the
Manor of Manchester," which, as we shall see, closely resembled
what the lawyers thought that a Court Leet ought to be.　It
is true that at this Court the Jury elected a Boroughreeve, an
officer whose title would have led us rather to expect his
election at the Court Baron.　But the Boroughreeve of
Manchester had nothing to do with collecting the Lord's rents
and dues from his burgage or other tenants, nor had he even
to manage any of the common affairs of the tenants of the
Manor.　For the period with which we are concerned he was
merely the head police officer,[2] superintending the two Constables and representing the little community to the rest of the
world.　Whatever inter-mixture of the agricultural or other
common interests of the tenants of the Manor there may have
been in preceding centuries, the Manchester Court Leet between
1689 and 1835 was concerned exclusively with the suppression
of the ever-increasing urban nuisances, the making of the
usual By-laws for the regulation of the streets, and the appoint-

---

[1] Particulars as to the actual work and character of the Court Baron for
Manchester are scanty ; see the Fifth Report of the Royal Commission on the
Courts of Common Law, 1833, pp. 53a, 75a, 78a, and especially 1-5b ; *A Picture
of Manchester*, by Joseph Aston, 1816, p. 30 ; *History of Lancashire*, by John
Corry, 1825, vol. ii. p. 477.

[2] "We came on to Manchester, one of the greatest, if not the greatest mere
village in England.　It is neither a walled town, city, nor Corporation ; it sends
no members to Parliament ; and the highest magistrate there is a Constable
or Headborough ; and yet it has a Collegiate Church, besides several other
churches ; takes up a large space of ground ; and, including the suburbs, or that
part of the town on the other side of the bridge [Salford], it is said to contain
above 50,000 people. . . . I cannot doubt but this increasing town will, some
time or other, obtain some better face of government and be incorporated, as it
very well deserves to be" (*A Tour through the whole Island of Great Britain*,
by D. Defoe, vol. iii. pp. 219, 220 of edition of 1742).　Defoe greatly exaggerated
the population of Manchester and Salford, which on his visit probably did not
reach 20,000.　In 1689 Manchester alone was put at about 6000 ; in 1774 at
41,000 ; in 1801 it was 84,000, and in 1831, 122,000.

ment of the multitudinous public officers requisite for these objects.[1]

The Court Leet of the Manor of Manchester is remarkable for its highly developed organisation. Held always by the Steward of the Lord of the Manor, with a Jury appointed at the preceding Court, it seems from the earliest recorded times to have claimed the attendance of every " Burgess " of the Township of Manchester, or his eldest son or wife, under penalty of threepence fine. This obligation on every holder of a burgage tenement may be connected with the grant of the charter of 1301 and the practice of the Portmanmoot of the Township.[2] In the eighteenth century, when the meaning of the custom had been forgotten, it seems to have been assumed by the Court that every male resident over twelve years of age was under obligation to attend ; and we have evidence that an immense list of names was actually called over, with a view to imposing, for the profit of some of the officers, a fine of threepence each on those who did not answer to their names.[3]

---

[1] We must leave to the historians of earlier centuries to decide whether the Court Baron and Court Leet of Manchester, as we find them in 1689, were descended from one Court of the Manor or from more than one Court. In the fourteenth century there had been a Court Baron of Manchester, sitting from three weeks to three weeks, exercising jurisdiction over the whole Barony of Manchester. Professor Tait supposes this Court, in shrinking in jurisdiction to the township of Manchester, to have become what we find, in 1552, as the Court Leet (*Mediæval Manchester and the Beginnings of Lancashire*, by James Tait, 1904, p. 35). On the other hand, the Charter of 1301 gave the inhabitants of the township a "curia burgi," "Portmanmoot," or Borough Court of their own, which elected the head officer or Reeve, and had jurisdiction over the Burgesses of the narrower area of the township in debt and assault. This Court seems to us more likely to have been the ancestor of the Court Leet of the earliest records of 1552. What is revealed in those records is exactly a Borough Court. It is never described as a Court Baron. We suspect that the Court of the Barony of Manchester at no time coalesced with the Portmanmoot, Borough Court, or Court Leet of the Township. The so-called "Court Baron of Manchester" of the eighteenth century may have been the direct descendant of the Court of the Barony. On the other hand, it is possible that the Great Court of the Barony was simply discontinued. We suggest that the Court Baron that we find in the eighteenth century, exercising jurisdiction only over the Township, may be the descendant of the Halmote Court held by the Lord for the Manor of the Township alone, the Court Baron side of which he retained in his own hands when he granted to his new Burgesses the right to hold a separate Portmanmoot.

[2] There was a similar obligation at Salford and Stockport, which had received baronial Charters in the thirteenth century, on which the Manchester Charter of 1301 was probably modelled (*Mediæval Manchester and the Beginnings of Lancashire*, by James Tait, 1904, p. 51).

[3] In the formal charge to the Jury of the Steward for 1788 (Roberts) we have it stated that the poorer inhabitants, "to avoid payment of the threepence,

But the distinguishing feature of the Manchester Court was the unusually large number of officers who were nominated by the Jury and formally appointed by the Court. These officers were required to serve their term of twelve months, all of them originally without remuneration. At their head was the Boroughreeve, the executive chief of the little community, who presided at all public meetings, and though without any of the authority of a Justice of the Peace, in many ways acted as the representative of the town. "In no Corporation," says a writer of 1816, "is the Mayor for the time being treated with more respect, the paraphernalia of a mace-bearer excepted, than the Boroughreeve of Manchester."[1] Second only to the Boroughreeve were the two Constables, who were always appointed together, and who acted jointly and severally as his principal lieutenants, without, so far as we can ascertain, any distinction of function. But besides these dignitaries, the Court appointed annually an ever-increasing array of other officers, who, by 1689, had come to number over one hundred.[2] Among these were the usual Aleconners and Scavengers, with innumerable others, such as Market-lookers and Muzzlers of Mastiff Dogs. It seems long to have been the practice, whenever the need for any new function or any particular nuisance or abuse forced itself upon the attention of the Jury, for a new and compulsorily serving officer to be appointed[3] to see that

attend the Court and listen to the calling over an immense roll of names, until they answer to their own, by which the greater part of the day is lost. . . . As to the common practice of calling over all the names of so populous a Manor as Manchester, it occasions loss of time to the poor, is productive of no advantage, no emolument but a trifling perquisite to the inferior officers of the Court, and the liberality of the present Lord of the Manor would induce him to correct this practice" ("Charge of 1788," reprinted in *The Court Leet Records of the Manor of Manchester*, vol. ix. p. 244).

[1] *A Picture of Manchester*, by Joseph Aston, 1816, p. 27. At Birmingham and Bolton, as well as at Salford, the Chief Officer of the Lord's Court bore the same title, which we have not found elsewhere, though Portreeve is not uncommon in the South of England, and Headborough, Boroughhead, and Borsholder are frequently met with.

[2] Already in the earliest record, that of 4th October 1552, we find 59 officers appointed (*The Court Leet Records of the Manor of Manchester*, vol. i. p. 1); the number rising to 110 on 5th October 1686 (vol. vi. p. 241), and to 138 on 15th October 1756 (vol. viii. p. 1).

[3] The Burgesses had possessed a right to pasture their pigs in the woods and on the waste of the manor. "In the sixteenth century pigs wandering about the streets and even into the churchyard became such a nuisance that a public swineherd was started, who assembled his charges with a horn in the morning, and led them out to the Lord's waste at Collyhurst" (*Mediæval Man-*

the regulations of the Court were enforced; and once an office was created, it continued to be filled year after year, even if its functions had become obsolete. These compulsory offices were, however, rapidly becoming merely honorary sinecures. "Many of these offices," said the learned Steward of the Manor in 1788, "have an appearance of throwing a degree of indignity on the possessors, and it not infrequently happens that the muscles of the gravest are relaxed when they hear the most respectable names being annexed to the offices of Scavengers, Market-lookers, and Muzzlers of Mastiff Dogs." But the duties, he explained, were more easy and dignified than the titles implied. "If a Scavenger see any person obstructing the streets in any manner whatever; or if a Market-looker find any unwholesome meat exposed for sale, he has nothing to do but to make a memorandum of the offender's name, and the time of committing the offence, and to give information thereat at the next Court Leet, and the offender will be amerced."[1]   Unlike most other Manorial Courts, that of Manchester levied a rate on the inhabitants—we find "Mysegatherers" appointed as early as 1554, and the "Town Lay" is regularly mentioned down to 1780, when it was merged in the Poor Rate levied by the Overseers.[2]   Either out of this rate, or else by customary

chester and the Beginnings of Lancashire, by James Tait, 1904, p. 49).   The Court even appointed its own public musicians in the form of the "Town Waits," who were ordered by the Court to play through the town on every Thursday evening "according to the ancient custom."   They were evidently remunerated by voluntary gifts from the inhabitants (*The Court Leet Records of the Manor of Manchester*, 5th October 1669 and 16th April 1672, vol. v. pp. vi, 99, 166).

[1] *A Charge to the Grand Jury of the Court Leet of the Manor of Manchester*, by William Roberts, 1788 ; reprinted in *The Court Leet Records of the Manor of Manchester*, vol. ix., Appendix I., p. 251.

[2] Thus, in 1590, the Jury present the stairs leading to the river as in a bad state, and they order the "Myselayers for the time being, calling unto them the Constables, with six other honest neighbours, shall assess the inhabitants of the town for the repairing of the stairs ; and have appointed A. B., etc., to receive the same moneys so gathered, and to bestow the same, and give an account of the remainder to the next Jury" (*ibid*. vol. ii. p. 50).   It was probable that such "Town Rates" or "Constables' Rates" were elsewhere levied by the Lord's Court (instead of by the Vestry as Church Rates), but the only other case of which we have definite mention is that of Lewes (Sussex), where, in 1772, at the "Lawday" it was "resolved that the Constables and Jury at the Court Leet or Lawday chosen shall and do continue to have power to make and collect a town tax for defraying the necessary expenses of the borough" (signed by 86 inhabitants). In 1822-1823 the Constables were still levying a "town tax" of a shilling in the pound (*The History and Antiquities of Lewes*, by T. W. Horsfield, 1824-1832, p. 211 ; see *infra*, p. 173).

fees, paid officers could be remunerated, and already in the first half of the seventeenth century there were evidently such deputies in existence. In 1648 we see the Court appointing a permanent officer, the Deputy Constable,[1] who serves continuously year after year, on whom most of the work is gradually devolved, and to whom an ever-rising annual salary is awarded.[2] Presently other salaried officers are added, in the shape of one, two, and eventually four Beadles, resplendent, a century ago, in " livery of brown, with scarlet collars, coat, waistcoat, breeches, and leggings." [3]

The Court thus constituted and served attempted courageously to cope with all the needs of the growing town. " Cows, horses, sheep, pigs, dogs all required regulation, and had it. Pigs, as the most perverse animals, required the firmest and most rigorous handling ; and hundreds of folio pages of Jury orders relate to swine alone and their numerous misdeeds and nuisances, their eating corn in the market and desecrating the churchyard." [4] We see the Jury not only enforcing the Assize of Bread and Beer, but also insisting that all the innumerable officers should duly make the presentments incidental to their several offices, from the use of unlawful weights and measures and the exposure for sale of " unbaited " beef, up to the enforcement of the obligation

---

[1] 10th October 1648. " It is ordered by this Jury that whereas there is found much inconveniences by paying Deputy Constables' wages per particular, and that the said Deputy Constable, that shall be made choice of by and for the assistance of these Constables, shall have for all the service and attendance due and appertaining to the said office of Deputy Constable the sum of ten pounds per annum, and that to be paid by fifty shillings per quarter " (*The Court Leet Records of the Manor of Manchester*, vol. iv. p. 25).

[2] It was £20 in 1756, £30 in 1762, £80 in 1778, £150 in 1786, the same in 1802 when Nadin was appointed ; £200 in 1805 ; in 1821 Lavender was appointed at £350, and raised in 1822 to £600, at which figure it remained until his death in 1833. Beadles, at first one and ultimately four, begin at £5 only, but end with £78 a year each (*ibid.* vols. iv. to x.). These salaries and many other expenses were charged in the Boroughreeve's accounts, which were annually submitted to the Court and passed by the Jury (for these accounts from 1612 to 1776, see *The Constables' Accounts of the Manor of Manchester*, by J. P. Earwaker, 3 vols., 1891-1892). In the nineteenth century, as described in a previous volume, we find them presented to and passed by the Open Vestry, prior to their inclusion in the Poor Rate, in accordance with 18 George III. c. 19 of 1778, which prescribed this for the accounts of the ordinary Parish Constables.

[3] *Reminiscences of Old Manchester and Salford*, by an Octogenarian, 1887, p. 18.

[4] *Manchester Court Leet Records*, by John Harland, Chetham Society, vol. 63, 1864, p. viii.

to keep watch in turn, and the execution of various new By-laws forbidding waggons to stand in the streets or the playing of football or "tipcat" in the streets.[1] We gather that the presentments were made either by the Jury as a whole, by any of the officers, or even by individuals not officers, whose complaints occasionally led directly to orders by the Jury.[2] The majority of the presentments and orders between 1731 and 1846 relate either to market offences, the sale of unwhole-some or "unmarketable" meat or fish, "blowing veal," the use of deficient weights or short measures, or the cutting or gashing of hides; or, on the other hand, to the innumerable nuisances of a growing city, from allowing swine to roam in the streets, or not repairing or cleaning the pavement, up to such modern annoyances as excessive factory smoke,[3] the stench from gas lime,[4] mock auctions, and the firing of pistols.[5] What is remarkable in the Manchester Court is the freedom with which it used what it conceived to be its power of making By-laws, by which it did not scruple to create new punishable offences. Thus in 1731 we find the Jury, "upon complaint made by several persons of people bringing milk to town suffering their horses to stand in the street with their cans on, whilst they sell their milk," peremptorily ordering the milk-sellers "that they shall not suffer them to stand in the streets, but that they shall set down their cans and put their horses in some stables; or we do amerce them five shillings apiece."[6] In 1732 the Jury orders that "the Scavengers do see that the

---

[1] *The Court Leet Records of the Manor of Manchester*, 12th October 1608, vol. ii. pp. vi, 239-240.

[2] Thus, 18th April 1733, " whereas complaint hath been made to us that W. B. . . . suffers his large bull-dog to go abroad unmuzzled," the Jury orders that the dog is to be muzzled in future, or that in default W. B. shall be fined twenty shillings" (*ibid.* vol. vii. p. 20).

[3] In 1801, as a local annalist records, " the Court Leet Jury presented eleven owners of factories for not consuming their smoke; they were fined respectively £100, but the fines were respited to allow time for their being altered " (*Manchester Historical Recorder*, 1874, p. 65).

[4] *The Court Leet Records of the Manor of Manchester*, 20th October 1820 (vol. xi. p. 6).

[5] *Ibid.* 21st October 1831 (vol. xi. pp. 257-258).

[6] 1st October 1731 (*ibid.* vol. vii. p. 7). The By-law is repeated two years later, when the fine is raised to ten shillings, and the Jury "order that the Bellman shall publish this order three several times, in one week's time, at the Milk Market, and that the Constable pay him for his pains " (*ibid.* vol. vii. p. 26). It is again repeated in 1744, when the fine is raised to thirty-nine shillings (*ibid.* vol. vii. p. 131).

dirt swept together shall not be left in heaps, but orders to be given to the usual inhabitants to remove the same, and not suffered to lie in heaps in the middle of the street." [1]   At the same Court it is recorded that "we . . . upon complaint made to us of servants and persons employed in looking after horses do frequently bring their horses into the public streets, and there dress them, which becomes a nuisance . . . do order that no person shall presume to do the like for the future, and that this be made public." [2]   Next year it is commanded that "no person does for the future break any hogsheads . . . in the street called Millgate . . . or any other hogsheads within this Manor, without immediately cleansing and sweeping the same, on penalty of forty shillings for each offence." [3]   In 1737 it is ordained that "for the future no tanner or other person shall lay down raw hides in the street or passage beside the shambles," under penalty of twenty shillings for each offence. [4]

The Court had also, in a sense, important administrative functions. The most valuable incidents of the Manor were the profits of the Soke Mill and Oven, [5] and of the Market. The large and growing revenues yielded to the Lord by these

---

[1] *The Court Leet Records of the Manor of Manchester*, 5th May 1732 (vol. vii. p. 11).

[2] *Ibid.* 5th May 1732 (vol. vii. p. 10).

[3] *Ibid.* 18th April 1733 (vol. vii. p. 20). "Long Millgate was," down to Victorian times, "a leading thoroughfare, the highway to the North of England" (*Reminiscences of Old Manchester and Salford*, by an Octogenarian, 1887, p. 43).

[4] *The Court Leet Records of the Manor of Manchester*, 6th October 1737 (vol. vii. p. 66).

[5] The Charter of 1301 had continued the obligation of the Burgesses to grind their corn at the Lord's mill, to dry their malt at his kiln, and bake their bread at his oven. These monopolies continued to be actively enforced, for his profit, by his lessees and agents, giving rise, in the seventeenth and eighteenth centuries, to constant friction ; and, it is said, between 1550 and 1758 to no fewer than sixty lawsuits. The exactions of the lessees of the Soke Mill in 1757 provoked the serious riots of that year, which led, in 1758, to a Local Act restricting the monopoly to the drying of malt. The monopoly had passed to the Trustees of the Manchester Grammar School, who were accorded, in partial compensation, a perpetual exemption from all local rates and taxes (32 George II. c. 61). The remaining monopoly of the malt kiln continued in their hands, their profit or tax being twopence a bushel. This was said to induce brewers to settle outside the boundary (*A Picture of Manchester*, by Joseph Aston, 1816, p. 168). Nevertheless it was, in 1825, productive of no less than £2250 a year (*Mediæval Manchester and the beginnings of Lancashire*, by James Tait, 1904, p. 50). This impost continued until the premises were sold to a railway company and the mill was discontinued (*History of Corn-milling*, by R. Bennett and J. Elton, 1898-1904).

monopolies were either leased or else collected under the direction of the Steward, who himself appointed his toll-gatherers and other agents.[1] But the Burgesses, the jurymen, and the officers of the Lord's Court had also their part to play. The annual Fair, for instance, held under a grant of 1227 at "Four Acres" or "Acrefield," represented, it is clear, an interference with ancient rights of commonfield agriculture and common pasture.[2] In the course of the eighteenth century this three-days' Fair became in the main a popular holiday, and in the nineteenth century a saturnalia. It yielded, however, no small revenue to the Lord, and was therefore continued in ancient form.[3] "On the second day the Steward of the Lord of the Manor (accompanied in procession by the Boroughreeve, the two Constables, and a few persons who represent Burgesses who owe suit to the Court of the Lord) proclaims the right of the Lord of the Manor to hold the Fair in that place."[4] More important was the participation of the Court in the administration of the ancient prescriptive Market, which had been held weekly since at any rate 1282. Though the Lord collected his own dues, it would seem that the actual management of the various market-places and the making of market rules and By-laws were, like the presentment of offenders against them, in the hands of the Court. We find the Jury deciding the hour at which the markets for flour, wheat, and oats respectively shall be opened by the ringing of a bell, and ordering "that no person does hereafter presume to sell any

---

[1] In 1731 the Court amerced the "Receiver of the Tolls" ten shillings, for not keeping a certain street clear (*The Court Leet Records of the Manor of Manchester*, vol. vii. p. 8).

[2] "An ancient custom obtained of pelting the first animal driven into the Fair with acorns and striking it with whips. This has been very conjecturally explained as a survival of an original protest of the inhabitants against the interference with their grazing rights by the establishment of the Fair" (*Mediæval Manchester and the Beginnings of Lancashire*, by James Tait, 1904, p. 45). The Fair days were the 20th, 21st, and 22nd of September. From fair-time till February the Acrefield was common pasture; from February till fair-time under arable cultivation. "As late as the beginning of the eighteenth century, corn growing on Acrefield had sometimes to be hastily cut and carried away before the fair or the people would have trampled it down" (*ibid.* p. 45).

[3] In 1708 Lady Ann Bland got a private Act enabling her to enclose the Acrefield and build St. Ann's Church; but she had to submit to the condition that a space 30 yards wide should be left open for the Fair.

[4] *A Picture of Manchester*, by Joseph Aston, 1816, p. 215. The Fair grew to be such a nuisance in the nineteenth century that it was moved, first to Shudehill, and then to Campfield; but it was not finally abolished until 1876.

meal before such bell rings, on pain of punishment."[1]   They
order the "cheese market" to be removed from one place, and
the "fish market" from another, assigning new sites at their
discretion.[2]   They insist on stopping the butchers from selling
meat right into the night of Saturday, and even on Sunday
morning, imposing a closing time of eleven o'clock at night.[3]
They forbid, under penalty of a fine, any sack of oats to be
offered for sale that contains less than 18 strokes, Winchester
measure; or any horseload of coal weighing less than two
hundred pounds, six score to the hundred, sack included; or
any cartload less than twelve hundred pounds.[4]   They prohibit
fruit stalls at this place or that, and exclude hucksters from
the market.[5]   In 1774 they remove the earthenware market
which had grown up "in the street called Smithy Door" to
the north side of the old churchyard.[6]   They exclude all dogs,
whether "male or female," from the flesh market.[7]

How far these administrative decisions with regard to such
important a source of Manorial revenue as the Manchester
market were really left to the discretion of the Jury, and
how far they represented only a convenient method of
strengthening and promulgating the decisions of the Manorial
officers, we cannot now determine.   What is clear from the
records is that year by year the Court went on appointing
its officers, making its presentments, and imposing its fines
with unslackened zeal, and doing an undiminished amount of
work right down to the nineteenth century.   Meanwhile
the township of Manchester—which had in 1774 still only
41,000 inhabitants—had sprung rapidly into a densely
crowded, populous city.   The mere "keeping the peace" in
this heterogeneous aggregation of factory operatives, newly
gathered together from all parts, soon transcended the scanty
powers wielded by the Boroughreeve and his two Constables.
As officers of the Court Leet they were not Justices of the

[1] *The Court Leet Records of the Manor of Manchester*, 16th April 1735,
vol. vii. p. 38.

[2] *Ibid.* 29th April 1736, vol. vii. p. 48.

[3] *Ibid.* 27th April 1738, vol. vii. p. 70.

[4] *Ibid.* 29th April 1736, vol. vii. p. 49.

[5] *Ibid.* 6th October 1737, vol. vii. p. 66; 22nd October 1741, vol. vii.
p. 110.

[6] *Ibid.* 12th October 1774, vol. vii. p. 159.

[7] *Ibid.* 14th April 1828, vol. xi. p. 189.

Peace, and the whole city had to depend for a police court on the good pleasure of half a dozen of the neighbouring country gentlemen, who took it in turns to ride into the town and commit offenders to the County gaol.[1] The nightly "watching" of such a town was utterly beyond the power of the two wealthy warehousemen or merchants who had been appointed Constables; and the obligation—really enforced in the seventeenth century—on all the inhabitants to "watch" in turn, bringing "each a Jack, a Sallet, and a Bill,"[2] "or hire some sufficient person to do it,"[3] was manifestly impracticable among a wage-earning, factory-working population. In 1765, and again in 1792, Acts of Parliament were obtained by the principal inhabitants establishing a body of Police Commissioners for Manchester and Salford, with power to appoint paid watchmen, light the streets, and levy a police rate; but so great was apparently the reluctance to these new measures that until 1797 practically nothing was done, and the dignity of the Court Leet remained unimpaired by any rival authority. As late as 1799 we find the Steward declaring the "new constitution of local government" to have been a failure, and urging the Jury to be active and all-embracing in their presentments.[4]

[1] "The towns of Manchester and Salford and the adjacent towns and villages now united with them by contiguous streets and buildings comprise a population far exceeding 100,000, and form together the largest provincial town in Great Britain; yet among this vast community there is not one resident Magistrate nor any Municipal government but the officers of the Court Leet, among whom there is no permanent authority above that of a Petty Constable. . . . For the local administration of justice, five Magistrates of the County residing nearest to the place have, much to their honour, undertaken the whole of this burthensome duty; one of them resorting to the town for this purpose every Monday, and two every Thursday, by a rotation among themselves" (*Report of the Committee appointed to secure Reforms, etc.*, 1808).

[2] *The Court Leet Records of the Manor of Manchester*, 6th October 1568, vol. i. p. 123.

[3] *Ibid.* vol. vi.

[4] "Now, Gentlemen," said the Steward to the Jury in 1799, "what has happened since the erection of the new constitution of local government ? During the wet and dark winter months the streets have remained uncleansed and without lights; for some time no watchmen or patrols were appointed—security and temptation were thus afforded to plunder, and none could pass through the streets in safety; escaping personal violence, they were in imminent personal danger from the numerous unguarded cellar-pits and various obstructions that everywhere interrupted their passage. . . . Though innumerable buildings are everywhere rising up and crowded together . . . no party walls have been erected. . . . Streets are still crowded with annoyances which the power of the new Act was calculated to remove. Offenders are everywhere encouraged by

A new period opens for Manchester with the nineteenth century. In its opening years, as we shall describe in a subsequent volume, the Police Commissioners began at last actively to bestir themselves, and they gradually organised something like an efficient service of watching, cleansing, and lighting the town. For the first eighteen years of the century the Police Commissioners were, however, completely dominated by the officers of the Lord's Court. The Borough-reeve for the time being not only presided at all the meetings, but also acted as Treasurer and as Chairman of the General or Finance Committee; whilst the two Constables acted as Chairmen of the two principal administrative departments, namely, the Watch Committee and the Committee for Lighting and Scavengering. Such police force as existed, either night-watchmen or "patrols," was thus under their personal command. Many of the offences which had formerly been presented at the Lord's Court had now been forbidden by explicit clauses in the Police Commissioners' Acts, and were therefore summarily dealt with by the Justices, but the Commissioners went on making use also of the Lord's Court as a convenient tribunal, and the Jury did not discontinue its own activity, especially with regard to false weights and measures and unwholesome food. We even find this energetic Court at the beginning of the nineteenth century presenting and fining mill-owners for letting their cotton factories get into a dirty condition, whilst the most common of all nuisances punished at this date was the emitting of large quantities of smoke by the new steam engines. The Lord's Court remained, in fact, a dignified and influential tribunal. The Steward was a learned barrister, who opened the six-monthly "Court Leet and View of Frankpledge" with an elaborate proclamation. The jurymen were chosen by the Steward from among the wealthy leaders of the commercial and manufacturing class, always predominantly Tory and Anglican in opinion. The annually nominated Constables were invariably local magnates belonging to the industrial aristocracy of the town. In turn one of the past Constables served as Boroughreeve.[1] Down to

the impunity with which their trespasses are committed" ("Charge of John Cross, Esquire," reprinted in *The Court Leet Records of the Manor of Manchester*, vol. ix. Appendix II.).

[1] "It has long been a rule in the choice of the Boroughreeve to select those

1818, at any rate, all the "police and sanitary" government of Manchester remained unchallenged in the hands practically of the little knot of leading inhabitants who were summoned as jurymen to the Lord's Court and who took it in turns to serve as Boroughreeve. This supremacy was made possible, first, by the genuine public spirit which they showed in discharging the onerous duties of the Manorial offices; and, secondly, by their practical wisdom in admitting into the governing circle not only the Churchwardens, Overseers, and Surveyors of Highways, but also the principal Whig and Nonconformist merchants and warehousemen.

We have already described the advent, at Manchester in 1818, of a turbulent Democracy, which first showed itself in tumultuous Vestry meetings at the Collegiate Church, and proceeded, about 1827, to swamp the Police Commissioners by qualifying, in hundreds, for membership of that body. This Democracy, made up for the most part of the small shopkeepers and publicans, felt itself completely excluded from the choice of Boroughreeve and Constables. The Steward did not summon its members as jurymen to the Lord's Court, still less were they appointed to any of the Manorial offices or as special constables. But the Constables' accounts, including the salary of the Deputy Constable, had, by statute, to be presented by the Overseers to the Vestry meeting, and had to be passed by that assembly. We have seen, in a preceding chapter, how eagerly the Radicals seized, from 1820 onward, this opportunity of cavilling at every item of the expenditure of such "unrepresentative" authorities as the Boroughreeve and Constables. At Leeds, it will be remembered, it was the action of the "unrepresentative" Mayor and Corporation that was similarly objected to. The Manchester officers had neither the authority of Justices of the Peace nor the power to levy a County Rate. But they were backed up by the neighbouring County Justices, and above all, they were supported by the opulent Whigs of Manchester itself—a class which at Leeds, where it was excluded from the Corporation, had made common cause with the Democracy. The result was that, though between 1818

gentlemen who have already served the office of Constable" (*A Picture of Manchester*, by Joseph Aston, 1816, p. 27).

and 1837 there were uproarious scenes at the Vestry and
Police Commissioners' meetings, from which the Boroughreeve
was once forcibly ejected,[1] the governing circle of the Lord's
Court held its own to the end.   When in 1828 the constitution of the Police Commissioners was reformed by a new Act,
the Boroughreeve and Constables dominated the new elective
body as successfully as they had the old one.   The growing
force of night and day police remained effectively under their
control.   The Lord's Court went on presenting offenders and
enforcing its fines.   Finally, with the change in public feeling
which came with the Reform Bill, and perhaps still more with
the change in social habits which was inducing the wealthier
inhabitants more and more to live outside the town, this
opulent governing circle became tired of its duties.   It was
found increasingly difficult to find a suitable person to act
as Boroughreeve,[2] and in 1836 and 1837 the individuals
nominated preferred to pay heavy fines, running up to £100,
rather than serve.[3]   Richard Cobden, then a young but
prosperous calico printer, summoned as a juryman in 1837,
drew up a protest calling for some change, which his
colleagues on the Jury consented to sign.[4]   Out of this

[1] "At a meeting of the Commissioners (1827) party spirit ran so high that
the Boroughreeve, C. Cross, Esquire, who presided, was assaulted and forcibly
ejected " (*The Manchester Historical Recorder*, 1874, p. 92).
[2] We have already mentioned (Vol. I. *The Parish and the County*, pp. 19, 63)
that the Tyburn Ticket, exempting the holder from parish offices, fetched a much
higher price in Manchester than elsewhere. In 1804 the two persons appointed
Constables claimed exemption as holders of such tickets, but the Court refused to
allow it.   The case was carried to the King's Bench, which maintained the
exemption (Mosley *v.* Stonehouse and Railton, 11th February 1806 ; *The Court
Leet Records of the Manor of Manchester*, vol. ix. pp. 215, 216).
[3] *Manchester Guardian*, 12th October 1836.
[4] We append this protest, which is of interest as the earliest publication by
Cobden, as published in the *Manchester Guardian*, 25th·October 1837.   "The
Jury serving at the Court Leet of the Lord of the Manor of Manchester cannot
separate without publicly making known the very great difficulties they have had
to encounter in the discharge of their most important duty, the selection of a
Boroughreeve for this township.   From the great increase of the trade of the
places and the consequent conversion of the dwelling-houses situated in the centre
of the town into warehouses, the manufacturers, merchants, and other principal
inhabitants of Manchester have, with a very few exceptions, removed their
residences into the out-townships ; but as the jurisdiction of this Court does not
extend beyond the ancient and circumscribed limits of Manchester, the Jury have
been placed in a difficult position, owing to the very restricted number of residents
who are eligible to serve the office of Boroughreeve, and the difficulty is materi-
ally increased by the aversion which now and for some time past has been manifested by the individuals selected to fill the office.   In proof of which, at the

grew the movement, headed by Cobden and the Brothers Potter, for the incorporation of the Borough. "Is Manchester," indignantly asked Cobden at a public meeting, "to be governed from Rolleston Hall, in Staffordshire?"[1]

last Court Leet the person named for Boroughreeve voluntarily incurred a large pecuniary penalty rather than accept the office ; and again, on the present occasion the individual appointed has declined to serve, and thus subjected himself to a still heavier fine. But so far from there being a prospect of any diminution of this difficulty in future, the Court has deemed it necessary to declare that, seeing the fear of pecuniary penalties is insufficient, it will proceed by indictment against all such as may refuse to accept its appointment. In the meanwhile the changes of abode referred to are still going on, and it is known that many individuals, to escape from the jurisdiction of this Court, are now preparing to remove to the out-townships ; from which the Jury are of opinion that the difficulties of their successors at the next Court Leet will be much increased, and possibly they may be compelled, in the absence of proper persons, to make choice of an unfit individual to hold the most important office in the town. The Jury regard such a state of things as highly inimical to the best interests, and derogatory to the just dignity, of this the second town of the Empire, and they earnestly hope and recommend that immediate steps may be taken to remedy the evil." This was signed by the whole fifteen jurymen, among them being such leading industrial magnates as Daniel Broadhurst, William M'Connel, and Edmund Potter, as well as Richard Cobden himself.

[1] *Manchester Guardian*, 10th February 1838. Rolleston Hall was the residence of the Lord of the Manor. A Charter was granted in 1838, but, owing to political and legal difficulties, it was not until 1842 that it was confirmed by Act of Parliament. In 1846 the Town Council bought from Sir Oswald Mosley, for the enormous sum of £200,000, the Manor and all the rights and incidents ; and the Lord's Court, regarded as a symbol of feudalism and a remnant of the past Tory supremacy, was allowed quietly to lapse. The Manor had been worth in 1282, £181 ; in 1665 (with shrunken area), £212 ; in 1579 it was sold for £3000 ; in 1596 a Mosley bought it for £3500 ; the town might have bought it in 1808 for £90,000, but thought the price excessive ; by 1846 unearned increment had brought it to £200,000 ! (see figures given in *Mediæval Manchester and the Beginnings of Lancashire*, by James Tait, 1904, p. 37).

Some of the smaller towns of Lancashire seem to have had, between 1689 and 1835, a local government under the Lord's Court, on the same lines as that of Manchester. "The towns of Great and Little Bolton—the two Boltons, as they were commonly called—had from time immemorial . . . been subject to the local authority of the Lords of the respective Manors. . . . Once a year in each place there was a Court Leet, the agent of the Lord of the Manor being the presiding authority, and this Court would proceed to appoint a Boroughreeve as head officer, and a staff of officials as Constables, Ale-tasters, Pig-ringers, Bellmen, and other functionaries." As at Manchester, "the powers of the Courts Leet were not extinguished or absorbed on the establishment in 1792 of a statutory body of Street Commissioners, and the annual Court Leet visit to Church on the first Sunday morning after election, preceded as it was by a grand breakfast the same morning at one of the leading inns, used to be a ceremonial invested with much consequence" (*Annals of Bolton*, by James Clegg, 1888, sec. 2, p. 9). Latterly, at any rate, there was a paid Deputy Constable with paid assistants (*Autobiography of a Lancashire Lawyer*, by John Taylor, 1883, p. 32). Much the same conditions existed at Rochdale, though we do not gather that its chief officer was styled Boroughreeve (*History of Rochdale*, by Henry Fishwick, 1889, p. 62) ; and at other towns in South Lancashire and Cheshire.

In the ancient town of Ashton-under-Lyne, we have an instance of the

(d) The Prevalence and Decay of the Lord's Court

We have now set before the reader a description of each of the types of Lord's Courts that we find exercising any of the functions of Local Government between 1689 and 1835. It remains to be considered how widely these types prevailed in the England and Wales of that period, and at what rate their activities gradually dwindled away.   On these points we

effective survival of the Court of the Manor as a local governing authority. The owner of the township in the nineteenth century was the Earl of Stamford and Warrington, drawing, in 1844, a rental of £30,000 a year from some two thousand tenants.   Though a body of Street Commissioners had been established under Local Acts, the admirably preserved records of the "Court Leet and View of Frankpledge and Court Baron of the Manor of Ashton-under-Lyne," confirmed by a full account of its proceedings for the year 1844, make it clear that, down to the middle of the nineteenth century at any rate, it was this Court that was the most important local governing authority.

What we may call its Court Baron side,—the trial of civil actions,—though mentioned as active by Aikin (1795) and Corry (1825), had apparently fallen into disuse after the establishment of a Court of Requests by Local Act of 1808. The ancient Manorial sokemill had long been disused.   But throughout the whole of the nineteenth century the Steward annually proclaimed, by placards and advertisements in the newspapers, the date of the approaching Court at the ancient Manor Courthouse, issuing special summonses to the existing Jury and officers, and also to the persons elected by him to serve as jurymen for the ensuing twelve months.   At nine o'clock, we are told in 1844, " the Court is opened by proclamation.   The Foreman of the Jury delivers in a written verdict," in which, at the Michaelmas Court, proper persons are "presented" to serve.   The "verdict" of the Jury then proceeds to present "the several offences that had been inspected during the preceding six months, which the Steward reads in a loud voice in the hearing of every one present ; and at the conclusion of the reading undertakes, as far as Lord Stamford is concerned, to remedy without unnecessary delay the grievances presented in the verdict."   The presentments (which, when they related to freehold property, were sometimes "traversed" by the defendant ; see a case, 29th April 1795) were numerous and important.   The Manor contained a considerable number of small freeholders, or holders of leases for long terms or several lives, who, in their sub-lettings, often proved "careless or avaricious landlords, whom neither the Local Acts nor common law could effectually reach." Hence the presentments of the Jury were used, both by Lord Stamford's agents and by the Street Commissioners, as convenient means of compelling such landlords to provide proper sanitary conveniences, to maintain pavements and fencing, to provide and cleanse drains, and to repair the roads.   "When the Steward had finished the reading of the verdict, he uniformly directs one of the officers of the Leet to call over the names of the suitors which comprehend all the tenants of Lord Stamford, and also all the freeholders (or frankpledgers, as they were anciently called) without the Manor, whether they be tenants of his Lordship or not.   In cases where the suitors appear by proxy, when their names are called in Court a charge of twopence per head is exacted as an acknowledgment, and one of the Bailiffs of the Court receives the same in a leathern purse attached to the end of a rod ten or twelve feet in length. . . . The Steward then addresses the Jury from the bench on the matters to be

do not find ourselves able to give any very accurate information. No list or other systematic record of these Courts has ever been made. Their proceedings were never reported in the newspapers nor recorded by any superior tribunal. There is reason to believe that the Steward, interested only in the business relating to the properties of the several tenants of the

inquired of by them, embracing the subjects laid down in the law books (see Kitchin on Courts) as coming under the cognisance of Courts Leet; and as occasion requires, he directs their attention to special circumstances like a Judge of Assize. . . . It is customary for about sixty or eighty of the gentlemen of the town and neighbourhood to dine together at the Commercial Hotel, the Steward of the Manor in the chair. The interchange of goodfellowship that takes place on these occasions between the representative of Lord Stamford and his tenantry contributes in no small degree to diffuse in Ashtonunder-Lyne a feeling of attachment to his Lordship's person and family ; and to perpetuate from one generation to another a tacit acquiescence in the verdicts of his Court Leet Jury, and to preserve from oblivion and extinction many of the ancient rights, liberties, and customs of the Manor." The decisions of the Court were, in fact, fully enforced. The fines imposed on defaulters and offenders were included in a Manorial distress warrant, given to the Bailiffs after every Court by the Steward. When any person contumaciously refused to pay, the Bailiff of the Manor simply seized his goods without further authority and sold them under the hammer.

The Ashton Court is remarkable as continuing down to the present day (1907) not only to be held, but actually to exercise local government functions. Every year the Court is held in ancient form, a "Mayor of the Manor, two High Constables, four Constables, twelve Bylaw-men, one Inspector of Weights and Measures, one Pounder, one Ale-taster, and three Bellmen" being appointed, together with a Jury of thirteen and a foreman. Presentments of nuisances are still regularly made by the Jury, to the number of half a dozen or so annually, and the persons in default are amerced. What is perhaps more remarkable is that the proceedings are still fully effective. The persons presented pay the fines imposed and remedy the nuisances complained of. No resistance is met with, but in case of default we are informed by the Steward of the Manor that he would have no hesitation in issuing a warrant and distraining for the fine. The presentments now refer usually to the highways, the persons presented being the Municipal Corporations, district councils, and other highway authorities, or occasionally private individuals. Even such great potentates as the Town Council of Manchester and the London and North-Western Railway Company are similarly treated (MS. Records, Manor Court of Ashton-under-Lyne, 1795-1906, for access to which we are indebted to the present Earl of Stamford and the trustees of the estate, and to Mr. Hall, the courteous Steward of the Manor ; the graphic account of the actual proceedings of the Court in 1844, given by the then Steward for the Royal Commission of Inquiry into the State of Large Towns and Populous Districts, Appendix to First Report, vol. ii. pp. 71-73 ; *Description of the Country from Thirty to Forty Miles Round Manchester*, by J. Aikin, 1795 ; *History of Ashton-under-Lyne*, by J. Butterworth, 1823 ; another, by the same, 1827 ; *Historical Account of Ashton*, by E. Butterworth, 1842 ; *Illustrations of the Customs of a Manor in the North of England*, by S. Hibbert-Ware, 1822 ; *Custom-Roll and Rental of the Manor of Ashton*, 1422, by J. Harland (Chetham Society, vol. lxxiv. 1869) ; *History of the County Palatine and Duchy of Lancaster*, by Edward Baines, vol. ii. pp. 300-329 of edition of 1888-1893 ; *History of Lancashire*, by John Corry, 1825, vol. ii. pp. 497-523 ; *Mediæval Manchester and the Beginnings of Lancashire*, by James Tait, 1904).

Manor, often omitted to enter the lengthy presentments of
the Jury about the management of the commonfield agriculture,
the petty nuisances of the hamlet, and the appointment of
Fieldsmen and Pinders. Such scanty archives as the Stewards
did keep are now for the most part hidden away among title
deeds of property in family muniment rooms or solicitors'
offices.[1] Even where antiquarian zeal has led to the printing
and publication of Manor Rolls, this has, in almost all cases,
chosen rather the earlier periods and has stopped short of the
eighteenth century.

At the outset of our inquiries we shared the common
opinion that these Manorial jurisdictions had, so far at any
rate as Local Government functions were concerned, come
silently to an end before our period.[2] But as we extended
our researches from County to County this impression wore off.
We are even inclined to suggest that, in 1689, the holding of
a Manorial Court for the suppression of nuisances, the management of the common pasture, and, less frequently, of the
commonfield agriculture and the appointment of Constables
and other officers for the district, was, in the thousands of
Manors that must still have existed, the rule rather than the
exception.   It is true that already in the middle of the
seventeenth century we hear that the Lord's Court is held "in
some lazy lordships not at all, but left as a thing obsolete and
useless." [3]   At the Restoration it was even thought necessary

---

[1] The collections of Manor Rolls of the eighteenth and nineteenth centuries
most easily accessible to the student are those of the Manors in the hands of
such public authorities as the Commissioners of Woods, Forests, and Land
Revenues (a list of about 100 of whose Manors is given in a Parliamentary Paper
of 6th July 1845), and the Ecclesiastical Commissioners, who have in their
London offices at least as many.   To both collections we have most courteously
been permitted access.   The extensive collections at the Public Record Office
(see its List and Index, No. 6), the British Museum, Lambeth Palace, the
Bodleian Library, and the Oxford and Cambridge Colleges seem to relate
principally to the earlier centuries.   A useful list of Manor records in the
principal public depositories is given in *The Manor and Manorial Records*, by
N. J. Hone, 1906, pp. 243-301.

[2] So competent an antiquarian as the late F. B. Bickley could state that by
1700, "and indeed as early as the middle of the seventeenth century, the Lords
of the Manor had lost the jurisdiction they possessed in earlier times, and the
rolls become merely registers of the transfer of land by succession, surrender,
sale, or mortgage" (*History of Dulwich College*, by W. Young, 1889, vol. ii.
chap. ii. on the Court Rolls, by F. B. Bickley, p. 266).

[3] *Pacis Consultum, a Directory to the Public Peace, briefly describing the
Antiquity, Extent, Practice, and Jurisdiction of Several Country Corporation
Courts, especially the Court Leet,* by Judge Jenkins, 1657, p. 2.

to provide that where the Lord's Court had for any reason not appointed a Constable, two Justices might temporarily exercise that power " until the Lord of the Leet shall hold his Court." [1] A somewhat later writer complains that "through the ignorance of unskilful Stewards this Court is almost become a shadow, so that in many places Justices of the Peace swear the Constables, and the inhabitants present the nuisances at the Sessions which ought to be presented here, whereby the Lord loses the benefits of his fines and amercements, and in time may totally be divested of the whole jurisdiction and profit of his Leet, of which inconveniences some Lords are less sensible because they never knew the true value and benefit of this jurisdiction." [2]   On the other hand, as evidence that these Courts had not become a negligible quantity, we may note that the celebrated " Orders and Directions " of the Privy Council of 1630 definitely placed no small share of the responsibility for the enforcement of local police regulations upon the Stewards of the Lord's Courts. [3] These Courts had, indeed, still so much vitality in 1659 that an ardent Utopian of that date thought it necessary to propose " that all Lords of Manors keeping constant Courts Baron and Courts Leet or either of them shall discontinue the same, and shall have the value of the profits of their Courts," on a ten years' average, paid to them out of public funds ; whilst it was also to be

---

[1] 13 and 14 Charles II. c. 12, sec. 15.

[2] *Historical Antiquities of Hertfordshire*, by Sir Henry Chauncy, 1700, p. 100.

[3] Among these " Orders and Directions " were the following : — " That Stewards to Lords and Gentlemen, in keeping their Leets twice a year, do specially inquire upon those articles that tend to the reformation or punishment of common offences and abuses : as of Bakers and Brewers for breaking of Assizes ; of Forestallers and Regraters ; against Tradesmen of all sorts for selling with under weights, or at excessive prices, or things unwholesome, or things made in deceipt. Of people, breakers of houses ; common thieves and their receivers ; haunters of Taverns or Alehouses ; those that go in good clothes and fare well, and none know whereof they live ; those that be night-walkers ; builders of Cottages and takers in of inmates ; offences of Victuallers, Artificers, Workmen, and Labourers. That the petty Constables in all Parishes be chosen of the abler sort of Parishioners, and the office not to be put upon the poorer sort, if it may be : Watching in the night and Warding by day, and to be appointed in every Town and Village for apprehension of rogues and vagabonds and for safety and good order" (MS. Register, Privy Council, 1631 ; *Orders and Directions, together with a Commission for the Better Administration of Justice*, 1630 ; see *The State of the Poor*, by Sir F. M. Eden, 1797, vol. i. p. 156 ; *History of Vagrants and Vagrancy*, by C. J. Ribton-Turner, 1887, p. 152 ; *Early History of English Poor Relief*, by E. M. Leonard, 1900, p. 158).

ordained that "all Hundred Courts" were "to cease, and to be for ever hereafter discontinued."[1]   And we have indirect evidence of the continued activity of the Lord's Court in the fact that neither the Minutes of Vestries nor the orders of Petty and Quarter Sessions during the seventeenth century contain, so far as we have noticed, any references to the appointments of Constables by the Justices.[2] The proceedings of the Middlesex Justices at the end of the seventeenth and the beginning of the eighteenth century contain, indeed, frequent references to the Constables appointed, not by the Justices but by the various Lord's Courts.   In 1727 Parliament expressly directed the Turnpike Act of that year "to be read at every Leet."[3]   Even as late as 1788-1793 we find the Quarter Sessions of Somersetshire and Oxfordshire thinking it worth while formally to recommend "to Lords of Leets" and "to Stewards of Courts" that they should take care to appoint none but efficient and trustworthy Constables.[4]

Nevertheless, though thousands of Manorial Courts were being held, no student of the records can fail to become aware, from the very beginning of the eighteenth century, that these ancient tribunals were being rapidly superseded by other forms of social organisation.   To take first the Court Baron side.   The progress of enclosure during the sixteenth and seventeenth centuries must have greatly diminished the business of the Courts.   The lack of any standing administrative machinery, and of explicit Corporate rights to the land—even the absence of publicity and the want of Corporate personality and perpetual succession—disabled the tenants of the Manor and the Jury of the Court from withstanding the constant pressure for the substitution of complete individual ownership for the ancient communal management of the cornfields and the hay meadows.   In the course of the eighteenth century, the rapid succession of Inclosure Acts, of

---

[1] *Chaos*, an interesting anonymous scheme for reconstruction, 1659, p. 26.

[2] In 1706, in the Vestry of St. Giles-in-the-Fields, "the Foreman of the Leet Jury is desired to move the Court that another Constable and Headborough be added for the first and second divisions of the parish" (*Account of the Hospital and Parish of St. Giles-in-the-Fields*, by J. Parton, 1822, p. 282).

[3] 1 George II. c. 19.

[4] MS. Minutes, Quarter Sessions, Somerset, Epiphany, 1788 ; *Bristol Gazette*, 24th January 1788 ; *Oxford Journal*, 18th May 1793

which, between 1689 and 1835, over 4000 were passed,[1] deprived thousands of Manorial Courts of their business connected with the co-operative management of agriculture, which had once formed so large a part of the Local Government of the village.[2] Along with this agricultural revolution must be noted the steady decline in the number of copyholds and customary freeholds, which in Sir Edward Coke's time had made up one-third of England,[3] but which, in the course of the next two centuries, were always becoming enfranchised into complete freeholds, or merged in larger properties. There remained to many a Court Baron only one public function, that of the decision of petty actions for debt and trespass. But the "Homage" of freeholders and copyholders, even when freeholders and copyholders still attended the Lord's Court, hardly afforded the best judicial tribunal for civil suits. Moreover, in the vast majority of Manors there came to be no freehold tenants liable to escheat to the Lord, and the copyholders shrunk up in number, or entirely ceased to exist. Whether or not from this cause, the hearing of petty debt cases was generally discontinued;[4] and we see this function passing

---

[1] Report of House of Commons Committee on Agricultural Distress, 1836, p. 501.

[2] "A strangely large proportion of the Inclosure Acts . . . sounded the death-knell each for one Manorial Court" (*North Riding Quarter Sessions Records*, by Rev. J. C. Atkinson, vol. vii. p. xxiii). It must be remembered that, over a large part of England, the enclosure of the commonfields had taken place without statutory authority (see *The Domesday of Inclosures*, 1517-1518, by I. S. Leadam (Royal Historical Society, 1897); "The Movements for the Inclosure and Preservation of Open Lands," by Sir R. Hunter, in *Journal of the Royal Statistical Society*, June 1897). Of the 2000 Inclosure Acts of the eighteenth century, a large proportion related to south-east England; and this is true, though to a lesser extent, of the 2000 Acts of 1800-1835. These Inclosure Acts, and the facts with which they deal, have, until lately, escaped proper study. Much light is thrown upon them by the work of Dr. Gilbert Slater, *The English Peasantry and the Enclosure of Commonfields* (1907).

[3] Bagnall *v.* Tucker, in *Reports of Divers Choice Cases, etc.*, by R. Brownlow, 1675, vol. ii. p. 156; *Treatise on Copyholds*, by C. Watkins, 4th edition, 1825, vol. i. p. 6.

[4] The history of petty debt courts does not fall within our scope, but we may mention that we have found it impossible (as we did also in the analogous cases of the County Courts and Hundred Courts) to form any idea of the extent to which the Manorial Courts continued actually to serve in this capacity between 1689 and 1835, or how they fulfilled this duty. Our first impression was that this particular function of the Lord's Court had become almost entirely disused. Thus we find the Privy Council in 1664 establishing, by a grant under the Great Seal, "a Court of Record to try small actions," in response to a petition from the inhabitants of Stepney and Hackney, who alleged that these Manors formed "a Liberty exempt both from the Sheriff's Bailiffs or the Knight

silently away to the "Courts of Conscience" or "Courts of Requests," established by particular statutes of the eighteenth century. Presently the Lord's Court, as a Court Baron, in distinction from a Customary Court and a Court Leet, comes to be held only in the exceptional cases (such as Epworth)

Marshal's men " (MS. Acts of Privy Council, 14th and 21st September 1664). The Manorial Courts were not mentioned, although we know that they were held ; and we can only assume that they did not then deal with pleas of debt. We read indeed, in 1728, that "of late this authority is seldom executed in some Manors, for that Courts Baron, which at first were held every three weeks, are now held no oftener than Courts Leet, viz. twice in the year. But . . . many Manors still retain their ancient power and authority in this particular" (*Practice of Courts Leet and Courts Baron*, by Sir William Scroggs, 4th edition, 1728, pp. 195-200). Further investigation into Manor records showed us that a large number of Courts continued in vigorous activity as petty debt tribunals. In not a few cases (as we have mentioned in the case of Bamburgh, Northumberland) we find tenants of the Manor fined for venturing to take their petty debt cases to any other tribunal. In 1774 we hear that the Court Baron sits every three weeks in the Manor of Trematon, Cornwall, and we see its Bailiff arresting a defendant who had been condemned to pay over £14 for damages and costs. On appeal its action was upheld by the King's Bench (Rowland *v.* Veale, in *Reports of Cases* by H. Cowper, 1783, pp. 18-22). "Down to about 1800," says the historian of an Oxfordshire Manor, "it appears from the Court books cognisance was taken of causes under forty shillings at Courts held in Bampton " (*History of Bampton*, by J. A. Giles, 1st edition, 1847, p. 104). On the other hand, when, in 1764, the Lord of the Manor of Warrington, Cheshire, sought to revive the jurisdiction in civil suits, his action seems to have been resisted as an innovation (*Annals of the Lords of Warrington and Bewsey from 1587*, by W. Beamont, 1873, pp. 116-117). We see the civil suits gradually falling into desuetude in the Manor of Havering atte Bower in Essex, where its Court, in 1822, had heard no pleas of debt since 1776, none of replevin since 1790, and none of ejectment since 1806 ; but was, as we have already mentioned, nevertheless required by the Court of King's Bench in 1822 to entertain a petty debt suit (R. *v.* Steward of Havering atte Bower ; see p. 18). So, in 1817, the Court Baron of the great Manor of Wakefield, Yorkshire, was found in full activity as a civil debt court (Holroyd *v.* Breare and Holmes, in *Reports of Cases, etc.*, by R. V. Barnewall and E. H. Alderson, 1822, vol. ii. p. 473). Up and down the country, it is clear, there were, especially in the North of England, scores of such Courts still hearing pleas of debt and trespass up to forty shillings, right down to the reign of Victoria. Yet so little was heard of them that it could be said by a great authority in 1825 that actions were at that date "now very rarely, indeed, if ever brought" in the Court Baron (*Treatise on Copyholds*, by C. Watkins, 4th edition, 1825, vol. ii. p. 382). In 1833 these tribunals were included in the inquiries of a Royal Commission, and they were incidentally reported as deciding civil actions in scores of places from Northumberland to Cornwall (Fifth Report of Royal Commission on Courts of Common Law, 1833, pp. 6, 20, 69, 77, 103, 133, 146, 191, etc.). In 1840 a return describes more than fifty Courts Baron in Northumberland, more than a score in Durham, half a dozen in Yorkshire, half a dozen in Wales, and half a dozen elsewhere (besides Hundred Courts, Honour Courts, and Borough Courts), still acting as petty debt Courts, and dealing, in some instances, with hundreds of pleas annually (House of Commons Return of Courts of Request, 1840). The County Courts Act of 1846 (9 and 10 Vic. c. 95) allowed Lords to surrender their civil jurisdictions, to be merged in the new County Courts ; and the amending Act of 1867 (30 and 31 Vic. c. 142) formally deprived them of any

" where a body of freeholders have a set of customs relating to fines, heriots, regulation of commons, and the like, resembling the customs of copyhold tenants." [1]

The Court Leet function of the Manorial Court—the suppression of public nuisances, the enforcement of personal obligations, and the appointment of police officers—was simultaneously being eaten into by newer forms of social organisation. After the first quarter of the seventeenth century we do not find Parliament conferring any jurisdiction upon

outstanding jurisdiction in matters falling within that of these Courts (*Treatise on the Law of Copyholds*, by John Scriven, 7th edition, 1896, p. 434 ; see article in *Nineteenth Century*, October 1897 ; *A History of English Law*, by Prof. W. S. Holdsworth, 1903, p. 418).

[1] *Law of Copyholds*, by C. I. Elton and H. J. H. Mackay, 2nd edition, 1893, p. 300. Where the Lord's Court has long since abandoned any functions of Local Government, and has become purely formal, we sometimes find it still making presentments of encroachments on the " Waste " of the Manor. Thus in the records of the " General Court Baron " of the Manor of Titburst and Kendalls in Hertfordshire (access to which we owe to the kindness of Mr. R. C. Phillimore), though any local government work had long before fallen into desuetude, we find, on 22nd June 1801, two presentments of persons making enclosures of the waste of the Manor. So at Barnes (Surrey), where the Lord's Court is still (1906) held, we read of a proclamation of the Court on 27th July 1894 against a tenant illegally digging gravel, and of his being " fined " £50 by the Lord of the Manor (*History of the Parish of Barnes*, by J. E. Anderson, 1900, p. 11).

More usually the Lord's Court became simply an opportunity for recording alienations of copyhold property, when a complacent Steward entertained at dinner a score of the Lord's tenantry. The Court was sometimes revived for this purpose after long desuetude. Thus " the Reeve and Constable of the Leet of Tunstall, . . . important civil officers in their day," had apparently ceased to be appointed after 1691. " But in the year 1826," the Lord's Court " was revived and has been since held annually as an audit for chief rents, for swearing in Constables, etc., and as a festive meeting and bond of connection between the Lord and his tenants" (*The Borough of Stoke on Trent*, by John Ward, 1843, p. 78). It is interesting to note that as early as three centuries ago the dinner had already become an important part of the ceremony. At Worplesdon (Surrey) the customs of the Manor formally recite that " the Homage and officers attending the Court and the Lawday have their dinner at the Queen's charge,"—the Queen owned the Manor,—" but on a special Court at the charge of the party desiring it." Similarly, at Dymock (Gloucestershire), Whiston and Claines (Worcestershire), Alvechurch (ditto), and many other Manors. In the Manor of Earl's Court (Middlesex), it is expressly provided that " any tenant may call a Court at his own charge, without suit unto the Lord ; the Steward and tenants to have their dinner provided and the Steward to be pleased for his pains " (*Treatise on Copyholds*, by C. Watkins, 4th edition, 1825, pp. 487, 545, 548, 549, 559). In the Manor of Bishopstoke (Hants), in 1752, the Jury " present that the Lord Bishop of the Manor ought at every Court to find and allow unto the Jury and Homage a dinner of plain butcher's meat and something in moderation to drink, in lieu of the pains and trouble they are at in attending and doing the business of the same Court, agreeably to the customs of this and other Manors belonging to the bishopric " (MS. Manor Rolls, Bishopstoke, 1752).

the Court Leet.[1]   From the very beginning of the eighteenth
century we become aware of the rapid supersession of its
functions, sometimes by new statutory bodies of Street
Commissioners or Turnpike Trustees to be hereafter described; sometimes by the Vestry of the Parish; sometimes
by the Justices of the County.   The presentments at the
Lord's Court become steadily more perfunctory, often de-
generating into a careless return of "omnia bene," or, as
in a Welsh Manor in 1804, "all well but the pigs." [2]
In some large and relatively populous parishes, such as
Woolwich and Tooting, we see the Vestry assuming the
right to pass the By-laws which elsewhere would have been
considered the business of the Lord's Court.[3]   In the same
years the Middlesex Justices in Quarter Sessions were taking
upon themselves freely to quash particular appointments of
Constables made by the Lord's Courts, discharging some
persons [4] and appointing others as they thought fit.   Towards
the end of the eighteenth century it is not uncommon to find
Vestries nominating Constables.   Presently their appointment by the Justices, in default of the Lord's Court, became
the common form.   In 1800, for instance, we gather that in
the extensive district of the Newport Three Hundreds of
Buckinghamshire, there were only four parishes in which the
Constables were still appointed at the Lord's Court.[5]   By
1829 we are told that "Petty Constables, though sometimes
appointed in Court Leet according to ancient practice, and
occasionally sworn into office either by the Lord of such

---

[1] The last instance is 21 James I. c. 21 (1623), as to innkeepers' offences.

[2] MS. Manor Roll, Maenol (in Diocese of Bangor), 1804, among the archives
of the Ecclesiastical Commissioners.

[3] See our preceding volume, *The Parish and the County*, pp. 56-60, 105, etc.

[4] In contrast, we may note that when, in 1652, a Constable for the Hundred
of King's Wimborne in Hampshire complained to the Judge at Assizes that he
had not been relieved of his office, though his year had expired, the Court would
not do more than direct the Steward for the Manor of King's Wimborne to
choose another person (MS. Circuit Books, Western Circuit, 9th July 1662).

[5] These were Bow, Brickhill, Castlethorpe, Haversham, and Stoke Ham-
mond.   The words "Court Leet" are written against these in MS. Minutes,
Quarter Sessions, Buckinghamshire, Easter, 1800.   Nevertheless in Gloucestershire, and doubtless elsewhere, every appointment by the Justices continued formally to be made only "until the Lord of the Leet shall hold his Court and
appoint another in his stead" (MS. Minutes, Quarter Sessions, Gloucestershire,
Epiphany, 1825; see for a similar form, *A Guide to the Practice of the Court of
Quarter Sessions for the County of Somerset*, by John Jesse, Junior, 1815, p. 22).

Court or by Justices out of session, are now generally nominated by their respective Parish Vestries, and sworn into office by the Justices at the Quarter Sessions, which is, on every account, the better and more regular mode."[1] "In the rural districts," wrote Chadwick only a few years later, "the Courts Leet have generally fallen into desuetude."[2] Here and there some valuable source of revenue kept the Lord's Court alive right down to Victorian times; it might be, as in the case of the Great Court of the Manor of Wakefield, the right to inspect and exact fees for standardising the weights and measures over an area of 230 square miles;[3] it might, as at Bradford,[4] Devonport,[5] and various other places, be a profitable market, with its power to levy toll; it might, as at Farringdon in Berkshire, be a prescriptive right to levy a "toll traverse" on cheese and corn arriving in the Manor;[6] or it might, as at Manchester, Leeds, Wake-

---

[1] *Practical Guide to the Quarter Sessions*, by W. Dickinson and T. N. Talfourd, 1829, p. 60.

[2] Poor Law Commissioners' General Report on the Sanitary Condition of the Labouring Population, 1842, p. 296.

[3] See *Court Rolls of the Manor of Wakefield*, by W. P. Baildon, vol. i. (1274-1297), 1901; *History of Wakefield*, by Thomas Taylor, 1886. The Manorial rights to this inspection of weights and measures, when actually exercised, were preserved in 22 and 23 Vic. c. 56, sec. 10 (1859), and 41 and 42 Vic. c. 49, sec. 49 (1878). The Act 55 and 56 Vic. c. 18 enabled local authorities to buy out the owners of such rights. The West Riding County Council had to pay £5000 in compensation in 1892 to get the function into its own hands (*Our Weights and Measures*, by H. J. Chaney, 1897, pp. 54-55). In the Manors of St. Giles-in-the-Fields and Stepney, Middlesex, the Manorial officers continued to be chosen for this purpose during the eighteenth century, and to levy fees and fines on persons using faulty weights and measures. These rights were upheld in the Court of King's Bench; see Duke of Bedford *v.* Alcock, 1 Wils. 248; Sheppard *v.* Hall in *Reports of Cases, etc.*, by R. V. Barnewall and J. L. Adolphus, 1833, vol. iii. p. 433; *Morning Advertiser*, 4th January 1806; *Treatise on Copyholds*, by John Scriven, 7th edition, 1896, p. 435. Similar jurisdictions continued to be exercised in these and other London Manors during the early part of the nineteenth century (see, for instance, a case in Clerkenwell, in 1832, Wilcock *v.* Windsor and Others, in *Reports of Cases, etc.*, by R. V. Barnewall and J. L. Adolphus, 1833, vol. iii. pp. 43-50).

[4] *Historical Notes on the Bradford Corporation*, by W. Cudworth, 1881, citing the case, Rawson *v.* Wright, in which this monopoly was successfully maintained in 1825.

[5] It is interesting to note that at Devonport, where the market yielded to the Lord of the Manor in 1830 a profit of nearly £3000 a year, the Lord's Court continued to appoint annually twelve "Constables for the Manor," even after the local Justices in Petty Sessions had taken to appointing fifteen Constables of their own (Brindley's *Plymouth, Devonport, and Stonehouse Directory*, 1830).

[6] In this case the Lord of the Manor in 1822 successfully maintained his right to exact and distrain summarily for sixpence on every ton of cheese and a

field, Bradford, and Ossett, be a Soke Mill, in which the Lord had known how to maintain a lucrative monopoly.[1]

It is, of course, impossible to ascribe to any one cause, or to assign to any one year, the setting in of the decay of the Lord's Court as an organ of Local Government. Just as no statute had created it, or endowed it with jurisdiction, so no statute ever abolished it, or even abrogated its powers. Its gradual fading away was, in fact, spread over several centuries. The persistent hostility of the King's Courts at Westminster, to be traced even in the thirteenth century, became specially accentuated in Sir Edward Coke, and was strengthened by the influences of the Commonwealth, which gave a shake to all feudal forms from which they never recovered. But apart from this disfavour of the King's Courts, at all times the jealous rivals of local jurisdictions, and apart from the disintegrating influences of seventeenth-century politics, the very ideas on which the Court of the Manor was based became ever more out of harmony with the new conceptions of social organisation. The principle of Government by the Common Agreement of the persons immediately concerned—the principle which lay at the root of such local autonomy as existed in the Court Baron—was ever more undermined by the growing tendency to base all civil relations on the strictly ascertained legal rights of the individual as an individual. Moreover, the Common Agreement on which the Court Baron rested was, as we have mentioned, essentially that of an Association of Producers, enjoying in individual ownership the use of the land, coupled with the power to levy taxes on the landless residents, who presently became the bulk of the population, and naturally resented their exclusion.

The Court Leet side of the Manorial Court was, as we may now see, equally out of harmony with the ideas and the needs of the eighteenth century. The limitation of the Leet to

penny on every quarter of corn ; he had in return to maintain market-house, lock-up house, pound, two pairs of stocks, and the stalls of the market ; to provide a brass bushel measure, and to repair half a bridge over the Thames (Rickards *v.* Bennett and Another, 1822, in *Reports of Cases, etc.*, by J. Dowling and A. Ryland, 1823, vol. ii. pp. 389-398).

[1] *History of Cornmilling*, by R. Bennett and J. Elton, 1898-1904, vol. iii. chap. viii., "Feudal Laws and Customs."

yearly or half-yearly meetings was specially inapplicable to the suppression of urban nuisances.[1] Its whole procedure, in its successive stages of presentment, amercement, affeering, and distraining for small fines was cumbrous and often ineffective; and the absence of any provision against a recurrence of the offence gave the locality the very minimum of protection. But we suggest that the break-up of the Court Leet is to be attributed, in the main, to the abandonment by the English people of the root-principle on which the Court depended. This principle, to put it shortly, was that, however men might differ in faculties or desires, they were all under an equal obligation to serve the community, by undertaking, in turn, all the offices required for its healthy life. This principle is manifested in the annual nomination of officers, their compulsory service, and its limitation to a single year. It is seen in the supremacy of the Jury, taken haphazard from the neighbours, and deciding, without experts, and even without witnesses, "on their own view and knowledge." It lies at the base of the usual absence of any permanent staff or Corporate revenue, and of the inability to see the necessity for more frequent meetings of the Court, or for its separation into committees. It accounts for the fact that Parliament was disinclined to endow this shifting Jury and perpetually changing group of amateur officers with any new functions, even if it ever occurred to any year's Court to ask for new powers, to be executed in future years by successive new groups of jurymen and officers whose character no one could foresee. We may recognise a noble element in this idea of universal equality of social obligation—the opposite, be it observed, of the eighteenth-century idea of universal equality of civil and political rights. But when this universal equality of social obligation meant each citizen taking, in turn, an "equal and identical" share in the service of the community, it proved impracticable for any but the most primitive society. Division of labour, implying specialisation of structure and

---

[1] The Court might have sat more frequently by the device of adjournment, but this was a device it seldom learned to use, and which had certainly not been contemplated in Magna Carta. In a case in 1832, an adjournment of a Court Leet from May to December was held to be not improper (Wilcock *v.* Windsor and Others, in *Reports of Cases, etc.*, by R. V. Barnewall and J. L. Adolphus, 1833, vol. iii. pp. 43-50).

function, became in fact a necessity of progress. Yet the twentieth-century student will perhaps regret that it was not the element of an identical equality, but the very notion of social obligation itself, which was swept away by the rival panacea of universality of civil and political rights.

CHAPTER III

THE MANORIAL BOROUGH

WE have now to describe a somewhat heterogeneous collection of local governing authorities which appear to us to be intermediate between the Lord's Court and the autonomous Municipal Corporation creating its own Justices of the Peace. The bulk of these authorities are plainly "Manorial" in their constitution. They are made up of such familiar parts as the Jury of Presentment, nominating or appointing Reeves, Constables, and other officers; they transact the public business at "Courts," called indifferently Leets, Views of Frankpledge, Courts Baron, Courts of Pleas, Courts of Record, Three Weeks' Courts, or Burghmotes; they exercise seignorial powers over the inhabitants at large—often absorbing indeed all the privileges of the Lord. They are frequently, we might almost say usually, termed "Boroughs" or "Free Boroughs." But we shall find, as Professor Maitland indicates, that "the Borough community will be closely related to the village community." [1] In some instances the so-called Boroughs are members of the seignorial Hierarchies of Courts that we have already described. In other places they are merely the urban parts of large Manors, becoming, by the grant of a measure of autonomy, what we shall term "Lord's Boroughs," the rest of the Manor being often designated "the Foreign." In a small minority of cases we find functions analogous to those of the Lord's Borough exercised by rudimentary authorities, which, so far as the accessible evidence is concerned, cannot actually be proved to have ever had any connection with a Lord's Court. But all these authorities, whether demonstrably seignorial in origin, or

[1] *Township and Borough*, by F. W. Maitland, 1898, p. 51.

127

doubtfully so, occupy, between 1689 and 1835, a similar
position in the local government of the country, between the
Parish and its officers on the one hand, and the Lord-Lieutenant,
High Sheriff, and Justices of the County on the other.   Hence
we group the whole of these authorities under the loose
designation of Manorial Boroughs—a phrase which we use
merely to distinguish them from the Municipal Corporations
empowered to create their own Corporate Justices of the Peace.[1]
We must leave it to the historian of the Manor to decide
whether some of the authorities which, between 1689 and
1835, fell within this class are appropriately designated
" Manorial."   In order that the student may bear this
reservation in mind, we begin with those instances which seem
to have least connection with the Lord's Court, and in which
the constitutional structure is most rudimentary.

(a) The Village Meeting

The most rudimentary—it may possibly be the least
significant—of quasi-manorial administrations existing in 1689
were the recurring village meetings, unchartered and unnamed,
that regulated the commonfield agriculture, the town's plough,
the customary privilege of gleaning,[2] the bull and boar, the
common herd, the pasturage on the commons and the waste,
and sometimes the quarry and the fishing grounds, without
any obvious relation to any Lord of the Manor.   No one has
yet explored the extent to which such customary sharings of
user of land, with or without legal ownership, have existed

---

[1] We know of no general description of the class of local authorities that
we term Manorial Boroughs.   The phrase " Manorial Corporations " was used
in the analytic index and tables of the Municipal Corporation Commission's
Report, 1835-1838, to designate some of the towns which they excluded from
their list of Municipal Corporations ; but they did not define its scope.   Their
separate reports on such of the Manorial Boroughs as they investigated, together
with those of the Commission of 1876-1880, are the principal accessible
materials ; but, as will be seen, we have made great use of the MS. archives of
such towns as Alnwick, Alresford, Altrincham, Arundel, Beccles, Birmingham,
Christchurch, Godmanchester, Lymington, Tetbury, and Wisbech ; and of the
local histories.   See also Miss Bateson's articles in *English Historical Review*,
1900-1902 ; and her *Borough Customs* (Selden Society, 1904 and 1906).

[2] The gleaning rules of Helpston in Lincolnshire in 1722 seem to have been
the following :—" That no person shall glean peas or beans till the peas or
beans be carried by the owners thereof, nor to carry away grain in sheets or
blankets, but to glean in bands only " (*Fenland Notes and Queries*, vol. iii. p. 304).

up and down England and Wales; nor enumerated the different forms under which some assembly or committee of the "commorants" arranged for the enjoyment of these "dolewoods" or "oxgangs," these "cattlegates" or "sheepheaves," these "stints" and "horseleazes," these "pasturegates" and "cowsgrasses."[1]

An interesting example of village government of this sort is afforded by the little village of Berwick in Sussex. Here, as we gather, nothing in the nature of a Manorial Court has been held for centuries. The inhabitants in 1721 are found governing themselves by voluntary agreement, then embodied in writing, in which the Rector joins. The arable fields, known as "tenantry-land," were unenclosed, and owned in severalty in the usual scattered strips. We have no record of decisions, like those of the Lord's Court of Great Tew, as to the crops to be sown. But each owner was to contribute a certain quota of sheep[2] to a common flock, to be placed in charge of a shepherd, and folded on the cornfields after a certain date. From information that we have gathered privately, we learn that, for the pasture lands, the Commoners cast lots annually for the parts of the common meadow they were severally to use during the ensuing year. As it was not thought seemly for the Rector to cast lots, he was allowed to use always the lot next to the brook. These rights to use the common lands seem to have been gradually bought up and exchanged by the principal landowner. But to this day (1907), as we are informed by the daughter of the late incumbent, the Parish Clerk has, by virtue of his office, the right to turn out one bullock upon what was formerly a commonfield, between certain fixed dates in the year; and this "right" is annually purchased from him by the farmer of those particular fields.[3]

Another curious survival is seen in the ancient village of

---

[1] See *The Law of Copyholds*, by C. I. Elton and H. J. H. Mackay, 2nd edition, 1893, p. 16.

[2] "Agreed that the sheep that are stocked for the Tye shall be stocked in this proportion, namely [the Rector] 16 for his privileges there; Widow Godly, 16; S. Stace, 8; Thomas Susan, 14; and those which have no land but their privileges shall keep only 3 ewes to their privileges, and no more."

[3] "Berwick Parochial Records," by Rev. G. M. Cooper, in *Sussex Archæological Collections*, vol. vi., 1853, pp. 240-241; supplemented by private information.

Yarnton in Oxfordshire, where there are three so-called "Lot Meadows," containing over 200 acres of valuable hay-fields. These have, time out of mind, been divided among the two tithe owners and the thirteen owners of shares, some of which are still appurtenant to neighbouring farms, whilst others are held by persons neither owning nor farming land. What is interesting is that, with the exception of the two "tidals" or "tithals," the shares of the co-owners, although all bearing distinct names, such as "Dun," "William of Bladon," "Rothe," etc., and dealt with as incorporeal hereditaments, are not represented by any definite pieces of land, but only by the right to draw lots annually for a thirteenth part in each of the "drafts" or sections into which the fields are then and there divided. The following description is by one who witnessed in 1905 a ceremony that was plainly of ancient usage :—

"On the day on which the meadows are appointed to be drawn . . . the Meadsman meets the owners of these shares at the tidals in Oxhey. He has with him a bag containing thirteen boxwood balls of about $1\frac{1}{2}$ in. in diameter, on each of which is written the name of one of these shares. At the first post, one of those present dips his hand into the bag and withdraws one of the balls; the name on the ball is called out, and a man with a scythe cuts half a dozen swathes to make a bare place, on which the owner of the lot cuts his initial. The whole company then walks on to the next stake, and a second ball is withdrawn. The man with the scythe again cuts half a dozen swathes, and the owner cuts his initial in the turf; and the performance is repeated till all the thirteen balls have been withdrawn, and every one of the thirteen owners has obtained his lot in the first draft. . . . In order to divide the lots, a man walks through the high grass from one post to the corresponding post on the other side of the field, and the track thus trodden shows the boundary. . . . It is obvious that this is the best way to divide the growing grass on unenclosed meadows. Every owner has his lot in each of the eight drafts, and the chance of the lot renders it most improbable that one man will get the pick of the field while his neighbour gets all the worst portions. As one of the farmers present said to me, 'They must have been clever old folk who thought this out.' To show how the lot works out, it will be sufficient to state that the owner of the share called Dun drew Lot 1 in the first draft of Oxhey, 9 in the second, 12 in the third, 4 in the first draft of the West Mead, 3 in the second, 11 in the third, 11 in the fourth, and 8 in the fifth." [1]

Similar village organisations connected with common agricultural interests may be found by the explorer in other parts of England.[2] It is, however, rare to find them getting

[1] "Till the beginning of the last century all three fields had to be cut the same day as they were drawn ; Oxhey on the first Monday after old St. Peter's Day, West Mead on the second Monday, and Pixey on the third. This custom was the cause of much disturbance and riot : outside labour had to be employed, and there was an influx of disorderly harvesters into the village ; but, in 1817, the vicar of Yarnton persuaded all parties to agree to a change, allowing the grass to be cut at any time before the cattle are turned into the meadow.

"The owner of each complete share is entitled to turn on to the meadows ten beasts after the grass is cut, but in so doing he must be careful to send no sheep or entire animals. The meadows are thrown open for stock on the Monday after August 12th, but there appears to be no rule fixing the date when the meadows are again laid up for hay ; in practice it is found, however, that as the meadows are very liable to floods, the cattle begin to lose flesh before the end of October, and they are, therefore, taken off" ("Lot Meadows, an interesting survival," by Adolphus Ballard, *Country Life*, 18th Nov. 1905 ; see also *Three Oxfordshire Parishes*, by Mrs. Stapleton, Oxford Historical Society, 1893, pp. 307-310). "Traces of a similar sharing of meadows by lot are said to be found to-day in the Lammas grounds in Hackney Marshes ; and old deeds of the thirteenth century in the chartulary of Godstow speak of Lot meadows at Cassington, the adjacent parish to Yarnton, and at Bletchingdon in the Cherwell Valley. The St. Frideswide's chartulary speaks of Lot meadows at Eynsham, which is the next parish to Cassington."

We have already mentioned elsewhere the common organisation of the four villages in Northamptonshire that share among them the Ashe Meadow ; appointing six "Fieldmen" to lay out the meadow in lots, which were drawn for at an annual gathering, and mown under the direction of "Crocusmen" (*History and Antiquities of Northamptonshire*, by John Bridges, 1791, vol. i. p. 219 ; *The Village Community*, by G. L. Gomme, 1890, p. 269). Similar lot meadows existed at Bestmoor (Oxon) ; see *The English Peasantry and the Enclosure of Common Fields*, by Gilbert Slater, 1907, p. 35.

[2] For instance, near the villages of Congresbury and Puxton in Somerset, there was, down to 1811, an extensive common, called the Dolmoors, running into both the parishes, the householders of which had the right of pasturage. This common was divided into twenty-four parts, and was managed by two officers, called Overseers of the Dolmoors, who served for one year and then nominated their successors. Every year, on the Saturday before Midsummer Day, a meeting was held in Puxton Church, by sound of bell, in the early morning, at which the villagers attended. The business was to draw lots for the privilege of having the use of twenty-three of the parts for the ensuing year, and to let by auction, by "inch of candle," the twenty-fourth part, "the Outdrift" or "the Outlet," for a sum of money varying from about one to three pounds, which was devoted to defraying the incidental expenses of the year. This ancient custom was only terminated by the 1816 award under the Inclosure Act of 1811 (*History and Antiquities of the County of Somerset*, by J. Collinson, 1791 ; *Delineations of the North-West Division of the County of Somersetshire*

beyond the undeviating maintenance of an ancient custom, without other administrative machinery than a public meeting and an officer—the " Meadsman," Common Herd, Fieldsman, or "Overseer,"—paid by customary fees or contributions.[1] But "between village and Borough," as Professor Maitland tells us, "there is no insuperable gulf, and if our villages had remained lordless they might perhaps in course of time have exhibited the decisive symptoms of Corporate unity." [2]

The first step in such an evolution might be the establishment of a standing committee. Of this the leading case is that of Aston and Cote,[3] two hamlets in the parish of Bampton, Oxfordshire, where the commoners had, time out of mind, down to Victorian days, maintained a " Sixteens," or standing administrative committee, on which each served in turn, every four yardlands annually furnishing one member. This body, as we learn from the case which the Lord of the Manor submitted to Counsel in 1657, had, from time immemorial, been accustomed " to make orders, set penalties, choose officers, and lot the meadows, and do all such things as are usually performed or done in the Courts Baron of other

---

by J. Rutter, 1829, p. 36 ; *The Sea-Board of Mendip*, by F. A. Knight, 1902, pp. 228-232 ; *The Village Community*, by G. L. Gomme, 1890, pp. 268-269 ; *Archæologia*, vol. xxxv. p. 471 ; *Notes and Queries for Somerset and Dorset*, vol. vi. p. 109).

[1] We ought not to forget that Domesday Book itself testifies to the existence of some entirely "lordless" villages (*Domesday Book and Beyond*, by F. W. Maitland, 1897, p. 133 ; *The Domesday Inquest*, by A. Ballard, 1906, pp. 138, 146 ; article by J. H. Round in *Victoria County History of Hertfordshire*, vol. i. 1905). Moreover, it seems worth considering whether some of these apparently autonomous village organisations may not have been, as the "berewicks" of Domesday possibly were, colonies or off-shoots from a Manor, forming distinct agricultural units in new settlements, and gaining a practical autonomy as they removed from the parent stock (see *Domesday Book and Beyond*, by F. W. Maitland, 1897, p. 114 ; *The Growth of the Manor*, by P. Vinogradoff, 1905, p. 224 ; *History of Municipal Government in Liverpool*, by Ramsay Muir, 1906, p. 3 ; article by F. M. Stenton in *Victoria County History of Derbyshire*, vol. i., 1905, p. 311).   [2] *Township and Borough*, by F. W. Maitland, 1898, p. 35.

[3] For the discussion of this interesting case, see Professor F. W. Maitland's article, "The Survival of Archaic Communities," in *Law Quarterly Review*, vol. ix., July 1893 ; *The Village Community*, by G. L. Gomme, 1890, pp. 158-170 ; *Villainage in England*, by P. Vinogradoff, 1892, pp. 392, 450 ; *History of Bampton*, by J. A. Giles, 1847, p. 79 ; *The Manor and Manorial Records*, by N. J. Hone, 1906, pp. 12-13 ; *Archæologia*, vol. xxxiii. p. 269 and vol. xxxv. p. 470 ; *The Jurist*, New Series, vol. xii. part ii. p. 108. *Journal of Archæological Institute*, vol. xliv. p. 405 ; *Gentleman's Magazine*, 1839, vol. ii. p. 640 ; *Proceedings of Society of Antiquities*, vol. ii. p. 52, vol. iii. pp. 54, 86 ; and the Inclosure Award, 1855.

Manors." The orders of the Sixteens were formally proclaimed from the Town Cross, and were then universally accepted as binding on the community. Four of the most influential members of the Sixteens were annually chosen to be Grass Stewards, and also to represent the men of Aston and Cote at the Lord's Court of Bampton, to which the hamlets apparently owed suit of court. The Sixteens had also to provide every season four two-year-old bulls to run on the common pasture. In return they were authorised to levy a fee for each cow placed on the Common, and to sell the bulls at the end of the season. The Sixteens appointed all the officers of the village, allotting to each the particular share of the " Town Hams " that custom assigned for the remuneration of the post—the Constable's Ham, the Herd's Ham, the two Water Stewards' Hams, the Hayward's Ham, the Water Hayward's Ham, and so on. The remainder of the " Town Hams " were " disposed of at the discretion of the Sixteens, some for the public use of the Town, as for making of gates, bridges, etc., and some sold to make ale for the merry meeting of the inhabitants." We need not in this work describe the elaborate arrangements that were still in force in 1657 for the annual sharing out by lot of the common meadow among the owners of strips in the commonfield; the gathering of the villagers under the direction of the Grass Stewards and the Sixteens, when the grass was ripe to cut, and the eager rushing of each man with his scythe to mow the part allotted to him. Nor does it enter into the plan of this work to go into the hotly debated question of the probable origin of this remarkable organisation, or to discuss whether it can be sufficiently accounted for by the supposition that it represented a district shared between three separate Manors.[1] It suffices us to note that the

---

[1] It may be important to trace the constitutional influence of "intercommoning," or the use of pasture lands more or less jointly by several villages, parishes, or Manors ; of which traces may be found in Marshland Fen (Norfolk) and in Lincolnshire fenlands, and also in the Essex marshes (see *Domesday Book and Beyond*, by F. W. Maitland, 1897, p. 367 ; *The Forest of Essex*, by W. R. Fisher, 1887, pp. 265, 277, 289 ; and the article by J. H. Round in *Victoria County History of Essex*, vol. i. pp. 369-374).

We may briefly note some other cases of village organisation. "The people of Ibthorpe," we read of a hamlet in the parish of Hurstbourn Tarrant, Hampshire, "are Lords of their own Manor, and to this day exercise their Manorial rights, in respect of which they have exclusive common rights on the seventy acres of common land at Pillheath, including a right to everything that

attempt made in 1657 to reduce the inhabitants to a position of ordinary Manorial dependence did not succeed; and that the rule of the Sixteens, curiously resembling, as we shall see, that of the simplest Manorial Boroughs, continued until the middle of the nineteenth century.

(b) *The Chartered Township*

If the Village Meeting, desiring legal authority for the management of its common estate, obtained a Royal Charter, it might develop, out of a rudimentary constitution analogous to that of Aston and Cote, a form of government even approaching a Municipal Corporation.

Among the possessions of the wealthy Abbey of St. Edmund was a fen or marsh of 1400 acres near the village of Beccles in Suffolk, which the Abbot had been accustomed for centuries to let to the townsfolk, getting his annual rent from four "Fenreeves" whom they elected at a public meeting. At the

grows on this common, with liberty to take it away for their use in Ibthorpe, but not for sale" (Paper by Mr. T. W. Shore, in *The Antiquary*, vol. xvii. p. 52, 1888; *The Village Community*, by G. L. Gomme, 1890, p. 260). In other villages we find ancient regulations resting on the agreement of a public meeting of the villagers. Thus the inhabitants of Winteringham in Lincolnshire framed in 1685 a formal code of By-laws, said to be agreed to "at a parish meeting." "Item," it was ordained, "that none shall burne or bake at any unlawful time of night, on paine of 3/4. Item, none shall dry any hempe or flax by the fire upon paine of 3/4. Item, none shall smoke tobacco on the streets upon paine of 2/- for every default" (*History of Winterton and the Adjoining Villages*, by W. Andrew, 1836, p. 105). Similar "fire rules" are found in other villages, though whether promulgated at the Lord's Court or Parish Vestry or merely by common agreement it is not easy to determine. At Helpston, in Lincolnshire, it was ordered in 1722 that no person was to "fetch fire from any neighbouring house without the same being carried in a lanthorn or warming pan, for every offence to pay ten shillings." Also it was ordered "that no person whatsoever shall smoke tobacco in the town, street, or in any stable, barn, or outhouse, without a sufficient muzzle, hood, or cover for the same, under the penalty for every offence of five shillings" (*Fenland Notes and Queries*, vol. iii. pp. 303-306).

Other villages had "Gild Halls" and "Town Bailiffs." At Leverington, in the Isle of Ely, there was an ancient "Gild Hall," used latterly as free tenements for paupers, and an annually chosen "Town Bailiff." This distinction seems to have been due to its possession of "townlands," producing no less than £300 a year, which were vested in trustees, one of whom served annually as Town Bailiff (*Historical Account of Wisbech*, by W. Watson, 1827, p. 471; *History of Wisbech*, by N. Walker and T. Cradock, 1849, p. 503; *History of Wisbech*, by F. J. Gardiner, 1898, p. 380). It is now, with a population in 1901 of 1124, governed by a Parish Council, with its endowments held for charitable purposes by separate trustees.

dissolution of the abbey, the townsfolk, by judicious payments to the King, got this arrangement continued in slightly varied form, the position being regularised by Royal Letters Patent and Charter of 1584 and 1605 respectively, which definitely established a Corporate body of "the Portreeve, Surveyors, and Commonalty of Beccles Fen." [1] This anomalous Corporation, created primarily to regulate a large common pasture rather than to govern a town, consisted of two Chambers, one of twelve and the other of twenty-four members, each filling vacancies by co-option. The members of the Twelve were alone eligible to serve as Portreeve, on election by the two Chambers of the Corporation voting together. The whole body of the commonalty, including the members of the two Chambers, met to enact "statutes, laws, articles, rules, and orders touching the pasture and fen," which made up all their property, and "also concerning the good rule, state, and government of the Commoners of or in the same fen"—who seem to have been all the householders of Beccles, for whose "common benefit and utility" the revenue was to be expended. The Charter had granted or continued to this Corporation the right to hold, quite apart from the Manorial Courts, its own Court of Justice,—the so-called "Fen Court,"—at which the Portreeve and the two or three Surveyors were the judges, and in which the principal part was played by the "Common Clerk" of the Corporation, and by the Inquest or Jury of the Commoners. This was a Court of Record for "plaints concerning the Fen," having power to punish by fine or imprisonment, or by exclusion from "commoning in the Fen." But neither the Portreeve nor the Corporation had ever been granted magisterial powers or regulative authority in anything beyond the management of the Fen.

Notwithstanding this limitation of their legal authority, we see the Portreeve, Surveyors, and Common Council of Beccles Fen gradually slipping into the position of administer-

---

[1] The MS. records of the Beccles Corporation are imperfect, no book of minutes having been found, and we were able to consult only a collection of scraps of orders, etc., from 1719 to 1832, and various presentments, charges, orders, etc., of the Manorial Court, 1628-1842. See also First Report of Municipal Corporation Commission, 1835, Appendix, vol. iv. p. 2133 ; *Some Account of the Corporation of Beccles Fen*, 1807 ; and the *History and Antiquities of the County of Suffolk*, by Rev. A. Suckling, 1846, vol. i. pp. 1-35.

ing much more than their common pasture. Their property, which came eventually to yield over £1000 a year, made them practically the dominant influence in this little town of a couple of thousand inhabitants. The Lord of the Manor had, indeed, the stallage of the market, and held his Courts—a Court Baron, a "Land Leet,"[1] and also (for the regulation of the fishing and navigation of the River Waveney) a "Water Leet." But the Manorial Courts evidently became very perfunctory, the presentments of the Homage and Juries steadily declining in number and importance, and the sessions of the Courts becoming less frequent.[2] After the middle of the eighteenth century, these Manorial Courts do practically nothing but present persons to serve as Constables, Flesh-searchers, and Ale-founders, with occasionally a Headborough. As the need for some more regulative authority becomes felt, we see the Corporation and its Portreeve coming more and more to the front. Their "Fen Court" is, indeed, abandoned, the last sessions having been in 1741.[3] But it is the Portreeve and his two Serjeants at Mace who enforce such of the Fen By-laws of 1613 as are not obsolete. It is the Portreeve, Surveyors, and Commonalty who in 1740 make the new regulations necessitated by the growing habit of keeping geese to supply the London market,[4] and who in 1762 revise the stint for sojourners, "certificate-men," householders "not paying task," and those who "pay task to the king" respectively.[5] It is the Portreeve's Feast, provided annually at the Corporate expense, which is the great event of the year in Beccles. In 1785 it is the Portreeve who, by the Deputy Steward of the Corporation and out of the Corporation funds, prosecutes before the County Justices those inhabitants who commit encroachments and nuisances in the streets.[6] It is

---

[1] This "Land Leet" called its Jury "The Jury of Headboroughs" (MS. records, Beccles Manor, 23rd September 1728, 24th September 1729), which may be compared with the Jury of Constables mentioned in *The Parish and the County*, Book I. Chap. III. "The Court of Quarter Sessions," pp. 464-466.

[2] Between 1750 and 1800 there were, for instance, only five "Water Leets."

[3] First Report of Municipal Corporation Commission, 1835, Appendix, vol. iv. p. 2138.

[4] MS. records, Beccles Corporation, 31st March 1740.   [5] *Ibid.* 1762.

[6] *Ibid.* 1st September 1785. It is interesting to notice that, in 1760, the Chief Constable for the Hundred of Wangford had—before the Corporation of Beccles Fen had taken up this Municipal duty—presented Beccles nuisances at Quarter Sessions (MS. Minutes, Quarter Sessions, Suffolk, 6th October 1760).

the Corporation revenue which provides most of the relief of the poor and maintenance of the roads. At last, in 1796, legal authority is given to this government by a Local Act for paving, lighting, cleaning, watching, and improving the streets of Beccles,[1] under which the Portreeve and Surveyors, *ex officio*, with several other members of the Corporation named in the Act, were made Commissioners to carry out the new duties, with power to levy a rate on the inhabitants.

From 1796 to 1835, when the population of the town was increasing from 2500 to nearly 4000,[2] the activities of the Corporation of Beccles Fen were indistinguishable from those of the Beccles Street Commissioners, who were, in fact, practically the same persons. When in 1804 the Commissioners decided to pave the town, the Corporation sold part of the Fen for £3000 to meet the cost. The payments for watchmen, fire engines, lamps, and repairing the pavements come sometimes out of one fund and sometimes out of another. This was the less material in that practically all that was left over of the Corporate income was paid " in relief of the town for Poor, Lamp, Church, and (Highway) Composition Rates," this subsidy amounting, on an average, to £792 a year.[3] By 1835, in short, the Portreeve, Surveyors, and Commonalty of Beccles Fen, originally only the managing committee of an extensive common pasture, had, whilst letting slip even such judicial powers as they had once exercised, assumed practically the whole government of the town, and were accordingly recognised as such and reformed by the Municipal Corporations Act of 1835.[4]

[1] 36 George III. c. 51.
[2] *History of Suffolk*, by Rev. A. Suckling, 1846, vol. i. p. 34.
[3] MS. Records, Beccles Corporation, 7th April 1831.
[4] We may name here the Corporation of the "Warden, Assistants, and Commonalty" of Godalming in Surrey, incorporated by successive Royal Charters, evidently governing the little town, but apparently entirely unconnected with any of the Courts of the several Manors that existed in the parish. Without property, taxing power, or magisterial jurisdiction its position in the town became, already by the end of the seventeenth century, titular and honorary only, the government passing to the Justices and to a body of Street Commissioners established by Local Act in 1825 (First Report of Municipal Corporation Commission, 1835, Appendix, vol. ii. p. 735 ; *Parish and Church of Godalming*, by S. Welman, 1900).

Such a Corporation of "Bailiff and Burgesses" existed, too, at Great Dunmow in Essex, under sixteenth-century Royal Charters—a self-renewing Society of Twelve, who owned the markets, collected such tolls as they could, and gave themselves an annual feast—entirely unconnected with the Manor. It remained

An even more remarkable instauce of the development of a committee for managing a landed estate into something very near to a fully developed Municipal Corporation is presented by the "ancient seaport" of Wisbech, in the Isle of Ely, with its Town Bailiff, ten Capital Burgesses, and Commonalty of forty-shilling freeholders—a quasi-municipal government which may with some warrant claim, to have furnished between 1689 and 1835 the most pure, energetic, and enlightened urban administration in the Kingdom.[1]

We do not need in this work to trace the origin of the Wisbech town government in the religious Gild of the Holy Trinity, the richest of all the Wisbech Gilds, that dominated the town from at least 1379 down to 1549.[2]   Here it suffices to relate that on the dissolution of this fraternity by the reforming zeal of Edward VI. the townsfolk succeeded in obtaining, or rather in purchasing, through the good offices of their Lord, the Bishop of Ely, not only the property of the Gild, but also a Royal Charter which incorporated them for the purpose of managing this landed estate, maintaining the Grammar School, providing for the poor, and looking after "banks, shores, and streams," with an implied authority to uphold and enforce the customs of the little community. Perhaps because it primarily concerned the management of a common property, and did not expressly convey any powers

unreformed in 1835, and was dissolved only after the Municipal Corporations Act of 1883.   This town of nearly 3000 inhabitants, having been twice refused a Charter of incorporation, is now (1907) governed only by a parish council (First Report of Municipal Corporation Commission, 1835, Appendix, vol. iv. p. 2215; ditto, 1880, part i. p. 37, part ii. p. 294 ; *History of Dunmow*, by J. W. Savill, 1865).

[1] For Wisbech we have had the advantage of examining the well-kept records from 1616 to 1835 ; see also Report of House of Commons Committee on Corporations, 1833 ; First Report of Municipal Corporation Commission, 1835, Appendix, vol. iv. p. 2551 ; Report of Historical Manuscripts Commission, 1883 ; *Reasons . . . against embanking the Salt Marsh belonging to Sutton*, 1720 ; *Introduction to the Charter of Wisbech*, by Mann Hutchesson, 1791 ; *Historical Account of the Ancient Town of Wisbech*, by W. Watson, 1827 ; *History of Wisbech, with an Historical Sketch of the Fens* (Anon.), 1833 ; *History of Wisbech and the Fens*, by Neil Walker and T. Cradock, 1849 ; *History of Wisbech, 1848-1898*, by F. J. Gardiner, 1898.   The population, said to have been 1705 in 1676, was 4710 in 1801, and 8777 in 1831.

[2] The existing records of the Gild begin in 1379 ; see Report of Public Record Commissioners, 1837 ; Report of Historical Manuscripts Commission, vol. ix. p. 293 ; *Introduction to the Charter of Wisbech*, by Mann Hutchesson, 1791 ; *History of Wisbech and the Fens*, by N. Walker and T. Cradock, chap. iii. pp. 280-301.

of government, this Charter was, for a Tudor instrument, unusually democratic in form. Ten of the "better, more honest, and more discreet inhabitants "[1]—called at first "the Company of the Ten," and afterwards "Capital Burgesses "— were to be freely elected at an annual assembly, or Common Hall, of all the inhabitant householders. During the next century and a half this simple constitution was rendered somewhat more definite, the choice of Capital Burgesses being first confined by agreement of the householders to forty· shilling freeholders, and then the constituency, by Charter of 1611,[2] being at the instance of the Corporation itself, alarmed at the disorder of the public assemblies, similarly limited. This franchise, whilst it excluded the mere hired man, cottager, and temporary sojourner, still admitted, as we believe, most of the independent householders of the little fishing and trading port, which had, by 1689, a population under two thousand. In contravention of the common legal theory, no provision was made in the Charters for any head of the Corporation, but local custom, transmitted from the Gild, had established a Town Bailiff, an officer who represented the township to the County and executed the decisions of the Capital Burgesses and assemblies of freeholders.[3] Between 1689 and 1835 we find the office filled by the Capital Burgesses in annual rotation, though in some cases a successful and public-spirited administrator remained for several years in succession.[4] We find no trace of the Lord of the Manor—the Bishop of Ely— holding any Court in Wisbech after the dissolution of the Gild.[5] The townsfolk themselves levied tolls and dues, took the waste on long lease, and in 1786 acquired the lease of the market rights. The parish officers, whether Churchwardens, Overseers, or Surveyors, appear, throughout the eighteenth century, as humble subordinates of the Bailiff and Burgesses; and it is only at the beginning of the nineteenth century that

[1] The terms used at first were "gratia eminentiae" and "de melioribus" (*Introduction to the Charter of Wisbech*, by Mann Hutchesson, 1791, pp. 8, 15).

[2] *History of Wisbech*, by N. Walker and T. Cradock, 1849, pp. 319-321.

[3] A Town Clerk was first appointed in 1679.

[4] In a few instances—one in 1565—the Town Bailiff seems not himself to have been a Capital Burgess (*History of Wisbech*, by N. Walker and T. Cradock, 1849, p. 306).

[5] The "Company of the Ten" themselves heard civil cases during the six-teenth century as a sort of voluntary arbitration tribunal (*ibid.* pp. 308-310).

the Open Vestry of inhabitants rises to any position of importance. Above all these authorities we are conscious of the Justices of the Peace of the Isle of Ely, meeting in Quarter Sessions at Ely and holding Petty Sessions at Wisbech, but only intervening in the affairs of the town when requested to do so by the Town Bailiff and Capital Burgesses. The records from 1689 to 1835 make it clear that the freeholders obeyed the directions of their first Charter in electing and re-electing at the Annual Meetings that were always held in the Gothic hall of the ancient Grammar School the ten " of the better, more honest, and more discreet inhabitants," the Vicar figuring nearly always in the list, the others comprising several " Esquires," " Gentlemen," and " Captains," whilst a few only, designated " Mr.," served to represent the shopkeepers or farmers of the township.

It would be an interesting subject for special inquiry why it was that this simple constitution produced, for the whole century and a half that we are considering, a government of remarkable excellence. About the fact the student of all the available evidence can, we think, have no doubt. The elaborately kept records, coupled with current traditions and the actual state of the town, demonstrate the existence of an administration which—possibly first taking on a distinctively Municipal and governmental character in the emergency of the plague in 1586 [1]—combined, from decade to decade, the three great qualities of popular assent, purity of administration, and continuity of enlightened policy. The note of what the historians of the town term the " direct control of the people " [2] is particularly strong. Even in 1669, at an epoch when Municipal Corporations were being stripped of all popular features, the freeholders of Wisbech managed, by prompt and vigorous action at Court, to prevent the transformation of their ten Capital Burgesses into a Close Body,[3] and, whilst retaining their privilege of popular election, even secured the definite recognition, in the new Charter, of the obligation of the Capital Burgesses, not only to allow in-

---

[1] *Historical Account of . . . Wisbech*, by W. Watson, 1827, p. 207.
[2] *History of Wisbech*, by N. Walker and T. Cradock, 1849, p. 347.
[3] *Historical Account of . . . Wisbech*, by W. Watson, 1827, p. 219; *History of Wisbech*, by N. Walker and T. Cradock, 1849, pp. 329-331 ; First Report of Municipal Corporation Commission, 1835, Appendix, vol. iv. p. 2551.

spection of all their accounts, but also to submit them to the " Common Hall " for its approval.[1] It was perhaps a persistence of this pugnacious watchfulness that induced successive Capital Burgesses to consider themselves the ministers, and not the masters, of the town.[2] Though the Charter made necessary only one meeting of the freeholders annually, we find a frequent consultation by the Capital Burgesses of their fellow-freeholders or the inhabitants at large. Thus even when they have to appoint a schoolmaster in 1690, this is done "at a meeting in the Town Hall . . . the Capital Burgesses being seven in number, by and with the consent of eleven others of the Burgesses."[3] When in 1699 the Capital Burgesses think it necessary to prohibit the squatting of cottagers upon the Lord's Waste, and to arrange for the erection of a wall at the Town Bridewell, they lay these matters before Assemblies of Burgesses, and obtain their express consent, and even their active co-operation in the work.[4] So intimate and informal was the relationship between the Capital Burgesses and the Burgesses at large, that it is often impossible to distinguish from the records which of the meetings were confined to the smaller and which were open to the larger body of governors; our own impression being that whenever any important new departure was contemplated, the Capital Burgesses made a point of calling their constituents into council to approve the proposal. Nor did the Capital Burgesses always confine their consultations to the freeholders. When in 1775 a local drainage Bill before Parliament seemed likely injuriously to affect the interests of the town, the Capital Burgesses summoned all the merchants and tradesmen to a Public Meeting, for which a special report was prepared, and from which authority was obtained to oppose the Bill at

[1] Charter of 21 Car. II. 1669 ; see First Report of Municipal Corporation Commission, 1835, Appendix, vol. iv. p. 2552. From 1818 the accounts were printed and published.

[2] Thus it was formally resolved in 1826 that no alterations should be made in the Free Grammar School "without the direction of the Burgesses at large being taken thereon at a public meeting " ; that a similar meeting should be held before any Bill was promoted altering the existing Local Act, or effecting any improvement in the town, or in the navigation (MS. Minutes, Wisbech Corporation, 2nd November 1826).

[3] *Ibid.* 6th June 1690 ; so again, 31st January 1707.

[4] *Ibid.* 1699 ; 22nd February 1700 ; 6th November 1720.

an estimated cost of £200 from the Corporate funds.[1]   It was after friendly consultation with "the clergy and some of the principal inhabitants of the town" that the Capital Burgesses submitted to the assembly of freeholders resolutions "for considering the best means of extending education among children of the poor," and started a "Lancastrian" School.[2] From 1809 onwards we find coming in the inhabitants in Vestry assembled, the Capital Burgesses habitually deferring to any express resolution of this public meeting.   It was in consistency with this constant reliance on popular assent that we find the Bailiff and Burgesses of Wisbech in 1833 warm in their welcome of the Municipal Corporation Commissioners, and uncompromisingly outspoken in their advocacy of a popularly elected Town Council as the leading feature of the Municipal Corporations Reform Bill, against which the governing bodies of nearly all the Municipalities in the land were protesting.[3]

This dominant fact of popular control does not seem at any time to have impaired the executive efficiency of the Capital Burgesses.   Though the "Company of the Ten" was annually elected by the public meeting of freeholders, which seems to have been an occasion of some public interest,—even the scene of sharp electoral contests lasting till midnight, at which between one and two hundred freeholders voted,[4]—it appears to have been fairly stable in its membership.   At no time was it the close preserve of party exclusiveness[5] or the plaything of political struggles; the substantial inhabitants, indeed, took their share of service as a public obligation and not as a private advantage.   And their duties were far from

[1] MS. Minutes, Wisbech Corporation, 21st December 1775; 8th January 1776.

[2] *Ibid.* 27th March and 19th April 1811.

[3] *Ibid.* 16th and 28th March 1833; 6th January 1834; Report of House of Commons Committee on Corporations, 1833; First Report of Municipal Corporation Commission, 1835, vol. iv. p. 2551; *History of Wisbech*, by N. Walker and T. Cradock, 1849, p. 337; *History of Wisbech* (anon.), 1833, p. 150.

[4] The quaint customs of the election are described in the *Historical Account of . . . Wisbech*, by W. Watson, 1827, pp. 230-233; *History of Wisbech* (anon.), 1833, pp. 145-146.

[5] As the Test Act applied to the Wisbech Corporation, the Capital Burgesses had to be at least "occasional conformists"; and when in 1819, 1821, and 1822 an avowed Nonconformist was elected, he was passed over (*ibid.* (anon.) 1833, p. 150; *ibid.* by N. Walker and T. Cradock, 1849, p. 335; *ibid.* by F. G. Gardiner, 1898, p. 93).

light. They met frequently—sometimes twenty times in a year—and attended regularly, deciding such issues as arose, or formulating them for submission to the popular assembly. But it was on the one among them who served as Town Bailiff that they relied for the daily task of town administration. It was the Town Bailiff whom they ordered to set the poor to work, pave the streets, scour the ditches, cleanse the market-place, collect the rents, and promote or oppose Bills in Parliament, exactly as if he had been their salaried servant, though such phrases as "at his convenience," "as he shall judge necessary," "at his discretion," or "as occasion offers" soften the peremptory tone of their multitudinous orders. Over the financial transactions of the Town Bailiff the Capital Burgesses throughout maintained the strictest censorship. "Ordered that no Town Bailiff shall expend upon any one work above forty shillings without a particular order from the Hall, and also that no workman's bill that exceeds the sum of forty shillings shall be paid by the Town Bailiff without being first perused and having the consent of the Hall thereto."[1] He was not even allowed to let the smallest tenement without the consent of his colleagues.[2] On the two occasions in 150 years on which a Town Bailiff neglected to deliver up, on quitting his office, a precise account of his stewardship, he was prosecuted with relentless rigour.[3] In 1774 we note the beginning of a system of executive committees, always consisting of the Town Bailiff and two other Capital Burgesses. From this date committees to light the town, to settle the rates of tolls and dues, to audit the accounts, and to let the lands become practically continuous. These committees seem to have been little more than devices for strengthening the authority of the Town Bailiff, for, as decade follows decade, we find the activity and importance of this dignitary constantly increasing. We gather, indeed, that towards the end of our period his official work became so

---

[1] MS. Minutes, Wisbech Corporation, 8th November 1694, 9th November 1725, 26th October 1730.

[2] "Ordered that no Town Bailiff do put any person into any town house without the consent of the Hall" (*ibid.* 8th November 1765).

[3] *Ibid.* 1752-1756, 26th October 1778; *History of Wisbech*, by N. Walker and T. Cradock, 1849, p. 332. Subsequent Bailiffs were required to give security for £500 (MS. Minutes, Wisbech Corporation, 26th October 1778).

continuous that it was not easy to keep up the succession of citizens with sufficient leisure, ability, and public spirit to undertake this onerous unpaid office—a difficulty which, in 1829, nearly brought the government of the little town to a standstill,[1] and may have accounted for the enthusiasm with which the Capital Burgesses accepted the reforms of 1835.

When we survey the administrative results obtained by Wisbech in the course of a century and a half, we are able to appreciate the pride and satisfaction of the whole body of inhabitants in their local government. At no time and for no purpose did the Corporation levy a rate. From first to last the Capital Burgesses, in a spirit of what their historians call "a healthy poverty,"[2] made shift with the rents of the Gild property, together with the ancient tolls and dues yielded by the trade of the port. Already in 1689 we find them managing their landed estate on the most approved modern principles. At a time when other Corporations were dealing with their property in secret conclave, conceding to their members beneficial leases, granting long terms for trifling fines, and improvidently alienating their freeholds, the Capital Burgesses of Wisbech were habitually letting their farms and town tenements by public auction for a term of twenty years, with carefully drafted covenants, which seem to have been strictly enforced. In 1751 they were quick to take advantage of the lowering in the current rate of interest, successfully negotiating a reduction of the rate on their loans to 4 per cent; and in 1774, alarmed at the slow rate at which this bonded debt was being reduced, they arranged for its conversion into life annuities.[3] Unlike the practice of so many other towns, in restricting contracts to members of the Municipal Corporation, the Capital Burgesses forbade any of their own number to be pecuniarily interested in the Corporation work or directly or indirectly to undertake the work of a paid office.[4] At no time did the Burgesses put forward any claim to exclude non-freemen from trading.[5] Such Corporate feasting as the habits of the time demanded were enjoyed by all the Burgesses in

[1] MS. Minutes, Wisbech Corporation, 14th November 1829.
[2] *History of Wisbech*, by N. Walker and T. Cradock, 1849, p. 347.
[3] *Ibid.* pp. 333-334.
[4] MS. Minutes, Wisbech Corporation, 14th December 1795.
[5] *History of Wisbech*, by N. Walker and T. Cradock, 1849, p. 338.

common ; the maximum sum to be spent was carefully limited,[1] and the whole of them were finally discontinued in 1767 owing to a growing sense of decorum. After that date, at any rate, the Capital Burgesses paid even for the annual dinner that they allowed themselves.[2] To the same growth of decorum we may perhaps attribute their success in suppressing, in 1786, the annual custom of "bull running," which had prevailed at Wisbech, as at Stamford and elsewhere, "time out of mind," and had degenerated into a carnival of brutal disorder.[3]

This strict and economical administration of the Corporate revenues was combined with an active policy according to the best light of the time. When the relief of the poor was the main function of the Capital Burgesses, we see them, instead of giving doles and pensions, providing hemp on which to set the poor to work ; building a workhouse in 1720 out of bricks made on their own land; establishing in 1691, and again in 1764, regular schools of spinning ; and supplying the children with both religious and industrial instruction.[4] When most other towns were still relying for their Municipal services on the performance by each individual householder of his ancient personal service, Wisbech was already being paved, sewered, cleansed, lighted, watched—no doubt very imperfectly, but at least on some general plan—by paid officers or public contracts, at the expense of the Corporate funds.[5] But the householder was not allowed to escape. From the middle of the eighteenth century onward, we find the Town Bailiff issuing printed notices to the inhabitants, insisting on the cessation of this or

[1] MS. Minutes, Wisbech Corporation, 26th October 1692 ; 5th November 1767 ; *History of Wisbech*, by N. Walker and T. Cradock, 1849, pp. 324-325.

[2] *Historical Account of Wisbech*, by W. Watson, 1827, p. 230.

[3] *History of Wisbech*, by F. J. Gardiner, 1898, p. 25.

[4] MS. Minutes, Wisbech Corporation, 20th February 1622, 7th July 1691, 14th November 1720, 1764, etc. ; *History of Wisbech*, by N. Walker and T. Cradock, 1849, pp. 327, 424 ; *ibid.* by F. J. Gardiner, 1898, p. 312. They even anticipated by seventeen years the statute requiring the outdoor paupers to wear a badge, resolving in 1680, "to pay for the stamp and 180 badges provided for the poor" (*ibid.* p. 327).

[5] Items for paving the streets, repairing the causeways, and maintaining bridges occur in the minutes in 1689, 1690, 1692, 1694, 1697, 1699, 1700, 1703, 1705, 1709, etc. ; for sewers to carry away waste water in 1698 and 1715 ; for the maintenance of the five town pumps in 1696, 1708, 1714, etc. ; for sinking a new well and erecting a new pump in 1714 ; for cleansing the streets and scavenging in 1621, 1705, 1721, 1723, 1725, etc.; for repairing the town's fire engines in 1707 ; for increasing the number of fire buckets in 1716 ; for watching the town in 1618, 1708, 1733, 1735 ; for lighting the town in 1715 ;

that street nuisance or encroachment, and following up these notices by prosecutions before the Justices of those who disobey such injunctions.[1] In 1810, when the population and trade were rapidly increasing, the Capital Burgesses strengthened the police powers thus exercised by the Town Bailiff by obtaining a Local Act, in which, among other things, the definition of public nuisance was enlarged and a more speedy summary remedy provided. A paid Town Inspector was then appointed to enforce the law.[2] Meanwhile the navigation of the tidal river, on which the prosperity of the town depended, was, from 1710 onwards, constantly being improved at the public expense. The buoys and beacons were the object of continual attention; a special officer, the "Beaconer," was appointed to look after them; the channels, always liable to be silted up, were dredged and deepened; pilots were licensed and a harbour-master was appointed; a public crane was erected as early as 1719, a public warehouse built in 1788, and a special timber wharf constructed in 1795;[3] a more commodious "custom house" was provided in 1801, whilst throughout the whole period we see the Capital Burgesses carefully watching the numerous drainage schemes or canal Bills promoted by the neighbouring Fenland authorities, lest any new project should interfere with the depth of the river channel.[4] The "ancient seaport," as we find it described in 1720, remained for a century more one of the most important of English havens for the coasting trade, with several scores of ships belonging to it, exporting to London, it was said, more oats and vegetable oil than any other port, and sometimes as much as 8000 firkins of butter in a year.[5] In 1786 the Capital Burgesses succeeded in buying up the lease of the

and so on. It was about this time that Defoe found Wisbech "a well-built market town . . . esteemed the best trading town in the Isle (of Ely), as having the convenience of good water-carriage to London, whither they send great quantities of oil and butter (*A Tour Through the Whole Island of Great Britain*, by D. Defoe, vol. i. p. 84 of 1748 edition).

[1] MS. Minutes, Wisbech Corporation, 10th November 1785 (as to deposit of dirt) ; 28th June 1785 (as to hogs wandering in the streets).

[2] MS. Minutes, Wisbech Corporation, 16th July 1810 ; 50 George III. c. 206 ; *History of Wisbech*, by N. Walker and T. Cradock, 1849, pp. 339-340.

[3] MS. Minutes, Wisbech Corporation, 5th June 1795.

[4] *Ibid.* 13th July 1719, 12th February 1744, 26th December 1749 ; *Reasons . . . against embanking the Salt Marsh belonging to Sutton*, 1720.

[5] *Ibid.; History of Wisbech* (anon.), 1833, p. 249.

market rights, which had been granted by the Bishop of Ely to a private lessee, when they at once provided standard Weights and Measures and set to work to enforce market regulations. At first they let the tolls by public auction. In 1810, however, their Local Act [1] gave them increased market powers, and during the next few years, when agricultural prices and rents were alike high, the Capital Burgesses used these powers to erect a public exchange and commodious market buildings for corn and fat cattle respectively; they freed the shambles; [2] they established a fish market; they provided a spacious public warehouse for the storage of wool; they contrived an elaborate system of allotting the stalls in the corn market by ballot, so as to avoid favouritism; [3] they appointed their own collectors of market tolls and a Market Beadle; and in 1829 they were far-sighted enough to decide "with a view to increase the beneficial purposes of the several markets, and to induce the public to resort to the town in greater numbers," on a policy of drastic reduction in the amount of the market tolls.[4] Space does not permit us even to mention all the manifold public enterprises successfully administered by these Wisbech Burgesses—their constant struggle to reclaim the "drowned lands" of their estate; their replacing of the old wooden bridge in 1756-1758 by a handsome stone one; [5] their erection of public stairs at a precipitous descent; [6] their provision of flat pavements for their footways in 1811; their active and generous co-operation in the provision of facilities for religious worship; and their liberal subscriptions to such enlightened enterprises as the provision in 1826 for public use of hot and cold salt-water baths, the maintenance of an iceboat to prevent any stoppage of the drainage current by frost,[7] and the provision of a savings bank. But it was perhaps in their zeal for public education that the Capital Burgesses of Wisbech were most in advance of the rulers of other towns. The Grammar School, for the maintenance of which they had been originally incorporated, was always the subject of their liveliest interest and constant attention. The master whom they

---

[1] 50 George III. c. 206.
[2] MS. Minutes, Wisbech Corporation, 16th July 1816.
[3] *Ibid.* 13th September 1811.   [4] *Ibid.* 2nd November 1829.
[5] *Ibid.* October 1756, 21st October 1757.
[6] *Ibid.* 21st March 1690.   [7] *Ibid.* 6th January 1802.

appointed, though always in holy orders, was expressly forbidden to accept a living, or even to officiate as a clergyman. He was not allowed to become a Magistrate or even a Capital Burgess. He was, relatively to the standard of the times, paid a liberal salary and provided with skilled assistance.[1]   In addition to this ancient Grammar School, the Capital Burgesses started a Sunday school in 1786, and, in co-operation with some of the principal inhabitants, in 1811-1813, also a "Lancastrian school" for the children of the poor.[2]   They were even so exceptionally enlightened, at the very early date of 1714, as to rearrange and open to the public a library of books, apparently provided by a voluntary book club in the seventeenth century, which was subsequently expressly designated a "public library";[3] providing new shelving, getting the books catalogued, and appointing a paid librarian, whose catalogue was "to be lodged in the Town Hall for the public use."

(c) *The Lordless Court*

We pass now to the bulk of Manorial Boroughs, a heterogeneous crowd of authorities exhibiting in 1689 every variety of constitutional structure, but all alike falling short of autonomous Corporate Magistracy, and all connected in some way with the Manorial jurisdiction, from which they may probably have sprung.   We group these into the three sub-classes, not very clearly distinguishable, that we term respectively the Lordless Court (where there was practically no Municipal structure), the Lord's Borough (where Municipal structure had been developed, but this had remained connected with the Lord's Court), and, derivative from one or other of these, the Enfranchised Manorial Borough.

An interesting example of the Lordless Court is furnished by the little "Borough" of Newbiggin-by-the-Sea in Northumberland, which held its markets and fairs by Royal grants of 1309 and 1319 and had in 1382 even sent members to Parliament.   This little port, in 1689 a mere fishing village, had shaken itself loose from any control or

---

[1] MS. Minutes, Wisbech Corporation, 1st November 1689, 6th November 1704.
[2] *Ibid.* 27th March and 19th April 1811.
[3] *Ibid.* 6th August 1714; *History of Wisbech* (anon.), 1833, p. 164; *ibid.* by F. J. Gardiner, 1898, p. 214.

interference by the Lord of the Manor. It had been incorporated by no Charter, either from the King or from its Lord. But the Lord of the Manor, Lord Widdrington, had apparently let slip his rights; and after his attainder in 1715, no Courts were held on behalf of any Lord until 1741. This long abandonment of the village to an unchecked autonomy, and the confusion and uncertainty into which the seignorial rights had fallen, seem to have led to the assumption by the Freeholders that they had no superior but the King. Accordingly these proprietors of the ancient "freeledges" or farms, into which the township had been divided from time immemorial, themselves held an annual "Court," which we can trace, from about 1730, continuously for at least a hundred years. During the eighteenth century, at any rate, they held the markets and fairs for their own profit, and even levied "quayage" dues on all ships entering their little harbour, according to Royal Letters Patent of 1316. To the Crown they paid an ancient fee-farm rent of a little more than £10 a year. "Whereas," they declared, "the Freeholders of the Town of Newbiggin . . . have time out of mind made orders among themselves for the stinting and eating of the Common Town Green and Loaning belonging to Newbiggin aforesaid, we whose hands are hereunto subscribed and put, being the present Freeholders of the said Town . . . in pursuance of the said custom, do unanimously consent and agree" to various orders and regulations. In 1720 Lord Widdrington's estates and Manors were bought by the York Buildings Water Company of London, apparently as a speculative investment; and in due course the Company took steps to reduce the Freeholders of Newbiggin to due Manorial subjection. In 1731 we see the Freeholders contributing "a shilling a freehold" to defend their rights and privileges. But more expensive proceedings were at hand. In 1733 a long Chancery suit was begun against them, which lasted ten years, but ended in some inconclusive way, leaving their privileges unimpaired.

"The proceedings of this suit," writes Dr. Creighton, "show us a community completely self-governed, with no interference from a Lord, and little from the Crown. . . . In 1730, back to which date the Freeholders' books survived, we find the arable land already divided, but the pasture land still held in common. The Freeholders meet and make By-laws for the pasturage. They appoint Constables, Ale-tasters, and Bread-weighers. They levy tolls on boats and ships, and receive payments for carts loading seaweed from the shore, for lobster-tanks in the rocks, for stones quarried on the fore-shore. The money they receive from these rents is divided among the Freeholders in proportion to the ancient freeledges or farms."[1] They even took to themselves all wrecks thrown upon their rocky coast, and sold the privilege of gathering seaweed. For nearly a century after the Chancery suit we find them governing the little town; declaring, in 1730, that the Ale-tasters whom they appointed "are to have at every alehouse in the town one quart"; in 1753 ordaining "no ducks to be kept in town"; in 1762 "that the Constable weigh all butter and bread that shall be offered for sale in the said township." Similar entries occur down to 1829. This humble government remained undiscovered by the Municipal Corporation Commissioners of 1835, and even by those of 1876-1880. The little group of Freeholders seems gradually to have let drop its public functions, whilst retaining, and even enlarging, its proprietary rights. It has enclosed parcels of land, let them on lease, and allowed quarries to be opened. The shares have (1907) gradually become con-centrated, it is said, in the hands of a couple of owners, who have bought up many of the "stints" of their colleagues, separately from their freeholds, taking conveyances of these separated "stints" as transferring all rights in the collective ownership. Meanwhile the little town, growing again into a port with some little trade and a population of a couple of thousands, has equipped itself with the commonplace machin-ery of an Urban District Council under the Public Health Acts, apparently leaving all its quondam public possessions to become exclusively the private property of these two proprietors.[2]

---

[1] "The Northumbrian Border," by Mandell Creighton, in *Archæological Journal*, vol. xlii., 1885, p. 62.

[2] The two Freeholders who are reputed to have got control of all the shares find, it is said, some difficulty in disposing of the property, owing to the ambiguity of their title, and we believe that litigation is pending (1907). To a similar difficulty experienced by their predecessors we owe much of our information.

The origin of some of the governments that we have called Lordless Courts may be suggested by the history of the so-called Borough of Tetbury in Gloucestershire.[1] Here we find a large Manor owned by the Berkeleys, extending five miles by three, and divided into two parts, "the Borough" and "the Foreign." Early in the seventeenth century "the Borough" had already, under successive seignorial Charters, acquired a certain degree of independence. At the Court held by the Lord's Steward every October, the Jury presented the names of three persons, out of which the Steward had to choose one as "King's Bailiff," whilst the other officers—Constables, "Wardsmen" (who were "Assistants to the Constables"), Carnals, Ale-tasters or "Assizemen," and a Searcher and Sealer of Leather—were freely elected by the Jury. The market tolls were strictly limited by ancient custom; the Lord had granted "common of pasture" over Tetbury Warren between certain

Copy of the case submitted to counsel two generations ago passed into the hands of the late Mr. Woodman, and furnished Dr. Creighton with his facts. That copy has disappeared from among the Woodman MSS. ; but Mr. J. Crawford Hodgson has another copy of it, which he kindly allowed us to see. The Chancery suit was Gregory *v.* Pattinson, 1733 to 18th June 1743. See also *The History of Northumberland*, by Rev. J. Hodgson, vol. ii. part ii., 1832, pp. 213-220; paper on "The Northumbrian Border," by Rev. M. Creighton, in *Archæological Journal*, vol. xlii., 1885, p. 62.

[1] For the history of Tetbury we have had the advantage of consulting the MS. records of the Feoffees, including minutes, accounts, and records of the Manorial Courts, etc. ; a unique copy of the presentments of the Court in 1623, setting forth the then constitution of the Borough ; *Articles of Agreement anno VII. Car. I. for the purchase of the Manor, Tolls . . . with Judge Coxe's opinion on some cases concerning the same*, 1782 ; By-laws made for the Borough, *London Gazette*, 12th September 1687 ; a "Case on the Tolls of the Fairs and Markets," 1790 ; 54 George III. cap. cxliv. (Tetbury Inclosure Act, 1814); 57 George III. cap. ii. (Tetbury Paving Act, 1817) ; 2 and 3 Vic. c. 7 (Sale of Advowson Act, 1839) ; Further Report of Commissioners to inquire into Charities, 1828, p. 351 ; *History of the Town and Parish of Tetbury*, by Rev. Alfred T. Lee, 1857 ; also *New History of Gloucestershire*, by Samuel Rudder, 1779, pp. 727-733.

Gloucestershire had other reputed Boroughs, such as Chipping Sodbury, which had between 1681 and 1688 Mayor, Aldermen, and Burgesses, and afterwards a Bailiff nominated by the Homage Jury at the Lord's Court; Dursley, with much the same organisation ; Newnham, electing annually a Mayor and six Aldermen, but actually governed by two "Beams" or Constables (First Report of Municipal Corporation Commission, 1835, Appendix, vol. i. pp. 37, 49 ; ditto, 1880, part i. p. 33, part ii. p. 406 ; *Ancient and Present State of Gloucestershire*, by R. Atkyns, 1768, pp. 347-354 ; *New History of Gloucestershire*, by S. Rudder, 1779 (for Chipping Sodbury, pp. 671-676); *Chapters of Parochial History* (Dursley), by J. H. Blunt, 1877 ; "Notes on the Borough and Manor of Newnham," by R. J. Kerr, in *Transactions of Bristol and Gloucestershire Archæological Society*, vol. xviii., 1893). We refer separately to Chipping Campden (p. 180).

dates, and there was also pasturage all the year round on certain other wastes of the Manor.[1]

This Manorial constitution was destined during the seventeenth century to be developed, by the gradual transfer of the Lord's rights, into an almost complete autonomy. A wealthy Alderman of the City of London, Sir William Romney, first took the market on lease from the Lord, at a substantial rent, together with the ancient "Tolzey"; and then in 1610 bequeathed the remainder of his lease, partly for charitable purposes and partly for the common good, to a body of trustees for the town, of whom he named the first thirteen, empowering them to co-opt their successors. Some years later we find this charitable trust made the subject of inquiry by commissioners for the Court of Chancery, who were, in fact, some of the neighbouring magnates, with a view to placing it on a more permanent basis. In consultation with the "King's Bailiff" for the time being (who was elected, it will be remembered, at the annual Court of the Manor), and the principal inhabitants, the Commissioners recommended the consolidation of the authorities of the town into a recognised governing body,[2] consisting of the Bailiff and twelve "Brethren and Assistants," known as the "Thirteen," representing, we may assume, the original trustees, and a "company or society called the Four-and-Twenty"; the Thirteen to fill vacancies by co-option from out of the Four-and-Twenty; and recruits for the Four-and-Twenty to be chosen by the two bodies jointly. The Thirteen were, by a provision as to which the legal authority might be questioned, to have the power to levy a rate upon the inhabitants, in supplement of their trust funds, and to appoint the Schoolmaster, the Lecturer, and the inmates of the almshouses. This constitution was sanctioned by the Court of Chancery, and embodied in an instrument under the Great Seal.[3]

But a further stage was yet to come. In 1632 the Lady Berkeley and her son, Lord Berkeley, being concerned to promote the welfare of their principal Borough of Berkeley,

---

[1] This constitution is described in the presentments of the Court held in October 1623, of which a unique MS. copy has been placed at our disposal.

[2] The resemblance of this constitution to that of Beccles should be noted.

[3] Further Report of Royal Commission to inquire into Charities, 1828, p. 851.

and needing ready money, offered to sell the Manor of
Tetbury, both "the Borough" and "the Foreign." It seems
that, possibly because there was no large estate within the
Manor, but four or five score small occupying freeholders, the
noble owners intimated their willingness "not only that every
particular tenant . . . might for their own particular and
private uses buy the inheritance of their several tenements
. . . but also that such parts thereof as might be convenient
and necessary might be bought and purchased for the public
and general good of the said Borough to have continuance
for ever for their public good and benefit." "Therefore," we
are told, "the Bailiff and the rest of the Thirteen and other
of the inhabitants of the said Borough . . . did consider and
treat among themselves what might be fit for them to do . . .
and upon mature and deliberate consideration had at several
meetings in public, they did think it fit for the general good
of the said Borough" to subscribe among themselves the sum
of £840, with which to buy not only the whole Manor with
its Courts, warren, waste lands, rents, royalties, liberties, and
franchises, but also an existing lease of the warren, and even
the advowson of the living, so that the Borough might appoint
its own clergyman. The "Articles of Agreement" then
concluded between the Lord and Lady Berkeley on the one
hand and the principal inhabitants of Tetbury on the other,[1]
afford a charming vision of a great deal of public-spirited
activity in the town. Unlike most Charters and other
instruments of this period, this agreement aimed at placing
the property in trust, not for the members of the governing
body, or of any Corporation, or even for a class of Burgesses,
Freeholders, or Freemen, but for all the inhabitant householders for the time being. Thus all the residents were free
to trade, to use the market, and to worship in the church.
The existing Commoners agreed to forgo their rights of
pasture over certain lands, in order to permit these to be
ploughed and sown with corn until the proceeds had sufficed
to complete the reimbursement to the trustees of any sums

---

[1] The MS. copy of the Articles of Agreement in our possession shows that
the formal agreement was made with (*a*) four trustees, (*b*) the Bailiff and the
rest of the Thirteen, (*c*) "the company or society called the Four-and-Twenty,"
and (*d*) 44 persons "all of the number called the Commonalty" (who were possibly
the freeholders).

that they had expended. The pasturage was subsequently to be enjoyed, not only by the owners of "the ancient messuages," but also by those of "newly erected messuages or cottages," and even by immigrants into the Borough after they had lived there seven years, or on payment of the sum of £5, immediately they took up residence.[1] This remarkable co-operative purchase of the Manor, under carefully drawn Articles of Agreement, incidentally, and possibly unintentionally, led to a change in the constitution. The legal ownership was vested in seven Feoffees, filling vacancies among themselves by co-option, who were jointly Lords of the Manor, and as such held the Courts. These became, it is clear, along with the Bailiff, the Executive of the Borough, acting in more or less consultation with the Thirteen, who were, we are told, always "the gravest, chiefest, and discreetest townsmen"; and who continued to audit the accounts and give a sort of confirmatory authority to the actions of the Feoffees and the Bailiff. The Bailiff was "usually the senior Thirteen who had not yet served that office." The Four-and-Twenty seems to have had no function beyond that of furnishing recruits to the Thirteen, and we do not gather that it continued to meet otherwise than as the Jury which the Bailiff summoned to the Court of the Feoffees, with which it is believed to have become identical.[2]

Under this Corporate government Tetbury continued to flourish, growing in population from about 1200 in 1700 to about 3500 in 1779, when it ranked as "the third town in Gloucestershire,"[3] building for itself in 1655 a market hall, setting up public pumps, and even widening its streets, out of its not inconsiderable Manorial revenues. The Feoffees' six-monthly Courts, with the two Juries, one for "the Borough," the other for "the Foreign," occasionally included among their presentments orders to the Feoffees not to dispose of any of the "Town's Stock" without the consent of the inhabitants, complaints as to the condition of the streets, and formal indictments of

---

[1] In 1640 the last remnant of the Lord's rights was got rid of by the purchase, for £1400, of the reversion of the Markets and Fairs after the expiry of the lease. This purchase had been provided for, by anticipation, in the Articles of 1632, and the trustees had saved up money for it.

[2] MS. note recording old tradition.

[3] *New History of Gloucestershire*, by S. Rudder, 1779, pp. 727-733.

officers for neglect of duty. This Court was also used by the Feoffees publicly to let by auction to the highest bidder both the tolls of the market and the manure of the streets. But from a case submitted to Counsel in 1790 we gather that the Feoffees found difficulty at that date in enforcing their authority, and were doubtful as to the powers that either they or their " Court Leet and Court Baron " could actually put in force against nuisance-mongers. How far and how rapidly the Feoffees, the Jury, and the Bailiff were, in the early decades of the nineteenth century, superseded by the County Justices, who had come to hold regular Petty and Special Sessions in the Borough, or by the inhabitants in Vestry assembled, we have been unable to ascertain. In 1814 the Feoffees cordially assisted in obtaining an Inclosure Act, and in 1817 a Paving and Lighting Act.

Meanwhile the little town of Tetbury was being rapidly left behind by the changing course of trade and industry. The market had been, at the beginning of the eighteenth century, the most frequented in the district, large quantities of wool, yarn, and serge, as well as of corn, bacon, cheese, and cattle, changing hands : so much as £1000 being dealt with on a single day. Gradually, however, it decayed ; the population declined to half the total of 1779 ; the Corporate revenues fell away to a few pounds annually ; the functions of the Bailiff, the Feoffees, and the Thirteen silently diminished to next to nothing, until the so-called " Borough " of Tetbury became almost indistinguishable in its government from the neighbouring villages.[1]

---

[1] It was not discovered by the Municipal Corporation Commissions of 1835 and 1876-1880. It became first a Local Board and then an Urban District Council, under the Public Health Act (population in 1901, 1989, or little over half the highest point reached more than a century previously). The Feoffees now regard themselves exclusively as trustees of a small charitable endowment.

Melton Mowbray, in Leicestershire, may be cited as an analogous case of a benefaction to the town becoming the basis of local autonomy (see *An Essay on English Municipal History*, by James Thompson, 1867, pp. 146-152 ; the various papers by Thomas North in the *Transactions of the Leicestershire Architectural and Archæological Society*, vols. iii. and iv., 1874-1875). Here lands were leased and purchased by the inhabitants in 1549-1565 and vested in Feoffees, the money being found by a quite extra-legal special levy. At first we gather that Town Wardens and "Spinny Wardens," Overseers for Pavements and Bridgemasters, Constables and Swineherds, a Hayward and a "Town's Husband," were all elected annually at a public meeting of the inhabitants.

Here and there we discover examples of Lordless Courts of less obvious origin than the Borough of Tetbury. In the wild and mountainous region that separates the verdures of Windermere from the spreading sands of Morecambe Bay, we find a "Society and Fellowship of the Four-and-Twenty," a Close Body meeting at the ancient abbey church of Cartmel, which we have assumed to be a Parish Vestry analogous to that of Braintree in Essex, and have already described it as such.[1] It seems, however, to have itself possessed Manorial jurisdiction over the seven townships of the parish, and to have held its own Manorial Courts for the appointment of officers and the regulation of the life of the inhabitants.[2] How the Four-and-Twenty "Sidesmen" of Cartmel, as they were eventually termed, came to possess this great Manor; how the unincorporated parish could legally hold it without its being vested in feoffees or trustees; how the Sidesmen got the right to receive the fines and amercements of the Courts held by a Steward on their

But an executive committee was chosen in 1582, and in 1628 we find "ten or twelve of the principal men of the parish" acting as a Close Body, which seems to have ruled, with the Trustees and Town Wardens, for over a century. By 1775, however, even this Close Body had fallen into desuetude, and discontent began to be manifested at the Trustees ruling alone. After some years' struggle a deed of compromise was signed in 1793, by which the town gave itself a new constitution, the whole authority resting in the annual public meeting, which chose all the officers. This, though a troublesome and occasionally turbulent authority, continued without legal warrant for three quarters of a century, until the administration passed under the Public Health Acts, first to a Local Board and then to an Urban District Council (population in 1901, 7454).

As possibly analogous to Tetbury and Melton Mowbray, we may cite the so-called Borough of Clitheroe, one of the townships of the great parish of Whalley in Lancashire, and formerly part of the extensive Honour of Clitheroe, with a population increasing from 1368 in 1801 to 5213 in 1831, which had received a seignorial Charter in the twelfth century. Here the government was in the hands of the owners of the ancient burgage hereditaments, who, having been duly admitted as Burgesses, elected annually two of themselves as Bailiffs, and were eligible to be summoned by the Bailiffs on an "Inquiry Jury," which served as a sort of occasional council. The Bailiffs acted as Lords of the Manor, holding (with their Recorder) a Borough Court for the trial of personal actions of any amount, and (by their Town Clerk as Steward) a Court Leet, at which a series of Manorial officers were appointed (including a paid "Well-cleaner"). See First Report of Municipal Corporation Commission, 1835, Appendix, vol. iii. p. 1488; *Ancient Charters and other Muniments of the Borough of Clitheroe*, by J. Harland, 1851; *History of the original Parish of Whalley*, by T. D. Whitaker, vol. ii., 1876, pp. 68-99; and pp. 48, 205 of the present work.

[1] *The Parish and the County*, Book I. Chap. V. Section (a), The Close Vestry by Immemorial Custom.

[2] *Annals of Cartmel*, by James Stockdale, 1872; *Cartmeltoniana*, by Rev. W. ffoliott, 1854; *The Rural Deanery of Cartmel*, edited by R. H. Kirby, 1892.

behalf ;[1] what exactly had been their relation to one particular township of their great parish, Flookburgh by name, which possessed ancient Municipal regalia and a sword of office and was reputed once to have been a Chartered Borough ;[2] how they acquired the power of disposing at their will of the waste and commons, eventually dividing up the whole area under Inclosure Acts among some 300 freeholders ;[3] how they managed to take deodands and forfeitures,[4] and even to appropriate the proceeds of wrecks upon the shore,[5] we must leave as interesting inquiries to the historian of a preceding period.

But government by a Lordless Court was not always confined to small and isolated communities. The best example of such a government is furnished, indeed, by the Manorial Borough of Birmingham.[6] The town of Birmingham, having in 1689 probably under 12,000 inhabitants, and fifty years later not more than twice that number, sprang, like Manchester, in the second half of the eighteenth century, from a mere manufacturing village, which had forgotten that it was ever called a Borough, into a densely crowded, great industrial

---

[1] *Annals of Cartmel*, by James Stockdale, 1872, p. 168.

[2] *Ibid.* pp. 121, 291.   [3] *Ibid.* pp. 326-384.

[4] "It is ordered that (three names) shall be appointed to collect these sums of money hereafter mentioned, being deodands and forfeited goods, viz. of J. F. 53/- ; of R. S. 40/- for horse and wheels ; W. H. for the running gear of Staveley watermill, 48/4 ; of C. B. for £10 lent by M. N. for L. R.'s horse and saddle ; and that these sums be paid before Christmas next or else the same be put in suit. Also that the men aforesaid do view a cockboat at N. and do sell the same" (Minute of 1653, *ibid.* p. 88).

[5] *Ibid.* pp. 298-295. Cartmel was not inquired into either by the Municipal Corporation Commissioners of 1833-1835 or by those of 1876-1880.

[6] *Throkmorton's Survey of the Borough and Manor of Birmingham*, 1553, by W. B. Bickley and Joseph Hill, 1891 ; *Memorials of Old Birmingham*, by J. Toulmin Smith, 1863 ; *The Gild of Holy Cross, Birmingham*, by Lucy Toulmin Smith, 1894 ; *History of Birmingham*, by William Hutton, 1st edition, 1781, 7th edition, 1840 ; *Hints for a History of Birmingham*, by James Jaffray, 1855 (?) ; *History of the Corporation of Birmingham*, by J. T. Bunce, vol. i., 1878 ; *The Duty of the Respective Officers appointed by the Court Leet in the Manor of Birmingham*, 1789 ; *A Concise History of Birmingham*, 1817 (?) ; *The Picture of Birmingham*, by James Drake, 1825 ; *Historical and Descriptive Sketch of Birmingham*, 1830 ; *The State of the Court of Requests and the Public Office of Birmingham*, by Joseph Parkes, 1828. The Court Leet records exist only from 1799, and are unimportant ; the MS. Minutes of the Street Commissioners are available from 1776 ; whilst we have only been able to find MS. Vestry Minutes for St. Martin's (the principal) parish back to 1795. On the other hand much may be gleaned from the newspapers (of which a large sample is to be found in *A Century of Birmingham Life* (1741-1841), by J. A. Langford, 1868) ; and contemporary references.

centre, containing by 1835 a population of more than 150,000.
Like Manchester, too, it had no Municipal Corporation, and
was dependent for all magisterial authority on the Justices
of the Peace of the County. But though Birmingham
remained, equally with Manchester, under a Manorial form
of government, the actual working of it was very different.
It was not merely that at Birmingham the more important
Municipal services had, from 1776 onwards, increasingly passed
into the hands of a statutory body of Street Commissioners,
which we shall subsequently describe.[1] What was even more
important, Birmingham had, already at the end of the seventeenth century, shaken off nearly all the authority of the Lord
of the Manor, and, by the beginning of the nineteenth century,
had ousted him from the last remnant of power. The government, nominally Manorial, took the form of what was practically a Lordless Court. As at Manchester, the chief officers
of the town were chosen annually at the Court Leet,[2] presided
over by the Lord's Steward. But by long tradition the
selection of the Jury was not in the hands of the Steward,
but was left to the "Low Bailiff" chosen at the previous
Court.[3] The Lord of the Manor had, in fact, let slip all
his authority over the Court Leet, except the formal presiding
of his Steward; and the Court itself had, in the nineteenth
century,[4] allowed its own powers to lapse. There was a busy
Manorial market, but in 1806 the Street Commissioners

---

[1] Book IV. Chap. IV. The Street Commissioners.

[2] The formal procedure of the Court Leet is given in *The Duty of the Respective Officers appointed by the Court Leet in the Manor of Birmingham*, by Thomas
Lee, Steward of the Manor, 1789, partly reprinted in the *History of the Corporation of Birmingham*, by J. T. Bunce, 1878, vol. i. pp. 4, 19, where the Court
Leet is described.

[3] "The function of the Low Bailiff is to summon an annual Court Leet, at
which he chooses a Jury, who elect all the officers for the ensuing year. . . .
The choice, therefore, of all these virtually rests with the Low Bailiff, as holding
the absolute choice of the electing Jury" (*The Picture of Birmingham*, by James
Drake, 1825, p. 18). In 1722, and again in 1792, this custom of leaving the
selection of the Jury to the Low Bailiff was contested. In order to secure the
election of Church and Tory officers, the Steward on each occasion chose the Jury
and elected his nominees. On each occasion the Whig Nonconformists fought
the issue at the assizes, with the result of establishing the customary right of the
Low Bailiff (*History of the Corporation of Birmingham*, by J. T. Bunce, 1878,
vol. i. pp. 17, 19).

[4] Hutton, writing in 1794, observes that the "duties of office are little
known except that of taking a generous dinner, which is punctually observed.
It is too early to begin business till the table is well stored with bottles and too
late afterwards" (*History of Birmingham*, 3rd edition, 1795, p. 144).

farmed the tolls and the management from the Lord, who thus lost all interest in the appointment of officers, and the Court Leet itself lost all practical control over market regulation. It continued to appoint annually a whole hierarchy of Manorial officers, as it was said, "to govern the town." "A High Bailiff, who inspects the markets and sees that justice is observed between buyer and seller, rectifying the weights and dry measures; a Low Bailiff, who summons a Jury who choose all the other officers, viz. two Constables and one Headborough; two High Tasters, who "examine the goodness of the beer and its measure; and two Low Tasters, or Meat Conners, who inspect the meat exposed for sale, and cause that to be destroyed which is unfit for food. Deritend, being a hamlet of Birmingham, sends its inhabitants to the Birmingham Court Leet, where a Constable is elected for them, and at which all the Town Officers are chosen and sworn in; the whole in the name of the Lord of the Manor." [1] But these officers did not in practice pay any attention to their nominal duties. After the end of the eighteenth century, at any rate,[2] they reported no offenders, the Jury made no presentments, and the Court levied no fines. The annual holding of the Court was transformed into an elaborate luncheon given by the retiring Low Bailiff to his friends and the principal inhabitants, at which the formal appointment of officers for the ensuing year was made.[3] There was not even the interest of religious or political rivalry, it having long been "customary to chose the High Bailiff from the Churchmen and the Low Bailiff from the Dissenters." The only functions really performed were ceremonial. "To the High Bailiff," we are told, "is conceded by custom the duty formerly exercised by the Constables of convening and conducting the business of all public meetings in the town. . . . He proclaims the two fairs, one at Whitsuntide, the other at Michaelmas, going in procession with the other town officers,

---

[1] *A Concise History of Birmingham* (anon.), 5th edition, 1817, pp. 38-39.

[2] *The History of the Corporation of Birmingham*, by J. T. Bunce, 1878, vol. i. p. 13, gives a few instances of amercements for market offences between 1779 and 1796.

[3] Thus, in 1825, "the Court Leet assembled . . . at the Public Office about 12 o'clock and proceeded from thence to the Royal Hotel, where they partook of a sumptuous cold collation, after which the following gentlemen were chosen to fill the offices" (*Birmingham Journal*, 29th October 1825).

the Jury of the Court Leet, and a retinue of his personal friends, attended by a band of music to enliven the scene." [1] Yet in the eyes of the Birmingham Radicals of 1830 the Court Leet and the High Bailiff loomed large as a relic of feudal tyranny, "a close, self-elected, in-and-in body, irresponsible to or uncontrolled by public opinion." [2] . . . "It is true that they have no power in the vulgar acceptation of the word. . . . But the assumed power of conferring on public meetings a character of Town's Meetings, and stigmatising other meetings regularly and openly convened by public requisition as not Town's Meetings; of defraying the expenses of some and refusing the costs of others—is a species of bastard power which must and will be soon extirpated. This rusty machinery may, in fact, be said to have usurped the right of petition and public meetings. It was aforetime always necessary to ask the Manager of the Court Leet whether he would let his man-servant the High Bailiff call such and such a meeting, and if cold water was thrown upon the meeting by the power behind the throne no meeting was called." [3] Yet the annual Courts Leet continued nominally to be held, and High and Low Bailiffs to be appointed for Birmingham, after the town had been definitely incorporated as a Municipal Borough, and, in fact, down to 1854, when the practice was silently discontinued. [4]

(d) The Lord's Borough

From the Lordless Court we pass by slight distinctions to the Lord's Borough, itself developing with almost imperceptible gradations into the Enfranchised Manorial Borough. Of the Lord's Borough the specimens range themselves in a practically

---

[1] *An Historical and Descriptive Sketch of Birmingham*, 1830, pp. 85-87. This "proclaiming the fair" is described in the *Birmingham Journal*, 20th May 1826, from which it appears that the function ended with a "sumptuous" dinner, given by the High Bailiff.

[2] *Birmingham Journal*, 16th October 1830.

[3] *Ibid.* 30th October 1830. The High Bailiff "became chairman of all Town's Meetings and the nominal leader of the town in all public affairs" (*Birmingham Journal*, 26th November 1864; *Modern Birmingham and its Institutions*, by J. A. Langford, vol. ii. p. 266).

[4] The Town Clerk informs us that the Birmingham Corporation, though owning the market rights, has never bought the Manor, which remains, as mere property, in private hands.

continuous series, from merely rudimentary examples, through the so-called Boroughs of Berkeley and Wotton, described in the last chapter as mere subordinate parts of a Hierarchy of Courts, up to the Borough of Arundel, where the dependence on the Court of the Lord was more nominal than real. What marks this series off from the Lordless Court is the presence, even in its lowest members, of new constitutional structure, additional to that of the most highly evolved Lord's Court: constitutional structure, which, in the highest members of the series, becomes itself the supreme, if not the only governmental authority of the town.

We may take as a specimen of the merest rudiment of a Lord's Borough the tiny community of Holy Island, off the Northumberland coast. Passing over all its celebrity in ecclesiastical history, we find Holy Island in 1689 under a primitive constitution. There are two Bailiffs, twenty-four Burgesses, and an unlimited number of Stallingers.[1] The Burgesses, called also "Freemen," are the owners of the ancient freehold tenements of the Island, which are twenty-four in number. They claim and are accorded an exceptionally large "stint" of pasturage on the commons of the Island. They alone elect one of the Bailiffs, the other being the nominee of the Lord. The Stallingers have no share in the election of a Bailiff, and but small stints of pasturage. But they have to attend the Lord's Court, and there they may possibly serve on the Jury, which presents nuisances and nominates a Serjeant, Constables, Aleconners, Bread-weighers, and other petty officers, though whether they may share in the trial of petty debt cases is less certain. This constitution went on until 1793, when an Inclosure Act ignored the distinction between Burgesses and Stallingers, which faded away.[2]

If a village community such as Holy Island had "received a few Chartered privileges from a mediæval baron," it might,

---

[1] "Stallangiator" is used about 1270 for "a staller, or tenser, a foreigner who paid for a stand in the market and did not enter the Freedom of the Borough" (*Borough Customs*, by Mary Bateson, vol. i., 1904, p. 112). The student will not fail to notice the close analogy between the twenty-four "Burgesses" of Holy Island and the usual "Four-and-Twenty" of a Northumberland parish (see *The Parish and the County*, 1906, pp. 179-181).

[2] *History of North Durham*, by T. Raine, 1852, p. 161. Holy Island (population in 1901, 405) is now governed by a Parish Council of its own.

as Professor Maitland points out, even be "allowed a precarious place on the roll of English Boroughs."[1]   But such Chartered Boroughs, for all their pretensions, might amount, in fact, constitutionally, to no more than Holy Island.   Thus, the ancient "Borough of Petersfield," in Hampshire, returning two Members of Parliament, was, in 1689, hardly to be distinguished from a mere Court of the Manor.   But at the Annual Leet or Lawday the officers appointed comprised (in addition to the Bailiff, Constables and Tithingmen) a Mayor, and two Ale-tasters, who were called Aldermen.   The Jury was selected and summoned by the Lord's Steward, so that the Mayor and Aldermen, like the other officers, might be said to be indirectly the mere nominees of the Lord.   Moreover, the Lord retained in his own hands all the jurisdiction, the profits of the Courts, and the administration of the market.   Yet the Mayor and Burgesses of Petersfield claimed to be a Corporation; the town called itself a Borough and returned Members to Parliament as a Borough; it seems once to have had a Merchant Gild; and the Mayor and Burgesses had, in the past, even asserted that their Corporation owned the Borough, and had been, time out of mind, legally seized of its fairs and markets.   The Burgesses of Petersfield had received seignorial grants and Charters of the fifteenth century, purporting to give them the same rights as were enjoyed by the citizens of Winchester; and but for the fact that a case was decided against them in 1613, might eventually have made their Manorial Borough independent of the Lord of the Manor.[2]

[1] *Township and Borough*, by F. W. Maitland, 1898, pp. 16-17.

[2] We have not been able to discover any MS. archives of Petersfield, beyond the Charters.   Most information is to be found in the *Report of the Case of the Borough of Petersfield . . . determined by . . . the House of Commons in 1820 and 1821*, by R. S. Atcheson, 1831, and the volumes on Parliamentary election cases by Thomas Carew (1755), Douglas (1775-77), Cockburn and Rowe (1833), and Perry and Knapp (1833); First Report of Municipal Corporation Commissions, 1835, Appendix, vol. ii. p. 797; Report of ditto, 1880, Part I. p. 90; Evidence, p. 76; *The Gild Merchant*, by C. Gross, vol. ii. p. 387.   See also *General History of Hampshire*, by B. B. Woodward, T. C. Wilks, and C. Lockhart, 1861-69, vol. iii. pp. 317-322.

In much the same position as Petersfield were, we imagine, several small Manorial Boroughs of Devonshire, such as Bovey Tracey, which had a Portreeve or Mayor, as well as a Bailiff, annually chosen at the Lord's Court, with a "Mayor's Riding," or "Mayor's Show," on "Roodmass Day," and a "Portreeve's Park," or field, of which the Mayor for the year had the profits; or Harton or Hartland, where the Portreeve was chosen at the Court Leet; or Modbury, with a great nine days' fair, proclaimed by the Portreeve and Borough Jury at the

The men of Alresford, only twelve miles distant from Petersfield, counted themselves more fortunate.[1] Here the ecclesiastical potentate of the south of England, the Bishop of Winchester, had, in 1570 or 1572, granted a written constitution to "our Borough and Town of New Alresford," making the local governing authority independent of the Manorial Court. "Know ye therefore," runs this verbose seignorial Charter, "that we, the said Bishop, have granted, and for us and our successors for ever ordained, that for the future there shall be for ever within our Town and Borough of New Alresford aforesaid one Bailiff and eight Burgesses of the better and more creditable inhabitants." In the involved legal phraseology of the day, the Bishop proceeds to name the first holders of these offices, but he provides that they shall choose from among themselves the Bailiff year by year, and fill vacancies in their own number by co-option. The Bishop does more than this. He starts this seignorial Corporation with two Courts of its own: one termed a Court Baron or Three Weeks' Court, for the settlement of disputes and debts among the inhabitants, and the other, a Court of Pie Powder, for the regulation of the great fair of Alresford to which the whole country-side then resorted. Moreover, he expressly relinquishes to his nascent Corporation certain of the powers usually connected with the holding of the Court Leet or Lawday, such as "Bloodshed, together with the amercements and pains thereof"; the "Assize of Bread, Ale and Wine"; the making orders "and constitutions among the

---

site of the old market cross; or Newton Abbot and Newton Bushell, two moieties of one parish, each governed by its own Portreeve, chosen annually at the Lord's Court (*History of Devonshire*, by R. N. Worth, 1895, pp. 240, 307, 319; "Early History of the Manor of Hartland," by R. P. Chope, in *Proceedings of Devonshire Association*, 1902, vol. xxxiv. pp. 418-454; *Modbury*, by G. A. Cawse, 1860; Report of Municipal Corporation Commission, 1880, Part I. pp. 17, 37, Part II. pp. 840, 860 (Bovey Tracey and Harton)). Such, too, may have been Colyford in Dorsetshire, reputed to have been a chartered Borough, and having a Mayor who took the profits of the fair (*The Book of the Axe*, by G. P. R. Pulman, 4th edition, 1875, pp. 789-790).

[1] For Alresford we have seen only MS. copies of the Charters; the MS. archives of the Manorial courts, 1657-1720, 1781-1835; and sundry unconsecutive archives of 1628-1705, jurors' book, 1825, etc. A minute book of the Corporation, mentioned in 1880, was not found. See also Report of Municipal Corporation Commission, 1880, Part I. pp. 8, 141; report of local inquiry by the Charity Commissioners in *Hampshire Chronicle*, 26th March 1887; also *Sketches of Hampshire*, by John Duthy, 1839, pp. 107-108.

artificers and other inhabitants of the Borough "; the " controlling and correction of weights and measures "; and the
making of By-laws " for the public good " and their enforcement
by fine and distress. The Corporation was to act as Reeve,
and thus secure to its own officers the collection of the
Bishop's rents. The Bishop even ceded the fair and the
markets, with their profits and tolls. Yet he retained his
Hundred Court and his Court Leet or Lawday, at which the
Bailiff and Burgesses, together with all the adult male inhabitants, were bound to appear.

Notwithstanding these liberal concessions and express
stipulations of autonomy, fortified by all the paraphernalia
of parchment and seal, we do not find, in actual practice, that
the Bailiff and Burgesses of Alresford amounted to much more
than the Mayor and Aldermen of Petersfield. Discouraged
by a great fire in 1689, which swept away church, market
buildings, and council house, they gave up holding the Three
Weeks' Court, which was their only machinery for making
By-laws, etc. Throughout the eighteenth century we see
them, without jurisdiction of their own, contentedly using the
Bishop's Court to get their officers—including even the
Bailiff—appointed and their regulations enforced. The
markets and fairs became steadily less frequented and less
valuable. But the little Corporate body still derived some
revenue from stallage and tolls, and retained the ownership
of a few cottages, which kept up some fragments of Municipal
dignity, allowed of a few charities, and provided an annual
feast. Undiscovered by the Municipal Corporation Commissioners of 1835, this miniature Corporation, having only
one paid officer, the Deputy Hayward, with twenty shillings
a year, lingered on until 1887, when its property was, by
scheme of the Charity Commission, transferred to trustees for
charitable purposes, and the Corporation itself was finally
dissolved.[1]

---

[1] The Bishop of Winchester created other Manorial Boroughs on his vast
estates, enjoying various degrees of autonomy. One of these was Gosport, which
always styled itself a Borough, and in 1684 strenuously defended its independence against the claim of the Mayor of the adjoining Borough of Portsmouth to
exercise jurisdiction and take certain ancient dues. From the MS. records
of the Bishop's "Court Leet and Court Baron" which we have consulted from
1623 to 1835, we gather that this Court was held by the Bishop's Steward
twice a year. There was, however, also a "Three Weeks' Court" held by the

In the little "Borough" of Altrincham[1] in Cheshire—in 1689, and for long after, probably numbering only a few hundreds of families—we have an interesting example of a Lord's Borough of great antiquity, having, in strict law very little autonomy, and still less of independent Municipal structure, and yet contriving to perform, throughout the eighteenth century, practically the whole civil government of the town, including most of the work done elsewhere by the Parish Vestry and the Justices in Petty Sessions. The "Court Leet and Court of Pleas," which we may regard as the descendant of the Portmanmoot or Borough Court conceded by Seignorial Charter about 1290, was one of the Hierarchy of Courts of the Barony of Dunham Massey.[2] Held every six months

Clerk or Bailiff, nominally on behalf of the Lord of the Manor. The principal part was played by the Homage or "Grand Jury," the members of which were, we imagine, summoned by the officers whom the former Jury had itself nominated. This Jury submitted annually the names of persons to fill the offices of "Bailiff" (called also Beadle in 1701), Constable (at first one only, latterly twelve), Overseer of the Ferry or Passage, Ale-taster or Aleconner, Coal-meter, and Cryer. We find the Jury in 1623 levying a rate for erecting a cage and stocks, and making various regulations for the cleansing of the streets and ditches. A sixty years' gap in the records at this point may have coincided with the encroachments of Portsmouth. From 1684 to the middle of the eighteenth century the presentments show us a government of the ordinary type, the Jury struggling to maintain the authority of the Court, fining absentees, presenting the common nuisances of obstruction of the streets, filthy hogsties, dirt and dung left unremoved, pigs wandering at large, etc. In 1698 "a standing law" is made that "every housekeeper do once every week for ever cleanse the kennel"; and another that "no person do from henceforth keep above one boat to let, to work" in the passage or ferry by which so many of the men of Gosport lived, and then to let it only to "settled inhabitants." From about 1750 the presentments become rapidly fewer, and the Court sinks to a mere apparatus for annually appointing the Bailiff and Constables. Without Charter, without property, and without a Corporate Magistracy, the claims of Gosport to be a Borough seem to have been forgotten; it was not discovered by the Municipal Corporation Commission in 1835; and it remained without effective local autonomy until the formation of a Local Board (now Urban District Council) under the Public Health Acts.

[1] For Altrincham the student should consult the MS. records of the Courts of the Barony of Dunham Massey, 1689-1835, and of Altrincham, 1658-1835, for access to which we are indebted to the Earl of Stamford and to Mr. Hall, the courteous Steward of the estate; First Report of Municipal Corporation Commission, 1835, vol. iv. p. 2575; ditto, 1880, pp. 9 and 652; *Historical Antiquities*, by Sir Peter Leycester, 1673, pp. 203-204; *History of Cheshire*, by G. Ormerod, 1819, vol. i. pp. 399, 417; in 1828 edition, vol. i. p. 536, etc.; *History of Altrincham and Bowden*, by A. Ingham, 1879.

[2] At the Court of the Barony of Dunham Massey we see amerced inhabitants and officers (*e.g.* Surveyors of Highways) of Altrincham among other places. New Freeholders are presented by the "Freehold Jury." Among the names of the "Leet Jury" we note those of Altrincham residents.

before the Lord's Steward and the "Mayor of the Borough," and attended by a "Grand Jury" or Grand Inquest of Freeholders of the Borough, it elected annually all the officers of the town; presenting, in the case of the Mayor, three names from which the Steward chose one.   Besides a Mayor, a Bailiff, and two Constables, along with such usual officers as Burleymen, Pinders, Ale-tasters, Dog-muzzlers, Scavengers, and Market-lookers, we see this tribunal appointing its own "Laylayers" to assess and collect the rates that it levied; and even, throughout the eighteenth century, the Surveyors of Highways and the Overseers of the Poor.[1]   In the background (just as we were at Bamburgh) we are conscious of separate meetings of the Burgesses or Freeholders—sometimes of "the Mayor and Burgesses"—who may perhaps have carried on the executive government between the six-monthly Courts.   These Burgesses were, for the first half of the eighteenth century, systematically "admitted" by the Jury at the Lord's Court, and sworn by the Steward, on their succession to their burgages, serving in due course the various offices in rotation.   After 1759 this formal admission seems to have been disused, and the Freeholders fade out of sight.   A remnant of the former custom was, however, preserved, in the presentment, year by year, of one Freeholder as a "colt" or recruit to the Grand Jury.

What was remarkable at Altrincham, down to the latter part of the eighteenth century, was the amplitude of the jurisdiction of the Borough Court.   It not only regulated its extensive Town Field, cultivated in the usual strips, and the wide common pastures,[2] but also sanctioned the enclosure and

---

[1] The appointment of "Laylayers" or Assessors at the Court continued down to 1839, at least. Assessors of the Land Tax were also appointed by the Court. We suspect that the nomination or appointment of Overseers of the Poor and Surveyors of Highways passed out of its hands early in the nineteenth century, when a church was built at Altrincham, and we assume that local Vestry meetings then began to be held.

[2] "Ordered that the Town Field be enclosed . . . on the 2nd of February each year, and that person that neglects making up his payments by that time appointed shall be amerced in ten shillings. . . . That the Pinners of the Town Field neglecting doing his office from the 2nd day of February yearly till such time as the last or least parcel of corn or hay therein shall safely be gotten out by the owner thereof; that if any damages should happen by either horse, cow, sheep, or swine, etc., . . . the Pinners shall be liable to make good treble damage, . . . and that for every default made by tethering, or leasowing in the

improvement of successive portions of land by individual owners. It closed footpaths when it thought fit upon any lands within the Borough. It was exceptionally active in enforcing the scouring of ditches, and also in defining the boundaries between individual properties.[1] But the same Grand Jury of Freeholders paid equal attention to what we may call police and sanitary functions. They dealt with tumults and affrays, finding in 1716 that one J. R. "has made a disturbance and tumult of a high nature," for which they "do amerce him in ten shillings."[2] The Altrincham Court even rivalled the Manchester Court Leet in the elaborateness of its By-laws regulating the personal conduct of the inhabitants, especially as regards Sabbath breaking, the harbouring of "inmates," carrying "fire from house to house uncovered,"[3] and the fouling of the Town Wells.[4] It gradually accumulated a long array of officers, each charged to enforce some particular obligation. The Court was a particularly active Market authority, though all the profits of the Market, like those of the Cornmill,[5] went to the Lord. It even performed various Municipal services, paving and lighting the streets, maintaining a water-supply by public pumps and fountains, keeping a fire-engine,[6] and undertaking, by a Municipal Bakehouse, to provide accommodation for all the baking for hire within the Borough—even enforcing, for the sake of regulating the hours, etc., a strict monopoly of this service, and laying down the "rules of baking."[7]

night, shall forfeit ten shillings" (MS. Records, Altrincham Corporation, 26th April 1699).

In 1698 the Pinners of the Town Field present persons for "tethering his little blind mare in the same Town Field and breaking the tether, and going loose eating George Clayton Junior's pease," and for "tethering his nag and breaking the tether in the Town Field in the open day to the damage of the corn" (*ibid.* 12th October 1698).

[1] *Ibid.* 20th October 1773 ; 14th October 1778.

[2] *Ibid.* 25th April 1716.   [3] *Ibid.* 15th April 1719.

[4] "If any one wash his hands or feet at the Town Well [he] shall pay twelvepence" (*ibid.*).

[5] In 1712 various persons were amerced for "withdrawing their grist from," or "not grinding at" the Lord's mill at Dunham (*ibid.* 23rd April and 1st October 1712).

[6] *Ibid.* 15th April 1762.

[7] "We do make an order that no one do make a common practice to allow others to bake in his oven to the hindrance of the Common Bakehouse of the Town, on pain of sixpence" (*ibid.* 21st October 1696).

"We find by a former order that the Baker of the Bakehouse has disregarded

But what distinguishes Altrincham, so far as we know, from the Lord's Courts and Manorial Boroughs in other parts of England, was its curious usurpation of all the civil powers of the Parish and its Vestry. The Court, by its Grand Jury, not only appointed, in flagrant disregard of the statutes, the Surveyors of Highways and the Overseers of the Poor,[1] but also received and allowed their accounts, and gave them frequent and peremptory orders.[2] We find the Court even deciding what Statute Labour and Team Duty should be exacted for the roads, and contracting in the matter with the Turnpike Trustees. The Court took repeated action against the harbouring of inmates.[3] It governed the poor, ordering those in receipt of relief to be "badged,"[4] directing particular children to be apprenticed,[5] compounding with putative fathers for bastard children,[5] appointing a salaried Overseer, and, in 1750, contracting at eighteenpence per week per head for the maintenance of all the inmates of the workhouse.[6] We discover the same all-embracing Court ordering the destruction of sparrows ("a very injurious bird within the limits of this Township")[7]; paying for the prose-

the order of drawing it at such an hour, being six o'clock in the evening ; and do make a further order that the said Baker of the Common Bakehouse for the future do heat the oven at a sufficient time that he may draw for supper at six o'clock " (MS. Records, Altrincham Corporation, 4th April 1711).

In 1741 the Baker was again peremptorily ordered "to set bread in the public oven at seven o'clock" in summer, and eight o'clock in winter, "and not before" (*ibid.* 14th October 1741).

In 1743 the tenant of the Bakehouse was ordered to bake "so early in the morning as that the inhabitants . . . may have their puddings, pies, and other eatables out of the oven precisely at twelve o'clock" (*ibid.* 12th October 1743).

Owing to the "Public Bakehouse" being insufficient, a new one is ordered to be built, and the prohibition of other baking for hire is repeated (*ibid.* 19th April 1769). The Baker continued to be negligent, and was amerced (*ibid.* 21st October 1772). Two Jurymen were deputed to inspect, and "to regulate the rules of baking" (*ibid.* 6th May 1778).

[1] *Ibid.* 26th April 1720.

[2] See, for appointment of Surveyors, *ibid.* 15th May 1717 ; for instructions to them, 7th October 1725 ; for regulation of Team Duty and Statute Labour, 22nd October 1760 ; for agreement with the local Turnpike Trustees, 20th October 1773.

[3] In 1709, for instance four Aldermen were ordered to "go through the Town and review what inmates are come into the Town, and give a full account to the Overseers" (*ibid.* 12th October 1709).

[4] *Ibid.* 15th April 1719.   [5] *Ibid.* 26th April 1720.

[6] *Ibid.* 13th April 1758.

[7] *Ibid.* 16th October 1755, 19th April 1763, and 22nd April 1789.

cution of felons [1]; and finding (by hiring substitutes) the quota of militiamen demanded from the Township or Borough.[2] There was, in fact, throughout the eighteenth century no Vestry meeting in Altrincham.

The Altrincham Court continued to be held long after the close of the eighteenth century—continues, in fact, even to this day (1907), formally to elect its " Mayor " and other officers. But after the close of the eighteenth century we see its functions shrinking gradually into those of a mere Leet, presenting petty nuisances. The trial of civil suits, which we find down to 1662 recorded in the same minutes as the other business, seems, in the course of the eighteenth century, to have become detached as a separate Court Baron,[3] which went on hearing an ever-dwindling number of pleas down to 1793. The regulation of the commonfields gradually ceases, presumably with the progress of enclosure. From the first quarter of the eighteenth century we are conscious of " Town's Meetings " of inhabitants, occasionally ordered and paid for by the Borough Court, at which various common deci-- sions were taken.[4] Towards the end of the eighteenth century the Constables, the Surveyors, and the Overseers seem increasingly to have regarded these Town's Meetings as their real superiors, rather than the Borough Court, with its Jury of Burgesses, now representing only a small minority of the residents. In 1802 the Borough got a church built—having hitherto worshipped at the church of the extensive Parish of Bowden—and presently started Churchwardens of its own, and formal Vestry meetings, with which the Town's Meetings probably became merged.[5] As the local organ of civil government, the Borough Court had been superseded by the Township Vestry and the Petty and Special Sessions of the County Justices of the Peace.[6]

---

[1] MS. Records, Altrincham Corporation,12th May 1736.

[2] Ibid. 15th October 1759.

[3] In 1712 the Borough Court fines a man twenty shillings " for proceeding at law against R. O."—presumably before some other tribunal—" contrary to several orders of this Court " (ibid. 1st October 1712).

[4] " We agree to have no more Town's Meetings but what's at the expense of those that appear, and to meet at the Court-house " (ibid. 5th May 1742).

[5] We see them, for instance, adopting the Lighting Act, just like an ancient autonomous parish. Provision was specially made in the Municipal Corporations Act of 1883 for a continuance of the ancient appointments of Mayor, etc., at Altrincham (46 and 47 Vict. c. 18, sec. 23).

[6] The neighbouring Borough of Stockport, also established by Seignorial

More remarkable in various respects was the working
constitution of Lewes, an ancient market-place and " Borough

Charter in the thirteenth century, had many features in common with Altrincham.   Down to the middle of the eighteenth century, whilst their formal constitutions were almost identical, the Lord's Steward seems, at Stockport, to have
retained the real power.   It was the Steward who selected the Jury of the Great
Court Leet or Portmote, from among the freeholders (who were all required to
be sworn and admitted as Burgesses) ; the Steward chose annually four persons
as suitable to be Mayor, of whom the Jury elected one ; the Steward paid the
Mayor a small salary from the Lord's funds, and required him to be in attendance at the Lord's Court ; the Steward even selected the Constables, for formal
appointment by the Court.   But the industrial development which, in the latter
part of the eighteenth century, transformed the two square miles of rural township around the village of Stockport into an irregular agglomeration of mills,
factories, and workmen's cottages, and numbering, by 1801, more than 14,000,
and by 1831, more than 25,000 persons, deprived the Lord of the Manor of all
control over anything but his actual rents.   The jurisdiction of his Court Baron
in petty debt cases quietly faded away about 1764 ; the presentments of nuisances
at his Court Leet became steadily more perfunctory and less respected, partly, no
doubt, because the disparity between them and the actual needs of the town
became ever more glaring ; an Inclosure Act in 1805 and a Court of Requests Act
in 1806 incidentally superseded ancient seignorial rights ; until finally, in 1826,
the principal inhabitants completed the decay of the Manorial authority by
obtaining a Local Act, under which the paving, cleansing, lighting and watching
the town was taken over by a body of Street Commissioners.   As at Altrincham,
there had been, at Stockport, no Vestry meetings ; not even for the great parish
of which the township formed only a part.   By a peculiar custom the four
Churchwardens were, down to our own day, chosen annually by the four Lords
of Manors in the parish, who were called (from 1464 at least), the " præpositi "
or "the four posts" of the parish.   This was all the more remarkable in that
the lands of these proprietors were exempt from the Church Rate, their share
being paid out of the Poor Rate for the whole parish.   The Churchwardens so
chosen rendered no accounts to any Vestry (*Stockport Ancient and Modern*,
by H. Heginbotham, vol. i., 1877, pp. 199, 211, 268).
      Notwithstanding the absence of any Royal Charter or Corporate Justices,
and the complete decay into which had fallen any powers that this Manorial
Borough may once have exercised, Stockport was included in the Municipal
Corporations Act of 1835 as a Municipal Borough, whilst Manchester and
Salford, having similar thirteenth - century Seignorial Charters, were, like
Altrincham, denied this privilege.   We attribute this distinction partly to the
insignificant fact that Stockport's chief officer was called a Mayor, and not
a Boroughreeve ; and partly to the accident that the Municipal Corporation
Commissioners had no detailed information showing the purely Manorial
character of Stockport before them, owing to the refusal of T. J. Hogg, one of
their number, to present, with what he considered undue haste, the reports on
the towns that he had visited.
      For Stockport we have relied on the Report on Certain Boroughs by T. J.
Hogg (Municipal Corporation Commission), 1888, p. 129 ; Home Office Domestic
State Papers and Magistrates Book (in Public Record Office) for 1818-1819 and
1835 ; *Stockport Ancient and Modern*, by H. Heginbotham, 1882-1892 ; *History
of the County Palatine and City of Chester*, by G. Ormerod, vol. iii. pp. 788-806,
edition of 1882 ; *East Cheshire*, by J. P. Earwaker, vol. i., 1877, pp. 329-421 ;
Stockport Inclosure Act, 45 George III. c. 91 (1805) ; Stockport Court of
Requests Act, 46 George III. c. 114 (1806) ; Stockport Paving and Lighting
Act, 7 George IV. c. 118 (1826).

Town" of Sussex, once of considerable importance, and in 1689, though much decayed, still sharing with Chichester the honour of being the capital of the county.[1] We find it at that date without anything in the nature of a Chartered Corporation, divided into four parishes; styled a Borough, and governed for all Municipal purposes as a single unit, under a peculiar close body. "There is, and always hath been," records the Steward of the Manor in 1662, "time out of mind within this Borough a Society of the wealthier and discreeter sort of the townsmen, commonly called 'The Twelve,' out of which society the Constables are always chosen, the elder, of course, according to his seniority; the younger is chosen by the elder, with the consent of the greater part of the Jury (sworn at the Lawday), out of such of the Society as were never formerly Constables within this Borough; for never was it known that any man was twice younger Constable or twice Headborough; and these Constables then elected make choice of their Headboroughs with consent as aforesaid (of the greater part of the Jury) and of the other officers before remembered, at the Lawday, without any contradiction or altercation by the Steward. The Society known as 'The Twelve' are never so few as twelve, nor more than twenty-four, and upon death or removal are supplied by election of the greater part of the subsisting Society. Town charges disbursed by the Constables for the common good of the inhabitants are yearly viewed, examined, allowed, and taxed in August or September by the Twelve, who in confirmation thereof subscribe their names to the Assessment, which is a sufficient warrant to the Headboroughs for the collection thereof. Now, town charges are of this or the like nature, viz. 40s. per annum to the Clock-keeper and

---

[1] We have not examined the MS. records of Lewes, which have been well extracted in *Ancient and Modern History of Lewes and Brighthelmston*, by William Lee, 1795, and *The History and Antiquities of Lewes*, by T. W. Horsfield, 1824-1827; see also the papers by W. Figg and Rev. E. Turner on "Old Lewes" and "The Ancient Merchant Gild of Lewes and the subsequent Municipal Regulations of the Town" in *Sussex Archæological Society's Collections*, vol. xiii., 1861, and vol. xxi., 1869, pp. 90-107; *The Gild Merchant*, by C. Gross, 1890, vol. ii. p. 145; *History . . . of Sussex*, by T. W. Horsfield, 1835, vol. i. p. 201; *Historical . . . Account of the Coast of Sussex*, by J. D. Parry, 1833, p. 325; *History of . . . Surrey and Sussex*, by Thomas Allen, 1829-1830, vol. ii. p. 543; *Victoria County History of Sussex*, vol. i., 1905, pp. 382-383. It was overlooked by the Municipal Corporation Commission of 1835, but was reported on by that of 1880 (Report, Part I. pp. 60, 144-145).

Bell-ringer; payment for mending and repairing the market-house, sessions house, bridge, stocks, cucking-stool, pillory, butts for whipping rogues, conveying malefactors to gaol, for the suppression of disorders and restraining offenders; also of later times disbursements for King's provision of wheat, oats, coals, carriages, etc.; brazen weights and measures; charges on the shire town."[1]

What may once have been the exact distribution of authority in Lewes between the Manorial Court and the peculiar Fellowship of the Twelve, is not easy to determine. During the seventeenth century, at any rate, we see the power of the Twelve steadily waning, their functions of passing By-laws and taxing the town being gradually assumed by the Leet Jury. Towards the end of that century, we are told, "political and religious divisions . . . seem to have paved the way for the above-noted encroachments on the ancient rights of the Fellowship," until in 1709 the record of their meetings comes to an end, and in 1720 their last surviving member dies. From this time forth Lewes was governed by its two "High Constables," annually presented by the Jury at the Lord's Court, and sworn in by the Steward; by the Head-boroughs nominated by the High Constables; by the Lord's Court itself, which occasionally made By-laws and suppressed nuisances; and by quite "extra-legal" meetings of the inhabitants, "publicly convened in their Town Hall" by the High Constables. The government of Lewes, in fact, during the seventeenth and eighteenth centuries bears a singular resemblance to that which we have described at Braintree, which did not claim to be a Borough, but which had the same kind of Fellowship or Company, working in close connection with the Lord's Court, equally coming to an end at the beginning of the eighteenth century, to be in both cases succeeded by public meetings of the inhabitants. But Braintree was a single parish, and its Fellowship was regarded as merely

---

[1] *History of Lewes*, by T. W. Horsfield, 1824, p. 174, quoting an account of, 1662. "The Constables, in conjunction with the Twelve, exercised the privilege of decreeing laws for the due regulation of the town, and even pushed their authority so far as to commit to prison, or to the stocks, those who ventured to question the legality of their decrees, and refused to conform to their requirements" (*ibid.* p. 176). There had also been a subordinate body called the Twenty-four ("The Ancient Merchant Gild of Lewes," by Rev. E. Turner, *Sussex Archæological Collections*, vol. xxi., 1869, pp. 90-107).

a Close Vestry, to be in due course replaced by an Open Vestry.[1] The four little parishes of Lewes, claiming collectively to rank as a Hundred, cannot be supposed to have had one Vestry in common, either close or open. Moreover, the Lewes Fellowship levied a " Town Tax " upon the whole Borough for the Constables' expenses, including whatever was laid out for the common purposes of the town, whenever the little property of the Borough did not suffice. Payment of this rate—which certainly seems of doubtful legality—was apparently usually made without question, but it was spasmodically resisted as early as 1584, when it was enforced, as it had been "time out of mind," by distraint and sale.[2] We find it again resisted in

---

[1] So too, at Brighthelmston, the little fishing village whose development into the fashionable seaside resort of Brighton we have already described, there seems to have been in the sixteenth century a government like that of Lewes or Braintree—we know not whether to call it a Manorial Borough. "From time immemorial the government of the Borough (or Lower Town) with which the [Upper] Town was connected, was entrusted to two . . . Headboroughs who sat alternately in the Borough Court, or together if necessity required it, and the Jurors, or sworn Assessors of this Court, were selected from such of the Decenners or Frankpledges as were in attendance, having no causes to be tried. Hence the origin of the Society of the Twelve, of whom such frequent mention is made in the Books of Customs, and whose duty it appears to have been to act as a Committee of Counsel to the Headboroughs, thereby securing to themselves rights and privileges which 'the landmen' [of the Upper Town] did not possess. . . . They claimed the exclusive right of composing the Jury of the Borough Court, and on the Lawday. The choice of the Constable, as well as of the Headboroughs, rested chiefly with them. They filled up vacancies in their own body, and pleaded immunity from the Borough Common Fine." But this supremacy of the fishermen did not endure. The Elizabethan Commissioners of 1580 revised the "customs" so that the government was shared equally between those "of the sea" and those "of the land." The prosperity of the Lower Town seems, however, rapidly to have declined, and it was finally ruined by the great storm of 1703. The Society of the Twelve—each of whom, as at Braintree, had once had his own "street or circuit" to superintend—came to an end about 1772 ("The Early History of Brighton," by Rev. E. Turner, in *Sussex Archæological Collections*, vol. ii., 1849, pp. 38-52). As at Braintree, the fact that Brighton formed but one parish resulted in the quasi-municipal powers lapsing to the Open Vestry already described. Another case of connection between the Lord's Court and a "Twelve" is afforded by East Stonehouse, Devonshire, a Manor included in the parish of St. Andrew's, Plymouth, but never in Plymouth Borough. In 1594 it was completely under the rule of its Lord, but regulations were made with "the consent and frank assent of twelve discreet and able persons of and within the said town and liberties" (*History of Devonshire*, by R. N. Worth, 1895, pp. 226-229).

[2] "Here I think fit to remember," says an old authority, "that about the twenty-sixth year of Queen Elizabeth, ten of the most aged of the Twelve came to John Shirley, Esq., afterwards Serjeant at Law, whose clerk I then was, to have his opinion what course might be taken against such refractory persons as refused to pay town charges assessed as aforesaid. But before he delivered

1721, when the members of the Court Leet Jury agree to indemnify the Constables for any costs they might be put to in enforcing it.[1]   In 1765, when the Borough had lost most of its property, and the Town Tax was more than ever needed, an adjourned Lawday results in a similar indemnity by " fifty-six of the most respectable inhabitants of the Borough." [2] Finally, in 1772, the public meeting resolves "that the Constables and Jury at the Court Leet or Lawday chosen, shall and do continue to have power to make and collect a Town Tax for defraying the necessary expenses of the Borough." [3] Thus fortified, the High Constables and Jury seem to have gone on levying such a Town Tax as was required, in 1822-1823 amounting even to as much as one shilling in the pound.[4]

Another variety of the Lord's Borough—one exhibiting all the worst features of the close Municipal Corporations that we shall hereafter describe—is seen in the Mayor and Burgesses of Arundel, the little town nestling under the ancient Sussex castle of the Duke of Norfolk.[5]   Here the

---

his resolution he demanded of them what they used to do formerly in the like cases.   Their answer was that, time out of mind, they had ever levied such taxation by distress after three days, the tax not satisfied, to sell the goods distrained, rendering the overplus to the owners thereof—which course he told them was warrantable by usage, and so justifiable by law.   Distresses, by opinion of Serjeant Heath and Mr. Foster, are justifiable by law, and may legally be maintained, being made and confirmed by common consent of the inhabitants of the whole Borough time beyond all memory, consisting of four parishes, attendant at one Lawday, and that the charges are public, lying upon the whole inhabitants as in one Borough, and not as divided parishes" (*Ancient and Modern History of Lewes and Brighthelmston*, by William Lee, 1795, pp. 191-192).

[1] *Ibid.* p. 211.   [2] *Ibid.* p. 212.
[3] *History of Lewes*, by T. W. Horsfield, 1824, p. 211.
[4] *Ibid.* p. 229.   This little Manorial Borough, not being reported on in 1835, went on unchanged, the High Constables and Jury levying annually their extra-legal Town Tax to eke out the Corporate revenues.   By 1880, when the population had grown to 6000, it yielded £70 a year.   In 1806 the principal inhabitants had obtained a Local Act constituting a body of Street Commissioners to pave, light, cleanse, and watch the Borough (*ibid.* p. 223, and Appendix, p. xliii).   Lewes was created an ordinary Municipal Corporation in 1881, contrary to the recommendation of the Municipal Corporation Commission of 1880 (Report, Part I. p. xi).
[5] MS. Minutes, Arundel Corporation, 1539-1835 ; ditto of "Borough Court," 1758-1835 ; MS. Archives, Court Leet, 1722-1740 ; First Report of Municipal Corporation Commission, 1835, Appendix, vol. ii. p. 672 ; *History and Antiquities of the Castle and Town of Arundel*, by Rev. M. A. Tierney, 1834 ; *Sussex Archæological Collections*, vol. vii. 1854 ; *History of* . . . *Western* . . . *Sussex*, by J. Dallaway, 1815-30, vol. ii. Part I. pp. 90-183 ; *History* . . . *of Sussex*, by T. W. Horsfield, 1835, vol. ii. pp. 122-132 ;

organisation of an ancient "Borough," mentioned in Domesday, had been defined by "articles of agreement" ratified and recorded by two of the Judges of Queen Elizabeth's reign, on the occasion of some dispute,[1] and this working constitution, unfortified by any Charter, remained practically intact down to 1835. In the various manuscript records of the old Corporation between 1689 and 1835, we can watch the administration carried on in the name of the Borough by the "Company" or "Society" of Burgesses, a close body of indefinite number,[2] consisting in practice only of about a dozen members, and open only to those whom the existing members chose to admit. This body, existing independently of any other authority, owned valuable water meadows, cottages, market and quay dues, and the Town Shambles. It held the "Borough Court" every three weeks, which—like the Court Baron granted to the men of Alresford—not only determined pleas of debt and trespass, but also made By-laws, confirmed the appointment of officers, and received and acted on presentments of nuisances, short weights and measures, and individual defaults.

Meanwhile the Lawday, or Court Leet and View of Frankpledge of the Earl of Arundel, was being held annually by his Steward. At this Court the members of the "Company" or "Society" of Burgesses, and indeed all the adult male inhabitants, were bound to attend, and the Mayor was chosen. But the members of the Jury, who, as we have seen, were the *primum mobile* of such a Court, were selected by the outgoing Mayor, who was expressly bound to return to the Steward a majority of the Company or Society of Burgesses, adding to them "so many other of the principal inhabitants as shall make up the full number of four-and-twenty according to the ancient custom."[3] Thus

---

History of the Counties of Surrey and Sussex, by T. Allen, 1829-1830, vol. ii. pp. 520-524 ; *Victoria County History of Sussex,* vol. i., 1905, pp. 383-384.

[1] In these "articles" (to be found in the MS. records of the Borough) the men of Arundel make good their claim to be free from any interference from the officers of the Hundred Court of the Earl of Arundel, thereby reminding us of the existence of a Hierarchy of Courts in the once more extensive Honour of Arundel, which, in the eleventh century, included the two whole Rapes of Chichester and Arundel, and more than 90 square miles.

[2] There are traces of its having been twenty-four in number.

[3] Compare the similar custom at Alnwick, described at p. 191.

it was the Close Body of the Company or Society of Burgesses that controlled the Jury. The Jury chose two of the Close Body, out of whom "the Commons, not being of the Jury," or, as we read later, "the scot and lot men," elected one to be Mayor for the ensuing year. All the other officers—two Constables, two Portreeves, two Aleconners, two Searchers and Sealers of Leather, and two Affeerors—were nominated by the Jury, which also "presented" the usual urban nuisances.

We need not describe the complicated interaction of the Company or Society of Burgesses and the Lord's Court. To all intents and purposes this exclusive little group of Burgesses, though preserving the form of subordination to the Lord's Court, had become the sole Municipal authority of the town, and completely master of their own proceedings. We cannot discover that, beyond maintaining a certain Municipal pomp and ceremony, this Company or Society of Burgesses was of any appreciable utility to the inhabitants. It is true that they held the Borough Court, but they charged high fees to suitors, and they let both the civil and criminal sides of this tribunal gradually sink to mere forms.[1] At one time half the Church Rate was contributed from Corporate funds, to the ease of the inhabitants, but this was refused after 1822. The Mayor and Burgesses claimed to be the "Bridgemasters" of the ancient stone bridge over the Arun, but they threw the cost of its repair upon the Poor Rate. They levied all the dues they could on the scanty market. They owned the quay, and exacted tolls on all goods landed from the river.[2] They reserved for themselves the filling of all the local offices, the ex-Mayor even by custom always becoming one of the parish Overseers for a year.[3] But all this became, during the eighteenth century, mainly a matter of ceremony and routine, the duties being neglected or left to the two or

[1] It seems from the scanty records that the so-called "Borough Court" took over from the Court Leet after about 1740 the work of dealing with the presentments of the usual urban nuisances and defaults, which we find the Constables and Portreeves making between 1758 and 1800 in the Borough Court, after which these, too, become perfunctory and formal.

[2] The paving, cleansing, lighting, watching, and improving the town had been abandoned to a body of Street Commissioners, established by Local Act (25 George III. c. 90) in 1785. The Mayor and Burgesses were *ex officio* Commissioners, along with other citizens named in the Act, and qualified by property ownership.

[3] MS. Minutes, Arundel Corporation, 4th April 1769.

three paid subordinates. The scanty manuscript records of their proceedings make it plain that the Burgesses regarded themselves, not as trustees, but as absolute owners of their revenues, which they shamelessly shared among their members. The pasturage on the water meadows was reserved exclusively for the members' cattle; the members got profitable allotments in severalty and beneficial leases.[1] Serving the office of Mayor, a privilege which came round to each Burgess every eight or ten years, was rewarded by an allowance of £100, " the profits, dues, rents, and benefits arising from the quay and the butchers' shambles," and other perquisites.[2] The " feastings " of the little company were almost incessant. At each three-weekly meeting of the Borough Court there was a feast to the Burgesses and their wives and all the officers. At every meeting of the Burgesses there was a dinner. At the annual Court Leet there was a dinner for the Burgesses and Jury. On the annual receipt of a buck from the Duke of Norfolk there was a " venison feast."[3] At "the going forth " of the retiring Mayor there was a " great feast." At every admission of a new Burgess there was " a handsome entertainment of eatables and drinkables for the Mayor and old Burgesses and their wives."[4] If we mistake not, the Mayor and Burgesses of Arundel must have provided themselves with a costly banquet nearly every other week throughout the year. Nor were these feasts extended to the town at large. The Burgesses repeatedly instruct the Mayor not to invite non-burgesses, under penalty of a fine.[5] So profitable and attractive was membership of this convivial Company, closely cemented by family relationship, identity of religious creed and similarity of political opinions, that the fee exacted from those who were favoured with the privilege of admission was gradually raised from £7 in 1726 to no less than a hundred guineas in 1828, in addition to a sumptuous banquet.[6] By 1833 the Company, now styling

[1] MS. Minutes, Arundel Corporation, 30th April 1744; *History of* . . . *Arundel*, by Rev. M. A. Tierney, 1884, p. 709.

[2] See the list of Mayors, 1798-1826, in MS. Minutes, Arundel Corporation.

[3] Discontinued after 1831, *ibid.* 7th June 1831.

[4] *Ibid.* 8th Oct. 1741 and 27th Nov. 1830.

[5] *Ibid.* 12th Sept. 1649 ; ditto, 1701.

[6] *Ibid.* 3rd Oct. 1726, 21st Sept. 1738, 11th March 1789, 17th Nov. 1796, 17th April 1828, and 27th Nov. 1830.

itself a Municipal Corporation, though claiming no Corporate Magistracy, had definitely shrunk to a fixed number of thirteen Burgesses, one of whom served as a Mayor. Their admitted Corporate revenues seem then to have amounted to about £300 a year. With the record that we have indicated it is not surprising that the Mayor and Burgesses of Arundel thought it prudent, in 1833, to keep all inquiries at arm's length. They refused to allow even the Duke of Norfolk's chaplain to complete his ducal history from their records.[1] The Government fared only slightly better. The Mayor and Burgesses of Arundel formally declared that they regarded the issue of a Royal Commission for an inquiry into the Municipal Corporations as "an exercise of the prerogative which they are advised is illegal, and which they think would be dangerous to the liberty of the subject . . . a violation of the Bill of Rights, an intrusion on the rights of Englishmen "; and though they did not persist in refusing to have anything to do with the Commission, they confined their information to the barest minimum.[2]

(e) The Enfranchised Manorial Borough

It is, as we already stated, not easy to draw a line between a Manorial Borough in which the Corporate body was as practically autonomous as that of Arundel, and those Boroughs, demonstrably Manorial in their origin, in which the connection with the Lord's Court had become only formal. In the two neighbouring Boroughs of Christchurch and Lymington, in Hampshire,[3] where the population in 1831 was between one

---

[1] History and Antiquities of the Castle and Town of Arundel, by Rev. M. A. Tierney, 1834, preface, p. vii.

[2] First Report of Municipal Corporation Commission, 1835, Appendix, vol. ii. p. 667.

[3] For Christchurch, see the large MS. volume in which an extensive series of miscellaneous records (1485-1857) is bound up; MS. Acts of Privy Council, 9th and 18th November 1670 ; First Report of Municipal Corporation Commission, 1835, Appendix, vol. ii. p. 1251 ; ditto, 1880, part i. p. 24; part ii. p. 108 ; The Antiquities of the Priory of Christchurch . . . with some general particulars of the Castle and Borough, by Benjamin Ferrey and E. W. Bayley, 1834 and 1841. For Lymington, see MS. Minutes of Corporation, 1574-1835 ; First Report of Municipal Corporation Commission, 1835, Appendix, vol. ii. p. 743 ; History of Lymington, by David Garrow, 1825 ; Records of the Corporation of the Borough of New Lymington, by C. S. Barbe, 1848 ; Old Times revisited in the Borough and Parish of Lymington, by Edward King, 1879 and 1900. See

and two thousand, the connection with the Lord of the Manor had, by the end of the seventeenth century, sunk into nothing more substantial than the ceremonial swearing in of the independently chosen Mayor and other officers at the Lord's Court, and the payment of a fee-farm rent to the representative of some ancient grantor. In each of these Boroughs there was a Close Body of Mayor and Burgesses, of unknown origin, existing by prescription independently of any other authority, occasionally called " the Company," appointing all the officers,[1] and disposing of the trifling town lands and the equally insignificant tolls and dues of market and harbour. Neither Corporation held any Court, though there are traces of informal arrangements among the Burgesses for compulsory arbitration in disputes.[2] During the seventeenth century both these Corporations had been active in making By-laws for the good government of their Boroughs, organising the " Watch and Ward," setting the Assize of Bread, repairing bridges and causeways, paving the streets, and even " paying the poor." In the latter part of that century we see their activities dwindle away. They continued, however, to control their markets and their little harbours, and maintain some Municipal dignity.[3] By the end of the eighteenth century they had still

also, for both these and other neighbouring Boroughs, the paper on " Early Boroughs in Hampshire," by T. W. Shore, in *Archæological Review*, vol. iv. 1889 ; *Topographical Remarks relating to . . . Hampshire*, by Richard Warner, 1793 ; *General History of Hampshire*, by B. B. Woodward, T. C. Wilks, and C. Lockhart, 1861-1869.

[1] At Christchurch the earlier dependence of the Borough had left a mark in the oath of the Burgesses, who swore on admission to " maintain all accustomed and ancient services of right belonging to the Lord of the Castle of the Honour of Christchurch, and now in the inheritance of the Right Honourable Henry Earl of Clarendon, whose Burgesses you are " (MS. Records, Corporation of Christchurch, 20th September 1693, etc.). There seems originally to have been only " a Portreeve or Prepositus, of late time," it was said in 1670, " for better credit called a Mayor," but merely the " sworn servant " of the Lord (MS. Acts of Privy Council, 9th November 1670). In the eighteenth century we find the Company of Burgesses nominating three of their number for Mayor, of whom the " Commonalty " or resident householders chose one (see the full description in MS. Minutes, Christchurch, 19th November 1805 ; and First Report of Municipal Corporation Commission, 1835, Appendix, vol. ii. p. 1254).

[2] MS. Minutes, Christchurch Corporation, 25th January 1641.

[3] At Lymington the Corporation exacted a licence fee (in 1563 and 1699) from any person who should " drag for oysters upon the haven " (MS. Minutes, Lymington Corporation, 1699) ; and from 1711 onwards this fishery was let on lease, with reservation to the Corporation of power " to set a moderate price for all such oysters " (*ibid*. 3rd December 1711).

further declined, existing thenceforth only for the election of members of Parliament, the periodical leasing of the remnant of their property and their dues, and the expenditure of the proceeds on an annual "Mayor's Breakfast" or other festivity,[1] latterly paid for by the "patron" of the Parliamentary seat.[2]

At the very top of our series of Manorial Boroughs we place the little rural township of Godmanchester in Huntingdonshire, for many centuries completely enfranchised from seignorial influence, fortified by successive Royal Charters, occasionally enjoying a Commission of the Peace of its own, and only falling short of the full status of a Municipal Corporation in never actually acquiring the power of creating its own Corporate Magistracy.[3] Yet, looked at from another

---

[1] *History of Lymington*, by David Garrow, 1825, p. 48.

[2] First Report of Municipal Corporation Commission, 1835, Appendix, vol. ii. p. 1255.

Chipping Campden, in North Gloucestershire—once an important woolstapling centre—received a Royal Charter in 1604, confirming a then existing prescriptive Corporation of the Bailiffs and Burgesses. This Corporation consisted of a Common Council, made up of fourteen Capital Burgesses (two of them serving as Bailiffs) and twelve Inferior Burgesses. The Capital Burgesses were alone eligible for election as Bailiffs, and it was they alone who elected the Bailiffs, and filled vacancies among the Capital and Inferior Burgesses alike. But there was also a body of Freemen, recruited by Birth and Apprenticeship, and the payment of half a crown as fee. In ancient times the privilege of trading or pursuing any craft had been confined to the Freemen, and in 1780 and 1794 the Common Council vainly strove to enforce this monopoly. There was a Court of Record, held every four weeks, at which civil actions up to £6 : 13 : 4 had once been tried, but which had come by 1689 to be merely a name for the periodical meetings of the Bailiffs and Burgesses. The town was by this time in slow but continuous decay; the revenues of the Corporation gradually sank to next to nothing; and it came more and more under the influence of the chief local landowner, the Earl of Gainsborough, who was always appointed High Steward. Undiscovered by the Municipal Corporation Commissioners in 1835, it lingered on, with population dwindling to under 2000, until 1886, when it was finally dissolved under the Municipal Corporations Act of 1883 (46 and 47 Vict. c. 18), and its little property vested by scheme of the Charity Commissioners in 1889. See MS. Minutes, Chipping Campden Corporation and Town Trust and also those of Vestry; Report of Municipal Corporation Commission, 1880, part i. pp. 23-24; "The Manor and Borough of Chipping Campden," by Rev. S. E. Bartleet, in *Transactions of the Bristol and Gloucestershire Archæological Society*, vol. ix., 1884, pp. 184-195; *Ancient and Present State of Gloucestershire*, by R. Atkyns, 1768, pp. 161-168; *New History of Gloucestershire*, by S. Rudder, 1779, pp. 319-324 and Appendix.

[3] Our chief sources of information as to Godmanchester have been the elaborate MS. Archives ("Stock Book," "Book of Entries," and "Court Book") of the Corporation from the sixteenth to the nineteenth centuries; see also First Report of Municipal Corporation Commission, 1835, Appendix, vol. iv. p. 2235; and *History of Godmanchester*, by Robert Fox, 1831.

standpoint, the Parish and Borough of Godmanchester is only one step removed from the Chartered Township, such as we have seen in Beccles and Wisbech, or from such Lordless Courts as Cartmel and Newbiggin-by-the-Sea; full, indeed, of survivals from the still more rudimentary Village Meeting or Court of the Manor of the primitive agricultural community.

It does not fall within the plan of this work to trace the rise of Godmanchester from its position as a Manor in Ancient Demesne, nor to describe how its residents got from King John, in return for the substantial fee-farm rent of £120 a year, a grant of the Manor itself, with all its profits and prerogatives. Confirmed by various subsequent Royal Charters and Letters Patent, the "men of Godmanchester" maintained their privileges and immunities until, by Charter of 1604, they were expressly incorporated as the Bailiffs, Assistants, and Commonalty of the Borough of Godmanchester. From that time forth we find the Borough governed by two Bailiffs, chosen annually out of their own number by a Close Body made up of the two Bailiffs for the time being and twelve Assistants, which met as a "Burghmote," recruited itself by co-option, and was served by a Sub-Bailiff, Recorder, Deputy Recorder, and Town Clerk of its own appointment. The Borough had its own Coroners by prescription, this office being always filled for a year by the retiring Bailiffs; its own three-weekly "Court of Pleas" for civil suits of trespass and debt, as well as for conveyances of property; its own annual Court Leet, View of Frankpledge, and Court Baron; and its own Fair or Mart, with the customary Court of Pie Powder. Within the wide area of the Borough, which extended over seven square miles of cornfield and meadow, there was—except the somewhat distant jurisdiction of the County Justices—no competing authority.[1] The Borough Corporation had not even to fear the rivalry of the Parish Vestry, for by a peculiar and almost unique custom, the Bailiffs and Assistants of Godmanchester were themselves the Vestry of the conterminous parish, appointing the Churchwardens and Sexton, nominating the Overseers and Surveyors, making the Church Rate, and acting

---

[1] The Bailiffs and Coroners were even sworn in at the Borough's own Court, though they were afterwards resworn, and their names enrolled, at Quarter Sessions (*History of Godmanchester*, by R. Fox, 1831, p. 152).

in all respects on behalf of the parishioners.[1] Finally, we
have to add that this all-embracing little Corporation took for
itself escheats and deodands within its own area; and as Lord
of the Manor owned all the extensive wastes and commons.

It is the popular administration and collective use of the
seven square miles of commonfields, water meadows, and
valuable pastures that form the characteristic feature of the
Godmanchester of the seventeenth and eighteenth centuries.
The Borough, as James the First declared in his Charter, consisted "altogether, or for the most part, of agriculture and
husbandry," the few hundred families concentrated in the four
ancient streets [2] proudly turning out in procession, if we may
believe Cotton and Camden, no fewer than "nine score ploughs
in a rural pomp" to welcome any monarch who passed through
their little village community.[3] The Borough records abundantly
reveal the character of the local industry. Much the most
important part of the work of the Bailiffs and Assistants
between 1604 and 1803 was connected with the commonfield
agriculture and the management of the town lands,—the
elaborate stinting of the common pastures, the sharing of "the
Freemen's Fen" between the separate herds of the two sides
of the town,[4] the preservation of the "wood, willows, or

---

[1] In this combination of Select Vestry with Manor ownership Godmanchester
comes near to Cartmel, with its sixteenth-century "Fellowship of the Four-
and-Twenty"; it has obvious resemblances to Braintree on the one hand and
Lewes on the other; in some respects we are reminded of Newbiggin-by-the-
Sea; but the only other case known to us in which a definitely incorporated
Municipal body acted as the Select Vestry is that of St. Ives in Cornwall
(*History of St. Ives, Lelant, and Zennor*, etc., by J. H. Matthews, 1892). We
have not investigated the actual origin of the Select Vestry in either of these
cases. In Godmanchester the habit of the Bailiffs and Assistants to act as the
Vestry was challenged in the ecclesiastical court in 1712; but they "appeared,
justifying the custom for sixty, seventy, or eighty years, so that the prosecution
slept" (MS. Minutes, Godmanchester Corporation, 14th October 1712; a
precedent of 1624 is printed in the *History of Godmanchester* by R. Fox, 1831).

[2] We do not know how far the traces of ancient divisions in the Borough
may be significant; there was a "West Side" and an "East Side," each having
its own Coroner, its own "cow-commons," and its own common herd daily
driven out and home by its own Neatherd; moreover, at the annual Court, when
twelve Jurors were sworn, three were taken from each of the four streets.

[3] *History of Godmanchester*, by R. Fox, 1831, p. 322.

[4] MS. Records, Godmanchester Corporation, 7th May 1707. It is not quite
clear to us who exactly were the Freemen, or what were their peculiar privileges.
The Municipal Corporation Commissioners of 1833-35 seem to have been
convinced that the Freemen comprised all sons or daughters of Freemen, as well
as persons admitted by purchase; and that Freemen were alone eligible to be
Assistants, alone entitled to trade within the Borough, alone eligible to serve as

bushes,"[1] and the discreet felling or cutting of these " to hedge in calves' pasture " or " to hedge the causeway."[2] As the arable land, though owned in severalty by the possessors of the "nine score ploughs," was divided into the usual innumerable strips, parted only by green grass balks, and cultivated in great commonfields, we see the Bailiffs in 1700 summoning "all the farmers to appear at Court Hall to appoint a Hadland Day according to the old custom; who did agree that none should sow barley [in the commonfield] before Friday 21st March, and that day only hadlands [headlands ?]."[3] In 1792 it is still necessary that the Bailiffs, Assistants, and inhabitants generally, in public meeting assembled, should agree, " in order to secure the grain from trespass," to obtain more control over the use of the commonfield for pasture, by imposing a tax of two shillings for each horse turned out.[4] As in the more primitive village communities, some of the meadows were annually divided up by lot for individual mowing; and we see the Bailiffs and Assistants solemnly ordaining in 1728 that " no Lot Grass shall be mowed for the year ensuing."[5] They make formal order " that no gleaners do go into the [Corn] Field to glean until Wednesday next, and that they come not into the Pease Field until harvest be done."[6] They have also to regulate and, when they will, to let on lease the profitable

Free Suitors in the Court of Pleas, and alone entitled—if they owned or occupied "commonable" houses, being ancient tenements within the Borough—to share in the common pastures. But the Charter of 1604 does not create " Freemen," but only " Burgesses," and mentions none of the above privileges. It expressly authorises the co-option of Assistants from among the " Burgesses and inhabitants." It was the inhabitants (or at any rate the owners or occupiers of the ancient tenements) who were entitled to the immunity from toll anywhere in England, and exemption from Jury service outside the Borough, as Tenants in Ancient Demesne. We noticed no trace in the records of the enforcement of any exclusive right of trading. It was probably the owners and occupiers of the ancient tenements who were referred to as Burgesses. It was to them—not their sons and daughters residing elsewhere—that the full privileges of commoners on the Borough pastures had been originally confined, but during the seventeenth and eighteenth centuries the owners and occupiers of divided and new tenements were more and more admitted. In 1803 the Inclosure Award "assigned the right to the owners and occupiers of commonable houses without reference to the qualification of Freedom," and this was confirmed by a judgment of the Court of Common Pleas, 20th November 1830 (*History of Godmanchester*, by R. Fox, 1831, p. 154).

[1] MS. Records, Godmanchester Corporation, 13th December 1697.
[2] *Ibid.* 14th April 1698 and 13th February 1699.
[3] *Ibid.* 12th March 1700. [4] *Ibid.* 7th August 1792.
[5] *Ibid.* 3rd October 1728. [6] *Ibid.* 23rd July 1691.

common fishery in the Ouse,[1] to insist on the millers down
stream opening the sluices in due time to prevent floods;[2] and
to construct proper "overshots or water flashes" to keep their
water meadows irrigated and yet not drowned.[3]   The most
important Municipal enterprise in the whole history of the
Borough is, in 1792, the draining of the flooded meadows,
which is carried out at the expense of "an equal acre tax on
all and singular meadows" within the Borough.[4]   The busiest
officers of the little community during the seventeenth and
eighteenth centuries were not the Constables or the Ale-tasters,
but the Haywards, Field Reeves, Grasshirers, Holmekeepers or
Greenkeepers, Neatherds, Gamekeepers, and Mole-catchers.   The
presentments which these officers make to the Borough Courts
relate, not to the usual urban nuisances, but to such offences as
"turning his horse foot-loose into the meadows,"[5] "for his horse
being stalled upon a common balk before the grain was carried
away on both sides,"[6] "turning his horse into the holmes
contrary to the Constitutions ";[7] "going into the stubble with
his sheep, being twice taken . . . before Michaelmas,"[8]
"keeping two calves upon the waste-ground before Ascension
Day ";[9] "not keeping a bull upon the commons," or "keeping an
insufficient bull ";[10] "setting his fold in the tilth-field after
Michaelmas ";[11] or "feeding his flock of sheep in the Pease
Field before Martinmas ";[12] or "mowing a balk . . . abutting
against West Gores."[13]   Almost the only nuisance that may be
called urban in its character is the "chimney out of repair, and
very dangerous of fire" in the street of thatched cottages, that
the Jury was constantly presenting at the beginning of the
seventeenth century.[14]

With the high price of corn, and the desire for improvements in agriculture, the temptation to the Burgesses of
Godmanchester to obtain an Inclosure Act became at last
irresistible, and in 1803 all the commonfields were redivided

---

[1] MS. Records, Godmanchester Corporation, 7th October 1725.
[2] *Ibid.* December 1689, 22nd October 1725.
[3] *Ibid.* 4th February 1726.   [4] *Ibid.* 13th December 1792.
[5] *Ibid.* 10th July 1690.   [6] *Ibid.* 7th and 28th August 1707.
[7] *Ibid.* 21st September 1699.   [8] *Ibid.* 7th August 1707.
[9] *Ibid.* 30th April 1691.   [10] *Ibid.* 12th May 1692, 7th July 1698.
[11] *Ibid.* 9th November 1693.   [12] *Ibid.* 4th November 1714.
[13] *Ibid.* 12th August 1714
[14] *Ibid.* 15th January 1691, 12th October 1732.

among the owners of the strips and enclosed in distinct freeholds. With them seems to have gone most of the vitality of
the Corporation. The business of the " Court of Pleas "
dwindled away to a few petty debt cases, and after 1805 the
meetings became formal. The Court Leet continued to be
held twice a year, chiefly for the appointment of Bailiffs,
Coroners, and Constables, the presentments becoming more and
more perfunctory. There still remained roadside wastes and
five separate commons to be regulated, weights and measures
to be occasionally inspected, and various ancient charities to be
administered. Godmanchester increased between 1801 and
1831 in population, and presumably in material productivity,
if not in prosperity. Yet it is impossible for those who have
read its seventeenth and eighteenth century records to watch
without regret the passing away of the earlier life, when these
couple of hundred little farmers, with their nine score ploughs,
pastured their common herds, drew lots annually for the
privilege of mowing the several plots of meadow grass, in Open
Court decided what crops to sow in each part of their common
demesne, simultaneously ploughed and sowed and reaped their
scattered strips in the common tilth-fields, and made what use
they could of the long grass balks by which the strips were
divided. This collective agriculture may have been primitive
and uneconomic in its character. The agricultural revolution
which we saw taking place at Great Tew may have been
difficult to accomplish. Yet as we watch the common life in
the little community of Godmanchester, and watch the dying
out of the spirit of fellowship, of the sense of common interests,
and of what we may call a communal consciousness, that the
common agriculture cannot fail to have promoted, we must
realise how grievous was the accompanying social loss, when it
was replaced, in the English rural village, by capitalistic
farming on an exclusively commercial basis.[1]

[1] The class of Enfranchised Manorial Boroughs seems to have included, by
1835, about a score of other towns in different parts of England, having
populations in 1831 of between 500 and 3500. The governing authority was
either a close council or officers practically nominating each other, without any
real control by a Lord of the Manor, but without, on the other hand, any
Corporate Magistracy. Such, we imagine, were Appleby (Westmoreland) ;
Brackley (Northamptonshire) ; Calne, Chippenham, and Westbury in Wiltshire ;
Camelford, Grampound, Marazion, and St. Ives in Cornwall ; Chard, Ilchester,
and Yeovil in Somerset ; Garstang (Lancashire) ; Newtown and Yarmouth in

(f) Manor and Gild

We pass now to a little group of Boroughs in which the government was shared between a Manorial Court and one or more Trade Gilds. The existence of Merchant or Trade Gilds or Companies was, as we shall presently show, characteristic in 1689 of a small but important class of Municipal Corporations, including the City of London. Even in the other Municipal Corporations we find, as a rule, a class of Freemen recruited by Apprenticeship—an institution from which it may possibly be argued that Trade Gilds must have once existed. But whether in a fully developed form, or only as a rudiment or remnant, Gild structure is almost universally absent from the scores of Manorial Boroughs of which we have given samples. In so far as there existed, within these jurisdictions, any class of Burgesses or Freemen, these were connected either with the tenure of land or with mere inhabitancy—the "suitors" of a Court Baron or the "resiants" of a Court Leet. To this generalisation the Manorial Boroughs of Northumberland and Durham present a remarkable exception.

The most interesting example of this group is the Borough

---

the Isle of Wight (Hampshire) ; Ruyton in Shropshire ; Sudbury (Suffolk), and Tenterden (Kent), to the latter of which we have already referred (p. 60). As to most of these, see First Report of Municipal Corporation Commission, 1835, Appendix, vols. i.-iv. ; Report of Municipal Corporation Commission, 1880 ; for Chard (not then reported on) see *Proceedings of Somersetshire Archæological and Natural History Society*, vol. xxvii. parts i. and ii., 1882-1883, and *The Book of the Axe*, by G. P. R. Pulman, fourth edition, 1875 ; for Sudbury (also not reported on) see R. v. Mayor of Sudbury, in *Reports of Cases, etc.*, by J. Dowling and A. Ryland, vol. ii., 1823, pp. 651, 660 ; and *Election Cases*, by J. Phillipps, 1782, pp. 131-216. A town might acquire not only the Manorial rights, but also a Charter from the King, and yet not develop. James I. incorporated the town of Blandford in Dorsetshire, and granted it the Manor, but conferred upon it no magisterial authority. The Bailiff and Burgesses continued until 1835 a Close Body, recruiting themselves by co-option, holding, by their Steward, their own Court Leet, but letting their Court of Record go into desuetude about 1780. Without any important Municipal functions, they were kept alive by possessing a revenue of a hundred pounds a year or so from rents and market tolls which was spent mainly in paying a few subordinate officers, with some Corporate feasting. With an unprogressive population of between two and three thousand, it is not easy to understand why this Manorial Borough was included in 1835 as a Municipal Corporation, whilst others were omitted (First Report of Municipal Corporation Commission, 1835, vol. ii. pp. 1133 ; *History and Antiquities of the County of Dorset*, by J. Hutchins, vol. i., 1861, pp. 214-246). Hemel Hempstead (Herts), chartered by Henry VIII., remains to this day (1907) unincorporated (*History of Hertfordshire*, by N. Salmon, 1728, p. 116).

of Alnwick—already mentioned as part of a Hierarchy of Courts—which, except for the interpolation of a Trade Gild, would have been included in the common class of Lord's Boroughs. But even as a Lord's Borough Alnwick would have had a distinguishing characteristic. Instead of showing any progressive emancipation from its Lord, it was, between 1689 and 1835, brought more completely under his control. It might, indeed, by 1835 almost have claimed a class by itself, as a disfranchised Lord's Borough.[1]

What exactly had been the status of the Burgesses of Alnwick in former centuries, and at what period of their history the Trade Gild or Gilds had been added to the Manorial structure, we are not here concerned to discover. At the Revolution the government of the little town was shared between two distinct but closely interwoven authorities—the Chamberlains, "Four-and-Twenty," and "Common Gild" of Freemen on the one hand, and on the other the Court Leet and Court Baron of the Earl of Northumberland for the "Manor and Borough."

The constitution of the extra-manorial body, the Chamberlains, "Four-and-Twenty," and "Common Gild," was determined by no Charter or other instrument. It had apparently been developed in the course of centuries by mere usage. The base was the whole body of Freemen of the Borough, recruited by Birth, Apprenticeship, and occasional co-option. At the end of

---

[1] We have sought to unravel the intricacies of the constitutional history of Alnwick from the voluminous MS. Records of the Corporation, which extend over three centuries ; from the scanty MS. Records of one of the Trade Companies (the Tanners) ; the "Articles of Agreement" between the Borough and the Duke of Northumberland, 1762 ; *Seven Letters to the Freemen of Alnwick respecting their differences with the Four-and-Twenty upon Borough affairs*, by an Old Craftsman, 1782 ; *Address to the Burgesses and Freemen of the Borough of Alnwick*, by the Chamberlains, 1782 ; *An Address to the Freemen of the Borough of Alnwick*, by T. H. Bell, 1815 ; *Address to the Freemen of Alnwick*, 1816 ; *An Appeal to the Public on the present existing Grievances of the Burgesses or Freemen of the Borough of Alnwick*, 1819 ; 3 George IV. c. 27 (Alnwick Paving Act, 1822) ; an anonymous *History of Alnwick*, 1822, in the Newcastle Public Library ; *Historical . . . View of Northumberland*, by E. Mackenzie, 1825, vol. i. pp. 433-484 ; First Report of Municipal Corporation Commission, 1835, vol. iii. pp. 1411-1419 ; "Feudal and Military Antiquities of Northumberland, etc.," by Rev. C. H. Hartshorne, 1858 (vol. ii. of *Memoirs of Archæological Institute* for 1852) ; the valuable *History of the Borough, Castle, and Barony of Alnwick*, by George Tate, 1866-1869 ; Report of Municipal Corporation Commission, 1880, part i. pp. 6-8 ; *The Alnwick Corporation Act*, 1882 (1901) ; and the recent Annual Accounts of the Chamberlains now printed for the information of the Freemen.

the seventeenth century these Freemen apparently included most of the householders of the town, and probably all the journeymen who were not householders.[1]   They were—like the Freemen of Newcastle and Durham, Morpeth and Hexham —grouped in separate Trade Companies,[2] each with its own Alderman and other officers, its own Corporate funds, its own periodical meetings, and its own internal regulations.   The rule was that a candidate for the "Freeledge,"[3] or Freedom of the Borough, had first to be admitted to one of the Trade Companies, and then passed as qualified by the "Four-and-Twenty."   In the seventeenth century, at any rate, and during the first decade of the eighteenth, this body of Freemen was occasionally also convened in "Common" or "Public" Gild, for the purpose of deliberating upon and assenting to the projects of the "Four-and-Twenty."[4]

[1] From 1650 to 1835 the number of Freemen seems always to have been between 250 and 300.   In 1801 there may have been 700 or 800 houses ; in 1689 probably not more than half that number.

[2] Of these Companies, ten were still existing in 1833 (those of the Merchants, Cordwainers, Skinners and Glovers, Weavers, Black and White Smiths, Tailors, Butchers, Carpenters and Joiners, Tanners and Coopers).   A detailed study of these Companies, in connection with those of Morpeth and Hexham, Durham and Gateshead, and in comparison with those of Newcastle-on-Tyne, might prove of interest and value.   Their old records are to be found in the custody of surviving members ; see also *History of . . . Alnwick*, by G. Tate, 1866-1869, vol. ii. ch. xvii. pp. 320-350.

[3] This use of "Freeledge" as equivalent to "Freedom" of a Borough or a Trade Company seems peculiar to Northumberland and Cumberland ; see the cases of Newbiggin and Holy Island, pp. 149, 161.,   It may be of significance that the ancient "farms" of Northumberland were called "freeledges" (see the preceding volume, *The Parish and the County*, pp. 179-181).

[4] From a cursory inspection of the MS. Records prior to 1689, as well as from what is in print, we gather that Common Gilds were held fairly frequently in the first half of the seventeenth century, both for passing the Chamberlains' accounts and for sanctioning the proposals of the Four-and-Twenty.   After the Restoration they seem to have been held less frequently, and to have been restricted to making By-laws as to the "stint" of the Town Moor.   After 1711, as we shall explain, they ceased to be held.   From that date, whenever the Four-and-Twenty (now calling themselves the Common Council) desired the opinion of the Freemen, we see the Aldermen of the Companies invited to call meetings of their several Companies, and to submit the question to them. In 1815 we notice the Four-and-Twenty inviting the Aldermen only to meet at the Town Hall and deliberate on their proposals (*An Address to the Freemen of the Borough of Alnwick*, by T. H. Bell, 1815).   We are told that "very early and frequent opposition was made to this assumed authority, as appears from the Order Books of the different trades, wherever the Freemen are threatening that if the Four-and-Twenty neglected to hold the Common Gilds, they would throw down the inclosures, and lay into common again those parts that had been taken in" (*History of Alnwick*, anon., 1822, pp. 328-329).

By 1689 the "Gentlemen of the Four-and-Twenty" had absorbed into their own hands at any rate all the executive authority of the Borough and much of the legislative power. It was the Four-and-Twenty that annually selected from among its own members four persons to serve as Chamberlains, who were, in fact, the executive officers of the Borough. It was the Chamberlains and Four-and-Twenty that enacted By-laws on all sort of subjects, even determining their own constitution and the rights of the Freemen at large.[1] It was this body that managed the Town Moor and the charitable endowments, the school and the place in which the market was held. It was this body that appointed the "Minister," Clerk, and Sexton of the parish church; that chose the Surveyors of Highways;[2] that raised the money required for the train-bands ordered by the Deputy-Lieutenants of the County,[3] and levied rates upon the inhabitants for the repair of the highways and the primitive requirements of an urban community.[4] It was the "Four-and-Twenty" who were the sole judges of the validity of the claims to the "Freeledge," as well as the sole grantors of the privilege of admission to persons other than those entitled by Birth or Apprenticeship.[5] Finally, it was the members for the time being of this mysterious "Four-and-Twenty," which often comprised twice that number, who alone filled vacancies in their own ranks, and increased or limited the total membership of this governing clique.[6]

---

[1] MS. Book of Orders, Corporation of Alnwick, 7th August 1677.

[2] *Ibid.* 9th April 1675.

[3] *Ibid.* 17th October 1690.

[4] For instance, in 1694, a "Sess laid on all the houses and lands . . . three times according to the Book of Rates," for water-supply (*ibid.* 7th August 1694) ; "four times the Book of Rates" for the highways (*ibid.* 23rd April 1729).

[5] *History of* . . . *Alnwick*, by G. Tate, 1866-1869, vol. ii. p. 239.

[6] In 1623 the body numbered 24 ; in 1647, 28 ; in 1667, no fewer than 57 ; in 1690 and 1694 there were at least 43 and 35 members respectively, and in 1709 there were at least 38 (*History of Alnwick*, by G. Tate, vol. ii. p. 256). In 1717 it is "ordered by the Chamberlains and Four-and-Twenty that no man be admitted a Four-and-Twenty man for the future till the death of another, and that upon the death of any of the present Four-and-Twenty so many new ones shall be chosen in the room or stead of such dying" (MS. Book of Orders, Corporation of Alnwick, 7th October 1717). "In the Borough books," we are told, "there is an order to this effect, We, the Chamberlains and Four-and-Twenty, sensible of the inconvenience of a too extended Executive, and disregarding the vulgar opinion that there is wisdom in a multitude of counsellors, do hereby agree that the Four-and-Twenty shall for the time to come consist of

Meanwhile the other governing authority of the town—the Court Leet and Court Baron of the Earl of Northumberland, with its Steward, its Bailiff, and its Jury for the Earl and for the King—was nominally in a position of superior dignity. It was the Bailiff appointed by the Lord who was the nominal head of the town,[1] and who is found, at any rate from 1537 down to 1697, joining with the Chamberlains and Four-and-Twenty in the administration of Borough affairs.[2]   It is at the Lord's Court that the Chamberlains and all the other Borough officers—the Constables, the Keepers of the Causeway, the Tasters of Ale, Overlookers of Bread and Flesh, the Moorgrieves, the Herds, the Market-lookers, the Keeper of the Pinfold, the Manager of the Town Clock, and the Keepers of Pants and Pumps, are presented, appointed, and sworn.   It is the Jury of this Court that, in the seventeenth century, passes By-laws[3] for the good government of the Borough, and even gives specific orders to the Chamberlains and Four-and-Twenty.   It was this Court that, throughout the whole period from 1689 to 1835, punished those who committed nuisances and decided civil actions between the inhabitants.   But in spite of all this show of power, the Lord's Court had sunk, by 1689, into being a mere appanage of the Chamberlains and "Four-and-

no more than seven-and-twenty" (*History of Alnwick*, anon., p. 324).   We have not found such an order ; and from other allusions (see *An Appeal to the Public on the Present Existing Grievances, etc.*, 1819), we infer that the order of 7th October 1717 is that referred to.   At no time (until the modern revolution of 1882) was the body elected either by the Freemen at large or by the Companies.

[1] It was part of the Earl's case in 1758 that his Bailiff "ought to be the chief officer and the person of greatest pre-eminence and authority in the government of the Town and Borough."   This pre-eminence and precedence was conceded by the Four-and-Twenty in the Articles of 1762, though it was stipulated that he should not be a member of the Four-and-Twenty unless he was a Freeman (*History of . . . Alnwick*, by G. Tate, 1868-1869, vol. ii. pp. 291, 295). In 1799, when the Lord insisted on this pre-eminence being recognised, the Four-and-Twenty took counsel's opinion "whether the Acts of Parliament which come directed 'To the Chief Magistrate or Head Officer of Alnwick' shall be received by the Chamberlains or given up to his Grace the Duke of Northumberland's Bailiff."   The answer may be inferred from the fact that the Four-and-Twenty presently ordered such communications to be delivered to the Bailiff (MS. Book of Orders, Corporation of Alnwick, 18th and 28th January 1799).

[2] *Ibid.* vol. ii. p. 255.

[3] On 17th April 1654, for instance, the Court Leet and Court Baron made regulations as to the customary annual horse-races, the enjoyment of the common pasture, and paving and cleansing the streets (MS. Book of Accounts and Orders, among Alnwick Corporation Records).

Twenty." The Jury, upon whose presentments and verdicts everything depended, was, by ancient usage, confined to Freemen of the Borough, and, in practice, to members of the " Four-and-Twenty." [1] So long, therefore, as the " Gentlemen of the Four-and-Twenty " were united among themselves, and retained a preponderating influence among the Freemen, their practical autonomy was tolerably secure from interference by the Lord's officers. But there was a weak point in the claim of the Borough to this autonomy. The powerful family of the Percies had, it was true, somehow or another, permitted an extra-manorial constitution to grow up at the very gates of the Castle. They had apparently conceded to the Burgesses, at some period or another, undefined rights of user over the " Forest of Aydon," or Town Moor, a large tract of land outside the walls of the Borough. But none of the ordinary franchises had been parted with ; " Markets and fairs, tolls and wastes of the town, and all other royalties," [2] the Manor and its Courts, belonged to the Lord and to the Lord alone. Moreover, the Lord owned the public bakehouses, and even when others were allowed to grow up he exacted an

---

[1] "At these early periods," says the local historian, "most of the jurors, if not all of them, were members of the Four-and-Twenty. . . . At an early period the Court Leet Jury and the Four-and-Twenty may have been the same body. . . . A Corporate record . . . says 'a note of the Twenty-four, as the addition is put to them for making up the number at the Court holden the 27th day of April 1647,' and this is followed by twenty-eight names." . . . "Early in the seventeenth century . . . the Jury of the Court Leet . . . were . . . the Four-and-Twenty " (*History of . . . Alnwick*, by G. Tate, 1868-1869, vol. i. p. 348, vol. ii. pp. 239, 256). This, however, is not proved. All that is certain is that, in the eighteenth century, it could be said that " the Freemen exclude all freeholders who are not Freemen from the Juries " (*ibid.* vol. ii. p. 256).

[2] Case submitted to counsel on behalf of the Lord in 1753 (*History of . . . Alnwick*, by George Tate, 1868-1869, vol. ii. p. 289).

"Though the tolls of the markets and fairs were claimed by the Lord of the Manor, the Market Place belonged to the Corporation, who exercised control and directive power both over it and over the streets of the town. They paid to Thomas Harvies, in 1637, ' 1s. for going with the drum at the fair both Sunday and Monday ' ; at an earlier period, in 1612, market keepers were paid by them. The Common Bellman, or Town's Servant, enjoyed a perquisite from stalls in the Market Place, for when one was appointed in 1675, it is said ' he shall have all the perquisites to that office excepting six stalls to Jane Grey.' They were at the expense of cleaning the Market Place and keeping it in repair ; in 1720 it was paved for them, and at the same time the old and new 'crosses were repaired. 'The Corn Market' was paved in 1755 at the cost of £5 : 8 : 0 ; in the following year they paved ' the Horse Market' ; in 1761, 'paving the Market Place' cost £10 : 12 : 4 ; and in 1765, 'for Market Place paved round the Shambles' £17 : 18 : 9 were paid " (*ibid.* vol. i. p. 447).

annual fee from each of them.¹ He had owned the public brewhouse, and he still levied a similar annual fee on every alehouse in the Borough.² He even claimed a toll on salt, and exacted a small annual fee from every retail shop that sold this necessary article, as an acknowledgment of his ancient feudal claim.³

From 1689 to 1750 we see in the manuscript records the "Four-and-Twenty" successfully pursuing their policy of concentrating in their own hands all the government of the Borough. Throughout this period the Castle dominating the town lay in a ruinous condition, and the heirs of the Percies were absentees. The representatives of the Lord of the Manor evidently became the boon companions of the principal Burgesses who made up the Four-and-Twenty, who, as the accounts show, "treated the officers of the Lord of the Manor, even in Alnwick Castle itself, with no meagre supply of wine and other spirituous liquors."⁴ In return, the Steward and the Bailiff evidently failed to inquire too curiously by what right the Four-and-Twenty sank shafts for coal in the Town Moor,⁵ took money for the quarrying of freestone there, and even, in order "to augment and increase . . . the revenues belonging to our Town . . . for the good of the said Town, and for the maintaining of its rights and privileges," enclosed hundreds of

---

¹ This fee continued to be taken until about 1800 (*History of . . . Alnwick*, by G. Tate, 1868-1869, vol. i. p. 448).

² Not relinquished until 1860 (*ibid.* vol. i. p. 448).

³ Down to about 1830 (*ibid.*).

⁴ *Ibid.* vol. ii. p. 264. Here are a few specimens out of many :—

"1635. For a gallon of burnt wine bestowed on the Lord's Commissioners, 4/.

"1658. Wine bestowed on my Lord's officers, 6/.

"1718. To the Castle three quarts canary, 7/6 ; 3 quarts white wine, 6/6 ; 3 bottles claret, 7/6.

"1728. Sent down to the Castle, 6 bottles of arrack punch, 18/ ; 4 bottles of French wine, 10/ ; 3 bottles of white wine, 4/.

"1748. One dozen of French claret, £2 : 5 : 0 ; paid to servants at the Castle, 11/."

After 1753, when, as we shall see, the Lord and the Borough went to war, these payments ceased.

⁵ In 1693 it was ordered by the Four-and-Twenty, "Whereas there was a former order . . . that every several Trade of the Town was to pay out of their respective Trade Monies for the carrying on of winning a colliery in our Common, . . . that . . . those that have not paid such sums to the Chamberlains shall pay in the said sums that is behind to the present Chamberlains . . . that upon refusal . . . the Chamberlains shall sue every such Alderman for such offence in the sum of 38/ by way of action" (MS. Book of Orders, Corporation of Alnwick, 22nd May 1693).

acres of this common pasture, and let them in farms,[1] without any compensation to the Lord of the Manor. They even went so far as publicly to declare, without contradiction by the Lord or his officers, that "time out of mind the Freemen or Burgesses of the Town and Borough . . . have had and now have the freehold and inheritance of Alnwick Moor or the Forest of Aydon."[2]

In this policy of improvement the Four-and-Twenty sometimes found themselves out of harmony with the general body of Freemen. The enclosure of so much of the Town Moor, and the letting of the farms to the highest bidder, for instance, roused in 1711 a storm of indignation. "Idle and disorderly persons," noted the Four-and-Twenty, "enemies to the well-being and good government of our Town and Borough, on two several times in the night privately pulled down great part of the inclosures.[3] The Four-and-Twenty put down this rebellion with vigour, not merely prosecuting and disfranchising the rioters and their abettors, but also ceasing, from that time forward, to summon any "Common Gild," so that the Freemen lost even their last remnant of control over the administration. "Quiet men," writes the apologist of the Four-and-Twenty, "disliked Gilds, which tradition said presented scenes of uproar and confusion . . . So bad a fame, indeed, did Gilds enjoy as to become proverbial; often when boys were engaged in noisy, uproarious play have I heard the exclamation, 'Bairns, what a gild ye are making!'"[4]

For the first half of the eighteenth century we may watch the vigorous little oligarchy of the Four-and-Twenty administering the affairs of the Borough at its own will and discretion—regulating the common pasture, letting the farms, providing a water-supply by a rate, rebuilding the shambles, widening streets, and erecting ornamental gates out of the Town Stock, subscribing £400 towards a turnpike road on condition that the gates were placed some distance away from the town,[5] scrutinising the indentures of apprenticeship to prevent the multiplication of Freemen,[6] maintaining the

---

[1] MS. Book of Orders, Corporation of Alnwick, 24th June 1698.
[2] *Ibid.* 3rd May 1711.
[3] *History of . . . Alnwick*, by G. Tate, 1868-1869, vol. ii. 276.
[4] *Ibid.* vol. ii. p. 272.
[5] MS. Book of Orders, Corporation of Alnwick, 23rd and 28th August 1752.
[6] It was found that youths living in the country were being nominally

Freemen's monopoly of carrying on trade, protecting the humbler members of the Trade Companies from oppression by the "Great Brethren,"[1] administering the common school, wrangling with the Four-and-Twenty, or Select Vestry, of the Parish as to the choice of a clergyman, and successfully insisting, by threatening to withdraw the stipend, upon the appointment of an Englishman and no Scot;[2] supporting, by fair means or foul, their own candidates for the representation of the County;[3] expelling members of their own body for misbehaviour, and disfranchising Freemen who dared to dispute their will.[4]   But this autocracy was tempered throughout by a good-natured sympathy with popular amusements. "Jolly men," it was said, "were the authorities of the town in these days, and diligent in seizing on public events as occasions for indulgence in drinking, feasting, and uproarious enjoyment; . . . they had one unvarying creed : whoever was king, and whatever occurred, they must be jolly. Though modest in amount at first, these indulgences reached a pitch of extravagance towards the middle of the eighteenth century."[5]

Horse-racing, bull-baiting,[6] the music of the Town Waits,

apprenticed to Freemen, in order to gain admission ; and it was ordered "that forever hereafter no man shall take an apprentice unless the said apprentice serve his master in his own house in the Town for five years" (MS. Book of Orders, Corporation of Alnwick, 25th April 1695 ; see also Orders of 22nd February and 25th April 1698, 21st November 1699, and 25th April 1705).

[1] "Whereas there hath a great difference happened between the Free Tailors of this Borough and the Great Brethren of that trade, for the determining of which, according to the ancient custom of this town, the Free Tailors have appealed to the Chamberlains and Four-and-Twenty, who upon a full hearing of the Free Tailors and the Great Brethren, . . . ordered . . . that the box, orders, and other writings belonging to the said Company of Tailors be forthwith delivered to the Free Tailors, and shall from henceforth be ever kept by the Freemen and their successors" (ibid. 2nd October 1691).

[2] Ibid. 12th September 1660, 29th September 1697, and 8th August 1722. It adds to the difficulty of understanding the government of Alnwick, that there was from at any rate 1693, and probably for a century earlier, a "Four-and-Twenty of the Parish," which we have described as a Select Vestry (The Parish and the County, 1906, pp. 179-181), quite distinct from the Four-and-Twenty of the Borough ; and that it was nevertheless the latter body which provided the salary of the clergyman, and chose both him and the Parish Clerk and Sexton.

[3] MS. Book of Orders, Corporation of Alnwick, 4th February 1748 ; History of . . . Alnwick, by G. Tate, vol. i. p. 474.

[4] MS. Book of Orders, Corporation of Alnwick, 18th June 1700.

[5] History of . . . Alnwick, by G. Tate, vol. i. p. 321.

[6] The Alnwick bull-baiting was renowned. "When a bull was baited, the Market Place was crowded with spectators—thousands were sometimes there ; and such exhibitions were not infrequent ; towards the close of last century as

who were perpetually parading the Borough in yellow plush breeches, blue coats, and gold lace, and above all, the annual carnival on St. Mark's Day, when the boundaries were ridden, and the curious ceremony of the admission of young Freemen by their "leaping the well"[1] was performed, were all provided for the entertainment of the inhabitants at the expense of the Borough funds. If the Chamberlains and the other "Gentlemen of the Four-and-Twenty" brightened their wits at the tavern almost every Thursday at the public expense,[2] they were certainly not niggardly in their provision of popular amusements. And they were, at any rate, stalwart guardians of the independence of the Borough and the rights of the Freemen, perpetually stretching these to the utmost possible point.

But an evil day was at hand for the independence of the Borough of Alnwick. In 1749 Sir Hugh Smithson,

many as seven bulls were baited in the course of one winter. . . . The rope by which the bull was fastened to the ring was tied around the root of the horns, and was about fifteen feet long, and dog after dog was let loose upon him and endeavoured to tear his flesh, till, maddened with rage, he sought to gore his aggressor or toss him into the air. Sporting men then kept and trained bull-dogs and gloried in their achievements, and the masters were careful and watchful of them while engaged in the fight ; and if any was likely to fall exhausted before the power of the bull, the master would rush forward, and drag the dog away all foaming at the mouth, and covered with sweat and blood, and plunge him into the cool water of St. Michael's Trough ; and then, refreshed it may be with the bath, back he would be brought to try again his prowess with the bull. Sport this may have been to vitiated tastes ; but cruel sport it was—to the bull, and to many of the dogs it was death. On October 25th, 1773, a bull was baited in Alnwick, and treated with such brutal wantonness that he lay down and expired. On November 11th, 1783, another was so baited, that enraged he threw down two tradesmen, one of whom had his leg broken, and the other received a severe wound in the head. One bull broke loose and galloped wildly through the streets, tossing dogs lifeless into the air, and trampling down those blocking his way. . . . I recollect the two last bull-baitings in Alnwick. Though a miserable, it was an exciting scene ; the market was crowded with women as well as men ; they were clustered in the windows, on the cross, on the Town Hall stairs, and on the Shambles. I still seem to hear the loud bellowings of the bull, the deep barkings of the dogs, the shoutings of the men, mingled with the shrieking of the women, as the crowd swayed to and fro with the changing fortunes of the fight" (*History of . . . Alnwick*, by G. Tate, 1866-1869, vol. i. p. 432).

[1] For contemporary notices of this somewhat ridiculous ceremony, which was made the occasion for a popular festival, see Report of Historical Manuscripts Commission on the Portland MSS., vol. vi. p. 108 ; *Gentleman's Magazine*, February 1756, vol. xxvi. p. 73 ; *Journal of John Wesley*, 25th May 1752 ; *Observations on Popular Antiquities*, by John Brand, vol. i. p. 240 of 1841 edition ; *The Provincial Souvenir*, by W. W. Fyfe, 1845 ; and *History of . . . Alnwick*, by G. Tate, 1866-1869, vol. ii. pp. 241, 251.

[2] Thirty meetings are expressly mentioned in 1771, with tavern expenses (*ibid.* vol. ii. p. 266).

inheriting through his marriage the north-country estates of
the Percies, and becoming Earl (and presently Duke) of
Northumberland, fixed on Alnwick Castle as his residence.
Combining the business habits of a successful London doctor
with an overweening sense of the importance of the Percies,
he started to define and enforce his powers as Lord of the
Manor. We need not enter into the intricacies of the nine
years' litigation that followed, when semi-mythical Charters
were invoked against casual inquisitions by County Juries;
ancient customs pleaded in opposition to feudal rights, and
the arbitrary usurpations of one of the parties balanced
against the mean encroachments of the other.[1] But the
Four-and-Twenty, with their scanty store of Town's Stock,
were no match for the great nobleman's unlimited resources
in money and patronage. As might have been expected, he
soon found agents, even among the Four-and-Twenty, for
securing his will. A compromise became inevitable, and
"Articles of Agreement" were made in 1762 between the
Lord on the one hand and the Common Council on the other.
It is characteristic of the eighteenth century that both the
Municipal Constitution of the Borough and the property rights
of the Freemen were settled by these Articles for more than
a century, without any decision either of the Legislature or
of the judicial tribunals on the subject. Broadly speaking,
the then existing Constitution was confirmed.[2] The close
body of the Four-and-Twenty was to continue to govern the
Borough without the intervention of the Freemen. In
return, the Four-and-Twenty had to admit that the Earl of
Northumberland was, in the fullest sense, Lord of the Borough
and Manor. His Bailiff, though not necessarily one of the
Four-and-Twenty, was to be the titular head of the Borough.
The soil and the "royalties" of the whole Borough, and of
the Forest of Aydon, which the Burgesses called the Town
Moor, were acknowledged to be vested in the Earl, the rights
of the Freemen over the Moor being definitely limited to
certain specified uses. It followed that no part of this

---

[1] *History of . . . Alnwick*, by G. Tate, 1866-1869, vol. ii. pp. 288-293.

[2] The principal constitutional alteration was that, instead of four only, eight
persons were annually to be presented for Chamberlains, of whom the Steward
chose four.

extensive area could thenceforth be enclosed or improved without his consent.

What remains of the history of the Borough of Alnwick is not exhilarating reading. For a few more decades the " Gentlemen of the Four-and-Twenty " persist in their attempt to develop the Municipal revenue, but they find themselves perpetually thwarted in any proposals of inclosure by the Lord's insistence on the lion's share of the advantage to be gained. Meanwhile, partly, it is said, at the instigation of the Lord's agents,[1] the Freemen once more strove to recover their control over the Borough affairs. From 1780 onwards we see the Four-and-Twenty repeatedly assailed by the discontented townsfolk.[2] For the last quarter of the eighteenth and first two decades of the nineteenth centuries, there raged in the little town a war of pamphlets and excited controversy for and against the autocratic rule of the Four-and-Twenty. This eventually led to years of tumult and litigation, from which the Close Body in 1819 emerged triumphant.[3] But in the contest its spirit had been broken; and though it triumphed over the Freemen (whose ancient monopoly of trade had gradually become unenforceable and disused), it found itself definitely in a position of subserviency to the Lord of Alnwick. From this time forward, far from claiming to be the government of the Borough, the members of the Common Council welcomed every occasion of abandoning

---

[1] "About three years ago," it was said in 1781, "several of the Freemen were sent for in a private manner at different times by some agents of the Duke to a certain public-house, and their minds were poisoned with artful insinuations, and alarmed with apprehensions as to their rights and privileges " (*Seven Letters to the Freemen of Alnwick*, by an Old Craftsman, 1782, Letter III.). This able pamphlet was written by the Clerk of the Corporation, and paid for by it (*History of . . . Alnwick*, by G. Tate, vol. ii. p. 299).

[2] Apart from accusations of secrecy and irresponsibility, with some occasional extravagance, we gather that the differences between the Four-and-Twenty and the rank and file of the Freemen turned on the policy to be pursued with the Town Moor. The Four-and-Twenty wished to effect permanent improvements, even at the cost of some immediate sacrifice of income, and to spend a part of the income on public objects needed by the Borough as a whole. The rank and file of Freemen resented anything that curtailed the present use of the Moor by themselves, and they objected to any expenditure, whether on the improvement of their property for the future or on objects of public utility, which diminished the sum to be divided in the current year. We shall describe subsequently the calamitous results of a similar attitude of the Freemen of Berwick-on-Tweed (see Chap. IX.).

[3] *History of . . . Alnwick*, by G. Tate, vol. ii. pp. 296-305.

public obligation and public authority. In 1822, with the help of their patron, they got passed a Local Act, throwing upon the rates various services formerly paid for out of the Town's Stock, and incidentally establishing a body of Street Commissioners,[1] which became the effective governing authority of the Borough. When in 1833 the Municipal Corporation Commissioners came to Alnwick, the Four-and-Twenty and their officers loudly protested that they were not a Municipal Corporation at all. With their enthusiastic approval the Duke of Northumberland managed, in spite of the fact that Alnwick was now a crowded town of nearly 7000 inhabitants, to get it struck out of the schedule of Boroughs to which the Municipal Corporations Act applied.[2] The statutory body of Street Commissioners accordingly went on ruling the town, and levying rates for services once performed by the ancient Corporation.[3] In 1854, after fourteen years' renewed agitation, the long dispute with the Duke as to his rights in the Town Moor was brought to an end by an Inclosure award, which conceded to him, in compensation for his purely honorific rights as Lord, no less than 237 acres as his own unincumbered freehold, and vested the remainder, discharged from any pasturage rights, in trust for the Freemen and their widows.[4] The final stage in the century-long process of disfranchisement of the ancient Corporation of Alnwick was reached in a Parliamentary committee room in 1882. Here the ignorance of the Legislature and the indifference of the Government Departments concerned, permitted, in direct contradiction of the recommendation of the Municipal Corporation Commission of 1876-1880, the passage into law of a Bill[5] which converted the Corporation into nothing but the trustee

---

[1] 3 George IV. c. 27 (Alnwick Paving Act, 1822). The population had grown in 1821 to 5927.

[2] *History of . . . Alnwick*, by G. Tate, vol. ii. pp. 305-307.

[3] This body of Street Commissioners was eventually merged in an Urban District Council, established as a Local Board in 1850 under the Public Health Acts. The Municipal Corporation Commission of 1876-1880 recommended the incorporation of Alnwick as an ordinary Municipal Borough, but this course has not been adopted. On the contrary, the Municipal Corporations Act, 1883 (46 and 47 Vict. c. 18, sec. 19), expressly exempted it.

[4] Award of 27th February 1854, confirmed by the Inclosure Commissioners, 2nd March 1854 ; for the preceding agitation, see *History of . . . Alnwick*, by G. Tate, vol. ii. pp. 307-315.

[5] 45 and 46 Vict. c. 23 (Alnwick Corporation Act, 1882).

of a group of property owners, and finally transformed what
had once been the Corporate inheritance of the town into
the private freehold, subject only to devoting £500 a year
to keep up the Freemen's School, of the existing Freemen,
with their widows and descendants.[1]

[1] The County of Northumberland had a number of other towns which
claimed to be "Boroughs by prescription," and may at one time have possessed
some of the characteristics of Manorial Boroughs. The principal were Hexham,
Haltwhistle, Mitford, Corbridge, Alnmouth, Bamburgh, and Warkworth, some
of which had had old Seignorial Charters. Practically no remnant of Municipal
structure remained in 1689 in any of them, except Hexham, which still had its
four Craft Gilds or Trade Companies, each electing annually its Alderman and
other officers, like those of Alnwick and Morpeth. The Borough was divided
into four Wards, from each of which six members were taken to form a "Four-and-
Twenty"—remarkably like the Fellowships of Braintree and Lewes respectively
—which greatly declined towards the close of the seventeenth century, up to
which time it had been levying rates, and (in conjunction with the Bailiff,
Constables, the Companies, and the Lord's Court) governing the Borough. The
Bailiff, the former Seneschal of the Archbishop for the Palatine Liberty of
Hexhamshire, was appointed by the Lord for life, and continued during the
eighteenth century to be the principal authority in the Borough. At the Hierarchy of Courts which he held for the Manor of the whole Liberty, and especially
at the Court for the Borough of Hexham, a whole array of officers were appointed, usually one for each of the four Wards, including Constables, Market-
keepers, Appraisers and Sealers, Ale-tasters, Surveyors of Highways, Pounders,
Townherds, Waits, and Scavengers. The Steward held twice a year a Court of
Record, styling itself Court of Pleas, claiming power to try all civil actions
without limit, which is mentioned in the House of Commons Returns of Courts
of Law of 1828 and 1840. There was also a "Side Court," or Court Baron,
held before the Bailiff quarterly, or oftener if required, for petty debt cases.
But the Courts and Companies of Hexham rapidly faded into insignificance
during the eighteenth century, until there was little more than the survival of
ancient titles to distinguish it from a mere parochial and Manorial administration. It was not inquired into by the Municipal Corporation Commissions of
1835 or 1880, any more than the other extinct Northumbrian Boroughs, and to
this day it has no more than an Urban District Council (*An Essay towards a
History of Hexham*, by A. B. Wright, 1823 ; *Historical . . . View of Northumberland*, by E. Mackenzie, 1825, vol. ii. pp. 267-284 ; *Northumberland County History*, vol. iii., 1896, by A. B. Hinds, pp. 20-104, 254-295).

In the ancient City of Durham we have a Manorial Borough exhibiting some
of the peculiarities of Alnwick. We have the same curious intermingling of
Manor and Gild, the same independent existence of Craft Gilds or Trade Companies, and the same practical supersession of seignorial authority by a popular
body. But at Durham the evolution had been registered by successive Charters
of the Bishop, whose power as Lord of the Manor was merged in his authority
as Palatine Lord, which enabled him to create recognised Municipal Corporations. The last of these Charters established in 1780 a Council of twelve Aldermen and twenty-four Common Councillors, annually electing one of the Aldermen
to be Mayor for the year. The Aldermen served for life, vacancies being filled
by the Council as a whole. The Common Councillors, on the other hand, were
to be chosen annually by the Mayor and Aldermen from among the twelve Companies, two from each. The Companies had their own several administrations,
annually electing officers to enforce the By-laws, which were in 1728 formally
revised and re-enacted by the Corporation as a whole. None were permitted to

(g) Arrested Development and Decay

To present any accurate summary of this long series of pseudo-municipal authorities is no easy task. We find them, as has been shown, all over England; from Northumberland

trade unless free of one or other of these Companies. Those entitled to become Freemen had to be proposed at three successive quarterly Courts of the Corporation, and to be approved by the Mayor, Aldermen, and Councillors. All this rigidity and exclusiveness, upheld in the Court of King's Bench in 1756 (Green v. Mayor, etc., of Durham, *Reports of Cases, etc.*, by Sir J. Burrow, vol. i. p. 127), broke down in 1761 under the temptation to create new Parliamentary electors ; when we gather that all trade restrictions ceased to be enforced. The Bishop had even ceded to the Corporation in 1602 his right to hold the Manorial Courts in that part of the Borough which was in his own Manor ; and what was called the Court Leet, View of Frankpledge, and Court Baron of the Borough, was regularly held at the Gildhall twice a year, when all the Burgesses had to answer to their names, some minor Manorial business was formally transacted, and petty debt cases were tried—the Town-Clerk, and not any Manorial officer, issuing the summonses and taking the fees. The administration of the market and the revenue from tolls had equally passed into the hands of the Borough authorities. The Bishop even included the Mayor for the year, together with the Mayors of his other Manorial Boroughs of Stockton and Hartlepool, in the Commission of the Peace for the County, and appointed him one of the Judges of the Court of Pleas.

Local Acts had been obtained in 1790 (30 George III. c. 67) and 1822 (3 George IV. c. 26) establishing a body of Street Commissioners, of which the Mayor, Aldermen, and Councillors were members *ex officio.*

We were informed that no minutes or other records of the Corporation exist of a date prior to 1835, or indeed prior to the present generation. See the First Report of Municipal Corporation Commission, 1835, Appendix, vol. iii. pp. 1511-1512 ; *History and Antiquities of Durham*, by W. Hutchinson, 1787, vol. ii. pp. 13-36 ; *General View of the Agriculture of Durham*, by J. Granger, 1794, p. 9 ; *Historical and Descriptive View of the City of Durham*, 1824, pp. 63-80 ; *Historical . . . View of Durham*, by E. Mackenzie and M. Ross, 1834, vol. ii. pp. 419-427 ; *History of Durham*, by R. Surtees, vol. iv. 1840, pp. 72-78 ; *Extracts from the Halmote Court of the Prior of Durham*, 1296-1384 (Surtees Society, vol. lxxxii., 1889) ; *Memorials of St. Giles, Durham* (*ibid.* vol. xcv., 1896) ; *The County Palatine of Durham*, by G. T. Lapsley, 1900 ; *Victoria County History of Durham*, by the same, vol. i., 1905, pp. 306-309.

The Bishop of Durham, as Lord Palatine, created other Boroughs, such as Barnard Castle, Darlington, Gateshead, Hartlepool, Northallerton (in Yorkshire), Stockton, and Sunderland, which seem to have had the characteristics of what we term Manorial Boroughs, none of them having their own Corporate Magistracy, and all of them being connected in some way with the Lord's Court. In Barnard Castle, Darlington, and Northallerton, practically no remnant of Municipal organisation survived to 1689, the government during the eighteenth century being purely Manorial and parochial. Darlington was made a Municipal Corporation in 1867 ; the other two have still only Urban District Councils. In Sunderland a new Charter of 1634 was allowed to lapse, and though the "Capital Burgesses" and "Stallingers" continued to exist, and to maintain rights of common on the Town Moor (Hicks v. Clark, 1722, in *Reports of Cases, etc.*, by Sir C. Levinz, vol. ii. p. 252), the government of the Borough was carried on by the Lord's Court, with its Bailiff, and (from 1717) by the Harbour Com-to Cornwall, from Lancashire to Kent; on the borders of Wales, amid the fens of the Eastern counties, and in the heart of the Midlands. In respect of their number and of the area of their jurisdiction, these Manorial Boroughs stand, as a class, midway between the thousands of active Lords' Courts and the

missioners under a series of Local Acts. In Gateshead, where there were even separately incorporated Craft Gilds or Trade Companies chartered between 1557 and 1671, analogous to those of Durham, the Borough organisation had been crushed by the jealousy of Newcastle-on-Tyne, to which it was actually annexed in 1553 by the short-lived statute 7 Edward VI. No. 10. When this was repealed the Bishop leased the Manor and its Courts, the Borough Tolls, and the valuable "Salt meadows," in such a way that these all fell into the hands of the Corporation of Newcastle. The last Bailiff was appointed in 1681. Between 1626 and 1740 there were four "Wainmen" appointed to collect a small toll on loaded waggons, but this was resisted in 1740 and abandoned. Nothing remained to the Burgesses or burgage owners of Gateshead but their rights of common, the only local officers being the two Stewards and the four Grassmen whom, from 1695 onwards, they annually appointed in public meeting; the Reeve and Hayward of the purely Manorial Halmote Court held by the lessee of the Manor; and the parochial officers appointed by the Close Vestry of the Four-and-Twenty that we have already described. Hartlepool and Stockton were more fortunate in having "Mayors" whom the Bishop could include in the Commission of the Peace for the County, and appoint to be Judges in his Court of Pleas. At Stockton, indeed, the Burgesses or burgage owners elected the Mayor annually, though this had to be done at the Bishop's Court Leet; and the Steward of the Bishop acted as Recorder, and sat with the Mayor at the other Manorial Courts of the year. Ex-mayors were styled Aldermen, but seem to have had no powers or duties. There was a Town's Serjeant, who was appointed Constable, and walked in procession before the Mayor "in a large wrapping cloak trimmed with lace." Stockton, Sunderland, and Gateshead were accepted as Municipal Corporations in 1835, and made such and duly reformed by the Act of that year. Hartlepool was not so accepted, and was only incorporated in 1851. See *History and Antiquities of Durham*, by W. Hutchinson, 1794; *History of Durham*, by R. Surtees, 1816-1840; *Historical . . . View of Durham*, by E. Mackenzie and M. Ross, 1834; *History and Antiquities of Durham*, by W. Fordyce, 1857; First Report of Municipal Corporation Commission, 1835; *Antiquities of Gainford . . . comprising the . . . history of . . . Barnard Castle*, by J. R. Walbran, 1846; *History and Antiquities of the Parish of Darlington*, by W. H. D. Longstaffe, 1854; paper by the same on "The Trade Companies of Gateshead" in *Gentleman's Magazine*, vol. xiii. 1862; *Memorials of the Life of Mr. Ambrose Barnes* (Surtees Society, 1866); *History of Hartlepool*, by Sir Cuthbert Sharp, 1851; *History and Antiquities of Northallerton*, by C. J. D. Ingledew, 1858; *History of Northallerton*, by J. L. Saywell, 1885; *Parochial History and Antiquities of Stockton-on-Tees*, by J. Drewster, 1796 and 1829; *Historical View of Monkwearmouth . . . and . . . Sunderland*, by George Garbutt, 1819; *History of Sunderland*, by J. Burnett, 1830; *History and Antiquities of Sunderland*, by J. W. Summers, 1858; *Sunderland*, by T. Potts, 1892.

Sheffield—already in 1689 a town of several thousands of people, and destined to reach, by 1835, a population of nearly 80,000—presents us with a remarkable example of unco-ordinated local jurisdictions. This Manorial Borough had a very early Seignorial Charter analogous to those of Manchester and Stockport; yet it resembles Beccles in getting also a Royal Charter in Elizabethan times; Wisbech in its government by the Freeholders; Tetbury in its connection with

couple of hundred of Municipal Corporations, in the Cities and Boroughs that were entitled to create their own Justices of the Peace. In diversity and complexity of constitution these Manorial Boroughs occupy a similar intermediate position. What is remarkable is the almost fantastically minute gradua-

trust property, and Alnwick both in its relations with the Lord of the Manor and in the interpolation of a Gild. At Sheffield, however, all the various jurisdictions remained distinct. In 1297 the Lord Furnival conceded by Charter to his "free tenants" of Sheffield, that they should hold in fee farm, on payment of a small annual sum, all the lands they had hitherto held of him upon other obligations. Whether from this origin or from older date, we find various pieces of land in the town owned and administered by what was called the "Common Burgery" of Sheffield, meaning, apparently, public meetings of Freeholders or "Burgesses" electing a "Town Collector." A Royal Charter of 1554 established a second body, the "Twelve Capital Burgesses and Commonalty of the Town and Parish of Sheffield," a close council of twelve, renewing itself by co-option, to administer certain property which had been forfeited under Edward VI. as being for superstitious uses, and which was then restored. The Capital Burgesses and the Common Burgery, though distinct in their origin, their membership, their property, and the purposes to which this was devoted, were apparently long closely connected. They even used the same seal. The Capital Burgesses were in effect, we are told, a self-elect "Court of Aldermen." They remained, however, a distinct Corporation, and came more and more to regard themselves as an ecclesiastical body, having as their primary duty the repair of the parish church and the provision of stipends for three clergymen. Accordingly they were eventually often styled the "Church Burgesses." But they always devoted part of their income to relieving the poor and repairing bridges and highways. There was a third Corporate body, the Cutlers' Company, under Act of Parliament of 1624, empowered not only to make regulations for the trade of cutlery, but to enforce such regulations over the whole of Hallamshire. Meanwhile the Duke of Norfolk, as Lord of the Manor, continued not only to administer the market and to take the other profits of the Manor, but also to hold both a six-monthly "Court Leet, Grand Court Baron, and Court of the Honour or Assembly Inquest,"—called briefly the "Sembly Court" —and regular Three Weeks' Courts for petty debt cases. "Upon every Sembly Tuesday," we read in 1637, "is assembled upon Sembly Green, where the Court is kept, . . . at least 139 horsemen with horse and harness provided by the . . . tenants to appear before the Lord of the Manor." The Common Burgery, as the Freeholders of the Manor, and the Homage, retained, notwithstanding their separate organisation, also a close connection with the Lords' Courts. Their accounts, from 1567 onwards, show that they paid for the dinner and the writing out of the lengthy presentments of the "Jury of the Sembly Quest," which was probably (as at Alnwick), composed exclusively of their members. The Jury appointed two Constables, two Searchers of Flesh, Fish, Bread, and Ale, two officers to compel all butter and eggs to be sold only in the market, two others to do the same for corn, six Overseers for mending Highways, four Searchers and Sealers of Leather, three officers to protect the town wells from pollution, two persons to see that swine were ringed, and four more to collect the Swineherd's wages. The Jury also made By-laws and dealt with nuisances. During the seventeenth century (as at Tetbury), Commissioners inquired into the administration of the trust property, and a decree was made in 1681 vesting the property of the Common Burgery in thirteen persons, vacancies among whom were (unlike Tetbury) to be filled by election of the "inhabitants," by which (as was eventually settled in 1817) was to be under-

tion of the steps by which the different members of the series pass one into another. There is, as Miss Bateson pointed out, "every gradation from a subjection only very slightly modified by privilege to a complete system of burghal self-government."[1] If a single highly evolved organisation had, at all the various stages of its development from the Lord's Court of a rural Manor right up to the most fully developed Municipal Corporation, been successively photographed for the information of future generations, these different pictures could hardly have represented the several stages more strikingly than do the hundreds of distinct local authorities simultaneously existing in the eighteenth century. We seem to see crystallised before us at various stages organisms that were proceeding along two converging lines of development. As compared with the subordination to the Lord and his officers, which is the mark of the Lord's Court, both series

stood freeholders. In the eighteenth century one of these "Town Trustees" was called "Town Regent" or "Town Collector," and the others were known as Assistants. Occasional "Town's Meetings" of Freeholders were held to choose a Collector, to elect new Assistants to fill vacancies, to appoint a Town Clerk (in 1707), and, now and again, to pass some resolution as to the property. These meetings seem to have been attended only by between ten and a hundred persons. There was a Beadle; there were Town Waits; there were presently Town Scavengers.

Exactly how the functions of government were divided among these four distinct authorities (in addition to the Parish Vestry and its Poor Law and Highway Officers) varied from generation to generation. What is remarkable is that they all remained in full and separate activity right down to 1835, and, it may almost be said, down to the present day. A Local Act in 1818 established a fifth authority, a body of Street Commissioners, and relieved the Burgery of its obligations in cleaning, lighting, and watching the streets. Another Local Act of 1827 regulated the procedure of the Burgery, and compelled publication of its accounts. A Charter established, as a sixth authority, an ordinary Municipal Corporation in 1843, which presently absorbed the Street Commissioners, but left all the other jurisdictions unimpaired. For Sheffield, we have not seen the MS. records, which have been fully extracted in *Records of the Burgery of Sheffield*, by J. D. Leader, 1897; see also Add. MSS. 27,538 in British Museum, as to the negotiations with the Lord of the Manor, 1719-1727; *Hallamshire*, by J. Hunter, 1st edition, 1819, 2nd edition, 1869; *New and Complete History of the County of York*, by T. Allen, 1828-1831, vol. iii.; *The Picture of Sheffield*, 1824; various papers in *Associated Architectural Societies' Reports and Papers*, vols. xii. and xiii., 1874-1876; *Yorkshire Past and Present*, by T. Baines, vol. ii., 1877; *Extracts from the Earliest Book of Accounts belonging to the Town Trustees of Sheffield*, by J. D. Leader, 1879; *Chapters in the History of Sheffield*, 1832-1849, by J. Parker, 1884; *Characteristics of some Inhabitants of Sheffield at the close of the Eighteenth Century*, by W. Smith, 1889; *Old Sheffield Jottings*, by J. D. Leader, 1891; *The House of Waltheof*, by S. O. Addy, 1893; *Sheffield in the Eighteenth Century*, by R. E. Leader, 1901.

[1] *Mediæval England*, by Mary Bateson, 1903, p. 395.

exhibit an ever-growing autonomy. Both series exhibit also a steady increase in extra-manorial or pseudo-municipal structure, especially in the form of a standing administrative organisation existing between the meetings of the Courts. In one set of cases autonomy seems to precede the growth of structure; in the other set of cases, the growth of new structure antedates any kind of autonomy. Thus, at Chipping Sodbury we see the beginning of a partial autonomy in the right conceded to the Jury of the Lord's Court to present three persons for the appointment of one of them by the Steward to be head of the town, with the correlative right of this head, whether called Bailiff, Portreeve, or Mayor, to select the Jury for the following year. Even Birmingham in 1800, for all its importance and magnitude, is constitutionally to be distinguished from a Lord's Court only by the fact that, somehow or another, the Bailiffs had come to choose the Jury and the Jury to elect the Bailiffs, independently of the will of the Lord or his Steward.[1] At Gosport and Clun, where exactly the same arrangement prevailed within the Lord's Court, the Bailiffs held also a separate Court for the settlement of civil actions among the inhabitants. At Alresford this separate Court had been expressly granted by Seignorial Charter, along with the Fairs and Markets, the Court of Pie Powder, and a great deal of Leet jurisdiction, though the Lord still held his View of Frankpledge or Lawday. Finally, at Tetbury, where the sixteenth-century constitution was almost identical with that of Birmingham in 1800, we may actually watch the development in the course of the seventeenth century of a bicameral Close Body, strangely similar to that of many Municipal Corporations, entirely replacing the Lord of the Manor, and concentrating in itself the whole of the Manorial powers. We may trace a similar growth of autonomy, leading to a development of new structure,

[1] We may see something like local autonomy conceded even with regard to the appointment, not only of the Bailiff, but even of the Steward of the Court. In the Privy Council in 1676, "a report from Attorney General, about appointing a Steward to hold a Leet on Whitmonday yearly at Kingsborough, within the Isle of Sheppey, as also a certificate under the hands of the most substantial inhabitants, principal land occupiers, and ancient jurymen of the Court called Kingsborough . . . representing P. T., gentleman, as a fit person to be Steward of the said Court, was read. Ordered that the Chancellor of the Exchequer determine as to the fitness of P. T., and pass a grant under the seal of the Exchequer under such small rent as he shall think fit" (MS. Acts of Privy Council, 17th May 1676).

in a series of cases in which the Lord of the Manor had either been non-existent, or had let his powers fall into abeyance. From such mere village communities as Berwick in Sussex, and Aston and Cote in Oxfordshire, we ascend by examples like Newbiggin-by-the-Sea, to such Chartered autonomous townships as Beccles and Wisbech, the powers of which are indistinguishable from those of a Municipal Corporation except for their inability to create their own Justices of the Peace. On the other hand, a different series begins with Holy Island, with its standing "Four-and-Twenty," existing by virtue of tenure, and yet in attendance as a Jury at the Lord's Court. We might adduce scores of interesting variations dependent upon the ownership of certain ancient burgage tenements, developing into self-renewing "Common Councils," with more or less connection with the Jury of the Lord's Court, and more or less the creatures of the Lord's Steward.[1] More interesting is it to trace the series through Lewes, with its "Company of the Twelve" of unknown origin; and Arundel, with its "Fellowship" gradually taking on all the paraphernalia of Municipal pomp, but still revolving round the Lord's Court; up to Christchurch, where the connection with the Lord of the Manor had by 1689 become shadowy; and Lymington, electing its own member of Parliament, and virtually identical with the common type of Municipal Corporation, but for the lack of Corporate Justices. Elsewhere we may see the new structure beginning, not with any development of the Homage Jury, but with a glorification of the Reeve and Headboroughs into a Mayor and Aldermen,[2] at first combined, as at Wotton and Berkeley, or as at Altrincham, with complete subordination to the Lord. This may be carried a stage farther, with growing autonomy, in instances such as Chipping Campden and Stockport. Finally, in Godmanchester and Blandford Forum, with Royal Charters, we have this type of Manorial Borough attaining complete emancipation from any Lord, and wielding all the Manorial powers, but not those of Justices of the Peace. In one

---

[1] Thus at Clitheroe, in Lancashire, it is the two Bailiffs and "the Inquiry Jury" which acts as a permanent Common Council; vacancies on the "Inquiry Jury" being filled by co-option from among the "Freemen," that is, those occupiers of "Free Borough Houses" who have been duly "presented" as Freemen by the "Inquiry Jury" in the Borough Court (First Report of Municipal Corporation Commission, 1835, vol. iii. p. 1485; and *supra*, pp. 48, 156).   [2] Or elsewhere Portreeve or Bailiffs.

small group of Manorial Boroughs, concentrated in Northumberland and Durham, we may even see this progressive autonomy and growth of extra-manorial structure associated with a constitutional development peculiarly typical of the most advanced of the Municipal Corporations, namely, a body of Freemen, recruited by apprenticeship to Freemen, and organised in Gilds or Trade Companies for the regulation of their several crafts.[1] It is a curious paradox, significant of the way in which the Manorial Borough runs into the Municipal Corporation, that one town, Morpeth, merely because it happens to have assumed the power of creating its own Corporate Justices, has to be omitted altogether from the class of Manorial Boroughs; though it was even more dependent on its Lord than Alnwick, and was, in fact, the Borough in which the special peculiarities of the Northumberland and Durham group of towns were most markedly developed. And throughout the Principality of Wales the combination of subordination to the Lord, with rudimentary Gild structure and the power to create Corporate Justices of the Peace, is so frequent, that we have found it impracticable to draw any line at all between the different Boroughs, which we leave to be described together in a separate chapter.[2]

It is interesting to note that, if we may assume the Manorial Borough to have arisen out of the Lord's Court, it is the Court Baron side, not the Court Leet, which, at any rate in the great majority of instances, furnished the opportunity and the means of pseudo-municipal development.[3]

[1] Apart from the Northumberland and Durham towns, we may almost say that apprenticeship, as a method of admission to Borough or Corporation privileges, is unknown in the Manorial Boroughs. The burgess-ship or "freeledge" is usually connected with an estate in land; sometimes, as at Clitheroe and Godmanchester, in certain ancient tenements; sometimes, as at Stockport and Wisbech, in any freehold. Very occasionally, as at Alresford and Tetbury, it is the whole body of inhabitant householders who are regarded as Burgesses, but in these cases the governing authority is always a close body, renewing itself by co-option. Only in two or three cases (outside Northumberland and Durham) do we find, in a Manorial Borough, any mention of apprenticeship in connection with civic rights, and then only (as at Chipping Campden and Berkeley) in the form of apprenticeship to any inhabitant householder of the Borough, which may be regarded as no more than a method of "gaining a Settlement" under the Poor Law, entitling the apprentice eventually only to the rights of a settled inhabitant.

[2] See pp. 232-260, Chap. V. "The Boroughs of Wales."

[3] The incident in this connection puzzled a learned lawyer well versed in the practice of the Lord's Court. "How the Mayor of a Corporation comes to

This applies both to the function of hearing pleas of debt and to that of managing the common interests in the land. In many cases, as at Clun, Gosport, and Arundel, we find the Manorial Borough holding a "Three Weeks' Court," or other tribunal for the settlement of disputes, whilst the Lord continues to hold his own Court Leet and View of Frankpledge. At Alresford we actually see the Lord granting to his "Free Borough" the privilege of holding the Court Baron, whilst retaining for himself the View of Frankpledge or Lawday. At Christchurch and Wisbech there is evidence that the nascent Manorial Borough found it desirable to take to itself the power of settling disputes among the inhabitants, even without definite authority, by establishing a voluntary arbitration tribunal. Elsewhere, as at Chipping Campden, the Manorial Borough would get a similar jurisdiction conferred upon it by Royal Charter, under the name of a Court of Record, whilst leaving unimpaired the Lord's Court Leet. It is only in a few cases, such as Tetbury, Clitheroe, and Godmanchester, that we find the Manorial Borough attaining to the dignity of holding its own Court Leet for the presentment of nuisances and amercement of offenders ; and then only as an incident of the ownership of the Manor itself. And, corresponding with this course of development, we shall see when we come to the Municipal Corporation that it was almost invariable that the Corporate body should possess what we may call Court Baron powers, and hold a civil debt Court, whilst in some instances the Court Leet would still be held by an external Lord of the Manor.

The connection of the Manorial Borough with the Court Baron, rather than with the Court Leet, is still more clearly seen on the property side. Practically all the Manorial Boroughs had commons and wastes to manage, even if few were in the position of Godmanchester, with its commonfield agriculture. It is, in fact, these common rights to landed property that gave substance and strength to the embryo Corporate body. "Not much is involved," says an able

be elected in this Court by the burgage-holders, suitors to the Court Baron, is a paradox which the editor is unable to solve " (*Jurisdiction of the Courts Leet*, by J. Ritson, 3rd edition, 1816, p. 8). The learned Steward of the Savoy could have discovered the explanation in the development of the Manorial Borough from the Lord's Court.

modern historian, "in being a Free Borough. Any little rural township became a Free Borough so soon as its Lord turned the holdings of his serfs into burgages, abolished villein services, and took money rents instead." [1] But to convert this nominal " Free Borough " into a continuously existing Corporate entity, with perpetual succession, what was needed in practice was the guardianship and administration of a common stock. Professor Maitland tells us in fact, that " the evolution of a Borough Corporation is very closely connected with . . . the emergence of a freely disposable revenue which the Burgesses will treat as the income of the town." [2] This common stock might, as at Tetbury, begin in a charitable donation. It might, as at Melton Mowbray and Wisbech, arise in a co-operative purchase by the inhabitants. But in the great bulk of instances the common stock consisted of the proceeds of the rights of user of the commons and wastes, or even the ownership of lands and tenements at a quit rent. " A Corporate personality," observes Professor Maitland, " is hardly required until there is a Corporate income "; and it was the agricultural interests administered by the Homage Jury of the Lord's Court, not the jurisdiction over the conduct of the inhabitants furnished by the Jury of the King, that, as at Beccles, provided the earliest Corporate income. And it was these interests in land that were often destined to increase in value. " A considerable part," in the change from a loose aggregate of joint owners to the evolution of a Borough Fund, says Professor Maitland, was " played by those leases of waste and common land which the community begins to grant in answer to an increasing demand for building sites."

Whether the governing council of a Manorial Borough, where such existed, developed out of the Homage Jury, and the ownership of ancient burgages; or out of a Leet Jury of resiants perpetuating itself into a Common Council, we watch it always tending to become a Close Body, renewing itself by co-option. This was, we can now see, constitutionally inevitable. The ownership of rights of common, or of the ancient

---

[1] *A History of Municipal Government in Liverpool to* 1835, by Professor Ramsay Muir, 1906, p. 15 ; see also *History of English Law*, by Sir F. Pollock and F. W. Maitland, 1895, vol. i. p. 640 ; *Mediæval Manchester and the Beginnings of Lancashire*, by J. Tait, 1904 p. 62.

[2] *Township and Borough*, by F. W. Maitland, 1898, p. 204.

burgage tenements, was concentrated in a definite section of the population, which exhibited no inclination to lessen its possessions by admitting new-comers to participation. On the contrary, we see the descendants of the original co-owners taxing the "foreigner" or "stallinger" by market tolls, fees for opening shops, and wharf dues.[1] Even when the governing authority of a Manorial Borough had little or no common property, and had arisen merely from the absence or indifference of the Lord of the Manor, possibly from the Court Leet of resiants, the fact that (as at Birmingham) this Jury was summoned by the Bailiffs, and the Bailiffs were chosen by the Jury, necessarily created a permanent body into which no outsider could force himself. And except in the little group of Northumberland and Durham Boroughs, the oligarchy which arose out of the Court of the Manor was, in the Manorial Boroughs, not widened by the existence of a class of Freemen. In many of the Municipal Corporations, as we shall see, it was this class of Freemen, into which outsiders were always entering by the humble portal of trade apprenticeship, that established, and in a few cases preserved to the last, a Democracy of craftsmen as the very base of the Corporate structure.

But the Manorial Borough drew from the Court of the Manor also the seeds of decay. Its very separation from the Lord of the Manor lessened its authority. The fact that it

---

[1] In the Manorial Boroughs, at any rate, there is no connection to be traced (outside Northumberland and Durham) between the exceptional taxation of "foreigners" and the maintenance of a monopoly of trading by a Gild or Gilds of merchants or craftsmen. Where "foreigners" were required to pay a fee on opening a shop (as at Berkeley, Gosport, Godmanchester, etc.), or where exceptional tolls were exacted from them in market or on the landing stage, this exaction was, in its intention, fiscal and not prohibitory. It represented either the claim of those who had entered into obligations (as, for instance, to pay a fee farm rent for the Borough) to compel others to contribute, or else (where the Borough owned the land in fee simple or the Manorial rights) merely the assertion of proprietary rights. It was not that the co-owners were not monopolistic; we find them, in fact, not only eager to exclude from their Borough "inmates" or lodgers, and the non-settled poor generally, but also perpetually striving to prohibit the assignment of "stints" to foreigners (as at Arundel), and even the letting of the freeholder's right to ferry passengers for hire (as at Gosport). We find no trace of any particular Craft defending a monopoly. In fact, almost the only trace of Municipal craft regulations in these Boroughs is that at Alresford, in 1570, the Lord expressly granted to his new Borough the power to make orders and regulations amongst artificers, though in whose interest it is not clear.

seldom acquired the Court Leet powers, and the growing insufficiency of these powers even where it possessed them, prevented it from building up the police authority over negligent or turbulent citizens, which the growth of an urban population required. Moreover, the Homage Jury which had made By-laws and levied contributions without question, so long as it coincided approximately with all the principal inhabitants, lost both these powers when it became a Close Body in the midst of a large population excluded from its counsels. These Twelves or Four - and - Twenties, these "Companies" and "Fellowships"—the direct descendants of the Homage Jury—drew their authority to regulate and tax from the ancient principle that a common agreement among a majority of the freehold tenants of the Manor was binding on the whole of them. This authority could hardly be stretched, even by the assumption of the title of Common Council, to cover a regulation and taxation of persons quite unconnected with the Manor. But perhaps the greatest blow to the authority of the Manorial Boroughs as to the Lord's Court was the Inclosure Act, which in so many cases transformed common uses into unrestricted individual ownership, and thus made unnecessary any collective administration of the land. Finally, in the constant aggrandisement by Acts of Parliament of the Justices of the Peace, the Parish Vestry, and the new Statutory Authorities for Special Purposes, the Manorial Borough found itself progressively superseded in its quasi-municipal functions, and tended to revert to the status of a mere Lord's Court.[1] Of this reversion the City and Borough of Westminster offers the most complete instance ;

---

[1] In some cases this reversion had taken place before 1689, and the town accordingly finds mention in our preceding chapter. Thus, if we had been describing Manchester in the fourteenth century, with its Seignorial Charter, granting to the Burgesses the right of electing the Boroughreeve, the privilege of deciding civil suits among themselves, and of holding their own Port-manmote, we must have included this among our Manorial Boroughs. But by the end of the seventeenth century the Manchester Burgesses had for some reason lost their autonomy, and the Manorial Borough had become no more than a highly evolved specimen of a Lord's Court. Thus, Miss Bateson says that "many village groups, Boroughs in little else but name, showed no commercial vitality, and became Manors again both in fact and in name, when villainage had lost its onerous character. Manchester is a case in point" (*Mediæval England*, 1066-1350, by Mary Bateson, 1903, p. 895). It thus affords an interesting analogy to other cases of reversion, such as the so-called City and Borough of Westminster.

one all the more striking, because the Manorial Borough in this case was the seat of the National Legislature and the home of a swarming urban population; because it had been dignified by the higher title of City; and because its pseudo-municipal structure was of comparatively modern growth, and its constitution had been deliberately fortified by the authority of an Act of Parliament.

CHAPTER IV

THE CITY AND BOROUGH OF WESTMINSTER

WE end our survey of Manorial Boroughs by the most anomalous of them all, the so - called " City and Borough of
Westminster." [1]   We shall not inquire how it had come about,
as was subsequently recited, that " the government of the
Borough of Westminster and the Liberty thereof was, by
several grants of princes and by immemorial usage, in the
Abbot and Convent of Westminster, and was in all times
executed by officers by them appointed and in the Courts to
them belonging." [2]   What seems to have existed, in the early
part of the reign of Elizabeth, was a highly developed Manorial
government, of which no actual records have yet been found,

---

[1] The constitutional history of Westminster appears to have been very
inadequately investigated by the numerous authors who have dealt with its
more picturesque features.   Besides the abundant MS. Minutes of the Vestries,
the Paving Commissioners, and the Court of Sewers, elsewhere referred to, the
student will consult those of the Court of Burgesses, which exist (imperfectly)
from 1611.; the " Act for the Good Government of the City and Borough of
Westminster," 27 Elizabeth, c. 17 (1585) ; the Orders and Ordinances made
under it, 1585, 1719, and 1720, reprinted in House of Commons paper, No. 666,
of 27th June 1853 ; the Acts 29 George II. c. 25 (1756), and 31 George II. c. 17
(1758) ; *A Brief Account of the Powers given to and exercised by the Burgess
Court of Westminster, by an Inhabitant* (n.d., about 1720) ; *The Case of the Dean
and Chapter . . . with regard to the Bill for regulating the Nightly Watch,*
1720 ; *A Letter to a Member of Parliament concerning the Bill for regulating the
Nightly Watch,* 1720 ; *Instructions and Orders given in charge by the Deputy
Steward . . . to the Jury,* 1734 ; *The Power and Practice of the Court Leet of
the City and Liberty of Westminster displayed,* 1743 (attributed to Sir Matthew
Hale) ; *Observations on the Police or Civil Government of Westminster,* by E.
Sayer, 1784 ; *Inquiry into the Nature and Duties of the Office of Inquest Juryman
. . . also the law for . . . Westminster,* by a Citizen (James Newell), 1824 ;
Report of House of Commons Committee on the State of the Nightly Watch,
1812 ; ditto, on the State of the Police of the Metropolis, 1816 ; ditto, 1822 ;
Report of Westminster City Council for 1902-1903.
[2] *The Case of the Dean and Chapter of Westminster with respect to the Bill
for Regulating the Nightly Watch,* 1720.

but which evidently had a High Steward, a Deputy Steward, a High Bailiff who exercised within the Liberty all the authority of a Sheriff, a High Constable, a Town Clerk, a Clerk of the Market, a "Searcher of the Sanctuary," and the "Mayor, Society and Clerk of the Staple."[1] The so-called "City and Borough" was at that time divided into twelve Wards, and was served by at least two Juries, and a bevy of Scavengers and Constables. In the year 1585 the office of High Steward happened to be filled by the Queen's principal minister, Lord Burleigh, and he seems to have been concerned, as well he might be, at the rapid increase of houses; "the parting and dividing of . . . tenements"; the aggregation, around the ancient Sanctuary, of people "without trade or mystery . . . given to vice and idleness, living in contempt of all manner of officers within the said City"; the wandering of unringed hogs on "the common at Tuthill," and even in the streets; the unchecked depositing of dung and filth in all public places, and the utter lack of any provision for cleansing or lighting the noisome thoroughfares. The powers of the Manorial officers to "correct and reform" these abuses being "not sufficient in law," Burleigh induced Parliament to reinforce them by a statutory enactment.

(a) Burleigh's Constitution

The Act of 1585, whilst recognising and implicitly confirming all the existing authorities, established, as part of the Manorial constitution, an entirely new Court. This tribunal, the Court of Burgesses, consisted of twelve Westminster tradesmen—two of them designated Chief Burgesses—appointed for life by the High Steward, with twelve others as Assistant Burgesses, appointed by the whole Court. Both Burgesses and Assistants were unpaid, and obliged to serve for at least one year under penalty of a fine To each Burgess there was committed the entire charge of one Ward, it being expressly enacted that he should, with his Assistant, "do and deal in everything and things as Aldermen's Deputies in the City of London lawfully do or may do." Sitting as a Court, the Burgesses were to make "Orders and Ordinances," and to "hear, examine, determine, and punish according to

[1] All referred to as already existing in 27 Elizabeth, c. 17 (1585).

the laws of this Realm, or laudable and lawful custom of the City of London," certain limited classes of offences—" matters of incontinencies, common scolds, and of inmates, and common annoyances " only. The Act was only to continue until the end of the next ensuing Parliament.[1]

What Burleigh had in view in this experiment was to make some provision for the prevention of nuisances in Westminster, without setting up at the gates of the Royal Palace any such independent Corporation as the City of London, or even as the ordinary Enfranchised Manorial Borough that we have described. With this object the appointment of the Burgesses was left in the hands of the High Steward, without any intermixture of popular election, or even of co-option. Neither individually nor as a Court were the Burgesses made Justices of the Peace, the full authority of the Middlesex magistrates being expressly preserved intact. The Burgesses, who were to be "merchants, artificers, or persons using any trade of buying or selling," were, in fact, given the powers, not of Aldermen of the City of London, but of the Aldermen's Deputies only. What these Westminster shopkeepers were intended to do, as appears from their first "Orders and Ordinances," evidently drawn up under the direction of Burleigh himself,[2] was, Ward by Ward, to keep a constant supervision over their neighbours, to report to the Court the delinquencies of these neighbours in the grievous matter of the "harbouring of inmates"; in the use of unlawful weights and measures, the sale of diseased meat, and other market offences; in the neglect of the householder's obligation to pave, cleanse, and light the street opposite his frontage; and in the constant failure of duty of such of them as served as Constables and Scavengers. Above all, they were peremptorily to put down the wandering hogs, the festering dung-heaps, and the manifold other nuisances of the streets.

We have been unable to explore the early history of this

---

[1] This Statute, treated as a private Act, "being omitted from the Statute Book and very little known" (*The Power and Practice of the Court Leet of the City and Liberty of Westminster displayed*, 1743, p. 7), was separately published in 1730 and 1806, and included in *A Collection of Acts of Parliament relating to the Local Government of . . . Westminster*, 1837.

[2] Orders and Ordinances of 27th May 1585, reprinted in H. C., No. 666, of 27th June 1853.

interesting experiment. The Act of 1585 was seven times successively renewed for short terms, until, in 1640, it was — possibly, it seems, by legislative inadvertence — made permanent.[1] From the scanty records that we have seen, we derive the impression of a body of no little activity, meeting every Tuesday as a Court of petty police, receiving abundant presentments from individual Burgesses and the officers, and severely fining, whipping, and imprisoning offenders against their By-laws.[2] In the dislocations of the Rebellion the Westminster Court of Burgesses evidently suffered from its dependence on the Dean and Chapter, and may even have gone for a time into abeyance.[3] When in 1705 the records enable us to resume the story, the Court is again at work, but with sadly diminished authority. The power of making By-laws had become practically disused.[4] There had grown up in the meantime, in the powerful Close Vestries on the one hand, and in the Westminster Commission of the Peace on the other, two rivals for the government of Westminster, between which Burleigh's makeshift supplement to the Manorial authority was destined to be flattened into a mere formality. During the first half of the eighteenth century we may watch the gradual failure of the Court of Burgesses to maintain its position, and the supersession of this or that part of its authority by the Vestries or the Justices. This

---

[1] 31 Elizabeth, c. 10 (1589) ; 35 Elizabeth, c. 7 (1593); 39 Elizabeth, c. 18 (1597) ; 43 Elizabeth, c. 9 (1601) ; 1 James I. c. 25 (1603) ; 21 James I. c. 28 (1624) ; 3 Charles I. c. 4 (1627) ; 16 Charles I. c. 4 (1640).

[2] MS. Minutes, Westminster Court of Burgesses, 1611-1616.

[3] In 1645 an Ordinance of the Long Parliament made the provision required by the cessation of the Dean and Chapter (see *The Pageant of London*, by R. Davey, 1906, vol. ii. p. 240). Between 1660 and 1689 the Privy Council displayed great and constant activity with regard to Westminster affairs. We find it perpetually intervening to secure the better paving and cleansing of the streets, the organisation of the Scavengers and their relation to the Raker, the measures to be taken in visitations of the plague, the repair of the highways, and the multiplication of vagrants and beggars. But the Council deals always with the Justices and the Vestries, and never once alludes to the Court of Burgesses (MS. Acts of Privy Council, 1660-1689). We may note that the High Constable of Westminster successfully petitioned for the grant of a scarlet cloak to wear at the coronation of James II. (*ibid.* 8th April 1685).

[4] "This power," it was said later, "has seldom been exercised to any great extent. . . . Most probably this neglect arose from the refusal of the inhabitants to comply with the Ordinances of the Court of Burgesses, and the want of a fund in that Court to support the expense of enforcing the observance of them" (*Observations on the Police or Civil Government of Westminster*, by E. Sayer, 1784, p. 8).

failure was due, no doubt, in great part, to the change of principle that we have elsewhere described, which was everywhere gradually superseding the obligatory service of the householder, enforced merely by Manorial authority, by a rate-paid staff of professional subordinates, under the supervision of the Justices of the Peace, the Vestry, and the Parish Officers. But Burleigh's experimental constitution had its own inherent weaknesses.   Government by the Westminster shopkeepers, especially when it took the form of the exercise of individual authority behind the screen of a Corporate jurisdiction,—though this, as was afterwards noted, had "neither a power to make Freemen, nor erect a Corporation of Trade"[1]—was, in the early years of the eighteenth century, found to rival in corruption and petty oppression the analogous administration of the contemporary Trading Justices themselves.

During the first half of the eighteenth century, at any rate, the Court of Burgesses kept up both the paraphernalia of a judicial tribunal and the dignified ceremonial of the Court of an ecclesiastical potentate.   On a stated day in November of every year, "the Deputy Steward, Burgesses and Assistants, High Constable and Clerk, met in Court between the hours of 10 and 11 in the forenoon, where, after they had put on their gowns, they went (all the Beadles belonging to the several Wards[2] . . . going before them with their silver-headed staves . . .) to the Deanery of Westminster, where, when they came, they were immediately admitted into his Lordship's presence in the Jerusalem Chamber, whereupon his Lordship, with his attendants and the whole Court following him, went to the Court House."[3]   At this annual sessions the Dean himself presided, and there would be received any important communications from the great nobleman who filled the office of High Steward; a new Deputy Steward or new Town Clerk would occasionally be sworn in; messages from Ministers of State would be transmitted by the High

---

[1] *A New and Complete Survey of London*, by a Citizen and Native of London, 1742, vol. ii. p. 1198.

[2] It was "ordered that no Beadle belonging to this Court do presume to appear in Court without his blue livery coat on" (MS. Minutes, Westminster Court of Burgesses, 25th September 1705).

[3] *Ibid.* 24th November 1718.   The Dean of Westminster· was at this date also Bishop of Rochester.

Steward for consideration, and other formal business would be transacted. Of more practical importance was the less dignified sessions of the Court in October, when, under the presidence of the Deputy Steward, the "Leet Jury and Jury of Annoyance" would be sworn and formally charged, and the forty or fifty Constables, together with various Scavengers and other officers, would be appointed. By December of the same year this "Leet Jury and Jury of Annoyance" would have handed in to the Court the last of its several rolls of presentments, and would be discharged. At the same meeting another Jury, called the "Wardmote or Christmas Jury," would be appointed, apparently to collect certain monies allocated to the discharge of poor debtors, the feeding of poor prisoners, and the relief of the poor generally.[1] This Jury was, in its turn, discharged early in the following January. At an April sessions of the Court another "Leet Jury and Jury of Annoyance" would be sworn to make the same sort of presentments as its autumnal predecessor. For the next two months these presentments would come before successive meetings of the Court, some of them being allowed to be traversed, when we presume they were tried before an ordinary Traverse Jury.[2] Besides ceremonial business and the suppression of nuisances, the Court dealt, now and again, with other matters appertaining elsewhere to a Municipal Corporation. We find it, now and again, setting the Assize of Bread.[3] It licensed the twenty-four Members of the Society of Bridge-porters who alone enjoyed the privilege of transporting burdens to and from "the Queen's Bridge" in New Palace Yard and all the wharves of the City.[4] There was even a body of Waits, or town musicians, who were sworn into office, and enjoined to provide themselves with silver

---

[1] High Steward's letter, in MS. Minutes, Westminster Court of Burgesses, 20th December 1726.

[2] See, for instance, a case in which a woman was presented on the 24th January 1710 by the Jury of Annoyance for the combined offence of "keeping a disorderly house" and "also for a house of office very nauseous and offensive"; and her traverse was tried on 31st January 1710, when she was found not guilty (*ibid.* 24th and 31st January 1710).

[3] *Ibid.* 28th April 1710; 20th March 1741, etc. A broadsheet of the Assize so set in 1735 is in the British Museum.

[4] *Ibid.* 9th December 1707; 28th July and 11th August 1713. The "Queen's Bridge" was a landing-place—probably a short pier—close to the Palace of Westminster.

badges bearing the Westminster arms, that they might be known as entitled to the privilege of playing in the streets.[1] For the transaction of all this business we reckon that there were some thirty sessions of the Court in each year, always held on a Tuesday at the ancient Court House.

But the individual work of the Burgesses must far have exceeded that done by them as a Court. At the beginning of the eighteenth century the extensive duties that Burleigh had originally cast upon them in the way of personal inspection of street and market had, it is true, to some extent been superseded. It was now for the Constables and Beadles, together with the members of the " Jury of Annoyances," to clear the Wards of "inmates" and vagrants; to discover broken pavements, heaps of muck, encroachments on the thoroughfares, and other nuisances, and to present the various market offences. But new and important duties had been placed upon the individual Burgesses and Assistant Burgesses. The drunken revels and brutal manners of the citizens of the Restoration, together with the robberies and assaults committed by the criminals of an unpoliced city then approaching 100,000 in population, had become sufficiently scandalous to make imperative the systematic organisation of "watch and ward" in the streets by night and by day. The appointment, payment, direction, and superintendence of this force was, for each of the Wards into which the City continued to be divided,[2] left entirely in the hands of the Ward Burgess and Assistant Burgess. The only paid assistance at their command was

---

[1] Their privileges are protected against certain parochial rivals (MS. Minutes, Westminster Court of Burgesses, 17th and 24th January 1710); they ask to have their particular "walks" rearranged (21st October 1735, 8th December 1741); and are ordered to share equally all their receipts (22nd December 1741). Fifteen years later they are divided into five divisions, each consisting of "two hautboys and a bassoon," allocated to a particular "walk" (*ibid.* 9th December 1756).

[2] The twelve ancient Wards were increased to sixteen on the creation of separate new parishes in the seventeenth century. Gradually, as it was found necessary to augment the staff of Constables, Beadles, etc., a multiplication of Wards took place without any change in the number of Burgesses, the word being thenceforth used in a new sense for a smaller division, more analogous to that of the Precinct of the City of London. "Of late years," it was complained in 1743, "since the increase of buildings, they have of their own accord divided each parish into almost as many Wards as twelve, and they don't choose the Burgesses for any particular Ward, but, in general, for the Liberty " (*The Power and Practice of the Court Leet of the City and Liberty of Westminster displayed,* 1743, p. 11).

that of the Beadles, several of whom were appointed by the Court, apparently on the nomination of the Ward Burgess, and paid between £25 and £45 a year each. Meanwhile the number of householders who were annually compelled to serve as Constables (or to provide deputies) had been steadily augmented; and it was the Ward Burgess who had to determine which householders should be summoned to the October meeting of the Court, and forced to accept this onerous office under penalty of a fine. The nightly watch, too, had been greatly increased, and the individual Burgesses were ordered to enforce on every householder the performance of this unpaid service; and to bring to the Court "the number of houses in their respective Wards that do pay to watch [in lieu of personal service], what number of [paid] Watch[men] are maintained, and what further number is fit to be increased."[1] It was the Burgess of the Ward who had to organise, inspect, and command this primitive police force. He had to "appoint in writing the courses and turns of the Constables and of the said watch, and the order wherein the several persons . . . shall appear and keep watch." He had even to turn out at night to inspect them, and to see that the watch was "kept with men of strong and able bodies"; and that "the Constables, Beadles, and Watchmen" duly attended to their work night by night. He had to assess, according to his discretion, the sums to be paid by the householders who wished to escape personal service; to organise the collection of this optional rate; to record and account for the proceeds; and to direct the expenditure of this money, over and above the salaries of the Beadles, in the hire of suitable Watchmen, paid by the night, whom the Burgess had himself to appoint.[2] To the obligation imposed by Burleigh on the selected Westminster shopkeeper of acting as Inspector of Nuisances and forming part of a petty tribunal, there had accordingly been added, between 1660 and 1720, the responsible duties of Superintendent of Police and Collector of Rates—involving,

---

[1] MS. Minutes, Westminster Court of Burgesses, 9th July 1706.

[2] The Burgesses evidently clung to their authority. A Constable who had taken upon himself to appoint a new Watchman in place of one who had resigned, was formally reprimanded by the Court (*ibid.* 25th July 1717). They refused to admit the Parish Beadle of St. Clements Danes as a paid Watchman (*ibid.* 20th November 1750).

day by day and night by night, the personal direction of an untrained and incompetent force of Ward police, as well as the assessment, collection, and expenditure of the semi-compulsory levy by which alone the service could be maintained.

Such being the kind and amount of unpaid public work exacted, at the beginning of the eighteenth century, from every member of the Court of Burgesses, we might have expected to find the shopkeepers and artificers of Westminster pleading excuses, or paying the statutory penalty of £10 to escape this onerous service, or at any rate refusing to continue in office beyond the obligatory year. The records reveal exactly the opposite. At a time when the citizens of Westminster were perpetually evading, or "fining" for, the offices of Constable, Churchwarden, and Overseer, we find no one ever refusing to serve as Burgess or Assistant Burgess. No Burgess is found laying down his office until advanced age or infirmity absolutely compels retirement, whilst there are plaintive appeals from Burgesses and Assistant Burgesses against being removed from office for neglect or misbehaviour.[1] Admission to the Court of Burgesses became, in fact, a coveted privilege. From 1706 onward we find it ordered that every new Burgess or Assistant Burgess shall "pay his footing" to the extent of £10 and £5 respectively, euphemistically called "the necessary" charges of the Court, and apparently devoted to some form of conviviality.[2]

What exactly formed the attractiveness of the office of Burgess we can only conjecture from indirect evidence. The Westminster Court of Burgesses, unlike most Close Corporations, had no Corporate property,[3] and levied as a Court no rate. The Burgesses had only power, but of this a profitable use could be made. From a communication of the High Steward in 1726, it appears that every Westminster citizen had still to pay "head money"—perhaps as "essoin pence"[4] —formerly a revenue of the Manorial authorities, but now

---

[1] MS. Minutes, Westminster Court of Burgesses, 3rd April 1711.

[2] *Ibid.* 4th March 1706.

[3] The Burgesses complained of their Corporate poverty. "There is," it was said, "no public fund out of which the Burgess Court can defend their authority against . . . contemners, as in most other Cities and Corporations" (*A Brief Account of the Powers given to and exercised by the Burgess Court of Westminster*, 1720, p. 16).

[4] MS. Minutes, Westminster Court of Burgesses, 5th October 1714.

devoted to charitable purposes; and that this was collected and distributed by the Burgesses. The High Steward had to appeal to them not to abstract more than £100 a year from this charitable fund as their own personal perquisites.[1] We catch occasional glimpses of such unexplained items as "paid to sixteen Burgesses £1 : 5s. each."[2] Of far greater amount was the levy for the expenses of the watch, "than which," we are told in 1714, "nothing is more abused."[3] In the absence of any fixed basis of assessment, of any definite pound rate, of any regular system of collection, of any adequate book-keeping, and of any effective audit, each Burgess was, it seems, left to raise what he liked, or rather what he could, from the grumbling householders of his Ward. The expenditure of this Ward revenue was equally uncontrolled. The Burgess seems to have appointed whom he chose as Watchmen, to have paid them what he thought fit, and to have dismissed them at his pleasure. What happened to the payments which the house-holders nearly always preferred to make rather than serve as Constable is not clear, except that the Court displayed a most suspicious eagerness to swell this source of revenue, levying (as was said in 1720) "great sums on the inhabitants under colour of fines."[4] "If a man pays his fine," it was com-plained in 1743, "the payment they pretend does not excuse him from serving the office except for that year, but he is eligible and may be elected in the following or any other succeeding year, as if he had never fined, by which means they harass any inhabitant of the Liberty they have a mind to in a most extraordinary manner, for most people will sooner fine than serve the office, because it requires so continual an attendance that a man acting as Constable can do nothing else. This choice is no way confined to take the oldest or properest inhabitants, but a man just come in is often chosen, when people who have lived there half their lives (by coming down properly) are omitted and forgotten."[5]

---

[1] MS. Minutes, Westminster Court of Burgesses, 20th December 1726.
[2] *Ibid.* March 1711.
[3] *Parochial Tyranny*, by Andrew Moreton (*i.e.* Daniel Defoe), 1714, p. 13.
[4] *A Letter to a Member of Parliament concerning the Bill for regulating the Nightly Watch in the City and Liberties of Westminster*, 1720, p. 25.
[5] *The Power and Practice of the Court Leet of the City and Liberty of Westminster displayed*, 1743, p. 18. In 1726 the Court resisted an attempt of

But besides the fines exacted by the Court, there is evidence of a system by which the individual Burgess levied blackmail on householders, who willingly gave bribes in order to escape being nominated as Constables or jurors.[1]   Such corrupt dealings of the Burgesses and Assistant Burgesses led naturally to corruption among the jurymen and the officers, high and low.   It was fondly supposed "that no method can be more just to inquire into offences than by such a Jury" as that of the Westminster shopkeepers, for, it was said, "they see the offences themselves and do not trust the evidence of others, so that they cannot be imposed upon by false evidence, or aggravating circumstances, or misrepresentations of things by partial and prejudiced persons."[2]   But the members of the Annoyance Jury could, it is only too plain, be placated, and induced not to cause trouble by presenting particular nuisances.[3]   The High Bailiff and the High Constable became notorious in their several spheres for systematic blackmail and oppression—taking bribes for passing over jurors, " compounding fines with the keepers of gaming and other disorderly houses,"[4] favouring publicans in the billeting of soldiers,[5] and

the High Bailiff to take these fines for himself (MS. Minutes, Westminster Court of Burgesses, 8th September 1726).

[1] *Ibid.* 6th November 1716, 21st October and 20th December 1718.

[2] *A Brief Account of the Powers given to and exercised by the Burgess Court of Westminster*, 1720, p. 14.

[3] The Court investigated in 1726 "a complaint . . . against the Foreman of the Annoyance Jury and other jurymen for corruption and a notorious breach of their oaths as jurymen."   One of the extensive "keepers of hogs," who were fed on the waste products of the London distilleries, had been amerced by the Jury for this nuisance, but had induced the Jury subsequently to withdraw this interference with his business.   The Foreman and some other members of the Jury confessed their guilt, and were fined £10 and £5 each (MS. Minutes, Westminster Court of Burgesses, 9th February 1726).

[4] *An Account of the Endeavours that have been used to suppress Gaming Houses*, 1722, p. 9.   The special position occupied by the High Bailiff made him, in many respects, virtually an independent officer, controlled neither by the High Sheriffs of London and Middlesex, nor by Quarter Sessions, with results that were sometimes scandalous.   Thus it was reported to the Prime Minister about 1760, that " William Morris or Morrice . . . son-in-law to Bishop Atterbury, whilst High Bailiff . . . acted in that office in a very vile and scandalous manner, taking yearly pensions of gaming houses and bawdy houses to remit their fines when convicted at the Sessions " (Add. MS. 33,053, p. 223).

[5] " Your Memorialists during the time of their being Constables have had frequent opportunities to hear, and have found several oppressions on the victuallers by the undue and illegal billeting or quartering of soldiers by Mr. Arthur Rawlinson, High Constable of the City and Liberty.   Your Memorialists have found that the said Arthur Rawlinson hath quartered two soldiers upon

exacting excessive costs in all the proceedings of the Court. At the bottom of the hierarchy the venality of Under Bailiffs,[1] Beadles, Constables, and Watchmen became proverbial.

(b) Municipal Atrophy

The eighteenth century saw a continuous shrinking up of the Court of Burgesses that we now proceed to describe. We wish that we could attribute this shrinking up to any recognition, by Parliament or public opinion, of the defects inherent in the very form of Burleigh's experimental constitution—to a conviction, for instance, of the inevitability of the misuse of power when entrusted to uncontrolled individuals " of mean degree," each acting in and for his own neighbourhood. Unfortunately, the local authorities by which, between 1720 and 1756, the Court of Burgesses was gradually superseded—the local Justices of the Peace and the Close Vestries—were equally defective in their constitution, and no less corrupt—perhaps even more oppressive—in their administration.

some poor people who retail beer, not near the quantity of others who have one and some no soldiers quartered on them, and hath been guilty of other irregularities and oppressions in his office " (MS. Minutes, Westminster Court of Burgesses, 27th October 1741 ; see also 20th April 1725). At the Parliamentary election of 1741, the High Constable ordered all the Petty Constables to vote for the two candidates that he favoured, and threatened all the publicans with extra billeting if they dared to vote for any one else (*Review of the late Election of Members of Parliament for the City of Westminster*, 1741).

[1] "The summoning Bailiffs pay £20 per annum each to the High Bailiff . . . for liberty to summon the Juries. So great a power being lodged in such low hands, the Justices found the consequences ; for at a Quarter Sessions, where several (keepers of gaming houses) were to be prosecuted, the summoning Bailiff did (as he has since declared upon oath), by the direction of two Burgesses, summon ten persons, and those ten persons . . . who . . . were found to be, several of them, tradesmen that were daily employed by those very persons that were to be prosecuted ; others were bail for the prosecuted. . . . And he owned that he knew them so to be when he returned the panel " (*An Account of the Endeavours to suppress Gaming Houses*, etc., 1722, p. 10). It is therefore not surprising to read, a little later, that "by having all fines and forfeitures belonging to him, his place is rendered very profitable " (*A New and Complete Survey of London*, by a Citizen and Native of London, 1742, vol. ii. p. 1198). The High Bailiff usually bought the office from the previous holder —latterly for as much as £4000—and paid £150 a year rent for it to the Dean and Chapter, making out of the fees, so it was alleged, only £450 a year (Report of House of Commons Committee on the Office of High Bailiff, see Hansard, vol. xx., Appendix lxv. 1811). It is clear that, as Horne Tooke declared in 1806, "the High Bailiff's office is a very lucrative one ; it is purchased openly of the Dean and Chapter ; they have great emoluments, and the holding of the election is one of their privileges "—one which enabled the High Bailiff to mulct Horne Tooke, as a candidate in 1794, of nearly £400 (*Horne Tooke refuted*, by Veritas, 1807).

Burleigh had expressly reserved to the Justices of Middlesex their general County jurisdiction over the City and Borough of Westminster. Down to the Rebellion these Justices seem to have refrained, as a rule, from encroaching on the sphere assigned to the Court of Burgesses. Under the Protectorate, however—possibly because of the abeyance of a Court dependent on an ecclesiastical potentate—we gather that a separate Commission of the Peace was issued for Westminster. We hear of "His Highness's Justices assigned to keep the public peace within the Liberty of the late Dean and Chapter," meeting periodically to deal with vagrants, ale-houses, etc.[1] After the Restoration this separate Commission of the Peace continued to be issued, and though we find the Court of Burgesses again sitting, the Justices of the Peace, whether acting for Westminster or for Middlesex as a whole, never relinquished the authority over the Westminster inhabitants which they had assumed. They seem, in fact, constantly to have sought to abstract additional powers from what they regarded as an upstart rival jurisdiction.

We note first the growth and activity of the Westminster Justices in Petty and Quarter Sessions. The Minutes that exist from 1707 onwards show them, as we have elsewhere described, to have met frequently, and to have exercised an active and minute control over the Overseers of the Poor and the Surveyors of Highways of the several Westminster parishes. But they were also exercising authority over the Constables, who, as we have seen, were the officers of the Court of Burgesses; we find them, too, supervising the Scavengers whom the Burgesses considered as exclusively their own servants; whilst the entire control of alehouses, vagrants, and "inmates" had evidently passed to Quarter and Petty Sessions.[2] By 1720 we see the Justices taking upon themselves freely to remove from office Constables whom the Court of Burgesses had appointed; to audit the accounts of

---

[1] *Several Orders made and agreed upon by the Justices of the Peace for the City and Liberty of Westminster*, 1655.

[2] It was noted, about 1720, in defence of the Court of Burgesses, that whereas their unrepealed By-law of 1586 fixed the maximum number of ale-houses in Westminster at 100, the Justices had permitted them to increase to over 2000 (*A Brief Account of the Powers given to and exercised by the Burgess Court of Westminster, circa* 1720, p. 12).

Scavengers,[1] and to punish them for neglect of duty; and to insist that the Constables for Westminster, like those for other parts of the County, should make regular presentments to Petty and Quarter Sessions.[2]   In 1720, when London was alarmed at the approach of the Plague, then raging in Marseilles, the Justices, both in Quarter and Petty Sessions, took up the whole range of street nuisances, and—entirely ignoring the Court of Burgesses—set themselves to discover what steps could be taken to improve the public health.   In a remarkable report laid before the Middlesex Quarter Sessions in 1721, we see the Justices dealing with exactly the kinds of nuisances for the suppression of which Burleigh had, more than a century before, created the Court of Burgesses—the dangerous harbouring of "inmates" in the overcrowded tenements, the myriads of hogs, the noisome accompaniments of the slaughterhouses, the accumulation of dung and filth in the streets, the broken pavements and unscoured kennels, and so forth.[3]   The Westminster Justices even took upon themselves to order the Constables and Beadles to make a complete survey, street by street, of the pavements of particular parishes, and report all defects to them.[4]   The Constables, Beadles, and Scavengers did not know which authority to obey; and we find them refusing to execute the orders of Justices, whilst more than ever neglecting the duties assigned to them by the Burgesses.[5]   In 1722 the conflict comes to a head in an almost insolent resolution of the Middlesex Justices which directly challenged the right of the Court of Burgesses even to exist.   The Court of Quarter Sessions, "being informed that the Burgesses within the City and Liberty of Westminster in this County do keep Courts and set fines on several of His Majesty's liege subjects . . . and also appoint Scavengers,

---

[1] MS. Minutes Petty Sessions, Westminster, 27th October 1720.

[2] MS. Minutes, Quarter Sessions, Middlesex, 16th April 1718.   The Government in 1719 seems to have been on the side of the Justices.   In that year the Secretary of State took counsel's opinion as to whether the Justices could not themselves appoint Constables, ignoring the Court of Burgesses.   The opinion was in the negative (Home Office Domestic Entry Book, in Public Record Office).

[3] MS. Minutes, Quarter Sessions, Middlesex, 12th October 1721.

[4] MS. Minutes, Petty Sessions, Westminster, 29th September 1721.

[5] The Court complains that "many of the Constables and Beadles have thought fit to return to the Court *omnia bene*" (MS. Minutes, Westminster Court of Burgesses, 19th December 1723).

make rates, and collect great sums of money on pretence of cleaning the streets within the said Liberty without any legal authority so to do,"[1] refers it to a committee of its own members to inquire what Courts are actually so held, and by what authority.

Meanwhile a struggle had been going on as to which body should exercise the new statutory powers that Parliament was, in this generation, conferring. Over Watch and Ward the Court of Burgesses maintained its authority for three-quarters of a century after the Restoration. When, for instance, in 1678 and 1685 the new parishes of St. Anne, Soho, and St. James's, Westminster, were created, "new Wards and new Burgesses . . . for the government thereof" were duly constituted, and new Watchmen appointed.[2] In 1706, and again in 1720, Bills for a reorganisation of the service under the control of the Justices and the several parishes were rejected by the House of Commons.[3] In the latter year the "Lords Justices"—then administering the government in the absence of the King on the Continent—called upon the Court of Burgesses for a report of its organisation of the Watch, suggesting certain improvements, which the Burgesses adopted, and were then able to claim to have, as against the Magistrates, the support of the Lords Justices' approval.[4] But the Justices of the Peace presently made a flanking movement. When at last public opinion was prepared to substitute a rate-paid staff for individual personal service, the most plausible proposition was to entrust the direction of the new force to bodies claiming to represent the inhabitants of each locality, and already levying "pound rates." Thus, when Bills were put forward by the Vestries of the several parishes of Westminster— bodies which, as we have described, were in close alliance with many Justices and Members of Parliament—we find the Legislature, in spite of constant protests by the Dean and Chapter and the Court of Burgesses, endowing one parish after another with full and complete power to organise, under the

---

[1] MS. Minutes, Quarter Sessions, Middlesex, 7th December 1722.

[2] *The Case of the Dean and Chapter of Westminster with respect to the Bill for regulating the Nightly Watch now depending in Parliament,* 1720.

[3] House of Commons Journals, 7th February 1706, etc.

[4] Additional Rules and Ordinances of 22nd September 1720 ; reprinted in H. C. No. 666, of 27th June 1853.

general supervision of the Justices, its own parochial Watch.[1] Before the middle of the eighteenth century the authority of the once-powerful Burgesses over the Watch was treated as entirely at an end, and they had to content themselves with the power of annually selecting about fifty of their neighbours to fill the hated office of Constable—a power which was evidently made to yield an income to the Court in the shape of fines apparently appropriated to the so-called expenses of the Court meetings.

With regard to paving and cleaning the streets the Burgesses were more quickly routed. Already in 1662 an Act of Parliament, confirmed by others in 1670, 1690, and 1697,[2] had entrusted, not to the Burgesses, but first to Special Commissioners and then to the Justices, the enforcement of the householder's obligation to pave and cleanse in front of his house down to the kennel. The authority of the Burgesses under their Act of 1585 was, however, not thereby abrogated; and between 1720 and 1730, in particular, we watch the two rival powers striving one against the other for the control of this service. When it was proposed to have two Surveyors for each Ward to see to the scavengering, under the control of the Justices, the Court of Burgesses retorted that the streets outside Westminster over which the Justices already had control were worse than those within its boundaries.[3] The Justices insisted that the Constables should make presentments to Sessions of all negligent householders, whilst the Burgesses

---

[1] House of Commons Journals, 28th February, 18th and 28th March 1735, 8 George II. c. 15 (St. George's, Hanover Square, and St. James', Piccadilly), 1735, amended as regards St. George's by 29 George III. c. 75 (1789), 7 George IV. c. 121 (1826); 9 Geo. II. c. 8 (St. Martin's-in-the-Fields), 1736; 9 George II. c. 13 (St. Paul's, Covent Garden), 1736, amended by 10 Geo. IV. c. 68 (1829), House of Commons Journals, 16th February 1736; 9 George II. c. 17 (St. Margaret's and St. John's), 1736; 9 George II. c. 19 (St. Anne's, Soho), 1736; 4 George III. c. 55 (St. Clement Danes), 1764, amended by 49 George III. c. 113 (1809).; 14 George III. c. 90 (St. Mary le Strand and Precinct of the Savoy), 1774, which also amended the prior Acts of the other Westminster parishes; 50 Geo. III. c. 84 (Liberty of the Rolls), 1810. See Report of the Westminster City Council for 1902-1903, pp. 33-36. An attempt to reorganise the Watch under the Burgesses, with new powers, did not succeed (*A Proposal for Regulating the Nightly Watch within the City and Liberty of Westminster*, 1755).

[2] 13 and 14 Charles II. c. 2; amended by 22 Charles II. c. 12; 2 William and Mary, sess. 2, c. 8; 8 and 9 William III. c. 37.

[3] *The Case of the Inhabitants of the Liberty of Westminster against the Clauses proposed by the Justices . . . to a Bill now passing to require Quarantine*, 1700 or 1720 (?).

required the Jury of Annoyances to present them to the Court of Burgesses.[1]   We need not here describe the stages by which the service of scavengering was transferred [2]—either by agreement between the Close Vestries and the Justices, or later on by Local Act [3]—from the unpaid Scavengers, enforcing the householder's obligation and co-operating with the " Raker," who contracted to take away the heaps of filth, to Committees of the Vestries, employing contractors or their own labourers to sweep the streets and remove the whole refuse of the City.   Nor can we here recount the similar evolution of the service of street lighting.[4]   What, however, we have to notice is the conviction, gradually forced upon Parliament, that the substitution, for the irregular pavements laid down by the householders—defective and constantly in bad repair—of a complete and uniform roadway for the ever-growing wheeled traffic, was an operation far beyond the means and capacity of any of these authorities.   A special statutory body had at last to be established by Acts of 1761-1765, entitled the Westminster Paving Commissioners,[5] with rating and borrowing powers more nearly adequate to what turned out to be the most costly Municipal enterprise of the eighteenth century.[6]

By the middle of the eighteenth century the Court of

---

[1] In 1724 the authority of the Burgesses to appoint Scavengers was disputed, the parish of St. Margaret's taking upon itself to appoint its own.   The Grand Jury thereupon presented the parish officers, and claimed that the appointment of Scavengers ought to be made by two Justices.   Against this view the Court of Burgesses indignantly protested (MS. Minutes, Westminster Court of Burgesses, 30th June 1724).

[2] In 1728 the Court of Burgesses tried to strengthen itself by new officers, appointing, in imitation of the Corporation of the City of London, two " Serjeants or Yeomen of the Channel "—an office which does not seem to have lasted long.

[3] Among such local Acts were 12 George I. c. 25. (St. James's Square), 1725 ; 24 George II. c. 27 (Golden Square), 1751 ; 25 George II. c. 23 (St. Margaret's and St. John's), 1752, see House of Commons Journals, 28th March, 10th April 1753 ; 6 George III. c. 56, private (Berkeley Square), 1766 ; 14 George III. c. 52 (Grosvenor Square), 1774.

[4] When, in 1737-1738, the Court of Burgesses contemplated getting powers to put up lamps to light the streets, the Vestries protested that this service "should be parochial and not general " (MS. Vestry Minutes, St. Martin's-in-the-Fields, 9th and 17th March 1738).

[5] 2 George III. c. 21 (1761); 3 George III. c. 23 (1763) ; 4 George III. c. 39 (1764), and 5 George III. c. 50 (1765).

[6] We trace the history of the Westminster Paving Commissioners in our subsequent volume, Book IV. Chapter IV. (" Street Commissioners ").

Burgesses had shrunk, we are told, to "but a shadow of power." They had become "unable to chastise the insults offered to them in their own Court."[1] Parliament now made a last attempt to galvanise into activity the ancient method of local administration—the enforcement by a Jury of Presentment, of the householder's obligation to do all that the common good requires, and to refrain from doing anything that is injurious to the King's subjects. By the Act of 1756 the Juries of the Court of Burgesses were placed on a new statutory footing. Twice a year the Court was to appoint an "Annoyance Jury" of not more than forty-eight householders, who were expressly empowered to present all manner of nuisances, active and passive. It was significant of the low estimation into which the Burgesses had fallen that Parliament expressly transferred from them to a second Jury, to be called the "Leet Jury," made up of one or more householders from each parish, not exceeding thirty, the selection and nomination of the whole of the Constables for Westminster, now grown to eighty in number; and required these to be formally appointed, with the High Constable, at a "Court Leet," to which the Burgesses might be invited if the High Steward chose.[2] The Burgesses thus lost the last remnant of their profitable power, and the pseudo-municipal government set up by Burleigh reverted to what was practically a Lord's Court, equipped with two statutory Juries and a statutory power of adjournment, to which the once potent Burgesses and Assistant Burgesses formed no more than a sort of honorary council.

For a few years this Annoyance Jury, summoned by the High Bailiff and prodded on by the Deputy Steward—these officers sharing between them a large part of the amercements[3] —annually paraded the streets of Westminster. Divided into three detachments, each under its own foreman, these forty-

---

[1] *Reasons for the Petition for better Paving, Cleansing, and Lighting the Streets of Westminster*, 1753 (?).

[2] 29 George II. c. 25 (1756), amended by 31 George II. c. 17 (1758) and 3 George III. c. 23 (1763).

[3] By the Act of 1758 (31 George II. c. 17) the High Bailiff was entitled to retain for himself one-fourth of the amercements. By order of the Court of Burgesses of 1757 small salaries and gratuities were assigned out of the balance to the Town Clerk, the Deputy Bailiff, and the Cryer and Mace-bearer; and the remainder was to be divided equally between the Deputy Steward and the Chief Burgesses "for the use of the Court" (MS. Minutes 5th April 1757).

eight Westminster shopkeepers went up and down for a fortnight, inspecting Weights and Measures and viewing "encroachments," handing in long rolls of presentments at successive Courts.   But as decade follows decade the rolls grow shorter and more perfunctory, and the annual perambulation becomes increasingly a mere occasion for a convivial meeting; so that it could be said in 1812 that the Jury was made up of favoured householders put on in order to enable them to escape service as Constables.[1]   Already in 1784, when a careful writer set out to describe "the Police or Civil Government of Westminster," he could omit all reference to this Jury, and dismiss the Court of Burgesses itself as a mere Leet at which the ceremony of swearing in the Constables was gone through.   The Constables themselves, he said, were under no effective direction.[2]   The High Steward in Court Leet could fine them for neglect, but had no authority to give them orders.   The Justices assumed a right to give them orders, but had neither power to appoint nor power to punish them.   The prevention of street nuisances became year by year increasingly the subject of specific legislative enactment, enforced by parochial officers and the summary jurisdiction of the Magistrates,—first under various clauses in the Local Acts which the Vestries and other local bodies were promoting, and then under the general statute for the Metropolis which Michael Angelo Taylor piloted through Parliament in 1817.   By this time, at any rate, if not before, it was clear that all the real powers of government had passed away from the statutory supplement which Burleigh had added to the Manorial structure of the so-called "City and Borough" of Westminster.   But the anomalous Court of Burgesses was not swept away, nor even formally stripped of its statutory or customary powers.   Right into Victorian times the High Steward, the High Bailiff, the High Constable,[3] the Leet Jury,

---

[1] Report of House of Commons Committee on the State of the Nightly Watch, 1812, pp. 36, 80, etc.

[2] *Observations on the Police or Civil Government of Westminster, with a Proposal for a Reform*, by Edward Sayer, 1784, p. 12.

[3] Early in the nineteenth century the High Constable continued to be appointed by the High Steward and Court of Burgesses, and received a small stipend (apparently £30 a year) from the Deputy Steward for relieving him of part of his work.   He had under his supervision the thousands of public-houses in Westminster.   "The inadequacy of the sum to the performance of the duty

the Annoyance Jury, and even the Burgesses and Assistant Burgesses, continued to exist and to walk through their parts, their position and functions becoming ever more exclusively ceremonial. In 1766 they were provided, by the generosity of the Duke of Northumberland (who purchased the ancient Guildhall for the purpose) with a permanent meeting-place.[1] On every possible occasion they laid loyal addresses at the foot of the throne. The last important entry that we find in their Minutes is a pompous protest, extending over many pages, at the negligence of some Court official in omitting formally to notify to "this ancient jurisdiction, coeval with our very monarchy itself," the arrangements made for Nelson's funeral in St. Paul's Cathedral.[2]

of the office," reports a Stipendiary Magistrate in 1812, "occasions that officer to resort to other means. The moment, therefore, he is appointed, he commences coal merchant and dealer in tobacco for the express purpose of serving the public-houses with these articles, thereby placing himself under obligations to the very people whose conduct he ought jealously to watch. . . . The last High Constable about eighteen months ago absconded with some public money in his hands, and his brother, quite a youth, has been appointed" (Sir R. Birnie to Home Secretary, 14th January 1812, Home Office Domestic State Papers in Public Record Office, No. 845 of 1812). This office was allowed to fall into abeyance in the middle of the nineteenth century, but cannot be said to have been abolished until the final abolition of the Court of Burgesses in 1901 (Annual Report of the Council of the City of Westminster for 1902-1903, pp. 31-32).

[1] MS. Minutes, Westminster Court of Burgesses, 23rd October 1766.

[2] *Ibid.* 20th January 1806. The Annoyance Jury continued until 1861, when it was abolished by 24 and 25 Vict. c. 78, which authorised the Court of Burgesses to appoint instead one or more Inspectors of Weights and Measures, a power itself superseded by 52 and 53 Vict. c. 21 (1889), which made the London County Council the authority for this purpose. The Court of Burgesses itself went on meeting, as a friendly social gathering, maintained by an annual subvention of £500 from the Government, the object or origin of which had been forgotten. By the Court of Burgesses' Scheme, 1901, made under the London Government Act, 1899, this obsolete and anomalous tribunal was finally abolished, and its property—a mace, a loving-cup, a snuff-box—transferred to the Metropolitan Borough Council of the then newly created "City of Westminster" (Report of the Westminster City Council, 1902-1903, p. 31).

CHAPTER V

THE BOROUGHS OF WALES

So far we have dealt only with local governing authorities which fell short of the powers of full Municipal Corporations in not being able to create their own Corporate Justices of the Peace. We have seen by what minute gradations the various classes of authorities were separated from each other, and how markedly they resembled a continuous series. Even the line dividing what we have termed the Manorial Borough from the Municipal Corporation will be seen, on closer examination, to be blurred by intermediate forms. It is, we think, a confirmation of this view that, when we come to consider the fifty or sixty so-called Boroughs in Wales, we find them exhibiting these very characteristics to an even greater degree than the Boroughs of England,—to such a degree, indeed, that we have been unable to make any lines of division among them. The different specimens, as we find them co-existing between 1689 and 1835, creep so closely one on the heels of the other that we are compelled to include, in a single chapter, the whole continuous series, from the most rudimentary village constitutions, scarcely to be distinguished from the Lord's Court of a rural Manor, up to fully fledged Municipal Corporations, with their own Quarter Sessions and their own Sheriffs; sometimes Counties in themselves; and in one case—unique among Boroughs anywhere in England or in Wales—even having a separate Custos Rotulorum and Lord-Lieutenant.

We accord the more willingly a separate chapter to the Welsh Boroughs, notwithstanding their resemblance to those of England, in that they formed, between 1689 and 1835 at any rate, an exceptionally important part, and a specially characteristic feature of the Local Government of the Principality. Whether owing to the late introduction of English Manorial forms, or to the systematic organisation that followed the conquests of Edward I., we find the privileges of a " Free Borough " scattered more lavishly about Wales than about England,—possibly with the view of attracting settlers round the castles and creating English garrisons,[1]—whilst these " Free Boroughs," nevertheless, remained more generally under the rule of the Lord of the Manor or of the Lordship, the Constable of whose great castle was frequently the titular Mayor of the Borough. Thus we see among the Welsh Boroughs, much more frequently than among the English, a relatively high development of Municipal structure coupled with a low degree of autonomy. We find Boroughs with elaborate constitutions, a full array of Municipal officers and Borough Courts of their own, returning members to Parliament, and possessing Royal Charters, remaining nevertheless in strict subordination to the Lord of the Manor. We may even find fully fledged Chartered Municipal Corporations, with their own Justices of the Peace and their own Quarter Sessions—sometimes even excluding the officers of the County—and nevertheless subject to a very real control by the Lord. The burgageship was, except in half a dozen Boroughs, closely connected with the tenure of property, the new Burgess being admitted at the Lord's Court, sometimes only with the Lord's express sanction. Only in half a dozen cases could admission be claimed by Birth or Apprenticeship.[2] The Lord's Steward, who was often the Constable or Deputy Constable of the Castle around which the Borough had been founded, usually

---

[1] "One of the features of Welsh society . . . was the marked distinction between the people of the towns and the country districts." The towns, once "practically Norman-English garrisons," only slowly became assimilated by the Welsh-speaking rural districts ; "and it was not difficult, even at the commencement of the (nineteenth) century, to find a market town distinctly English, while the surrounding country was occupied by people who habitually spoke the Welsh language" (*The Welsh People*, by J. Rhys and D. Brynmor-Jones, 1900, p. 479).

[2] In the following Welsh Boroughs there were, between 1689 and 1835, Trade Gilds or Companies, viz.: Haverfordwest, Carmarthen, Brecon, Cardiff, Denbigh, and (a mere remnant) Ruthin. On the other hand, Dr. Gross finds evidence of the existence in the fourteenth century of the Merchant Gild in no fewer than thirty Welsh towns, among which Brecon and Ruthin do not occur (*The Gild Merchant*, by C. Gross, 1890, vol. i. pp. 16-18).

performed the functions of a Recorder, and his Deputy sometimes even bore that title. In marked contrast with England,
this general Manorial supremacy throughout all Wales was
recognised and confirmed by Act of Parliament as late as
1535-1543,[1] when the Stewards of Manors and Lordships
were expressly authorised to hold their Courts Leet and Courts
Baron and Lawdays; to decide civil suits up to forty shillings;
and to exercise full Manorial jurisdiction even if they had not
formerly done so, without any words exempting from such
jurisdiction the Boroughs within the Lordships or Manors.
On the other hand, the same statutes conferred generally upon
the Mayors, Bailiffs, and head officers of Corporate towns in
Wales, whether subject to the authority of the Lord of the
Manor or not, a privilege never generally conferred by statute
upon the English Boroughs, viz. the right to try personal
actions by Juries of six men. The result was to increase, in
the fifty or sixty tiny "Boroughs," each numbering in 1689
only a few score or a few hundred families, a confusion of
Manorial and Municipal jurisdictions and rights that was
already almost beyond unravelling.[2]

[1] 27 Henry VIII. c. 26 (1535) and 34 and 35 Henry VIII. c. 26 (1543);
The Welsh People, by J. Rhys and D. Brynmor-Jones, 1900, pp. 368-383.

[2] Exactly how many Welsh Boroughs there were in existence between 1689
and 1835, and precisely which of them enjoyed an independent Corporate
Magistracy, we have been unable to determine. Their title of Borough, and to
some extent their status, was confirmed by the legislation of 1535-1543. The
statute providing for the Parliamentary representation of Wales (27 Henry VIII.
c. 26, 1535) established one Member for each "Borough being a shire-town,"
their pay being collected from all the "ancient Boroughs." This was apparently felt as an injustice by the Boroughs which were not shire towns, and
35 Henry VIII. c. 11 (1543) enabled all the Cities and Boroughs in each
county to share in the election of the Borough Member assigned to that county
(*History of the Parliamentary Representation of the County of Cardigan*, by John
Hughes, 1849). There were, we gather, nearly sixty places reputed to be
Boroughs and sharing as such in electing Members of Parliament. (See the
various papers relating to the *Charters to Welsh Boroughs*, by Henry Taylor,
R. W. Banks, G. G. Francis, and others, in *Archæologia Cambrensis*, especially
vols. iv. ix. and x. of 4th series, and vol. ix. of 5th series; *The Parliamentary
History of the Principality of Wales*, by W. R. Williams, 1895; *The Representative History of Great Britain*, by T. H. B. Oldfield, 1816, vol. vi. p. 118).
But these Boroughs must have been extremely small. The whole population of
Wales in 1689 cannot have exceeded 350,000; and it only rose, by 1801, to
550,000 (without Monmouthshire). It seems doubtful whether there was, in
1689, any Borough of 3000 population. Even in 1831, after great expansion,
there were only eight Boroughs with more than 5000 population, whilst the
most populous of all (Carmarthen) did not reach 10,000. Eighteen Boroughs
in Wales were confirmed as Municipal Corporations, and reformed, by the Act
of 1835.

(a) Incipient Autonomy

It is difficult, amid the dozens of decrepit little hamlets among the Welsh hills that called themselves Boroughs, to know which to pitch upon as the most embryonic specimen. We ignore for this purpose the dozen or more of tiny villages in which Borough privileges had become obsolete, leaving behind them nothing more than the memory of ancient grants or Charters, and perhaps a titular Mayor, without powers or functions,—it might be, as at Prendergast in Pembrokeshire (which is said to have once been a separate jurisdiction excluding the County officers), nothing more than a custom to elect as Mayor him "who had been oftenest drunk through the year."[1] Perhaps the least to be distinguished from a mere rural Manor was the Bailiwick of Gladestry and Colfa, a part of the Hierarchy of Courts of the Lordship or Manor of Cantref Moelynaidd in Radnorshire, that we have already referred to. Here the Lord's annual Court Leet and monthly Court Baron was the sole governing authority. But by prescription "the right of the estrays" belonged, we are told, "to the Freeholders, and a Freeholder in one of the said town-

---

[1] *Haverfordwest and its Story*, 1882, p. 128; Abergwilly, too, elected a Portreeve (*Carmarthen Journal*, 15th October 1830). Among such entirely obsolete Boroughs may be classed the town of Mold (Flint), which, even in the days of Leland, had but "the name of a Mayor," and continued throughout the eighteenth century to hold a burlesque election of a "mock Mayor" in the "Wake week" (*Cambro-Briton*, March 1820, p. 259); Overton, in the same county, Chartered in the thirteenth century (First Report of Municipal Corporation Commission, 1835, vol. iv. p. 2819; ditto, 1880; *Overton in Days Gone By*, by G. J. Howson, 1883); Abergele, in Denbighshire (see *Records of Denbigh and its Lordship*, by J. Williams, 1860, p. 225); Bala, in Merionethshire (see *Topographical Dictionary of Wales*, by S. Lewis, 1849, vol. i.); Builth, in Brecknockshire (*ibid.*); Caerphilly, in Glamorganshire (*ibid.*); Caerleon, in Monmouthshire ("Caerleon," by T. Wakeman, *Archæologia Cambrensis*, vol. iii. 1848, pp. 328-344); Fishguard, conjectured to have been Chartered by John ("Antiquities of Northern Pembrokeshire," by Idrison in *ibid.* 3rd series, vol. i., 1855, p. 271); Harlech, in Merionethshire, "reduced to a few poor cottages" ("Documents relating to the Town and Castle of Harlech," by W. W. E. Wynne, in *ibid.* vol. i., 1845, and vol. iii., 1848; "Letters concerning Harlech," by the same, *ibid.* vol. iv., 1858); Holt, in Denbighshire, with a Mayor chosen at the Court Leet (R. *v.* Roland, *Reports of Cases, etc.*, by R. V. Barnewall and Alderson, vol. iii. p. 130); Nevin, in Carnarvonshire (*Report on Certain Boroughs*, by T. J. Hogg, 1838, pp. 97-105); Newport, in Pembrokeshire, a mere Lord's Leet appointing a Mayor (First Report of Municipal Corporation Commission, 1835, vol. i. p. 353; *Description of Pembrokeshire*, by G. Owen, edited by H. Owen, 1892, preface, p. x), and Newtown, in Montgomeryshire (*Report on Certain Boroughs*, by T. J. Hogg, 1838, pp. 107-112; "Newtown, its Ancient Charter and Town Hall," by R. Williams, in *Powysland Club Collections*, vol. xi., 1879).

ships was alternately and annually returned at the Court Leet to take the estrays, as also to serve the office of Chief Constable." In the person of this representative of the Freeholders, keeping for them a common purse, we seem to have the merest germ of autonomous structure. Within the same Lordship we find several Boroughs, with minutely graduated increases in complexity and independence.[1] Presteign, a Borough by prescription, was hardly more advanced than Gladestry and Colfa. It had no Burgesses entitled to vote for Members of Parliament, and its Bailiff, the Head of the town, was appointed at the Lord's Court. At Rhayader and Knighton the Boroughs had Burgesses, being Freeholders admitted and sworn at the Lord's Court, but no more elaborate organisation than a Bailiff, who collected the rents, estrays, and fines, and governed the town. But there was a beginning of autonomy in the constitution of the Court. In both Boroughs the practice was for the Bailiff for the time being to present two other names with his own, and for the Steward to choose one of them; but if any of the Burgesses made another nomination of three persons, the choice of which trio should be presented to the Steward was made by vote of the resident Burgesses, still leaving the final selection to the Steward. The Burgesses of Knighton had the further privilege that any two of them present at the Court Leet might object to the admission of any new Burgess; that the eldest son of a deceased Burgess could claim admission; and that the Burgesses collectively might nominate any person

[1] For the Radnorshire Boroughs, see *supra*, p. 48 ; First Report of Municipal Corporation Commission, vol. i. p. 355; "History of Radnorshire," by J. Williams, in *Archæologia Cambrensis*, 3rd series, vol. iv. Another of them, New Radnor, which covered a fifth of the whole County, but had, even in 1833, only 2461 inhabitants, was much further advanced in Municipal structure. It had an independent Close Body of a Bailiff, two Aldermen, and twenty-two other Capital Burgesses, renewing itself by co-option. The Bailiff and the Aldermen acted as Justices, and the Borough had a Recorder who presided at Quarter Sessions. But for all this show of autonomy, the Corporation was, throughout the eighteenth century, absolutely subservient to the family of Lewis, a member of which filled the post of Recorder for generation after generation. In the survey of the Manor of Avan Wallia in 1659, we see a Borough (Avan Burgus) where a Court was held monthly before a Portreeve, and there were Burgesses who placed three names before the Lord's Constable, who appointed one of them to be Portreeve ("Manorial Particulars of the County of Glamorgan," by G. T. C. in *Archæologia Cambrensis*, 4th series, 1879, vol. ix. pp. 125-127). There were probably many such incipient Borough organisations in the Wales of the sixteenth and seventeenth centuries

to be a Burgess, whether a freeholder or not. They were also exempt from the tolls of the Borough Market; their Bailiff had the profit of the wool weights in the Town Hall and half the "pitching dues" at markets; and they had once owned a wood and exercised powers over the wastes of the Manor.[1]

More elaborate structure than these Radnorshire Boroughs, but scarcely greater autonomy, is seen at Caerwys[2] in the County of Flint, Chartered by Edward I. in 1290, a little market town sharing with the other Flintshire Boroughs in the privilege of electing a Member of Parliament, but of which the population can never have exceeded a few hundreds. Here we find a Recorder, two Bailiffs, a Cryer, and a body of Burgesses forming what claimed to be a Borough. But it was the King, or his agent, who appointed both the Recorder and the Cryer, to hold office during his pleasure; it was the Recorder

---

[1] Laugharne, in Carmarthenshire, may perhaps be classed with these Radnorshire Boroughs, though there the Portreeve was, by 1833, beginning to take upon himself some of the minor functions of a Justice of the Peace (First Report of Municipal Corporation Commission, 1835, vol. i. pp. 287-288). Its ancient dignities were specially preserved by the Municipal Corporation Act, 1883 (46 and 47 Vict. c. 18, sec. 20). The Boroughs of Hay and Crickhowell, in Brecknockshire, had nothing but Bailiffs appointed at the Lord's Court (*History of Brecknockshire*, by E. Poole, 1886, pp. 210, 220).

At this grade of structure and autonomy, though with numerous minute variations, we may place Newborough in Anglesey, which once had a Merchant Gild and a Hanse, but had dwindled by the end of the seventeenth century into no more than a village possessing a Mayor, and some Burgesses, with a rapidly decaying civil Court. Deprived of the parliamentary Franchise in 1709, by 1833 it was all but obsolete (*Topographical Dictionary of Wales*, by S. Lewis, 1849, vol. i. (under Beaumaris); "Antiquitates Parochiales," by Rev. H. Rowlands, in *Archæologia Cambrensis*, vol. i., 1846, pp. 305-307; First Report of Municipal Corporation Commission, 1835, vol. iv. p. 2807). On the other hand, though Bardsey, on the island of the same name, off the coast of Carnarvonshire, had a Recorder as well as a Bailiff and a Constable, appointed at the Lord's Court, it was not called a Borough (*Short History of Bardsey*, by Evan Richard, in *Cambrian Register*, vol. iii., 1818, p. 198). Tregaron, in Cardiganshire, had really been a Borough with a Mayor, its Burgesses voting for Parliamentary representatives, but we cannot find that it had any other Municipal structure at all ; and, 1742, the House of Commons decided that it had forfeited its Charter (*Cardiganshire*, by G. E. Evans, 1903, p. 101 ; *Parliamentary History of Cardiganshire*, by John Hughes, 1849 ; "Account of the Parish of Caron" in *Cambrian Register*, vol. ii., 1796, p. 386). Wiston, in Pembrokeshire, was also a Parliamentary Borough, and had a Mayor and a Grand Jury of Burgesses, but the Lord of the Manor was supreme, and the government was practically that of an ordinary Manor (First Report of Municipal Corporation Commission, 1835, vol. i. p. 421).

[2] "The Place of Caerwys in Welsh History," by E. Owen, in *Archæologia Cambrensis*, vol. viii. of 5th series, pp. 166-183 ; First Report of Municipal Corporation Commission, 1835, Appendix, vol. iv. p. 2610 ; ditto of 1880, p. 21 ; *Topographical Dictionary of Wales*, by S. Lewis, 1849, vol. i.

who held the Court which transacted all the business; it was the Cryer who nominated the Bailiffs; the Bailiffs selected the Burgesses who were to form the Jury; and the Jury admitted at its pleasure other inhabitants to be Burgesses.[1] Sometimes the Lord's authority was manifested both at the base and at the head of the Corporation. Thus, at Llanelly, in Carmarthenshire, in 1689 a tiny fishing village of a few hundred inhabitants, but nevertheless an ancient Borough, it was the Lord's Steward who selected the Jury, which presented persons to serve as Portreeve, Serjeants at Mace, "Layerkeeper," Town Cryer, Haywards and Ale-tasters—as well as inhabitants to be Burgesses—for appointment or admission by the Steward. Practically all the interest of the Burgesses was concentrated in the administration of the commonfields; and when in 1807 an Inclosure Act vested these in a body of trustees, no new Burgesses were admitted.[2]

[1] Similar conditions existed at Rhuddlan (Flint), also a Royal Borough, Chartered in 1284 (First Report of Municipal Corporation Commission, 1835, vol. iv. pp. 2835-2840 ; ditto of 1880, p. 100). We gather from the scanty MS. records of Aberavon in Glamorganshire, a decrepit little fishing port of a few score families, that this ancient prescriptive Borough, Chartered by the Lords of Glamorgan, had no more elaborate structure or greater autonomy. The Lord's Steward chose the Portreeve out of three persons nominated by the Jury of the Lord's Court. The twenty-five senior Burgesses enjoyed each three acres of Borough Land (MS. Minutes, Corporation of Aberavon, 1847-1863, preserved in a volume of extracts only ; First Report of Municipal Corporation Commission, 1835, vol. i. p. 163 ; "Lords of Avan," in *Archæologia Cambrensis*, 3rd series, vol. xiii., 1867, p. 3 ; *Topographical Dictionary of Wales*, by S. Lewis, 1849, vol. i.). Here, too, we may place Pwllheli, in Carnarvonshire, though the townsmen are said to have elected the Bailiffs and Town Steward (Report on Certain Boroughs, by T. J. Hogg, 1838, pp. 113-125 ; *Carnarvon Herald*, 11th October 1834). In a similar position was Llanidloes, in Montgomeryshire, an ancient reputed Borough, which had once done a great trade in flannel, but chose its Mayor at the Lord's Court, and was entirely subjected to the Mostyns and the Wynns (Report on Certain Boroughs, by T. J. Hogg, 1838, pp. 43-56 ; "Parochial Account of Llanidloes," by E. Hamer, in *Powysland Club Collections*, vols. iii., iv., v., vi., vii., viii., and ix., 1871-1876).

Scarcely more advanced beyond the mere Lord's Court was the ancient Borough of Flint, with Royal Charters, a population in 1831 of 2216, and all the paraphernalia of Mayor, Bailiffs, and Burgesses. These all depended on the Court Leet of the Constable of the Castle, who was himself Mayor ; his Deputy was Recorder, chose the Jury, and made all appointments (First Report of Municipal Corporation Commission, 1835, vol. iv. pp. 2679-2682 ; *Historic Notices of Flint*, by Henry Taylor, 1883).

At Criccieth, "a pleasant fishing village" in Carnarvonshire, an ancient prescriptive Borough, the office of Mayor was said to be hereditary in the family of Ormsby, Constables of the Castle and Lords of the Manor (Report on Certain Boroughs, by T. J. Hogg, 1838, pp. 24-28 ; *North Wales Chronicle*, 9th October 1832).

[2] Llanelly Inclosure Act, 1807 ; *Cambrian*, 18th September 1818 ; *Car-*

In the little fishing port of Swansea—with a population of some 1700 persons, and as yet unconscious of its destiny as a great metallurgical and mercantile centre—the Lord's authority was at the end of the seventeenth century less apparent.[1] There was a considerable development of Municipal structure, and under Charters of the Commonwealth the head officer of the town had even presumed to call himself Mayor. Besides the Court Baron of the Lord there was an independent Court of Pleas of the Borough, having a civil jurisdiction unlimited in amount, which was held from three weeks to three weeks. There was throughout the eighteenth century what was unusual in Welsh Boroughs, an indefinite body of Burgesses, admitted by rights of Birth, Marriage, and Apprenticeship, as well as by simple gift. There was an independently existing Close Body—a Portreeve and twelve Aldermen—recruiting themselves by co-option from the Burgesses. There existed Corporate property yielding £1800 a year, and a revenue from tolls of £1000 a year, burdened, however, by a debt which, in 1833, seems to have amounted to over £20,000. On the surface the Corporation maintained the appearance of independence, subject only to a right in the Lord of the Manor to veto any improper appointment. But it is clear that, beneath the

narron Herald, 24th May 1834 ; First Report of Municipal Corporation Commission, 1835, Appendix, vol. i. pp. 305-810 ; ditto of 1880, pp. 61-62 ; Old Llanelly, by J. Innes, 1902. Llanelly became in the nineteenth century an important port and metallurgical centre—the subject of no fewer than twenty-four Local Acts and Provisional Orders—with a population in 1881 of 4173, and in 1901 of 25,617. It obtained a Local Board (now an Urban District Council) in 1850.

An example of the same type is furnished by the little Borough of Usk, in Monmouthshire, where we see the Lord's Court attended by an indefinite body of Burgesses who elected a Portreeve, but these Burgesses were themselves recruited by the nominees of the Lord. It was at his Court that the Bailiff was appointed. The Lord also had the appointment of the Recorder, who held his Court, summoned to it which jurymen he chose, and evidently controlled the Portreeve, under whose direction the Bailiff and Constables acted. When in 1821 the Jury wanted to present a new Burgess, the Recorder declined to admit him on the ground that the "Lord of the Borough" (the Duke of Beaufort) had given him no instructions to admit additional Burgesses (Cambrian, 3rd November 1821). See Report of House of Commons Committee on Corporations, 1833 ; First Report of Municipal Corporation Commission, 1835, Appendix, vol. i. p. 413 ; ditto of 1880, pp. 117-118.

[1] Swansea Charters, by G. G. Francis, 1867 ; Siluriana, by D. L. Isaac, 1859, p. 244 ; Contributions towards a History of Swansea, L. W. Dillwyn, 1840 ; First Report of Municipal Corporation Commission, 1835, Appendix, vol. i. p. 383 ; House of Commons Return as to Freemen, 1840 ; Cambrian for 1818-1834. Swansea was included as a Municipal Corporation under the Act of 1835.

surface, the Lord enforced his will whenever he chose to do so. Legally he may have let lapse all beyond the right, through his Steward, of vetoing any appointment of an Alderman to be Portreeve, a Burgess to be Alderman, or any person to be Common Attorney, Layerkeeper, or Water Bailiff. But this right of veto sufficed to make him the supreme authority in every department. These various positions entitled their holders to what became, with the growth of the port, lucrative privileges and emoluments. The result, if we read the story aright, was simply a scramble among Burgesses and Aldermen for the Lord's favour.[1]

---

[1] By 1801 the population had increased to 6099, and by 1831, if we include certain suburbs, to more than twice that figure. Other Boroughs at about this grade were Loughor (Glamorganshire), with a Recorder, Portreeve, Serjeants at Mace, and other officers, chosen at the Court Leet of the Lord (First Report of Municipal Corporation Commission, 1835, vol. i. p. 315); Newport (Pembrokeshire), with a Mayor and a Court Leet Jury selected by him, the Jury admitting new Burgesses, and the Lord appointing the Mayor from among three persons nominated by the Jury (*ibid.* vol. i. p. 353; "Description of Pembrokeshire" by G. Owen, in *Cymmrodorion Record Series*, No. 1, 1891); Llantrissant (Glamorganshire), population in 1831, 956, with a Portreeve appointed in much the same way, twelve Aldermen, and other officers ("Llantrissant Castle," by J. S. Corbett, in *Archæologia Cambrensis*, 6th series, vol. i., 1901, p. 5; First Report of Municipal Corporation Commission, 1835, vol. i. p. 311); Kenfig (Glamorganshire), with a somewhat elaborate Municipal structure, ultimately dependent on the Constable of the Castle, who was the Lord's agent (*ibid.* vol. i. p. 269; "Kenfig Charters" in *Archæologia Cambrensis*, 4th series, vol. ii. 1871; "The Borough of Kenfig," by R. W. Llewellyn, *ibid.* 5th series, vol. xv.); Lampeter, in Cardiganshire, with a population in 1831 of 1197, with a Portreeve and Burgesses chosen at the Lord's Court; re-established as a Borough by a new Charter of 1814, but practically subject to the Lord of the Manor (First Report of Municipal Corporation Commission 1835, vol. i. pp. 283-285; "Charters connected with Lampeter," by Rev. W. H. Davey, in *Archæologia Cambrensis*, 5th series, vol. xv., 1892, pp. 308-314; *Lampeter*, by G. Eyre Evans, 1905; MS. Acts of Privy Council, 27th May, 14th August, and 13th December 1813).

On the other hand, the prescriptive Borough of Kilgerran, in Pembrokeshire, had become independent of any Lord, though without progressing far in structure. This "Lordless Court" was presided over by a Portreeve whom the last Jury of Burgesses had appointed, and who himself summoned the new Jury, and appointed Bailiffs (First Report of Municipal Corporation Commission, 1835, vol. i. p. 279). Much the same seems to have been the position of St. Clears, in Carmarthenshire, with a population of 1083 under a Portreeve and Court Leet (*ibid.* vol. i. p. 377). Llandovery (Carmarthenshire), with a population in 1831 of 1766, had secured great autonomy by its Charter of 1485, the Burgesses freely choosing their Bailiff, who held "Hundred Courts" monthly for trial of civil and criminal cases. But all this had long before fallen into decay, none but the annual Court of the Lord was held, and practically no other Municipal structure existed in 1833 than a Bailiff, elected by the Burgesses at the Lord's Court, who appointed six Constables, committed offenders for trial, and administered the Town Hall and the Markets (First Report of Municipal Corporation Commission, 1835, vol. i. p. 301).

(b) The Welsh Manorial Borough

We select from our materials two of the most typical of the Welsh Manorial Boroughs, of which we happen to have explored the manuscript records between 1689 and 1835, for that more detailed description which alone can convey an impression of the actual working of these quaint constitutions. The little Denbighshire town of Ruthin, clustering round the castle built by Edward the First, was one of the places at which the County Justices met in Quarter Sessions, using an ancient building known as the Town Hall.[1] At the same Town Hall the Steward of the Lord held his Court twice a year " for the Lordship and Borough of Ruthin." This Court was served by two separate Juries called by the Steward; and two sets of officers presented by the Juries for the Lordship and the Borough respectively. There was the " Grand Jury " or " Grand Inquest " of the Lordship, acting for an extensive district, attended by Constables and Tithingmen for the several townships; nominating persons—sometimes by custom from house to house[2]—to serve as Constables; presenting roads and bridges out of repair, defective stocks and pinfolds, footways stopped up, gates and fences lying low between neighbours,[3] ditches and sewers unscoured and overflowing, landowners enclosing commons, cottagers squatting on the wastes, and Freeholders " abstracting " their suit of Court. Within the Lordship was the little town of Ruthin, which had been made a " Free Borough " by Charter of Henry VII., but had fallen into decay as early as 1636. It is not easy to make out from the scanty records of the Court what exactly was the relation of the Borough government, the jurisdiction of which extended for " half a league " in all directions from the centre of the town, to the Courts of the Lordship. There was a Borough Jury, or " Borough Inquest," nominating two of the inhabitants to serve as " Aldermen and Chief Magistrates "[4] for the en-

---

[1] MS. Records of the Manor of Ruthin, 1722-1798, in the Public Record Office; Court Rolls of the Lordship of Ruthin, by R. A. Roberts (Cymmrodorion Record Society (1893)); First Report of the Municipal Corporation Commission, 1835, vol. iv. p. 2849; papers in Byegones relating to Wales and the Border Counties, 1876-1877; An Account of the Castle and Town of Ruthin, by R. Newcome, 1st edition, 1829; 2nd edition, 1836. Ruthin was included in the Act of 1835.   [2] MS. Minutes, Ruthin Court, 20th October 1759.

[3] " For wanting of a gate that is necessary to keep neighbourhood between neighbours " (ibid. 17th April 1755).   [4] Ibid. 22nd October 1754.

suing year; presenting four others as Constables, four as Town
Serjeants, and two as "Leavelookers"; amercing Burgesses and
resiants who failed to attend the Court; making their own set
of presentments, distinct from those of the Grand Jury of the
Lordship; fining innkeepers without licences, and butchers
selling "blown" meat; presenting dangerous structures, defective causeways or pavements,[1] noxious smells, outstanding
steps, uncovered cellars, filthy hogsties, and the innumerous
other nuisances of a little town.   The Aldermen were assisted
by a Close Body of "Capital Men" or Common Councillors,
sixteen in number, who were chosen jointly by the two
Aldermen immediately after their own election, and who
assumed the right to be summoned to serve on the Jury which
chose the Aldermen.   By immemorial custom they were all so
summoned, and most of them attended—claiming, indeed, that
the proceedings would be invalid unless the Jury was composed,
to the extent of at least a majority, of Common Councillors.
The two Aldermen for the year received and controlled all the
funds of the little Corporation; they had the privilege of
nominating the two Churchwardens of the parish, and their
joint consent was necessary to the admission of any new
Burgesses by the Council.   Whether the two Burgesses
annually chosen as Aldermen had any right to act as Magistrates is far from clear.   The County Justices disputed their
jurisdiction, but the action that was brought did not con-
clusively decide the point.   It was reported in 1835 that the
Aldermen had, during the eighteenth century, held Petty
Sessions, but we do not feel sure whether such magisterial
action as they occasionally took went beyond committing
offenders for trial, and exercising the sort of authority that we
find often used by a Mayor.   The four Constables, one for each
Ward, were appointed by the Aldermen and Common Council
jointly, and sworn in at the Court.   In 1766 one of the Constables presented the Borough "for not erecting a pillory and
stocks," when "the sum of four pounds will build the same";
and in this sum the Borough was apparently amerced.[2]   More
real, perhaps, was the quaint array of "Javelin Men," perhaps
identical with the Town Serjeants, whom the Town main-

---

[1] MS. Minutes, Ruthin Court, 17th April and 18th October 1735.
[2] *Ibid.* 27th April 1766.

tained, "dressed in handsome liveries, armed with old-fashioned halberts," to give a little colour to the Aldermanic processions. In a single entry of 1748 we catch a glimpse—rare in these Welsh Boroughs—of Gild organisation, confirmed, it appears, by Charter of Henry VII., and also centring in the Lord's Court, at which "encroachers" upon the privileges of the duly apprenticed Company-members are presented for amercement.[1] There was evidently a well-frequented market, which had at one time yielded a considerable revenue to the Borough; and the tolls were, even in 1835, leased for £110 a year. How the actual administration of this Manorial Borough was divided among the Recorder, the Aldermen for the year, the Common Councillors, the Borough Jury, the several Trade Companies, and their officers, and how far during the eighteenth century all alike stood in subordination to the Lord's Steward, who presided at the Court, and to the County Justice who rode in to hold Sessions in the Town Hall, we must leave to be unravelled by the local antiquary. By 1835, it is clear, the owner of the Manor had come to possess overwhelming influence: nominating inhabitants to be Burgesses, addressing a letter to the Foreman of the Jury recommending the two persons to be chosen as Aldermen, continuing the same persons in that office year after year, giving one of the two places to the deputy Steward of the Manor, who had in

---

[1] "We, the Stewards of the Companies of Grocers, Tailors, Hatters, and Smiths, and in behalf of all the several traders of the said Companies and Fraternity of the whole, do present the persons as under-named that have not served their apprenticeships with any of the said Fraternity, nor have gained their settlement within this Borough or the Liberties thereof, who are now at this time encroachers upon the said Fraternity (ten names)" (*ibid.* 7th May 1748). One of the Companies continued to exist down to 1835; this was that of the Cordwainers, which had apparently absorbed the former Companies of Tanners, Curriers, Skinners, and Saddlers.

We might class as a decayed or undeveloped Ruthin, the tiny Borough of Dinas Mawddwy, in Merionethshire, in 1793 a mere cluster of "mud cottages with rush-clad roofs" (*Letters written during a Tour through North Wales*, by Rev. J. Evans, 3rd edition, 1804, p. 75); which had a "Mayor" who claimed to be a magistrate, and who did actually participate in the licensing of beershops. He was in effect appointed by the Lord of the Manor, and in form chosen at an annual assembly of Burgesses grandiloquently called "the General Sessions of the Peace," which was in fact a Court of the Manor, from three persons nominated by the Lord. The Steward of the Lord acted as Recorder and held the Manorial Courts (First Report of Municipal Corporation Commission, 1835, vol. iv. pp. 2673-2674; "Relics of Dinas Mawddwy," by E. L. Barnwell, in *Archæologia Cambrensis*, 3rd series, vol. xiv., 1868, p. 202).

practice the selecting of the Jury; and appointing the Recorder (who acted as Clerk to the Aldermen) during pleasure.

But the best vision of these Welsh Manorial Boroughs is afforded by the archives of the little port and market town of Aberystwyth in Cardiganshire, of which the population in 1689 was probably only a few hundreds; in 1801, 1758; and in 1831, 4128.[1] To the little community that gathered round the new castle, erected at the mouth of the River Rheidol by Edward I., there had been granted by him in 1278 a Charter, making the town a " Free Borough," with two fairs and a weekly market, and an exclusive right of trading in the persons admitted as Burgesses. This Charter of 1278, confirmed and extended by several others, does not refer specifically to any organisation for government. What Edward the First conceded to the fishermen and traders of Aberystwyth in this respect was apparently the privilege of holding the Manorial Court (heretofore, we assume, held by a Steward for the King), exercising its jurisdiction without seignorial interference, and taking its profits for the local communal purposes. The lordship or ownership of the Manor itself, apart from its profitable Court, seems never to have been formally conveyed. Nor is it clear whence was derived the title and office of Mayor. The earliest recorded mention of such an officer is in 1615, and in 1673 the town is described as " governed by a Mayor and other sub-officers." [2] In 1689, and annually down to 1834, we find the Mayor for the time being issuing at Easter and Michaelmas, in the name of the King, a writ to the two Bailiffs of the Borough, requiring them to proclaim the holding of the Court Leet and View of Frankpledge; and to summon between thirty and forty of the leading Burgesses,

---

[1] See MS. Presentment Book, Court Leet, Aberystwyth (Cardiganshire) (extant only from 1690); MS. Minutes, Quarter Sessions, Cardiganshire, 1739-1835; First Report of Municipal Corporation Commissioners, 1835, Appendix, vol. i. p. 171; *Aberystwyth Guide*, 1816; *Aberystwyth and its Court Leet*, by Rev. G. Eyre Evans, 1902; *The New Aberystwyth Guide*, by T. J. Llewellyn Prichard, 1824; *Topographical Dictionary of Wales*, by S. Lewis, 1849, vol. i.; *New Guide to Aberystwyth*, by Thomas Owen Morgan, 1848; *Old Aberystwyth*, by David Samuel, 1890; *History of Cardiganshire*, by S. R. Meyrick, 1810; *Carmarthen Journal*, 17th October 1834, 8th May and 27th November 1835; *Carnarvon Herald*, 29th November 1834; *A History of the Parliamentary Representation of the County of Cardigan, etc.*, by John Hughes, 1849.

[2] *Aberystwyth and its Court Leet*, by Rev. G. E. Evans, 1902, p. 9; *Britannia*, by Richard Blome, 1673, p. 268.

whom the Mayor himself designated in the writ.[1] At the "Easter Leet" and "Michaelmas Leet," thus held by the Mayor in person, the Jury, consisting of such of those summoned as attended, the number being made up in Court to at least twelve persons,—calling themselves, by the way, the "Grand Jury for the Town, Liberty, and Borough of Aberystwyth,"[2]—admitted new Burgesses, heard complaints from any one who chose to prefer them, and made presentments. At "the Michaelmas Leet" the Jury annually "presented" the persons to be appointed officers of the town for the ensuing year—the Mayor, the Coroner, and the two Bailiffs and the two Constables.[3] Apparently the choice of the Jury was, in fact, final. But the phraseology is merely that of submission of a name for confirmation. "We, the said Jury, do present A. B., etc., to be a fit person to be Mayor of the said town," etc. We see, as a matter of fact, the Mayor-Elect always presenting himself to the next Court of Quarter Sessions of the County for the purpose of taking the oaths of allegiance and supremacy;[4] but there seems no case in which the selection made by the Jury, for this or any other office, was objected to. The Mayor was not a Justice of the Peace *ex officio*, nor was the person chosen usually (or possibly ever) included in the Commission for the County. This Court Leet, meeting normally only twice a year (and not, in fact, making any effective use of the power of adjournment), was, with the officers that it annually appointed, the only governing authority[5] belonging to the town, other than the usual institutions of the parish. Hence it is not surprising to find that the County Justices in Quarter, Petty, or Special Sessions, and the High Sheriff himself, had, as a matter of fact, no less jurisdiction in the "Town, Liberty, and Burgh of

---

[1] From the lists of 1737-8 it seems that the same persons did not, at that date, serve year after year; though this seems, later, to have become the practice.

[2] *Aberystwyth and its Court Leet*, by Rev. G. E. Evans, 1902, p. 5; MS. Presentment Book, 13th October 1809.

[3] In 1708 we see the Court Leet appointing two "Searchers and Sealers of Leather," under Act of 1 James I. (*ibid.* 18th May 1708). Occasionally it selects persons to be Constables.

[4] MS. Minutes, Quarter Sessions, Cardiganshire, 11th January 1786.

[5] Between 1736 and 1835 various persons are, in the contemporary documents, designated Aldermen (*Aberystwyth and its Court Leet*, by Rev. G. E. Evans, 1902, pp. 10-14). It does not appear how these were appointed, or what position they held, but they were presumably those who had served as Mayor.

Aberystwyth " than elsewhere in Cardiganshire ; except that the Borough chose its own Coroner, and claimed to be exempt from the jurisdiction of the County Coroner ;[1] and except that it formed a district outside those of the High Constables of the County, and that its own Mayor seems to have acted as High Constable.[2]

We shall realise more clearly the position of this " Free Borough " if we run over the various functions of the local government in such a town, and see by whom they were performed between 1689 and 1835. In many respects the most important of these functions, as we see them in the contemporary English Boroughs, were those exercisable only by Justices of the Peace. In Aberystwyth there were no Municipal Justices. For all the services of the " Single Justice " and the " Double Justice," the town was dependent on the nearest resident gentry who happened to be in the County Commission of the Peace. Without their help the profane swearer could not be fined, the drunkard set in the stocks, or the vagrant whipped. We do not find that the Mayor had even the power of committing to the county gaol, for trial by Quarter Sessions, or to the next " Grand Sessions of Wales " (which took the place of the English Assizes), persons accused of larceny, assault, or felony. The only offences which the town dealt with by its own officers were the nuisances cognisable by the Court Leet, such as failing to fulfil the householder's common obligations to keep the street pavement clean and in repair, and disobeying the numerous regulations as to the enjoyment of the common pasture. Unlike many Boroughs, Aberystwyth had not even a lock-up,

---

[1] Though the Court Leet had elected a Coroner from the date of the earliest extant records, his right to act did not go unchallenged. In 1810 the Jury indignantly " presents " that one of the Coroners of the County " has encroached upon the rights and privileges of this Town, Burgh, and Liberty by holding three several inquisitions within the limits and boundaries thereof." The Court thereupon amerces him in the sum of £2 (MS. Presentment Book, Aberystwyth, 14th May 1810). We do not gather what was the result of the dispute, but the Court Leet continued to appoint its Coroner to the last.

[2] The Mayor of Aberystwyth, like the Mayor of Cardigan and the Portreeve of Lampeter—the two other " Boroughs " within the county—was always reported to the Court by the Sheriff, in obedience to the command in the writ issued to him and recorded on the Sessions Roll, along with the five High Constables of the Hundreds of the County, and the five Bailiffs for these divisions. (See, *e.g.*, MS. Sessions Rolls, Quarter Sessions, Cardiganshire, Trinity 1765 ; *ibid.*, Easter 1775, from which the Portreeve of Lampeter is omitted.)

or any sort of prison under its own administration, the House
of Correction in the town being erected, maintained, and
administered by Quarter Sessions.[1] Similarly, we see the
town unable to license its own alehouses, or to authorise the
performance of stage plays [2] in the building that was called
the Gild Hall or Town Hall, though it was the County that
owned it, and paid its keeper, as it had paid for its erection.[3]
It was, too, the County Magistrates who appointed the Overseers
of the parish, supervised their relief of the poor, gave them
instructions, and allowed their accounts. It was the County
Magistrates who appointed the Surveyor of Highways, instructed
him what streets to repair, enforced for him the performance
of Statute Labour, and authorised now and again his levy of a
Highway Rate.[4] When we turn to the specially urban services
of paving, cleansing, lighting, and watching the streets, we see
the town making shift with the powers of the Court Leet;
presenting and fining householders "for want of mending and
clearing the gutter" in the cobblestone pavement in front of
their respective houses, for making dunghills in the public
street, for not making the gutters level with the rest of the
pavement, for "not clearing their mixen from the street," for
leaving carts and waggons in the street, or "for laying of
rubbish, dirt, dust, or dunghills before their respective doors."[5]
But it is long before the town ventures upon any collective
service of this kind. When the inhabitants wish to have a
Scavenger it is to the County Justices that they resort, and
Quarter Sessions appoints such officers for the town, under the

---

[1] It had its own stocks and whipping-post, which (like any mere parish) it
had to maintain. The Jury, in 1708, "present the stocks, whipping-post, and
common ground . . . to be out of repair, and ought to be repaired by the
inhabitants of the said town and liberty" (MS. Presentment Book, Aberystwyth, 18th May 1708). The whipping-post is not mentioned after 1761, and
after this date we hear, too, no more of the want of a ducking-stool, but
presentments as to the stocks occur down to 1810, and they were not removed
until 1821 (*Aberystwyth and its Court Leet*, by Rev. G. E. Evans, 1902, pp.
97-104).

[2] MS. Minutes, Quarter Sessions, Cardiganshire, 15th July 1812.

[3] *Ibid.*, 11th January 1786, 10th January and 11th July 1821.

[4] MS. Minutes, Quarter Sessions, Cardiganshire, 3rd April 1832, authorising a rate of a shilling in the pound on the whole town for the repair of the
Marine Terrace.

[5] MS. Presentment Book, Aberystwyth, 21st April 1812; *Aberystwyth and
its Court Leet*, by Rev. G. E. Evans, 1902, pp. 110-115 under dates 1713-
1774.

powers provided for unincorporated towns by the Act of 1715.[1]
Presently the Court Leet takes it upon itself to appoint a
Scavenger, who seems to have served without payment.[2]   Even
after 1801, when the town increased by leaps and bounds,
doubling its population within thirty years, it failed to accomplish
any paving or lighting at the public expense, or the provision
of night watchmen.   Its power of organising Municipal
services was, indeed, limited, for the Court Leet could levy no
rate.   The income from the town property was small, and it
does not seem to have occurred to any one that, if no influential
person seriously objected to the expenditure, the Parish Vestry
might have included any necessary item in the Church Rate, if
not in the Poor Rate.   We see, however, no indication that
there was any desire for the organisation of such common
services.   By far the largest part of the business of the
Court Leet was concerned with the management of the
common pasturage and wastes adjoining the town, over
which their Royal Charters had given the Burgesses inde-
feasible rights, not, however, differing in kind or degree from
those exercised elsewhere by Manorial authorities.[3]   Next in
importance to the common pasturage were the markets and
fairs and the haven afforded by the river.   Over all these
the Court Leet exercised such scanty regulative power as in
fact existed.   We see the Jury vainly striving, by repeating
its general denunciation of offenders, to get the weights and
measures inspected.[4]   It was the Justices in Quarter Sessions
who appointed and paid the Clerk of the Market and Inspector
of Corn Returns; and the Justices at last instruct him to
procure standard weights and measures and to inspect those

[1] 1 George I. stat. 2, c. 52 ; MS. Minutes, Quarter Sessions, Cardiganshire,
13th January 1747 ; 10th January 1759, 11th January 1786.
[2] It is interesting in 1811-1815 to find the Scavenger paying £8 or £10 for
the privilege of holding the office—doubtless for the value of the manure and
ashes.   Later on we see the Churchwardens and Overseers for the year formally
appointed Scavengers, in order that they may employ the paupers on the work
(MS. Presentment Book, 22nd October 1811 ; *Aberystwyth and its Court Leet*,
1902, p. 26).
[3] *Aberystwyth and its Court Leet*, by Rev. G. E. Evans, 1902, pp. 157-164.
In 1740 the Court Leet appoints an officer to "survey" the common lands to
prevent geese, swine, and mangy horses being placed upon them (MS. Presentment Book, Aberystwyth, 10th April 1740); and in 1812 two such officers are
appointed "to oversee the wastes," the Mayor "to pay them that which he
thinks reasonable" (*ibid*. 21st April 1812).
[4] *Aberystwyth and its Court Leet*, by Rev. G. E. Evans, 1902, pp. 79-81.

in use.[1]   In order to get any expensive improvements effected in the Market or the Harbour, these had both to be placed in other hands: the market, in 1823, by lease to six inhabitants who undertook to erect a building; and the harbour, in 1780, by a Local Act vesting it in trustees.[2]   Though the Court Leet had, by Charter, the right to exclude all but Burgesses from trading, and to admit new Burgesses only at its own will,[3] we see this exclusive privilege becoming obsolete early in the eighteenth century.   The Court Leet makes spasmodically a few presentments against "foreigners," which evidently fail to be enforced.[4]   In fact, from 1740 onwards, practically the only valuable incident of the status of Burgess—apart from the right to turn out beasts on the common—was the Parliamentary Franchise that it carried.   The main importance of the Court Leet lay in its power of admitting new Burgesses, and thus controlling the share of the town (along with the four other Boroughs of Cardiganshire)[5] in the election of a Borough Member.   Between 1740 and 1778, and again between 1812 and 1817, such new Burgesses were admitted in great batches; over nine hundred, mostly not resident, on payment by each of two pounds eleven and sixpence in fees, being thus introduced just prior to particular elections.[6]

The scanty records that alone exist of the Municipal government of Aberystwyth do not permit us to infer with any

[1] MS. Minutes, Quarter Sessions, Cardiganshire, 11th January 1786, 15th July 1795.

[2] *Aberystwyth and its Court Leet*, by Rev. G. E. Evans, 1902, pp. 88; 20 George III. c. 26; *New Guide to Aberystwyth*, by T. O. Morgan, 1848.

[3] In 1734, three of the persons "presented" by the Jury for admission as Burgesses were "not allowed by the Mayor" (MS. Presentment Book, Aberystwyth, 1734; *Aberystwyth and its Court Leet*, by Rev. G. E. Evans, 1902, p. 144), which we do not understand.

[4] "We present D. R. and J. L. for buying sheep and goat skins, lamb and kid skins within the said Town and Liberty aforesaid, not being qualified as Burgesses and Freemen of the said Town, to the nuisance and inconvenience of those that are so qualified and exercise the trade of Skinners" (MS. Presentment Book, Aberystwyth, 18th May 1708).   We have found but one other case of a person specifically presented for this offence, viz. a "periwig-maker and barber" in 1739 (*Aberystwyth and its Court Leet*, by Rev. G. E. Evans, 1902, p. 79), but general presentments of "foreigners" are made at intervals down to 1743, after which the Burgesses' trading privilege is not mentioned.

[5] Viz. Cardigan, Lampeter, Adpar (disfranchised in 1742), and Tregaron (disfranchised in 1730) (House of Commons Journals, 7th May 1730; *History of Cardiganshire*, by S. R. Meyrick, 1810; *History of the Parliamentary Representation of the County of Cardigan*, by John Hughes, 1849, p. 8).

[6] *Aberystwyth and its Court Leet*, by Rev. G. E. Evans, 1902, pp. 145-156.

confidence how the constitution actually worked, or whether it underwent between 1689 and 1835 any important change. From first to last the fishermen and little traders who made up the resident Burgesses appear to have been overshadowed by the neighbouring gentry, notably by the family of Pryse of Gogerthan. Down to about 1730 we gather that the government was in the hands of the gentry; a Pryse is frequently Mayor; the office is held by other landed proprietors; and the jurors all sign their names and affix their seals. Between 1730 and 1780 a great change takes place, probably not unconnected with two separate proceedings in the Court of King's Bench on writ of *quo warranto*, and a more strict enforcement of the oaths of allegiance and supremacy.[1] From 1730 the mayoralty comes apparently more and more to be filled by the middle-class folk of the town, though for a generation the Jury continues to be made up of persons who could at least sign their names and affix their seals. From the middle of the eighteenth century we see the administration putting on more and more of the forms of the close Municipal Boroughs of the period. The presentments of the Jury at the Court Leet are made to serve as resolutions of a Town Council. No longer confined to the designation of persons to serve offices, neglects and defaults to be remedied or punished, and offenders to be amerced, they take on both legislative and executive form. New rules are made, decisions on policy are formulated, expenditure is ordered to be incurred, bills are directed to be paid, and even leases of land are granted—all under the ancient formula of presentment. The Court takes it upon itself to create new offices, and to give new titles to the old ones. A Chamberlain is appointed from 1763 to hold the funds of the "Corporation of Aberystwyth."[2] The Bailiffs become "Serjeants at Mace," and one of them eventually the Bellman. At last there is even appointed a Town Clerk, an office created towards the end of the eighteenth century, and filled by the chief Tory solicitor of the town.[3] At the same time we see a distinct worsening in the status of the members of the Jury, who evidently become more than ever subservient to the real rulers of the town. Out of the seventeen members

---

[1] *Aberystwyth and its Court Leet*, by Rev. G. E. Evans, 1902, pp. 20-21, 170-171.　　　　[2] *Ibid.* p. 25.　　　　[3] *Ibid.* p. 26.

of the Jury of 1779 only six can sign their names, the others making their marks. From the latter part of the eighteenth century, at any rate—possibly from an earlier period—the whole administration was evidently in the hands of a small clique of well-to-do merchants and shopkeepers, mainly Tory in politics and largely Anglican in religion, who took it in turns to fill the different offices, summoned the same persons (principally non-resident tenants of the local squire and Member for the Borough) year after year to serve on the Jury, and perpetuated their own rule, to the exclusion of all the other inhabitants,[1] until an elected Town Council was established by the Municipal Corporations Act. It is to be recorded to their credit that, under the influence of the leading local merchant, they kept all their little communal property together, refusing always to sell the freehold, and granting, even to their own members, only leases for terms of years.[2] That such leases were sometimes granted on unduly favourable terms to members of the ruling clique was the subject of popular allegation in 1834,[3] which the records now show to have been not without foundation.[4] It is needless to say that the accounts were not published; nor, save for being perfunctorily laid before the Jury at the Michaelmas Leet, either audited or inspected.[5]

[1] During the fifty years 1786-1835, the mayoralty was monopolised by fifteen persons only—one, the leading merchant, serving at least twelve times.

[2] *Aberystwyth and its Court Leet*, by Rev. G. E. Evans, 1902, p. 15.

[3] First Report of Municipal Corporation Commissions, 1835, Appendix, vol. i. p. 173.

[4] The Court Leet Jury of 1780 presented that a lease for ninety-nine years of a plot of land should be granted to the Mayor for the time being, without any entry of the presentment being made. The Mayor promptly sold the lease for £100, and this sum was never credited to the town. It was found necessary in 1828 to buy back the lease at the town's expense (*Aberystwyth and its Court Leet*, by Rev. G. E. Evans, 1902, p. 49).

[5] First Report of Municipal Corporation Commission, 1835, Appendix, vol. i. p. 173.

A stage further than Aberystwyth was, perhaps, the shire town of Cardigan, the population of which by 1831 was only 2795. Here, too, there were no Corporate Justices, and the only Court was the Court Leet of the Manor, which the Corporation owned, which it designated the Mayor's Court, and at which new Burgesses were admitted. At the Michaelmas Court the Mayor and Coroner, together with the Constables, were appointed, on the presentment of the Jury or "Grand Inquest" of Burgesses, summoned by the two Bailiffs, whom the outgoing Mayor had appointed. But, unlike Aberystwyth, Cardigan had also the characteristically Municipal feature of a standing Common Council, of thirteen Burgesses, serving for life, which appointed the Town Clerk, administered the 200 acres of uninclosed common land, and transacted all the

Whilst the Municipal Government of Aberystwyth arose out of the Court Leet aspect of the Lord's Court, that of Neath in Glamorganshire seems to have been closely inter-woven with the Court Baron jurisdiction and its Municipal analogue, the Court of Pleas. From the scanty MS. records we infer that this reputed Borough Corporation, admitted as such by the Municipal Corporations Act of 1835, had been gradually developed from a series of Courts, one styled a Court Baron; one, less subordinate to the Lord's Steward,

business of the Corporation. It so happens that we have recorded the be-ginning of this Common Council, and can see its simple development from the Jury of the Court of the Manor. In 1653 it was presented at the Lady-day Court "that it was necessary that a Council of Twelve, being Aldermen and sufficient Burgesses of the said town, should be added to the Mayor for the time being, to advise him for the good of the Corporation." Twelve persons were accordingly named by the Jury as the first Council; and vacancies subsequently occurring from time to time were filled by presentment of the "Grand Inquest" (First Report of Municipal Corporation Commission, 1835, vol. i. pp. 197-200; *History and Antiquities of the County of Cardigan*, by S. R. Meyrick, 1810; *Cardiganshire*, by G. Eyre Evans, 1903, pp. 6-14; *Lampeter*, by the same, 1905, p. 197; *Carmarthen Journal*, 21st March and 2nd May 1828, 3rd, 17th, and 31st July 1835).

At Carnarvon, on the other hand, autonomy had progressed further than struc-ture. This ancient shire town, with Charters from 1284, was in form governed by the Constable of the Castle, appointed by the Crown to be Mayor during its pleasure. There was no Council, and there were no Courts beyond the Court Leet (designated the Borough Court), no Corporate magistrates, and legally no Municipal officers but a Recorder or Town Clerk, whom the Mayor appointed and who acted as Deputy Mayor; and two Bailiffs. But there was an indefinite number of Burgesses who had to be admitted at the Court, and who were entitled to various immunities; and the Crown had tacitly devolved on them all the current administration. At the Court Leet the Burgesses at large elected the two Bailiffs, who really governed the Borough, together with Town Stewards, who acted as Treasurers, a Coroner, Serjeants at Mace, Constables, etc. Under this simple organisation, Carnarvon, from the opening of the nineteenth century, advanced in population and trade, having, in 1831, 6877 inhabitants. The Corporation bought fire engines, made new gates through the old walls, built markets, provided a new water-supply, and (in 1832) even followed Manchester in erecting its own gasworks—piling up, it must be added, a debt of £9000 (First Report of Municipal Corporation Commission, 1835, in summary tables only; *Account of Dolgelly and Carnarvon*, anon., 1820 (?); *Old Karnarvon*, by W. H. Jones, 1882 and 1889; "Charter granted by Edward I. to the Town of Carnarvon, 1284," by H. L. J., in *Archæologia Cambrensis*, 3rd series, vol. iii., 1857, pp. 173-178; *Carnarvon Herald*, 1832-1834, *passim*; *North Wales Chronicle*, 20th March and 2nd October 1832).

The little Borough of Conway in the same county seems to have been in a similar constitutional position, but remained on a much smaller scale (Report on Certain Boroughs, by T. J. Hogg, 1838, pp. 14-21; "Conway Municipal Records," by E. Owen, in *Archæologia Cambrensis*, 5th series, vol. vii., 1890, p. 226; *History and Antiquities of the Town of Aberconway*, by R. Williams, 1835, p. 96; *Topographical Dictionary of Wales*, by S. Lewis, 1849; *Conway Parish Register*, by A. Hadley, 1900, p. xi).

called a Borough Court; and one termed a Court of Pleas, forming part of a Hierarchy of Courts in the wide domains of the Abbey of Neath. We catch a glimpse at the end of the seventeenth century of a Court held before "the Constable of the Castle and the Portreeve," a Court at that time styling itself a Court Leet, at which "the Grand Jury and Homage" make the usual presentments, admit Burgesses, and appoint a Portreeve and the ordinary officers. We have a vision of a thriving little town, having its own Court apart from that of the Lord, owning Corporate property, maintaining an organised Watch, and enjoying a large measure of autonomy. But the Lord encroaches on their rights and seeks to bring them into subjection to his own Court; and, in spite of resistance, apparently succeeds in his aim, the records between 1759 to 1797 showing the town business as transacted at the Lord's "Court Baron." Meanwhile there was also being held every month "His Majesty's Court of Pleas," also before the Steward and Portreeve, at which the Aldermen and Burgesses attended. At this Court occasional civil suits were tried before a Jury, Constables were appointed, the rota of inhabitants to serve the Watch was regulated, and defaulters were fined. By 1813 the meetings are called "Hall Days," the trial of actions is silently dropped, and we read definitely of the election of officers for the Borough—of three persons being chosen, out of which one is appointed Portreeve, and similarly in the case of Aldermen, Common Councillors, Common Attorneys, Serjeants at Mace, Ale-tasters, Sealers and Searchers of Leather, Layerkeepers, Constables, and Burgesses. In 1818 the minutes become styled "Minutes of the Corporation of Neath"; the meetings are uniformly called "Hall Days," except that formal entries of a "Court of Pleas" are interpolated, without any but formal business being recorded; and for the ensuing seventeen years, down to 1835, the proceedings become more and more assimilated to those of an ordinary close Corporation.[1]

---

[1] MS. archives of the Corporation of Neath (old notebook without date; proceedings of the "Court Baron," 1759-1797; ditto of 'he "Court of Pleas," 1759-1818; Minutes of the Corporation, 1818-1835); *Cartæ et alia munimenta*, by G. T. Clark, vol. ii. ; *Original Charters and Materials for a History of Neath and its Abbey*, by G. G. Francis, 1835 ; First Report of Municipal Corporation Commission, 1835, vol. i. p. 333.

(c) The Welsh Municipal Corporation

In the ancient Borough of Cardiff—population in 1689 only a few hundreds, and even by 1801 no more than 1870[1] —we see a transitional form between Swansea and Aberystwyth on the one hand, and (as we shall presently describe) Brecon and Carmarthen on the other. We need not recount the foundation of Cardiff as a "Free Borough" by Seignorial Charter of 1183, or the gradual elaboration of its privileges.[2] By Royal Charters of 1600 and 1608, the Bailiffs, Aldermen, and Burgesses of the Town of Cardiff became a close Corporation. "The Aldermen," we are told, "fill up their own body; the Common Council fill up the vacancies among the Chief Burgesses; and the sole power that is exercised by the Burgesses at large (who may themselves be appointed in any number by the Bailiffs) is that of electing four of the self-elected Aldermen, out of whom the Constable of the Castle is to appoint the two Bailiffs."[3] To this close Corporation more extensive powers had been accorded than to any of the Welsh Boroughs that we have hitherto described. The Bailiffs, Aldermen, and Burgesses of Cardiff held the markets and fairs, took the tolls, administered the little harbour and the river, and collected tonnage dues on shipping, and an import duty on slates, owned houses and lands within the Borough, and hundreds of acres of heath in the neighbourhood, and enjoyed a Municipal income that, by 1833, reached over £1000 a year—all upon a nominal quit rent to the Lord of the

---

[1] Even in 1796 Cardiff "was chiefly an agricultural centre for the surrounding district . . . a centre for markets and fairs" (The Welsh People, by J. Rhys and D. Brynmor-Jones, 1900, p. 525). By 1831 its population had risen to 6187, and the transformation had just begun.

[2] We have not examined the MS. records of Cardiff, four volumes of which have been elaborately printed by the Corporation (Cardiff Records, edited by J. H. Matthews, the "Archivist to the Corporation"; see the review in English Historical Review, vol. xvi. p. 550, by W. H. Stevenson). See also House of Commons Journals, 20th January 1774, and the Paving and Lighting Act of 1774 ; Cambrian, 15th and 22nd May and 2nd October 1818, 31st July 1819, and 15th December 1821 ; Topographical Dictionary of Wales, by S. Lewis, 1849, vol. i. ; First Report of Municipal Corporation Commission, 1835, vol. i. p. 187 ; History of the Town and Castle of Cardiff, by W. L. Jenkins, 1854 ; Growth of Cardiff from 1875 to 1880, with some Particulars of Cardiff in the last Century, 1880 ; Cartæ et alia munimenta quæ ad dominium de Glamorgan pertinent, by G. T. Clark, vol. ii. ; The Gild Merchant, by C. Gross, 1890.

[3] First Report of Municipal Corporation Commission, 1835, vol. i. p. 190.

Borough.[1] There was an independent body of Burgesses or Freemen, recruited by Birth, Marriage, and Apprenticeship, as well as by gift, organised in Gilds or Trade Companies, each under its own Master and Assistants.[2] The Freemen were not only exempt from the tolls and dues levied by the Corporation, but also from most of those levied in other cities and towns—an exemption which Cardiff dealers successfully maintained "in various parts of England in the first half of the nineteenth century . . . on production of a Certificate showing that the claimants were Freemen."[3] Finally, the Corporation had large magisterial powers independent of the County. The two Bailiffs were the Judges of the Court of Record, the Coroners for the Borough, and the Returning Officers at the Parliamentary election. The Corporation had its own Borough gaol; it alone held Courts within the Borough; its monthly Court of Record under the Bailiffs had unlimited jurisdiction to determine civil suits, whilst its two Bailiffs, its Steward, and the senior of its Aldermen were (with the Constable of the Castle) Justices of the Peace, with jurisdiction exclusive of the County Justices, and power to hold Quarter as well as Petty and Special Sessions. Yet, with all these large and indefinite powers of a full Municipal Corporation, Cardiff combined a subjection to the Lord of the Borough greater, in fact, than that in which lay many a humbler Borough. Some of the steps by which the little community of Burgesses had during the fifteenth and sixteenth centuries gradually attained the forms of constitutional autonomy are, indeed, still to be traced. The Constable of the Castle (or, as some said, the Lord's Deputy Constable), who was the Lord's nominee and agent, was, according to the terms of the earlier Charters, himself the Mayor of the Borough and its chief officer, and long presided over the "Town Court" or Common Council. He was the first magistrate of the town, and he remained throughout a necessary part of the quorum of the Bench, the other Justices being, in fact, merely additional to himself. The

---

[1] In the seventeenth century the Earls of Pembroke ; from 1683 to 1775 the Viscounts Windsor ; from 1775 the Marquises of Bute, were successively Lords of Cardiff.

[2] *Cardiff Records*, by J. H. Matthews.

[3] *Ibid.* vol. i., 1898, p. 3.

Court of Quarter Sessions itself, which the Cardiff Justices came to hold, seems to have arisen merely by a silent and imperceptible transformation of the Court Leet of the Lord.[1] All the elaborate Municipal structure of the Borough depended on appointment by his Constable. The Town Clerk, who was the officer of the Court of Record, and seems to date only from 1729, was his own nominee, appointed under his seal. Most of the other officers of the Borough—the Ale-taster, the Serjeants at Mace, the Water Bailiffs, the Toll-Gatherers, the Keepers and Clerks of the Markets, Shambles, and Fairs, the Common Attorneys of the Court of Record—were finally chosen by him from a list of persons submitted by the Bailiffs. Even the Bailiffs themselves were similarly selected by him, out of a list of four of the Aldermen submitted by the Burgesses on Charter Day. The Lord was thus able, through the Constable or Deputy Constable of his Castle, to favour those Burgesses who forwarded his views, and especially to exclude permanently from lucrative or honourable office any person whose action or opinions he disliked.[2] The result was, as we are told, that "from the reign of Anne to that of George the Fourth, the vitality of the Corporation lay dormant, while the Lords were increasingly strengthening the

---

[1] The Borough, as we learn from a memorandum by the Town Clerk of 1818-1825, was "divided into four Wards, and the Jury presented in each. . . . The parties presented generally submit and pay three-and-fourpence each, together with the fees of process, by way of fine" (*Cardiff Records*, by J. H. Matthews, vol. ii., 1900, p. 128). The uniform amercement is, as we have seen, characteristic of Courts Leet. In the seventeenth century the "Grand Jury" of the Court was diligently presenting nuisances, and "intruders in the Town"; we find it also presenting the boundaries of the Borough, and by no means restricting itself to finding true bills. In 1666, indeed, we see the Court held as a Court of Survey of the Lord, declaring the customs of the Manor, including the obligation of every Burgess to do suit and service (*ibid.* vol. ii. p. 68). Only later does the Court take on the distinctive characteristics of Quarter Sessions. This Cardiff Court, expressly reported in 1824 the ablest Municipal lawyer of the day (H. A. Merewether), "considering the matters presented by the Jury, will, I have no doubt, upon proper inquiry and accurate search, be found to be also the Court Leet; and the ancient title of the Court will, I imagine, be found to have been *Sessio Pacis et Curia Domini Regis.*" To this opinion the editor of the published records appends the footnote, "This surmise is undoubtedly correct" (*ibid.* vol. ii. p. 130). In the following chapter we shall describe a similar evolution, by imperceptible gradation, of the Court of Quarter Sessions out of the Leet jurisdiction of the Manorial Court, in Dorchester, Pevensey, and other English Boroughs (pp. 350-355).

[2] For a spasm of rebellion in 1818, see *Cambrian*, 8th, 15th, and 22nd May 1818; and *Cardiff Records*, by J. H. Matthews.

ties which bound the town to the Castle. The Council Chamber in the Gildhall became an office for the transaction of Castle business ; and the rarely held meetings were occupied with little more than the installation of Bailiffs and Aldermen, who were nominees of the Lord, and devoted to his service." [1]

[1] *Cardiff Records*, by J. H. Matthews, 1900, vol. ii. pp. 112-118.

Various other Welsh Boroughs in which there were Chartered Justices of the Peace were in a position of real dependency similar to that of Cardiff. Thus, at Montgomery the Burgesses, who obtained their burgess rights by birth, claimed to own the Manor, and nominally elected their two Bailiffs, who licensed the beershops and did a few other magisterial acts. But the Lord of the Lordship disputed this claim, and unquestionably appointed the High Steward, who (along with the Coroner) presented a list of six persons, from among whom the Burgesses made their choice. The High Steward or his deputy held the Court Leet, which was the only tribunal of the town (after a three-weekly Court of Record had become disused in the middle of the eighteenth century) ; and the County Justices dealt with all the offences. In practice, the Borough was entirely under the thumb of the Lord of the Lordship (Mr. Hogg's Report on Certain Municipal Corporations, 1888, pp. 85-89 ; *Antiquities of Shropshire*, by R. W. Eyton, vol. xi. ; "Ancient Charters of the Borough of Montgomery," in *Powysland Club Collections*, vol. xxi., 1887). We gather that Cowbridge in Glamorganshire was in a similar constitutional position to Montgomery (First Report of Municipal Corporation Commission, 1835, vol. i. pp. 221-224 ; *Cambrian*, 15th September, 2nd October, and 20th November 1834). So, too, may have been Llanfyllin, in Montgomeryshire, with a somewhat complicated constitution (Report on Certain Boroughs, by T. J. Hogg, 1838, p. 35 ; "Llanfyllin, some Additional Items of Municipal History," in *Powysland Club Collections*, vol. xxiii. p. 121).

The Borough of Welshpool in Montgomeryshire had two Bailiffs, a Recorder, and a Steward, who were Justices of the Peace, and held both civil and criminal Courts. They were nominally elected by the Burgesses, but were chosen in practice by the Jury of Burgesses at the Court of the Lord of the Lordship, by whom they were really appointed (Report on Certain Boroughs, by T. J. Hogg, 1838, pp. 140-145 ; Correspondence in *Archæologia Cambrensis*, vol. xiii., 1882 ; "Welshpool : Materials for the History of," by M. C. Jones, in *Powysland Club Collections*, vols. vii., xii., xiii., xiv., xv., xvii., xix., xxi., and xxiv.).

We have little information as to the actual position of Beaumaris in Anglesea ; in 1831 a Borough of 2500 inhabitants, with a close body of "Mayor, Bailiffs, and Burgesses," which exercised the powers of the Lord of the Manor, but held no Manorial Courts. By Charter the Mayor, Bailiffs, and Recorder were Justices of the Peace. A Court of Record was held down to 1779 (*Topographical Dictionary of Wales*, by S. Lewis, 1849, vol. i. ; First Report of Municipal Corporation Commission, 1835, vol. iv. pp. 2583-2590).

So, too, at Kidwelly in Carmarthenshire (population in 1801, 1150 ; and in 1831, 1435) there was a Chartered Corporation of Mayor, Aldermen, Bailiffs, and Burgesses ; with a close body, recruiting itself by co-option, and admitting new Burgesses by birth or gift ; and a Corporate magistracy, with Quarter Sessions, besides a disused Court of Record and an obsolete Hundred Court (First Report of Municipal Corporation Commission, 1835, vol. i. pp. 273-276 ; "Kidwelly Castle," by G. T. Clark, in *Archæologia Cambrensis*, 2nd series, vol. iii., 1852, p. 3 ; *Description and History of the Castles of Kidwelly, etc.*, by G. T. Clark, 1852 ; *The Welsh People*, by J. Rhys and D. Brynmor-Jones, 1900, p. 428).

The neighbouring Boroughs of Pembroke and Tenby in Pembrokeshire

Few and far between were the Welsh Boroughs that had
attained to greater heights of real autonomy, to a more elaborate
Municipal Constitution, or to a larger independence of the
County Magistracy than Aberystwyth or Cardiff. But although
differing from these in working constitution only by minute
gradations, Brecon, Denbigh, Carmarthen, and Haverfordwest
reach, in form, a level more closely corresponding with that of
the English Municipal Corporations that we shall presently
describe. In each of these Boroughs there was a Corporation
nominally independent of any Manorial Lord; each had Trade
Gilds or Companies of Freemen; each held its own civil and
criminal Courts, and took the fees and fines for its own
Corporate purposes; each created within itself its own Justices
of the Peace, with whom the County Justices could not
interfere. Carmarthen, moreover, which was between 1689
and 1835 the most populous town in all Wales,[1] was a County
of itself; and Haverfordwest,—in 1791 "the handsomest, the
largest, and genteelest town in South Wales"[2]—which had a
body of nearly 300 Freemen, recruited by Birth, Apprenticeship, Marriage and gift, who met in Common Hall, and elected
their Mayor, Sheriffs, Bailiffs, and Common Councillors by
popular vote, was not only a County of itself, but also had its own
Custos Rotulorum and Lord Lieutenant, thus reaching a degree
of independence of the County attained in England only by the
City of London.[3] These four Corporations so closely resembled

present a curious twin autonomy, the same persons long continuing to be the
dominant members of both Corporations, which had practically emancipated
themselves from seignorial control. Nominally the Mayor was elected by the
Burgesses, but practically the whole power was in the hands of a Close Body in
each case, which was more interested in maintaining its influence in electing
the Member of Parliament for the Pembroke Boroughs than in Municipal
administration, which became, however, of importance when the population of
Pembroke rose, by 1831, to 6511, whilst that of Tenby only reached 1942. In
both Boroughs the Mayor was chosen alternately from "town and country,"
and acted as Magistrate (First Report of Municipal Corporation Commission,
1835, vol. i. pp. 365, 402; *History of Little England beyond Wales*, by E. Laws,
1888; *Welshman*, 1832-1834).

[1] Population in 1801, 5548; rising by 1831 to 9955, beyond which it has,
in over seventy years, scarcely increased.

[2] *A Tour to Milford Haven*, by Mrs. Morgan, 1791, p. 195, etc. The
population in 1831 was 5240, beyond which it has during seventy years scarcely
increased.

[3] As we have already explained ("The Parish and the County," Book II.
pp. 311-312), all the English Boroughs, even those that were Counties of themselves, were nevertheless in some respects within the jurisdiction of the Lord

in form the English Municipal Corporations about to be described that we spare the reader any detailed description of their constitutions. What need here be said is that they all reveal traces of an earlier Manorial status not essentially dissimilar from that of Swansea or Cardiff, out of which they had in some way or another emerged. The Men of Brecon had, down to the sixteenth century, had a Bailiff appointed by the Lord, and though they bought their Manor for a substantial fee farm rent, they seem to have parted with many of their Manorial rights; and though their Royal Charter gave the Corporation great apparent autonomy, we find it, in practice at any rate, after 1754 as abjectly subservient to the Morgans as Aberystwyth was to the Pryses.[1] Denbigh, which had started with a Seignorial Charter, fortified this by nearly a dozen Royal Charters, extending over three centuries, and made itself independent of any Lord, and even of the County Sheriffs ; and the Corporation exercised all the Manorial powers, as well as holding Petty and Quarter Sessions.[2] Carmarthen, which had formerly had Provosts and Bailiffs for the two halves of the Borough appointed by their respective Lords, became apparently completely emancipated, but sank into such chaos in 1762 that its Corporation lapsed by non-appointment to fill vacancies, and a new Charter had to be obtained from the King, establishing a Corporation exactly like those of the English Boroughs.[3] Finally, Haverfordwest, which chose its

Lieutenant of the County at large in which they were geographically situated, though the Liberty of the Cinque Ports ranked in this respect as a County. The City of London, the only exception, had no Custos Rotulorum or Lord Lieutenant, but a Commission of Lieutenancy under the Lord Mayor.

[1] "The Corporation," it was said in 1828, like all the other Corporations in Wales, "are . . . the tools of the patron, who conducts all their motions like figures in a puppet show " (Article on "Welsh Boroughs" in *Carmarthen Journal*, 19th September 1828). See MS. Minutes, Corporation of Brecon, 1668-1807; First Report of Municipal Corporation Commission, 1835, vol. i. p. 177; *History of the County of Brecknock*, by T. Jones, 1805, vol. ii.; *Topographical Dictionary of Wales*, by S. Lewis, 1849, vol. i.; *Illustrated History of Brecknockshire*, by E. Poole, 1886; *Carnarvon Herald*, 18th October 1834; *Welshman*, 12th December 1834.

[2] First Report of Municipal Corporation Commission, 1835, vol. iv. pp. 2661-2669; *An Account of the Castle and Town of Denbigh*, by R. Newcome, 1829; *Ancient and Modern Denbigh*, by J. Williams, 1856; Review of this in *Archæologia Cambrensis*, 3rd series, vol. i., 1855, pp. 69-72, 185-190; *Records of Denbigh and its Lordship*, by J. Williams, 1860; *Carnarvon Herald*, 6th, 13th, and 20th December 1834.

[3] *Cambrian*, 1819-1822; *Carmarthen Journal*, 1824-1836; *Welshman*, 1832-1834; First Report of Municipal Corporation Commission, 1835, vol. i.

Mayor and other officers at what was called a Hundred Court, found itself governed, in practice, for all its apparent Democracy and autonomy, by a set of Justices of the Peace commissioned by the King and nominated by the Lord Lieutenant whom the King had appointed to rule over the "County of the Borough";[1] and this potentate seems, indeed, to have exercised as dominating an influence in the actual working of its constitution as did the Constable of the Castle at Cardiff.[2]

p. 203; *Royal Charters and Historical Documents relating to the Town and County of Carmarthen*, by J. R. Daniel-Tyssen and A. C. Evans, 1878; *Carmarthen and its Neighbourhood*, by W. Spurrell, 1860 and 1879.

[1] Although the Mayor, Sheriffs, and Recorder, whom the Burgesses chose at the "Hundred Court," were, by Charter, Justices of the Peace, the King issued his own Commission of the Peace for the County of the Borough of Haverfordwest, including the leading notables of the town; and as the persons appointed to the Chartered offices were, as a matter of fact, always taken from those in this Commission, they never acted as Justices by Charter, but always with their colleagues as Justices by Commission.

[2] *Haverfordwest and its Story* (anon.), 1882; First Report of Municipal Corporation Commission, 1835, vol. i. p. 233; House of Commons Return as to Freemen, 1840; *Carmarthen Journal*, 1829-1835; *Welshman*, 4th May 1832 and 3rd October 1834. It is interesting to see the Town Council of Haverfordwest, in evident succession to a Manorial Court, deciding (like the Lord's Court of Great Tew) upon the course of cultivation of its commons, and making a levy to defray the working expenses. In 1665 it is "ordered that the commons called Portfield be set out for ryeland; Burgesses to pay 6s. 8d. per acre, and strangers 13s. 4d. per acre, and inhabitants paying in the Royal Aid 8s. per acre" (Town Council Minutes, 2nd March 1665, in *Haverfordwest and its Story*, p. 100).

CHAPTER VI

THE MUNICIPAL CORPORATION

OUR survey of the ascending series of partially enfranchised communities, enjoying various degrees of privilege or of exemption from County jurisdiction—from the rural Manor under its Lord's Court up to such essentially Municipal governments as Arundel or Alnwick—brings us at last to the Municipal Corporation. In this chapter we abandon, for the time, our presentation of individual type specimens, in order to lay before the student a systematic analysis of the constitutional elements of the Municipal Corporation as it existed at the Revolution, and of its development between 1689 and 1835. And this analysis must, we fear, be long; for it is true to-day, as Madox quaintly said nearly two centuries ago, that "whoso desireth to discourse in a proper manner concerning Corporated Towns and communities must take in a great variety of matter, and should be allowed a great deal of time and preparation." [1]

[1] *Firma Burgi*, by T. Madox, 1726, preface. Perhaps because the sources for an account of the Municipal Corporations between 1689 and 1835, though abundant, are bewildering in their extent, variety, and local dispersion, we have not found any previous analysis of much use. The MS. Minutes are in nearly all cases preserved and accessible to the student. Especially at Liverpool, Leeds, Bristol, Plymouth, Norwich, Beverley, Newbury, Gloucester, York, Nottingham, Leicester, Southampton, Derby, Coventry, Exeter, Ipswich, Berwick-on-Tweed, Penzance, Deal, Cambridge, Reading, Winchester, Romsey, Oxford, Chipping Norton, Woodstock, Dorchester, and above all, the City of London, have we found these admirably kept volumes of great use. Some of the Corporations (among which those of London, Leicester, Northampton, Cardiff, Bristol, Norwich, Nottingham, and Colchester may be honourably mentioned) are proceeding to print and publish their earlier records. In other cases (as at Liverpool, Southampton, Bath, and Carlisle) this is being done by voluntary effort. It is to be hoped that these enterprises will be continued down to at least 1835. The numerous town histories, so conveniently catalogued in Dr Gross's *Bibliography of English Municipal History*, unfortunately seldom contain much information about local government in the eighteenth and nineteenth centuries.

Our first difficulty was to arrive at any precise definition of the subject-matter. When in 1833 the Whig Government appointed the well-known Royal Commission to inquire into all the Municipal Corporations of England and Wales, it was found impossible even to frame an exact list of those which were in existence, still less to give any precise definition of what constituted a Municipal Borough or a Municipal Corpora-

An exception must be made for the quite admirable *History of Municipal Government in Liverpool*, by Professor Ramsay Muir, 1906. On the other hand, the voluminous report and appendices of the Municipal Corporation Commissioners, comprising nearly 4000 pages, afford a picture of the constitution and working of the boroughs reported on, as they were in 1833, unparalleled in extent, systematic completeness, and elaboration of detail. The actual evidence taken by the Commissioners was not officially recorded, but local summaries exist, in more or less detail, of that given at Boston, Cambridge, Dover, Gateshead, Hull, King's Lynn, Liverpool (two versions), Newcastle-on-Tyne (two versions), Norwich, Nottingham, Poole, Reading, Warwick, and Yarmouth. No reports were published on Carnarvon, Colchester, New Romney, Saffron Walden, Sudbury, or Yarmouth, though for the last-named we have the summary of the evidence. The whole report is summarised, not very accurately, in A. J. E. Cockburn's *Corporations of England and Wales*, 1835, and Sir J. R. Somers Vine's *English Municipal Institutions*, 1879. More valuable is the paper contributed by Joseph Fletcher (who had worked as assistant secretary to the Commissioners) to the *Journal of the Royal Statistical Society* (vol. v., 1842) ; and the elaborate analytic index to the First Report and its four volumes of appendices, which was published in 1839 (unfortunately not invariably accurate). The Second Report (1837), relating to the City of London, and the Report on Certain Boroughs, by T. J. Hogg (1838), were not included in this index. The Report and Evidence of the House of Commons Select Committee on Municipal Corporations, 1833, must also be referred to. References to other material for particular towns, and to the Municipal Corporation Reform Act itself, are given elsewhere, though we have preferred, in this chapter, to cite principally the 1835 Report (as being most accessible), on those points as to which we have ground for belief that its description applied equally to 1689 as to 1833. The titles of the principal general treatises on English Borough Corporations will be found in Dr Gross's *Bibliography* (pp. 15-48), to which must be added the various works of Mary Bateson and F. W. Maitland—both lost, alas ! to English historical scholarship in 1906—which we have found of the greatest use. We must mention, too, Mrs. J. R. Green's brilliant *Town Life in the Fifteenth Century*, 1894 ; the admirable work done by Professors Ramsay Muir and James Tait on Liverpool and Manchester respectively ; that of Rev. W. Hudson on Norwich ; and that of Mr. Adolphus Ballard on *The Domesday Boroughs*. Of French and German authors, Gneist, in his *Self-Government*, 1871, gives a good historical, legal, and statistical analysis of Municipal history, and of the situation before and after the 1835 Act ; and Dr. Joseph Redlich's *Englische Local-Verwaltung* (1901 ; translated as *English Local Government*, by J. Redlich and F. W. Hirst, 1903) affords an admirable critical survey. The English reader will find in *Surveys Historic and Economic*, by Professor W. J. Ashley, 1900, pp. 167-249, and in the *History of Modern Liberty*, by J. Mackinnon, 1906, vol. i. pp. 142-144, a brief summary of the Municipal theories of Savigny, Arnold, Nitsch, Gierke, Hegel, von Maurer, Keutgen, Flach, Varges, von Below, Wilda, and Sohm ; see also "L'Origine des Constitutions Urbaines au Moyen Age," by H. Pirenne (*Revue Historique*, vol. liii., 1893, and vol. lvii., 1895).

tion.[1] The privilege of incorporation, with the rights of legal personality and perpetual succession, and the use of a common seal, had been granted by Charter or statute to all sorts of bodies, religious, commercial, or educational, having no connection with local government. We cannot be sure that all the existing or reputed Charters were genuine; still less is it beyond dispute what exactly they meant. The muniments of Municipal Corporations are obviously incomplete, and have not always been in proper custody. Moreover, many Corporations, like those of the City of London, Bedford, and Oxford, claimed to exist by mere prescription, and to have possessed Mayors, Aldermen, or Burgesses, wielding extensive powers of government, and enjoying large privileges, long prior to their receipt of a Charter recognising their incorporation. It may possibly be true, as Miss Bateson has urged, that, in strict law, some formal act was necessary for the formation of a Borough. "In the Middle Ages," it is said, "towns did not grow, but were made. A village, just because it was a large one, could not gradually come to be called a Borough any more than it can nowadays. A definite legal act was necessary to sever it from a Hundred, and give it a Hundred Court of its own. Wherever we can go back to the beginning this formal act of creation can be traced."[2] The trouble is that, just in those cases in which we find no such legal act, there is no beginning to go back to; and we cannot simply assume that every Municipal Corporation had its own Hundred Court. Many towns, as we know, "long ago received a few Chartered privileges from a mediæval baron," who had declared that they

[1] A list of 302 "cities, boroughs, and towns corporate" was appended to the House of Commons Committee Report on Promulgation of the Statutes (Dec. 1796), but it does not seem to have been supplied to the Commissioners or known by them, as it includes places into which they did not inquire, and excludes others into which they did inquire. At least a third of the total cannot be said to have had Municipal Corporations. The Commissioners themselves found the definition quite impossible. It would have been equally impossible, we are told, to give any precise definition of a Municipal Borough or a Municipal Corporation in the thirteenth century (*History of English Law*, by Sir F. Pollock and F. W. Maitland, 1895, vol. i. p. 653). Comyns' *Digest* could give no better definition than that "Borough imports an ancient town of principal note, and which enjoys particular privileges" (first edition, 1762, vol. i. p. 613). "No accurately exhaustive list of our Corporate Boroughs ever was or ever could be made" (*Township and Borough*, by F. W. Maitland, 1898, p. 23).

[2] *Mediæval England*, 1066-1356, by Mary Bateson, 1903, p. 125.

should be "Free Boroughs," and they were accordingly, though without Hundred Courts of their own, "allowed a precarious place on the roll of English Boroughs,"[1] which might harden into permanence.   Others, again, like that of Arundel, did in fact possess all the attributes of incorporation without having at any time received any Charter whatsoever.   "There were," it is true, things which a Borough "could not do unless it obtained a privilege from the King.   It could not, for example, institute Coroners, for that would have disturbed the justiciary scheme of the shire of which the Borough formed a part.   It could not declare that its own officers should do that work of summoning, distraining, and arresting which had theretofore been done, even within Borough walls, by the Sheriff.   Nor could it take from the Sheriff the power and duty of collecting those rents and tolls which were due to the King."[2]   But none of these rights, as will hereafter abundantly appear, was indispensable to a Borough or to a Municipal Corporation. We might have expected to find some line of demarcation in the completeness with which the particular urban community had actually enfranchised itself, whether with or without a Charter, from the control of its Lord.[3]   But this, as we have seen, would compel us to rank as Municipal Corporations Birmingham and Newbiggin, where the Lord had long ceased to intervene, and to omit from this class such Chartered Municipalities as Morpeth and Cardiff, where the Lord of the Manor, notwithstanding the existence of Borough Justices of the Peace, and even of Borough Quarter Sessions, was still the mainspring of the constitution.   Nor does the right to return representatives to the House of Commons afford us any guidance. Members of Parliament were elected by places which had never been imagined to be Municipal Boroughs, or to possess any sort of Corporate government, whilst many undoubted Municipal Corporations never exercised this privilege.   The terms used in the various communities are equally distracting.

[1] *Township and Borough*, by F. W. Maitland, 1898, p. 17.
[2] *The Charters of the Borough of Cambridge*, by Mary Bateson, with introduction by F. W. Maitland, 1901, pp. viii-ix.
[3] Comparatively few of the couple of hundred undoubted Municipal Corporations of 1689 were in towns which, like "the Leicester of Domesday Book, stood, *as a Free Borough should*, on no man's land, and in no Hundred" (*Records of the Borough of Leicester*, by Mary Bateson, vol. i., 1899, p. xii). See *The Domesday Boroughs*, by A. Ballard, 1904.

Some obvious Municipal Corporations had no Mayors and no Aldermen, but merely a Bailiff just as Tetbury had; a Port-reeve like many a Devonshire village; a Warden recalling a hospital or a college; or a pair of Bailiffs just as Birmingham had. On the other hand, many a village, like Fishguard and Overton, completely dependent on its Lord, and without magisterial jurisdiction, called the petty officers appointed at the Lord's Court by the high-sounding titles of Mayor and Aldermen. Similarly, whilst some Municipal Corporations knew nothing of burgage tenure, nor of Freemen or Burgesses, Lords' Courts up and down the country swore in new Free-holders and other immigrants as Burgesses or Freemen; whilst at Alnwick, which can rank only as a Manorial Borough, there was, as we have seen, a numerous body of Freemen, recruited by Birth, Apprenticeship, Marriage, and Co-option, and organised into Trade Gilds, which dominated the town government down to the middle of the nineteenth century. Nor was the size or population of the town any certain guide. There were Municipal Corporations in villages of a few hundreds, or even of a few scores, of inhabitants; whilst flourishing communities, like Blakeney in Norfolk, during the Middle Ages, and Manchester and Sheffield in the eighteenth century, had none. Not all Municipal Corporations possessed markets, whilst many places without pretension to incorpora-tion had enjoyed them from time immemorial.[1] It may be that, in the Middle Ages, the distinction turned on whether or not the place paid to the subsidies at the rate of one-fifteenth (like the rest of the County), or, as a Borough which the King himself had created or recognised as existing by prescription, at the rate of one-tenth.[2] But this arbitrary distinction, which affords us, in the absence of complete lists of the

---

[1] "Considering the great part that the market plays in certain theories as to the origin of Boroughs, it is noteworthy that of the forty-two markets mentioned in Domesday Book, only eleven are situate in places that are called Boroughs" (*The Domesday Inquest*, by A. Ballard, 1906, p. 181).

[2] *Mediæval Manchester and the Beginnings of Lancashire*, by James Tait, 1904, p. 54. Thus the town of Stretton, in Rutland, being charged as a Borough with its share of a tenth, appealed in 1453, and produced Royal Letters Patent conceding to the inhabitants that they should not be charged to tenths "with the King's Burghs and Towns of Ancient Demesne," notwith-standing that they may have paid such in the past, but that they should be "taxed and charged to all Quinzimes and Quotas of Quinzimes together with the men of the Geldable" (*Firma Burgi*, by T. Madox, 1726, pp. 80, 81).

places which paid tenths instead of fifteenths, but little
historical guidance, fails us completely by 1689, when tenths
and fifteenths were alike obsolete.   Similarly, we cannot, in
1689, take as our test the assumed distinction in the representation at the ancient County Court or at the Assizes, where
the Township, it is said, appeared by the Reeve and four men,
whilst the Borough came as an independent Hundred by its
own twelve men.[1]   We come at last to the fact of enfranchise-
ment from the County officers, and this we think the really
significant attribute.   Even this proves too indefinite to mark
off with any precision the Municipal Corporation from the
Manor.   The whole of the individual type specimens that we
have described in the preceding five chapters resemble each
other and the true Municipal Corporations to be presently
analysed, in enjoying exemption from the jurisdiction of one
or other of the officers of the County.   None of them, nor yet
the Municipal Corporations themselves (with the exceptions of
Haverfordwest, Berwick on Tweed, the City of London, and the
Liberty of the Cinque Ports), were wholly exempt from County
jurisdiction—just as none of them, not even the City of
London, could exclude either the King's Judges on their
circuits, or the officers of the King's Courts at Westminster.
Nevertheless it is in this direction that we find the line of
demarcation for the period between 1689 and 1835, between
those members of the series which can, and those which
cannot, conveniently be classed as Municipal Corporations.
As we saw in our preceding volume,[2] it was the Justices of
the Peace who became, in the eighteenth century, the real
rulers of the County.   Similarly, we find that it was the
Borough Justices of the Peace who, in this period, more and
more became the dominant influence in the Municipal Corporation.   We shall therefore, in the following chapters, include as
true Municipal Corporations all those communities which,
whether by prescription or Charter, actually enjoyed the
privilege of clothing one or more of their members or officers,

---

[1] In the sixteenth century St. Albans pleaded that it was a Borough
because it had sent members to Parliament.   " A test by which, perhaps, they
really set more store was the sending of a Jury of twelve Burgesses to answer
for the Borough before the Justices in Eyre" (*Mediæval England*, 1066-1550,
by Mary Bateson, 1903, p. 396).

[2] *English Local Government*, Vol. I., "The Parish and the County," Book II.

within the limits of the Borough, without personal appointment by the Crown, with the well-known powers elsewhere given by the Commission of the Peace.[1] It is upon these Boroughs—numbering in England and Wales about two hundred—that we shall, for the rest of this volume, focus our attention,[2] though we shall not abstain from citing the many features in which the members of the series below this arbitrary line resembled those above it.

(a) *The Instrument of Incorporation*

To the lawyer of the seventeenth century, as to his successor of to-day, it seemed clear that the privilege of incorporation—the creation of a fictitious person, as a legal entity having perpetual succession—could be obtained only from some legal instrument; in fact, omitting the mediæval possibility of incorporation by the Pope and the modern intervention of an Act of Parliament,[3] only by a grant from the

---

[1] Merewether pointed out in 1822 that the holding of Petty Sessions has been typical of incorporated Boroughs since, at any rate,'the sixteenth century, when the "tourn or leet" lost its criminal jurisdiction. A "usual clause in Queen Elizabeth's Charters . . . is that which makes the Mayor and some of the Aldermen Justices of the Peace, and gives the Borough the power of holding Sessions of the Peace" (*A Sketch of the History of Boroughs and of the Corporate Right of Election, etc.*, by H. A. Merewether, 1822, p. 22). Maitland, too, drew attention to the importance of the special Royal Peace conferred on fortified places as marking off the Borough from the village (*English Historical Review*, vol. xi., 1896; *Domesday Book and Beyond*, 1897, pp. 184-185, 192-193).

[2] We estimate the number in England and Wales in 1689 as between 199 and 205, according to the view taken of certain anomalous cases. For even the possession of magisterial jurisdiction does not afford an absolutely certain test. In some cases, as we have seen among the Boroughs of Wales, it cannot be stated with certainty whether any Corporate member or officer actually exercised, or was legally entitled to exercise, magisterial powers. In a few other cases (Brackley, Clun, Thornbury, etc.) magisterial powers had fallen completely into disuse. In some Boroughs (those of the County of Durham, for instance) the Corporate body could not create a Justice ; but its Mayor for the time being was, as a matter of fact, always included, *virtute officio*, in the Commission of the Peace for the County. Omitting all these cases, we make the total of true Municipal Corporations in 1689 to have been 199.

[3] Statutes determining or modifying the constitutions of Municipal Corporations were, of course, not unknown prior to 1689. The early Acts relating to Southampton, Plymouth, Hull, and the City of London are notable examples, whilst the governing Council of Northampton was changed from an elective to a close body by Act of 1487. But such cases of statutory intervention were, prior to 1689, comparatively rare. Nor must we quite ignore other formal instruments. The whole question of the Instrument of Incorporation, and its

Crown, which was usually expressed in a Royal Charter. It might, therefore, be supposed that the constitutions of the couple of hundred of Municipal Corporations of 1689 were all definitely fixed and easily to be ascertained. This was very far from being the case. By 1689 most Boroughs had received successive Charters inconsistent with each other, and it became open to question which of them was the more authoritative.[1] This uncertainty as to which among several Charters was to be considered the "Governing Charter" was immensely increased by the events immediately preceding the accession of William and Mary.[2] It does not fall within the plan of this work to describe the assaults which had been made, first, by Charles the Second, and then by James the Second, upon the independence of the Municipal Corporations. The proceedings taken against the Corporation of the City of

variation from age to age—the relative prevalence and the particular degrees of validity and scope of Seignorial Charters confirmed or unconfirmed by Royal authority, Palatine Charters, Royal mandates directing constitutional changes, Royal grants, Royal Letters Patent, Royal Charters of original grant or of confirmation, or of *inspeximus* of lost Charters, accepted or not accepted, surrendered and enrolled or not enrolled, authorised or not authorised by statute, charitable trusts or agreements enrolled in the Court of Chancery, decrees of that Court, Gild ordinances enrolled by the Lord Chancellor or the Lord Chief Justice pursuant to statute of 19 Henry VII. c. 7 (1503) or not so enrolled—requires further investigation. We have taken the Royal Charter as the most common instrument. What we say as to the uncertainty as to what it prescribed, its omissions, its frequent failure to prevail over contrary "immemorial" custom, and its subsequent supersession by mere usage or the enactment of a By-law, all applies equally, as far as we can make out, to the other formal documents by which particular groups of persons assumed to become Corporations. The Municipal Corporation Commissioners of 1835 obtained particulars of 1357 Royal Charters to Municipal Corporations, to which a few more might be added. Of those analysed, 61 dated from before the time of King John (1199) ; 566 from between 1199 and 1485 ; 598 from between 1485 and 1688 (the Tudors and Stuarts), making 1297 in all prior to the Revolution. Between 1689 and 1835 only 60 were issued (Index to First Report of Municipal Corporation Commission, 1839, p. 104).

[1] Thus, no fewer than nine Royal Charters had been granted to the Corporation of Havering-atte-Bower in Essex, from 1465 to 1665 ; but the Corporation elected to act under those of 1465 and 1559, and ignored whatever in the others was inconsistent with them (First Report of Municipal Corporation Commission, 1835, vol. v. p. 2878). At Carlisle there had been "two Charters subsequent to the Governing Charter, viz. 16 Charles II. and 36 Charles II. These, however, were not accepted, and the Corporation always continued to act under the former Charter, 13 Charles I." (*ibid.* vol. iii. p. 1469 ; compare S. R. Gardiner's *Commonwealth*, vol. iii., 1901, p. 260, etc.).

[2] *History of My Own Time*, by Gilbert Burnet, 1833, vol. ii. p. 332 ; *History of England*, by L. von Ranke, 1875, vol. iv. pp. 169-171 ; *State Trials*, vol. viii., 1810, pp. 1039-1388.

London in 1683, when the servile judges, on a writ of *Quo Warranto*, pronounced the Corporation to have forfeited, not only its privileges, but also its very existence, struck terror into the hearts of Mayors, Aldermen, and Common Councillors all over the kingdom. Most of the Corporations were induced voluntarily to surrender their Charters, on the assumption that they were in some way forfeit; and to solicit new ones from the Crown, in which power was reserved to remove members or officers at will, whilst the appointment of the more important officers was often made subject to the Royal approval. Nor would it be worth while attempting to unravel the complicated proceedings in the several Corporations during these seven years. Charters were declared forfeit or were voluntarily surrendered. " It was much questioned," says Burnet, " whether these surrenders were good in law, or not." [1] New Charters were given, and again revoked. Sometimes the surrenders of the old Charters were formally enrolled; sometimes this registration, supposed to be necessary to the validity of the surrender, was neglected. Sometimes the new Charters were formally accepted, sometimes not. In some cases they were acted upon, in others not. Mayors, Aldermen, and Councillors were sometimes appointed according to the new constitutions, sometimes under the old ones. Those who were obnoxious to Charles the Second, as being disaffected to the Court, were removed in 1683-84; those who were obnoxious to James the Second, as being hostile to Roman Catholicism and the dispensing power, were removed in 1686-87; and it was often uncertain whether the removals, together with the consequent new appointments, were valid. When the invasion of the Prince of Orange became imminent, James the Second hastily restored the old Charters of the City of London, and issued a proclamation purporting to restore the constitutions of all the other Corporations, except those of which the Charters had been declared forfeited by legal judgments, and those of which deeds of surrender had been formally enrolled.[2]

---

[1] *History of My Own Time*, by G. Burnet, 1833, vol. ii. p. 332.
[2] MS. Acts of Privy Council, 17th October and 1st November 1688. The Charters of the Boroughs incorporated since 1679 were annulled. All Corporations of which deeds of surrender had not been enrolled, and which had not had judgments entered against them, were to continue as Corporations, and were to fill up vacancies, notwithstanding that the time for so doing had elapsed; all

Some of them acted on this proclamation and some did not. Those that were excluded from the proclamation were left in a position of exceptionally doubtful legality. Some continued to act on the Charters of James the Second, while others treated them as null and void.[1] Eventually an Act of Parliament declared the illegality of the judgment against the Corporation of the City of London, and restored its rights and privileges in the widest terms; whilst for the next few years the student of the archives of the Privy Council finds that body busy with petitions about new Charters, or Letters Patent deciding various points in dispute.[2] It was a necessary consequence of the destructive proceedings of the seven years 1682-1688 that, for the whole of the eighteenth century, hardly any Municipal Corporation could feel assured that any particular element in its constitution, or any particular form that it affected in its practice, would be upheld by the Courts at Westminster, if any person chose to dispute an election.[3]

members of such Corporations claiming by Charter, Letters Patent, or Grant, since the surrender or judgment, were to be removed; the Attorney-General was to cancel the surrenders made but not enrolled; all Corporations of which deeds of surrender had been enrolled, or against which judgment had been duly entered, were to have their ancient Charters restored, and the former members and officers reinstated, etc. It is not clear exactly how much was supposed to be effected by the proclamation itself as distinguished from the steps which it promised should be taken. By a second proclamation, a fortnight after the first, the Corporation of Exeter, which had been excepted from the first by mistake, was declared to be within its terms; and the ancient Charters of four other Corporations, against which judgment had actually been entered, or the surrenders of which had actually been enrolled, were nevertheless declared to be restored.

[1] The Corporation of Oxford, which, besides older instruments, had Royal Charters of 1606 and 1684, chose to ignore the latter, and only partially to act on the former. On an information "filed by the Attorney-General in 1697 for the purpose of enforcing a clause contained in it, the Corporation, in their answer, disclaimed the obligation of that Charter, in any points which abridged their previous liberties and privileges, and were supported in their position by the judgment of the Court" (First Report of Municipal Corporation Commission, 1835, vol. i. p. 98).

[2] MS. Acts of Privy Council, 1689-1699, relating to Winchester, Coventry, Nottingham, Dunwich, Colchester, Plymouth, Bewdley, Southwold, Deal, Tewkesbury, etc.

[3] Thus Portsmouth found its Charter of 1684 upset when litigation arose, on the technical point that the surrender of the previous Charter had not been enrolled, and was therefore invalid; whilst the invalidity of this surrender, which had been recited as forming the consideration for the new Charter, made the latter fail for want of consideration, and rendered its acceptance a nullity (Butler *v.* Palmer, in *Reports of Cases, etc.*, by William Salkeld, pp. 190-191; see *Practical Treatise on the Law of Corporations*, by James Grant, 1850, p. 46). The Corporation thereupon resumed under the old Charter (First Report of

But there was a further ground for uncertainty as to what was legally the constitution of a Municipal Corporation. "During the Middle Ages," wrote Maitland, "the function of the Royal Charter was not that of ' erecting a Corporation,' or regulating a Corporation which already existed, but that of bestowing liberties and franchises upon a body which, within large limits, was free to give itself a constitution from time to time.[1] . . . It was very free . . . to develop a conciliar organ, one council or two councils, to define the modes in which burgherhood should be acquired, to adopt the ballot or the open vote, and generally to be as oligarchic or as democratic as it thought fit. And at least from the fourteenth century onwards a large use was made of this liberty. Elaborate constitutions were established, and after a few years abolished, and some of our Boroughs had revolutions enough to satisfy a South American Republic."[2] Nor did these revolutions come

---

Municipal Corporation Commission, 1835, vol. ii. p. 802). At Bewdley the new Charter of 1685 was acted upon as valid for thirteen years, until, in the keen struggle for power between the two great families of the town in 1708, a flaw was discovered, litigation ensued, the Charter was declared void, and the old Charter of 1606 was reverted to. In 1708, "At the single instance of a noble lord, a new Charter was forced upon an ancient Corporation " (*Speech made in the House of Commons upon the late Ministry's forcing a New Charter on the Town of Bewdley without a surrender of the Old*, 1710, Somers' Tracts, vol. xii., 1814, p. 671). The other party did not relinquish its hold, and " for two years, in consequence of the Charters, Bewdley had two Corporations, and two Bailiffs who fulminated against each other like rival Popes " (*History of Bewdley*, by John R. Burton, 1883, pp. 44-45). With the change in the political complexion of the House of Commons in 1710 came a resolution declaring the Charter of 1708 to be void. Steps were taken for its repeal ; but the restoration of Whig power in 1714 found it still in being, and it was not subsequently disputed (First Report of Municipal Corporation Commission, 1835, vol. iii. p. 1771).

[1] The " men " of Bedford, for instance, had received numerous Royal Charters and Letters Patent varying and increasing their Corporate powers and privileges, but none of them had defined the constitution (*ibid.* vol. iv. pp. 2103-2105). The ancient Borough of Ludlow, governed by a " Twelve and Twenty-Five " from time immemorial, and furnished with an array of Royal Charters granting to the Bailiffs, Burgesses, and Commonalty the widest range of liberties, franchises, and immunities, had no constitution fixed by Royal Charter until that of 38 Elizabeth (1596). " Know ye that we, willing that the aforesaid old and ancient manner and form of governing in the Town or Borough aforesaid be from henceforth for ever inviolably in all respects duly observed " appears as the preamble of the elaborate constitution prescribed in that year (*Copies of the Charters and Grants to the town of Ludlow*, n.d. pp. 103-104). In 1537 Henry VIII. had issued what was called a " Decretal Order," confirming the ancient usage, and in 1597 the Court of Exchequer pronounced another " Decretal Order " to the same effect (*ibid.* pp. 213, 222).

[2] *Cambridge Charters*, by Mary Bateson, with introduction by F. W. Maitland, 1901, pp. viii, ix. The student of Charters will note that in all Charters

to an end in the sixteenth or the seventeenth century. Only a small number of Corporations thought it worth while to strengthen their position during the eighteenth century by applying for new Charters.[1]   But we could give innumerable instances, in both the seventeenth and eighteenth centuries, of radical changes in the constitution of particular Municipal Corporations, brought about merely by the adoption of a new By-law or standing order.

The most common of these changes during the sixteenth and seventeenth centuries was exactly similar to that which we have shown to have taken place at this very period in numerous urban and rural Parish Vestries—the establishment of a Close Body to stand in the place of the general body of Burgesses. The " Twenty-Four," recites one of these Municipal By-laws, " shall be instead of the whole commonalty, and no other of the commonalty to intermeddle upon pain of five pound." [2]   A lesser revolution might be effected by a By-law relating to the election or qualifications of the Common Council, the Aldermen, or the Justices of the Peace; usually of a restrictive tendency, either in transferring the right to appoint to a smaller body, or limiting the persons eligible for

after the Restoration—not only in the Charters granted by Charles II. and James II. but also in those granted by William and Mary and by the subsequent monarchs—the exact constitution of the Municipal Corporation is the dominant consideration. Few Municipal Corporations were, however, governed by these later Charters, which usually effected only particular amendments of the local constitutions.

[1] Among them, Minehead in 1716, Pontefract in 1717, Lostwithiel in 1731, Tiverton in 1737, Maidstone in 1743, Colchester in 1757, and Saltash in 1774. Most of these applications for new Charters to existing Municipal Corporations were occasioned by some lapse in the succession of members or officers, or some failure to fulfil the obligations of the Corporation. See, for Minehead, Home Office Domestic State Papers in Public Record Office, vol. v., 1716 ; for Pontefract, *ibid.* vol. x. 30th September 1717, and MS. Acts of Privy Council, vol. ii. p. 45, 17th October 1717 ; for Lostwithiel, *ibid.* vol. ii. pp. 460, 624, 25th October 1731 and 20th April 1732 ; for Tiverton, new Charter of 1737 ; for Maidstone, MS. Acts of Privy Council, vol. viii. pp. 316, 580, 617, etc., 15th February 1743, 7th November 1744, 8th January, 8th and 17th July 1745, 14th May 1747 ; for Colchester, *ibid.* vol. xvi. p. 620, etc., 8th November 1757 and 9th February 1758, 21st December 1761, 2nd January 1762, and 29th April 1763 ; for Saltash, new Charter of 1774.

[2] MS. Minutes, Corporation of Romney Marsh (Kent), 1604. By its ancient Charter this Corporation comprised the whole commonalty of the Marsh, who had, down to 1604, administered their affairs in public meeting, and chosen from among themselves a Bailiff and ten Jurats. From that date the whole work was done by the Close Body, filling vacancies in its own ranks by co-option.

appointment.¹ Many of the officers actually at work in the Municipal Corporations, exacting fees and controlling the conduct of the inhabitants, had no better sanction for their existence and activities than resolutions of the governing body or immemorial custom.² And with regard to the qualification to be required in a Burgess or Freeman, though this was, in a sense, the very foundation of the Corporation, the changes were so frequent and so casual that it is clear that they were hardly regarded as alterations in the constitution.³ In the early years of the nineteenth century the spirit of the age led a few close Corporations voluntarily to open their ranks to a somewhat larger circle, by resolutions reviving the assembly of Freemen in Common Hall, and by a transfer to such assemblies of the election of some of the great officers, and more or less of the administrative control.⁴

¹ Thus, at Maidstone, in 1764, the Common Council made a By-law abrogating the right of Burgesses to vote either for Common Councillors or on the admission of new Burgesses. This, however, was set aside by the Courts in 1766 (*The Charters and other Documents relating to the King's Town and Parish of Maidstone*, by W. R. James, 1825, p. 228). A By-law of the Municipal Corporation of Chester in the reign of Henry VIII. confined the choice of Aldermen to members of the Close Body, although neither the previous nor the subsequent Charters contained any such limitation. Notwithstanding litigation on the point in 1735, the By-law continued in force down to 1835 (*Gentleman's Magazine*, April 1735, vol. v. p. 217 ; First Report of Municipal Corporation Commission, 1835, vol. iv. p. 2622). So at Romsey, Hampshire, the Municipal Corporation did not scruple, in 1742, to enact by By-law that the Aldermen should henceforth be chosen only from among the Capital Burgesses, and the Mayor only from among the Aldermen, although the Governing Charter of 1608 had imposed no such limitation, and had expressly made every Burgess eligible for either place (*ibid.* vol. ii. p. 1331). At Cambridge, which had received numerous Charters from the reign of Henry I. to that of Charles I., an extremely complicated method of choosing the Mayor had been arranged by By-law as early as 1345. This was varied by another in 1568, which was abrogated in 1786, when the old method was reverted to (Newling *v.* Francis, in *Reports of Cases, etc.*, by Durnford and East, vol. iii. p. 189 ; First Report of Municipal Corporation Commission, 1835, vol. iv. p. 2185 ; *Practical Treatise on the Law of Corporations*, by James Grant, 1850, p. 81).

² This does not apply merely to Constables, Ale-tasters, or Beadles inherited from the Lord's Court or accreted from the Gilds and Companies, but also to such powerful functionaries as the Chamberlains and Town Clerks of some Municipal Corporations.

³ Thus, at Monmouth, where the Charters contained no provision as to the admission of new Burgesses, both the method of admission and the qualifications were altered from decade to decade according to the will of the dominant majority (First Report of Municipal Corporation Commission, 1835, vol. i. p. 324). The Corporation of Poole, Dorset, made residence obligatory (*ibid.* vol. ii. p. 1321).

⁴ Thus, at Plymouth, Devon, a By-law of 1803 led to the four or five hundred Freemen being summoned to Common Hall nearly every month, to elect the

There were, however, some Corporations, and not a few institutions in many others, for which no better warrant was claimed than prescription.   Many of these, as we found to be the case with the Close Vestries, we suspect to have had their origin in By-laws adopted at comparatively recent dates, the record of which had been lost or forgotten.   "It was," we are told, "in the fortieth year of Queen Elizabeth's reign that the judges, upon the application of the Privy Council, determined that from usage, within time of memory, a By-law may be presumed, restraining to a select body the right of election of the principal corporators, though vested by the ancient constitution in the popular assembly."[1]   The Courts of the seventeenth and eighteenth centuries continued to accept long-sustained usage as evidence of there having been a By-law instituting the practice.[2]   We have accordingly to relinquish the idea of discovering the constitutions of the Municipal Corporations from their Charters, or of confining our examination of them to what may be supposed to have been the strict law.   To the student of English Local Government between 1689 and 1835, what is important is what actually existed, not what subsequent lawyers might eventually decide ought legally to have existed.   With the Municipal Corporation as with the Parish and the County, it was the actual local usage that was significant, rather than law and the lawyers.[3]

Mayor, Recorder, Aldermen, etc., and a standing Committee of twenty-one (MS. Records, Plymouth Corporation, 1803-1835 ; First Report of Municipal Corporation Commission, 1835, vol. i. pp. 579, 581).   At Chipping Wycombe (Bucks) a similar change was made in 1832 with regard to the election of new Burgesses (*ibid.* vol. i. p. 41).

[1] *The Law of Municipal Corporations*, by J. W. Willcock, 1827, p. 8.

[2] Thus, at Nottingham, the choice of Aldermen was, in practice, confined to members of the Close Body, with a tradition of a By-law prior to the earliest records, which commence in 1575.   "In 1810 this mode of election was called in question in the case of the King against Ashwell, in which an information *Quo Warranto* was granted."   In proof of the alleged By-law, which could not be produced, the defendant "gave evidence of the usage of the Corporation as far back as the records of the Corporation went.   A verdict was given for the defendant as to the fact of such a By-law having existed, and the Court of King's Bench . . . held the By-law to be reasonable" (First Report of Municipal Corporation Commission, 1835, vol. iii. p. 1990 ; *Reports of Cases, etc.*, by East, vol. xii. p. 22 ; *Practical Treatise on the Law of Corporations*, by James Grant, 1850, p. 81).

[3] In the nineteenth century, on the other hand, we find the Courts upholding the words of the Charters, as against the constant usage of the Corporation.   At Truro, for instance, when a Capital Burgess had been elected

(b) Corporate Jurisdictions

Although not defining constitutions, the legal instruments —whether Seignorial Grants, Royal Charters and Letters Patent, or deeds of agreement or trust enrolled in the Court of Chancery—were highly valued by the corporators who so jealously preserved them under threefold lock and key in ancient town chests. What these documents conveyed was not only real estate, but also acquittances, immunities, franchises, privileges, and jurisdictions. The character and the constitution of the Corporate body was, as Maitland suggests, largely left to shape itself according to the concessions made to it. The area over which the Municipal Corporation extended, its membership, and the number and character of its officers, for instance, were, as we shall see, dependent on the kind and extent of the powers which it possessed. The development, and even the structure of its governing body, between 1689 and 1835, was, as will subsequently appear, largely influenced by the amount of its property and by its obligation or privilege of electing " Burgesses " to sit in the House of Commons. Hence, before we proceed to our analysis of the constitution of the Municipal Corporations, we must make a rapid survey of the general character of the jurisdictions that they exercised. Some Corporations, as we shall see, possessed all these jurisdictions; some only a selection among them, with every variety of combination; and some, again, literally only one of them. The only jurisdiction, in fact, that was universal to all Municipal Corporations, as we have defined them, as it was the only one that was peculiar to them, was that involved in the possession of a Corporate Magistracy.

One of the most important of the powers of the Municipal Corporation of 1689 was that connected with real estate, within or without the Borough; a power which had come to include a varied series of Corporate rights, amounting, over certain lands in nearly every Borough, to complete ownership

according to custom, but contrary to the directions of the Charter of 1589, his election, on being objected to, was, in 1823, declared void (First Report of Municipal Corporation Commission, 1835, vol. i. p. 657). So at Monmouth, where the Common Council had long usurped the right to elect the Mayor, which a Charter of 1550 had given to the Burgesses at large, the Courts, on appeal made in 1818, upheld the right of the Burgesses, in spite of long-continued usage (*ibid.* vol. i. p. 322).

in fee simple. There might still be traces, in the form of burgage tenements held at fixed quit-rents which had become nominal, of the earliest seignorial commutation of villein service into money payments; there might be remnants of Corporate accountability for such quit-rents to the Crown or other superior Lord; the Borough itself might be held in fee farm upon an annual payment. Moreover, among the successive concessions by the Lord of the Borough there would usually have been various Manorial customs as to the administration of the commonfields, the stinting of the pastures, and the utilisation of the waste, out of which the emerging Corporation would have built up autonomous and vaguely defined rights over all the land within its area, so far as this had not been reduced to complete individual management.[1] The entire complex of rights that we term the Manor might even have been acquired by the Corporation, and with it, therefore, not only the power to hold Courts, to which we shall presently allude, but also the right to estrays, escheats, and other profitable incidents connected with land. But the Corporation might own other real estate—properly acquired from a dissolved Gild or religious house, or simply purchased from the King or other owner, or inherited from some pious founder for the fulfilment of a trust or merely for the "common good." It was for greater assurance in these cases that the Charters so often expressly gave the Corporations the right of holding, administering, and selling real estate.

But although the Borough had, even in 1689, nearly always some interest in agriculture, it was, of course, predominantly a community of traders, master craftsmen, retail shopkeepers or dealers of one sort or another, together with

---

[1] It must not be forgotten that the typical Borough of 1689, like that of the thirteenth century, still had, within its boundaries, "fields as the neighbouring villages had fields; vast, hedgeless, fenceless tracts of arable land, in which the strips of divers owners lay interspersed 'hide meal and acre meal'" (*Township and Borough*, by F. W. Maitland, 1898, p. 4). The Borough of Nottingham, for instance, extended over no less than 15 square miles, and included, even as late as 1833, "a considerable quantity of forest, meadow, and common land without the walls of the town" (First Report of Municipal Corporation Commission, 1835, vol. iii. p. 1985). The Borough of Queenborough, in Kent, included about 240 acres of open land (*ibid.* vol. ii. p. 823); the Corporation of Canterbury exercised jurisdiction over 4 square miles of rural "liberties" (*ibid.* vol. ii. p. 709); that of Coventry over agricultural areas 20 miles in circumference (*ibid.* vol. iii. p. 1795).

their journeymen or assistants. Thus the "Association of Producers" in agriculture had become gradually transformed into an "Association of Producers" in commerce and manufacture. This transformation was reflected in the Corporate jurisdictions. To the control of the land there was gradually added a control of trading. We have seen this in its simplest form in some of the most rudimentary Manorial Boroughs, innocent of anything like Gild organisation, where the Mayor would exact a fee from every newcomer who opened a shop. We need not consider such vexed questions as, what was implied in the grant of a Merchant Gild so frequent in the thirteenth century, or in the rise of the Craft Gilds; or how far the Gild orders were confirmed by the clauses giving the Corporations the right to regulate artificers; or superseded by the Statute of Apprentices under which, as a matter of fact, the eighteenth-century Corporation usually preferred to take its proceedings to prevent "foreigners" (by which was meant simply persons not "free" of the Corporation) from interfering with the profits of the Burgesses.

The Burgesses of the Borough desired, however, to attract to their town, under certain conditions, both sellers and buyers from outside its area. This could best be done by the Borough obtaining the right to have a Market on certain days of the week or month, or a Mart or Fair on certain days in the year. Hence we find this concession frequently made by Lord or King to the Municipal Corporation, though, as we have mentioned, it was by no means exclusively confined to Corporate towns. The privilege might be the right to establish a new Market or Fair, or merely the transfer of the ownership in a previously existing Market or Fair. This Franchise was, even after the Restoration, still an object of ambition in a town aspiring to become a Municipal Corporation. "Our being dependent on Sandwich," said the inhabitants of Deal, in 1698, "for every article of food, places the people in a very great strait, incapacitates the ship-agents and boatmen in sending daily supplies to the shipping, and enhances the price, causing general complaint among the whole population, now exceeding three thousand souls."[1] But it was more than

---

[1] *Reasons for seeking a Charter for Deal*, 1698; reprinted in *History of Deal*, by S. Pritchard, 1864, p. 146.

a matter of convenience. A weekly market not only saved the inhabitants the trouble and expense of taking their wares or their custom to another centre, but also furnished the Corporation with new sources of revenue and power.

But in the period between 1689 and 1835, the most notorious of all the privileges and franchises of a Municipal Corporation, was that possessed by the majority of them of returning their own "Burgesses" to sit in the House of Commons. This had formerly been an onerous obligation, or, if an advantage, it was mainly in being exempt in the matter from the jurisdiction of the County Sheriff and from the duty of contributing to the expenses of the Knights of the Shire. By 1689, however, and still more between 1760 and 1832, it had become a valuable privilege, with important results, to be afterwards described, upon the constitution and administration of those Corporations which possessed it.

We pass now to the administration of justice in its various branches, the most prized among Municipal jurisdictions. It was, as we shall subsequently show, this function more than any other that determined the evolution of the working constitution of the Municipal Corporation and its relation to the local inhabitants. For the moment it must suffice to point out that the right to hold a Court of Justice was an integral part of many of the Franchises that we have already described. The mere concession by the Lord to his tenants of any measure of autonomy in the administration of their land was frequently accompanied by permission to hold their own Court for the settlement of cases of debt and trespass among themselves.[1] When the Burgesses acquired the Manor itself, they obtained with it the right to hold the Court Leet, View of Frankpledge, and Court Baron. Similarly, the grant of a Market or a Fair implied the right to determine the disputes and punish the defaults of buyers and sellers, either in distinct tribunals, such as the Court of Pie Powder

---

[1] Jurisdiction in civil suits—often limited to personal actions, and still more frequently to actions of small amount, but in about fifty towns extending to all actions of any amount—was exercised in 1689 by nearly all Municipal Corporations, there being, as far as we can make out, only about a dozen exceptions. Among these were Bossiney, Brading, Chesterfield, Glastonbury, Kidderminster, Louth, Macclesfield, Pembroke, and Pevensey. In some Boroughs the Court Baron of the Lord still exercised civil jurisdiction.

or the Court of the Clerk of the Market, or in such other Courts as the Borough possessed. Nor did the jurisdiction of the Borough Courts stop at those Borough boundaries which were annually perambulated with so much ceremony. Some of the market jurisdictions, for instance, extended miles beyond. A Municipal Corporation, too, might own land outside its own Borough, and might even be, in its corporate capacity, Lord of a Manor, the Bailiff to whom a " Bailiwick " had been granted, or the Steward or Lord of a Hundred. The King, moreover, had often conceded to the Corporation express jurisdiction of particular kinds over wide stretches of land, many miles of river, and even adjacent parts of the sea. The Mayor might be " Conservator " of this or that river, or " Admiral " over a whole estuary, entitled to exercise specific civil and criminal jurisdiction even over other Boroughs.

The investment of one or more members of a Municipal Corporation with the well-known powers and authorities else-where conferred by the Commission of the Peace brings us to a new range of jurisdiction. The function of creating a Magistracy for the town—of holding Petty Sessions, and even Quarter Sessions — was, as our subsequent chapters will abundantly show, the most potent of Municipal Franchises. To say that it characterised all Municipal Corporations whatsoever, is merely to repeat that we have made the possession of this Franchise the logical *differentia* of the class. However elaborate may have been the organisation of a Borough and however complete its autonomy, we have left it behind us as a Manorial Borough unless it could clothe one or more of its citizens with the jurisdiction of a Justice of the Peace. After 1689, indeed, the desire of a town to have its own Magistrates was the most frequent reason for seeking a Charter.[1] But even this essential characteristic does not furnish us with a sharp dividing line. The Portreeve or

---

[1] The inhabitants of Deal, in their *Reasons for seeking a Charter* (1698), stated " that they are obliged to go to . . . Sandwich, whenever they need a J.P. for signing Poor's Cess, removal of paupers, etc. ; and sometimes from caprice these things have been denied us ; . . . that Sandwich puts upon us fines for licences of public-houses and does whatever it pleases, and keeps that money, and returns none of it to us, which would assist our rates if we were separated from that place ; . . . Sandwich monopolises all law and justice " (MS. Records, Corporation of Deal ; *History of Deal*, by S. Pritchard, 1864, pp. 144, 146).

Bailiff of many a Manor or " Lord's Borough "—often assuming
the title of Mayor—claimed vague rights of acting as " Conservator of the Peace," whatever this might mean; and even
felt himself warranted, by the ambiguous way in which the
statutes had sometimes referred to the Mayors, in acting as a
Justice.[1]   Even more perplexing from the standpoint of
classification were those Boroughs which had no right to
create their own Corporate Justices, but which had, as a
matter of fact, acquired the privilege of having the Mayor
for the time being, and even some other members of the
Corporation, invariably included in the Commission of the
Peace for the County at large.   There might even be a
separate Commission of the Peace issued for the Borough;
and if this separate Commission was continued decade after
decade, it might make the Manorial Borough almost indistinguishable in practical working from a Municipal Corporation.   On the other hand, there were genuine Municipal Corporations in which, although a Corporate Magistracy nominally
existed, this had become attenuated by disuse, or had even
fallen into abeyance.   The Borough Court of Quarter Sessions
was not infrequently allowed to lapse.   Sometimes even the
Borough Petty Sessions became merged in that held in the
town by the County Justices for the surrounding district.
Such Municipal Corporations were in process of retrograding
to the status of a Manorial Borough, or even to that of a
mere Lord's Court.

The criminal jurisdiction exercised by these Corporate
Justices varied greatly in scope.   At the bottom of the scale
stood those Corporations—nearly forty in number—which
had no Court of Quarter Sessions and had been granted power
to try and punish only such offences as fell within the jurisdiction of Petty Sessions; such as drunkenness and disorderly
conduct, minor assaults, and the ever-growing series of
nuisances which the statutes allowed to be dealt with
summarily.   Persons accused of graver offences had to be
committed for trial at the County Quarter Sessions or the

---

[1] Thus Dinas Mawddwy, a place which had no Charter, and was governed by
its Lord's Court, had a Mayor, chosen by the Leet Jury from among three
persons named by the Lord's Steward.   This Mayor granted ale-house licences
as if he were a Justice (First Report of Municipal Corporation Commission, 1835,
vol. iv. p. 2673).

Assizes.[1]   Next in order came those Corporations [2] where the Justices could try and punish all misdemeanours, however grave, but not even the smallest felonies.   Others [3] could try and punish all felonies "not affecting life or member," or all felonies except manslaughter and murder.[4]   Above these stood the Corporations [5] in which the Justices could deal with all felonies whatsoever—in one case [6] even expressly including high treason.

A more definite sliding scale of jurisdictions, by which one Municipal Corporation was distinguished from another, was the degree of its emancipation from the jurisdiction of the Justices of the County at large.   The lowest grade of Municipal Corporations in this respect were those—about

[1] Among the Corporations which had no higher jurisdiction than this were Chesterfield (First Report of Municipal Corporation Commission, 1835, vol. iii. p. 1790); Gravesend (ibid. vol. v. p. 2866); Ripon (ibid. vol. iii. p. 1710); and Truro (ibid. vol. i. p. 657).   But it is to be noted that, however restricted might be the criminal jurisdiction of the Borough Justices, they had, in all other respects, the full powers of a County Justice so far as the Borough area was concerned.   In one respect, indeed, the Justices of the Peace of the most insignificant Borough were in a superior position.   "The authority of these is not revocable as the Commission of the Peace is" (The Justice of Peace, by Theodore Barlow, 1745, p. x).

[2] About fifteen in number, in all but four of which the jurisdiction was exclusive.

[3] About eighty-seven in number, in two-thirds of which the jurisdiction was exclusive.

[4] Leeds (First Report of Municipal Corporation Commission, 1835, vol. iii. p. 1621).

[5] About forty-seven in number, all but three (Boston, Buckingham, and Wallingford) having exclusive jurisdiction.

[6] Chester (ibid. vol. iv. p. 2623), by the so-called "Crown-mote Court."   It is to be noted that the extent of the criminal jurisdiction enjoyed by a Municipal Corporation was often out of all proportion to its size and importance in 1689, still more so in 1835.   Among the Corporations entitled to try all felonies were not only those of most of the English shire towns, Counties Corporate, and Cinque Ports (though some of each of these classes were restricted to felonies not touching life or limb), but also such small towns as Dunwich, Evesham, Maldon, Romney Marsh, and Southwold, and (concurrently with the County Justices) Buckingham and Wallingford.   The tiny Corporation of Banbury in Oxfordshire had had a gallows formally granted to it, and its Justices at the Borough Quarter Sessions long tried even capital cases.   An execution by their sentence took place about 1746 (ibid. vol. i. p. 11).   On the other hand, Carmarthen (a County Corporate), Maidstone (a shire town), and so important a residential centre as Bath, were restricted to misdemeanours.   "The want of all power to try felonies," we are told in 1833, "has been long felt at Bath, as an evil of serious importance.   With a population exceeding 50,000 in the city and immediate neighbourhood the most trifling case of larceny must be sent to be tried at the County Quarter Sessions or Assizes, which are held at Wells, Bridgwater, and Taunton, at the distance of 18, 39, and 50 miles respectively from Bath" (ibid. vol. ii. p. 1116).

thirty-five in number—in which the Borough Justices had only concurrent jurisdiction in the town along with the County Justices, and could only hold Petty and Special Sessions. A higher stage was that of having exclusive jurisdiction within the Borough for a Borough Court of Quarter Sessions, whether in respect of misdemeanours only, or also of felonies. The highest of all these Corporate jurisdictions was possessed by those Boroughs—over forty in number—which absolutely excluded the Justices of the County at large from any inter-meddling with cases of even the gravest felonies that arose within the Borough ; three or four of which not only held their own Courts of Quarter Sessions, but also regular Sessions of Oyer and Terminer and of Gaol Delivery.[1]

From the standpoint of the Municipal Corporation, the right to administer civil and criminal justice carried with it three inestimable privileges—immunity from attendance at the Courts held in other places and by other authorities, the settlement of all cases by the Corporate officers themselves, and the retention by the Corporation of the fees, fines, and other compulsory payments by plaintiffs and defendants. What those inhabitants who were not members of the Corporation most appreciated was the saving in time, trouble, and expense caused by having a tribunal on the spot, with magistrates always at hand. It was the popular appreciation of this Municipal service that inspired most of the petitions for incorporation between 1689 and 1835. On the other hand, the monopoly of this magisterial power possessed by the Close Body, together with the partiality and oppression to which, in a few of the worst cases, this gave rise, were among the grievances of the Municipal Reformers of 1832-35.

An incident in this local administration of justice, as we have already seen in the Court of the Manor and in the

---

[1] Exeter held sessions of Gaol Delivery (First Report of Municipal Corpora-tion Commission, 1835, vol. i. p. 490) ; Bristol, of Oyer and Terminer and Gaol Delivery (*ibid.* vol. ii. p. 1171). Southampton held sessions of Oyer and Terminer and Gaol Delivery, apparently under a special Commission from the Crown, down to 1725 ; and claimed that its Town Clerk should officiate, without the Clerk of Assize. We see the Corporation arranging for such separate sessions, possibly held by the Recorder, from time to time. Since 1725, however, the town has been simply included in the Western Circuit of the Judges (Speed MSS. pp. 73-74, in MS. Records, Southampton Corporation ; *History of Southampton*, by J. S. Davies, 1883, p. 188).

Manorial Borough, was the power of prescribing in advance what should be the obligations of the inhabitants. It was, as we have seen, taken for granted that the Court which dealt with individual cases should also formulate By-laws. Nor do we find, in fact, that the autonomous Courts of the Municipal Corporation exercised in this capacity any more extensive legislative powers than did the Courts of the Manorial Borough, or even those of the Hundred or the Manor. All alike regulated the use of the common lands. All alike defined what would be punished as a public nuisance. All alike formulated particular obligations of the individual inhabitant to do what the common good required. If the Municipal Corporation had obtained the insertion, in one of its Charters, of a clause giving express power to make By-laws, this gave no new sanction, and did not even extend the scope of its law-making power beyond that actually exercised by a Lord's Court. In one direction, it may be thought that the Municipal Corporation had an additional By-law-making power, namely, in the regulation of artificers. We do, indeed, find that By-laws made by the Corporate body, or by a Gild with its sanction, regulating apprenticeship, the right to trade, the quality of the wares, and the charges to be made for specific services, were, between 1689 and 1835, much more frequently characteristic of Municipal Corporations than of Manorial Boroughs; whilst such regulations were almost unknown in the Courts of Manors. We find, too, the Municipal Corporations, even in the eighteenth century, making new constitutions for their Trade Companies, and actually incorporating new ones for the regulation of particular trades.[1] But the examples of Alnwick and Sheffield sufficiently prove that both Gild structure and trade regulation might exist in places dependent only upon Seignorial Charters, and still under the dominion of the Lord of the Manor. The only real advance in the legislative power of the Municipal Corporation, as compared with that of a Lord's Court or a Manorial Borough, was, in

---

[1] As in the City of London, Dover (MS. Records, Dover Corporation, 23rd July 1718), Bristol (MS. Records, Bristol Corporation, 17th November 1714), and Exeter (MS. Records, Exeter Corporation, 30th March and 22nd December 1685, 23rd August 1737). At Gateshead, as perhaps at other Boroughs in the County of Durham, which we have classed as Manorial Boroughs, Gilds had been incorporated by separate Charters from the Bishop as Lord Palatine.

fact, that exercised by its Justices of the Peace, and this was analogous to that already described in the Quarter Sessions of the County.

The power of the Municipal Corporation to levy taxation sprang, it need hardly be said, from the jurisdictions that we have described. We may pass rapidly over the right of the Corporation to assess upon its own members or upon the burgage tenants, their shares of fee farm rent or other Corporate liability; and no less rapidly over such mediæval powers of levying taxation over all the householders of the Borough as were involved in the Royal or statutory grants of murage or pavage. More significant to us, as regards the Municipal Corporation of 1689, is its power to levy taxes within its area on the persons buying or selling, or exercising a craft. This fiscal power might be connected either with the concourse of traders and customers at its Market or Fair, or with the monopoly of trading enjoyed by its Burgesses. We may regard as merely a development of this power of levying contributions upon the operations of traders, such not infrequent Corporate rights as the exaction of petty customs, " thorough toll " or " toll traverse," and various forms of *octroi*, whether derived merely from prescription, from ancient Manorial rights, or from Royal grant. What is significant in all these Municipal taxes on trading is the series of exemptions from them enjoyed by the members of the Corporation, or by other privileged groups of traders, master craftsmen, or journeymen; coupled with powers, in one or other authority, of regulating admission to these privileged circles, or of levying extra taxation on those who were excluded from them. Closely connected with these powers and immunities within the area of the Corporation was a series of immunities, enjoyed by members of the Corporation under Royal grants, from some or all of the analogous powers of taxation exercised by the Corporations of other Boroughs,—an exemption some- times so extensive as to free the privileged citizens from such local taxation throughout the King's dominions. Hence by 1689, though the widest of these exemptions was becoming somewhat difficult to enforce, there was not only a prefer- entially taxed class within the Borough, but also, in strict law, small and scattered sets of licensed " free traders " passing to and fro amid an intricate network of local *octrois* covering no small proportion of the Kingdom. But, just as we have seen with the By-law-making power, all these taxes and immunities occur among Manorial Boroughs, and even mere Manors—for instance, those in Ancient Demesne [1]—as well as among Municipal Corporations. What was peculiar to Municipal Corporations, and that only to those which could hold Courts of Quarter Sessions to the exclusion of the County Justices, was the power to tax for gaols, maintenance of prisoners, vagrants, etc., by a County Rate; or (in the case of Boroughs not being Counties of themselves) by a rate " of the nature of a County Rate."

(c) Corporate Obligations

To the member of a Municipal Corporation this organisation seemed, as we have indicated, a complex of immunities and franchises, rights and privileges, which might, in their extent and variety, be equivalent to a valuable Corporate income. To the King and his ministers, as we may believe, the Municipal Corporation appeared in another light. Besides the Corporate jurisdictions, which were sources of advantage and privilege, there were onerous Corporate duties to be performed and burdensome Corporate responsibilities to be fulfilled. To the mediæval statesman, we may imagine, the Municipal Corporation was, like the County and the Parish, primarily an organ of obligation, by means of which, in particular localities, the services required by the community as a whole could be performed and exacted. There was, to begin with, some Corporate payment to be made in commutation of, or in substitution for, the tribute formerly exacted from individuals.[2] The exemption from the jurisdiction of the County Sheriff was accompanied by a corresponding

[1] For the peculiar privileges of Manors in Ancient Demesne, see pp. 22, 183.

[2] The Corporation of Southampton, which had in the Middle Ages enjoyed a valuable trade with the Mediterranean, paid £200 a year. " In 1552 the King ordered that when the customs of the port did not amount to £200, and no ships called carracks of Genoa and galleys of Venice should enter the port to load or unload, the town should . . . pay . . . only £50. To this day certificates are still prepared every year on 9th November that no carracks of Genoa nor galleys of Venice have arrived at the port " (*Town Life in the Fifteenth Century*, by A. S. Green, 1894, vol. ii. p. 305 n. ; *History of the Customs Revenue*, by Hubert Hall, 1885, vol. i. pp. 134, 310, vol. ii. p. 114).

obligation to collect the King's revenue and to execute the King's writs within the limits of the Borough. The Head of the Corporation, if he enjoyed precedence and social consideration inside his Borough, was also the officer to whom the King addressed his orders, and upon whom rested the responsibility for the Borough. In the Middle Ages the Municipal Corporation had been responsible, if not for the defence of the Borough against a foreign enemy, at any rate for the upkeep of the wall and the provision of the necessary " harness " and arms to equip the citizens ; an obligation succeeded by that of duly keeping the Nightly Watch, and above all of maintaining the King's Peace within the Borough and enforcing the laws of the land. The obligation to send one or two Burgesses to sit in Parliament, and to pay their wages, was part of the burden of the Corporation ; special obligations were incurred in connection with grants of Pavage and Murage,[1] of Lastage and Pontage, of Markets and Fairs, of Bridge Tolls and Ferries. It was in order to enable the Municipal Corporation to fulfil its Corporate obligations that it was empowered to command and enforce the personal service of its members in any of its offices, and to levy upon them such taxation as might be necessary. Nor was this Corporate obligation only nominal. Frequent cases show that any failure of a Municipal Corporation to fulfil any of its responsibilities, or neglect of any of its duties, might be sharply punished by a fine leviable on any member of the Corporation, by imprisonment of its Head or other officers, by the Borough being temporarily " taken into the King's hands " and exposed to the tyrannies and exactions of his officers, and even by the forfeiture of the privilege of incorporation itself.[2] Moreover, in addition to these national obligations, the Municipal Corporation had, in nearly every case,

---

[1] The grant of petty customs or other dues might be coupled with an obligation to perform particular services ; thus it was alleged that the valuable dues levied by the Bristol Corporation had originally been granted " for the paving of the city, for the repairs of the city walls and of the Quays—purposes and objects which have all long ceased, or for which other and most ample rates are provided by the Legislature " (*Felix Farley's Journal*, 1826).

[2] In 1341, as the Municipal Corporations of Hythe and Romney had not provided the ships which they were required to find, " the collector of the subsidy as well as the King's collectors of wool in Kent, were ordered to ignore their Franchises, and tax them just like other men " (*Cinque Ports*, by Montagu Burrows, 1888, pp. 140-141).

undertaken more or less responsibility in the capacity of what we may call Public Trustee. It had often received grants of land or bequests, charged with payments for this or that charitable and public object, or left generally in trust for the poor. It had in many towns succeeded to, or stepped into the shoes of, religious Gilds, and had made itself more or less responsible for continuing part of their work. A large part of what afterwards became the statutory provision for the poor was, down to the sixteenth century, provided by the Municipal Corporation.[1] It had established, often by means of gifts, collections, or bequests, causeways and bridges, hospitals for the aged, schools for boys, and other public services, for the maintenance of which it had incurred a moral if not a legal responsibility. Down to the end of the sixteenth century, when the administrative functions of the Parish and the County were still small in amount, the couple of hundred Municipal Corporations were performing, we may estimate, the greater part of all the services of Local Government that existed.

By 1689, however, though considerable remnants of these Corporate responsibilities still remained, they had very largely lapsed. The particular duties which the Municipal Corporation had undertaken had, one after another, become attenuated or entirely disappeared. The old duty of the defence of the Borough against a foreign enemy had passed out of memory. The fee farm rent, or other annual payment for the Borough, had, with the alteration in the value of money, become almost a nominal charge, and had often been redeemed. The maintenance of the poor had been taken over by the Overseers of the parishes under the Elizabethan statute. The obligation of finding Burgesses to sit in Parliament had changed from being a costly burden into a much valued privilege, which might be profitable to the Borough, if not even a source of pecuniary gain to the Corporation itself. Many other obligations had become obsolete, or continued only as matters of routine. The King, moreover, and his ministers no longer importuned the Municipal Corporations with commands; and ceased, in the eighteenth century, even to hold them in any practical way responsible for the Boroughs.

[1] *Early History of English Poor Relief*, by Miss E. M. Leonard, 1900.

To the Hanoverian Monarchs, as to Sir Robert Walpole and his successors, it never occurred to connect the existence of a Municipal Corporation with any responsibility for meeting even the long-standing requirements of its Borough, still less the new or changing needs of the inhabitants. The one duty of the Corporation that was still recognised was that of providing the local Magistracy, and even this was not enforced. If a Municipal Corporation let this duty drop, and allowed its criminal jurisdiction, like its civil tribunals, to fall into abeyance—if it ceased to hold Quarter Sessions, and let its Petty Sessions dwindle into mere opportunities for committing offenders for trial elsewhere—the County Justices were always ready to take up the work, and virtually to reabsorb the Borough in the County. And apart from this provision of a Corporate Magistracy, the function of a Municipal Corporation as an organ of national obligation was, by the end of the eighteenth century, almost forgotten.

(d) *The Area of the Corporation*

Paradoxical as it may seem, the Municipal Corporation had, in the vast majority of cases, no one area over which it exercised authority. A Municipal Corporation, like the Manor and unlike the Parish and the County, was, in fact, not primarily a territorial expression. It was a bundle of jurisdictions relating to persons, and only incidentally to the place in which those persons happened to be. The persons were, it is true, always assumed to be connected with some geographical centre—they were the "Burgesses," the "Approved Men," the "Mayor, Masters, and Councillors," or "the Mayor, Jurats, and Commonalty," of some Borough or City. But it follows from our account of the acquittances, franchises, liberties, and immunities which comprised the total jurisdiction of a Municipal Corporation, that the areas over which authority was exercised might differ widely for the different powers, and might in some cases be susceptible of no geographical definition whatever. It is true that, where a Municipal Corporation had no other powers or functions than those of local Magistracy, its area may be said to have been strictly that part of the County within which its Justices exercised their authority. But beyond this simple form, every additional jurisdiction, it is scarcely too much to say, involved, for its operation, a separate and different geographical area. Thus we find Municipal Corporations wielding this or that power over the areas of one or more Manors; other powers over the areas of one or more Parishes.[1] Their Market, Conservancy, and Admiralty jurisdictions might extend for miles into adjacent Counties; far up rivers and creeks, and along estuaries and seas; including wide stretches of upland and commons, scattered hamlets and fishing-ports. The area within which some of their immunities might be enjoyed— to which, therefore, their power of securing exemption potentially extended—was actually co-extensive with the Kingdom. It was even wider. There was one at least of the Municipal Franchises that had no geographical limits whatever, though it is precisely the one which to-day we associate most directly with definite boundaries, namely, the right to return Burgesses to sit in Parliament. Not a few Municipal Corporations made wide use of their power of admitting to membership persons residing elsewhere, and they could have extended the right to share in their political franchise to all British subjects wherever domiciled. Thus, the geographical extension of a Municipal Corporation can be represented only by an indefinite number of circles, differing among themselves from jurisdiction to jurisdiction. One of these—as we think the most important—was the area over which the Corporate Justices exercised their magisterial powers. This it was, generally coincident with an older

---

[1] In a few exceptional instances one or other of the Chief Officers of a Municipal Corporation had even jurisdiction extending far beyond any of its ordinary boundaries. We shall mention subsequently the jurisdiction exercised by the Coroners and other officers of the Corporations of the Cinque Ports over their Non-Corporate "Limbs" or "Members." The Mayor of Wareham in Dorsetshire, who was *ex-officio* Coroner for that Borough, exercised the powers of Coroner also over Brownsea Island and the whole of the so-called Isle of Purbeck (First Report of Municipal Corporation Commission, 1835, vol. ii. p. 1360). We do not know whether this fact, or that of Poole being a County of itself, has any connection with there having occasionally been a separate Lord-Lieutenant for the Isle of Purbeck, and a separate Commission of the Peace for Poole. The Corporations of Wareham and Poole were always quarrelling about their respective rights in Poole Harbour, the one to be exempt from "Keyage," the other to levy it (see, for instance, MS. Acts of Privy Council, 10th February, 20th May, 15th June, and 20th July 1664).

U

Manorial or Parochial area,[1] that was usually regarded as specially the Borough or City, the boundaries of which were periodically perambulated with so much pomp. It is the area of this jurisdiction that we find some Municipal Corporations, both before and after 1689, intent on extending by Royal Charter, in order to prevent the upgrowth, sometimes of rival authorities, sometimes of lawless Alsatias, through the neglect of the County Justices, or their scarcity around the busy trading port or inland manufacturing centre.

This particular area it was, too, that, in two or three dozen towns, we find divided into Wards, divisions of great antiquity and unknown origin, which were, more frequently than not, non-coincident with the numerous small Parishes into which the larger Boroughs were usually parcelled out. The number of Wards might be two, four, five, six, eight, twelve, twenty-one, or twenty-five ; and, contrary to a common impression, we do not find that this division had, in the majority of cases, any connection with the Aldermen of the Corporation.[2]

---

[1] This area was sometimes (as at Leeds and Maidstone) coincident with a whole Parish ; sometimes, as in most of the older shire towns or cathedral cities, it included several Parishes (in the City of London, over a hundred) ; in many of the smaller Boroughs it was (as we have seen in the cases of so many Manorial Boroughs) confined to one Township of a Parish, or to one Manor. But occasionally the area was defined by Charter quite irrespective of any of these. The Municipal Corporation of Penzance, for instance, exercised its jurisdictions within exactly half a mile radius from a central point (*infra*, Chap. VIII. ; First Report of Municipal Corporation Commission, 1835, vol. i. p. 571).

[2] It may, of course, be true of those particular towns, that, " in London, as in Norwich, Yarmouth, Ipswich, and Canterbury, Aldermanries, Wards, and Leets were in fact synonymous " (*History of Boroughs and Municipal Corporations*, by H. A. Merewether and A. J. Stephens, 1835, vol. i. p. 549). But this does not nowadays appear quite so certain as it did. It is true that besides the better-known cases above mentioned, the Municipal Corporation of Salisbury had five persons called Aldermen, chosen by the Corporation on Charter Day, who, by tradition, ought to have presented all misdemeanours and disorders in the several Wards to which they were assigned, and who had formerly super-intended the "victualling" of the population. So at Wilton. At Canterbury the Aldermen were even more definitely connected with the Wards, to each of which two were assigned. In each Ward they held a Court annually, of the nature of a Court Leet or Wardmote, at which Constables and Borsholders were appointed. In "1719, the Aldermen were paid forty shillings each towards holding the Courts at their respective Wards" (*Canterbury in the Olden Time*, by John Brent, 1879, p. 105 ; First Report of Municipal Corporation Commission, 1835, vol. ii. p. 699). So, too, at Winchester, Aldermen were assigned one to each Ward ; and at Exeter, two to each Ward. On the other hand, no such connec-tion can be traced in various other Boroughs, such as Pembroke, which had two Wards ; Ruthin, St. Albans, Ludlow, and Monmouth, which each

What was, however, almost universal was a connection between the Ward, the provision of a Constable and the obligation of defence, or at least of service in the Nightly Watch. In one small Borough where the Corporation was at one time under obligation to find, when required, twenty-one ships for the King's service, the Borough was deliberately divided into twenty-one Wards for this purpose, each Ward being required to provide one ship, and being requited by the privilege of having one packet-boat in the profitable passage service to and from the French coast.[1] But however the Wards had been formed, they were, in 1689, commonly made use of for the appointment of Constables and the organisation of the Watch, and they were not infrequently each placed (as we have seen to be the case also in such an unincorporated Parish as Braintree and in such a Manorial Borough as the City of Westminster), under the individual charge of one of the Members of the Governing Council—it might be a Jurat or Alderman, it might be a mere Common Councilman [2]—who acted as "Captain of the Watch," or at any rate was responsible for "setting the Watch," and was exempted from

had four; Alnwick, Carmarthen, Oswestry, and Reading, which had five; Llandovery, which had six; or Haverfordwest, which had eight. York had only four Wards, though it had twelve Aldermen; Brecon had twelve Wards though it had fourteen Aldermen; Chester twelve Wards though it had twenty-four Aldermen; and Tenby twelve Wards with an indefinite number of Aldermen. At Cambridge there were four Wards, presided over, not by Aldermen, but by four Bailiffs. Though Bristol and Sandwich had each twelve Wards and placed each of them under an Alderman or Jurat, the Aldermen and Jurats were appointed quite independently of the Wards, which had originally numbered only five in one Borough and eight in the other. And at Norwich, where the twenty-four Aldermen were actually assigned to twelve districts of the City, these were themselves merely subdivisions of the four ancient Wards, apparently made expressly for the purpose. The City of London (where, as we shall subsequently describe, the twenty-five Wards were subdivided into Precincts, which were Constablewicks) may have been in a different position; though there seems some reason to suppose that, even there, the Wards were, as at Bristol, Norwich, and Sandwich, really made for the Aldermen, rather than that the Aldermen sprang from the Wards.

[1] Dover, see *Cinque Ports*, by Montagu Burrows, 1888, p. 82.

[2] Thus, at Dover, when all the householders were required to watch "in their turns," the Mayor, Jurats, and Common Councilmen were to be "Captains of the Watch," and "to set the Watch," but were exempt from other service (MS. Minutes, Dover Corporation, 1st July 1689). Sandwich "was formerly divided into eight Wards for purposes of defence, in each of which were two Constables; but from the year 1437 there have been twelve Wards or districts, and a Jurat presides over each of them, and annually nominates his Constable and Deputy Constable therein, who are sworn" (*Collections for a History of Sandwich*, by W. Boys, 1792, p. 787).

other service.   Or they might be made use of as magisterial districts, for the administration of justice within each of which a particular Borough Justice was made specially responsible.[1]

We must add, too, that within the Municipal boundaries there were often *enclaves*, wholly or partially exempt from the jurisdiction of the Municipal Corporation—sometimes connected with an ancient castle, a cathedral, a shire hall, or an ecclesiastical foundation—which were usually termed Precincts. These were to be found to a greater or less extent in most of the ancient shire towns and cathedral cities;[2] and they often led to a tangle of jurisdictions and a complication of responsibilities which it is impossible to unravel.   Occasionally, too, the limits of the various jurisdictions were so vaguely defined, and so much in doubt, as to be practically unknown.[3]

(e) The Membership of the Corporation

What may be termed the membership of the Municipal Corporation is as difficult to define as its area.   Who of right belonged to this "society of mortal men," by Charter or prescription rendered "immortal, invisible, and incorporeal"?   For, as it was said by Madox in 1726, "the Kings of England having in several ages past granted divers liberties to their towns, it became in some cases doubtful what persons were entitled to those liberties.   For men that lived together in a town were not all of a sort.   There were townsmen and suburbians, townsmen and co-inhabitants: in fine, some that were of the Gild or Gilds of that town and some that were not.   Many were willing to have the benefit of the common liberties but were unwilling to have a share in the common

---

[1] As at Southampton, MS. Ordinances, 1606 ; in MS. Records, Southampton Corporation.

[2] Also in the City of London, Ludlow, Pontefract, Scarborough, etc.   At Hereford the "Bishop's Fee" extended to half the city, and within it he alone had jurisdiction, held his own Courts, appointed his own Manorial Officers, and committed offenders to his own prison (*Collections towards the History and Antiquities of the County of Hereford*, by John Duncomb, 1804, vol. i. p. 293). The common use of the term Precinct for an exempted area must not be confused with its use, as we shall hereafter describe, in the City of London, for a subdivision of a Ward.   We know of no other town besides London and Norwich in which the Ward was subdivided.

[3] As at Kingston-on-Thames (First Report of Municipal Corporation Commission, 1835, vol. v. p. 2892).

burdens or payments." [1]   Occasionally, indeed, the membership
or method of constitution of the governing body of the
Corporation was set out in the legal instrument by which it
had been created or ratified.   But the recruiting of the
Corporation—that is, the admission of new Freemen or
Burgesses [2]—and the extent of the participation of these in the
Corporate immunities and Franchises, was seldom provided for,
except by local tradition, interpreted and amended by successive
By-laws.   And yet, as we shall see, it was exactly the
character of this membership—whether it was great or small
or resident or non-resident; and how far it included or
excluded one or other class or classes of the inhabitants—
that determined in each case the working constitution and the
nature of the administration of the couple of hundred Municipal
Corporations throughout the Kingdom.

It is, we think, significant of the course of development of
the Municipal Corporation that, just as the government of the
Manor rested almost wholly upon the Homage of the Court
Baron, and as the burgess-ship of many Manorial Boroughs
depended on the holding of land, so too, among Municipal

---

[1] *Firma Burgi*, by T. Madox, 1726, pp. 50, 279.

[2] "The fact is that none of the early Charters . . . provide for the admission of Freemen or Burgesses ; and very few of the more modern Charters"
(*History of the Boroughs and Municipal Corporations*, by H. A. Merewether and
A. J. Stevens, 1835, vol. i. p. 248).   We do not discuss the controversial point
as to whether, by the word "communitas" or otherwise, reference was ever made
in earlier times to any but a privileged class of inhabitants.   "Some hold," said
a learned antiquary of 1700, "communitas to be a general term that comprehended all persons whatsoever that resided within the Borough ; but the
Commonalty cannot be taken in this sense, for then they would extend to all
sorts of people, men, women, children, servants and labourers, who would have
equal right in the choice of officers and in the government of the Borough,
which was in no age known. . . . With us the word communitas comprehended
only a select company chosen for their wisdom and long experience to advise the
Chief Officer of the place " (*Historical Antiquities of Hertfordshire*, by Sir Henry
Chauncey, 1700, pp. 241-242).   Between 1689 and 1835, at any rate, it was
always authoritatively assumed that the privileges implied in Municipal incorporation were granted, not to all the inhabitants of the place mentioned, but to the
particular persons or classes designated.   See *Firma Burgi*, by Thomas Madox,
1726 ; *An Historical Treatise of Cities and Burghs or Boroughs*, by Robert Brady,
1704 ; *History of the Boroughs and Municipal Corporations*, by H. A. Merewether and A. J. Stephens, 1835 ; *Essay on English Municipal History*, by
James Thompson, 1867 ; *Town Life in the Fifteenth Century*, by A. S. Green,
1894 ; *History of English Law*, by Sir F. Pollock and F. W. Maitland,
1895 ; *Domesday Book and Beyond*, by F. W. Maitland, 1897 ; *Township and
Borough*, by the same, 1898 ; *The Domesday Boroughs*, by Adolphus Ballard,
1904.

Corporations, we find some limiting their membership to Free-holders within the Borough. It is true that these Municipal Corporations were, in 1689, few in number; but it is no less significant that they were among the most archaic in type, and characteristic of towns of small and stationary population. Membership of this kind sometimes extended to all the Free-holders of the Borough,[1] and in other cases only to the owners of certain ancient "burgage tenements," or immemorial hold-ings,[2] to the exclusion of newer houses or other holdings of land. Sometimes, the heir-at-law of a Free Burgess, succeeding to his freehold tenement within the Borough, was entitled to be admitted as a Free Burgess at the Manorial Court; though the purchaser of a freehold within the Borough had to be formally presented by the Jury before he could obtain admission. In one or two other cases succession to, or acquisition of, a freehold tenement within the Borough, though, by 1689, no longer the only avenue to membership of the Municipal Corporation, was one among several ways by which the Freedom could be obtained.[3] In practically all these cases, the Freeholders had to go through the ceremony of admission to the burgess-ship (including an oath of fealty) at a Manorial Court—a Court sometimes owned and held by the Corporation, sometimes by an individual Lord of the Manor.

In a large class of Municipal Corporations—about two-fifths of the whole—Servitude of Apprenticeship in the Borough was one of the ways by which the Freedom could be acquired. This apprenticeship had always to be to a master who was, at the date of its beginning, himself a Freeman, and usually a resident in the Borough. Occasionally there would be further restrictions. The apprentice might not be entitled to "take up his Freedom," unless his servitude had been for seven complete years entirely within the Borough; unless he had lived in his master's household; unless his master had remained a Freeman during the whole period; unless his master had himself in his time served a similar apprentice-

[1] As at Bossiney (First Report of Municipal Corporation Commission, 1835, vol. i. p. 453), Havering-atte-Bower (*ibid.* vol. v. p. 2878).
[2] As at Pontefract (*ibid.* vol. iii. p. 1876).
[3] As at Carmarthen (*ibid.* vol. i. p. 207), Dover (*ibid.* vol. ii. p. 944), and Sandwich (*ibid.* vol. ii. p. 1046).

ship; or unless he paid a substantial fee.[1] How far the system of Corporate recruiting by apprenticeship to a craft may be considered as a remnant of previous Gild structure, or how far it was merely analogous to the acquisition of a parochial settlement under the Poor Law by service of apprenticeship within the parish, we must perforce leave to be settled by the historian of the Middle Ages. What is clear is that, by 1689, this method of recruiting by Servitude was, in some Boroughs, rapidly disappearing, and in others it was losing its reality. We shall notice hereafter the persistent efforts made by one Municipal Corporation after another, between 1689 and 1835, to tighten up the conditions, with a view either of preventing merely colourable apprenticeships or of absolutely restricting their number. But in spite of the tendency of this avenue to membership to close up, it continued right down to 1835 in all the populous towns in which Municipal Corporations existed, and must therefore be ranked as one of their most typical characteristics. It was to this method of recruiting the Municipal Corporation that England owed its patches of exuberant low-grade Democracy which gave a peculiar flavour to the electoral history of the principal populous ports and trading centres.[2]

The recruitment of Corporate Membership by Apprenticeship had the peculiarity that, so far as the Municipal Corporations of 1689 are concerned, it never stood alone, as the only avenue to admission. The acquisition of the Freedom by Apprenticeship was nearly always supplemented by a power in the Corporation, usually exercised by the Governing Council, to admit other persons by co-option, with or without the

---

[1] As at Aldeburgh (First Report of Municipal Corporation Commission, 1835, vol. iv. pp. 2093-2094). In the Corporation of Queenborough, in Kent, it was even enacted by By-law that no person should take an apprentice until he had himself been nine years a Freeman; and in 1824 also that no Freeman should take a second apprentice until the expiration of the term of the first, even if his indentures were cancelled (*ibid.* vol. ii. p. 827).

[2] At Liverpool, where there were between three and four thousand Freemen, nearly all admitted by apprenticeship to the various handicrafts connected with shipbuilding, the discontented bankers, merchants, and householders asserted in 1833 that the " restrictions on obtaining the Franchise have the natural effect of limiting it chiefly to mechanics and labourers, and to persons of very limited education and property, who are consequently very much dependent on the will of others, and peculiarly exposed at elections to the temptations of bribery and undue influence " (*ibid.* vol. iv. p. 2705).

exaction of a substantial fee. And along with admission by Apprenticeship, we find nearly always admission by Right of Birth, and sometimes also admission by Right of Marriage. The sons of Freemen—sometimes only sons born within the Borough or after the father's own admission to the Freedom, sometimes only the eldest son or the first born after the father's admission—were entitled on coming of age to take up their Freedom. The husband of a Freeman's widow or daughter acquired in some Corporations a like privilege.[1]

A small but very important class of Municipal Corporations based their membership upon local Gilds or Trade Companies. We cannot attempt to explore the history of the Merchant Gild or of the later organisations of the Crafts; or even to speculate upon the manner of their interpolation into Municipal constitutions, or the extent to which, in their prime, they influenced the working of the Corporations. Our impression is that the establishment of Gilds had affected the constitutions of the Corporations, as we see them in 1689, in four main features. It was, we imagine, the Gild which had, in many cases, given body to the nascent Corporation, by providing the "common stock" or corporate fund, which, as we have seen reason to suspect, was both a cause and a sign of the growth of the sense of Corporate personality.[2]   It may

---

[1] Admission was (besides frequent or occasional co-option) by Servitude of Apprenticeship only, in Aldeburgh, Coventry, and Daventry; by Apprenticeship or Birth in about sixty Corporations; by Apprenticeship, Birth, or Marriage in about seventeen. In Fordwich, Hythe, Kidwelly, Ludlow, Malmesbury, and Ruyton, admission was by Birth or Marriage, but not by Apprenticeship; in Dunwich, Hastings, Higham Ferrers, Huntingdon, Lyme Regis, Macclesfield, Montgomery, Pevensey, Preston, Rye, Welshpool, and Wenlock, it was by Birth alone (together with co-option). The Right by Birth was confined at Boston to the sons of Aldermen and the eldest sons of Common Councilmen (First Report of Municipal Corporation Commission, 1835, vol. iv. p. 2152); and at Lyme Regis to the sons of Capital Burgesses (ibid. vol. ii. p. 1306). The Right by Marriage might be confined to the widow, or to a daughter, or to a daughter born after her father's admission, or to the eldest daughter. At Hereford it was limited to the eldest living daughter in cases in which there was no son (ibid. vol. i. p. 257); at Exeter only to daughters of Aldermen (ibid. vol. i. p. 488).

[2] In Liverpool, at any rate, "the Gild . . . was from an early date, and perhaps from the first, simply an aspect of the Borough community. Its officers were the Borough officers; its Freemen were admitted in the Portmoot, and this admission gave them full burghal rights. . . . Until the creation of the Gild the Borough Court and officers would have no funds to dispose of. . . . The Gild had revenues. . . . It is the Gild, therefore, which gives birth to the first vague idea of the Borough as having a Corporate existence, distinct from the existence of the individuals who compose it" (History of Municipal Govern-

not improbably have been to the Gild that the Corporation owed some of its most distinctive administrative officers—its Chamberlains, Cofferers or Keymasters, its Common or Town Clerk, and, so far as titles are concerned, its Warden, and even possibly its Aldermen. It may have been to the Gild that the Corporation owed its transformation from an association of owners and occupiers of agricultural land—the Homage, the freeholders; the group of holders of burgages or " burgess parts "—into an association of traders and craftsmen, with the accession of members who had served an apprenticeship, or had otherwise acquired the " Freedom " of the Borough ; together with the consequent relative "democratisation" of what would otherwise have been an entirely Close Body. Finally it was, we think, from the Gild that the Corporation had derived the peculiar feature of the Court of Common Hall—the exercise, by a general assembly of Freemen, of the supreme or ultimate authority.   By 1689, however, the social importance of the Gilds had long since passed away, and the influences which they had exercised had either ceased or had been themselves transformed.   Nevertheless, in nearly a score of Boroughs definite Gild structure still existed, more or less interwoven with the Municipal Corporation.[1]   In

---

ment in Liverpool, by Ramsay Muir, 1906, pp. 34-35). And at Leicester, Miss Bateson thought that the Four-and-twenty Jurats of the Borough were probably identical with those of the Gild (*Records of the Borough of Leicester,* by Mary Bateson, vol. i., 1899, p. xlvi).

[1] Among these were Berwick-on-Tweed, Carlisle, Chester, Dorchester, Haverfordwest, Hereford, Kingston-on-Thames, Lichfield, London, Ludlow, Morpeth, Newcastle-on-Tyne, Richmond (Yorks), Ruthin, Shrewsbury, Southampton, Wells, Winchester, and York. It will be remembered that Gilds or Companies existed also in the Manorial Boroughs of Alnwick, Durham, Gateshead, and Sheffield. Other Boroughs in which Merchant Gilds or Trade Companies appear to have existed, but where we have been unable to trace any definite organic connection between them and the Municipal Corporation—at any rate between 1689 and 1835,—included Andover, Bath, Brecon, Bodmin, Bristol, Cambridge, Carmarthen, Chichester, Coventry, Daventry, Dover, Exeter, Faversham, Guildford, Hertford, Kingston-upon-Hull, Lancaster, Leeds, Lynn, Monmouth, Norwich, Preston, Reading, Salisbury, St. Albans, and Walsall. Thus, in about three-fourths of the two hundred Municipal Corporations of 1689 we have discovered no trace of Merchant or Craft Gilds or Trade Companies having played any part in the town life, or even existed, for at least three centuries. On the other hand, Dr Gross has shown (*The Gild Merchant,* 1890) that the Merchant Gild—possibly not the Craft Gilds or Trade Companies—existed at an earlier date in many other towns, without, however, necessarily being connected with the Municipal Corporation. Some of the Gilds of Bristol, Kingston-upon-Hull, Preston, Southampton, and York may have been survivals of this form. The whole subject of the Gild (to which we shall recur in our sub-

some of these places, including the greatest of all Municipalities,
admission to the Freedom of the Corporation was conditional
upon the applicant having already acquired the Freedom of
one of the Companies.   In other cases no person could
become "free" of a Company, and thus entitled to participate
in its privileges or immunities, unless he was already "free"
of the Municipal Corporation.   In other cases, again, the
Freedom of either body entitled the possessor to the Freedom
of the other.   Finally (as with the holding of land), we see
the Freedom of a Trade Company ranking only as one among,
various methods of acquiring the Freedom of the Corporation.
In the other cases (about a score) in which the Gilds can be
shown to have existed in the towns, we have not been able to
find any evidence that they were organically connected with
the Municipal Corporations.

In about forty of the Municipal Corporations of 1689—a
fifth of the whole number—whilst there was a distinct class
of Freemen or Burgesses, we can trace no connection between
the Freedom and either landholding or the exercise of a trade.
Admission to the Corporation was obtained, not by succession
to a tenement or by Apprenticeship, but solely by Gift,
Redemption, or Purchase—that is to say, by co-option—
usually exercised by the Governing Council at its discretion,
though sometimes qualified by traces of Right by Birth.   In
the great majority of Municipal Corporations, moreover,
admission by co-option accompanied and supplemented the
other avenues to the Freedom.[1]   In all these Boroughs, as
was pointed out in 1827, the Corporation "may make every
man in the Kingdom a Burgess and voter, and thereby
introduce universal suffrage, on the one hand; or by omitting
to elect new Burgesses as the old ones die off, they may, on

sequent chapters in connection with Morpeth, Berwick-on-Tweed, Ipswich,
Leeds, Coventry, Bristol, Norwich, and London) needs further study, and
especially further investigation of the MS. records.

[1] Admission by simple co-option, whether styled admission by Gift, by
Redemption, or by Purchase, prevailed in nine-tenths of the Corporations.   It
does not seem to have existed (at any rate between 1689 and 1835) in those of
Bishop's Castle (Right of Birth only); Malmesbury and Ruyton (Right of Birth
or of Marriage only); Carlisle, Lichfield, and Stafford (Apprenticeship or Right
of Birth only), or Abingdon, Bossiney, Brading, Clitheroe, Orford, Pontefract,
Romney Marsh, Southwold, Tregony, Warwick, and Weymouth, in which
various forms of ownership, occupancy, or payment of scot and lot alone constituted membership.

the other, establish the oligarchy of two or three persons only returning the representatives to Parliament," [1] and, as may be added, permanently filling all the offices in the Corporation, and disposing of its property. As we shall subsequently explain, the Corporations from 1689 to 1835 often passed successively from restriction to lavish admission. It is possibly owing to a policy of restriction in preceding centuries that we find many Corporations without any separate class of Burgesses or Freemen.

There were some fifty Municipal Corporations—a quarter of the whole—which had no Freemen or Burgesses; that is, the membership of the Corporation was identical with that of the Governing Council, a Close Body, filling vacancies by co-option from outsiders. In a few of these cases we have proof that a separate class of Burgesses or Freemen had once existed; [2] in others, the Charters contained provisions for the admission of persons to be Freemen which do not seem to have been acted upon; in others, again, the former existence of a separate class of Freemen may perhaps be inferred from the fact that the process of co-option to the Governing Council included a formal admission to the Freedom of the Corporation. In the majority of these cases, however, we are left doubting whether there ever had been in these Boroughs a distinct class of Burgesses or Freemen. All these fifty freeman-less Corporations had, in 1689, one attribute in common. They all belonged to small or stationary populations. Moreover, the bulk of them had distinct resemblances in their Manorial character to those archaic Municipal Corporations of which the Burgesses were occupying owners of land. But instead of bearing traces of connection with the Homage of the Court Baron, they seem to revolve round the Jury of the Court Leet. In many of these little Municipal Corpora-

---

[1] *A Collection of Ancient Records relating to the Borough of Huntingdon*, by Edward Griffith, 1827, p. 8 *n.*

[2] It is significant that, in the important Corporation of Leeds, established by Charter as late as the seventeenth century, the very existence of a separate class of Freemen had, by the end of the eighteenth century, become entirely forgotten; although the MS. Records reveal the existence, in the latter part of the seventeenth century, of incorporated Trade Companies, with apprentices and Freemen, and a "Common Assembly" of the Borough, which had to be summoned to make ordinances "touching the working, dyeing, or sale of woollen cloth within the Borough" (*infra*, Chap. VIII.; First Report of Municipal Corporation Commission, 1835, vol. iii. p. 1617).

tions of the South-Western Counties and the Welsh Border, we seem, in fact, to be not far removed from that large class of Manorial Boroughs that we have described as arising out of the Leet aspect of the Lord's Court. We might class with these the one or two Municipal Corporations in which the Close Body alone enjoyed the powers and privileges of the Corporation, but in which the Jury of the Manorial Court would admit to absolutely nominal membership any " resiant " within the borough, sometimes any person paying scot and lot, or any inhabitant householder, irrespective of landholding or apprenticeship, birth or marriage. In these cases the so-called " Freedom " of the Borough was little more than certified inhabitancy. It is this tiny fraction of the couple of hundred Municipal Corporations—a fraction which cannot even be elevated into a class—that alone bears out the far-fetched theory of Municipal freedom invented by the Whig lawyer Merewether on the eve of the Municipal Revolution of 1835. " No plausible solution," he says, " of that difficulty [of determining who was by right entitled to the Freedom] can be surmised, but that obvious one which the Common Law suggests—of their being admitted, sworn and enrolled at the Court Leet of the Borough, in respect of their resiancy within it—whereby being Freemen *of*, or *belonging to* the Borough, they were its Burgesses." [1]

It is characteristic of Municipal Corporations that wherever Freemen existed, the individuals had always to be formally " admitted " to membership of the Corporate body. This admission was, in the more archaic Corporations, by presentment of the Jury in a Manorial Court, which, as we have seen, might be of the nature either of a Court Baron, or of a Court Leet, held by the Corporation itself or by a private Lord; in a few of the Corporations of great towns, by the Court of a Trade Company; and in the great majority of Corporations, by one or other of the " Courts," or assemblies, of the Corporation itself. Just as recruits had to be formally admitted, so also could existing members be extruded from the Corporate body. This " disfranchisement " might be by consent, either through the desire for relief from Corporate

---

[1] *History of the Boroughs and Municipal Corporations,* by H. A. Merewether and A. J. Stephens, 1835, vol. i. p. 248.

obligations, or for a temporary purpose, such as giving evidence in a case in which the Corporation was a party. On the other hand, the disfranchisement might be penal in character, in retribution for some action deemed to be inimical to the Corporation. Provided that all the proper forms were observed, a Corporation could legally disfranchise a member for any reasonable cause; such as a breach of duty to the Corporation or even the commission of an infamous act or indictable crime.[1] The fact that members of a Municipal Corporation had to be formally admitted, and could be legally extruded, emphasises its character as an arbitrarily selected group of persons; in complete contrast, we may point out, with a modern Municipality, which is regarded as necessarily and irrevocably including all the inhabitants of a given geographical district.

By 1689 what was of importance to the Municipal Corporation was not so much the particular methods by which the Burgesses or Freemen of the Corporation were recruited, as the numerical strength of this class of inhabitants privileged in some way or another to participate in the Corporate administration or the Corporate advantages. The number of the Freemen had, however, a close connection with the method by which the Freedom could be acquired. When admission to the Freedom depended on the ownership of land, the Freemen necessarily remained only a tiny fraction of any growing urban population. Again, if the Freedom depended on the grant of consent of a Jury or of the Close Body of the Corporation, there was a tendency to restrict recruiting to the number required to supply candidates for the Corporation offices. Nor was the number of Freemen substantially increased by admissions by Right of Birth and Right of Marriage; the accessions in these cases being usually more than balanced by losses through the decay of families, migration, and the inability or unwillingness of qualified citizens to take up their Freedom. Hence, the

---

[1] Thus at Exeter, in 1692, three Freemen were disfranchised for refusing to watch, and two for accepting poor relief (MS. Records, Exeter Corporation, 28th March and 12th September 1692). In the next year it was "ordered that henceforth no Freeman who receives parish alms, or who . . . by reason of his poverty cannot perform his duty of Watch and Ward, shall give any voice at any election of Mayor or Barons to Parliament" (*ibid.* 11th September 1693).

Municipal Corporations which restricted their admissions to persons recruited in any or all of these ways were constantly slipping into the already extensive class of Corporations having no Freemen outside the membership of the Governing Council or Close Body. Moreover, all these ways of becoming free of a Municipal Corporation were compatible with non-residence, and did, as we shall see, lead to the creation of non-resident Freemen with no concern in the good government of the Borough. The only broad avenue to the Freedom of a Municipal Corporation—the only way in which a residential Democracy actually came into being—was, in fact, the device of Apprenticeship to a Freeman in order to exercise a trade within the Borough.[1] In those Municipal Corporations in which the Freedom acquired by Apprenticeship was accompanied by valuable privileges in connection with manufacture or trade, we find, as might have been expected, a constant pressure to get into the ranks of the Freemen. Thus, the Boroughs which had, in 1835, the largest number of Freemen relatively to the population—the only ones in which the population of Freemen exceeded ten per cent of the adult male householders—had Municipal Corporations in which Freedom by Apprenticeship was a reality, especially if the Freemen were organised also in active Trade Companies. How far these Freemen Democracies really shared in the responsibilities of government or the privileges of the Corporation we must leave to be considered in our section on Municipal Constitutions.

(f) The Servants of the Corporation

If we inquire what, to the rural inhabitant who came into the town, would have seemed most novel and strange in the Municipal Corporation of 1689, the answer may perhaps be the prominence and all-pervadingness of the public officers who concerned themselves about the little community. It

---

[1] The Corporation of Preston, though it had by 1833 no fewer than 3300 Burgesses, without recruiting by Apprenticeship, is hardly an exception. Over 3000 of these were non-residential, and admitted only for political purposes, whilst there were also 300 " Foreign Burgesses " or " Out Burgesses," admitted only for market privileges (First Report of Municipal Corporation Commission, 1835, vol. iii. pp. 1687-91 ; *Preston Court Leet Records*, by A. Hewitson, 1905).

was not that the particular officers would, taken one by one, be unfamiliar to him. Many of them, in fact, alike in title and in function, were common to both rural Manor and urban Corporation. The Municipal Borough, even as late as the eighteenth century, continued in most cases to be an agricultural community, sometimes keenly interested in arable commonfields and hay meadows, and nearly always in common pastures.[1] The Corporations had therefore a whole array of what we may call agricultural functionaries of one sort or another—Haymakers,[2] Grassmen,[3] Pound-keepers or Pound-drivers, Woodwards, Tenders of the Town Wood,[4] Neatherds, Pasturemasters [5] or Field-drivers,[6] Common-keepers or "Tenters of the Common,"[7] Mole-catchers, Swineherds or Hogdrivers.[8] Under some Municipal Corporations [9] he would even have found "Burleighmen," whom he would identify easily with the familiar "Burleymen" or "Bylawmen."

Nor would the most bucolic visitor be surprised to find as officers of the Municipal Corporation the usual Beadles and Constables, Borsholders and Tithingmen, who might be called "Dozeners" or Common Wardsmen, who would sometimes exercise also such offices as those of Pound-keepers, Ale-tasters, or Searchers of the Market. Moreover, if he had come from

---

[1] At Newcastle-on-Tyne, where every Freeman had his two cows on the Town Moor, the Corporation appointed a couple of Noltherds [Nowtherds or Neatherds], salaried officers of some importance, who provided two bulls for the Moor, and whose duty it was " to collect the herd twice a day at milking time, and drive them to the precincts of the town, where they . . . find their way of themselves to their several owners." Right down to the reign of Victoria, as we are told by a visitor, "five or six hundred, or more, of these matronly animals may be seen daily on their march homewards, in two grand divisions, the one of which enters the town by Percy Street, and the other by Gallowgate, all . . . immediately on their arrival in the town instinctively broke off into detachments, each departing through the cross streets as occasion required, and these again subdividing into twos and threes . . . through intricate streets and lanes to their places of abode" (*A Home Tour through the Manufacturing Districts*, by Sir George Head, 1840, vol. i. pp. 339-342 ; First Report of Municipal Corporation Commission, 1835, vol. iii. pp. 1646, 1647).

[2] As at Rochester (*ibid.* vol. ii. p. 848).

[3] As at Newcastle (*ibid.* vol. iii. p. 1646).

[4] As at Congleton (*ibid.* vol. iv. p. 2654).

[5] As at York and Beverley (*ibid.* vol. iii. pp. 1739, 1455).

[6] As at Bedford (*ibid.* vol. iv. p. 2108).

[7] As at Derby (*ibid.* vol. iii. p. 1851).

[8] The Town Swineherd was an important Municipal officer at Shrewsbury ; the Hogdriver at Hythe ; and the Swine-catcher at Congleton.

[9] As at Beaumaris (*ibid.* vol. iv. pp. 2583, 2585).

such a highly developed Manorial government as that of Manchester, he would have become accustomed, not only to such other Municipal officers as Scavengers and Street-wardens, but also to the multifarious officers concerned about the quality of the wares offered for sale and the management of the markets.   He would find in some towns " Breadweighers " to see that the loaf was of due weight, and " Butter-searchers " [1] to test the quality of the butter.   There would be Ale-tasters or Ale-conners or Ale-founders, enjoying, as a definite perquisite, a glass of ale yearly from each publican ; [2] or half a pint out of each brewing.[3]   Most Corporations, like many Manors, had their Searchers and Sealers of Leather ; or there would be general " Searchers of the Market," " Market Sayers," " Leave-Lookers," or " Markets-Lookers."   There might be Herring-Packers or Fish Washers.[4]   Under many Corporations we find Carnals or Carnivals, sometimes known as " Fish and Flesh Searchers," [5] or " Fleshwardens." [6]   In all markets people were accustomed to pay toll, and it was merely a slight peculiarity when the Corporation had a special Egg-Collector, who took the toll of one egg from each basket, which was the Mayor's perquisite ; [7] or when there was a Sample-man, who levied a similar perquisite of coals, called the Mayor's Sample, out of every consignment.[8]   The Municipal Corporations at the great ports would have their Coalmeters and Cornmeters, Cornmeasurers or Cornprizers ; some of them " Water Bailiffs," and others Bridgemen, Bridge-keepers or " Bridge Wardens." All these officers were either to be found in the more developed among the Manorial governments that we have already described, or were obvious variations of them.

But although the great majority of the minor officers of the Municipal Corporation of 1689 would be familiar to the denizen of the rural Manor—although, in fact, there was

---

[1] As at Stockton (First Report of Municipal Corporation Commission, 1835, vol. iii. p. 1729).

[2] As at Congleton (*ibid.* vol. iv. p. 2652).

[3] As at Barnstaple (*ibid.* vol. i. p. 431).

[4] As at Dover (MS. Records, Dover Corporation, 8th September 1701) and Rye respectively.

[5] As at Bedford (First Report of Municipal Corporation Commission, 1835, vol. iv. pp. 2103, 2109).

[6] As at Ipswich (*ibid.* vol. iv. pp. 2295, 2304).

[7] As at Newcastle-on-Tyne (*ibid.* vol. iii. p. 1646).

[8] As at Hull (*ibid.* vol. iii. p. 1548).

scarcely any among them who could not have been found in one or other of the Manorial Boroughs that we have described —the Municipal Corporations, as a whole, were distinguished alike by the greater number and variety of the officers at any one place, and by the more important part that they played in the town life, than in the rural Manor, or even in the typical Manorial Borough. This was connected with the fact that they held their offices continuously throughout the year; giving up their whole time to their duties, and being habitually paid, usually by fees, but sometimes by annual salaries. It is in the Municipal Corporation that we find them most frequently rejoicing in gorgeous uniforms, and equipped with wands or staves of office.[1] The Constable or humble Beadle develops into a Town Serjeant, a Mayor's Serjeant, a Serjeant at Mace,[2] or even a Sword-bearer. The Bellman becomes the "Town Crier" or the "Town Drummer." The amateur and honorary Scavenger develops into a "Street Keeper," an "Overseer of the Streets," or a "Street Warden," or into a "Scavenger to gather the money," having humbler subordinates to collect the dirt.[3] On the other hand, the primitive Scavenger might be specialised into an organised staff, a "Cleaner of the Castle Walks" at a shilling a week; a "Cleaner of Water Grates" at £4 a year; a "Cleaner of Flags" (foot pavements) at half that sum; a "Sweeper of Streets" at four guineas a year; a "Weeder of Footpaths" at threepence a week; and even a special "Cleaner of Chandeliers" at ten shillings a year.[4] The "Water Bailiff" would, in the Municipal Boroughs having ports, blossom into a "Water Treasurer," a "Haven Master" or a "Harbour Master," with

[1] At Sandwich "the Hogmace, or Serjeant at Brazen Mace, is first mentioned (as Overseer of the Streets) in 1471. He bears a stout staff with a brazen head, has a salary of £3 and a livery . . . a blue plaited vest with black velvet cuffs . . . and a gold-laced hat. . . . The Beadle . . . carries a stout staff with a brazen end at the top. His office is to take up vagrants and upon conviction to punish them ; and he is to look after hogs and other nuisances in the streets. His livery is a laced brown great-coat and a gold-laced hat" (*Collections for a History of Sandwich*, by W. Boys, 1792, pp. 785, 786).

[2] At Southampton, of the four Serjeants at Mace, two "were gaolers, one of the Debtors', the other of the Felons' Prison ; the third collected the tolls of the poultry and vegetable market; and the fourth was Water Bailiff" (*History of Southampton*, by J. S. Davies, 1883, p. 211).

[3] As at Rochester (First Report of Municipal Corporation Commission, 1835, vol. ii. p. 855).

[4] As at Richmond (Yorks, *ibid.* vol. iii. p. 1702).

the custody of the "Silver Oar," a mystic symbol which was always taken by him when he accompanied an officer charged to make an arrest, or to execute the process of the City Courts, on a ship in the current of the river.[1]   But in spite of the increase in the number and the variety, the dignity and the pomp of these officers—in spite, too, of their greatly extended power of interfering with the conduct of their fellow-citizens, and of exacting fees for their activities—they had, in the process of becoming permanent paid functionaries, lost their ancient independent status and authority.   The Constable or the Scavenger, the Dog-muzzler or the Pinder of the Lord's Court, was an independent citizen, under no man's orders from Leet to Leet, and even at the bi-annual Court acting more as an independent initiator of the Jury's presentments than as a subordinate official submitting his report.   In the Municipal Corporation those who bore the same, or even more dignified titles, were day by day under the orders of the Chief Officers, whom we have now to describe, and subjected to constant direction by the Governing Body.   The Officers of the Manor had, in fact, become the Servants of the Municipal Corporation.[2]

(g) The Chief Officers of the Corporation

There were in all Municipal Corporations certain great officers, usually belonging by virtue of their office to the Governing Body, and clothed by Charter or prescription with specific authority, for the due exercise of which they were responsible only to the law.   The number of these officers, with their titles and their powers, differed from Corporation to Corporation.   In some Municipalities we find scarcely more than the Head of the Corporation, whether styled

---

[1] As at Bristol (First Report of Municipal Corporation Commission, 1835, vol. ii. p. 1169).

[2] It may be mentioned that several Corporations, from the City of London down to the little Borough of Congleton in Cheshire, kept their packs of hounds, with a "Common Hunt," or a "Huntsman," and various "Dog Whippers" (ibid. 1835, vol. iv. p. 2652). The Corporation of Congleton long maintained its "Bearward," though we do not know whether the "Town Bear" outlived the Commonwealth (ibid. vol. iv. p. 2652 ; in 1621 it was ordered that a new bear should be obtained by the Bearward, the Town Bear having died). Various Municipal Corporations, too, had, like Nottingham, Hythe, and Doncaster, their Gamekeeper, or like Scarborough, their Warrener and Gamekeeper. Norwich had its "Swanner," to look after the Corporation swans in the River Yare (ibid. vol. iv. pp. 2461, 2465).

Portreeve or Warden, Alderman, Bailiff, or Mayor. At the other end of the scale stood those Municipal Corporations which had added to the important staff of the wealthiest and most autonomous Manorial Boroughs the responsible functionaries of a County at large. For the purpose of this analysis we can divide these great officers into three classes. First, we have officers with whom we have, in our series of Lord's Courts and Manorial Boroughs, already become familiar, as the recipients of the authority ceded by the Lord of the Manor—Bailiffs, Mayors, Recorders, Stewards. Secondly, there are those that we have watched developing in the more important Manorial Boroughs for the transaction of their business and the management of their property—Common or Town Clerks, Chamberlains or Treasurers, Attorneys or Remembrancers. Finally, we see emerging in the Municipal Corporation the functionaries of a County—the Sheriff, the Coroner, the Justices of the Peace and, quite exceptionally, the Lieutenancy. We do not wish to suggest that this rough-and-ready classification by functions necessarily corresponds to any rigid lines between officers. The Mayor and the Recorder, sometimes also the High Steward, the Bailiffs and the Town Clerk, of a Municipal Corporation would combine with their offices the powers and duties of Justices of the Peace ; the Mayor might also be the Coroner ; the Bailiff might perform the functions of Sheriff ; the Town Clerk might, as Steward, hold the Borough Courts, and act as Clerk of the Peace at the Borough Court of Quarter Sessions. Our third class of officers—those resembling the officers of the County at Large—had, in perhaps the majority of instances, no separate existence, the powers and obligations being added to those of one or other of the Chief Officers inherited from the Lord's Court or the Manorial Borough. Only in the most privileged Boroughs—sometimes the largest, sometimes merely those of ancient dignity or importance—do we find separate officers holding such County offices as those of Sheriff and Coroner.

To take first those Chief Officers who seem to have been developed from the Court of the Manor In our view of Lord's Courts, Lordless Courts, Lord's Boroughs, and Enfranchised Manorial Boroughs, we have watched, stage by stage, the gradual rise in activity and power of the nominees of the little community of tenants or residents; and the corresponding decline in influence of the representatives of the Lord of the Manor. Thus, in an ordinary Manor the Lord's Steward and the Lord's Bailiff are the rulers, the tenants having no other representatives than the Homage or the Jury, summoned by the Lord's officers. It was a step in advance when the Homage was allowed to present one of its number to be Reeve, who collected the sums due from the tenants, and executed the necessary distraints. Such an officer perhaps gained intangibly in dignity when he was called Portreeve or Boroughreeve, Bailiff, Alderman, or Mayor. It was a further stride in independence, perhaps coincident with the privilege of paying only a commuted lump sum in lieu of all demands, when the inhabitants were accorded the right to choose even the "King's Bailiff" (or the Lord's Bailiff), either as sole Bailiff, or in addition to the "Town's Bailiff." When this stage is reached, there may be practically complete autonomy, as it is the Jury which presents the Bailiff or Bailiffs by whom the Jury itself is selected and summoned—the Lord's Steward becoming a merely formal president of the Court, recording its will. It was usually only a recognition of this practical autonomy when the Lord permitted the Mayor or Bailiffs to hold a separate Portmanmote or Borough Court, for the settlement of disputes among the tenants, altogether independent of the Lord's Steward. The division of duties between the two Bailiffs now becomes decisive—one, usually termed the Mayor, becomes the president of the Court and the Head of the Corporation, whilst the other sinks to the position of a mere subordinate agent.[1] The cession to the Borough, by King or Lord, of the View of Frankpledge or right to hold a Court Leet, often led to the

---

[1] Thus, at Sandwich, when the Freemen acquired the privilege of electing the Head Bailiff or Mayor, "the King's Bailiff became a mere Custom House officer, subordinate to the Chief Magistrate" (*Cinque Ports*, by Montagu Burrows, 1888, p. 202). It may be that it was from this point that the office of Mayor took its origin. At Liverpool, for instance, "the Mayor . . . began by being simply the major ballivus, the chief of the two Bailiffs; but very soon an additional Bailiff was appointed, and the Mayor became a distinct and quite superior officer." Here, as elsewhere, we find one of the Bailiffs "called the 'Mayor's Bailiff' and . . . nominated by the Mayor after his election, the other Bailiff being popularly elected" (*History of Municipal Government in Liverpool*, by Ramsay Muir, 1906, p. 49).

appointment, by the nascent Corporation, of a Steward of its own—sometimes called a Recorder—to hold the Borough Court of criminal jurisdiction. The Lord's Steward was then apt to become a remote personage, only dealt with when some application to the Lord had to be made. What is interesting throughout this growth of autonomy is the transposition in importance of the officers of the Lord and those of the tenants, together with the tendency, in both alike, to a fission into several offices, each having its own specialised status and function. Instead of the Steward of the Manor, whom the Lord appointed, we often find, in a Municipal Corporation, an honorific personage dignified by the appellation of High Steward, and a working lawyer styled Recorder, both alike appointed by the Corporation.[1] Instead of the humble Reeve of the Manor, we see, in the Municipal Corporation, its real Head, whether styled Mayor or "the Bailiffs," and, as mere subordinate officers, one or more Bailiffs whose duty it was to execute the processes of the Courts over which the Head of the Corporation presided.

(*h*) *The Head of the Corporation*

The most distinctive officer of the Municipal Corporation was its Head—in the majority of the Boroughs styled the Mayor, but sometimes alternatively the Bailiff, or "the Bailiffs," the Portreeve, the Alderman, or the Warden [2]—who

---

[1] After the Restoration the appointment of Recorder was frequently made subject to the approval of the Crown, or was reserved to the Crown and made by a *congé d'élire*. These "approbations" are a familiar form of entry in the Royal Warrant Books of the eighteenth century (in Public Record Office).

[2] The normal title became that of Mayor ; in the Cities of London and York early dignified into Lord Mayor. Kidderminster had a High Bailiff, and more than a dozen Boroughs (among them Andover, Bewdley, Blandford, Brecon, Chippenham, Daventry, Leominster, Llandovery, Lydd, Pevensey, Romney Marsh, and Seaford) were presided over by a Bailiff. Some of the Welsh Boroughs (like Beccles, Chard, Langport and Yeovil among the Manorial Boroughs of England) called their head Portreeve. At Bury St. Edmunds, Grantham, and Wokingham he was styled Alderman ; at Godalming, Louth, and Sutton Coldfield, Warden. In more than a score of Boroughs—the most conspicuous being Ipswich, with its neighbours Aldeburgh, Dunwich, Eye, and Southwold ; also Cardiff, Ludlow, Montgomery, Welshpool, Tewkesbury, Tamworth, Droitwich, Wenlow, Bridgnorth, Lichfield, Scarborough, and East Retford —the headship of the Corporation was held by a pair of officers, the two Bailiffs (at Denbigh and Ruthin the two Aldermen), who were appointed simultaneously, and who exercised jointly all its powers and duties.

filled a large part in the town life, and on whom great power and dignity was heaped. There was, it is true, nothing in his title to distinguish him from the heads of many of the Manorial Boroughs, which also had their Bailiffs, their Portreeves, their Aldermen, and even their Mayors. But the head of the Municipal Corporation, whether styled Warden, Portreeve, Alderman, Bailiff, or Mayor, had always been named as such in the Charter, and specially invested by that instrument with large and indefinite powers. He presided at all the assemblies of the Corporation, whether meetings of Freemen or Burgesses, or sessions of the Council or other select body;[1] he acted, in the smaller Boroughs, as the Treasurer or Receiver of the Corporate revenue;[2] and in most of the important municipalities having Chamberlains or Treasurers he still retained, with or without the concurrence of these officers, large executive powers in the management of the Corporate estates between the meetings of the council.[3] He was, during his term of office and usually for some time afterwards, a Justice of the Peace; and he was always referred to as the "Chief Magistrate." He presided at the Borough Quarter Sessions. He held whatever Courts the Corporation maintained, often sitting alone as judge, or jointly with the Recorder; or deputing the Recorder or other officer to hold the Court on his behalf. He might unite in his person a number of offices connected with the various jurisdictions of the Corporation. He was usually *ex-officio* Coroner for the Borough, and Clerk of the Market, and sometimes also King's Escheator,[4] Keeper of the Borough Gaol, Examiner of Weights and Measures, and Admiral of the Port. But this was not all. The Head of the Corporation nearly always enjoyed the privilege during his year of office of making one or more persons "free of the Corporation." He invariably appointed some or all of the minor officials of the Corporation; and in a few cases all the offices, great or small, were in his gift,

---

[1] Except at Norwich.   [2] As at Bodmin and Bossiney.

[3] See the "Rules made to be observed by Mayor," 14th July 1665, in MS. Records, Winchester Corporation.

[4] Though the office of Escheator, which had, by 1689, become merely nominal, was mostly held by the Mayor or other Head of the Corporation, at Grantham, by exception, a separate Escheator was annually appointed (First Report of Municipal Corporation Commission, 1835, vol. iv. p. 2242).

with the exception of the half a dozen chief posts specifically named in the Charter.[1] In the Municipal Corporation of the latter part of the seventeenth century, though possibly not quite to the same extent as two centuries previously, it is not incorrect to say, that "the Mayor has taken the place of the Lord of the town."[2] And sometimes he was a vigilant Lord. We are told, for instance, of one Mayor in the latter part of the seventeenth century, that he "kept a strict eye on inferior officers that they did not unmercifully squeeze those whom they had in their custody. . . . [He] was a spy upon all base practices as amongst attorneys, serjeants, notaries, tidewaiters, wardens, gaolers, tollers, key-masters, chamberlains, and collectors. He was a terror to those who corrupted the meanest office. . . . [He] took order about the Assize of Bread and deserved no less than Minutius, by preventing the frauds of forestallers and regraters. No fish or flesh was brought to the shambles, but what was wholesome. Provision was made for the poor, there was no inequality of rates, the parishes were eased of foreigners and vagrants, public buildings kept in good repair, cozenage banished from the market, ale-houses limited, hospitals put under the tuition of honest, discreet overseers, public charities applied to the

---

[1] As at Rochester.

[2] *History of Municipal Government in Liverpool*, by Ramsay Muir, 1906, p. 49. "The vast extent of the powers exercised by the Mayor is among the most striking features. He is almost omnipotent, and all the other officials of the Borough are little more than his servants. He is the administrator of the property of the Borough, the president of its Courts, its chief judge, the regulator of its trade, the manager of its frequent co-operative trading enterprises" (*ibid.* p. 50). He was, to use the significant phrase of the Court of Plympton Earle, the "Head and Chief Governor of the Town" (First Report of Municipal Corporation Commission, 1835, vol. i. p. 600). "By our institutions," said the Town Clerk of Bristol in 1718, "the honour of the city subsists in the person of our Mayor, who within the boundaries is superior to and presides over our Lord-Lieutenant and every other subject; and also the supreme authority which runs through every branch of the government of this City subsists in his person" (MS. Records, Bristol Corporation, 26th June 1718). At Southampton it was expressly ordained in 1606, that "the Mayor shall be the principal officer of the Town, according to the grant, and shall be so reputed and taken as he hath been time out of mind; and he is principally to the uttermost of his power to have care, and to travail also, that the statutes, laws and ordinances of the Town and Franchise be observed and kept, and he shall have the first voice in all elections and other things that concern the town, and in case the Burgesses' voices be equal, then to have a second voice" (MS. Ordinances, 1606; among Records of Southampton Corporation. This is differently given in *History of Southampton*, by J. S. Davies, 1883).

uses they were intended for, and the coal trade put into such a method with the keelmen and fitters that the public has long after found the benefit of that regulation." [1] Occasionally, when a specially zealous fanatic became Mayor, he could become, temporarily, an effective *censor morum*. We cannot refrain from reproducing the naïve diary of 1703, in which a pious Mayor describes the manner in which he reformed the morals of his Borough, then a prosperous naval port and Admiralty centre, enjoying all the licence of war-time. On his election, as he writes, "the Bench were treated at my house, with the Commonalty and the Freemen. I ordered half a barrel of beer at four several houses. . . . Before I was sworn I caused the Queen's Proclamation to be nailed up in the Court Hall. Some of the Bench was very inquisitive to know what that was so nailed up. I told them it was the Queen's Proclamation to suppress vice and immorality, and that it was my purpose and resolution to put it into due execution. After I was sworn such an oppression and terror fell upon my spirits that I feared I should have sunk under it. However, I made a sort of speech to the officers of the Parish that were there present, and told them it should be my endeavour to do my duty in the office I was entrusted with ; and I should punish all officers under me who did not do theirs. . . . The same terror and amazement followed me several days, inasmuch that several persons questioned in themselves, as they have since told me, whether I might not wholly have gone beside my senses." His first step was to cause a proclamation against tippling and trading on Sunday to be called by the Common Crier. The following Sunday, he tells us, "I took a walk into the street with my staff in order to observe how far the Town had complied with my order. . . . I found the public-houses took no notice . . . but kept their doors open as formerly ; upon which I made them shut them. . . . I also met with several shop-keepers who had their doors half open, but I made them shut them. . . . I met with some turbulent spirits who opposed me, and told me this was a new thing they did not understand—why could they not have liberty to do as they pleased in their own

---

[1] *Memoirs of Mr. Ambrose Barnes* (Mayor of Newcastle-on-Tyne), Surtees Society, 1867, pp. 101-102.

houses ; and truly they would not shut up their doors to stifle themselves for want of air for any upstart, although the Mayor. I told them . . . I was resolved on a reformation in Deal. I charged the servants and the seamen, when I met them, that they took care they did not swear, get drunk, nor be disorderly as they had formerly been, for that this rod in my hand should be a severe scourge to all manner of vice, profaneness, and immorality. Thus I went through the three streets proclaiming my intentions: I did not pass one door that was open till, by argument and by threatening, I made some of the household shut it. . . . Saturday . . . I took a seaman by the collar amidst all the people in the market-place, and caused him to be put in the stocks for profane swearing, and gave him a charge to tell his companions of it. . . . I likewise gave notice to the market people that I would punish all disorders in all sorts of people, and especially any breaches of the peace committed in the market, of which I was then Clerk. On the same day, about an hour after, I took up a common prostitute, whose conduct was very offensive, brought her to the whipping-post—being about mid-market, where was present some hundreds of people—I caused her to have twelve lashes ; and at every third lash I parleyed with her, and bid her tell all the women of the like calling wheresoever she came that the Mayor of Deal would serve them as he had served her. . . . After which, I gave her a groat, and sent her, by a Constable, out of the Town. On the following morning, no less, as I was informed, than five-and-twenty such-like characters left the Town . . . uttering the most fearful oaths, and vowing vengeance on me for what I was doing, and declaring aloud that they would not come again to Deal till the present Mayor was dead and damned ; and then, whenever it should happen, they would come back. . . . In the afternoon (Sunday) the Jurats and Common Council came to my house to go with me to Church, as was the custom. . . . As I came by the 'India Arms' Inn, I saw a coach making ready to start for Canterbury. I sent for the coachman, and told him, if he was not upon the King's business, he should not go till the next morning. He complied with my request . . . When I came to Church I observed the clergyman . . . about to commence the service by reading the

Common Prayers, without his surplice; upon which I sent my Serjeant to him, and gave him my service, desiring him to put on the surplice. . . . After prayers, when we came to sing psalms, being part of the 75th Psalm, and at particular verses, which were very appropriate to certain persons present, I stood up, spreading my hands, pointing round the Church to some whose ill lives I knew, as well as their conversations, which this Psalm most peculiarly hinted at. After church, as we came home, I discovered some public-houses open; I made two men pay twelve pence each for being found in one of them; and threatened that, if on another Lord's Day any men were found there, I should fix a fine on the house. During the following week some of my Brethren on the Bench told me they were tired, and said they would not keep my company nor support me, if I took such extreme measures. I replied I had begun a good work and . . . would not abandon it. . . . I felt it a duty to be more zealous for that than my own worldly affairs, though I hoped I should find time to attend to both." He describes how he continued, Sunday after Sunday, to perambulate the Town with his Serjeant, shutting up public-houses and shops. "But at length," he continues, "I found they paid no attention to my orders nor to my threatenings, so I determined that, wherever I found any person in a public-house drinking, or selling of goods in shops, they should be fined. On one Sunday, I found six houses that had company, and three tradesmen selling goods. The next day I caused a warrant to be made out, and made them all pay a fine; which struck a terror over the rest. After this, I could walk through the Town on a Sunday and not see a door open, either in a public-house or shop. If any company is within, 'tis very privately done, whereas before they used to keep them open." He then relates how he had copies of the Queen's Proclamation against vice and immorality hung up in the public-houses and barbers' shops; and how he sent one to the schoolmaster, saying, "Which I desire you will affix in some convenient place in your school, letting your scholars know from me that, if any of your boys for the future shall be guilty of blaspheming the name of God, or be seen playing in the streets on a Sunday, or disturb the congregation at church, or shall be found robbing of orchards, or any other like crime,

I shall cause them to be severely punished—which is what is needful at this place." We need not be surprised to learn, as he adds, that "the strict observation of the Sabbath, the putting a stop to the tippling, trading, and profane swearing, etc., by the execution of the law, and my earnest zeal in all places of public resort, and in all companies wherever I came, made many persons I had a regard for slight me. Some took the liberty to lampoon me in song and verse, in no measured terms; while others resorted to ridicule and banter—all which I disregarded, but still kept on following the heat whilst it was hot, though it like to have proved very fatal to my own health. Upon divers occasions I received letters containing verses, reflecting on me harshly, but I did what I thought right, and that was my recompense."[1]

Between 1689 and 1835 we shall note a relative decline in the importance of the Mayoralty; owing partly to the ever-growing activity of the Borough Justices sitting as a Bench of Magistrates in Petty and Special Sessions, and partly to the ever-increasing minuteness of the Council's control of the Corporate property. But the reader of the wonderful day-by-day record of the travelling and preaching of John Wesley, between 1735 and 1790 will remember how frequently he comes in contact with the Mayors of the towns, who themselves permit or prohibit his preaching, command the local Constables, initiate or suspend proceedings, and generally act as local potentates.

With all this power and pomp of the Head of the Corporation, the question arises to what extent he was provided with a salary or allowance for expenses. In some archaic Corporations, the Head continued to receive the customary small emoluments of the Reeve of the Manor. He might enjoy during his term of office the use of the proceeds of a given piece of land, a larger "stint" on the Common, or three turns of the Town Fishery.[2] In most Corporations, as in some

---

[1] "The Sayings and Doings of Thomas Powell, Mayor of Deal in the year 1703, written by himself"; in *History of Deal*, by Stephen Pritchard, 1864, pp. 156-163. It should be added that Powell greatly distinguished himself in the great storm of 1703, when over 200 shipwrecked men were saved, largely by his "humane and spirited exertions" (*ibid*. p. 172). He was re-elected Mayor in 1708 (MS. Records, Deal Corporation).

[2] The Mayor of Fordwich in Kent had the right of fishing in the Corporation's river "until he takes a trout," and then "two nights together" in

Manorial Boroughs, the Mayor took for himself, if not the whole of particular tolls or dues, at any rate a part of these exactions—it might be a hundred oysters out of every barrel, the second-best fish out of every boat, a bushel of coals from every load. In many Corporations he received the profits of the Fair,[1] or the fees of the Borough Court, or shared with the Bailiffs the profits of executions. In the larger Municipalities these perquisites had been wholly or partially commuted for fixed allowances and were often supplemented by definite stipends, which in one or two instances came to exceed a thousand a year. But it may safely be assumed that even the largest of these allowances never did more than cover the out-of-pocket expenses of the holder of the office, and seldom sufficed to meet the innumerable charges in the way of fees, the salaries of an enlarged household, the liveries or uniforms of "the Mayor's servants," the maintenance of a State coach, and the incessant eatings and drinkings of Juries and committees, the banquets to the Assize Judges, the convivialities of the "Mayor's Counsellors" and the "Mayor's Brethren"—not to mention the hospitality to visitors of the Borough which custom required. The Headship of the Corporation, whatever its nominal emoluments, was, in fact, in 1689 as in 1835, always an honorary office of considerable personal labour, rewarded only by the prestige, power, and social consideration universally conceded to the Chief Magistrate of the Borough.

So important a part in the working constitution of the Municipal Corporation was played by its Head, that we must necessarily relegate the method of his appointment to our analysis of Municipal Constitutions. But whether he was

addition, whereas other Jurats and Freemen only had a night each "in course as they severally dwell according to the course of the sun, from the house of the Mayor for the time being." Moreover, the Mayor had the refusal of all fish caught for sale, until 1721, when it was agreed that he should "have one night before the outmen, in consideration of the Freemen having liberty to sell their fish or turns to whom they please" ("Book of Decrees," 1671; in "Fordwich Municipal Records," by Rev. C. E. Woodruff, in *Archæologia Cantiana*, vol. xviii., 1889, p. 96; Privy Council Register, 10th July 1685; *History of the Town and Port of Fordwich*, by the same, 1895, pp. 205-206). The excellence of the Fordwich trout and their great commercial value were commended by Isaac Walton (*The Complete Angler*, edition of 1823, pp. 68-69).

[1] As at Wareham (First Report of Municipal Corporation Commission, 1835, vol. ii. p. 1360).

simply "presented" at the Court of the Lord of the Manor, by the Homage or other Jury; whether he was selected by a Court of Aldermen or by a Common Council from among their own members; or whether he was elected by all the Burgesses or Freemen of the Corporation, or even by the householders of the Borough, it is, we think, significant of his ancestry that his appointment nearly always took place somewhere near Michaelmas in each year, after the arable crops had been got in, and the commonfields had been thrown open again to the Town Herd, exactly at the season when the Lord's Courts and Manorial Boroughs were appointing their Reeves or other officers. And however little was the participation of the mere inhabitants of the Borough in the selection of a new Head of the Municipal Corporation, it was perhaps a reminiscence of popular satisfaction at emancipation from the control of the Lord of the Manor—if not a reminiscence of the Anglo-Saxon theory that the King's Peace died with the monarch and had to be set up afresh by his successor —that the whole of the inhabitants shared, on "Charter Day, in a sort of Carnival of pleasurable disorder. In one Borough it was customary that "on the election of a Bailiff, the inhabitants assemble in the principal streets to throw cabbage-stalks at each other. The Town-house bell gives signal for the affray. This is called the *lawless hour*. This done (for it lasts an hour), the Bailiff-elect and Corporation in their robes, preceded by drums and fifes (for they have no Waits), visit the old and new Bailiff, Constables, etc., attended by the mob. In the meantime, the most respectable families in the neighbourhood are invited to meet and fling apples at them on their entrance. I have known forty pots of apples expended at one house."[1] In many other Boroughs public festivities on the annual appointment of the Mayor were maintained in full force. The accounts of the expenses, with their items for " the tenders [attendants] on the newly elected Jurat or Mayor; the band, consisting on the first occasion of four fiddles and two drummers; the women at sixpence a head strewing herbs in the path of the newly elected; the ribbon for cockades; the 'colourmen' [men bearing flags]; the Freemen paid for their votes even when absent from home;

[1] At Kidderminster. See *Gentleman's Magazine*, 1790, vol, lx. p. 1191.

and the winding up with a grand smash of broken windows, glasses, pots, and punch ladles, form altogether a vivid Hogarthian picture of the proceedings."[1]

(*i*) *The Bailiffs*

There is perhaps no more interesting proof of the haphazard development of the Municipal Corporation than the wide range in dignity and status of the personages who, in one or other Boroughs, were styled Bailiffs.[2]   As we have already seen, in forty Municipal Corporations, the Bailiffs— usually a pair—were actually the Heads of their several Corporations, with all the powers of Mayor.   In about a hundred Municipal Corporations, on the other hand, the officers termed Bailiffs were so insignificant that they appeared only as part of the subordinate staff of half-obsolete Courts, mentioned, if at all, among such petty officers as Constables, Poundkeepers, Cryers, and Serjeants.   In about thirty Municipal Corporations, however, the Bailiffs occupied an intermediate position.   Whilst not the Heads of their Corporations, their offices, as we shall presently describe, were named in the Charters, and clothed with independent jurisdictions.   But whether the Bailiffs were the Heads of their several Corporations, petty officers of the Borough Courts, or dignified functionaries of independent status, they always retained traces of an apparent descent from the Reeve or Bailiff of the Lord's Court.   As Head of the Municipal Corporation, the Bailiff was, as we have seen, nothing but a glorified Reeve.   As a petty officer of the Borough Court, the Bailiff retained the function of his Manorial ancestor in collecting fines and making distraints.   And when the Bailiff takes rank below the Mayor among the Chief Officers of the Municipal Corporation, he resembles, as we shall see, the Bailiff of a Franchise or Liberty, who, on behalf of his Lord, excludes the Sheriff or his officers from executing processes within the exempted area.

[1] " Extracts from the Account Book of Captain John Harvey, R.N., Mayor of Sandwich, 1774-1775," by Thomas Dorman ; in *Archæologia Cantiana*, vol. xx., 1893, p. 222.

[2] Possibly the wide use of the term Bailiff may be due to the loose terminology of early documents, especially translations.   The word " Bailivus " was nearly as general as " minister."

In nearly all the Boroughs in which the Bailiffs were Chief Officers of the Corporation subordinate to the Mayor, there were two Bailiffs, often distinguished from each other, as the High Bailiff and the Low Bailiff,[1] the Senior Bailiff and the Junior Bailiff,[2] Bailiff of the Brethren and Bailiff of the Commons,[3] the Land Bailiff and the Water Bailiff,[4] or — historically most significant — the King's Bailiff and the Town's Bailiff.[5] In fewer than a dozen Boroughs do we find any exception to this duality of the Bailiff; six Corporations had only a single Bailiff as a Chief Officer,[6] subordinate to the Mayor, whilst two rejoiced in four.[7]

The functions of the Bailiffs, in all these Corporations in which they were Chief Officers subordinate to the Mayor, had, by 1689, come to differ widely from town to town. We see them most frequently having some responsibility for the selection or summoning of Juries, and for the execution of the processes of one or other of the Borough Courts. They are often responsible for accounting for fines; for the collection of rents and fees; and sometimes for performing all the duties of Treasurer and Accountant.[8] We see them sometimes discharging the offices of Coroner, Keeper of the Borough Gaol, Clerk of the Market, and even those of Billet-master and Poundkeeper. But they were often, by Charter or by usage, clothed also with judicial powers; they were frequently included among the Justices of the Peace; they sat as Judges in the Court of Pleas or other Borough Court; they held the Court of Pie Powder. They often held the Corporation's Manor Courts, and exercised the powers of the Lord of the Manor. They sometimes acted, either alone or jointly with the Mayor, as Returning Officers for the

---

[1] Winchester.
[2] Southampton.
[3] Lancaster.
[4] Queenborough.
[5] Dartmouth.
[6] Lydd, Axbridge, Chichester, Plympton Earle, Salisbury, Sandwich.
[7] Exeter and Berwick-on-Tweed. At Cambridge also there were four, but they had by 1689 shrunk into Petty Officers.
[8] At Exeter we are told, in 1584, "the Receiver is always one of the four Bailiffs, and hath the like and the same charge as every one of them hath ; but the office of Receiver is particular to himself, and none is chosen thereunto except he be of the number of the Common Council or Four-and-Twenty " (*The Antique Description and Account of the City of Exeter*, by John Vowell, 1765, p. 165).

Borough.[1]   They reached, perhaps, their highest status and greatest dignity in those Boroughs in which they fulfilled the duties of Sheriffs in the return of writs and the execution of processes; sometimes to the exclusion, either wholly or partially, of the Sheriff of the County at large.[2]   In one Corporation at least—though the Borough was not a County in itself—the two Bailiffs were actually called Sheriffs of the Borough, and acted separately as such.[3]

By 1689 the Bailiff or Bailiffs who were Chief Officers had come to be chosen by the Corporation, and nearly always by its Governing Council or Close Body.   What is interesting is to notice the traces of a former duality in the method of their appointment.   Occasionally the Head of the Corporation nominated or appointed one of the pair and the Council the other.   Sometimes the two Bailiffs were chosen by different parts of the Corporation, perhaps by the Court of Aldermen and the Common Council respectively; sometimes even out of different sections of the Freemen.   It is impossible to refrain from the suggestion that, in this duality in the method of appointment, as in the duality in the familiar titles, there is a trace of the right of appointment of the two Bailiffs having been conceded at different dates, at successive stages of autonomy; the Town's Bailiff coming very early to represent the tenants, whilst the King's Bailiff remained much longer the nominee of the Lord, only passing later into the power of the Corporation.[4]

[1] We may note as exceptional that at Cambridge the four Bailiffs had formerly presided individually (like the Aldermen of London, Canterbury, and other places) over the Wards into which the Borough was divided, in which they had to keep the peace (First Report of Municipal Corporation Commission, 1835, vol. iv. p. 2188).

[2] As at Northampton, Great Grimsby, Oxford, Bath, Bridgwater, Sandwich, Winchester, etc.   At Great Grimsby the two Bailiffs were judges of the "Foreign Court of Pleas," joint Lords of the Manor along with the Mayor, joint Presidents with the Mayor and the High Steward at the Court Leet, and a necessary part of every Court of Mayor and Burgesses (ibid. vol. iv. p. 2252).

[3] Bath (ibid. vol. ii. p. 1115); so perhaps also at Winchester (ibid. vol. ii. p. 902).

[4] At Dartmouth the Bailiff usually served for two years, the King's Bailiff of one year becoming the Town's Bailiff of the next (ibid. vol. i. p. 478).   At Wenlock, ex-Bailiffs were styled Bailiffs' Peers (ibid. vol. iii. p. 2076).

(*j*) *The High Steward and the Recorder*

The tendency to fission, or to a duplication of offices, is seen also in the case of the Steward. In the Manorial Boroughs, as we have seen, it was usual for the Lord of the Manor to continue to hold a Court, at which his Steward presided. Such an arrangement occasionally continued, even after a fully developed Municipal Corporation had come into being.[1] Even when the Lord had ceased to take the profits of the Court, he might exceptionally retain the appointment of the Steward or Capital Seneschal, or, as he tended to be called, the High Steward.[2] More usually, however, we find the Corporation, by 1689, controlling all the Courts held within the Borough, and appointing, to preside at one or other of them, its own Steward or Chief Steward.[3] This officer or dignitary had evidently, at the outset, been supposed to be a lawyer, and was sometimes required by Charter to be a "discreet man learned in the law."[4] He was assumed to preside at the various Courts of the Borough, and was frequently, *ex officio*, one of its Justices of the Peace. His appointment might rest with the Crown, or with the Governing Council or Close Body of the Corporation, some-times subject to the approval of the Crown. But the office of Steward was, in nearly all cases, destined to undergo a change. In a few towns, the Steward became a mere subordinate officer of the Corporation, holding the Courts on its behalf as for an individual Lord.[5] In a few others he continued to be one of the Chief Officers of the Corporation, acting as one of its Justices and holding its Courts.[6] In a few more, his office became a mere sinecure, executed by a "sufficient deputy," who might be styled simply Deputy-Steward or Sub-Seneschal,[7]

---

[1] As at Morpeth, Salisbury, Ripon, etc. (see pp. 339, 500).

[2] As at Havering-atte-Bower (First Report of Municipal Corporation Commission, 1835, vol. v. p. 2878); Oswestry (*ibid.* vol. iv. p. 2825). At Gravesend the office of Capital Seneschal or High Steward was hereditary in the family of the Earl of Darnley (*History of Gravesend*, by R. P. Cruden, 1843, p. 307).

[3] As at Hereford (First Report of Municipal Corporation Commission, 1835, vol. i. p. 255).

[4] As at Oswestry (*ibid.* vol. iv. p. 2825).

[5] As at Berwick-on-Tweed (*ibid.* vol. iii. pp. 1438, 1442).

[6] As at Basingstoke (*ibid.* vol. ii. p. 1101); Congleton (*ibid.* vol. iv. p. 2651).

[7] As at Gravesend (*History of Gravesend*, by R. P. Cruden, 1843, pp. 307, 308; First Report of Municipal Corporation Commission, 1835, vol. v. p. 2865).

but whom we also find dignified by a title destined to become itself of importance, that of Recorder.[1] In one or two cases, at least, the Steward was considered to be himself the Recorder—these two names denoting, in fact, one and the same functionary.[2] In the vast majority of cases, however, we find the office split definitely into two. There is on the one hand, the Steward, Chief Steward, Capital Seneschal, High Steward, or Lord High Steward,[3] an officer of great dignity and some influence, but with practically no duties or emoluments; usually a gentleman of high position, perhaps the owner or the patron of the Borough; required, indeed, by the Charters of many towns to be an "eminent," an "illustrious," or a "distinguished" man;[4] occasionally at least a Knight, if not a peer of the realm.[5] This office, which we may suspect to have become differentiated with the object of obtaining an influential protector at Court, became exclusively honorary, though some of the archaic remuneration—a pipe of wine every third year,[6] or eighteen sugar loaves annually[7]—

---

[1] As frequently among the Boroughs of Wales. At Gravesend the High Steward nominated two barristers to the Governing Council of the Corporation, for one of them to be chosen as Recorder (First Report of Municipal Corporation Commission, 1835, vol. v. p. 2865). At Castle Rising the Recorder was appointed by the Lord of the Manor (*ibid.* vol. iv. p. 2211); so also at Clun (*ibid.* vol. iv. p. 2642); as frequently in Manorial Boroughs. The term Recorder is of high antiquity; such an officer is noticed at Bristol in the fourteenth century (*ibid.* vol. ii. p. 1158), and at Southampton in the fifteenth (Speed MSS., Southampton Corporation, p. 72; *History of Southampton*, by J. S. Davies, 1883, p. 185), where the form of oath taken by him in 1461 is given, showing that he was already both a judicial and an advisory officer. The rise of the Recorder to be a Chief Officer is, in a sense, analogous to the similar development of the Custos Rotulorum among the County Justices (see *The Parish and the County*, pp. 285-286).

[2] Andover (First Report of Municipal Corporation Commission, 1835, vol. ii. p. 1084); Maidenhead (*ibid.* vol. v. p. 2911); Southwold (*ibid.* vol. iv. p. 2516); Folkestone (*ibid.* vol. ii. p. 982). At Chipping Wycombe, on the other hand, the Recorder was required by the Charter to execute the office of Steward (*ibid.* vol. i. p. 42). Thus at Dover, when the office was held by so distinguished a person as the Lord Chancellor, the Earl of Hardwicke, it was still described on his death in 1764 as that of "Steward of the Corporation, and Assistant to the Mayor and Jurats at their Courts of Sessions and Trials" (MS. Records, Dover Corporation, 26th March 1764).

[3] As at Gloucester (First Report of Municipal Corporation Commission, 1835, vol. i. p. 59); Lynn (*ibid.* vol. iv. p. 2397).

[4] As at Newbury (*ibid.* vol. i. p. 90); Hertford (*ibid.* vol. v. p. 2886)'; Hereford (*ibid.* vol. i. p. 255); Maidenhead (*ibid.* vol. v. p. 2910); Wokingham (*ibid.* vol. v. p. 2939); Windsor (*ibid.* vol. v. p. 2933).

[5] As at Stratford-upon-Avon (*ibid.* vol. i. p. 119); Henley (*ibid.* vol. i. p. 72); Banbury (*ibid.* vol. i. p. 9).   [6] At Bristol (*ibid.* vol. ii. p. 1165).

[7] At Kingston-on-Thames (*ibid.* vol. v. p. 2896).

would occasionally be continued.   On the other hand, we have the Recorder (occasionally still styled also Deputy Steward), an "honest and discreet man, learned in the laws of England and of the degree of the utter barristers,"[1] whose duty it was to preside at one or other of the Borough Courts, occasionally to hold the Court Leet and View of Frankpledge in place of the Steward,[2] to administer the oath of office to the Mayor, to be present as a Justice at the Borough Court of Quarter Sessions when important criminal cases had to be tried, to sit with the Mayor as legal Assessor, and to advise the Corporation on any legal or constitutional point of difficulty.   He might receive a nominal stipend, or a fee for each attendance,[3] or more rarely a substantial salary.   On the other hand, there was a tendency —as with the High Steward—to make the office one of honour and dignity only, to be filled by a nobleman or gentleman of position, the work being performed either by deputy, or relegated to some other officer of the Corporation.[4] In the majority of Boroughs, however, the Recorder remained the principal legal adviser and the leading judicial functionary of the Corporation.   In one great Borough, in the eighteenth century, the Recorder, we are told, " was frequently a member of one of the great families of the district. . . . He took the leading part in the Mayor's Court, supplying, doubtless, the legal knowledge which the Mayor could not be expected to possess. But he was not, like the modern Recorder, a bird of passage, coming only for the Sessions of his Court.   He cast in his lot with the Borough, and his legal knowledge and skill in interpreting charters were often useful.   He sometimes goes up to London on legal business."[5]

[1] As at Aldeburgh (First Report of Municipal Corporation Commission, 1835, vol. iv. p. 2092).
[2] As at St. Albans (*ibid.* vol. v. p. 2921); Truro (*ibid.* vol. i. p. 656); Bury St. Edmunds (*ibid.* vol. iv. p. 2174).
[3] At Dorchester this fee was "two moidores," computed to be £2:14s. (*ibid.* vol. ii. p. 1275).   At Bristol it was as much as a hundred guineas a time, with a hogshead of port or sherry annually (*ibid.* vol. ii. p. 1165).   At Southampton there had usually been New Year's gifts of sugar, spices, wine or olives, but in 1688 a yearly fee of five pounds was fixed (Speed MSS. p. 72; MS. Records of Southampton Corporation; see also *History of Southampton*, by J. S. Davies, 1883, pp. 184-185).
[4] As at Penzance.
[5] *History of Municipal Government in Liverpool*, by Ramsay Muir, 1906, p. 83.

(k) The Chamberlain and the Town Clerk

We may pass lightly over the officers whom the Municipal Corporations gradually accumulated to perform the usual administrative work. It is interesting that the oldest of them, and in 1689 in one or two cases still the most prominent, was not, as we might nowadays expect, the Town Clerk, but the Chamberlain, Cofferer,[1] Receiver,[2] Chamber-reeve,[3] or Treasurer. In the most rudimentary Municipal Corporation, as in the simpler Manorial Boroughs, it was upon the Head of the Corporation that all the administrative work fell, just as it did upon the Reeve of the Manor. When the little community began to possess a Corporate fund, the Head of the Corporation, whether styled Reeve, Portreeve or Boroughreeve, Alderman, Bailiff, Warden or Mayor, himself often kept the cash.[4] Equally significant of the transition from the Manor is the fact that in some Municipal Corporations the Chamberlains, or Treasurers of the Corporation, were actually appointed by the Lord's Steward or other officer.[5] The next step, we infer, was for the Head of the Corporation to devolve the duties upon an officer or officers appointed by himself, a position in which half a dozen Municipal Corporations in 1689 still found themselves.[6] Finally, we have the arrangement at which the great majority of Municipal Corporations had, by 1689, arrived, by which the officers fulfilling the duties of Treasurer were appointed by the Corporation itself, nearly always by the Governing Council, but occasionally by presentment of a Jury at one or other of the Borough

---

[1] So styled at Bridport.

[2] So styled at Bury St. Edmunds, Dartmouth, Newcastle-under-Lyme, Saltash, Truro, and Warwick.   [3] So styled at Haverfordwest.

[4] This was the case at Altrincham, Arundel, Beccles, Berkeley, Chard, Dunmow, Durham, Godalming, Lymington, and Yeovil, among Manorial Boroughs. And at Bodmin, Liskeard, Penzance, Plympton Earle, Poole, Sutton Coldfield, and Morpeth, among Municipal Corporations; whilst it was equally characteristic of several Welsh Boroughs, such as Denbigh, Llandovery, and Llantrissant. At Alnwick there were four Chamberlains, who were (under the Lord's Bailiff) jointly Heads of this Manorial Borough.

[5] This was the case at Cardiff (First Report of Municipal Corporation Commission, 1835, vol. i. p. 189), and Swansea (ibid. vol. i. p. 391), as well as at Alnwick (vol. iii. pp. 1413, 1415).

[6] For instance, Barnstaple (ibid. vol. i. p. 430); Carlisle (ibid. vol. iii. p. 1471); Chester (ibid. vol. iv. p. 2621); Lincoln (ibid. vol. iv. p. 2347); Maidstone (ibid. vol. ii. p. 757); Wells (ibid. vol. ii. p. 1370).

Courts;[1] or by popular election by the suffrages of the whole body of Freemen.[2]

As its administrative work increased, we see the Municipal Corporation, like the Manorial Borough, creating an office unknown to the Manor,[3] that of the Common Clerk,[4] or Town Clerk. We infer that the office, like that of the Recorder, had gradually become differentiated from that of the Steward. In a few cases, even in 1689, we find it still combined with the Stewardship,[5] or the Recordership;[6] whilst in others it was combined with the post of Deputy Steward.[7] In some

[1] As at Grimsby (First Report of Municipal Corporation Commission, 1835, vol. iv. p. 2250), Laugharne (*ibid.* vol. i. p. 288), and Aberystwyth (*ibid.* vol. i. p. 171).

[2] As at Berwick-on-Tweed (*ibid.* vol. iii. p. 1438); Cambridge (*ibid.* vol. iv. p. 2186); Carmarthen (*ibid.* vol. i. p. 206); Hastings (*ibid.* vol. ii. p. 998); Ipswich (*ibid.* vol. iv. p. 2295); Pevensey (*ibid.* vol. ii. p. 1017); Plymouth (*ibid.* vol. i. p. 582); Romney Marsh (*ibid.* vol. ii. p. 1027); Rye (*ibid.* vol. ii. p. 1032); Sandwich (*ibid.* vol. ii. p. 1044); Southwold (*ibid.* vol. iv. p. 2517). In the City of London the election was by the superior grade of Freemen (the Liverymen). The Chamberlains of the City of London and Bristol were legally "corporations sole," and thus enjoyed the privilege of perpetual succession. They also exercised quasi-judicial functions in respect of apprentices, having power to adjudicate on complaints, cancel or vary indentures, compel masters to pay damages and even to imprison recalcitrant apprentices.

[3] At the highly developed Lord's Court of Epworth (Lincolnshire) there was, however, a Clerk of the Court.

[4] So styled at Carlisle (*ibid.* vol. iii. p. 1469); Grantham (*ibid.* vol. iv. p. 2242); Hereford (*ibid.* vol. i. p. 256); Liverpool (*ibid.* vol. iv. p. 2699); Tenterden (*ibid.* vol. ii. p. 1064); Tewkesbury (*ibid.* vol. i. p. 125); and Yarmouth, Isle of Wight (*ibid.* vol. ii. p. 916). For a good description of his office, see *Town Life in the Fifteenth Century*, by A. S. Green, 1894, vol. ii. pp. 257-264.

[5] As at Brading, Isle of Wight (First Report of Municipal Corporation Commission, 1835, vol. ii. p. 680); Liskeard (*ibid.* vol. i. p. 526); Devizes (*ibid.* vol. ii. p. 1265); Eye (*ibid.* vol. iv. p. 2229); Newtown, Isle of Wight (*ibid.* vol. ii. p. 794); Lampeter (*ibid.* vol. i. p. 283); Usk (*ibid.* vol. i. p. 416); Wiston (*ibid.* vol. i. p. 423); Westbury (*ibid.* vol. ii. p. 1378); Stockton (*ibid.* vol. iii. p. 1729); or, as at Neath, with the post of Constable of the Castle (*ibid.* vol. i. p. 334); or, as at Penzance, with that of Seneschal (*ibid.* vol. i. p. 572).

[6] As at Clun (*ibid.* vol. iv. p. 2642); Flint (*ibid.* vol. iv. p. 2681); Garstang (*ibid.* vol. iii. pp. 1520, 1521); Kenfig (*ibid.* vol. i. p. 269); Montgomery (Report on Certain Boroughs, by T. J. Hogg, 1838); Swansea (First Report of Municipal Corporation Commission, 1835, vol. i. p. 390); Wootton Bassett (*ibid.* vol. i. p. 147). At Southampton, as an eighteenth-century antiquary tells us, "there is little said of the Town Clerk in the ancient books of the Town, but in one of them, A.D. 1570, he is called Clerk of the Records of the Town, which seems to be expressive of his office, the Recorder being Keeper of the Records" (Speed MSS., Corporation of Southampton, p. 73; see also *History of Southampton*, by J. S. Davies, 1883, p. 186).

[7] As at Beccles (First Report of Municipal Corporation Commission, 1835, vol. iv. p. 2136); Sutton Coldfield (*ibid.* vol. iii. p. 2033); Newport, Shropshire (*ibid.* vol. iii. p. 1962); Windsor (*ibid.* vol. v. p. 2933); Andover (*ibid.*

cases the Town Clerk was appointed by the Lord of the Manor,[1] and in various others by the Steward,[2] or by the Recorder,[3] whom he often served as Deputy Recorder. In half a dozen cases the appointment was vested by Charter in the Crown, usually on petition from the Governing Council of the Corporation.[4] In the great majority of Municipal Corporations, however, the Town Clerk had, by 1689, acquired a leading place among the Chief Officers of the Corporation, though possibly he was not yet, as the Town Clerk of Launceston declared a century later, "to the Mayor of a Corporation what the Lord Chancellor is to the King, the chief adviser."[5] He was, by specific direction in the Charters, appointed by the Corporation itself; usually by the Governing Council,[6] but in a few cases by presentment of a

vol. ii. p. 1082); Blandford (*ibid.* vol. ii. p. 1134); East Retford (*ibid.* vol. iii. p. 1862).

[1] As at Cardiff (First Report of Municipal Corporation Commission, 1835, vol. i. p. 189); Cowbridge (*ibid.* vol. i. p. 221); Llandovery (*ibid.* vol. i. p. 302); Llantrissant (*ibid.* vol. i. p. 314); Oswestry (*ibid.* vol. iv. p. 2826); and Welshpool (Report on Certain Boroughs, by T. J. Hogg, 1838, p. 141).

[2] As at Andover (First Report of Municipal Corporation Commission, 1835, vol. ii. p. 1134); Buckingham (*ibid.* vol. i. p. 28); East Retford (*ibid.* vol. iii. p. 1862).

[3] As at Bradninch (*ibid.* vol. i. p. 458); Derby, subject to approval by the King (*ibid.* vol. iii. p. 1850); Helston (*ibid.* vol. i. p. 512); Launceston (*ibid.* vol. i. p. 518); East Looe (*ibid.* vol. i. p. 534); Penryn (*ibid.* vol. i. p. 563); Thetford (*ibid.* vol. iv. p. 2541); and Warwick (*ibid.* vol. iii. p. 2059).

[4] As at Falmouth (*ibid.* vol. i. p. 502); Kingston-upon-Hull (*ibid.* vol. iii. p. 1549); Leeds (*ibid.* vol. iii. p. 1618); Newport, Isle of Wight (*ibid.* vol. ii. p. 776); Wigan (Report on Certain Boroughs, by T. J. Hogg, 1838, p. 155). The appointment, or approval of appointment, was given by the Privy Council and latterly by the Home Office; and the student will find numerous instances recorded in the MS. Register of the Privy Council, 1660-1832; and in the Home Office Domestic State Papers and Entry Book, 1700-1832, in Public Record Office; for one such case concerning Sudbury, see Calendar of Home Office Papers, 1770-1772 (1881), pp. 243, 344-345.

[5] Town Clerk of Launceston to Town Clerk of Plymouth, 15th October 1804, in MS. Records, Plymouth Corporation. The Town Clerk of the fifteenth century had been, in many Boroughs, "a Municipal Chancellor in whom was embodied a continuous tradition of administration and a fixed jurisprudence" (*Town Life in the Fifteenth Century*, by A. S. Green, 1894, vol. ii. pp. 260-261).

[6] We give one such minute of appointment as typical. "This day J. K. of the Town and County of Southampton was, by the majority of votes, whereof Mr. Mayor and the Recorder were two, elected Town Clerk for the said Town of Southampton, he proposing to execute the office gratis, enjoying the usual perquisites; to gather the Town rents, dues and fines without any certain reward, which is to be left to the discretion of the Corporation when he shall account with them; to make up the Town accounts and account with them as often as they shall be pleased to require; and to go abroad upon the Corporation's business without any reward, the Corporation allowing him reasonable

Jury;[1] in a few other cases by the Head of the Corporation,[2] and sometimes by popular election of the whole body of Freemen.[3] We see the Town Clerk becoming the principal officer of the Corporation, and combining in his person many different offices. In one Borough or another we find him acting as Clerk of the Peace, Prothonotary, Clerk of Indictments, Clerk to the Magistrates, Registrar and Clerk of all the Borough Courts; he would sometimes be Coroner, Under Sheriff, Deputy Recorder, Corporation Solicitor, Keeper of the Records, Steward of the Corporation Manors, and Billetmaster. He might preside at the Court Leet, Court Baron, Borough Court or Court of Pleas, or sit as assessor in the Mayor's Court. Almost invariably he acted as solicitor and legal agent to the Corporation, and, in conjunction with the Recorder, as its legal adviser. He was often one of the Corporate Justices of the Peace; but, unlike the Recorder and the Chamberlain, not usually a member of the Governing Council, to which he acted as Clerk.[4]

charges and expenses" (MS. Records, Southampton Corporation, 30th September 1708).

[1] As at Aberystwyth (First Report of Municipal Corporation Commission, 1835, vol. i. p. 171); Bossiney (*ibid.* vol. i. p. 453); Laugharne (*ibid.* vol. i. p. 288); St. Clears (*ibid.* vol. i. p. 377); and Havering-atte-Bower (*ibid.* vol. v. p. 2878).

[2] As at Appleby (*ibid.* vol. iii. p. 1426); Huntingdon (*ibid.* vol. iv. p. 2287); Ilchester (*ibid.* vol. ii. p. 1290); Kilgerran (*ibid.* vol. i. p. 279); and Seaford (*ibid.* vol. ii. p. 1059).

[3] As at Bedford (*ibid.* vol. iv. p. 2107); Berwick-on-Tweed (*ibid.* vol. iii. p. 1438); Bridgnorth (*ibid.* vol. iii. p. 1781); Cambridge (*ibid.* vol. iv. p. 2187); Carmarthen (*ibid.* vol. i. p. 206); Hastings (*ibid.* vol. ii. p. 998); Ipswich (*ibid.* vol. iv. p. 2295); Macclesfield (Report on Certain Boroughs, by T. J. Hogg, 1838, p. 58); Pevensey (First Report of Municipal Corporation Commission, 1835, vol. ii. p. 1017); Plymouth (*ibid.* vol. i. p. 581); Romney Marsh (*ibid.* vol. ii. p. 1027); Sandwich (*ibid.* vol. ii. p. 1045); and Wenlock (*ibid.* vol. iii. p. 2077); also, subject to the approval of the Crown, at Grimsby (*ibid.* vol. iv. p. 2250); and Poole (*ibid.* vol. ii. p. 1322).

[4] He was, however, a member of the Council at Canterbury (*ibid.* vol. ii. p. 691); Chichester (*ibid.* vol. ii. p. 720); Faversham (*ibid.* vol. ii. p. 964). At Dover he might or might not be chosen a member of the Common Council by the Mayor and Jurats (MS. Records, Dover Corporation, 19th January 1688; First Report of Municipal Corporation Commission, 1835, vol. ii. p. 943). At Southampton, on a new appointment being made in 1774, it was resolved "that he shall not have any deliberative voice in the Common Council, nor enter into any public debate, unless his opinion be asked, or he shall find the Body going into error in point of law or in prejudice of their own privileges" (MS. Records, Corporation of Southampton, 5th March 1774).

(l) The County Officers of the Municipal Corporation

It was, as we have said, an object of the Municipal Corporation to free itself from external control, and particularly to exclude the officers of the County and their underlings. To obtain this privilege, Corporation after Corporation not only made large payments to the King, but also undertook to perform, within the boundaries of its Borough, all the various duties of the County officers, notably those of the Coroner, the Sheriff, and the Justices of the Peace, and, in a single quite exceptional case,[1] also the Lieutenancy. In the majority of cases these duties, with the corresponding powers and authorities, devolved upon the existing Corporate officers. The Head of the Corporation, whether Portreeve, Warden, Alderman, Bailiff or Mayor, was always, *ex officio*, a Justice of the Peace for the Borough, and often also Coroner; if the Corporation enjoyed the privilege of sending members to Parliament, it was its Head, not the County Sheriff, who acted as Returning Officer;[2] in the smaller Boroughs he often himself fulfilled such of the duties of Sheriff and High Constable[3] as the Corporation had become responsible for. But this work naturally usually devolved upon other Corporate officers. The Bailiffs usually saw to the return of writs, the impanelling of Juries, and sometimes also the custody of the gaol; in some Municipal Corporations, indeed, claiming to be fully equivalent to the Sheriffs of

---

[1] The City of London. Haverfordwest, Berwick-on-Tweed, and the Liberty of the Cinque Ports had separate Lieutenants appointed by the Crown.

[2] In the nineteen Cities or Boroughs which were Counties in themselves, the Sheriff or Sheriffs of the Municipal Corporations were the Returning Officers; at Berwick-on-Tweed, which was, between 1689 and 1835, in virtually the same position, it was the Mayor and Bailiffs jointly (First Report of Municipal Corporation Commission, 1835, vol. iii. p. 1440); this was the case also at Newcastle-under-Lyme (*ibid.* vol. iii. p. 1952); Bedford (*ibid.* vol. iv. p. 2106); Preston (*ibid.* vol. iii. p. 1689). In other Boroughs it was the Head of the Corporation, who was accordingly declared incapable of being himself elected as a Member of Parliament, or of returning himself as a member for the Borough (House of Commons Journals, 2nd June 1685).

[3] The exact position in the County organisation of those Boroughs which were not Counties in themselves seems to have varied from County to County, and from function to function. For most purposes, in most Counties, the Borough seems to have been treated as a separate Hundred; and in these cases the Municipal Corporation, by its Head or some other of its Chief Officers, performed the duties of High Constable.

Counties.[1]   Occasionally we find the Bailiffs discharging also the duties of the Coroner.[2]   In some other Boroughs the duties of Coroner devolved upon the Town Clerk,[3] or upon one or more of the Aldermen.[4]

The majority of Municipal Corporations, however, appointed a separate Officer as Coroner, usually under the specific authority of a Charter.; the appointment being frequently conferred habitually for a year upon the person who had served as Head of the Corporation during the preceding year,[5] or else made, either annually or for life, by the Governing Council; in a few cases by the Head of the Corporation,[6] or by election by the whole body of Freemen,[7] or (in one case) by the Freeholders of the city.[8]   In a few Corporations the same officer was appointed to discharge within the Borough both the duties of Coroner and, to some extent, those of Sheriff.[9]

---

[1] Notably at Bath (First Report of Municipal Corporation Commission, 1835, vol. ii. p. 1115); Grimsby (*ibid.* vol. iv. p. 2252); Liverpool (*ibid.* vol. iv. p. 2698); Northampton (*ibid.* vol. iii. p. 1967); Oxford (*ibid.* vol. i. p. 101).   There was, even in the eighteenth century, great difficulty in restraining the officers of the County Sheriff (who were eager for fees) from making executions and arrests in the Boroughs that were exempt from his jurisdiction. The Corporation of Northampton had, for instance, to complain in 1722, and again in 1728, of such action; and on 10th May 1722 formally ordered that any case should be promptly made the occasion for an action in defence of the franchise of the Borough (*Records of the Borough of Northampton*, vol. ii., by J. C. Cox, 1898, pp. 54-55).

[2] As at Liverpool (First Report of Municipal Corporation Commission, 1835, vol. iv. p. 2698).

[3] As at Banbury (*ibid.* vol. i. p. 10); Canterbury (*ibid.* vol. ii. p. 691); Derby (*ibid.* vol. iii. p. 1850); Harwich (*ibid.* vol. iv. p. 2264); Lichfield (*ibid.* vol. iii. p. 1927); Maldon (*ibid.* vol. iv. p. 2438); Newark (*ibid.* vol. iii. p. 1937); Plympton Earle (*ibid.* vol. i. p. 600).

[4] As at Barnstaple (*ibid.* vol. i. p. 429); Denbigh (*ibid.* vol. iv. p. 2662); Kendal (*ibid.* vol. iii. p. 1591).   At Romney Marsh the duties of Coroner were performed by the four elected Justices (*ibid.* vol. ii. p. 1027).

[5] As at Bridgnorth (*ibid.* vol. iii. p. 1781); Bury St. Edmunds (*ibid.* vol. iv. p. 2173); Daventry (*ibid.* vol. iii. p. 1843); Eye (*ibid.* vol. iv. p. 2229); Godmanchester (*ibid.* vol. iv. p. 2235); Grantham (*ibid.* vol. iv. p. 2242); Grimsby (*ibid.* vol. iv. p. 2250); Guildford (*ibid.* vol. v. p. 2872); Hedou (*ibid.* vol. iii. p. 1588); Kingston-on-Hull (*ibid.* vol. iii. p. 1549); Oswestry (*ibid.* vol. iv. p. 2826); Scarborough (*ibid.* vol. iii. p. 1714); Thetford (*ibid.* vol. iv. p. 2542).

[6] As at Appleby (*ibid.* vol. iii. p. 1426).

[7] As at Berwick-on-Tweed (*ibid.* vol. iii. p. 1438); Cardigan (*ibid.* vol. i. p. 198); Ipswich (*ibid.* vol. iv. p. 2295); Monmouth (*ibid.* vol. i. p. 323); Poole (*ibid.* vol. ii. p. 1322); Rochester (*ibid.* vol. ii. p. 847); Southwold (*ibid.* vol. iv. p. 2516).

[8] York (*ibid.* vol. iii. p. 1741).

[9] As at Ludlow (*ibid.* vol. iv. p. 2789); Lynn (*ibid.* vol. iv. p. 2398).

Only those Municipal Corporations which had been specifically granted by Royal Charter the privileges of their Boroughs or Cities being "Counties of themselves," could appoint Sheriffs of their own, though in three or four other towns, as we have mentioned, the Corporations enjoyed virtually equivalent immunities. The nineteen "Counties Corporate," [1] as they were called—the "citees, viles ou burghs queux sonnt countees encorporates de eux memes" of the Parliamentary scribe of 1439 [2]—were completely exempted from all jurisdictions of the County and its officers, with the exception of the Lieutenancy. The Municipal Corporation was therefore responsible to the Crown for the fulfilment, within the City or Borough, of all the obligations of a County at large, except only those relating to the militia, for which it was responsible to the Lord-Lieutenant. Thus, the Sheriffs of these Corporations had practically the same powers and duties as those of ordinary Counties. They were, however, never appointed by the Crown, but by the Municipal Corporation itself, usually by its Governing Council; but in a few cases, under more or less restriction of choice, by the whole body of Freemen. [3] It should, however, be noted that it was the Municipal Corporation itself, not its Sheriff or Sheriffs, which had undertaken the responsibilities of a County, and it was to the Head of the Corporation, not to the Sheriff or Sheriffs, that the Crown looked for their fulfilment. The Corporation Sheriffs, though irremovable by the Crown, were accordingly not equal in status or dignity to those of the Counties: they were, in fact, only subordinates to the Mayor —to use the quaint words of the old chronicler Stow, "the Mayor's eyes, seeing and supporting part of the care, which the person of the Mayor alone is not sufficient to bear." [4]

[1] They were Bristol, Carmarthen, Chester, Coventry, Gloucester, Lincoln, London, Norwich, Nottingham, and York, having each two Sheriffs; and Canterbury, Exeter, Haverfordwest, Kingston-on-Hull, Lichfield, Newcastle-on-Tyne, Poole, Southampton, and Worcester, having each one Sheriff. The origin and significance of this divergence of practice is quite unknown to us.

[2] Rot. Parl. v. 28a (18 Henry VI.).

[3] As at Carmarthen (First Report of Municipal Corporation Commission, 1835, vol. i. p. 205); Haverfordwest (*ibid.* vol. i. p. 235); Kingston-on-Hull (*ibid.* vol. iii. p. 1549); Norwich (*ibid.* vol. iv. p. 2460). In the City of London the election was by the superior grade of Freemen (the Livery).

[4] *Survey of London,* by John Stow, book v. chap. v. p. 89 of Strype's edition of 1720.

By 1689 they had come to have very varied functions in the different towns, but they were rapidly becoming merely ceremonial officers. In many Corporations they had to accompany the Mayor on all pageants and ceremonies, including his formal attendances at church—a duty occasionally refused by Nonconformists.[1] In the greatest of all the Corporations, as we shall subsequently describe,[2] the two Sheriffs moved in great pomp and had extensive and almost incessant duties, but these were chiefly formal and ceremonial. In other Boroughs the Sheriffs were supposed to preside, sometimes at the ancient Borough Court, sometimes at a Sheriffs' Monthly Court, at which minor litigation was dealt with. They had the superintendence of the gaol and the Bridewell, together with the appointment to various lucrative offices, such as those of Under Sheriff, Gaoler, Bridewell Keeper, Sheriff's Yeomen, Sheriff's Beadles, etc. In one or two Corporations they were furnished, for their attendance on the Mayor and the Assize Judges, with gorgeous State carriages. They provided sumptuous banquets at the Assizes, and they had occasionally to present the Corporation, or the Mayor for the time being, with a costly piece of plate.[3] In other Boroughs that were Counties Corporate the office of Sheriff served principally as an opportunity for the Corporation to confer temporary dignity, and often some perquisites, on one of its number.

The newer dignity of the Custos Rotulorum and Lord-Lieutenant was, as we have already mentioned, only exceptionally found connected with a town. Why the small Welsh Borough of Haverfordwest should, for several centuries, have enjoyed a Lord-Lieutenant to itself—appointed, however, by the Crown—we are unable to explain.[4] The exceptional position of Berwick, where the Governor was Lieutenant, and of the

---

[1] In 1660 information was given to the Privy Council "that George Steward, Esq., lately chosen Sheriff for the City of Norwich, since his oath taken, refused to accompany . . . the Mayor of the said City, according to custom, to the Cathedral Church"; whereupon he was summoned to appear, and made to promise due attendance in future (MS. Acts of Privy Council, 10th and 26th October 1660).

[2] See *post*, "The City of London," Chapter X.

[3] Notably in the City of London and Bristol.

[4] This unique status of Haverfordwest may possibly be connected in some way with the existence of a County Palatine of Pembrokeshire down to the sixteenth century; see *The Parish and the County*, p. 313.

City of London, is more easily understood. There is no evidence that the premier Municipality had ever formed part of the County organisation of Middlesex; and it may well have been considered too important an aggregation of population and wealth to be entrusted to any individual subject. The custom grew up of entrusting the duties of the Lieutenancy to a Commission appointed by the King, of whom the leading member was the Lord Mayor for the time being. In the Liberty of the Cinque Ports, comprising fifteen Municipal Corporations, all the duties of a Custos Rotulorum and Lord-Lieutenant were, as we shall subsequently describe, performed by the Lord Warden.

By 1689, however, as we have elsewhere described, the real Rulers of the County were not the Sheriff and Coroner, nor even the Custos Rotulorum and Lord-Lieutenant, but the Justices of the Peace in their General Sessions assembled. It was, as we have said, the distinctive mark of a Municipal Corporation that it created its own Justices of the Peace, who exercised within the boundaries of the Borough all the powers elsewhere conferred by the King's Commission. These Magisterial powers were nearly always combined with some high Municipal office. The Head of the Corporation, whether Portreeve, Bailiff, Alderman, Warden or Mayor, was invariably a Justice of the Peace *ex officio*. So, too, was the Recorder, wherever such an officer was appointed; less frequently also the Coroner, the Bailiffs, the Deputy Recorder and the Town Clerk. The Head of the Corporation for the preceding year was sometimes a magistrate for twelve months after quitting office, and was often specifically termed "the Justice." Occasionally the Bishop, or sometimes the Dean and a Prebendary or two, would be included among the Corporate Justices. Sometimes the Sheriffs were *ex officio* Justices: in the larger Boroughs one or more of the Aldermen or Jurats, sometimes those who had "passed the Chair," [1] and sometimes all of them. [2] Only rarely do we find the

---

[1] As at Chester (First Report of Municipal Corporation Commission, 1835, vol. iv. pp. 2620, 2622); Berwick-on-Tweed (*ibid.* vol. iii. p. 1436); Canterbury (*ibid.* vol. ii. p. 695); Lincoln (*ibid.* vol. iv. p. 2346); King's Lynn (*ibid.* vol. iv. p. 2391); Norwich (*ibid.* vol. iv. p. 2464); Liverpool (*ibid.* vol. iv. p. 2700); Boston (*ibid.* vol. iv. p. 2153).

[2] As at Bristol (*ibid.* vol. ii. p. 1165); Dover (*ibid.* vol. ii. p. 946); Faversham

Corporation appointing persons specifically to be Justices of the Peace; though in some Boroughs two, three, or four would be selected from among the Aldermen, or from such of them as had served as Head of the Corporation. In one Borough the whole body of Freemen elected annually four of the Jurats to serve as Justices.[1]

(m) *The Mayor's Brethren and the Mayor's Counsellors*

Closely associated with the Mayor, as Head of the Corporation and chief of its executive, were the Aldermen, the " Mayor's Peers " or " Mayor's Brethren," whom we find nearly everywhere serving him both as executive assistants, undertaking individually particular functions or supervising particular districts of the Borough, and also as a sort of consultative council.[2] In the Cinque Ports, at any rate, there are signs that their appointment had been, in earlier times, actually made by the Head of the Corporation.[3] Some-

(*ibid.* vol. ii. p. 966); Folkestone (*ibid.* vol. ii. p. 981); Gloucester, where the Bishop, the Dean, and two Prebendaries were also Justices (*ibid.* vol. i. p. 63); Hythe (*ibid.* vol. ii. p. 1008); Kingston-on-Hull (*ibid.* vol. iii. p. 1552); Rye (*ibid.* vol. ii. p. 1034); Sandwich (*ibid.* vol. ii. p. 1048); Seaford (*ibid.* vol. ii. p. 1059); Stamford (*ibid.* vol. iv. p. 2530); Winchelsea (*ibid.* vol. ii. p. 1074); Leeds (*ibid.* vol. iii. p. 1621); Beverley (*ibid.* vol. iii. p. 1458); Grantham (*ibid.* vol. iv. p. 2242); Hastings (*ibid.* vol. ii. p. 998); Lydd (*ibid.* vol. ii. p. 1013); and the City of London after the Charter of 1741, *infra*, Chap. X.

[1] Romney Marsh (First Report of Municipal Corporation Commission, 1835, vol. ii. p. 1027).

[2] In many Corporations, principally but not exclusively in the South-western counties—such as Abingdon, Aldeburgh, Bewdley, Bodmin, Blandford, Brecon, Bridgwater, Buckingham, Devizes, Dunwich, Eye, Glastonbury, Grantham, Haverfordwest, Lancaster, Leominster, Liskeard, East and West Looe, Lost-withiel, Marlborough, Marazion, Monmouth, Newcastle-under-Lyme, New Radnor, Okehampton, Penryn, Plympton Earle, St. Ives, Shaftesbury, Sutton Coldfield, Thetford, Tiverton, Tregony, Truro, Wareham, Westbury—the place of Aldermen is taken by " Capital Burgesses," or " Principal Burgesses," or " Capital Councillors," or " Common Burgesses." At Andover we have the " Approved Men "; at Bradninch, Dartmouth, Totnes and Wells, the ' Masters "; and at Ipswich and Orwell, the " Portmen." In nearly all the Kent and Sussex Boroughs, especially those which formed part of the Liberty of the Cinque Ports—Deal, Dover, Faversham, Folkestone, Fordwich, Hastings, Hythe, Lydd, Pevensey, Rye, Sandwich, Seaford, Tenterden, and Winchelsea, and also Gravesend and Romney Marsh—the title is " Jurat "; probably derived from the Norman towns. The title of Alderman is most usually found with that of Mayor; but in various Corporations, such as Bridgnorth, East Retford, and Kidderminster, Aldermen were presided over by a Bailiff; in that of Sutton Coldfield, by a Warden; and in that of Neath, by a Portreeve. Capital Burgesses and Jurats are found indifferently with Mayors or Bailiffs as Heads.

[3] They were, in fact, his lieutenants or assistants (see, for instance, Sandwich, *Cinque Ports*, by M. Burrows, 1888, p. 201).

times each Alderman, or each pair of Aldermen, was placed in charge of, or at the head of, a particular Ward of the Borough, for which he undertook a special responsibility. In one ancient Municipality, for instance, the Alderman was charged individually to inquire "whether there be any nuisance or purprestures in the City, as by setting of pales, walls, stalls, bulks, porches, windows, and such like, whereby any incroaching is used; or any timber, stones, dunghills, or heaps of dirt, or any other thing be cast and laid in the streets to the letting or hindering of any way, or to the annoyance of any person. Also whether any do keep slaughtering within the City, or do keep and feed any hogs, ducks, or any other filthy beast. Also whether the streets be kept clean and swept twice in the week at least. Also whether any house be ruinous and stand dangerously, and whether any chimney, oven or furnace, or backs or hearths for fire, do stand dangerously and in peril of fire, and the same not presented by the scavenger. Also whether there be crooks, ladders, and buckets in readiness to serve, if need should be, in peril of fire; and whether every man have in readiness a vessel of water at his door when any house is adventured with fire, and not advertised by the scavengers."[1] Gradually, however, the Ward duties, and indeed most of the executive functions of individual Aldermen, sank into the background, in comparison with their collective responsibility as a Court or Council. In some Boroughs they remained indefinite in number, existing merely by custom, being frequently those who had served as Mayor,[2] and partaking of the Mayor's dignity. In one Borough, for instance, we read, "their number varied widely, but there seems to have been a theory

---

[1] MS. Records, Exeter Corporation; *The Antique Description and Account of . . . Exeter*, by John Vowell, 1765, p. 172 (first printed 1584). At Bristol, we find the Mayor and Aldermen allotting the several Wards among themselves, and ordering "that the several Wards written after the names of the Mayor and Aldermen be under the care and inspection of each Justice of the Peace respectively" (MS. Minutes, Bristol Corporation, 30th September 1706).

[2] So in the Municipal Corporations of Bedford, Chichester, Guildford, Liverpool, Northampton, Poole, Southampton, Welshpool, and Weymouth, as well as in such Manorial Boroughs as Altrincham, Kenfig, Newport in Pembrokeshire, Stockport, and Stockton. In some other Corporations, such as Chester, Coventry, Derby, Hedon, and Hereford, the Aldermen were a definite number, serving for life, vacancies being filled from among those who had served as Head of the Corporation. This was the case also in such Manorial Boroughs as Dursley, Llantrissant, Longhor, Wickwar, and Wotton-under-Edge.

that they ought to number twelve. . . . They consisted of all
Mayors who had passed the chair, though, possibly, other
leading citizens were also admitted among them. They thus
held their position for life. . . . The front seats in the chapel
were reserved for them. The Town Waits played before their
doors. They sat on the Bench with the Mayor in his Court,
where all the multifarious judicial business was transacted.
They are repeatedly mentioned as sharing with the Mayor
responsibility for his acts; and not rare is the announcement
of a new edict on some important point, 'Ordered by the
Mayor and his Brethren with the consent of the Assembly.' " [1]
Only in two exceptional Corporations, to be subsequently
described [2]—the only ones in which the Aldermen were
elected by their Wards—do we find their positions as Captains
of the Watch and Heads of their Wards at all comparable in
dignity and importance with those enjoyed by them as
Members of the Court of Aldermen. By 1689 they had
come usually to be specified in the Charter as a permanent
select body, definite in number and in the method of their
appointment; in all cases forming part of the Court of
Common Council where any such Council existed; only in
two or three cases sitting also separately as a Court of
Aldermen, except for the special purpose of filling vacancies
in their own body, or among the Common Councilmen, and
for the execution of their duties as Justices of the Peace. For,
as we shall presently describe, it was upon some or all of the
Aldermen, in conjunction with the Head of the Corporation,
that were cast the duties of the Borough Magistracy. Even
if only some of them were, by Charter, Justices of the Peace,
we see all of them, nearly everywhere, performing collectively
some of the functions elsewhere exercised only by Justices,

---

[1] *History of Municipal Government in Liverpool*, by Ramsay Muir, 1906,
p. 82 ; see also the same author's *History of Liverpool*, 1907.

[2] London and, to a lesser degree, Norwich. At Bristol, though vacancies
among the Aldermen were filled by co-option without reference to the Wards of
the City, they were all assigned to particular Wards, of which they individually
took charge, especially as regards the supervision of the public-houses, the
collection of the Watch Rate, and the issuing and hearing of summonses for
non-payment of the Poor Rate. The Alderman presided, too, over meetings
of the Ward—as, for instance, those for the election of members of the
Corporation of the Poor—but held no Wardmote or other Court in the Ward.
See on this point *Town Life in the Fifteenth Century*, by A. S. Green, 1894,
vol. ii. p. 279.

such as licensing ale-houses, making rates, passing accounts, and appointing Constables; and they were evidently often considered to be members of the judicial bench. "Magistrates' posts," sometimes richly carved and ornamented, used, in the larger cities, to be set up outside their doors to indicate their residences, a picturesque usage which was in 1689 not yet wholly abandoned.[1] Sometimes we find them all entitled, whether magistrates or not, to sit as Judges in the Borough Court, and to take part in the trial of civil actions.[2]

To this variegated array of independent dignitaries, each with his own authority and his own sphere of operations, we might add the "Mayor's Counsellors," whom we find, in the majority of Municipal Corporations, specialised out of the Burgesses or Freemen, and forming, in more or less intimate association with the Aldermen and the Chief Officers, a standing Assembly or Court of Common Council. These Counsellors, usually twelve, four-and-twenty, or eight-and-forty in number, had no individual functions or status, and we accordingly leave them to be dealt with in our section on the Administrative Courts of the Corporation.[3]

---

[1] See reference to this custom in *The Widow*, by Beaumont and Fletcher, the paper by J. A. Repton, in *Archæologia*, vol. xix., 1821, pp. 383-385 ; the *Book of Days*, by R. Chambers, 1869, vol. i. pp. 161-162 ; *Remnants of Antiquity in Norwich*, 1843 ; *Norfolk and Norwich Notes and Queries*, 1897, pp. 195-196. A relic of the custom may be seen in Scotland to this day, in the decoration with the town arms of the lamp-post nearest to the house of the Provost (*e.g.* at Linlithgow).

[2] Here Aldermen are to be understood as the senior grade of members of the Governing Council of the Corporation. It should, however, be remembered that "Alderman" is used in various other senses. In the Municipal Corporations of Bury St. Edmunds and Grantham, as in the Manorial Borough of Wokingham, the Head was styled Alderman. In those of Barnstaple, Brecon, Bridgwater, Denbigh, Macclesfield, New Radnor, Ruthin, and Wootton Bassett, the Aldermen were one or two persons elected to be Justices. At Bridgnorth the ex-Chamberlain was so designated. At Aberavon the two Aldermen were petty officers. The title was formerly used in Sussex Manors for a mere Beadle. At Alnwick, Morpeth, and elsewhere the Aldermen were the heads of the Gilds or Trade Companies. At Salisbury, Southampton, and Wilton there were so-called "Aldermen of the Wards," distinct from the Mayor's Brethren.

[3] It must be remembered that service in all the ancient Corporation Offices, from the Headship down to the Beadleship (but not including the Town Clerkship), was compulsory. Refusal to serve was habitually punished by fine. Thus, at Southampton, "the House met, Mr. Recorder present, and fined T. B. forty pounds for refusing the office of Bailiff" (MS. Records, Southampton Corporation, 2nd November 1693). Another Burgess pays three guineas as fine for being excused from service as Beadle (*ibid.* 5th October 1703) ; another, five pounds for escaping the office of Constable (*ibid.* 2nd October 1702) ; another, ten pounds to avoid being Water Bailiff, and another, thirty pounds to " be excused

(*n*) *The Courts of the Corporation*

The immigrant from a rural Manor or a Manorial Borough would take for granted the existence of Courts, at which his obligations as a "resiant" or a Burgess, as a neighbour or a "foreigner," would be enforced.   In some of the smaller and more archaic Municipal Corporations he would find Courts bearing exactly the same names, and wielding exactly the same powers as those of rural Manors.   In a few instances he would even find one or other of the Courts in the Borough still continuing to be held by the Lord's Steward, in the name and for the profit of an individual Lord of the Manor.   But if our rural immigrant entered the jurisdiction of one of the more powerful of the Municipal Corporations, he would be surprised at the number and variety of the Courts held by the Mayor or one or other of the Chief Officers, at their strange titles, at their multifarious officials, and, above all, at the extent of the authority that they exercised over his conduct and his property.

What is interesting to the historical student is that, if we arrange the couple of hundred Municipal Corporations in a series, according to the nature of their Courts, we find the same tendency to fission and specialisation that we noticed in the case of the Chief Officers of the Corporation.   Just as we have found in the rural Manor an Undifferentiated Court which was not divided into the Court Leet, Court Baron, and Customary Court of the contemporary lawyers, so we discover in some of the Municipal Corporations an undifferentiated Portmote, Curia Burgi, or Borough Court, which combined

the several offices of Two Bailiffs and Sheriff" (*ibid.* 6th October 1696).   At Exeter, S. M. is fined forty pounds "for refusing the office of a Steward or Bailiff of this City being thereunto duly elected " (MS. Records, Exeter Corporation, 23rd January 1688).   The earlier form of penalty in the Cinque Ports had been the peculiar communal house demolition, which these Boroughs had in common with those of the North of France (*Feudal England*, by J. H. Round, 1895, pp. 552-571).   Moreover, there was often a custom of service in successive years of all the Corporate officers in a graded order.   A Freeman often served successively as Common Councilman, Alderman, Bailiff or Sheriff, and Head. It was proposed at Exeter in 1691 "that no person or persons whatsoever which have not served the offices of Low Bailiff, High Bailiff, High Constable, and Chamberlain of that City, or the major part of those offices," should be eligible for nomination as Mayor (MS. Records, Proposal Book, Exeter Corporation, 23rd February 1691).

judicial with administrative functions, and dealt with both criminal offences and civil suits between parties. This, indeed, almost follows from what we have already described. A town which became the seat of a Municipal Corporation did not thereby cease to be a Manor, or to be included in a Manor; nor did the Manorial Courts thereby cease to be held in and for such a town. In many cases the ownership of the Manor passed to the Municipal Corporation, which naturally continued to hold the accustomed Courts. These made the usual presentments, heard suits between parties, and amerced offenders—exercised, in fact, all the civil and criminal jurisdiction of the little community—and also made the primitive sanitary and other regulations for the Borough, administered its valuable commons, and appointed nearly all its officers, whether Haywards, Scavengers, Beadles, Watchmen, Bellmen, Constables, Inspectors of the Commons, Tithingmen, Ale-tasters, or Clerks of the Market.[1] Even when the Corporation did

[1] Thus, in the simple case of Chipping Norton in Oxfordshire, which had been incorporated by Charter in 1607, the Municipal Corporation bought the Manor in 1667, and continued down to 1846 to hold what was evidently an Undifferentiated Court, doing everything but decide civil suits, for which a separate Court of Record had been established by the Charter (MS. Records, Corporation of Chipping Norton; *Notes on the History of Chipping Norton*, by A. Ballard, 1893, pp. 10, 23, 24-28; First Report of Municipal Corporation Commission, 1835, vol. i. p. 35). As the Jury orders are of great interest, such orders being extremely rare in printed form, and as they significantly recall the decisions of the Court of Great Tew (see pp. 80-87), we append copious extracts.

"That the Great Common shall be hained from horses, cows, and all other great cattle on the 6th of November next, and shall not be broken with horses, cows, or other great cattle until the season will permit, viz. between the 1st and 12th days of May next, and then not before eight o'clock in the morning, and to be left to the discretion of the Inspectors, who will give public notice of the same. . . . That any persons putting any . . . beasts to dispasture upon . . . the said Commons, shall, before they are put on, take them to the Drivers to be branded. . . . That every person putting any cow . . . on the said Commons without previously having sufficient knobs on their horns shall for every offence incur a penalty of 2s. 6d. to the Lords. . . . That mares with sucking colts shall be put on Southcomb Common only . . . that the Inspectors shall let both the Commons to be stocked with sheep . . . to depasture thereon day and night, and one-third of the monies arising from the same to be expended in the improvement of the Common . . . that the Drivers shall drive the Commons from the time of breaking to the time of haining at least four times, and if they do their duty to the satisfaction of the Inspectors they shall receive ten shillings of them next Leet . . . that parishioners only be allowed to cut, take and carry away furse or gorse from off Southcombe or the Poor's Allotment, and that they shall not stock it up with a hoe or any other tool, but shall cut it with a bill or hatchet, and shall carry it home on their backs . . . that every person making a dunghill in the public streets or lanes within this Borough, and suffering it to remain after three days'

not acquire the ownership of the Manor, we see it holding, under one title or another, one or more Borough Courts, each combining heterogeneous functions.   Such a Borough Court might frequently unite a minor criminal jurisdiction with the appointment of officers, the admission of Freemen, the enrolment of apprentices, the regulation of the town by By-laws, and the management of the Corporate property.   It might, on the other hand, combine the hearing of civil suits between parties and the recovery of petty debts with similar administrative duties.   But we may notice a tendency to a more logical differentiation, until, in the large majority of our couple of hundred Municipal Corporations, what we have in 1689 is a set of separate Courts for civil and criminal jurisdiction respectively, with distinct organs for the administration of the Corporate property and the transaction of the other business.

(o) Courts of Civil Jurisdiction

A tribunal for the trial of civil actions was nearly always a feature of the Municipal Corporation of 1689.   In a very few instances, indeed, the right to hold such a Court—analogous to the Court Baron—had never been acquired by the Corporation itself, and the Court continued to be held by the Lord for his own profit.[1]   But in the vast majority of

notice from the Scavenger, the dunghill to become forfeited to him, and that R. B. be appointed Scavenger for the next year, who shall have the dirt to his own use, and five shillings besides for his trouble . . . that if any person shall call out the Jury for the inspection or decision of any matter or dispute or otherwise, he shall give notice to the Foreman in writing . . . and that a shilling shall be paid to each juryman by the person so calling them out, or by the Constable when called out on public business . . . that no house divided into two or more tenements since the passing of the Act of Inclosure . . . is entitled to more than one Common (the then original one), and that no house erected or built since that time . . . is entitled to common right . . . that R. B. shall be Watchman, Beadle, and Bellman . . . and that T. G. be appointed Nightly Watch . . . that J. A. . . . . Jury hereby appoint (to be Hayward)" (*Laws and Orders made by the Jury at a Court Leet and Court Baron and View of Frankpledge, holden by the Bailiffs and Burgesses of the Borough of Chipping Norton,* 1821).

[1] In the exceptional case of the old ecclesiastical City of Salisbury (First Report of Municipal Corporation Commission, 1835, vol. ii. pp. 1343-1344) this Court had never been ceded to the Municipal Corporation (except for a brief period during the Commonwealth, see *The Commonwealth Charter of the City of Salisbury,* by Hubert Hall, 1907); and continued to be held by the Bishop's Steward, and for his profit.   At Ripon the Steward of the Archbishop of York held the Court (First Report of Municipal Corporation Commission, 1835,

Municipal Corporations this civil jurisdiction had been handed over by the Lord, or expressly granted by the King to the incorporated body.   It is, we think, illustrative of the rise of such Boroughs from the Manor that we find this Court, so closely resembling the Court Baron, in the hands of Municipal Corporations which had not attained to other franchises, and where the Lord of the Manor still retained in his own hands the View of Frankpledge and some or all of the jurisdiction of the Court Leet.   But apart from these exceptions, the Municipal Corporations—however their Civil Courts may originally have been obtained—had, in one or other of their Charters, secured from the King an express grant of the right to exercise civil jurisdiction, in a Court that bore different names in the various Boroughs.   The most frequent name for this chartered tribunal was the Court of Record, which we find used in a hundred and twenty Boroughs; or "Three Weeks' Court"—occasionally "Three Weeken Court"—which we trace only in half a dozen towns;[1] more frequently the "Court of Pleas," a term used in a score of places.   In ten or a dozen cases it was called the Mayor's Court;[2] in two or three, the "Bailiff's Court"[3] or the "Provost's Court"; or (in the Counties Corporate) the "Sheriff's Court" or "County Court."[4]   We find it designated the "Town Court" or the "Borough Court,"[5] or the "Gildhall Court,"[6] or occasionally

vol. iii. p. 1710).   At Oswestry, where a Court of Record was held weekly before the Mayor, the Lord of the Manor was entitled to receive one-half of the fines arising in Court, and the attorneys who practised in it were appointed by the Mayor and Steward jointly.   At Buckingham, Shaftesbury, and Wilton, the Lord still retained in his own hands the View of Frankpledge and all the jurisdiction of the Leet, whilst permitting the Municipal Corporation to hold a Civil Court of the nature of a Court Baron.   In a few other Corporations, such as Wigan, Basingstoke, Havering-atte-Bower, and Ruthin, the Manorial origin of this Court is plainly visible in the retention of the title of Court Baron, Lordship Court, or "Court of Ancient Demesne"; in the participation, as "Suitors" or judges, of the freeholders, or other "tenants"; or in the limitation of the jurisdiction to sums under forty shillings.

[1] Such as Buckingham, Macclesfield, Yeovil.

[2] Such as the City of London, Bristol, Coventry, Exeter, Great Grimsby, Hereford, Marlborough, Newcastle-on-Tyne, and Plymouth.

[3] Such as Ipswich and Chichester.

[4] As at the City of London, Bristol, Newcastle-on-Tyne, Worcester, etc.

[5] As at Winchester, Monmouth, and Great Yarmouth.   By the ancient customs of the Manor, a "Burgh Court" had to be held weekly at Great Yarmouth and adjourned at the will of the Bailiff (*Treatise on Copyholds*, by C. Watkins, fourth edition, 1825, vol. ii. p. 557).

[6] As at Norwich and King's Lynn.

even the King's Court. There were even such uncouth titles as "Foreign Court"[1] or "Court of Burgess and Foreign,"[2] "Court of Passage"[3] or "Passage Court," "Pentice Court,"[4] "Tolzey Court,"[5] the "Court of our Lord the King called the "Portmouth,"[6] or, more simply, "Court of Portmote"[7] or "Portman's Mote."[8] But whatever might be the local appellation of this Municipal Court of civil jurisdiction, it had always certain invariable features in common with the Court Baron of the rural Manor. There was, at least in theory, a body of persons who acted as judges, all equally entitled to be present and to pronounce the decisions, even if, in practice, the actual holding of the Court was deputed to one or two Corporation officers, and even if a Jury summoned by the Mayor, Bailiff, or Serjeant at Mace could be impanelled to pronounce the verdict. These judges comprised usually the Mayor or Bailiff or other head of the Corporation, and the other principal personages named in the Charter; the Recorder and sometimes the Town Clerk; sometimes the whole of the Aldermen, Jurats, or Capital Burgesses; sometimes all the members of the Close Body. Another point of resemblance to the Court Baron was its habit of holding frequent sessions at regular short intervals, most frequently from three weeks to three weeks, but occasionally monthly, fortnightly, or even weekly.

The jurisdiction of this Municipal tribunal was always limited to suits in which the cause of action arose within the Borough, and occasionally to suits against Freemen of the Borough. In many towns the jurisdiction was limited to personal actions, but in many others it included actions relative to lands within the Borough, and in many others,

[1] Great Grimsby.   [2] Pontefract.   [3] Chester and Liverpool.
[4] Chester.   [5] Bristol.
[6] New Woodstock.   [7] Rochester, Chester, and Faversham.
[8] Ipswich. In some Municipal Corporations we see remnants or traces of ancient Hundred Courts, held on behalf of the Corporations, in respect either of their own territories, or of estates outside. Thus, in the City of Gloucester, between 1657 and 1796 at any rate, there was a "Hundred Court" held formally every week before the Mayor and the two Sheriffs. The minute-book contains, after 1680, practically nothing but the perpetual repetition of the names of the "suitors" of the Court, who included the Earls of Hereford and Gloucester, Lord Stafford, the Dean and Chapter of the Cathedral, and other large landowners. As late as 1791 it swore in not only Constables, but also the Master and Wardens of the Company of Butchers (*supra*, p. 51; MS. Hundred Court Minute-Book, 1657-1796; in Records of Corporation of Gloucester).

again, all sorts of actions could be tried.   In some towns there
was a limit to the amount of the debt or damages for which
an action might be brought.   In one or two cases this limit
is a minimum of forty shillings, possibly with the object of
protecting from Municipal competition a Lord's Court having
jurisdiction within the Borough.   More frequently there was no
minimum but a maximum, sometimes of about £10 or £20, but
ranging from £5 to as much as £200; presumably to protect
the interests of the King's Courts at Westminster.   Occasionally the grant would be to have cognisance of pleas in all
personal actions to an unlimited amount, or all pleas, real
or personal, arising within the Borough, unless either the
Crown or the Corporation was a party.   The Mayor, Bailiff,
or other head of the Corporation issued the process of the
Court, which, whether arrest or seizure and sale of goods,
was executed by the Serjeants at Mace or other officers of
the Corporation, who could only act within the narrow limits
of the particular Borough.

The tendency to fission and specialisation in the Courts
of civil jurisdiction is seen in the larger or more privileged
Municipalities, where the Corporation held several Courts,
dealing with different classes of actions.   Thus, some Municipal
Corporations had, besides a Petty Debt Court, a "Court of
Equity" for cases involving real estate;[1] a "Bailiff's Court"
or other tribunal at which minors could execute valid conveyances; and even a separate Court, sometimes called
Portmanmote or "Court of Hustings," at which fines and
recoveries could be levied, wills proved, and conveyances of
real estate executed by married women.   In other cases we
find Courts for actions against Freemen distinct from the
Courts for actions against non-Freemen;[2] or Courts for the
recovery of petty debts distinct from those in which more
important actions could be tried.[3]   In some towns, indeed, the
Corporation held several distinct Courts of civil jurisdiction,
under different officers, without, apparently, any differences in
scope or function, and acting merely as rivals for the litigation
of the Burgesses.[4]   But whatever may have been the origin

[1] As at Norwich.
[2] As at Newcastle-on-Tyne and Great Grimsby.
[3] As at Rye and Bury St. Edmunds.
[4] Thus, the Municipal Corporation of Ipswich had three distinct civil Courts:

or function of these Municipal Courts of civil jurisdiction; whatever, in particular Boroughs, were their numbers, titles, and scope, we see them nearly everywhere losing their business in the course of the eighteenth century, the decay often becoming rapidly marked in the last quarter of that century. The causes of this decay seem to have been partly the somewhat uncertain quality of the presiding judges, and occasionally, it was said, the suspicion caused by their belonging all to the same political party; but much more the defects in the organisation of the Court itself. It could not summon witnesses who were outside the limits of the Borough, and could only enforce its judgment by arrest or execution within the same narrow limits. Its scale of charges was always sufficiently heavy to discourage suitors, whilst the fees which it allowed to attorneys were far below those which they obtained in the superior Courts, so that in town after town we find them ceasing to attend at the Courts. Sometimes the procedure was antiquated and pedantic, involving great delays, as in one case, where the Court was held only once a month, and three "Court Days" had to intervene between every stage of the pleadings.[1] For all these reasons the King's Courts at Westminster were always very ready to grant writs of prohibition or allow cases to be removed by writ of certiorari or otherwise, so that the jurisdiction of the local tribunal lost its certainty and whatever celerity and cheapness it may have possessed.[2] Finally, the establishment, under Local Acts, of Courts of Request or Courts of Conscience provided in most places alternative tribunals for the recovery of petty debts, which offered superior advantages in the way of prompt hearing, simple procedure, and low fees.

its Court of Pleas, having jurisdiction in all pleas, real and personal, where the cause of action arose within the Borough; its Court of Requests under Local Act; and its Petty Court of the Bailiffs, at which minors over fourteen could execute valid conveyances of real estate. At Chester, too, the Corporation held three civil Courts: the Portmote Court, before the Mayor and Recorder; the Pentice Court, before the Sheriff; and the Passage Court, which was in the nature of an adjourned sessions of the Pentice Court. The Corporation of Bristol had its ancient "Mayor's Court," as well as the better-known "Tolzey Court" held by the Sheriffs, the two tribunals having at one time maintained an active rivalry, in which the Mayor's Court succumbed, and became entirely disused (*infra*, Chap. VIII.).   [1] Walsall.

[2] "The Courts of Westminster," as Counsel advised the Corporation of Deal in 1730, "keeping inferior jurisdictions very strict, especially if of new

(p) The Court Leet

In the great majority of Municipal Corporations of 1689, the tribunal most in use (otherwise than for civil actions) was the ancient Court Leet. In about a dozen Boroughs the right to hold this Court had never been acquired by the Corporation, and the Court was either held by the Lord's Steward or by a Municipal officer on behalf and for the profit of the Lord of the Manor. In nearly all the Municipalities, however, the Corporation had acquired the right to hold its own Court Leet, in a few cases by specific grant from the King, embodied in a Charter.[1] But it is interesting to notice how much more rarely this grant of a Court of petty police appears in the Charters obtained by the Municipal Corporations, in spite of the fact that it was nominally the Court of the King, to be holden only by his authority, than the Court of Civil Jurisdiction which (as Court Baron) the lawyers regarded only as a private tribunal, incident to every Manor. In the vast majority of Municipal Corporations the jurisdiction of the Leet had not been differentiated into a distinct tribunal separately granted or assigned, and had remained a mere incident to the ownership of the Manor. When the Corporation acquired the Manor, or took it on lease from the Lord,[2] the Court Leet and View of Frankpledge continued to be held by the Steward, for the new Lord of the Manor as for the old one.[3] We need not

creation" (MS. Records (Book of Counsel's Opinions, 1716-1776), Deal Corporation).

[1] At Beaumaris in Anglesey, for instance, we find the Charter giving "within the said Borough and the Liberties and precincts of the same, View of Frankpledge of all Burgesses, inhabitants and resiants twice by the year . . . and all that ever appertaineth to a View of Frankpledge together with summons, attachments, arrestments, issues, amerciaments, fines, ransoms, profits, commodities and other things whatsoever that might and ought to appertain to us, our heirs and successors in any wise." So in the Charters of Bewdley, Bodmin, Boston, Carlisle, Evesham, King's Lynn, Kendal, Liskeard, West Looe, Richmond (Yorks), St. Albans, Sutton Coldfield, Tamworth, Tenterden, Torrington, Truro, Worcester, etc.

[2] At Hertford, where the Corporation had been granted by Charter the right to hold certain Courts, the Earl of Salisbury received a subsequent grant of the Manor. He thereupon leased to the Corporation for twenty-one years, periodically renewed, the Court of the View of Frankpledge, with certain bridge tolls (*History of Hertfordshire*, by N. Salmon, 1728, p. 38).

[3] One of the best instances of such a Municipal Court of the Manor was that of the Corporation of Nottingham, held by its Town Clerk as Steward. This

repeat the description that we have already given of the Lord's Court. What is interesting is that, under the Municipal Corporations this Manorial tribunal often continued in the archaic form which we have termed the Undifferentiated Court, combining the exercise, in the name of the King, of minor criminal jurisdiction, with the making of Bylaws, the management of commons and wastes, the appointment of officers, and the admission of new tenants, freeholders or Burgesses. What distinguished the Undifferentiated Court of a Municipal Corporation from that of a rural Manor was the almost invariable abstraction of the petty debt business, for which, as we have mentioned, a separate Court had been set up by Charter.

But although the Court Leet was, in 1689, a feature of almost every Municipal Corporation, and although this Court when held by and for the Corporation did not appreciably differ in constitution or procedure from that which we find in the rural Manor or the Manorial Borough, we notice at once an all-round shrinkage in its functions, reducing it, in nearly all Boroughs, to a minor part of the machinery of the Corporation. In the rural Manor we see the Court Leet appointing, or the Jury presenting for appointment, all the officers of the Manor. At Birmingham and Manchester we see the Jury even choosing the head or heads of the town, in the High and Low Bailiffs or the Boroughreeve and

---

six-monthly "Court Leet and Court Baron of the Mayor and Burgesses . . . with respect to the Manor of Nottingham," under the name of the "Mickletorn Jury," perambulated the Borough, regulated the common lands, decided which rights of way should be abandoned and which obstacles should be removed, suppressed all sorts of nuisances, prevented encroachments, and imposed fines right and left on erring citizens, from the Mayor down to the humblest servant "not demeaning himself properly." The MS. presentments of this "Magnus Turnus," "Mickle Turn" or "Great Court Leet," extending intermittently from 1512 to 1857, are of great interest, and might well be published by the Corporation in full ; meanwhile the *Calendar of the Archives of the Borough of Nottingham*, by Stuart A. Moore, 1876-1877, gives a good description of them. *The Court Leet Records of Southampton* are now being published under the editorship of Professor Hearnshaw. The Corporation of Oxford held two such Courts—"the Court Leet and View of Frankpledge of the Four Aldermen, held for the four Wards of the said City," and "the Court Leet or View of Frankpledge and Court Baron" of the Corporation as Lord of the Hundred of Northgate. Both were tribunals of the usual Manorial type, appointing officers, presenting nuisances, amercing offenders, and fining absentee jurymen (MS. Records, Corporation of Oxford, Court Leet of the Four Aldermen, 1746-1839, and Court Leet of Northgate Hundred, 1746-1839).

Constables.   In one or two archaic Municipal Corporations
we see the whole constitution still revolving round the
Court Leet, the Jury presenting the Mayor as well as all
the petty officers, and admitting the new Burgesses.[1]   By
1689 this function of the Court Leet had, we suspect, in the
majority of the Municipal Corporations, passed away, either
entirely or except as regards the host of petty functionaries
under titles such as Borsholders, Tithingmen, Thirdboroughs,
Constables, Haywards, Common-drivers or Ale-tasters.   In
most cases, the annual choice of Mayor or Bailiffs, and the
appointment of all the important officers, had been transferred
to the Burgesses or to the Close Body acting in their name.
In other cases, this transfer took place in the course of the
eighteenth century, whilst the appointment of the Constables
was increasingly taken over by the Borough Quarter Sessions.
But traces of the old function of the Court Leet survived in the
formal presentment by the Jury of the persons otherwise
chosen to fill the various offices; or, still more frequently,
in the ceremony of the Mayor, Bailiffs, Constables and other
officers being formally sworn in at the "Law Day" in
the Autumn.[2]

[1] In the Corporation of Brading, Isle of Wight, for instance, all the officers,
from the Senior and Junior Bailiffs who were the Heads of the Corporation down
to the Hayward, were chosen at the Court Leet, by actual presentment of the
Jury ; though we are told that, in 1833, the choice was really that of the
retiring officers at a private meeting (First Report of Municipal Corporation
Commission, 1835, vol. ii. pp. 679-680).   So at Bossiney in Cornwall, where,
except the Recorder, all the officers from the Mayor down to the Ale-taster were
presented by the "Grand Jury" at the annual Court Leet (*ibid.* vol. i. p. 453).
So at Plympton Earle in Devonshire, and Welshpool in Shropshire, the Head of
the Municipal Corporation and a whole array of officers were appointed by the
Court Leet.   In the Corporation of Dorchester, down to 1756 at any rate, it was
the Michaelmas "Court Leet and View of Frankpledge" that chose the Mayor
as well as the Constables, Serjeants at Mace, Beadle, Assizers of Bread and Beer,
Viewers of Flesh and Hides, Hayward and other officers (MS. Records, Corporation of Dorchester, 1727-1756).   By 1833 this choice of the Mayor had passed
to a meeting of the Close Body, significantly held on the same date as that on
which the Court Leet had met for this purpose (First Report of Municipal Corporation Commission, 1835, vol. ii. p. 1274).   In the Corporation of Great
Grimsby in Lincolnshire, where the Court Leet was held annually, the Jury
continued, right down to 1835, to appoint six Auditors of the Chamberlains'
accounts, two of them being Aldermen, two Common Councilmen, and two
simple Freemen ; but all of them, in practice, being members of the Leet Jury
(*ibid.* vol. iv. p. 2251).

[2] Thus, in the ancient Corporation of Plympton Earle in Devonshire, the
Mayor, immediately after his election, annually held the "Fulfill-Court" or
"Customary Court," with a Jury of "suitors," or Freemen of the Borough.

Another change that had usually taken place by 1689 in the Court Leet of the Municipal Corporation, was the dwindling away of its functions of managing the common affairs of the inhabitants and of making By-laws for the good government of the Borough. This function had, in the course of the seventeenth century, been undertaken by the Administrative Courts or Councils which we shall presently describe. In the records of one Municipal Corporation we see a period of alternative or concurrent action by the Court Leet and Common Council, leading to the final supersession of the former by the latter authority. " The practice," reports an investigator of these records in 1833, " from the year 1661, the date of the earliest book that I saw, down to 1728, seems not to have been uniform. In the earlier part of this period almost the whole affairs of the Corporation seem to have been transacted at the Court Leet. This Court is held before the Mayor. At a Court Leet, held the 21st October 1661, Freemen were created; orders were made respecting dredging and fishing; a Deputy Mayor and a Justice of the Peace were elected; and victuallers were licensed. . . . These instances do not recur, but the election of Chamberlain by this Court took place many years later. Admissions to the Freedom, and regulations relating to the oyster and other fisheries, at the Court Leet . . . repeatedly occur down to the year 1728. During this period, however, the Mayor, Jurats, and Bailiffs were concurrently exercising the same functions. In some cases the order is stated to be made by the Court Leet on the presentment of the facts by the Jury." During these years, in fact, the management of the affairs of this Corporation was sometimes in the hands of the Court Leet, sometimes in those of the Mayor, Jurats, and Bailiffs, and sometimes, as in 1716

This Jury formally presented the Mayor to be "Head and Chief Governor of the Borough," certain other Freemen to be Ale-tasters, Pig-drivers, and Scavengers. The Court, by its president the Mayor, appointed four Constables. Those freeholders who owed "suit and service" to the Court—prosaically confined in practice to those whose chief-rents were in arrear—were summoned to attend, the absentees being presented by the Jury, and amerced threepence each (First Report of Municipal Corporation Commission, 1835, vol. i. p. 600). So, too, Lincoln held annually its "View of Frankpledge with the great Court Leet and Court Baron of the Mayor, Sheriffs, Citizens, and Commonalty of the City of Lincoln, together with the Sheriff's Turn of the same City," at which the Mayor and Coroners were sworn, and Chief Constables, Searchers and Sealers of Leather, and other officers were appointed (MS. Records, Corporation of Lincoln, 1689, etc.).

and 1717, in those of "the Court of Burghmote," at which all the Burgesses may have had the right to be present. Eventually, the Close Body of the Mayor, Jurats, and Bailiffs got the whole business; the Court of Burghmote was not summoned; and though the Court Leet continued to be held, its proceedings gradually became only formal.[1] In a flourishing Midland city the Court Leet of the Corporation had been particularly active throughout the sixteenth and for the first half of the seventeenth century in making By-laws, passing resolutions for the guidance of the Corporate Magistrates, making regulations as to carrying on trade and orders to be obeyed by the various Companies, and performing other acts of a legislative character, as well as participating in the administration of the market and the commons. We see all this activity beginning, under the Commonwealth, to dwindle, and rapidly sinking during the next half-century to merely sporadic interventions. After the Revolution the general orders and all other action of legislative character practically disappear, a few items at long intervals alone reminding us of the once incessant activity. After 1733 the orders altogether cease.[2] Sooner or later the same fate seems to have overtaken the Courts Leet of nearly all the other Municipal Corporations. Losing both the power of appointing officers and the power of making By-laws—the two functions which gave an authoritative position to the Courts of Bamburgh, Alnwick, Manchester, and Ashton-under-Lyne—the Court Leet of the Municipal Corporation sank, for the most part, in the course of the eighteenth century, either into a mere half-yearly formality, or into a

---

[1] The case is that of Queenborough (Kent); see First Report of Municipal Corporation Commission, 1835, vol. ii. pp. 829, 835. So in the Municipal Corporation of Huntingdon, where the enjoyment of the common pastures by the Burgesses constituted a privilege of some value, the "regulations respecting the time of stocking the commons, and the number of cattle, etc., to be put upon them, were made by the Leet Jury, and presented to the Mayor for his approval." After 1825, however, the Corporation ceased to hold the Court Leet, owing to the occurrence of disputes; and the Common Council, a Close Body, appointed a committee of its members and a "Foreman of the Commons" for the entire management of the property (*ibid.* vol. iv. pp. 2288, 2289).

[2] *Infra*, Chap. VIII. ; MS. Records, Court Leet, Coventry, 1588-1783. The nuisances at the Court Leet, once punished by amercement at the same Court, were presently made the subjects of formal prosecution before the Borough Justices. Thus, at Southampton in 1704, it was "this day ordered that the Town Clerk do prosecute all nuisances presented by the Court Leet Jury" (MS. Records, Southampton Corporation, 8th October 1704).

tribunal of petty police for the suppression of the minor urban nuisances.

(q) *The Borough Court of Quarter Sessions*

When the statute of Edward the Sixth directed all indictments found at the Turn 'or Leet to be transferred for trial to the General Sessions of the Peace, it became an object with the Municipal Corporations to secure or maintain their immunity from the jurisdiction of the Justices of the Peace of the County; and we find as a "usual clause in Queen Elizabeth's Charters . . . that which makes the Mayor and some of the Aldermen Justices of the Peace, and gives the Borough the power of holding Sessions of the Peace." [1] Wherever the Municipal Corporation had obtained the privilege of holding this "Court of Quarter Sessions," we see the new tribunal gradually absorbing, in addition to the ordinary criminal jurisdiction over thefts and assaults, much of the peculiar business of the Court Leet, such as the appointment of Constables, the ordering of the Watch, the prohibition of taking "inmates" or lodgers, the suppression of unlicensed ale-houses and of "bawdy houses," and even the punishment of nuisance-mongers. It was largely in consequence of this rivalry that the Courts Leet held by the Municipal Corporations gradually lost, as we have seen, the last remnant of their criminal jurisdiction, or became restricted to petty police offences.[2] This supersession of the Manorial Courts of the Borough by the Borough Justices of the Peace resembled, in its gradual but constant progress, the corresponding supersession of the Manorial Courts of West-

---

[1] *A Sketch of the History of Boroughs and of the Corporate Right of Election,* etc., by H. A. Merewether, 1822, p. 22. We know of no study of Borough Courts of Quarter Sessions, for which the materials exist in the considerable but miscellaneous collections of Sessions Rolls or Papers and Books of Orders or Minutes among the MS. archives of the various Corporations. We have found those of Bristol, Coventry, Southampton, and Winchester the most useful. The printed *Records of the County Borough of Cardiff,* by J. H. Matthews, 1898, etc., include (vol. ii.) material of this kind.

[2] The Corporation of Saltash in Cornwall held a "Water Court"—which recalls to us the "Water Leet" held in the Manorial Borough of Beccles—for the cognisance of offences committed on the water within the Liberties of the Borough. Some time before 1833 it had become disused, its functions being discharged by the Borough Court of Quarter Sessions (First Report of Municipal Corporation Commission, 1835, vol. i. p. 607).

minster, the Tower Hamlets, and Southwark, by the County
Justices of Middlesex and Surrey in the seventeenth century,
and did not differ from that taking place towards the close of
the eighteenth century throughout the rural districts.[1]   What,
however, is peculiar to the process in the Boroughs is the
curious intermingling of the structures of the two Courts—
almost simulating an evolutionary process—that we see
taking place.   We are, in fact, inclined to think that if the
proceedings of Courts Leet and General Sessions of the Peace
in the various Municipal Corporations during the sixteenth
and seventeenth centuries could be explored in detail, it
would be discovered that there was no fixed line of demarcation, either in function or in structure, between the " View of
Frankpledge and Court Leet" of the Borough, held by the
Mayor or other Corporate officer on behalf of the Corporation
as owner of the Manor, and the " General Sessions of the
Peace " held under Charter by the Corporate Magistrates.[2]
The Head of the Corporation, whether Mayor or Bailiff, or a
pair of Bailiffs, who frequently presided at all the Courts of
the Borough, whatever they were called, and who was often
accompanied on the Bench by his " brethren," the Aldermen,
Jurats, or Capital Burgesses,[3] sometimes regarded himself as
holding the Court of the Manor, sometimes the ancient
Portmanmote or Court of the Borough, and yet did not
resist the gradual description of his colleagues and himself as
" their Worships," as if they were sitting as Magistrates, and
was never indisposed to supplement his Manorial or Borough
Court powers by those which he could exercise as a Justice

---

[1] See the preceding volume on the Parish and the County ; also Chap. IV.
of the present volume, "The City and Borough of Westminster."

[2] At Cardiff, as already mentioned (p. 256), the actual identity of the two Courts
was asserted in 1824 by the Town Clerk. "The Quarter Sessions," he said,
"considering the matters presented by the Jury, will, I have no doubt, upon
proper inquiry and accurate search, be found to be also the Court Leet ; and
the ancient title of the Court will, I imagine, be found to have been 'Sessio
Pacis et Curia Domini Regis'" ; to which the modern archivist appends the
note, "This surmise is undoubtedly correct" (*Records of the County Borough
of Cardiff*, by J. H. Matthews, vol. ii., 1900, p. 130).

[3] At the Court of Quarter Sessions held by the little Corporation of Bideford
in Devonshire, all the members of the Close Body, comprising eighteen Aldermen and Capital Burgesses, were summoned to attend, and usually sat on the
Magistrates' Bench, though only the Mayor, Recorder, and one Alderman were
Justices of the Peace (First Report of Municipal Corporation Commission, 1835,
vol. i. pp. 437, 438).

of the Peace. In one important Municipal Corporation, for instance, the ancient " Portmoot Court " of the Borough and the " Mayor's Court," which corresponded to that formerly held by the private Lord of the Manor, seem actually to have both become merged in the Borough Court of Quarter Sessions, which long preserved some remnant of the names of these two Courts as part of its own title. " The Quarter Sessions," said the Town Clerk in 1833, "are still sometimes called the Portmoot." Within his memory the Jury of this Borough Court of Quarter Sessions had appointed some of the lesser officers of the Borough, though this power had latterly been taken over by the Town Council. The " Borough Court," " Mayor's Court," or " Court of Passage " gradually confined itself, under the last name, to civil suits. But in 1797, at any rate, it was, under the title of the " Mayor's Court," as we learn from a contemporary writer, enforcing local ordinances by criminal process, permitting " no infringements of the By-laws to pass with impunity ; neither wealth, distinction, nor power is any barrier to those amercements to which their irregularities may make them liable ; obstructions in the streets, wharves, and other improprieties by the most eminent man in the town, are on representation immediately punished by fine in common with the most ordinary porter or carman." [1] This jurisdiction is presently found exercised by the Borough Justices in Petty and Quarter Sessions. It seems that the sessions of this old Municipal Court, whatever was its title, were held for civil suits, by the Mayor, Recorder, and Bailiff immediately after those of the Mayor, Recorder, and Aldermen as Justices of the Peace, trying only criminal cases. For both sessions the Bailiffs summoned the Juries of Freemen only, as in the old Portmoot. It is impossible to avoid the inference that, in this particular Corporation at least, the various jurisdictions had, in the course of the eighteenth century, been, half unconsciously, merged and redistributed. " I conclude," says the latest historian, " that Sessions and Court of Passage taken together are to be regarded as the continuation of the old Portmoot about which we have heard so much." [2] In several of the ancient Municipal Corporations

---

[1] *General Description of the History, etc., of Liverpool*, 1797, pp. 275-276.
[2] *History of Municipal Government in Liverpool to 1835*, by Ramsay Muir,

forming part of the Liberty of the Cinque Ports, we see a
similar transition from the early Hundred Court, held by
the Head of the Corporation with "sectatores" or suitors, in
the presence of all the Freemen, into the Borough Court of
Quarter Sessions held by the Mayor and the Jurats, as
magistrates, but with summons to all the Freemen to attend.
In one after another of the Cinque Ports we may watch this
silent transition leaving its mark on the records, the proceedings
of what continued uninterruptedly one and the same tribunal
gradually beginning to add to the title of Hundred Court the
words "sive sessio pacis"; then calling it "Hundred Sessions";
and, finally, dropping altogether the earlier designation in
favour of General Quarter Sessions of the Peace.[1] We have
traces of exactly the same transition from a Hundred Court
into a Court of Quarter Sessions in other Boroughs.[2] In other
Municipal Corporations we see a similar confusion, leading to
an extraordinary intermingling of powers between the Borough
Court Leet and the Borough Court of Quarter Sessions. In
one Midland City, for instance, whilst the Court Leet at its
spring and autumn meetings was passing orders mandatory
on the City magistrates with regard to matters of petty
police, the Grand Jury of the Borough Court of Quarter
Sessions was "presenting" to these same dignitaries sitting as
Justices of the Peace, not merely highways out of repair and
nuisances annoying to the neighbours, but also such typically
Manorial defaults as the damaging of the commons by cutting
turf and removing gravel, and the failure of particular tenants
of the Manor to scour their ditches or keep their causeways in
repair.[3] In other Boroughs it is quite impossible to dis-

1906, p. 143 ; *Report of the Proceedings of a Court of Inquiry into the existing
State of the Corporation of Liverpool*, 1833, p. 57 ; First Report of Municipal
Corporation Commission, 1835, vol. iv. p. 2713. The history of the Liverpool
Courts is obscure. The forthcoming volume of documents relating to *The Court of
Passage*, which Professor Ramsay Muir is to edit, will probably clear up the matter.

[1] MS. Records, Pevensey Corporation, especially "Pevensey Hundred Court
Book," 1699-1778, when the transition is well marked, both in the character
of the business and in the terminology ; "Report on New Romney Records," by
E. Salisbury, in *Archæologia Cantiana*, vol. xvii., 1887, pp. 27, 30 ; *Collections
for a History of Sandwich*, by W. Boys, 1792, p. 784 ; *History of Kent*, by
E. Hasted, vol. x., 1800, p. 163 ; *History of Dover*, by Rev. J. Lyon, vol. i.
1813, pp. 227-228, 245 ; *History of Rye*, by W. Holloway, 1847, pp. 185, 187.

[2] See, for instance, the "Law Hundred Courts" of Colchester (*History of
Essex*, by P. Morant, 1768, vol. i. p. 3, *n.*).

[3] See the MS. Presentments by Grand Jury "at the General Sessions of the

tinguish, either in form or in substance, the presentments of nuisances which the Grand Jury made to the Justices in Quarter Sessions from those which the Jury—often called the Grand Jury—of the Borough Court Leet were simultaneously addressing to "their Worships," the Mayor and other Magistrates who held that ancient Manorial Court.[1] Occasionally we see the transition from the Court Leet to Quarter Sessions arrested by the embodiment of an intermediate form in the written constitution—a Corporation being specifically granted by Charter the right to hold a criminal Court under the name of "the View of Frankpledge and General Sessions of the Peace."[2] In such cases the Corpora-

Peace," 1629-1742, and MS. Records of Court Leet 1585-1733, both among the records of the Corporation of Coventry. So in the Corporation of Newbury in Berkshire we see the Court Leet, in the latter part of the seventeenth century, passing orders to the Tithingmen to search their tithings for "strangers," and enacting prohibitions of the reception of "stranger inmates without security to the Churchwardens and Overseers," under penalty of five shillings for each offence. In 1677 four persons were fined five shillings each for this new crime. In the very same year the Borough Court of Quarter Sessions enacts a similar ordinance, but with the penalty increased to 20s. The same concurrent exercise, both of legislative and judicial functions, by the Court Leet and the Court of Quarter Sessions occurred with regard to paving (MS. Records, Corporation of Newbury, 1660-1700 ; also *History of Newbury*, by W. Money, 1887, pp. 292-295).

[1] See, for instance, the MS. Sessions Rolls and Papers, 1592-1833, in records of Corporation of Southampton. The following are typical presentments of the Grand Jury at the Quarter Sessions : " We present the Cowherd for not performing his duty in riding the Common twice a day and not keeping a dog to drive out the cattle of foreigners. We present the Brickburner for not keeping his fences in repair. . . . We present [that] the pavement and the nastiness which is at New Corner are a great and common nuisance to the whole town and neighbourhood " (MS. Sessions Rolls, Southampton, July 1704).

[2] Charter to New Woodstock in 1665 ; see MS. Records, Corporation of Woodstock, 1665-1746. We owe this reference, and much other information, to Mr. Adolphus Ballard, Town Clerk of Woodstock. It is not easy to classify the Woodstock Court precisely. It was known locally, not as Quarter Sessions, but as the Court Leet ; it appointed the Constables and the Tithingmen, the Ale-tasters and the Clerk of the Market ; and the Jury made elaborate presentments of the Court Leet type, naming not only the offence committed, but also the penalty incurred, and sometimes making this dependent on the nuisance not being abated within a specified date. To take only one year, those for October 1673 included the following :—" We present . . . for not cleansing his brook . . . to cleanse the same under pain of five shillings. We present . . . for his muckhill before his door, etc. . . . We present Widow . . . for entertaining her daughter for the space of one month contrary to the statute. . . . We present . . . for not coming to church the last Sunday one shilling. . . . We present . . . for a disturber of the peace one shilling. . . . We present . . . for keeping an unlawful meeting in his house under pretence of religious worship " (MS. Records, Corporation of Woodstock). On the other hand, it was held not by the Steward of the Manor, nor by any officer on behalf of the

tion often continued to hold a criminal Court of a mixed nature, partly Court Leet, partly Sessions of the Peace, down to about the middle of the eighteenth century, after which the Court Leet features gradually drop out. In other Boroughs the transformation and merging of the Borough Court or Court Leet into the Court of Quarter Sessions seems to have taken place by the transitional form of adjournments, the October or November Sessions of the Peace being that at which the ancient business of the Court Leet was performed, and being therefore long distinguished from the adjourned Sessions on other dates by the title of "Law Day."[1]   Finally,

owner of the Manor, but by the Mayor, Deputy Recorder, and two Aldermen, sitting as Justices of the Peace; it was held at frequent intervals during the year, and it tried offenders upon indictments, though only for misdemeanours. Thus, in 1729, men were "indicted" before it for following the trade of a tailor in the Borough without being free; and fined in small sums.   In 1787 a man was indicted for assault.   In graver cases, it directed an indictment to be prepared, and committed prisoners to the County Gaol for trial at the County Quarter Sessions or the Assizes.   But it could itself sentence not only to a money penalty, but also to imprisonment, the stocks, whipping, or a ducking; and much of its work took the form of mandatory general orders by the Court without any presentment by the Jury.   Yet with the legal title and some of the attributes of a Court of Quarter Sessions, its jurisdiction was limited to misdemeanours, and in practice to little more than an enforcement of the Borough By-laws and Leet presentments, all grave crime being dealt with by the County Justices.   We may cite here also the Corporation of Stratford-on-Avon, where the Borough Justices had a so-called "Court of Quarter Sessions," which, in 1833 at any rate, was held only once a year, and then only for Court Leet purposes.   A Jury was sworn to make presentments upon which judicial action was taken, and though the officers of the Borough were appointed by the Close Body, they were sworn in at this annual Court (First Report of Municipal Corporation Commission, 1835, vol. i. p. 120).   So, too, at Chipping Norton in Oxfordshire, where the criminal jurisdiction of the Borough Justices as a Court of Quarter Sessions was in 1833 not exercised, the Court which we have already mentioned came latterly to be held formally four times a year—three times without business, but in October conjointly with the active and all-embracing "Court Leet and Court Baron and View of Frankpledge," held by the Corporation, as Lord of the Manor, that we have already described. Throughout the eighteenth century the two Courts were apparently thus virtually merged, and right down to 1846 the jurymen were always "charged" as being, simultaneously, (i.) the "Grand Jury" for "the General Quarter Sessions of the Peace for this Borough, which is lodged in the Bailiffs as Justices of the Peace, Oyer and Terminer by special grant by Charter"; (ii.) the Jury of the Court Leet; and (iii.) the Homage at the Court Baron (see the charge in *Notes on the History of Chipping Norton*, by A. Ballard, 1893, Appendix B).

[1] Thus, at Winchester, the ancient "Boroughmote Court" or "Lawday" had its jurisdiction enlarged by an Elizabethan Charter, and passed insensibly into the Borough Court of Quarter Sessions.   We see the Mayor, Aldermen, and Recorder assuming exclusive jurisdiction over all criminal offences (except murder and treason) committed within the City; sitting with the usual paraphernalia of Grand Jury and Traverse Juries; and sentencing prisoners to be

we may note a trace of the same evolution in the character
and titles of the Juries that were summoned to the Court.
The Jury of the Court Leet not infrequently appeared as two
Juries, which were actually called in some cases the Grand
Jury or Grand Inquest, which made presentments, and the
"Party Jury" or "Petty Jury," which tried actions; and
these seem insensibly to have passed into the Grand and
Petty Juries of the Borough Court of Quarter Sessions.[1]

whipped, imprisoned, and transported. Yet, during the earlier years, we see
this same tribunal—then still usually termed the Boroughmote Court or
"Lawday" (*e.g.* 22nd May 1691, in MS. Proposal Books)—at its September
and December sessions in each year doing a considerable amount of non-criminal
business which had evidently continued on from the earlier Court, such as
receiving the report of the Mayor and his brethren upon the Municipal accounts ;
ordering the levy of a Scavenger's Rate and appointing two persons to collect it ;
making all the usual presentments of a Court Leet ; declaring the ancient
customs of the City ; and accepting fines in lieu of service as Constable (MS.
Proposal Book and Minutes of Quarter Sessions, in records of Corporation of
Winchester). We may trace the similar merging of the Court Leet in the little
Corporation of Totnes. When, in 1596, the Mayor, Recorder, and ex-Mayor
were made Justices of the Peace, they exercised in their quarterly sessions the
usual jurisdiction of Quarter Sessions, with Juries summoned by the Town
Clerk and Serjeants at Mace, though, in 1833, remitting grave cases to the
Assizes. But these same Justices held also two "adjourned sessions" in
November of each year. At the first of these, which was also called a Court
Leet, similar Juries, also summoned by the Town Clerk and Serjeants at Mace,
made a formal presentment of the Mayor, who had really been chosen by the
Close Body of "the Masters and Counsellors" of the Borough ; and they also
presented persons for appointment by the Mayor and other magistrates, as
Constables, Serjeants at Mace, Clerk of the Market, and Wardens of certain
wells, conduits, etc. At the second "adjourned sessions" of the Justices, also
called a Court Leet, all these officers were formally sworn in (First Report of
Municipal Corporation Commission, 1835, vol. i. p. 642).

[1] In the transitional stage we see the same persons made use of as the Juries
of both Courts. At Andover in Hampshire, where the Court Leet, being held
separately for the "In-Hundred" and "Out-Hundred" respectively, retained
some little differentiation from the Borough Court of Quarter Sessions, "the Grand
Jury of the In-Hundred is detained to act as the Grand Jury of the Court of
Quarter Sessions" (First Report of Municipal Corporation Commission, 1835,
vol. ii. p. 1086). The MS. Records of the Corporation of Dorchester, in
like manner, give the names of the men, chosen from the three parishes of the
Borough, who served as "the Court Leet Jury, held Monday, 30th September
1776," with the following note : "The above to be the Grand Jury for the same
Leet, and the General or Quarter Sessions to be held at the Assize or Shire
Hall," on the subsequent Monday (MS. Bundle, 30th September 1776, records
of Corporation of Dorchester). At Portsmouth, Southwold, and Newport (Isle
of Wight) the case was reversed, the Petty Jury of the Quarter Sessions being
utilised as the Jury of the Court Leet (First Report of Municipal Corporation
Commission, 1835, vol. ii. pp. 781, 782, 812 ; vol. iv. p. 2518). At Faversham,
when the Court Leet was held simultaneously with the Court of Quarter Sessions,
one Jury served both as Grand Jury of the Sessions and Jury of the Leet ; in the
latter capacity making presentments of nuisances, upon which the Justices took
action ; and losing even this last Manorial function on the establishment of a

Other combinations of Leet structure with that of Quarter Sessions are to be traced in other Municipal Corporations. There may be found a Jury selected by the Town Clerk from those inhabitants who did not use weights and measures for purposes of trade, annually sworn and charged, not at a Court Leet, but by the Borough Justices of the Peace at a sessions specially held for the purpose. Such a Jury would perambulate the Borough, testing all weights and measures, and seizing those found defective. The offenders would then formally be "presented" by this Jury to the Borough Justices, who then and there convicted them of the misdemeanour, and sentenced them to money fines.[1]

The Borough Quarter Sessions, however it may have come into existence, differed in various respects from the corresponding General Sessions of the Peace of the Justices of the County, which we have elsewhere so fully described. We note at once the contrast in the membership of the Court. In the County, as we have seen, the Justices of the Peace, all of whom were summoned to, and were at least potential attenders at, Quarter Sessions, numbered from several scores up to several hundreds of country gentlemen and beneficed clergymen scattered all over the County. In the Municipal Corporation there were, as a rule, only half a dozen Justices of the Peace, all of whom held specific offices in the Borough—the Mayor, the Recorder or High Steward, the ex-Mayor or "Justice," occasionally the Common Clerk or Town Clerk, or the Coroner, and sometimes one or more of the Aldermen, Jurats, or Capital Burgesses. The Bench at the Borough Court of Quarter Sessions came thus to be usually occupied by the same three or four persons, and the fact that among them was, in the more important Boroughs, the salaried Recorder—nearly always a trained professional lawyer—necessarily made this tribunal much more like a modern Court of Justice than the amateur, shifting Bench at the Quarter Sessions of the County. The invariable participation of the Recorder, or his Deputy, when felonies were tried,

statutory body of Street Commissioners in 1789 (*ibid.* vol. ii. pp. 970-971). At Bodmin "the Courts of Sessions of the Peace are held . . . at the same time as the Court Leet. . . . The Grand Jury of the Court Leet act also as Grand Jury of the Sessions" (*ibid.* vol. i. p. 445).

[1] Hereford (*ibid.* vol. i. p. 260).

and the fact that he virtually laid down the law and prescribed
the limits of the sentence, made the attainments and character
of the Justices of comparatively little importance, so far as
the graver criminal business was concerned.

But the Borough Justices did not confine their General
Sessions of the Peace to the well-known quarterly meetings.
We find them, in town after town, sitting monthly, or even
weekly, in adjourned " sessions," which had, in strict law, all
the immense powers of Quarter Sessions.   We have described
how the County Justices in 1689 drew no sharp line of
demarcation between the cases dealt with by the " Double
Justice " in Petty Sessions, and those which they would hear
at the Quarterly General Sessions of the Peace, at which any
two magistrates made a quorum.   In various Municipal
Corporations we see a similar confusion between Quarter and
Petty Sessions, carried to a greater height and continuing
for a longer period.   At the " adjourned Sessions " held every
month, every fortnight, or every week—sometimes in the
Mayor's Parlour, sometimes at the " Tolzey " or Borough Court
House—we find the Constables, occasionally " the Constables'
Jury," [1] whatever this was, or even what was called a
" Grand Jury " or a " Grand Inquest," [2] making " presentments "
of nuisances of every kind, such as insanitary practices, selling
ale without a licence, " harbouring inmates," permitting
mastiff dogs to go unmuzzled, allowing chimneys to be in a
dangerous state, being a popish recusant, carrying on trade
without being free of the city, having cows feeding on the
common not being " neached "; and every species of neglect
of duty by Beadles, Constables, Surveyors, and even the
Bailiffs, Sheriffs, and the Mayor himself.   We have been quite
unable to distinguish which of these presentments, all made
to the General Sessions of the Peace, were of what we may
term the Court Leet character, the Quarter Sessions character,
and the Petty Sessions character respectively.   In many
cases the offences presented were, as we have already pointed
out, of distinctly Manorial type, and we think we see traces
of the Jury itself naming the customary fine.[3]   In other cases,

[1] At Coventry; see our preceding volume, *The Parish and the County*, pp.
464-465.   [2] At Bristol and Winchester.
[3] See, for instance, MS. Session Rolls, Corporation of Southampton, 1682
(presentment of persons failing to repair pavements).

the offences thus laid before the Court were evidently summarily disposed of by the infliction of a small money penalty, or a whipping. In others, again, especially some of those declared to be made by the Grand Jury, it may well be that indictments had to be framed, an opportunity for traverse given, true bills found, and Traverse Juries summoned. At the same meetings we find these Justices doing what was distinctly the work of the Single or Double Justice, such as ordering payments in relief of the poor, swearing-in Constables, hearing cases of recalcitrant apprentices and sentencing them to be whipped. We do not feel sure that at these intermediate Sessions—which the Recorder did not attend—there were "true bills" found or felonies tried. But the Justices would hear Poor Rate appeals, order (in Boroughs which were Counties Corporate) payments out of the "county stock" for the conveyance of vagrants; pass orders relating to the administration of the prisons; approve the rules of friendly societies; grant debtors their discharge under the Insolvent Debtors Acts; direct payments for the conveyance of "His Majesty's baggage," and perform various other functions of the Court of Quarter Sessions on its civil side. These Borough Justices, in fact, seem to have made even more orders of a legislative character than those of the County. In every respect they combined the functions of the Court of Quarter Sessions, not only, as we have seen, with many of those of the Court Leet or Borough Court, but also with those elsewhere exercised by the Single or the Double Justice technically "out of Sessions."

(r) *Courts of Specialised Jurisdiction*

Besides the Courts of Civil Jurisdiction and the Court Leet or Borough Court of Quarter Sessions, many Municipal Corporations had other Courts having particular reference to one or other of the special jurisdictions that we have described: a Court of Pie Powder or a Court of the Clerk of the Market, for dealing summarily with all cases among the frequenters of the Market or Fair; a Court of Orphans, for administering the estates of minors;[1] a Court of Conservancy,

---

[1] The principal Court of Orphans was that of the City of London. But the Southampton Corporation had also, by Charter of 1640, the right "to hold a

for enforcing customs and obligations relating to the river; a Court of Admiralty, for adjusting all matters connected with the harbour, the shipping, the fishing, and the adjoining shores of the sea.[1] It is significant that all these archaic Courts, held by the Head of the Corporation or on his behalf, were or had been of mixed character, dealing indifferently with civil actions brought by one person against another; criminal offences against the law or the local By-laws,[2] presented by officers or Juries; the enactment of new By-laws, or the issue of orders to officers; the perambulation of boundaries, and the maintenance of such things as sea-marks, sluices, embankments,

Court of Orphans . . . with authority over their persons and goods," which was not disused until the middle of the eighteenth century (*History of South-ampton*, by J. S. Davies, 1883, p. 239 ; see *Borough Customs*, by M. Bateson, 1904-6).

[1] There were Courts of Admiralty at Boston (First Report of Municipal Corporation Commission, 1835, vol. iv. p. 2155); Bristol (*ibid.* vol. ii. p. 1177); Carmarthen (*ibid.* vol. i. p. 212); the Liberty of the Cinque Ports (*ibid.* vol. ii. p. 927); Dunwich (*ibid.* vol. iv. p. 2223); Haverfordwest (*ibid.* vol. i. p. 239); Harwich (*ibid.* vol. iv. p. 2267); Ipswich (*ibid.* vol. iv. p. 2317); Kingston-on-Hull (*ibid.* vol. iii. p. 1549); Lynn (*ibid.* vol. iv. p. 2403); Maldon (*ibid.* vol. iv. p. 2447); Newport, Isle of Wight (*ibid.* vol. ii. p. 783); Poole (*ibid.* vol. ii. p. 1323); Rochester (*ibid.* vol. ii. p. 857); Southampton (*ibid.* vol. ii. p. 884); Southwold (*ibid.* vol. iv. p. 2518). The Court was held by the Mayor as "Admiral of the Port," sometimes assisted by other officers, such as the Ex-Mayor, the Recorder, and the Town Clerk, and occasionally (as at Rochester) also by Freemen nominated by the Mayor to sit with him as Judges of the Court. That for the Liberty of the Cinque Ports was held in the name of the Lord Warden by a Judge appointed by him. There was either one Jury for all purposes; or (as at Boston) two for the two several divisions of the port; or (as at Ipswich) a series of Juries for the various sessions of the Court, whether for perambulations, the trial of causes, or the presentment of offenders; usually chosen from among those Freemen of the Borough who were connected with the sea: at Maldon, always fishermen; at Rochester, oyster dredgers; at Poole, old shipmasters and pilots. The jurisdiction often extended far beyond the limits of the Borough: at Boston, for instance, it comprised not only the Borough and its port, but also the parts of the Wash known as "the Deeps," and all the streams and watercourses of "the washes" in and near the "Parts of Holland," or that portion of Lincolnshire named in the Charter. It was the claim of the Court of Admiralty of the Corporation of Dunwich to exercise jurisdiction over the Port of Southwold that led to the incorporation of the latter Borough, and the grant to it of its own Court of Admiralty. See on the whole subject of Admiralty jurisdiction, *Select Pleas in the Court of Admiralty*, by R. G. Marsden (Selden Society, 2 vols., 1894-1897), and *Burrell's Reports of Cases determined by the Court of Admiralty*, by the same, 1885.

[2] The powers of the Court of Admiralty of the Corporation of Bristol extended to all "thefts, frays, piracies, etc., upon the sea, or else river, creek, or haven within the compass and circuit of the jurisdiction . . . and of obstructions on the river . . . of fraud of the King's custom, . . . false weights and measures, wreck, royal fish, etc.; and also of the number of ships within the haven and jurisdiction, and the owners of them" (First Report of Municipal Corporation Commission, 1835, vol. ii. pp. 1177-1178)

etc.; and even, in ancient times, the management of property. But the administrative and legislative functions of these Courts had, by 1689, already passed almost entirely to the Governing Council or other organ of the Corporation, or were during the eighteenth century transferred to some statutory body for the management of the river, harbour, or market; leaving to the ancient Courts usually little more than a petty police jurisdiction. As parts of the Constitution of the Municipal Corporation they had, by 1835, become almost nominal.[1]

(s) The Administrative Courts of the Municipal Corporation

So far we have dealt with a series of Courts that were, in the main, judicial tribunals, largely if not entirely occupied with the settlement of disputes between individuals, the determination of the obligations of the various inhabitants towards the King, the Lord of the Manor, and the rest of the community, and, above all, with the keeping of the King's Peace within their jurisdictions. We pass now to the Courts that are in the present day usually termed Councils or Assemblies, which had been evolved for the specific purpose of administering the common affairs of the community. These Administrative Courts, like so much else of the constitutional structure of the Municipal Corporations, were not peculiar to

---

[1] At Ipswich the two Bailiffs, as jointly "Admirals of the Port," appointed a Steward of the Court in 1811, for the express purpose of formulating the presentments to be made by the Jury. At Harwich, right down to 1791, the Court received a report from the Water Bailiff, and made the "Assize of Fish." At Rochester, where the oyster fishing belonged to the Corporation, and was a profitable enterprise of some magnitude, its regulation and management was entirely in the hands of the local Court of Admiralty. The Jury of "free dredgers," annually selected by the Mayor, formally presented the rules for the government of the dredgers, which were confirmed and promulgated by the Mayor in the name of the Court. The Jury presented also every year a person to act as Chamberlain or Treasurer of the fishery. This Court of Admiralty acted also as a Court of Conservancy for the River Medway, the Mayor presiding at Courts held when required, at which Juries selected from those "free dredgers," who were Freemen of the Borough, made regulations and presented offenders in all matters relating to the "floating fish within the liberties." Sometimes, where no Court had been held for many years, the Mayor continued to act as arbitrator. In the little Corporation of Newport, Isle of Wight, "parties complain to the Mayor respecting matters belonging to this part of his jurisdiction; he determines them orally, and the parties submit" (First Report of Municipal Corporation Commission, 1835, vol. ii. p. 783).

them. It is true that in the Manor and the Hundred all the administrative decisions were made at the same Undifferentiated Court, which did the civil and criminal business, by the same Juries and officers, under the more or less authoritative control of the Lord's Steward. But already in some of these Lord's Courts we catch glimpses of occasional meetings of another body—sometimes, as we have mentioned, of "the Freeholders"[1]; sometimes of "twelve discreet and able persons"[2]—acting between the six-monthly sessions of the Court; helping the Steward and the Bailiff to frame the regulations, or carrying out the presentments of the Jury as to the management of the commonfields, the stinting of the pasture, and the assessment of rates for the repair of the well or the mending of the roads. In the lower members of our series of Manorial Boroughs, some of them scarcely to be distinguished from the Lord's Court, we see the occasional meetings of the Freeholders replaced by a standing body—a "Fellowship," a "Society," a "Company,"[3] a "Twelve," a "Thirteen," a "Sixteen," or most commonly a "Four-and-Twenty,"—closely connected with the Jury of the Lord's Court. We need not speculate as to the origin of such a body. In one case, at least, we may see it actually arising from a presentment of the Jury of the Court: "that it was necessary that a Council of Twelve, being Aldermen and sufficient Burgesses of the said Town, should be added to the Mayor for the time being, to advise him for the good of the Corporation."[4] In one archaic Municipal Corporation, as we have already mentioned, we have a meeting of all the Freeholders or Burgesses resolving that twenty-four of their number should henceforth "be instead of the whole commonalty, and no other of the commonalty to intermeddle under pain of five pounds,"[5] exactly as in the analogous instance of the Select Vestry of

---

[1] As at Bamburgh (*supra*, p. 94).

[2] At East Stonehouse, which never developed beyond being a mere Manor, we hear of the regulations of the Lord being made "with the consent and frank agreement of twelve discreet and able persons of and within the said town and liberties" (see Deed of 1594, quoted in *History of Devonshire*, by R. N. Worth, 1895, p. 228).

[3] As at Braintree (*supra*, p. 172); Lewes (*supra*, pp. 171-172); Brighton (*supra*, p. 173 *n*.).

[4] Presentment of the Jury at the Court Leet of Cardigan, 1653; in First Report of Municipal Corporation Commission, 1835, vol. i. p. 197.

[5] MS. Records, Corporation of Romney Marsh, 1604.

the Parish we have cases in which the Close Body was created by resolution of the inhabitants in Vestry assembled.[1] On the other hand, we have traces of the Council having originated from above, not from below. The Head of the Corporation may have a group of persons to assist him in his work, and these "Mayor's Peers" or "Mayor's Brethren" form his first standing Council. In Corporation after Corporation we see this little group calling to their aid selected Members of the Commonalty, as the "Mayor's Counsellors," the Common Councilmen becoming thus an adjunct to the Aldermen.[2] As we proceed along the ascending series we see this standing body, whether formed from above or from below, gradually shaking itself free from the Lord's Court,[3] acquiring funds of its own, possibly even the right to hold a separate Court, and presently becoming, instead of the creature of the Lord's Court, the master of that tribunal and of the officers there appointed. We suggest that the popular idea that the Municipal Corporation arose out of the Gild may be so far justified that in many cases it was the Gild, with its common stock, and even its Corporate trading ventures, that was the origin, if not of the Common Council itself, of some of the characteristic features of the Common Council as we see it in 1689; such as the abandonment of judicial forms and processes, the exclusion of the public, the

---

[1] *The Parish and the County*, pp. 184-188.

[2] At Folkestone, where the administration had been shared between the Mayor and Jurats and the General Assembly of Freemen, we see the former, in 1582, electing and choosing, "by the consent of the whole Commons, twenty-five Commoners, in the name of the whole Commonalty, to be a Town Council, to make and agree unto all such necessary laws as shall be thought good by the Mayor and Jurats" (*Account of Folkestone*, by S. J. Mackie, 1883, pp. 314-315). The same thing happened at Rye in 1574 (*History of Rye*, by W. Holloway, 1847, pp. 205-206). Similar developments seem to have taken place at Southampton and Plymouth in the seventeenth century.

[3] But, as we have already indicated, the development was not universal. A few places which obtained the privilege of making their own Justices of the Peace, and therefore come into our category of Municipal Corporations, never got beyond the organisation of a Lord's Court; leaving, for instance, the whole administration in the hands of the Steward appointed by the Lord of the Manor (as at Havering-atte-Bower, First Report of Municipal Corporation Commission, 1835, vol. v. p. 2878), or in those of the so-called Mayors, Bailiffs, Aldermen, or other officers presented by the Jury at the annual Court Leet of the Lord (as at Bossiney, *ibid.* vol. i. p. 458; Castle Rising, *ibid.* vol. iv. p. 2211; Over, *ibid.* vol. iv. p. 2816; Ruthin, *ibid.* vol. iv. p. 2849); or in those of private meetings of such officers (as at Brading, *ibid.* vol. ii. p. 679).

sworn secrecy of the meetings, the elaboration of the Standing Orders, and, above all, of the general assumption by Common Councilmen of the functions of an independent Legislature in all the Corporation affairs. Along with the growth of power and of work we see an elaboration of structure. The members of the Court of Common Council, in more than a hundred of the Corporations, including all those of any importance, became of two, and, in half a dozen instances, of three different grades.[1] The most common titles of these grades were those of Aldermen and Councillors respectively, though every possible combination seems to be represented of such alternatives as Jurats, Capital Burgesses, Assistants, Brothers,[2] Chief Benchers, Principal Burgesses, Com-Burgesses,[3] Masters,[4] and Portmen,[5] for the upper class or classes; and of Approved Men,[6] Burgesses or Capital Burgesses, Burgesses of the Common Council, Commoners, Chief or Capital Citizens,[7] the Commonalty,[8] Inferior Burgesses,[9] Capital Inhabitants,[10] Assistant Burgesses, Assistants,[11] and Secondary Burgesses,[12] for the lower class. With two striking exceptions, which we shall subsequently describe, we do not find these two or three grades of members forming distinct chambers or assemblies on anything like the bicameral system so common among National Legislatures everywhere, and among modern Municipalities in the United States. Nor did the Aldermen, with these two same exceptions, enjoy any power of veto or superior voice or vote in the Common Council, of which they, equally with the Councillors, formed a part.[13] We find them,

---

[1] Among the Municipal Corporations in which the Common Council included a third grade of members, besides the Head and often other Chief Officers, were Bury St. Edmunds (Assistants, Capital Burgesses and Burgesses of the Common Council, *ibid.* vol. iv. p. 2172); Chesterfield (Aldermen, Brothers and Capital Burgesses, *ibid.* vol. iii. p. 1789); Derby (Aldermen, Brothers and Capital Burgesses, *ibid.* vol. iii. p. 1849); Worcester (Aldermen, Capital Citizens and Councillors, and Capital Citizens, *ibid.* vol. i. p. 153); Scarborough (the First, Second, and Third Twelve, *ibid.* vol. iii. p. 1715); Windsor (Aldermen or Chief Benchers, Benchers and Younger Brethren, *ibid.* vol. v. p. 2932); Lancaster (Aldermen, Capital Burgesses and Common Councilmen, *ibid.* vol. iii. p. 1602).

[2] As at Chesterfield.   [3] As at Grantham.
[4] As at Wells.   [5] As at Ipswich and Orford.
[6] As at Guildford.   [7] As at Bath and Worcester.
[8] As at Daventry.   [9] As at Glastonbury.
[10] As at Marazion.   [11] As at Reading, Rochester, Salisbury, and Tiverton.
[12] As at Wokingham.
[13] The Aldermen sometimes sat apart as a Court to fill vacancies in their own body, and occasionally to appoint new Common Councilmen.

indeed, often clothed in gowns of superior stuff or more brilliant hue,[1] accorded precedence in Municipal processions, sitting on the front bench in the Council Chamber, and occupying, with their wives, special "Aldermen's seats" in the parish church.   But apart from these honorary distinctions, the superior position and influence of the Aldermen was really outside the Council Chamber.   Some or all of them, as we have seen, usually shared with the Head of the Corporation the dignity and the office of Justice of the Peace.   As Justices they had their own spheres of activity in the Courts of Quarter Sessions, on the Magisterial Bench at Petty and Special Sessions, and in the multifarious duties of the Single Justice.

There was often another element in the Common Council besides the Aldermen and Councillors.   Besides the Head of the Corporation, who always presided, some of the Chief Officers sat frequently as official members.   Among these the most usual were the Recorder and the Bailiffs; sometimes the Justice or Justices; sometimes the Sheriff or Sheriffs, and the Chamberlain or Chamberlains; occasionally the Steward or High Steward, the Coroner, and even the Town Clerk.[2]

The majority of the members of every Common Council were, however, the ordinary Councillors.   Whilst the typical number of Aldermen was twelve, or fewer, the Councillors were most usually the "Four and Twenty," though occasionally the "Eight and Forty."   And in about sixty Corporations, mostly connected with the smaller Boroughs, there was only one grade of members, termed indifferently Burgesses or Capital Burgesses, Aldermen, Brethren, Assistants or Common Councilmen, and these members, usually about a dozen or

---

[1] At Plymouth "the Aldermen seem first to have assumed scarlet gowns, which they wore by regulation sixteen times a year, in 1572, though the practice was subsequently dropped, to be renewed in 1598.   In 1669 the gowns of the Twenty-Four were of black cloth, guarded with black velvet, and having square collars lined with fur" (*History of Plymouth*, by R. N. Worth, 1890, p. 195 ; see MS. Records, Plymouth Corporation, 1572, 1598, 1669, etc.).

[2] At Henley-on-Thames and Maidenhead the two Bridgemen or Bridge-masters sat in the Council (First Report of Municipal Corporation Commission, 1835, vol. i. p. 71 and vol. v. p. 2909) ; at Ludlow, the two Capital Masters or Justices (*ibid.* vol. iv. p. 2787).   At York all the past Sheriffs were members (*ibid.* vol. iii. p. 1740) ; at Oxford, all the past Bailiffs and Chamberlains (*ibid.* vol. i. p. 98).   At Norwich there was a Speaker who presided.   These Chief Officers were often appointed from among the members of the Council ; and in those cases they were not an addition to the Council.

twenty-four in number, constituted, with the Head and occasionally other Chief Officers, the whole Governing Council.

The procedure of the Court was always elaborate and punctilious. All the members were sworn to secrecy, they were fined for absence,[1] they were forbidden to leave the Chamber before the close of the proceedings without permission from the Mayor, and they, with all the Chief Officers, were required to appear (and even to go and return along the streets)[2] in gowns of the prescribed colour and material. In all the more important Corporations regular committees of the Court were appointed, sometimes for special purposes, such as audit, but often to administer particular functions of the Corporation.[3] In the course of the sixteenth and seventeenth

---

[1] In 1692, for instance, at Dover, a Jurat was fined half a crown, and five Common Councilmen were fined eighteen pence, for absence from the Council; whilst two Common Councilmen were dismissed from office for failure to attend several meetings (MS. Records, Corporation of Dover, 27th June 1692). A Common Councilman was dismissed from office at Exeter, and even disfranchised, for refusing to attend "several times" (MS. Records, Corporation of Exeter, 21st December 1703). Aldermen or Common Councilmen were sometimes dismissed from office on their becoming bankrupt; see a case at Exeter in 1718 (*ibid.* 13th October 1718).

[2] In 1690 it is ordered in Exeter "that all the members of this House when they are summoned hither are to come from their own houses, and so to return, in their gowns, on payment of twelve pence on every default" (*ibid.* 14th October 1690).

[3] We append some typical Standing Orders of 1687 :—

"That Mr. Mayor declare to the House when assembled the end of their then meeting that that which is most material may be first brought into consideration.

"That the oath of the Common Councilman be read at every meeting of the House.

"That every person sitting in his place shall be silent, attending to the matter in debate, and not to speak or talk to any other member.

"That when any member hath a desire to speak he shall decently stand up, keeping his place, with his hat off, and shall address his speech to the Mayor, and not to any other person.

"That no member shall offer to speak before the other that is speaking shall have fully ended his speech and sat down in his place.

"That if two members shall happen to stand up together with their hats off, and desire to speak to the present business, that person which the Mayor shall observe to stand up first shall have priority of speaking.

"That if any thing or matter be proposed by any member of the House and seconded by another, Mr. Mayor shall give order that the same be debated and a question put for a vote before any other business be considered of.

"That no member shall speak above twice to any business without leave of Mr. Mayor.

"That the time of meeting be at nine of the clock, and an half-hour glass be put up; after the glass is out those who come to forfeit twelve pence.

"If any person offend in any to forfeit twelve pence" (prefixed to "Book of Orders" of Council 1687, in MS. Records, Bristol Corporation).

centuries, if not earlier, we see this Common Council drawing to itself all the authority of the Corporation, raising the revenue, enacting By-laws, giving orders to the Mayor, controlling the expenditure, and sometimes claiming inherent powers of legislation analogous to those of Parliament. It was this power of the Common Council, no less than that of the Chief Officers, that the statesmen of the Restoration sought to place in safe hands by the Test and Corporation Acts, which bequeathed a tradition of political partisanship and religious exclusiveness to the ensuing century and a half.

Besides the Court of Common Council there was, in 1689, in nearly a score of Corporations, an Administrative Court made up of the whole body of Burgesses or Freemen. These assemblies of Freemen were usually called Common Gilds or Common Halls, and were, in the most notable instances, organically connected with the Gilds or Trade Companies existing in the several Boroughs. In some cases the meeting of Freemen in Common Hall assembled was the only Administrative Court, itself electing the Head of the Corporation and its Chief Officers, admitting new Freemen, enacting and revising By-laws, managing the common lands, administering the property, voting the expenditure, determining the scale of tolls and dues, and, in fact, acting both as the Legislature and, along with the officers whom it had appointed, as the Executive of the Corporation.[1] In other Boroughs, Common Hall was only one among two or more Administrative Courts, and was summoned either to decide specially important issues, or merely to elect one or more of the Chief Officers, and to pass platonic resolutions for or against the policy of the National Government or the Corporation Executive.[2] This Executive

---

[1] The principal Corporation of this type was that of Berwick-on-Tweed, which we shall subsequently describe (see Chap. IX.). Among others may be cited Southwold (First Report of Municipal Corporation Commission, 1835, vol. iv. p. 2516); Welshpool (Report on Certain Boroughs, by T. J. Hogg, 1838, p. 139); Wenlock (First Report of Municipal Corporation Commission, 1835, vol. iii. p. 2077).

[2] It is in this class that we must place the City of London, to be subsequently described in detail (see Chap. X.), but with the peculiarity that its Freemen were of two grades, and its Court of Common Hall included only the superior grade (the Liverymen). Among others we may cite Bridgnorth (*ibid.* vol. iii. p. 1780); Carmarthen (*ibid.* vol. i. p. 204); Dunwich (*ibid.* vol. iv. p. 2220); Fordwich (*ibid.* vol. ii. p. 987); Great Grimsby (*ibid.* vol. iv. pp. 2250, 2251); Hastings (*ibid.* vol. ii. p. 997); Ipswich (*ibid.* vol iv. pp.

might, in such Corporations, be a Close Body of the ordinary type, or an Elective Council; in either case, it might be made up of members of one grade, or of two grades. If we were writing the history of the Municipal Corporations of the fourteenth and fifteenth centuries we should perhaps have to give a prominent place to this Court of Common Hall. But by 1689 it had, in most Corporations, sunk into the background;[1] it had, in many of them, even ceased to be summoned; and in only a very few do we find it acting as the only Administrative Court.

(t) *The Municipal Constitutions of 1689*

So all-important had become the Administrative Courts by 1689 that any exact description of the method of appointment of their several kinds of members must amount, in fact, to an analysis of the working constitutions of the Municipal Corporations themselves. At first sight this analysis appears to offer no difficulty, as it was to the constitution of the Administrative Courts that the later Charters had devoted most attention. Unfortunately not only were the constitutions so prescribed in many cases extraordinarily intricate,[2] but also, as we have seen, the Charters were frequently ignored or the Corporations selected which among several provisions they preferred. The result was an extraordinary diversity. "England," said a learned historian, "in very ancient times was productive of cunning framers of constitutions. Very few towns in the Kingdom are governed by the same laws; and while many of them have whimsical, many more have exceedingly beautiful schemes of government."[3] In sub-

2295, 2305-2306); Maidstone (*ibid.* vol. ii. p. 755); Pevensey (*ibid.* vol. ii. p. 1017); Romney Marsh (*ibid.* vol. ii. p. 1025); Rye (*ibid.* vol. ii. p. 1033); Sandwich (*ibid.* vol. ii. p. 1043); Seaford (*ibid.* vol. ii. p. 1059).

[1] We may perhaps trace, in the titles often assumed by the Governing Council, such as "the Hall," or even "the Common Hall," and in the right of the Freemen to hear the proceedings outside the open door (see p. 386), vestiges of the time when all the Freemen were entitled to be present and to take part. We have described (*The Parish and the County*, pp. 215-230), a quite analogous development of a Close Vestry side by side with occasional open meetings of householders.

[2] The student may take as examples of intricacy the constitutions of Cambridge, Doncaster, and Newcastle-on-Tyne.

[3] *History of Northumberland*, by Rev. J. Hodgson, part ii. vol. ii. 1832, p. 429. "Heartily do I wish," he continued, "for the happiness of this

sequent chapters we shall describe, in some detail, half a score of these constitutions, so as to enable the student to realise the nature of this diversity and complexity. Here it suffices to point out that, excluding innumerable minor variations, we may distinguish, among the 180 Corporations having Governing Councils, three main types, according to the extent to which they adopted any form of popular election of Council and Chief Officers. In the great majority of these Corporations (more than two-thirds of them) the members of the Governing Council served normally for life and the Council renewed itself by simple co-option, itself filling all the offices. In the second class, the ordinary members of the Council served normally for life and the Council filled vacancies by simple co-option; but the Head of the Corporation, and frequently some of the Chief Officers, were elected for one year by the Freemen or Burgesses. This popular election was, however, nearly always limited, the choice of the electors being restricted, as regards the Head of the Corporation, to members of the Common Council, or to those of the superior grade only, or even to two or more nominees of the Council. In the third class, the members of the Common Council were themselves elected, usually for life, as well as the Head and various Chief Officers annually, by the Freemen or Burgesses. We must, however, notice that the Corporations in which election by the Freemen played a part, whether in the choice of Mayor and Chief Officers or in that of the Governing Council, had constituencies differing widely in number and character. In some, the Freemen formed only a small class, occasionally not greatly exceeding the number of persons to be elected. In most of these, moreover, admission to the Freedom was so limited that the electors were, in effect, largely the nominees of those whom they elected. In these cases the Corporations, though nominally making use of the form of popular election, belonged essentially to the first of our classes in which recruiting was by co-option. Only in those Boroughs in which there was a relatively numerous body of Freemen—and

glorious country, that the theorising spirit of the present time, while it is abridging so many ancient Municipal franchises of important rights, may not be taking wheels out of the machine of the nation, which are still necessary for producing those harmonious and powerful movements for which Britain has been so long and so justly celebrated."

this meant, in practice, those in which Servitude of Apprenticeship opened a wide and independent avenue to the Freedom—
can popular election be said to have even approached to
reality.

There were about twenty Municipal Corporations in 1689
in which the whole body of Freemen in Common Hall
assembled constituted either the sole Administrative Court, or
one among two or more such Courts. What really determined
the essential character and influence of these different Courts
of Common Hall was the particular methods which their
Corporations pursued in the recruiting of the Freemen. If the
Freemen themselves formed a close circle, recruited merely by
simple co-option, the Corporation, notwithstanding its Court
of Common Hall, was equivalent to the ordinary type in
which the government was exclusively in the hands of a
co-opting Court of Common Council. Where, on the other
hand, the Freemen were widely recruited by Right of Birth or
Marriage, and especially by Servitude of Apprenticeship, we
get in these Courts of Common Hall a special kind of
Municipal Democracy, in which proportionately large numbers
of manual-working wage-earners come to play an important
part. Finally, where the Freemen, as in one or two
insignificant Boroughs, coincided with all the householders or
"Scot and lot" inhabitants, we find a form of Municipal
Government not essentially different from that of the Parish
under the rule of the ratepayers in Open Vestry assembled.

There was one particular development of the Municipal
constitution to which we must here call attention. We have
seen, in our examination of the Lord's Court and the Manorial
Borough, how the wide jurisdiction of the Lord of a Hundred,
an Honour or a Forest, coupled with the existence of, and the
practice of granting a certain degree of autonomy to, the
Courts of such local jurisdictions as the Manor, the Borough,
or "the Foreign," led to the formation of what we have called
Hierarchies of Courts. It is one more example of the close
connection between the evolution of the Municipal Corporation
and the course of development of the Manor and the Manorial
Borough that we are not without traces of a hierarchical
relation among Municipal Corporations themselves, and between
them and less highly evolved members of the ascending series.

We may note, to begin with, that the wide geographical extent of some of the Municipal Corporations led, almost inevitably, to a hierarchical relation with inferior authorities. It was not merely that, as we have seen, a Municipal Corporation might acquire the Lordship of a Manor outside its own ordinary boundaries, even in another County;[1] so that its Governing Council could hold and control a subordinate "Court Leet, with View of Frankpledge and Court Baron," like any private Lord. The Municipal Corporation might even receive the grant of a Hundred or a Bailiwick in the same or in another County, and exercise, in its Corporate capacity, a large and ill-defined authority over the Manors and Parishes of the Hundred or "Bailiwick."[2] At the capital of the Kingdom we have the case of a Municipal Corporation acquiring, and for centuries retaining, the Shrievalty of the whole County in which it was geographically situated; appointing the Sheriffs and, through them and their underlings, holding Courts, exercising jurisdiction, and executing processes in and over many scores of Manors and Parishes outside its own area.

More interesting in this connection is the quasi-hierarchical relation which sometimes arose from the extent of the jurisdiction which a Municipal Corporation possessed either as a County Corporate or in Markets, in River Conservancy, and in Admiralty. The County jurisdiction of the Municipal Corporation often extended to a wider district than that of the Borough proper. Its market regulations often ranged over considerable areas outside the Corporation boundaries.[3]

---

[1] Thus the Corporation of Winchester was, in 1745, paying its Solicitor a fee of five guineas for "going to the Manor of River in Sussex, and holding an annual audit there, for the better collecting and receiving the quit-rents issuing out of the said Manor to this Corporation" (MS. Records, Winchester Corporation, 22nd March 1745).

[2] Such a case is presented by York, when the Corporation possessed the Bailiwick of Ainsty ; but this Hundred or Wapentake was definitely made part of the County of the City of York, by Letters Patent of 27 Henry VI. (*Firma Burgi*, by T. Madox, 1726, p. 293).

[3] The jurisdiction of the Municipal Corporation of Canterbury extended for certain purposes over twelve entire parishes, and over parts of other parishes outside its walls, these districts being styled the "Liberties" (First Report of Municipal Corporation Commission, 1835, vol. ii. p. 685). A special Local Act confirmed to the Corporation of Dorchester "the right to weigh all goods within twelve miles of the town" (9 Henry VI. c. 6 ; *Town Life in the Fifteenth Century*, by A. S. Green, 1894, vol. i. p. 3 n.). The Municipal Corporation of York had been made, by Charter of 1463, the King's justiciaries for overlooking

The Corporation's Court of Admiralty was frequently held on the shore of adjacent Manors and Parishes, and even in neighbouring minor ports. The Corporation of Southampton, for instance, had been granted by Royal Charter the town of Portsmouth, which was included in its "farm." This historical relation of superiority lent force to the assertion of the Admiralty jurisdiction of the Southampton Corporation, not only over the Manorial Borough of Lymington, but also over Portsmouth waters, which lay within the ancient limits of the Port of Southampton. In 1707-1709 we see the Corporation vainly striving to maintain its ancient monopoly of jurisdiction over Portsmouth,[1] now granted a Municipal Corporation of its own. Meanwhile the Corporation of Portsmouth had successfully asserted its own jurisdiction over the ecclesiastical Manor of Gosport, over which, during a great part of the seventeenth century, it substituted its own authority for that of the episcopal Lord of the Manor.[2]

and preserving the main rivers of Yorkshire (*ibid.* p. 234 *n.*). The Corporation of Norwich was, by statutes of the fifteenth century, the oversight of weaving and worsted-making throughout Norfolk (*An Essay towards a Topographical History of the County of Norfolk*, by F. Blomefield, 1805-1810, vol. iii. p. 125). When a Borough had been granted the high immunities of a "County Corporate," the boundaries of the County usually transcended those of the Borough. Thus the Municipal Corporation of Kingston-on-Hull exercised its Borough jurisdiction over an area which had, in 1831, 15,996 inhabitants; whilst its County jurisdiction extended over a population of 32,958 (First Report of Municipal Corporation Commission, 1835, General Report, p. 31). Within the area of the "Corporate County" of Coventry, but outside the ten Wards of the City, were numerous villages of rural character, over which the Corporation exercised jurisdiction (*ibid.* vol. iii. p. 1795). So, too, even if the Borough was not a County of itself. The Justices and Coroners of Great Grimsby exercised jurisdiction over various townships outside the Borough (*ibid.* vol. iv. p. 2249). We have already mentioned the wide jurisdiction of the Coroner of Wareham (p. 289).

[1] The Corporation for centuries "exercised every branch of Admiralty power: they had in the Town an Admiralty Court and prison; they claimed all wrecks, took cognisance of fishing in the water within their precincts, which they suffered none to do but such fishermen as were licensed by them. And as by the Admiralty law it is sea everywhere to the first bridge, they claimed a right to exercise that power as far as Redbridge on the River Test, and as far as Wood Mill on the River Itchen." For centuries the Corporation held its Courts at the traditional places on the seashore, near Keyhaven, Lepe, and Hamble (Speed MSS. in archives of Southampton Corporation, pp. 60, 84-85; MS. Records of ditto of August 1706, 1707-1709, and 12th June 1798; *History of Southampton*, by J. S. Davies, 1883, pp. 221-224, 239-242; *Town Life in the Fifteenth Century*, by A. S. Green, 1894, vol. ii. p. 319). This Court of Admiralty was disused towards the latter part of the eighteenth century; an attempt to hold it in 1793 was not persisted in.

[2] The Corporation of Exeter exercised jurisdiction over the course of the

But the most remarkable example of a Municipal Hierarchy—an example unique in England and Wales—is that presented by the Liberty of the Cinque Ports. We cannot pretend to recount the glorious rise of this famous galaxy of towns from the eleventh to the fifteenth century, nor yet relate the story of its decline under the Tudors and the Stuarts; but seeing that it lingered on, as a definitely constituted Hierarchy of jurisdictions right down to Victorian times, and continues in extremely attenuated form even to the present day (1907), we cannot abstain from a brief analysis of its constitution and functions as they existed between 1689 and 1835.[1]

River Exe down to the sea, controlling the village and Port of Topsham, and elaborately regulating not only the pilotage, but also the fishing (MS. Records, Exeter Corporation, 23rd December 1686, 18th January, 12th February, 8th March, and 26th April 1687, 8th May 1708). It was to deliver it from the jurisdiction of a Court of Admiralty that "it was thought proper," says Madox, "to incorporate Southwold, to enable it to bear up the better against the town of Dunwich" (*Firma Burgi*, by T. Madox, 1726, p. 296). "The liberties and jurisdiction of Rochester on the Medway extend to Sheerness, a distance of twenty miles. Bristol has jurisdiction as far as the Holmes in the Bristol Channel, twenty-five miles from the town. Newcastle-on-Tyne has jurisdiction on ten miles of the river below the town, and seven above it. The jurisdiction of Ipswich extends over a considerable part of the harbour of Harwich" (First Report of Municipal Corporation Commission, 1835, p. 31).

[1] It is remarkable (and not creditable to English historical scholarship) that, in spite of abundant and easily accessible material, there exists nothing that can be called a constitutional history of the Liberty of the Cinque Ports, even twenty years after the admirable outline sketch of Montagu Burrows (*Cinque Ports*, 1888), to which we are exceptionally indebted, has both signalised the need and pointed out the way. The MS. Records (especially rich at Sandwich, Romney, Rye, Fordwich, and Lydd), including those of the Lord Warden's Courts from 1616, are still largely unexplored, and only very imperfectly printed. Many of those of Dover from 1365 to 1768 are in the British Museum. Among published sources we need indicate only the volumes of the Historical Manuscripts Commission relating to Lydd, Hastings, Romney, Fordwich, Folkestone, Hythe, Rye, and Sandwich (1873, 1876, 1892); the First Report of the Municipal Corporation Commission, 1835, ditto, 1880; the statutes, especially the "Cinque Ports Acts, 1811 to 1872," and the saving clauses in the Municipal Corporations Acts, 1882 and 1883; Chief Justice Hale's chapter in his *Treatise*, 1667, Part II. pp. 106-113; *Charters of the Cinque Ports*, by Samuel Jeake, 1728; *History . . . of the Isle of Tenet*, by John Lewis, 1736; *History of Faversham*, by Edward Jacob, 1774; *Collections for a History of Sandwich*, by William Boys, 1792; *History of the Town and Port of Dover*, by Rev. John Lyon, 1813-1814; *History of Hastings*, by W. G. Moss, 1824; *Oral Traditions of the Cinque Ports*, by Kennet B. Martin, 1832; *Chronicles of Pevensey*, by M. A. Lower, 1846; *History of Rye*, by W. Holloway, 1847; *History of Sandwich*, by Oscar Baker, 1848; *History of Winchelsea*, by W. D. Cooper, 1850; *History of Deal*, by Stephen Pritchard, 1864; *Visitors' Guide to Faversham*, by F. F. Giraud and C. E. Donne, 1876; *Descriptive and Historical Account of Folkestone*, by

We shall best understand the complicated constitution of the Liberty of Cinque Ports if we realise, at the outset, that the thirty-nine [1] Boroughs and villages comprised under that designation formed no part of the Counties of Kent or Sussex or Essex, by which they were severally surrounded, and were entirely exempt from the jurisdiction of these Counties, constituting in themselves, notwithstanding their geographical discreteness, one homogeneous County, ranking as a separate shire, paying as a shire a fifteenth instead of a tenth, but partaking also of the nature of a single Municipal Corporation —paying, for instance, unlike any County, its fifteenth in one lump sum—and endowed with Courts and jurisdictions exceeding those of either County or Borough.[2]   At the head

S. J. Mackie, 1883 ; *The Barons of the Cinque Ports and the Parliamentary Representation of Hythe*, by G. Wilks, 1892 ; *The Story of King Edward and New Winchelsea*, by F. A. Inderwick, 1892 ; *History of the Town and Port of Fordwich*, by C. E. Woodruff, 1895 ; *History of the Castle, Town, and Port of Dover*, by Rev. S. P. H. Statham, 1899 ; *The Cinque Ports*, by F. H. M. Hueffer, 1900 ; *Dover Charters, etc.*, by Rev. S. P. H. Statham, 1902 ; *The Cinque Ports, their History and Present Condition*, by J. B. Jones, 1903 ; *Dover, the Ancient Cinque Port*, by An Ancient Freeman, 1903 ; *Indexes of the Great White Book and the Black Book of the Cinque Ports*, 1905 ; *Dover, a Perambulation*, by J. B. Jones, 1907 ; *Sir Thomas Mantell's Tracts relative to Cinque Ports*, 1828 ; together with numerous valuable papers in *Archæologia Cantiana and Sussex Archæological Collections*, and some in the *Reliquary* (vol. xviii., 1877-1878) ; *Archæologia* (vol. xviii., 1817), *etc.* ; *Archæological Review* (vol. iv., 1890) ; *St. James's Magazine* (vol. ii., 1861) ; *History of Kent*, by Edward Hasted, 1797-1801 ; *History of the Weald of Kent*, by R. Furley, 1871-1874 ; *History of Sussex*, by T. W. Horsfield, 1835, vol. ii. App. pp. 58-75 ; *Feudal England*, by J. H. Round, 1895, pp. 552-571 ; and *Town Life in the Fifteenth Century*, by A. S. Green, 1894, vol. i. pp. 384-416.

[1] Besides the original five Ports (Hastings, Sandwich, Dover, Hythe, and Romney), and the two "Ancient Towns" added as equivalent constituents soon after the Norman Conquest (Winchelsea and Rye), there were, "under" or attached to one or other of these, eight corporate and twenty-four non-corporate "Limbs or Members" (under Hastings, the Corporations of Seaford and Pevensey, and the villages of Bulvarhythe, Hydney or Eastbourne, Petit Tham, Bekesbourn, Grange and Northeye ; under Sandwich, the Corporations of Fordwich and Deal, and the villages of Reculver, Sarre, Stonor, Ramsgate, Walmer, and Brightlingsea ; under Dover, the Corporations of Folkestone and Faversham, and the villages of Margate, St. John's, Goresend, now Birchington, Woodchurch, St. Peter's or Broadstairs, Kingsdown, and Ringswould ; under Romney, the Corporation of Lydd, and the villages of Old Romney, Bromehill, Dengemarsh, and Orwaldstone ; under Rye, the Corporation of Tenterden ; and under Hythe, the village of West Hythe).   Ramsgate and Margate were incorporated in 1884 and 1857 respectively.   The total population of the whole Liberty of the Cinque Ports in 1689 cannot have exceeded 25,000—a total which it may have reached six centuries before.   In 1835 it was still under 70,000, though it has now risen (1907) to over 150,000.

[2] The usual popular treatment of the Cinque Ports as a federation of independent town republics for the protection and development of their

of this unique Corporate County, called a Liberty, stood the Lord Warden of the Cinque Ports, an officer appointed for life by the Crown, and for many centuries combining his post with that of Constable of Dover Castle. This great dignitary united in himself the status and the functions, not only of Custos Rotulorum and Lord-Lieutenant of an ordinary County, but also those of High Sheriff. At the same time he was the Head of what was, in effect, a single Municipal Corporation; he had, like a newly elected Mayor, to take an oath of fidelity to its constitution, administered to him by the Speaker of its Legislative Assembly; he held, when he chose, its great "Court of Shepway"; he was Chancellor of what in the seventeenth century was described as its "mixed Court of Star

autonomy obscures, we think, the real nature of the organisation of this Liberty. It is doubtful whether it promoted Municipal freedom. "It is evident," says Mrs. Green, "that the bond which existed between the Chief Ports . . . had no influence whatever on the development of local liberties. . . . With . . . Municipal freedom the question of federal organisation had nothing whatever to do. . . . There is no evidence that the confederation of the Cinque Ports afforded to its members any security of Municipal freedom, or any extension of the rights to be won from their several Lords; and as a matter of fact, this group of favoured towns does not seem to have made the slightest advance on other English Boroughs, either in winning an earlier freedom, or in raising a higher standard of liberty" (*Town Life in the Fifteenth Century*, by A. S. Green, 1894, vol. i. pp. 409, 416). It was not even a confederation. It formed, as Mr. Round has rightly insisted, "a single community, possessing a single assembly, and receiving a joint Charter" (*Feudal England*, by J. H. Round, 1895, p. 560). In its combination of County and Municipal Corporation, and also possibly in the importance of the office of Chamberlain in Sandwich (*History of the Customs Revenue*, by Hubert Hall, 1885, vol. i. p. 64; vol. ii. pp. 31, 97, 162), the constitutional status of the Liberty of the Cinque Ports somewhat resembles that of the City of London. They are alike, too, in never having had a Merchant Gild (though Fordwich was granted one in the twelfth century); in being alone of local authorities specifically mentioned and guaranteed in their privileges in Magna Carta; in enjoying, also alone among local authorities, special honorary positions at a Royal Coronation; and in their complete exemption from the jurisdiction of the adjoining Counties. On the other hand, the City of London very early freed itself from any domination by the Constable of the Tower; whereas the Cinque Ports remained permanently under that of the Constable or Lieutenant of Dover Castle (as Lord Warden), whose position towards them recalls that of so many Constables of Castles in Wales to the little Boroughs clustering round them. The analogy with the Lord Warden of the Marches (of Wales), with his Court of the Marches exercising jurisdiction over many Municipal Corporations and other places, is worth notice (see *The Council of the Marches of Wales*, by Miss C. A. J. Skeel, 1904). The Cinque Ports ceased to be a separate County for civil administration under the Local Government Act of 1888, becoming (as Brightlingsea had long been in Essex) individually merged in Kent and Sussex respectively (except that Hastings became a County Borough). But there is still a separate Commission of the Peace for the Liberty, and the Lord Warden still acts as Lord-Lieutenant.

Chamber, Exchequer, and Chancery"; he was Admiral presiding at its Court of Admiralty, and likewise President of its peculiar "Court of Lodemanage," which was concerned with all that related to pilotage and sea passage for the entire Liberty.

The Lord Warden originally exercised his highest authority in the so-called "Court of Shepway," which had formerly been held by the King's itinerant Judges, but which obtained its autonomy in 1260. To constitute this Court there were summoned to meet, at the Cross at Shepway near Lympne, as "sectatores" or suitors, whenever the Lord Warden chose, the Heads and a certain number of Freemen or "Barons" [1] from each of the seven principal ports, and, if required, Juries from each of the Boroughs from which there were offenders to be tried. Its business had apparently comprised both judicial and legislative and even administrative questions. It became, however, limited to the work of a tribunal of appeal in a few great and rare issues,[2] and ceased, in fact, to be summoned except for the ceremonial purpose of swearing in a new Lord Warden.[3] Long before 1689 all its judicial business had passed to the other Courts held by the Lord Warden's officers from time immemorial in St. James's Church at Dover. The prison at Dover Castle was at his command, and the "Bodar," the Bidder or Summoner of the Ports, was stationed at Dover, and became his agent. The fees and fines, like the wrecks, enriched him and his officers. His "Court of Chancery" dealt with both civil and criminal cases down to the nineteenth century. His "Court of Lodemanage" regulated the ancient

---

[1] The term "Baron," as applied to the Freemen of the five Cinque Ports, the two "Ancient Towns" and their eight Corporate members, has survived as an honourable distinction from the time when it meant only *baro*, a free man ; being retained in legal documents throughout the centuries, possibly in view of the fact that these Freemen held their lands or shares in the Corporate lands on something analogous to military tenure from the Crown. At one moment it seems to have been even doubtful whether their representatives in Parliament should sit with the Peers or with the Commons.

[2] High treason, failure to render ship service, falsifying coin, false judgment, and treasure trove.

[3] At Shepway, whence this Court derived its name, it probably met in the open air. The last Court for ordinary business may have been that of 1471. For another century the formal Court at the installation of the Lord Warden was held at Shepway ; then once at Bekesbourn in 1597 ; then at Dover ; becoming obsolete in 1765, until the revival for the ceremony of 1861 (*An Account of the Grand Court of Shepway*, by E. Knocker, 1862).

"Fellowship of Pilots of the Cinque Ports"—a kind of Gild common to the whole Liberty—and administered, down to 1853,[1] the elaborately regulated pilotage system of the Goodwin Sands. His Court of Admiralty, though its criminal jurisdiction has been abolished, continues to this day (1907) to enforce along the whole coast-line from Shellness Point in Sheppey, or, as some say, even from Harwich, all the way round to Seaford, his rights to "flotsam, jetsam, and lagan," and to deal with salvage cases. To this day he nominally commands the local forces, and nominates to commissions in the Cinque Ports regiment of Militia; above all, he still presents to the Lord Chancellor the names of persons to be included in the separate Commission of the Peace which is issued for the Liberty as for a County.[2]

But just as we have seen that the Mayors of ordinary Municipal Corporations came to be assisted by "Mayor's Counsellors," and just as we have described, both in, the County and the Municipal Corporation, the processes of legislation and administration passing away from judicial to administrative bodies, so, in the Liberty or Corporate County of the Cinque Ports, we see developing a specialised Administrative Court. From the thirteenth or fourteenth century, at any rate, there had come to be an annual assembly held, not at Shepway, but at first near the watch-tower at Brodhill on Dymchurch beach, and then at Romney, consisting of some seventy representatives of the seven principal ports and their Corporate Members; at first to deal specially with the management of the jurisdiction over Yarmouth Fair[3] and

---

[1] It was then merged, together with the "Trinity House of Dover," in the corresponding national institution which bears the name of the Trinity House in London. The regulations of the Court of Lodemanage dated from 1495, and even then merely codified earlier custom. For incidental light upon its nineteenth-century working, see *Dover, the Ancient Cinque Port*, by An Ancient Freeman, 1903.

[2] By virtue of 51 George III. c. 36, secs. 1, 2 (1811), a separate Commission of the Peace was issued for the Liberty of the Cinque Ports, and the Justices of the Peace, who are nominated by the Lord Warden, were empowered to act in such places within the Liberty as were not within the jurisdiction of the Justices of particular Boroughs. In 1812, possibly in consequence of this statute, we hear of the Lord Warden holding a "Court of Lieutenancy" which is closely analogous to the Commission of Lieutenancy of the City of London (*Indexes of the Great White Book and the Black Book of the Cinque Ports*, 1905).

[3] The relation of the Liberty to the Great Fair at Yarmouth in Norfolk is full of interest. The fishing-fleet of the Cinque Ports had long been in the

such questions as the provision by each Port of its quota towards the ships for sea service and the assessment upon each of its share of the sums required for taxes. But these " Brotherhoods and Guestlings," [1] as the assemblies came to be called, in which the Lord Warden had no place, and over

habit of using the uninhabited shingle beach at the mouth of the Yare as a convenient centre, and had naturally exercised a rough jurisdiction over the crowds which were gradually attracted by what became a Michaelmas Fair. The modern student will be reminded of the use of the Newfoundland shore by the French fishermen, and of the still existing government of the Labrador coast by the "admiral" of the Newfoundland ships on their yearly visits. As the town of Great Yarmouth gradually grew up, the temporary jurisdiction of the Bailiffs annually appointed by the Cinque Ports inevitably led to conflicts which became accentuated when Great Yarmouth, in 1209, obtained a Municipal Corporation. For upwards of four centuries the "Yarmouth feud" continued, the Bailiffs of the Cinque Ports ever losing ground, until, in 1663, the Brotherhood and Guestling decided to discontinue their appointment, and to abandon the visit of its greatly diminished fishing-fleet. The MS. "Relations of the Bailiffs" to the Brotherhood for many years exist among the Romney Corporation archives ; see also *Cinque Ports*, by Montagu Burrows, 1888, pp. 166-176 ; *History of Great Yarmouth*, by Henry Manship (written 1619), 1854 ; *History and Antiquities of the Ancient Borough of Great Yarmouth*, by Henry Swinden, 1772.

[1] The better opinion to-day appears to be that these names are instances of mistaken derivation. The records show that the old name for this Administrative Court was "the Court of the Brodehull," or "the Brodehull" ; thence passing gradually into forms like "the Broderield," "Brotheryeld," "Brotherhylde," and "Brood" (1573), understood to be "the Brother Gild," and so translated at the end of the sixteenth century into "the Brotherhood" (found in 1572 ; *Indexes of the Great White Book and the Black Book of the Cinque Ports*, 1905). When the Corporate Members also sent representatives it was styled "the Guestling," the derivation of which is unknown. In view, however, of the fact that the names of both the Court of Shepway and the Brotherhood are really derived from the places where they originally met, it has been suggested that "the Guestling" takes its title from the little village of Gestlinges, in the same neighbourhood as Shepway and Brodhull. The regular annual sessions of this "Brotherhood and Guestling," long held at Romney in succession to Brodhull or Dymchurch, ceased in 1601 ; between 1633 and 1750 they were held irregularly at long intervals ; and the subsequent assemblies of 1771, 1811, 1828, 1866, and 1887 were almost entirely formal and ceremonial (see the MS. Minutes between 1558 and 1750 among the Dover Corporation Archives in British Museum ; *Calendar of Home Office Papers, 1770-2*, 1881, p. 283 ; *An Account of Cinque Ports Meetings called Brotherhoods and Guestlings*, by T. Mantell, 1811 ; *Court of Shepway* ; *Statement of the Right of Precedence of Hastings*, 1866). Yet it is said that the Hall and Brotherhood House at Romney, which had been acquired for the business of the Liberty in the sixteenth century, was rebuilt as late as 1728. The Brotherhoods and Guestlings of 1689-1835 had their "Ports' Clerk," their "Ports' Bailiff," two "Ports' Solicitors," and a "Ports' Counsel," who advised the Speaker. These officers were paid by fees. It is difficult to find any trace of a common revenue or common fund. The common expenses, like the shares of any tax or common charge, seem to have been allotted as soon as incurred among the several Ports, often by Circular Letters issued by the Speaker, and individually collected from them.

which the Mayors of the seven principal Ports acted in turn as "Speaker," though they took over from the "Court of Shepway" the legislative and administrative business of the Liberty as a whole, themselves fell into desuetude in the seventeenth century, and were subsequently held only at long intervals, for formal and ceremonial purposes. The Lord Warden and his Courts thus remained the only effective authorities of the Cinque Ports as a whole.

Subordinate to the organisation of the Liberty as a whole, each of the seven Ports had its own independent Municipal Corporation, with Mayor and Jurats, who all acted as Justices of the Peace for the Borough, often with some sort of Common Council, or Four-and-Twenty, subordinate to themselves; with an ancient "Hundred Court" of popular character passing into a Court of Quarter Sessions, having unlimited criminal jurisdiction;[1] with a Court of Record for civil actions of any amount; with ancient Corporate property in land and prescriptive revenues from tolls and dues; with mediæval "custumals" or elaborate codes of peculiar customs; with numerous officers bearing quaint titles; and with a body of Freemen or "Barons," "quit of shires and hundreds" and enjoying freedom from toll throughout the kingdom, recruited by Birth, Marriage, and Apprenticeship, as well as by simple co-option, and meeting in ancient popular assemblies known as "Hornblowings," which had once transacted indiscriminately all the judicial, legislative, and administrative business of the little communities, but had before 1689 for the most part gradually lost their control over all the various branches of the Municipal government. Here we can note only the relation of these fully developed Municipal Corporations to the other members of the Hierarchy. They were responsible to the Lord Warden and his Courts for the fulfilment of the services upon which their privileges depended; for the payment of their contributions to the "Purse"[2] for

[1] A murderer was executed in 1742, on the sentence of the Court of Quarter Sessions of the Borough of Rye (*History of Rye*, by W. Holloway, 1847, p. 377).

[2] The unit of levy was "a Purse"; settled in 1495 at £4 : 7s., when the contributions from each Head Port and Member were fixed at from one shilling to six and eightpence each. Later, when each of the seven Ports paid a pound, the eight Corporate Members paid thirteen and fourpence each, whilst the Non-Corporate Members dropped out of the list of contributories (*Cinque Ports*, by M. Burrows, 1888, pp. 182-183).

the maintenance of the King's Peace and the enforcement of the law of the land; and for the due execution of justice within their respective Boroughs. They had to do suit and service at the Court of Shepway, and by custom also send their representatives to the Brotherhood and Guestling on pain of fine. Under the designation of "false judgment," there was a practical appeal from any of the Borough Courts to the Lord Warden, nominally in the Court of Shepway, but actually to his own Court at Dover. And by custom, either the Court of Shepway or the Brotherhood and Guestling could make regulations binding throughout the whole Liberty of the Cinque Ports. On the other hand, the "Five Ports and the two Ancient Towns" had certain vaguely defined rights and jurisdiction over the "Limbs" or "Members," Corporate and Non-Corporate, which were severally attached to or "under" each of them.

Of these thirty-two "Limbs" or "Members," eight had independent Municipal Corporations of their own, and enjoyed an organisation almost as elaborate and an autonomy almost as complete as that of the Port to which they were attached. When the Liberty furnished its fifty-seven ships on the national service, the "Limbs" or "Members" helped their respective Ports by supplying one or more vessels towards its quota. Latterly, however, their subservience seems to have been limited to the payment of their ancient annual contributions (which some of them discontinued in the course of the seventeenth and eighteenth centuries) and the concession of a certain honorary suzerainty and ceremonial precedence.[1]

Over the twenty-four Non-Corporate "Limbs" or "Members"

---

[1] The "Corporate Members" appear mostly to have been incorporated between the twelfth and fourteenth centuries ; but the Municipal Corporation of Tenterden dates only from 1449, that of Seaford from 1544, and that of Deal from 1699. Of the "Limbs" or "Members" Seaford alone was represented in the House of Commons. Tenterden began to be irregular in its payments to Rye as early as 1689, but paid up arrears at intervals until 1749. An action by Rye in 1766 was dismissed with costs (*History of Rye*, by Wm. Holloway, 1847, p. 374). Faversham discontinued its payments to Dover about 1734 (*History of Faversham*, by E. Jacob, 1774, p. 21 *n.*). The payment by Folkestone being several years in arrear, Dover in 1752 demanded a remittance, which was refused, and the matter was allowed to drop (MS. Records, Dover Corporation, 29th June and 25th September 1752 ; *Descriptive and Historical Account of Folkestone*. by S. J. Mackie, 1883. pp. 835-837).

the several Head Ports exercised a more effective jurisdiction. These villages, which were never represented at the Brotherhood and Guestling, had no other government than that afforded by their superior authority, which had at one period occasionally held a Court there, and continued to appoint annually for each of them one of the leading residents as a so-called "Deputy," who was sworn to faithful allegiance to the Head Port. This Deputy was not a magistrate, and all criminal offenders, like all civil suits, had to be tried in the Courts of the Head Ports. Each member had once contributed its own tiny share—it might be as little as two men and two oars [1]—to the quota of ships which its Head Port had to furnish, and had long made an annual payment towards its expenses. To provide these annual payments to the Head Ports, and to meet other necessary local expenses, the Deputies seem formerly to have levied small assessments on their villages, but it is doubtful whether any of these survived the seventeenth century.[2] The Deputy called meetings of the inhabitants of his village, over which he presided; but such meetings were not Courts, and beyond making representations and sometimes submitting nominations for the office of Deputy, seem to have had no particular functions. But down to 1888, at any rate, these tiny villages bore, in their exclusion from the Counties of Kent and Sussex, as well as in their subordination to the Courts and officers of their several Head Ports, the mark of their humble position at the base of the Hierarchy of the famous Liberty of the Cinque Ports.[3]

[1] As from Grange.

[2] See, as to such assessments in Margate, *History of Kent*, by E. Hasted, 1800, vol. x. pp. 312-313.

[3] Long before 1689 many of these Non-Corporate Members had become decayed, and the relationship between them and their Head Port had become only nominal. During the eighteenth century the connection with the others fell rapidly into decay. Those that were still making their accustomed annual payments ceased gradually to do so, and the contributions were not enforced. The inhabitants of Deal broke away from Sandwich in 1699, and obtained a Municipal Corporation of their own, "being irritated to purchase their dear-bought privileges by the Mayor of Sandwich his too violent pressing for a market pursuant to the Lords Justices reviving an old statute for paying of toll, etc." (*Collections for a History of Sandwich*, by W. Boys, 1792, p. 718). The new Corporation ceased after 1702 to pay its annual contribution, which Sandwich sought in vain to enforce at the Brotherhood and Guestling of 1726, and finally abandoned in 1746. Even then the Sandwich Justices retained concurrent powers in Deal, and Deal citizens had to serve on Sandwich Juries. The Lord of the Manor of Stonor refused in 1771 to submit to the jurisdiction of

We may now attempt to sum up the Municipal Constitutions of 1689. The Municipal Corporation of that date was still essentially a bundle of "Acquittances, Franchises, Liberties, and Immunities," varying in number, kind, and extent, but, in pursuance of the arbitrary definition that we have adopted, always including the privilege of making its own Corporate Justices of the Peace. This bundle of rights was vested, by prescription or by some legal instrument, in a group of persons, assumed to belong to a particular place. The rights were exercised by officers and Courts, having jurisdictions of different kinds, and extending over widely differing areas, according to the nature of the Franchise. It was a feature of some of these Corporate jurisdictions, just as we have seen it to be of those of the Hundred and the Manor, that they constituted, in a few cases, Municipal Hierarchies. But nearly all the Municipal Corporations of 1689 had shaken themselves free, alike from the jurisdiction of individual Lords of Manors and Hundreds, and from that of any superior

the Sandwich Coroner, and successfully maintained the exemption of that decayed "Member." On the other hand, Ramsgate, in 1749, as the price of getting an Act to build its harbour, had to consent to yield £200 a year from its revenues in aid of the declining harbour of Sandwich Corporation, which continued to appoint a Deputy for its younger rival until that was incorporated in 1884. To this day the Recorder of Sandwich acts also for Ramsgate. Walmer also continued down to 1888 to have a Deputy appointed by Sandwich; and Brightlingsea in Essex did so down to 1804, the appointment being even formally revived in 1888. But Brightlingsea, with Bekesbourn (which had been without a Deputy since 1792) and Grange, had been virtually absorbed into their respective counties by 51 George III. c. 36 (1811), which, whilst nominally saving the rights of the Head Port, gave the County Justices and Coroner full jurisdiction. Margate, less fortunate than Deal, remained subject to its Head Port throughout the eighteenth century, having its Coal-meters and Coal-measurers appointed by Dover, to the expenses of which it annually contributed. It petitioned in vain in 1785 for a Charter of Incorporation, which it did not obtain till 1857. Dover continued, down to 1888, to appoint Deputies for St. John's, St. Peter's or Broadstairs, Woodchurch and Ringwould (MS. Minutes of the Corporations of Deal and Dover; *History of Rye*, by W. Holloway, 1847; *Collections for a History of Sandwich*, by W. Boys, 1792; *History of Dover*, by Rev. J. Lyon, 1813; *Cinque Ports*, by Montagu Burrows, 1888). It was one result of the Local Government Act of 1888, which merged these "Limbs" or "Members" in the Administrative Counties of Kent and Sussex respectively, that, with the exception of some of those of Dover, they finally ceased to have any effective connection with their respective Head Ports. The Non-Corporate "Limbs" of Dover in the Isle of Thanet remain to this day (1907) under the Justices of the Liberty; the Dover Coroner still holds the inquests there; and for purposes of licensing, and weights and measures, the Corporate Justices of Dover hold adjourned sessions at Broadstairs for these Non-Corporate Thanet "Limbs" (*The Cinque Ports, their History and Present Condition*, by J. B. Jones, 1903, p. 104).

Municipal Corporation; standing out as so many autonomous governments, themselves wielding one or more powers over the inhabitants of the localities concerned. To a greater or lesser extent most of the couple of hundred Municipal Corporations of 1689 had even freed themselves from the jurisdiction of the County at large. But in the degree of this immunity from the authority of the County, they differed among themselves to the utmost possible extent, and in a bewildering variety of shades; ranging, in fact, from no more than a concurrent jurisdiction of the Corporate Justices along with those of the County, and that only with regard to minor offences, up to the status and position of "Counties in themselves," with their own exclusive civil and criminal jurisdiction, their own Coroners, and Sheriffs, and, in four remarkable cases, even a distinct Lieutenancy.

With regard to the internal organisation of these couple of hundred Municipal Corporations, the differences were so innumerable, the gradations so minute, and the structure often so elaborate and complicated that it is difficult to make any general statement both succinct and accurate. Broadly speaking, these Corporations might have been classified in 1689 according to two outstanding features of their internal economy —the method by which their governing authority was appointed, and the devices by which their Freemen were recruited. The great majority, amounting to three-quarters of the whole, were governed each by a Close Body, which itself selected the Head of the Corporation, and filled vacancies in its own ranks by simple co-option. In these cases, even if there existed also a large body of Freemen, recruited by Apprenticeship, they were excluded from the government of the Corporation, and were merely humble participants in some of its profitable privileges, such as freedom from toll, eligibility for charities, and "stint of common." This kind of government it was that the Royal Commission of 1835, under the epithet of "the Corporation system," assumed to be representative of the whole. But there were two other classes of Municipal Corporations, in both of which a popular element played an important part. In a small but extremely important group of Corporations, including several of the largest Boroughs and the City of London itself there existed a large body of Freemen, effectively open to all comers by Servitude of Apprenticeship, which exercised annually some electoral rights, varying from the mere choice of a Mayor from among the members of the Close Body, up to the unrestricted election of the Governing Council and principal officers. In a still smaller, but extremely interesting group of Corporations, the whole body of Freemen, in Common Hall assembled, themselves exercised some or all of the powers of government. These two classes of Municipal Corporations, comprising together a quarter of the whole, may not unfairly be termed Municipal Democracies, with the important qualification that the Freemen, though in 1689 still relatively numerous, did not include even the whole of the householders, and had already begun to be made up in part of non-residents. In the succeeding chapters we shall select for special description Municipal Corporations illustrative of each of the three main classes, and of some of the varieties within the classes. But before plunging into this detailed description and criticism of Administration by Close Corporations and Administration by Municipal Democracies, we must first enumerate three main lines of disintegration which went on between 1689 and 1835 in all Corporations alike, whether governed by Close Bodies, by Elective Councils, or by the whole body of Freemen in Common Hall assembled.

CHAPTER VII

MUNICIPAL DISINTEGRATION

THE working constitution of the Municipal Corporation, based upon the structure that we have described in the preceding chapter, did not, between 1689 and 1835, remain unaltered. Under the influence of changing circumstances the different parts of the constitution swelled or contracted from decade to decade in varying degrees in different towns. We have already shown how the Lord's Court and the Manorial Borough were, during this very period, gradually being superseded, as local governing authorities, by the Parish Vestry and the County Justices on the one hand, and by the new Statutory Authorities on the other. An analogous transformation took place in the Corporate towns, with the significant difference that the change went on to a large extent within the four corners of the Municipal Corporation itself.[1]

(a) The Rise of the Corporate Magistracy

To take first the Corporate Magistracy. We have elsewhere[2] described in minute detail the growth of the work of a Justice of the Peace in the eighteenth century, and the way in which Parliament heaped upon him, by successive statutes,

---

[1] We do not attempt in this chapter to deal with the larger question of the cause of that general decay of town life which seems to have set in at the very beginning of the sixteenth century (see *Town Life in the Fifteenth Century*, by A. S. Green, 1894, vol. ii. pp. 437-448) ; for which various economic as well as political causes have been suggested, including even (by Dr. Jessopp) "the Great Pillage" of the Monasteries (preface to *The Story of our English Towns* by P. H. Ditchfield, 1897, p. xxi).

[2] *The Parish and the County*, 1906.

duty after duty, to be performed either as "Single" or as "Double Justice," or in Petty, Special, or Quarter Sessions. In all this legislation there was practically no distinction between the Justice of the Peace serving for the County under a Commission from the King, and the Justice of the Peace created by a Municipal Corporation under Royal Charter.[1] Thus, just as the country gentleman who had taken out his "Dedimus potestatem" found himself year by year more heavily burdened with magisterial business, so the Mayor and Aldermen of the Corporate Borough found their duties as Magistrates expanding relatively to those of the more antiquated Courts or officers. In some Municipal Corporations, as we shall see, the magisterial duties of the Mayor and Aldermen became so onerous and incessant as to take up the greater part of their time. At Liverpool, for instance by 1835, the mere police-court work had come to necessitate daily attendance. "Besides the business of a parochial nature," we are told, "each Magistrate has four weeks' duty in the year, upon the daily business of the town, and four weeks' attendance at the dock police-office, upon the daily business there. These attendances are regulated by formal routine lists kept for the purpose. Upon an average, full three hours a day are occupied upon the town business and about half that time at the docks; the daily average of business being about sixty cases requiring

---

[1] Though the terms of the numerous statutes clearly make no distinction between one kind of Justice and another, some doubt seems at first to have been entertained as to the full authority of a Corporate Justice. At any rate we have, in 1715, a statute expressly declaring that "the Justices of the Peace of all Cities, Corporations, Boroughs, and other places" were empowered to put all the Highway Acts in force within their respective jurisdictions (1 George I. St. 2, c. 52, 1715). Counsel advised the Deal Corporation in 1768 that the Borough Court of Quarter Sessions could, like the Quarter Sessions of a County, appoint under the statutes a Scavenger and make a Scavenger's Rate, distinct from that of the Surveyor of Highways (MS. Records, Book of Counsel's Opinions, 1716-1776, Deal Corporation). In a few Boroughs (such as Oxford, Haverfordwest, Poole, etc.) a separate Commission of the Peace was issued, which included, with the leading members of the Corporation, a few other local dignitaries who did not attend ; and it was in these cases under the Commission, rather than under the authority of the Borough Charters, that the Borough Court of Quarter Sessions was held. When County Justices and Corporate Justices came into conflict, the former tended to prevail. Thus, in the alarm about cattle plague in 1751, when "the Magistrates of some Corporations presumed to hold fairs and markets," when the County Justices had prohibited such fairs and markets in the County at large, a special statute made any such prohibition extend to all Corporations within or adjacent to the County, "any Charter, privilege, or exemption to the contrary notwithstanding" (24 George II. c. 54).

their adjudication." [1] Even where the jurisdiction of the Borough Justices in Quarter Sessions did not extend to felonies, the Court might find a great deal to do in trying misdemeanours, recording orders in bastardy, hearing appeals against convictions by Justices "out of Sessions," enrolling the rules of friendly societies, and dealing with a variety of Poor Law business.

In the administration of the criminal law, as we have already seen, this progressive enlargement of the jurisdiction of the Justices led, in the Municipal Corporations, to the rapid decay of the ancient authority of the Manorial Courts and the silent transformation of the tribunals once specially characteristic of a Borough—the Hundred Court or Portmanmote, the Borough Court or Curia Burgi—in which the whole Corporation had participated, into Sessions of the Peace, shared in only by the two or three or half a dozen Corporate Justices. [2] What had once been matters for presentment and amercement by a Jury of Freemen at an essentially popular assembly, [3] became subjects of summonses and indictments, prepared by the petty police-officers, and often dealt with by a couple of Corporate Justices either sitting as Quarter Sessions, or else summarily inflicting sentences of fine, imprisonment, or a whipping under their new statutory powers. Thus, those members of the Corporation who were Justices of the Peace found themselves wielding, both individually and collectively, an ever-growing authority over their fellow-citizens.

This exaltation of the Corporate Justices became all the

---

[1] First Report of Municipal Corporation Commission, 1835, vol. iv. p. 2700.

[2] We may, as already mentioned, see in the records this transformation of a Hundred or Borough Court into a Sessions of the Peace, silently taking place. Besides the case of Winchester, to which we have referred, we may note that the MS. volume entitled "Pevensey Hundred Court Book" (copy of which we owe to the Rev. W. Hudson) begins in 1698 as a record of the Hundred Courts acting on presentments, mostly of nuisances and defaults. It gradually passes, by 1778, into the record, on the one hand, of a "General Quarter Sessions of the Peace," acting on the bills of indictment found *billœ verœ* by a Grand Jury, dealing with felonies, and of a Petty Sessional Court doing ordinary magisterial business.

[3] We may perhaps suppose that it was to a recollection of the ancient popular participation in the Hundred Court, or Borough Court, that at Queenborough in Kent, when the Close Body of the Municipal Corporation held its meetings, "the doors were open and the Freemen came and stood without the place . . . in the curtilage"; though they did not take any part in the voting (*Report of the Trial of an Action of Debt brought by the Corporation of Queenborough against Edward Skey, etc.*, 1828, p. 163).

more marked owing to the narrow geographical area within which alone their authority was exercised. Unlike the County Justices, who could act all over their County, the jurisdiction of the Mayor and Aldermen was strictly confined within the boundaries of their Borough, from which the County Justices were either expressly excluded, or in which they had given up acting. In some cases, the jurisdiction of the Borough Justices was, in practice, further subdivided, each taking one Ward or one small district.[1] This limitation was, in some respects, a source of strength. There was in the Borough practically no way of evading the authority of a particular Magistrate, by choosing (as was frequently done in the county) to have the parish accounts passed, or get any necessary order made by another who was believed to be more favourable. Even the smallness of the Borough Quarter Sessions, by making it almost identical with Petty Sessions, enhanced the authority of each individual Justice.

It was a necessary consequence of the propinquity and intimate relationship of the Corporate Justice to his Ward or district of the Borough, that his interference with the parish government was frequently minute and incessant. We see the Mayor and Aldermen themselves attending the small Vestry Meetings,[2] and taking part in the nomination of the Overseers and Surveyors whom they afterwards, as Magistrates, formally appointed. We see them giving frequent orders for the relief of this or that poor person, or the repair of this or that road, and issuing peremptory instructions to the Overseers and Surveyors, whose accounts they would afterwards, as Magistrates, allow, and for whose reimbursement they would authorise the necessary rate. All the enactments by which successive Parliaments sought to place the administration of the rural parish more effectively under the control of the County Justices accrued to the benefit also of the Mayor and Aldermen of the Municipal Corporation. They gave directions

---

[1] This allocation of Aldermen to particular Wards was more frequent with regard to licensing business, the magisterial supervision of the parish officers and the Poor Law, and the control of the Constables and the Nightly Watch, than with regard to the actual trial of offenders. Even in the City of London, and at Bristol and Norwich, where, as we have seen, the allocation of Aldermen to particular Wards was most definite, the petty police tribunals of the Magistrates exercised criminal jurisdiction over the whole city.

[2] Notably at Leeds, Bristol, Reading.

to the Beadle about vagrants ; they prescribed the work to be created for the relief of the Unemployed ; they scrutinised the dietary of the workhouse.   Moreover, the necessary develop-ment, in a crowded urban community, of a paid official staff of Municipal officers, in itself greatly enlarged the practical authority of the Corporate Justices.   The country gentleman who was a Magistrate might give orders, but he had no paid subordinates whom he could command to carry them out. The Mayor and Aldermen of a Corporate Borough had at their command, not only the ordinary parish officers, but also such obedient dependents as salaried Beadles and Watchmen : possibly Street Keepers and Scavengers ; and at any rate a venal force of hireling Deputy Constables, who performed the service of Nightly Watch and Ward, which could no longer be exacted from the ordinary householder.   There was, too, a prison close at hand—the Borough Gaol or Bridewell, entirely under the Borough Justices' control—to which any recalcitrant person could be summarily committed by any Magistrate.

But the Corporate Justices did not confine themselves to their judicial and, so to speak, police powers.   Sitting as the Borough Court of Quarter Sessions they became, like the Justices of the Counties at large, virtually a local Legislature. We see them passing resolutions which were tantamount to By-laws as to what were to be considered nuisances, upon what conditions the ale-house licences should be granted, at what hours these ale-houses should close, and how many should be allowed in the Borough.[1]   Finally, in some Boroughs

---

[1] Thus, at Leeds the Borough Justices ordered that all public-houses must be closed at ten o'clock (*Leeds Intelligencer*, 18th June 1792).   At Derby the public-houses had no closing time until 1799, and then only on Saturday, when they were forbidden by the Borough Justices to remain open after 11 P.M. (*Derby Mercury*, 21st November 1799).   The Mayor of Plymouth, as Chief Magistrate, issued an order in 1809 to all the publicans, that they were to close these houses at 10 P.M., and not serve night watchmen (Fol. Misc. Papers, 1800-1835, in Plymouth Corporation Records).   More or less Sunday closing was occasionally enforced.   At Derby the Borough Justices ordered the sale of drink to cease, and all persons to be turned out, during Divine Service (*Derby Mercury*, 21st November 1799) ; those of Leeds made the same rule as to beer, but prohibited altogether the Sunday sale of "drams" of spirit (*Leeds Intelligencer*, 18th June 1792).   We may add that the Borough Justices usually limited the number of licences.   At Leeds, for instance, in 1790 and 1792, they passed emphatic resolutions against the grant of any additional licences, and declared their intention to reduce the number as licence-holders died or removed (*Leeds Intelligencer*, 11th May 1790 and 18th June 1792).   Occasion-ally the restrictive policy was due to the influence of local brewers, who did not

already in 1689 and in many more by 1835, we see the Borough Justices, in Quarter Sessions assembled, taking upon themselves, in imitation of the Justices of the Counties at large, the duty, not only of ordering specific payments for the maintenance of the gaol, the expenses of the Sessions, and the conveyance of vagrants, to be defrayed out of the Poor Rate,[1] but also the making and levying, on their own authority, of a separate rate upon all the householders of the Borough, " in the nature," as was said, " of a County Rate." [2]

This long array of varied powers and duties, between 1689 and 1835, gradually heaped upon those members of the Municipal Corporations who were Justices of the Peace, necessarily affected the balance of the various parts of the working constitution. We do not find that Parliament or the statesmen of the time ever gave a moment's consideration to the change which was being incidentally made in the Municipal Corporations by every statute that increased the functions or magnified the authority of the County Justices. The tendency to make the Magistrates of the Borough the dominant authority within it was, moreover, one with which the House of Commons of the eighteenth century would have thoroughly concurred. It was to the Borough Justices, and not to the Corporations, that the Privy Council and the Secretary of State came increasingly to look for the peace and good order, and freedom from sedition, of their respective Boroughs. It was to the Borough Justices that any warnings were addressed

---

want rivals : see a case at Canterbury in 1776 (*Charters destructive to Liberty and Property*, by Thomas Roch, 1776, pp. 85-93). See on the whole subject, our *History of Liquor Licensing in England principally from 1700 to 1830* (1903). In 1826, Estcourt brought in a Bill which incidentally proposed to transfer the licensing powers of Corporate Justices, in those Boroughs in which they had no exclusive criminal jurisdiction, to the County Justices. The Corporation of Oxford strenuously protested, and the measure was eventually abandoned (Domestic Entry Book, vol. lx., 7th April 1826, in MS. Home Office Records in Public Record Office ; MS. Records of Oxford Corporation, 11th May 1826).

[1] This power was extensively used at Bristol, and to a smaller extent at Banbury.

[2] Such a rate, under the name of a Borough Rate, a City Rate, a County Rate, a Liberty Rate, a Hundred Rate, a Marshalsea Rate, or a Gaol Rate, was made and levied by the Borough Justices, without participation of the Court of Common Council, in some fifty Boroughs, being one-fourth of the whole. This levy of taxation by the authority of the Borough Justices, in some towns an ancient custom, was an innovation of the nineteenth century in such Boroughs as Canterbury, Faversham, Maidstone, Maldon, Rochester, Sandwich, Winchelsea, and Winchester.

and any communications as to the regulation of liquor licensing, the management of the gaols, or the prevention of vagrancy, were made. Thus the Borough Justices, besides sitting on the judicial Bench, silently developed into an important legislative and executive authority for their town, more or less distinct from the Corporation as such ; tending to become, in fact, an influential private committee of the little group of leading members of the Corporation, which in nearly all matters wielded in the Borough the real power of government.

(b) *The Decline of the Common Council*

Along with the growth in activity and authority of the Corporate Magistracy we watch, during the eighteenth century, in the great majority of Municipal Corporations, a steady decline in the work and prestige of the Common Council. We infer that it was under the Commonwealth that this Administrative Court reached the height of its power in the Corporation ; dispensing with the meetings of the Burgesses in Common Hall, giving orders to the Mayor, disposing of the Corporate funds, and absorbing, as we have suggested, many of the functions of the ancient Manorial Courts—taking over the management of commons and fisheries, appointing both the servants and the Chief Officers of the Corporation, and enacting By-laws regulating the conduct of the citizens. How far the reaction at the Restoration and the arbitrary " regulation " and " new modelling " of the Corporations under Charles II. and James II., together with the growth of internal factions defending or denouncing the action of the King, may have contributed to shake the authority of the Municipal Corporations generally we leave to others to estimate. What is clear is that, within the Corporations, it was the Common Council that lost ground. The impression which the student derives from the records of the Councils for a whole generation after the Revolution is one of a series of mutual accusations and recriminations, between those who had favoured and those who had opposed, first, the surrender of the old Charters, and secondly, their resumption under William and Mary.[1] To

---

[1] At the Nottingham Common Council in 1690, we read of "the disaffected party" who were struggling with the "best and most loyal subjects . . . who

the decline in authority through faction was added the loss in influence caused by an ever-increasing exclusiveness. The Revolution Settlement had left unrepealed [1] the Corporation and Test Acts of 1661 and 1672, which required, from all persons admitted to Corporate office, the taking of the oaths of supremacy and allegiance, the signing of a declaration against the doctrine of transubstantiation, and the reception, within one year before their appointment, of the Sacrament according to the rites of the Anglican Church. The effect of this test, as was indeed intended, was to exclude all honest Roman Catholics and consistent Protestant Dissenters.[2] Moreover, as the Common Council was often either supreme in the election of the members to represent the Borough in Parliament, or at any rate very influential in their choice, the desire of the party in possession to retain what was becoming a valuable privilege, led to the persistent exclusion of recruits belonging to the opposite faction. Thus, Common Councils became, early in the eighteenth century, exclusively partisan in religion

. . . showed themselves well forward with their hands and purses" in promoting the Revolution (*Records of the Borough of Nottingham*, vol. v., 1900, p. 365). Those who opposed the Corporation policy of James II. were termed "the anti-surrenders" (*ibid.* p. 377). A generation later they were still in feud. In 1717 "the question being put whether or no Mr. Theodore Ffosbrooke shall be disenfranchised from being a Burgess of this Corporation, having been convicted of being disaffected to His Majesty King George, it was carried in the affirmative by the majority of votes, and he is hereby disenfranchised accordingly" (MS. Records, Nottingham Corporation, 7th June 1717).

[1] A Bill to repeal the Corporation Act was brought forward in 1689, but not proceeded with (*History of England*, by Lord Macaulay, chap. xi. vol. i. p. 709 of 1877 edition).

[2] The Corporation Act was 13 Charles II. sess. 2, c. 1 (1661); the Test Act, 25 Charles II. c. 2 (1672). The first was aimed principally at the Presbyterians, the second at the Roman Catholics. From 1727 onward, Parliament almost every year passed an Act of Indemnity (from 1760 a regular annual) for the protection of persons who had taken office without complying with the Corporation and Test Acts; and prosecutions under the Acts were at all times rare. This accounts for the fact that, in a few Corporations, such as those of the City of London, Nottingham, Gloucester, and Bristol (in the first part of the eighteenth century), we find not only "occasional Conformists," but also actual Nonconformists in the Common Council—even, by rare exception, occasionally in a majority. But the mere existence of the statutory disability, combined with the religious and political partisanship of the time, almost always served to exclude the definitely attached member of a Nonconformist body. The certificate of having taken the Sacrament, which the Act required, had to be paid for by a fee to the officiating clergyman. The taking of the oaths also involved a fee, and we find the Common Councils resolving to defray these expenses for their members (*e.g.* MS. Records, Winchester Corporation, 29th September 1759).

and politics; in the vast majority of Corporations, it need hardly be said, exclusively Anglican and Tory. By the exclusion of Dissenters the Borough lost the services of some of its best citizens. "Many grave, worthy magistrates," we read in 1716, "have been turned out, and more kept out." Though the average character of the membership of the Corporations was undoubtedly lowered by these exclusions, we need not necessarily believe, as the writer asserts of Newcastle-on-Tyne, that their places were "filled up with selfish drones, gamesters, and drunkards."[1] We note the result of the factious fighting of 1689-1725, and of the century of political and religious exclusiveness by which it was followed, in the growing difficulty experienced by many Corporations in inducing leading citizens to accept office or membership,[2] in the imposition of substantial fines for refusal to serve,[3] or neglect to attend. Coincidently with this decline in public estimation, the Common Councils were losing much of their

---

[1] *Memoirs of Mr. Ambrose Barnes* (Surtees Society, vol. i., 1867), p. 10.

[2] See, for instance, the successive refusals in MS. Records, Corporation of Dorchester, 1694-1696. At Winchester, in 1693, we see three persons being peremptorily ordered to become Freemen, "and in case they or either of them refuse the same, that they be put in election for Constables for the next year at the election of officers, or else to be prosecuted at law at the City charge" (MS. Records, Winchester Corporation, 7th November 1693). In 1788 the Common Council of Southampton found itself reduced to making an eloquent appeal to the "Gentlemen of the Grand Jury" to become members. After a lengthy description of the evils to be feared if the Corporation became extinct, this address continues as follows: "We call on you as good citizens to stand forth in support of those laws by which our lives and property are protected. We invite you as men of virtue and abilities to a participation of those powers and privileges which unworthy men are anxious to attain to. Diminished in number, we have lost nothing of that spirit which should ever accompany authority, and by which we are enabled to bear the burden of quick returning offices and to despise the unjust reproach of being tenacious of our rights. If animated by the same spirit you accede to our wishes that burden will become light, and that reproach will be heard no more" (MS. Records, Corporation of Southampton, 13th October 1788).

[3] Though Nonconformists were prevented by the Test Act from serving in Corporate offices, it was for a whole century assumed that this did not relieve them from their liability to accept office and serve if appointed. In the City of London, in particular, it was made a regular source of revenue by the Corporation to appoint to such Corporate offices as Sheriff, wealthy Nonconformists who might be counted on to pay heavy fines rather than accept office. Down to 1767, in fact, Nonconformists "were fined for not accepting Municipal offices, which they could not hold without receiving the Sacrament according to the rites of the Church of England. But Lord Mansfield, in his memorable judgment" (Chamberlain of London v. Allen Evans), "abolished these fines as illegal in the name and in the spirit of religious liberty" (*Recollections and Suggestions*, by John, Earl Russell, 1875, pp. 415-416, 420-422).

particular work. The extensive disappearance of the common-field agriculture in the neighbourhood of towns, and the gradual enclosure even of the commons and wastes, deprived the Common Councils of the agricultural business which they had inherited from the Court Baron. With the gradual abandonment of the old provision for local needs by personal services—the shrinkage of Watch and Ward, the failure of the householders to pave, cleanse, and light their particular parts of the streets,[1] the decay of authority and efficiency among Court Leet officers—the Common Council found itself ever less concerned with what we nowadays regard as the primary Municipal functions. Meanwhile successive statutes were enforcing and developing the obligations of the inhabitants in Vestry assembled to relieve the poor and maintain the high-ways. For the first few decades of the eighteenth century we still find Common Councils, mindful of the old obliga-tions of their Corporations, voting grants of land and money for the erecting of workhouses,[2] the provision of work for the unemployed,[3] the maintenance of orphan or neglected children, the suppression of vagrancy, the repair of roads and the paving of streets.[4] Very shortly, however, with the

[1] The function of the Municipal Corporation in these services had been confined, for the most part, to enforcing the obligations of the householders. Thus, at Oxford in 1694, "at this Council it is agreed that in the dark nights between this and Candlemas Day next, every inhabitant of the city shall hang out a lanthorn and lighted candle at his door, from 6 of the clock in the evening till 9, upon pain of forfeiting for every default, 6d." (MS. Records, Oxford Corporation, 27th November 1694).

[2] We hear, for instance, of the "setting up of a parish house" at Dover in 1725 (MS. Records, Corporation of Dover, 14th October 1725); the "Town Storehouse" was granted by the Corporation for the purpose, and was used until 1751 (*ibid.* 1st April 1751). The Common Council of Winchester had granted the "Market House" for the purpose in 1709 (MS. Records, Corporation of Winchester, 24th March 1709); and that of Reading a suitable place in 1702 (MS. Records, Corporation of Reading, 3rd April 1702).

[3] In 1661 the Nottingham Common Council was ordering the purchase of "so much flax as may conveniently keep forty poor people at work" (MS. Records, Corporation of Nottingham, 3rd December 1661). In 1710 it voted £10 a year "towards the spinning school . . . to commence when the school is established" (MS. Records, Corporation of Nottingham, 15th February 1710); in spite of the failure of a previous venture (*ibid.* 18th August 1697 ; see *Records of the Borough of Nottingham*, vol. v., 1900, p. 395). In 1709, the Winchester Common Council directed "Mr. Mayor" to provide "useful tools for the clothing trade for setting the poor to work" (MS. Records, Corporation of Winchester, 24th March 1709).

[4] In 1673 the Common Council of Rochester made a systematic attempt to get the whole work of keeping the Borough in order performed, as of old, by

constant multiplication of statutés, it came to be commonly assumed that such services were within the province of the Vestry and the Parish Officers, not within that of the Municipal Corporation ; and that their cost was rightly chargeable to the Poor Rate and the Highway Rate, not to the Corporation funds. Thus, we see the Common Council, relieved of its old obligations, and not undertaking new ones, shrinking on all sides, and in town after town declining (though to this the City of London, Liverpool, Bristol, and not a few other Corporations present noteworthy exceptions) into a mere committee for the management of the Corporate property. This property being seldom administered by the Corporation itself, but being almost invariably farmed to contractors, or let on leases, the minutes become frequently little more than a monotonous record of renewals of contracts and leases, together with admissions to the Freedom, the nomination of persons to receive the benefit of charitable trusts, and the formal annual appointment of the Corporate officers.[1]

(c) *The Establishment of New Statutory Authorities*

But in Borough after Borough, especially those in which the population was increasing, the need of a more extended and more efficient Municipal government was making itself felt in such matters as paving the streets, keeping them clean, providing lamps in the dark nights, reinforcing the amateur Nightly Watch by paid men, and effecting rudimentary street improvements. We shall describe in another volume the manner in which these newly felt needs led to the obtaining, by town after town, from about the middle of the eighteenth century onwards, of an almost continuous stream of special Acts of Parliament, conferring new powers of regulation, collective provision, and taxation, to enable the town to cope with the requirements of its growing population. These new

the householders, including cleansing, scavengering, and lighting. See the " By-laws made by the Mayor, Aldermen, and Assistants . . . 6th September 1673," in *An Authentic Copy of the Charter and By-laws of the City of Rochester*, 1809.

[1] This was notably the case—if we may include markets and water supply as property, when they were dealt with as such—at Plymouth, Leicester, Leeds, Gloucester, as well as in smaller Boroughs.

powers were, in a few cases, conferred upon the Corporation itself, and exercised by its Governing Council, or by bodies of Commissioners appointed and controlled by it.[1] This accretion of statutory powers and duties tended, in such Boroughs, to arrest the decay of the Court of Common Council as an administrative body ; in one exceptional instance that we shall presently describe these new responsibilities were so numerous and so extensive that they exalted the Court of Common Council and its statutory offshoots to a dominant position in the Corporation, overshadowing even the Corporate Magistracy itself. But in the vast majority of towns in which statutory powers were granted, Parliament preferred to entrust the new functions of regulation and taxation, not to the Municipal Corporations, but to entirely new bodies, established for the special purposes desired, on which the Mayor and some other representatives of the Corporation were merely *ex-officio* members in a permanent minority. We must postpone until another volume any description of these hundreds of "Ad Hoc" authorities, hitherto ignored by the historian, their extraordinary diversity of constitution, the extent and variety of their powers and duties, and the way in which they actually worked. Whether these new Statutory Authorities were formed by nomination, co-option, or popular election ; whether they were established to manage the relief of the poor, to pave, cleanse, light and watch the town, to erect markets or provide docks, or to maintain roads or embank rivers ; whether they drew their revenue from rates, tolls, dues, subscriptions, or from any combination of these ; whether they united in themselves both judicial and administrative powers, or had to resort to the Borough Justices to enforce their By-laws, the new bodies nearly everywhere tended to accelerate the decay of the Court of Common Council.[2] This result was foreseen

[1] Among such towns the principal, besides the City of London, were Liverpool and Bristol.

[2] "By entrusting to other bodies, groups of Commissioners and the like, those new powers and duties that were to answer new urban needs," Parliament, as Maitland pointed out, "fostered the notion that the property of the Corporation was morally the property of the Corporators. . . . The watching, paving, lighting of the town, these matters were no affair of the Corporation ; with the relief of the poor it had nothing to do. There was a vicious circle ; the Corporation was untrusted because untrustworthy, untrustworthy because untrusted. For what end then did its property exist ? For the election of the patron's nominee, and then for the 'common' good of the corporators ; and

by a shrewd member of the Corporation of Southampton in 1770, shortly after a body of Paving Commissioners had been established in his town. " The whole Common Council of the Corporation," said Dr. Speed, "are indeed to be always Commissioners, but then there are always to be five-and-twenty Commissioners distinct from the Corporation, a greater number than the acting part of the Common Council . . . usually amounts to, and these five-and-twenty are directed to be always kept full. . . . [The Corporation members] will upon any difference of opinion be always outvoted. . . . Besides which, this new Act takes in so many articles of the police and government of the town, and even of the Corporation's property, all of which are vested in them by their Charter, so that by promoting and consenting to this Act they have made themselves mere ciphers, and have nothing to do but to lend the sanction of their authority as Justices of the Peace." [1]   And the very fact that the Borough Justices were, in nearly all cases, made the judicial tribunal before which the new Commissioners had to bring the offenders against their regulations, or to which parties aggrieved by their action might appeal, in itself led to a gradual withdrawal of the principal members of the Corporation from any active participation in the work of the new bodies. As Justices these members had to adjudicate on the action of the Statutory Authorities, in which, therefore, they felt themselves unable to take a personal part.

(d) *The Passing of the Freemen*

The importance in the Municipal Corporation of the general body of Burgesses or Freemen had, with the decay of the Gilds and the discontinuance of the "General Assembly" or Common Hall during the sixteenth and seventeenth centuries, in the great majority of Boroughs steadily declined. But in spite of this degradation of constitutional status, we must remember that, in 1689, the Municipal Corporations of

that may mean dinners or a division of the income or even of the lands among them. Morally the town loses its personality ; for it loses the sense of duty " (*Township and Borough*, by F. W. Maitland, 1898, p. 95).

[1] Dr. Speed's MS. papers about paving, 1770, in the Speed MSS., pp. 28-29, among Southampton Corporation Records.

all the older Boroughs, and indeed of all the places then populous, had a relatively large body of Freemen, usually including all, or nearly all, the traders and shopkeepers, alehouse keepers and attorneys, and, in fact, a majority of the substantial householders along with many of the journeymen.[1] In the course of the ensuing century and a half we see, in all but half a dozen exceptional Corporations, the Freemen gradually passing out of the life of the town; in all cases declining relatively to the population; usually sinking steadily in absolute numbers, sometimes down to an insignificant handful; often becoming largely non-resident, and interested merely in returning to Parliament the nominee of the patron of the Borough; and in other cases degrading in social status from the shopkeeper and master craftsman down to a crowd of dependent weekly wage-earners and even almsmen and paupers.[2] In the manuscript minutes of Municipal Corporations all over the country we may easily recognise, in the light of the subsequent result, the threefold course of this passing of the Freemen.

There is every indication that the most effective binding force of the Municipal Corporation of the fifteenth century was the identification of its Freemen with the whole of the industry of the Borough, along with the Corporate regulation and profitable livelihood which this identification ensured. "Our forefathers," wrote the Emperor Sigismund in 1434,

---

[1] This was notably true of the City of London, Bristol, Norwich, Liverpool, Hull, Newcastle-on-Tyne, Worcester, Nottingham, Leicester, Berwick-on-Tweed, Beverley, Lancaster, Doncaster, Ripon, Preston, Oxford, Cambridge, Kingston-on-Thames, Dover, Queenborough, Gloucester, Chester, Maidstone, Canterbury, Rochester, Sandwich, Winchester, Bridgnorth, Evesham, Tewkesbury, Oswestry, Shrewsbury, Lincoln, Bedford, King's Lynn, Boston, Ipswich, Great Grimsby, Hertford, St. Albans, Plymouth, Barnstaple, and Wells.

[2] Thus, at Maidstone in 1825, it could be said that "of the 490 resident Freemen there are, and always have been, a great portion in a state of absolute pauperism, many actually residing in the parish workhouse. . . . It is a sort of tacit understanding . . . that the question of parish relief shall not be put to any of the voters" (*The Charters and other Documents relating to the King's Town and Parish of Maidstone*, by W. R. James, 1825, p. xiii). The poverty and corruption of the mass of the Norwich Freemen led to the grossest electoral scandals (First Report of Municipal Corporation Commission, 1835, vol. iv. p. 2484, etc.). At Oxford in 1833, "although there is a body of more than 1400 resident Freemen, the annual vacancies of Corporation offices are generally filled up by the votes of less than 500 persons, consisting of the inmates of the workhouse—who, on election days, have a holiday for this purpose—and of the most indigent, illiterate and worthless inhabitants of the city" (*ibid*. vol. i. p. 99).

"have not been fools. The Crafts have been devised for this purpose, that everybody by them should earn his daily bread, and nobody should interfere with the Craft of another. By this the world gets rid of its misery, and every one may find his livelihood."[1] We need not discuss here either the effectiveness or the justification of the mediæval regulations of Gild or Corporation by which this identification of the Freemen with the local industries was secured. Whether or not these regulations were beneficial to the community, they became, from the very beginning of the seventeenth century, more and more out of gear with the actual organisation of industry. The Chartered monopoly of the Freemen was usually expressed in such phrases as "opening shop," or "opening of their shop windows," which ceased to be applicable to the growing number of merchants and wholesale dealers, on the one hand; and on the other to the mere hireling journeyman, working for wages all his life long. The Civil War and the "new order" of the Commonwealth shattered many of the antiquated Gild and Corporation restrictions; and after 1689, at any rate, we find such Municipal Corporations as attempted to maintain the Freemen's trade monopoly often preferring to proceed against "foreigners" under the Statute of Apprentices,[2] for exercising a trade without having served a legal apprenticeship thereto, rather than under their Charters and By-laws confining trade to Freemen of the Borough. But the Elizabethan statute was held not to apply to any new industry or new process; in fact, magistrates and judges, under the influence of the growing bias against any restraint of trade, came more and more to find excuse for upsetting what were felt to be obsolete restrictions. Moreover, the Corporations had, with the decline of the Gilds, abandoned any effective regulation or supervision of the various trades, and what survived of their Chartered privileges was, in effect, merely the power to exact a fee from any non-freeman who opened a shop in the Town.[3] In the course of the eighteenth century,

---

[1] Goldasti's *Constitutiones Imperiales*, vol. iv. p. 189 ; quoted in *History of Trade Unionism*, by S. and B. Webb, 1894, p. 19.

[2] 5 Elizabeth, c. 4, 1562.

[3] It is, in fact, not clear whether the Freemen's so-called monopoly of trade had not—at any rate in many Boroughs—consisted less of an exclusive privilege than of an exemption from a tax upon traders. As we have seen in the case of

even this power of taxing the non-freemen was, in the great majority of towns, lost by desuetude or judicial decision.[1] Decade by decade we see, in one Borough or another, some recalcitrant shopkeeper refusing to pay the fee demanded of him, and successfully maintaining his position in the law courts.[2]

In one direction, at any rate, the Corporation ceased to wish to enforce the Freemen's monopoly. As the separation between employers and journeymen became more sharply marked, we see the Common Councils, made up exclusively of employers, discovering that the restriction of crafts to Freemen was, so far as journeymen were concerned, entirely without justification. Prosecutions against non-freemen journeymen become of rare occurrence. Whenever the question is raised, the masters insist on the abrogation of the restriction. Already in 1700 we see the Bristol Common Council authorising the Mayor and Alderman, in order to defeat " a confederacy " among the workmen " now in this city," to admit

such Manorial Boroughs as Wotton and Chipping Campden, a tax upon strangers is not necessarily connected with the existence of a privileged class of Freemen. So we find that, at Winchester, "by ancient usage . . . the Mayor and Alder-men" had "annually taxed and assessed the artificers and others inhabiting and using trades within this City, and not free thereof, as for the opening of their shop windows, according to their discretion." In 1650, "for that such custom seemeth to be too much arbitrary," it was ordered that the assessment of the non-freemen should be by the Council, and should not exceed £5 a year (MS. Records, Winchester Corporation, 17th January 1650).

[1] In 1722, for instance, the Common Council of Deal wanted to prosecute a Scotch pedlar who, duly furnished with a Government licence, was "selling goods in the Town on a considerable scale." They were advised that "Deal being a new Corporation lately made, and having no prescription to make By-laws, it is very much to be questioned how far they can make By-laws to exclude persons not free from using any trade there" (Book of Counsel's Opinions, 1716-1776, among MS. Records, Deal Corporation).

[2] The position was thus stated in 1826 by a despairing Kentish Mayor : "Under the circumstances that have been described most of the Municipal bodies within England and Wales exercise the authority assigned to them by the Crown, upon precarious tenure, and they cannot assure themselves of safety in their proceedings. They are at the mercy of contumacious, factious in-dividuals ; and cannot assume their Franchises, nor discharge their duties, with-out incurring the risk of being led into expensive legal proceedings of doubtful issue. The By-laws, which have for their object to ensure to the inhabitants of Corporate towns the services of individuals in public offices, are not only inoperative except by the means of very expensive prosecutions, but they are, or may be, rendered absolutely nugatory at the will of any individual, under the provisions of the statute law, as it has been decided in certain cases " (*Observations upon the Municipal Bodies in Cities and Towns, incorporated by Royal Charters*, by R. P. Cruden, 1826, p. 67).

"to the Freedom of the city," without fee or formality, any skilled workmen who could be got "from London."[1]   In 1747 the Mayor of Dover reported to the Common Council that the committee for building the gaol, "on account of the very high wages of the workmen of the Town, and their demands for allowances, had thought proper to offer 2s. 6d. a day to carpenters and bricklayers, and 1s. 6d. a day to labourers, without any allowances; and that the carpenters and labourers were willing to work at that price, but the bricklayers refused so to do."   The Common Council ordered "that such bricklayers as will work cheapest, whether they be Freemen or not, shall be employed to work about the said gaol."[2]   In 1750 the same issue was brought to a head in the City of London, where, after prolonged controversy between masters and workmen, the Court of Common Council, as we shall hereafter describe, passed an Act which practically enabled any employer to get leave to engage non-freemen journeymen whenever the Freemen were unreasonable.[3]

The most important feature of the Municipal Corporation of the eighteenth century was, in fact, not its connection with the trade of the Borough, but its power of returning members to sit in the House of Commons.   What had, in the sixteenth century, been an onerous burden, had, with the rise of Parliament in constitutional importance and the desire of rich men to become members, developed into a privilege worth struggling for.   In many Boroughs it was the Freemen who elected the members; and it became thus of great importance so to manipulate the admission of new Freemen by co-option as to ensure the continuance of the majority on the side of the dominant party.   In Borough after Borough we see the Common Council, usually just before a general election, exercising its prerogative of admitting batches of new Freemen, sometimes hundreds at a time, residing all over the country, and having no other connection with the Borough or qualification than a willingness to vote for the nominee of the patron or of the dominant party.[4]   This swamping of the

---

[1] MS. Records, Bristol Corporation, 10th December 1700.
[2] MS. Records, Corporation of Dover, 27th April 1747.
[3] See the subsequent chapter on "The City of London."
[4] The scandal was only slightly mitigated by an Act of 1763, which forbad the exercise of a vote as a Freeman in a Parliamentary election to those who

Freemen by political non-residents was inconsistent, it will be noted, with any attempt to maintain the Freemen's monopoly of trade. It became, in fact, unwelcome to the dominant party that any independent local shopkeeper or artificer should be able to apply to be admitted to the Freedom, as this tended to endanger the majority. We therefore always find the admission of batches of non-residents coincident with the abandonment of any restriction on trade, and usually also with a disuse of admission by Servitude of Apprenticeship. The number of Freemen might eventually be large, but by becoming practically nothing but non-resident "faggot voters," they passed out of the life of the town.

In many Boroughs, however, we see a tendency, not to enlarge, but actually to restrict the number of Freemen. When it was not any Governing Council but the Freemen themselves, in Common Hall assembled, who admitted new members to their own body, we see them acting on the principle of keeping their privileges as much as possible to themselves. This was especially the case where the Freemen shared among themselves pecuniary advantages of some value, such as pasturage on the Town Moor, fishing in the river, or participation in lucrative endowments. We see the Freemen in such cases more and more scrutinising the claims to admission by Right of Birth or Right of Marriage, or by Servitude of Apprenticeship; narrowly limiting or abandoning the exercise of their power of co-option; and sometimes raising the price exacted for this privilege to an almost prohibitive sum.[1]

There was, however, one method of recruitment of the membership of the Municipal Corporation which maintained a connection between its Freemen and the life of the Borough. When any duly apprenticed citizen could claim to be allowed

had been admitted within the preceding year, otherwise than by Right of Birth or Marriage or by Servitude of Apprenticeship (3 George III. c. 15).

[1] Already in 1772 Parliament found it necessary to come to the rescue of persons entitled to claim their Freedom, but who had been "refused to be admitted thereto," and could only enforce their rights at great expense without being able to recover costs. It was enacted that any Freemen should be entitled to inspect and take copies of entries of admission ; and that any Mayor or other officer refusing to admit to the Freedom a person legally entitled to it should pay all the costs of the consequent proceedings by Mandamus (12 George III. c. 21).

to take up his Freedom, neither the Common Council, nor even the body of Freemen in Common Hall assembled, had power to close the avenue, however much they might desire to do so. Moreover, though the whole body might see an advantage in restricting admissions, no individual Freeman would forgo his right to introduce his own sons and his own friends, as his apprentices, into the privileged circle. And if the Freemen were, as in the City of London, organised in Gilds or Trade Companies, the officers of these associations had their own reasons for encouraging fee-paying recruits. Hence we find, in 1835, in some Municipal Corporations, large bodies of resident Freemen, intimately associated with the industrial life of the Borough. But these bodies of Freemen were, for the most part, of a peculiar class. The vigilant scrutiny which the general tendency to exclusiveness kept up made a " colourable " apprenticeship usually impracticable. This open avenue to the Freedom was available, therefore, mainly for those who actually worked as craftsmen, or served behind the shopkeeper's counter. Moreover, what the Freeman obtained was, as we have seen, seldom any appreciable share in the government of the Corporation, but often small pecuniary advantages, such as " stints," doles, and saleable votes, attractive chiefly to an impecunious class. From all these causes, wherever a large body of Freemen remained in existence, we find it characterised by the predominance of manual-working wage-earners, together with a leaven of publicans, brokers, and practising attorneys of the Borough Courts (all of whom had to be Freemen as a condition of their licences), and, in a few Boroughs, a certain proportion of retail shopkeepers. In one notable instance, the City of London, the exceptionally numerous body of Freemen was, for reasons which will here-after appear, composed predominantly of the retail shopkeepers, along with a powerful contingent of Corporate officers and licensed professionals.[1]

(e) *The Mingling of Decay and Growth*

We may now attempt to summarise the general changes

[1] In this exceptional Corporation, the mere Freemen, as such, had, as we shall hereafter describe, little effective share in the government, this being confined either to the higher grade of " Liverymen," or to the Freemen ratepayers.

suffered by the Municipal Corporations as a whole in the period between 1689 and 1835. Already at the Revolution the constitution was in decay, and its spirit departed. As we have shown, the Municipal Corporation had been, in its origin and in its prime, essentially an " Association of Producers "— at first, of agriculturalists and then of craftsmen and traders. It was upon this aspect of the Corporation that depended some of its most important elements, such as its quasi-Manorial Courts and its open Democracy of Freemen. In 1689 these survived only in obsolescent or attenuated forms. What was important at that date was the Court of Common Council, usually fortified as a Close Body by Royal Charters, and the Corporate Magistracy, likewise established by Charter, but sharing in all the powers then beginning to be heaped by statute upon the County Justices of the Peace. In the next century and a half, the decay of the quasi-Manorial Courts was completed, and the Freemen either passed out of the life of the Borough by extinction or non-residence, or else sank to a position of venal dependence. The Court of Common Council clung to its property, but followed the Court Leet in the desuetude of its public functions. Out of this decay we see rising two disconnected new growths. The Borough Justices of the Peace, a tiny inner circle of the Corporation, found themselves endowed with an ever-increasing authority over their fellow-citizens, alike in a judicial, in an administrative, and in a taxing capacity. This little oligarchy—in the vast majority of Boroughs mysteriously renewing itself by complicated forms of co-option, but in a few cases resting on election by a degraded body of Freemen—became wholly detached from the general body of inhabitants. Meanwhile, other leading citizens had obtained from Parliament the statutory establishment of new authorities, which undertook the services of urban life, with which the Municipal Corporations had failed to grapple. What completed the disintegration was the fact, as will appear in our subsequent description, that these bodies of Paving Commissioners, Lamp Commissioners, Police Commissioners or Improvement Commissioners, were (in complete contrast with the ancient Municipal Corporation) essentially Associations of Consumers, established expressly to provide, at the common cost, services enjoyed by the whole body of citizens. To this general process of Municipal Disintegration there were, in particular Boroughs, as will appear in our next three chapters, exceptions and qualifications; whilst one Municipal Corporation, the greatest of them all, underwent an entirely different evolution.

END OF PART I. VOL. II

For Product Safety Concerns and Information please contact our EU
representative GPSR@taylorandfrancis.com
Taylor & Francis Verlag GmbH, Kaufingerstraße 24, 80331 München, Germany